1985 YEARBOOK
EVENTS OF 1984

FUNK & WAGNALLS NEW ENCYCLOPEDIA 1985 YEARBOOK

LEON L. BRAM
Vice-President and
Editorial Director

NORMA H. DICKEY
Editor in Chief

Funk & Wagnalls, Inc.

Publishers since 1876

CONTENTS

MEMBERS OF THE STAFF

FOREWORD: THE EVENTS OF 1984

The year 1984 was a highly eventful one politically. In the United States, President Ronald Reagan won reelection in a landslide, Democrat Walter Mondale and running mate Geraldine Ferraro, the first woman ever to run for the vice-presidency on a major party ticket, fought a hard campaign but proved unable to overcome the large lead enjoyed from the outset by Reagan, who was aided by the nation's continuing economic recovery and by his own personal popularity. In Canada, Prime Minister Pierre Elliott Trudeau resigned, after having led the nation for almost 16 years. His successor as Liberal Party leader and prime minister, John Turner, held office only briefly before calling new elections and going down to defeat in another landslide; Progressive Conservative Brian Mulroney took office as prime minister. Voters also went to the polls in other nations, including Israel, Australia, and New Zealand.

Deaths brought changes of government elsewhere. In the Soviet Union, Konstantin Chernenko became the new leader, following the death of Yuri Andropov after only 15 months in power. In India, Prime Minister Indira Gandhi was assassinated by Sikh bodyguards, apparently in revenge for the government's bloody attack on a Sikh temple harboring armed separatists. Her son, Rajiv, succeeded her.

India was not the only country beset by internal turmoil. Violence continued in Central America, Lebanon, and Soviet-occupied Afghanistan. In Great Britain, Prime Minister Margaret Thatcher narrowly escaped death when a bomb planted by IRA terrorists went off in her hotel. Relations between the United States and the Soviet Union remained at a low ebb, and the Soviets led a Communist-bloc boycott of the summer Olympic games in Los Angeles. Nevertheless, a record number of nations competed in the summer Olympics, which were marked by dramatic, often record-setting, performances and by an atmosphere of goodwill.

As U.S. space shuttles completed five new missions, attention focused on possibilities for exploring and exploiting space on a more ambitious scale; these plans and dreams are the subject of our first feature article. A second feature article focuses on dreams being realized by present-day explorers who search for priceless treasures of the past in shipwrecks on the ocean floor. A third feature looks at Toronto, one of the world's great contemporary cities, as it celebrated its 150th anniversary.   THE EDITORS

NEXT STEPS IN SPACE

by DAVE DOOLING

Dave Dooling is the science editor of the Huntsville (Ala.) Times and writes frequently on the U.S. space program.

We learned some years ago from the space program that the sky is no longer the limit, that only our imaginations—and pocketbooks—limit what we will do. Where, then, do we appear to be headed in space? Will the skies be filled with commerce, as the poet Tennyson dreamed more than a century ago? They may well be. In the next century, people may be living and working on Mars—even growing their own food in martian greenhouses. Colonists on the moon may be mining valuable minerals. Computer chips, new drugs, and parts for space vehicles themselves may be manufactured in space.

Before the end of this century, if present plans go according to schedule, a permanently manned U.S. space station will be in orbit around earth. This station will be the key to our longer-term future in space. Crew members will be conducting scientific experiments, testing on a small scale various manufacturing processes not feasible on earth, and monitoring the effects on the human body of living in space. Astronauts will be able to leave the station to retrieve and repair malfunctioning satellites. Space shuttles, including unmanned versions capable of lofting large payloads, will be routinely transporting cargo and crew to and from the station. Two space tugs—a large vehicle and a special "mini-tug"—will be available for moving loads already in orbit.

The Dream Takes Shape

In his 1984 State of the Union address, President Ronald Reagan called for a national commitment to the goal of a permanently manned, orbiting space station by the early 1990's. Although there has been criticism

9

of this goal, Reagan's support may help speed the project on its way. The cost to U.S. taxpayers is estimated at $8 billion. The project would produce a second-generation station, the first generation being represented by the smaller, less sophisticated U.S. Skylab and the Soviet Union's Salyut stations. The Soviets also are believed to be working on a second-generation space station and a shuttle.

The U.S. space station has already gone through a long—and still not completed—design period. National Aeronautics and Space Administration (NASA) officials say the problem is designing a space station that will be usable in the 21st century, that can grow as technology grows. This has meant avoiding detailed designs until late in the game. A general outline has developed, though. Current plans envision living quarters and working space for the crew, with laboratory areas for research in life sciences and materials processing. Outside there will be docking bays for the space tugs, propellant tanks for refueling them, hangars for repairing satellites, and a platform for developing new technologies for construction in space. The station itself is to be assembled from separate pieces, or modules, brought up by the shuttle. It will likely include a long "power tower" featuring an array of solar panels about half the size of a football field.

Daily Life in the Space Station

Life aboard the space station should be demanding but rewarding. A rough idea of what it might be like can be given, based in part on experience with Skylab.

There will be a crew of about seven, perhaps more. An odd number might well become the standard,

Dr. Rhea Sedden, a NASA physician-astronaut, demonstrates the preparation of frozen meat in a state-of-the-art space kitchen of 1980. The new generation of astronauts will be provided with a considerably more sophisticated galley, featuring a microwave oven and a dishwasher, that will allow them to prepare meals far less spartan than those available to their predecessors.

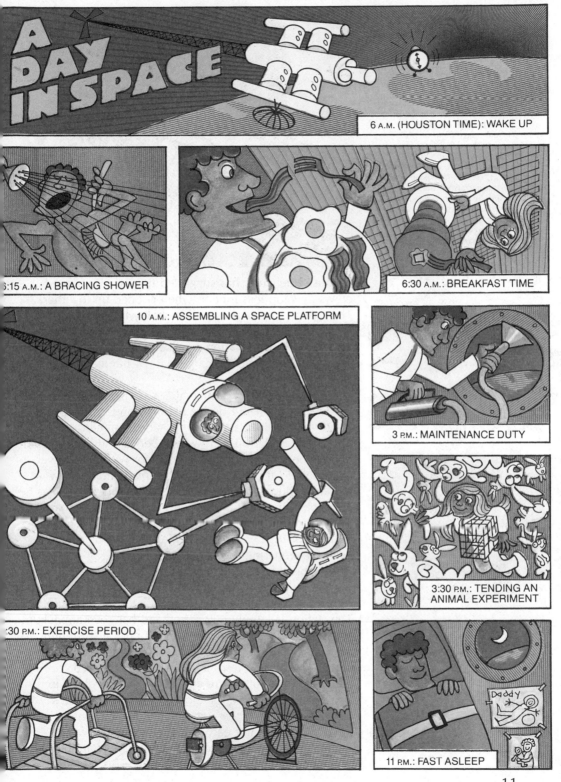

11

American astronaut William B. Lenoir suffered bouts of nausea aboard the space shuttle Columbia, and Soviet cosmonaut Anatoli Berezovoy was virtually unable to walk following his 211-day space flight in 1982. Because the side effects of weightlessness could pose serious problems, medical checks, such as the vision acuity self-test performed during a mission by Lenoir (right), and extensive physical examinations, such as the one received by Berezovoy (below) after his return to earth, are given a high priority by space program medical teams.

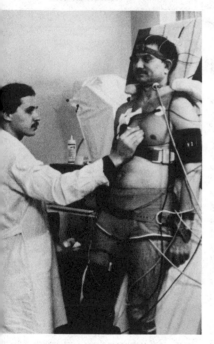

because one study has suggested that odd-numbered crews develop less friction when cooped up together. The typical tour of duty will probably be 90 days, the length of time between supply shipments, although visits to the space station are likely to be more frequent as the shuttle brings up cargoes to be handled by the crew.

A typical workday begins at 6 A.M., Houston time. (NASA in early 1984 designated the Johnson Space Center in Houston as the primary development center for the space station.) Crew members are allowed an hour of personal time to get ready for work. A shower is available—it plays a key part in maintaining crew morale—although water usage is sharply regulated, as on a ship. Breakfast and other meals are not as spartan as those of the early astronauts. The kitchen includes a refrigerator-freezer for perishable foods, a microwave oven for preparing them, and a dishwasher.

After breakfast, the crew assembles to check the day's duty plan. Some will be involved in routine maintenance of the station, but only for a few hours. The station is largely automated and has several backup systems so that the crew is not kept busy just running the place. Today, one person is using the large robot arm to assemble a test model of a large infrared telescope. Two other crew members are involved in a space walk to ensure the close fit of the telescope's mirror segments. Their suits, unlike the ones introduced on the shuttle in the early 1980's, are made of rigid sections that slide past each other and have an internal pressure of 8 pounds per square inch. This pressure allows them to take space walks without having to first breathe oxygen for 3 hours to prevent the bends, or decompression sickness. Another crew member is overseeing berthing of the mini-tug with the Space Infrared Telescope Facility, orbiting 200 miles higher than the space station. The mini-tug will bring the telescope back to the station, where its instrument module will be changed and its helium-coolant tank refilled.

After a quick lunch, everyone gets back to work. Dinner comes around 7 P.M., and then the crew has a couple of hours before bedding down for the night. Exercise is a regular part of this period, to avoid the deconditioning, or loss of physical fitness,that the crew members can experience during their three months of weightlessness aboard the station. After dinner the galley is turned into a small gymnasium, with the crew taking turns exercising on, for example, a treadmill and "weight lifting" equipment.

On the ninth day of each ten-day "week," crew members will be given a brief physical by the station surgeon and wear a miniature physiological data recorder during their activities. During the night, the recorder's contents will be sent to the ground, to be evaluated by physicians. On the tenth day the crew members will rest.

Space station crew members will perform regular maintenance on equipment that will look much like this drawing of a General Electric UARS (upper atmospheric research satellite). Using space tugs, station personnel will also place such satellites in orbit.

A favorite activity on the crew's rest day will probably be looking at the earth. When seen from an orbiting spacecraft, the globe presents an ever-changing vista as lighting angles and weather change. Other diversions will likely include playing laser discs of movies or music. Data-relay satellites might be used to pipe daily news reports up to the crew and, on rest days, for making private phone calls to families on earth. The station's decor will avoid the high-tech look so popular in science fiction movies: the living module will have its walls decorated with murals of scenes on earth, and the crew can add its own touches (a few sketches by astronauts' children have appeared on the shuttle). As space flight becomes relatively easy, astronauts on missions of particularly long duration may be allowed visits by their families.

Space Tugs

Of the two space tugs to be based at the station, the mini-tug will initially be based at the shuttle, serving as a small truck between the shuttle and satellites at higher altitudes. The mini-tug will be only 14 feet in diameter, in order to take little room in the shuttle payload bay.

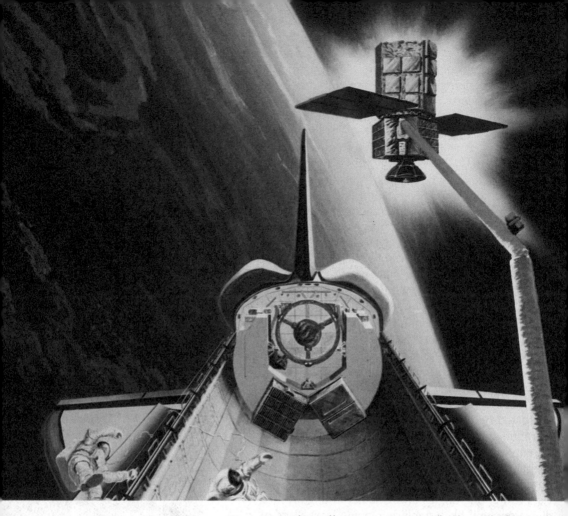

Since its tasks will not require it to fly through the lower atmosphere, it will need neither wings nor a heat shield. Later, the mini-tug will be based at the space station. Its functions will include bringing satellites in for regular maintenance checks and unscheduled repairs, and even collecting debris in the vicinity.

The larger tug would be used to carry heavy satellites up from the station to very high, geostationary orbit (an orbit around the equator at an altitude of about 22,300 miles in which a satellite moving from west to east always stays above the same spot on earth). It will be a most ungainly-looking craft, a collection of spherical propellant tanks held together by spindly metal frames.

The Technological Mission

A key role for the space station at first will be so-called technology development missions, intended to build a base of experience for the kinds of complex tasks ultimately planned for the station. Putting together

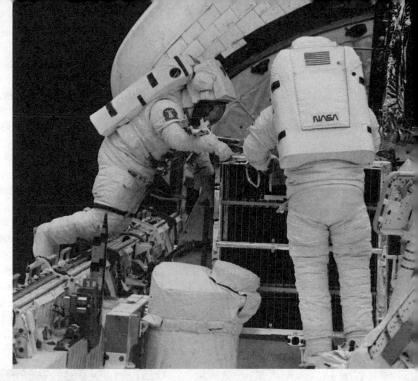

Work already performed in space—such as retrieval of crippled satellites with the shuttle's robot arm (artist's conception at left) and repair of damaged craft in the shuttle's cargo bay (right)—provide valuable lessons about the tasks that will be required of space station teams.

the test model of the large infrared telescope is one example. Another would be assembling and "refueling" a dummy space tug.

At least two platforms will probably accompany the space station, one in the same orbit and one in an orbit around earth's poles. The former would carry instruments for studying the stars and the sun. The family of instruments designed for the planned Advanced Solar Observatory, for instance, would study all the electromagnetic radiation emitted by the sun across the spectrum from radio waves through X rays. The centerpiece of the observatory would be the Solar Optical Telescope, slated for flight aboard the shuttle in the early 1990's, with a possible later transition to the station. With it, scientists hope to be able to learn how the sudden outbursts of radiation and gas from the sun's surface called solar flares are formed and what mechanisms drive the solar atmosphere lying below the visible surface.

The platform in polar orbit, meanwhile, would turn its sensors earthward. Radar would scan the waves to measure ocean currents, and also map the geology of the earth's surface. Special instruments would track the winds and monitor the atmosphere's chemical makeup and changes brought about by the seasons and by industrial pollution.

15

Mystery Drugs and Other Products

Curing the incurable may become one of the legacies of the space station. Experiments already started aboard the shuttle in 1982 are expected to lead to the marketing of a new, as yet secret, drug late in this decade. The manufacturing process now being tried out on the shuttle is called continuous flow electrophoresis, in which an electric field causes a fluid mixture's components, one of which is the desired drug, to separate from each other. The process is used on earth but is much less efficient there because of the effects of gravity.

Other types of manufacturing are also expected to benefit from the opportunities opened up by the space station. At the least, the behavior of materials under zero gravity should yield valuable knowledge about what happens when they are processed on earth, and may lead to improving those processes. At best, special high-value materials—such as, in electronics, nearly flawless gallium arsenide chips for fast, densely packed microcircuits—may be manufactured.

The "power tower" space station design, with solar energy panels attached to a long tower extending from the living and work areas, is expected to allow plenty of room for the station to grow as technology expands in the 21st century.

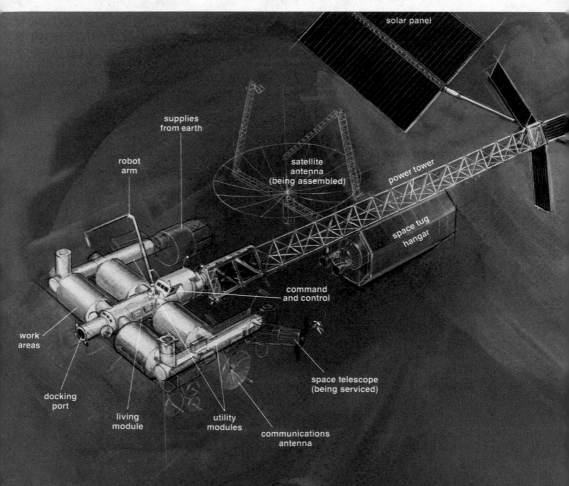

solar panel

supplies from earth

robot arm

satellite antenna (being assembled)

power tower

space tug hangar

command and control

work areas

docking port

living module

utility modules

space telescope (being serviced)

communications antenna

Beyond Earth's Orbit

The U.S. space program began sending unmanned probes to explore areas of the solar system far from the earth in the 1960's. The space station could serve as an assembly point for such missions. The moon would be the first destination, because it is the body closest to earth and has a valuable resource locked up in its soil: oxygen, which potentially could be extracted and used for life support in space and, in combination with hydrogen, for powering rocket engines. Next might come missions to comets and then to Mars.

Perhaps the mission that scientists want most for the near future is one that would bring back a sample of Mars. In the current scheme, the mission's lander would carry a small vehicle, or rover, that would crawl across 60 miles or so of martian surface, taking photos, making surface measurements, and digging up soil samples. After a three-month journey, the rover would be back at the lander, to which it would transfer the samples, then trundle off for good, to drive as far as its mechanical heart allows.

The capsule with the samples would be fired into orbit around Mars, where it would rendezvous with a larger spacecraft that would carry it back to earth orbit, but not to earth. Because of concerns that Mars might harbor life forms harmful to life on earth (an unknown virus, for example, could pose a staggering hazard), the capsule would enter the earth's upper atmosphere just to brake its speed, then be picked up by a space tug and taken to the space station. There it would be placed in a quarantine module, where extensive tests would be made, along with attempts to regenerate any life forms that might be hidden in the martian soil.

Just as the space station will be the end point for such missions, so it will be the start. The probes would be shipped to the station months ahead of their launch date and given extensive testing in space to ensure that everything worked as planned. They would then be placed atop a space tug and shot into deep space, the tug returning to earth orbit for reuse.

Mining the Moon

The U.S. space program's expected return to the moon would also be staged from the space station. On the first mission, a Polar Lunar Orbiter (appropriately called Polo) would map the moon's surface in greater detail than before. Next, a series of unmanned rovers would be sent to promising sites to measure, in detail, what elements make up the soil. After collecting

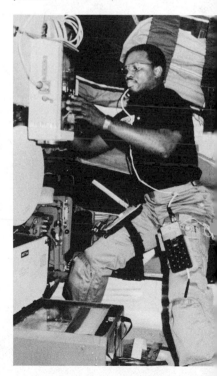

Taking advantage of zero-gravity, total-vacuum conditions, Charles D. Walker (above) operates an experimental device which is expected to permit the eventual manufacture of new lifesaving drugs. Below, astronaut Ronald E. McNair works with a minerals-processing experiment designed to develop identical-sized latex particles.

samples, the lunar rovers would fire them into orbit, where they would be gathered by a small manned lunar orbiting lab. After several weeks of exploring the lunar surface in this way, the crew would return to earth and a final unmanned rover would be readied, for use in bulldozing and excavating experiments at the most promising site for lunar mining.

A lunar refinery would follow, packaged as a single tug's payload. It would use a large mirror to focus sunlight on soil dropped into its hopper. As the soil heated up, the oxygen it contained would be liberated and, through another system, liquefied. Oxygen would not be the only useful product of the refinery. The leftover slag would be a valuable source of titanium, iron, and other metals.

People would arrive as the lunar refinery was going into operation. Several space tugs would haul modules similar to the space station's to the lunar surface, and an engineer rover would position them in a layout like that of the station, then cover them with 6 feet of lunar soil, the cheapest available insulation against solar and other radiation. Once covered, the base would look like a pattern dug in the soil by a giant mole. Little would protrude but radio antennas, a periscope or surveillance TV camera, and the doors of the air locks and garage.

Within two years, the lunar population might rise to a dozen. The primary purpose of establishing the lunar installations would be oxygen mining, but scientists would be able to use the operating base as a starting point for extensive lunar exploration. Wheeled versions of the space station modules would permit forays of two to four weeks away from the moon base, as scientific teams positioned remote measuring equipment, drilled for samples of the lunar subsurface, and ran various tests. In time, exploration would move to the far side of the moon, where a smaller base would be built. There, possibly using a crater as the foundation, a large radio telescope could be constructed. During the two weeks of lunar night it would be the premier radio observatory in the solar system, because it would be shielded from interference—"noise"—from radio waves produced on earth and by the sun.

An Industrial Revolution

With the moon colonized, the industrial revolution in space might be able to take off. It would be easier, in terms of energy expended, to bring materials from the

President Ronald Reagan (right), who has expressed the hope that a permanently manned, orbiting space station will become an international project, holds a briefing for Canadian Prime Minister Brian Mulroney (center) prior to the October flight of the space shuttle Challenger. Joining the two leaders in examining a model of Spacelab, first carried aloft by the shuttle Columbia in late 1983, are Challenger crew members Robert L. Crippen (left), Marc Garneau (Canada's first astronaut), and Kathryn Sullivan. Spacelab (below) is a European-built prototype for a space research station.

surface mini

ore in

hydroponic farm

garage

lunar rover

air lock

garage

lunar truck

pressurized lunar rover

Oxygen and metals may someday be mined on the moon; this artist's conception of a lunar mining base includes a hydroponic farm, where plants are grown in nutrient-containing solutions.

moon to geostationary orbit than to carry them up from the surface of the earth. In addition, packaging of materials for transport would be much simpler when free of the aerodynamic limitations imposed by the earth's atmosphere.

The minerals on the moon contain many of the metals required for building the sophisticated structures needed for the lunar base itself, as well as for large space systems such as solar power satellites and support structures for space bases. The dominant material is the compound of silicon and oxygen known as silicon dioxide (silicon is the foundation, literally, for most solar power cells and electronic chips). Other noteworthy minerals present include oxides of aluminum, calcium, iron, magnesium, and titanium, valuable as sources both of metals and of oxygen.

The principal product of the lunar camp might be a solar power satellite in geostationary orbit to beam energy to earth. The SPS system would in effect place a 22,300-mile extension cord between utility power grids on earth and solar cells in space. The electricity generated by the cells would be converted to microwaves and transmitted (unaffected by clouds or darkness) to earth, where it would be reconverted to electricity. The satellites required for this scheme would be gargantuan indeed, as large as the island of Manhattan (over 20 square miles), and the "rectennas" (receiving antennas) on the ground would be 20 miles across.

Studies conducted in the 1970's showed that while the SPS could be built, serious economic and environmental questions remain to be answered. They could, however, be tackled with the space station. A test model of the SPS built at the station would enable planners to produce more realistic cost estimates and also conduct environmental tests, transmitting power first from a low altitude, then from geostationary orbit.

As the space transportation and manufacturing system expands, the resource network may reach out to the asteroids for elements not readily available on the moon, and to the comets for hydrogen locked up in their ice. With both hydrogen and oxygen produced extraterrestrially, space travel would no longer depend on earth for propellant.

Colonizing Mars

Eventually, the resource network might be large enough to make it possible to send manned expeditions to Mars. Studies done in recent years have outlined how this could be done.

By the year 2057, the 100th anniversary of Sputnik 1, earth's first artificial satellite, our grandchildren may be living and working on Mars. Plans are already taking shape for a Mars base using hardware developed for the shuttle or anticipated for the space station. The base site would be one known to have water (probably near one of the poles). Soil and rocks would be mined for materials to build martian greenhouses for growing food. Argon, which makes up 1.6 percent of the martian atmosphere, might be used as a fuel (for so-called ion engines) by ships making the journey back to earth. In time, forays might even be made from Mars to the more distant asteroids to prospect for metals.

The benefits for life on earth may in fact be the most valuable result of the venture into space. Drawing on extraterrestrial resources for manufacturing products people need may make it possible to stop pillaging earth for minerals. Science and technology could then turn to re-creating lost forests, to restoring now-barren plains, and perhaps even to turning vast expanses of desert into habitable land—all using the technologies developed for making homes on Mars.

SUNKEN TREASURES

by PHILIP Z. TRUPP

Philip Z. Trupp is the Washington, D.C., editor of Oceans magazine and the director of communications of the Atlantic Alliance for Maritime Heritage.

With a half-dozen seasoned Atlantic shipwreck divers, I headed out of Morehead City, N.C., in the fall of 1982 to explore what had been described as a classic intact wreck—the *Papoose,* a 600-foot-long merchant vessel sent to the bottom in 1943 by a German U-boat lurking in the Gulf Stream. The divers carried hundreds of pounds of scuba-diving gear, cameras, tools, and measuring devices to study, document, and recover items from the ship—to bring a little of her back to life.

The Gulf Stream is a notoriously tricky body of water, and on this voyage its reputation held true. The wind was piping up, and the seas were rising and occasionally rolled over our stern, threatening to wash our gear overboard. It was slightly mad of us to be so far out of sight of land—a full five hours running off shore—on such a fickle day. But we had come this far, and we were prepared to take a few risks to see the sad and lonely *Papoose.*

Each diver had a specific task. One, an engineer, would photograph and measure the great wound inflicted by the U-boat's torpedo; he would include his findings in a book he was writing about World War II marine weapons. Another diver, wearing a necklace of cameras, was compiling a photomontage of World War II ships—before and *after* they had been sunk. A biologist would study the *Papoose* as a marine habitat for the tropical creatures living in the Gulf Stream. Also diving were a historian and his assistant, a young woman with more than 100 hours of bottom time on Atlantic wrecks. I was along to observe and gather material for a TV series.

A diver approaches the encrusted anchor of a sunken ship near the Bahamas. Marine salvors have estimated that, lying within U.S. coastal waters, there are at least 100,000 wrecked ships from before 1900 weighing 100 tons or more.

We anchored into the wreck, and our boat strained at its anchor chain; this far out in the Gulf Stream the current is strong, and the wind adds a nasty current of its own at the surface. One of our divers suited up, staggered under the weight of his gear on the heaving stern, and rolled overboard. He swam beneath our boat and attached a line to the anchor chain; the line would stream back toward us in the current, and we would use it to pull ourselves hand-over-hand to the point of our descent.

The water was surprisingly warm, and we struggled in single file down the line. It was exhausting work; the divers breathed heavily and released explosions of air bubbles. But the water was wonderfully clear. By the time I was 30 feet down, I could see the dim shape of the *Papoose* on the bottom, canted over on her side on the white sand. Slowly the ship came into sharper focus.

At a depth of 120 feet I touched down on a high railing along the main deck, now thickly carpeted with pink and white soft corals. I drifted weightlessly above the railing and swam easily over the sweep of her hull. Gaping holes where steel plates had collapsed exposed a jumble of debris piled inside the vessel. At some point beneath the blackened bridge, the ragged hole made by

the torpedo opened up like a cavern. It was a forbidding sight. The *Papoose* must have gone down very quickly, with a frightening loss of life.

At a depth of 120 feet we could stay only 15 minutes on the wreck; a longer time would require decompression to avoid the bends, a severely painful disorder caused by ascending too rapidly back to normal air pressure. We had come a long way for so little time on the bottom, but it was a successful and exciting venture for all of us.

Wrecks Upon Wrecks

Even in the computer age when we have access to vast stores of information, we can only speculate about how many ships like the *Papoose* lie hidden beneath the world's waters. Not even Lloyd's of London, the venerable marine insurance company, knows the full value of the world's lost vessels. There are only rough estimates. Marine archaeologist R. Duncan Mathewson III, of Treasure Salvors Inc., a marine salvage company based in Key West, Fla., claims that in U.S. waters there are at least 100,000 wrecks from before 1900 weighing 100 gross tons or more. Records are not kept on smaller vessels, but explorer/photographer Don Kincaid, who has spent more than two decades photographing sunken ships along the U.S. East Coast,

Treasures worth millions of dollars have been recovered from the Atocha and the Santa Margarita, two 17th-century Spanish galleons wrecked near Key West, Fla. Among the precious objects rescued from the deep are yards of valuable gold chain (far left) and an ornate "poison cup," on display at a New York City museum. Recovered artifacts, such as those viewed by archaeologists below, often have historical as well as monetary value.

Descending from the salvage ship Mariner, *a diver prepares to search out prizes from the British warship* De Braak, *sunk off the coast of Delaware in 1798. Among the riches recovered were handfuls of gold pieces, many of them sparkling as though newly minted (below, right), as well as weapons, crystal, and the engraved ring worn by the sloop's captain. Sent to the bottom by a summer squall, the 85-foot-long* De Braak *was filled with booty—worth perhaps $500 million—plundered from treasure-laden Spanish galleons.*

claims that there is a wreck every quarter of a mile—"and wrecks on top of wrecks!"—from the tip of Florida to the Canadian border.

These are only "local" figures. What about the number of wrecks worldwide? "There's no way to count them," says U.S. Navy historian John Jedrlinic, who in recent years has been putting together a data base on ship losses. Jedrlinic estimates that 1,000–2,000 ships were lost each year until 1900, when vessels became larger and were equipped with better navigational aids and weather instruments.

Wars add greatly to the ever-growing inventory of lost ships. U.S. Coast Guard historian Robert Scheina says the Allies lost at least 6,000 vessels during World War I. The figure exceeds 13,000 for World War II, a number that includes more than 7,000 merchant ships such as the *Papoose.*

Treasure Troves

There are as many ways to judge the value of these sunken vessels as there are vessels themselves. They carried cargoes ranging from coffee beans to gold bars. Some divers dream of finding the rare "treasure" wrecks laden with gleaming coins and jewels.

Melvin A. Fisher, president of Treasure Salvors, claims that the amount of gold mined in the New World and lost while bound for Spain in the 16th and 17th centuries is equal to all the gold found during the Klondike and California gold rushes combined. In 1971, after years of searching, Fisher discovered the 1622 Spanish galleon *Nuestra Señora de Atocha* some 40 miles from Key West; in 1980, Fisher found her sister ship, the *Santa Margarita.* So far, the vessels have yielded roughly $60 million worth of treasure, including gold and silver bars, thousands of coins, gold chains, one set with jewels and pearls, and a gold bosun's pipe valued at $120,000. But Fisher believes he has only scratched the surface.

Salvors around the world have recovered fabulous treasure troves, among them the Dutch East India Company vessel *Hollandia,* wrecked in 1743 off the Scilly Isles near Cornwall, England. More than 350,000 silver coins were brought up from the *Hollandia.* Another wreck that produced riches is the *Campen,* lost off the Isle of Wight in 1627, which yielded 8,000 silver coins. On today's collector's market, the coins are worth an average of about $350 each.

Famous treasure ships of more recent vintage include the White Star liner *Laurentic,* which was bound from Liverpool, England, to Halifax, Nova Scotia, during World War I when she struck a mine off Malin Head, Ireland. The *Laurentic* went down in 120 feet of turbulent sea with hundreds of tons of gold bars that were being sent to Canada to repay war debts. Captain G. C. C. Damant of the Royal Navy took charge of the recovery under a government contract in 1917. During the recovery effort, Damant's divers blasted away an outside cargo port and cleared tons of debris that had piled up in the passageway, to gain entry to the inner portion of the ship, where the gold was stored. As the work progressed, the *Laurentic* began to cave in and sink deeper into the ocean bottom. The steel decks fell into each other so that the passageway to the gold room was less than 2 feet high and a death trap of wires, plates, and steel girders. The way was cleared with explosives, but there was so much wreckage that Damant was forced to change his plans. Rather than burrow through the side of the ship to the gold, he decided it was safer to blast through the *Laurentic's* five decks, straight down into the storage room. Meanwhile, the ship continually moaned and shifted and threatened at any moment to collapse.

Seven years and 5,000 divers later (with all living to tell the tale), all but 25 of the gold bars were recovered and returned to the government. It was one of the most challenging and successful recoveries of the century.

More recently, in 1981, diver and filmmaker Peter Gimbel organized an exploration of the *Andrea Doria,* the Italian luxury liner that sank off Nantucket Island in 1956. Since it was thought that the liner went down with millions of dollars worth of cash, jewels, and bonds, numerous schemes had been hatched to recover the ship's treasures. Gimbel's plan was the only one to succeed; his crew retrieved one of the *Andrea Doria's* safes, as well as three doors, china, and ashtrays from the liner. Dramatically, the safe was at first placed in

Salvor Edward Michaud displays a picture of the Sindia *along with items he recovered from the four-masted square-rigger, which went down off the New Jersey coast in 1901. Built by the shipyard that later produced the* Titanic, *the 329-foot sailing ship was en route to New York from Japan, where she had picked up a cargo valued at up to $30 million. The chief obstacle to salvaging the* Sindia's *treasures was the wreck's location, just 100 feet off the Ocean City beach. "Surf," said Michaud, "can beat a man crazy."*

the shark tank at the New York Aquarium in Coney Island—with the sharks supplying security and the water providing protection against deterioration. The safe was later moved to a less exotic location there and was opened during a live television documentary on the *Andrea Doria* in August 1984. (It contained only bundles of waterlogged currency in small denominations.)

Also in 1981, salvor Keith Jessop pulled off a formidable recovery in very deep water. Using the most advanced underwater diving systems, his team recovered over $80 million in gold bars (5½ tons) from the British cruiser *Edinburgh*. During World War II, it had been sunk by a German U-boat, in approximately 800 feet of water, in the Barents Sea near the Soviet port of Murmansk. The gold was payment from the Soviets to Great Britain and the United States for war matériel. Salvor Jessop was awarded about $36 million for the recovery; the Soviet and British governments divided the rest. (U.S. claims had been settled earlier by insurance.)

Historical Revelations

Of the tens of thousands of ships on the ocean bottom, only a handful, less than 1 percent, contain

negotiable treasure, such as gold and jewels. Most give us a different, priceless treasure—history. A sunken ship lies in trust, preserved in the airless environment of the sea, and those in deep water are especially well protected. No dry land sites anywhere—except perhaps Egyptian tombs—are in a better state of preservation than a vessel far down in the ocean. A sunken ship, therefore, can be a rare window through which a moment in time is glimpsed.

This is not to imply that sunken ships are always found intact, upright on the botton, masts still standing, sails waving in the currents. Most ships break up on the way down, hit the bottom at about 100 miles per hour, and become a chaotic, confusing jumble. I recall the chagrin of a novice wreck diver who, after surfacing from an underwater tour of a 400-foot Liberty ship, asked his diving buddy, "Where was the wreck?" It takes experience to actually know a sunken ship when one sees it.

But no matter what its condition on the way down, a ship deteriorates much more slowly as it sinks deeper into protective layers of sand and mud. Ancient vessels have been found in remarkably good condition. For instance, near the northern coast of Cyprus archaeologists have recovered a well-perserved vessel that is nearly 2,300 years old. In 1977, a group of marine archaeologists excavating a 900-year-old wreck in the Aegean Sea, near Marmaris, Turkey, recovered engraved glassware, Greek coins, bronze kettles, and, amazingly, Greek jars containing seeds, almonds, and lentils—even a plate with chicken bones.

In another exciting find, a group of research divers organized in 1965 by Alexander McKee, a British historian, gained the cooperation of the British government and private investors and in 1982 raised large portions of the 16th-century Tudor vessel *Mary Rose*, a fighting ship of King Henry VIII. Her recovery off Portsmouth, where she sank during a battle with the French in 1545, carrying nearly 700 men to the bottom, revealed a cross section of contemporary society: pewter dinnerware for the officers of the vessel and rude wooden plates, or trenchers, for the men; pocket sundials; and gaming boards used by the officers. Skeletons of archers poised with arrows ready to fire proved that Henry insisted that his crack bowmen use their talents at sea as well as on land. The *Mary Rose* came back to life after centuries on the bottom—a true ghost of the past, and one bringing fascinating insights to the present.

Divers have also observed the eerie intact remains of two U.S. gunboats, the *Hamilton* and the *Scourge*, lost in Lake Ontario in August 1813, during the War of 1812, in a sudden storm. The National Geographic Society in 1982 used underwater robots equipped with cameras to photograph the two vessels standing upright, some 300 feet down on the bottom, guns in place, swords scattered across the deck beside the bones of sailors who went down with their ships.

Even more awesome in its state of preservation is the *Breadalbane,* a three-masted British ship built in 1843. The 123-foot vessel and its crew of 21 had been dispatched in 1853 in one of the greatest rescue attempts ever made—a constant convoy of ships and men from England to the Canadian Arctic in a fruitless search for the two lost ships and crew of the explorer Sir John Franklin, who had been searching for the Northwest Passage. In August 1853, the *Breadalbane* was 600 miles north of the Arctic Circle when ice closed in, shearing away her bottom and sinking her in 340 feet of water. (The crew members all survived, able to scramble up on the ice and wait for another ship to pick them up.) In 1980, famed Arctic diver Dr. Joseph

A diver surfaces from the waters of Bodrum in western Turkey with a valuable find: an ancient pottery vessel, still in good condition. The artifact is from a Roman ship believed to have been wrecked during the first century B.C.

Archaeologists examine the anchor of the Monitor, the Civil War ironclad that revolutionized naval battle. The anchor was recovered in 1983, ten years after a search expedition located the Monitor south of Cape Hatteras, N.C. Various other artifacts have also been raised from the ship, but the hull—and the vessel's famous gun turret—remain beneath the sea.

MacInnis, after three years of searching, found the *Breadalbane* upright and intact, in excellent condition as a result of the near-freezing temperature of the water.

Saving the Ships

Finding a sunken ship is one thing; working out what to do with it is another. For example, the U.S. National Oceanic and Atmospheric Administration (NOAA) has taken charge of the famous Civil War ironclad *Monitor*, 220 feet down in the rough currents of the Atlantic south of Cape Hatteras, N.C. After many years of exploration, in 1973 a *Monitor* search expedition from Duke University discovered the long-lost vessel. The *Monitor* and the Confederate ironclad *Merrimack*, with their iron plating, had ushered in the era of armored battleships. Soon after the two ships' historic battle, the *Monitor* and 16 crewmen were lost without a trace during a fierce storm on December 31, 1862, when she broke her towline while being moved to Beaufort, N.C. The shipwreck site is now an official NOAA marine sanctuary, giving the *Monitor* the same status as a national park and protecting the vessel for the public.

Ed Miller, an engineer with extensive experience in marine problem-solving, is director of the NOAA *Monitor* project, which is responsible for the conservation of the vessel and for deciding which parts of the *Monitor*, if any, should be brought up for study and public display. The *Monitor*'s hull is believed to be too fragile to be raised, but various artifacts, such as the ship's lantern, have been brought up from the wreck. The *Monitor*'s anchor was recovered in 1983. The raising of the famous revolving "cheesebox" gun turret was under consideration by the *Monitor* project, but it would be a risky and expensive undertaking. "You have to ask yourself," says Miller, "whether the criteria for removing things from the bottom are acceptable. Is it worth the costs and the risks?" He also makes the point that "you shouldn't recover anything unless you're prepared and able to preserve it, and with anything like the gun turret on the *Monitor* you're talking about a very sizable preservation job."

The skeleton of the Mary Rose was raised from the sea in 1982 after divers painstakingly attached what was left of the vessel to a specially constructed lifting frame. One of Henry VIII's prized warships, the Mary Rose had lain beneath the sea near Portsmouth since 1545.

If the turret is raised, it would take years before it could be displayed. When an object is removed from the seabed, the exposure to air can lead to its rapid deterioration. To prevent this, the turret would have to undergo expensive treatment in a wet tank, where the iron oxides could be stabilized.

Failing to preserve a ship or an artifact properly can be disastrous, as illustrated by the recovery in 1956 of the Civil War gunboat *Cairo* from the Yazoo River near Vicksburg, Miss. The vessel was found virtually intact, but when the *Cairo* was moved to dry storage, it rapidly disintegrated.

Public Parks and the Public Interest

Most shipwrecks, like the *Monitor*, remain as remote from the average citizen as a trip to the moon. There are notable exceptions, however, and the U.S. National Park Service maintains a number of fascinating underwater parks. The Isle Royale National Park in Lake Superior contains ten major charted shipwrecks on the bottom of the lake, some in pristine condition. Using a plastic underwater map as a guide, divers can, at leisure, explore one of the wrecks, the *Monarch*. (Of course, the NPS allows nothing to be removed.) A passenger and package freighter built in 1890 and wrecked 16 years later in a vicious storm, the *Monarch* now lies in two pieces, one in 20 feet and the other in 70 feet of crystal-clear, bone-chilling water. The ship displays classic turn-of-the-century marine technology. Deeper down and far more spellbinding is the *Kamloops*, built in 1924 as a package freighter and sunk only three years later. The packages are still onboard, but a diver must go dangerously deep—175 to 260 feet—to see them. The remains of the crew are also still there; the frigid lake bottom has preseved their soft tissues. It is a dive into the deep for only the most experienced underwater explorers with somewhat macabre appetites.

Dan Lenihan, chief of the NPS Submerged Cultural Resources Unit, says the NPS has begun a wide-ranging survey of ships in U.S. waters. "We're covering millions of acres, and it will take a couple of decades to finish." The NPS has already covered 6 miles of the California coastline, confirming a half-dozen wrecks in the area. The next step will be to investigate them to determine which vessels are important historically.

Protection or Private Enterprise?

At present, there is no general U.S. law or policy to protect sunken vessels from being emptied or taken

A gilded royal lion, its ferocity undimmed after more than three centuries at the bottom of Stockholm's harbor, was one of the prizes recovered by divers from the Swedish warship Vasa, *sunk in 1628.*

apart by anyone who finds them before the ships and their contents are studied by archaeologists and historians. Only ships in national parks or marine sanctuaries are under the jurisdiction of the federal government. Bills have been introduced in Congress since 1979 that would give either the federal or state governments title to all historic shipwrecks within specified distances of the U.S shoreline. The most recent version of the legislation, which passed in the U.S. House but was not voted on in the Senate, would give states control of certain historic vessels in, or buried beneath, lakes, rivers, and coastal waters.

Legislation of this kind is supported by many archaeologists, but it also has its opponents. Private treasure salvors, such as Mel Fisher, have fought lengthy court battles with the federal and state governments. To the salvors, government controls are a disincentive to those who seek to bring treasure and history from the sea at their own risk and expense. For example, after Fisher spent years and millions of dollars to find and recover the treasure of the *Atocha*, both Florida and the federal government laid claim to what he had found, necessitating a court battle. In a landmark 1978 decision, the U.S. District Court for the

The U.S. National Park Service administers many scenic and historical sites containing sunken ships. At far left, a diver circles the gun turret of a World War II amphibious tank at the War in the Pacific National Historical Park in Guam. At left, an NPS archaeologist examines the plans of a submerged World War I vessel between dives at Point Reyes National Seashore in California.

Southern District of Florida ruled in favor of Fisher's claim; the judge characterized claims to the treasure by governments as being based on "the most flimsy grounds." The U.S. Supreme Court upheld the ruling.

The search for sunken ships has created a sometimes bitter dispute between treasure hunters and marine archaeologists. The salvors, who use private capital to seek out shipwrecks, claim that many wreck sites would never be explored were it not for their efforts. Meanwhile, the archaeologists feel that a shipwreck is a public resource and an invaluable historical record that should not be plundered for private gain—or, for that matter, by sport divers who want to bring up souvenirs. Protective legislation may allow a compromise. The states, which would own the shipwrecks, would run preservation and study programs, allowing sport divers to explore but not take anything from the wrecks. The states would also award limited salvage permits to private concerns. Ideally, sport divers, archaeologists, and treasure salvors could work together. Given the size of the task of exploring the vast riches and history that lie on the floor of the sea, many feel it is reasonable to make use of every capable hand—public and private.

Toronto

Celebrating Success

by DAVID A. MILLER

David A. Miller is senior writer at The Sunday Star *in Toronto.*

Visitors enjoy Canada's Wonderland, a theme park north of Metro Toronto.

Until recently Toronto was one of the best-kept secrets in the world. The largest metropolitan region in Canada and the nation's financial center, the capital of the province of Ontario, the town that brought us Pablum and insulin, Toronto had quietly evolved into one of the world's great cities without blowing its horn or kicking up its heels.

In 1984, however, the city of 3 million on the shores of Lake Ontario threw a big old-fashioned birthday party to honor the 150th anniversary of its incorporation as a city on March 6, 1834. The year-long celebration, which coincided neatly with the 200th anniversary of Ontario's settlement, was the largest public party in Toronto's history. There was much to celebrate, as well as a good deal to show off to the millions of visitors who flocked to this rich and lively metropolis.

It wasn't always that way. In the early years of the 19th century, when the city was officially called York, it was generally referred to as "muddy York." Anna Jameson, a British writer who lived in Toronto for a brief and unhappy nine months in the 1830's, portrayed it as "a fourth- or fifth-rate provincial city." Many residents of "Hogtown"—another popular sobriquet of more recent years, inspired by both the meat-packing industry and the city's dominant position in Canada's economy—were apt to agree, and Torontonians looking for a night on the town often traveled to Buffalo for some excitement.

An Urban Success Story

The region of Metropolitan Toronto, which includes the city of Toronto and five adjoining cities and boroughs, encompasses 240 square miles on the northwest shore of Lake Ontario. That location and the excellent natural harbor it provides have been largely responsible for Toronto's emergence as Canada's financial, commercial, and industrial center.

As of 1983, an estimated 3,067,100 people lived in Metro Toronto; 600,000 resided in the city itself. Metro is one of North America's fastest growing urban centers. Yet Toronto has the atmosphere of a small town when it comes to neighborhood safety, social services, and overall quality of life. No one litters, and tourists have marveled at being stopped on the streets by citizens if they discard as much as a gum wrapper.

Toronto's "Sesqui"—the party the city threw for its 150th birthday—went on for months and included a visit from the sailing vessels known as the Tall Ships, which attracted millions of tourists and natives to Toronto's Lake Ontario waterfront.

The city also has one of the lowest crime rates in the world for a major urban area, thanks to the downtown residential areas called the neighborhoods. People jam the downtown streets late into the night because most live only steps away. Toronto has no ghettos and no real slum areas.

Toronto owes much of its success to the careful planning that went into its development in the past decades. The city began to boom after World War II, when waves of new residents from Europe and from elsewhere in Canada started to arrive. To coordinate solutions to the problems caused by this rapid growth, the Municipality of Metropolitan Toronto was created in 1954. (At the time, Metro consisted of the city of Toronto and 12 adjoining municipalities; the current organization came about as a result of a 1967 restructuring.) There were 1.17 million residents in 1954. To help them get around, the Toronto subway system—Canada's first—opened that year.

Hundreds of high-rise apartments sprung up everywhere during the 1960's to handle the influx of immigrants. The downtown got bigger and bigger, and skyscrapers soared to 50 and 60 stories. As if to symbolize Toronto's active new spirit, an international competition was launched to design a new City Hall. The award-winning structure, formally opened in 1965, features two semicircular office towers, which surround a huge, low, clam-shaped council chamber.

An immense geodesic dome, containing the largest IMAX movie theater in the world, is part of Ontario Place, a popular recreational park and entertainment complex built on struts over Lake Ontario.

The building boom continued unchecked until 1972, when Toronto elected a firebrand mayor named David Crombie. An alderman and a lecturer on urban affairs, at Toronto's Ryerson Polytechnical Institute, Crombie had successfully campaigned on a platform calling for controlled growth instead of "bulldozer development." He believed that development could not continue unabated without protection of the neighborhoods, of historic streets, and of the 100-year-old Victorian houses that were being razed for high-rise apartments. The mayor soon won enactment of a bylaw temporarily forbidding all construction of commercial buildings taller than 45 feet unless they included housing. The two-year freeze enraged the developers but pleased many planners interested in restoring the old neighborhoods and creating livable communities right next to commercial areas. By 1976, when a new zoning plan was passed, Toronto had become widely recognized as one of the pioneers of neighborhood protection, with people valued over concrete and steel. The developers learned to work with the zoning code, which simply required that commercial buildings be combined with residential space and parkland. One notable project begun in the 1970's was the revitalization of Toronto's historic waterfront on Lake Ontario. Located at the southern edge of the downtown area, the waterfront now includes the 92-acre Harbourfront, offering a wide variety of restaurants, art exhibits, and entertainment, as well as the new Queen's Quay Terminal, a blending of condominiums, offices, shops, and a dance theater. The entire downtown area has experienced a renaissance in recent years and now boasts 3 miles of climate-controlled underground walkways, with hundreds of shops, cafes, and gardens.

An extensive project expected to begin shortly is the large-scale development of 186 acres of land currently owned by the city, Canadian National Railways, and Canadian Pacific Ltd., and mainly occupied by an unappealing tangle of railroad tracks. The railway land, skirted by the revitalized Lake Ontario waterfront to the south and Toronto's busy downtown financial district to the north, effectively cuts the city off from its harbor area. Some building has already taken place in the area or on its outskirts. The CN Tower, which at 1,815 feet high is the world's tallest freestanding structure, was completed in 1975 on the tract itself. In 1980, work began on a 20,000-capacity convention center in the shadow of the CN Tower on the fringe of the railway

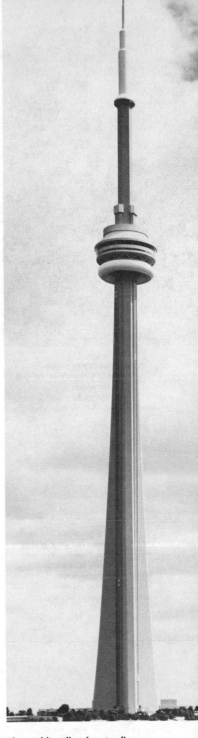

The world's tallest freestanding structure, the CN Tower, looms above downtown Toronto. Its observation decks offer an unparalleled view of the city.

land. The center and an adjoining hotel opened in 1984. The Royal Bank of Canada recently opened a new computer center on the northern edge of the tract.

In December 1983 the Toronto City Council approved a "development concept" outlining the general plan for the railway land project. Before complete clearance could be granted, both the Metro and provincial governments had to approve an official plan, being worked out by the city in 1984. Actual construction was not expected to begin until late 1985. The general outline for the 20-year, $2.5 billion project called for construction of a new financial core, office buildings, shops, theaters, a new road network, and up to 5,000 housing units. The railroad tracks were expected to be hidden in a new rail corridor with landscaped bridges over the trains, opening the waterfront to all of Metro. Concern had been expressed that the project would overcentralize Toronto's job opportunities, to the detriment of the rest of Metro. However, the regional Metro government was forging ahead with a series of new mini-downtowns to give the boroughs their own sense of identity and to reduce the number of commuters by enabling some suburbanites to work and live in the same area.

Toronto's policy of carefully controlled urban growth has led to the preservation of many of its fine 19th-century buildings, such as the old city hall above.

From Indians to Urban Center

Toronto traces its recorded history back to 1615, when Étienne Brulé, an interpreter for the French explorer Samuel de Champlain, became the first white man to see the huge inland Lake Ontario at the mouth of what is now the Humber River. Brulé was greeted by

A city whose residents are likely to work, shop, and play in the neighborhoods where they live, Toronto boasts an abundance of elegant boutiques and restaurants that serve a wide variety of ethnic cuisines.

a band of Mississauga Indians and learned that the area was called "Toronto," an Indian word meaning meeting place.

A small fur-trading outpost was established at Toronto in 1720, but the French did not take any real interest in the area until 1749, when they established the tiny Fort Rouillé on what is now the grounds of the Canadian National Exhibition, a huge annual fair. After the British victory in the French and Indian War, Britain gained control of all of Canada in 1763. Toronto began to take on increased importance under English rule. In 1787, the British officially bought the site from the Mississaugas for £1,700 worth of cash and goods, a purchase that established forever the staunch British roots of the area. Much of the groundwork for the British flavor of Toronto had been laid a few years earlier, with the arrival of Loyalists from the United States, where they had opposed the American Revolution. Their settlement of Ontario in 1784 was marked in the province's bicentennial celebration.

Toronto, which became the capital of the province (called Upper Canada) in 1793, was renamed York in

The twin towers of the award-winning new City Hall rise like a pair of giant parentheses behind Nathan Phillips Square, a popular spot for conversationalists and lunch-hour sun worshippers.

41

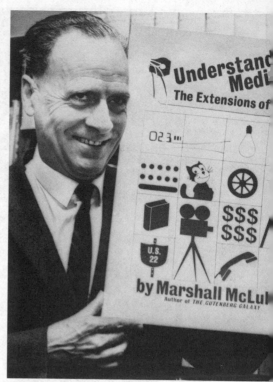

Toronto lays claim to luminaries in a variety of fields. Clockwise from lower left: Mary Pickford, the movie "sweetheart" of the 1920's; Dr. Frederick Banting, codiscoverer of insulin; communications theorist Marshall McLuhan; pianist Glenn Gould; and pop singer Anne Murray.

honor of the Duke of York. The provincial legislature did not meet in York until 1797, when work on a parliament building—the first brick building in the new community—was completed. The structure and the rest of York's public buildings were burned to the ground in 1813, when, during the War of 1812, some 1,700 U.S. troops invaded the town, killing 62. York survived, and within ten years it grew to a settlement of 209 houses and 27 stores, all fed by the St. Lawrence River supply route.

The town continued to grow and, at the time it was incorporated (and the name Toronto restored) in 1834, boasted 50 taverns and 34 firehalls—which may have said a lot about the society and construction of the day. The city went into a brief decline in 1841 when the provinces of Upper and Lower Canada were united and Kingston became the capital. But Toronto moved forward even in its slower years. By 1844, the population had grown to 18,420. King's College, the forerunner of the University of Toronto, was built in the 1840's. The St. Lawrence Hall, still standing today, opened in 1850 as the social and cultural center of Toronto. By the 1850's, Toronto was again the provincial capital, and the first railway serving the city

began operation. Toronto soon became a major commercial and manufacturing center.

When the Dominion of Canada was born in 1867, the population of Toronto was 45,000. The expanding railway system allowed Toronto to serve a huge area, and the city grew to 208,000 people as Toronto stepped quickly into the 20th century. The boom continued, thanks to the canny British bankers who established Canada's first stock exchange there and in effect ran the rest of the country from the shores of Lake Ontario.

Ginger Ale and Movie Stars

In the late 19th and 20th centuries, Toronto's natives and residents have made diverse contributions to society. Sir Sandford Fleming introduced the concept of standard time in 1884, and Canada Dry Ginger Ale was developed in 1904. Also in 1904, five-pin bowling, the most popular form of bowling in Canada, was invented by a Torontonian entrepreneur when the patrons at his bowling alley complained that they did not have time to play a regulation game in their short lunch break.

A sparkling history of medical and scientific firsts can be claimed. Sir William Osler, author of the 1891 classic *Principles and Practice of Medicine*, introduced

43

bedside teaching for medical students. In 1921 at the University of Toronto, Dr. Frederick G. Banting and graduate student Charles Best discovered insulin and were the first to use it to treat diabetes. Pablum was developed by a team of doctors at the world-famous Hospital for Sick Children in 1930. Dr. Gordon Murray, in 1946 at Toronto General Hospital, was among the first to develop the artificial kidney, and the cobalt "bomb" for cancer treatment (a capsule of radioactive cobalt that is placed under the patient's skin) was developed by biophysicist Harold Johns of Princess Margaret Hospital. North America's first high-power electron microscope was built at the University of Toronto during World War II, and both the first solid-state computer and the first pressure suit for pilots were developed there.

The city also has been home to a long list of celebrities. Mary Pickford, the motion picture actress known as America's Sweetheart, was born on University Avenue. Born in Toronto as well were actors

Christopher Plummer, Beatrice Lillie, and Raymond Massey; composer Percy Faith; pianist Glenn Gould; opera star Teresa Stratas; and rock singer Neil Young. Recording star Gordon Lightfoot lives in Toronto, and singer Anne Murray just north of Metro.

Also born in Toronto were newspaper executive Roy Thomson and Canadian statesman Lester Pearson. Writer Margaret Atwood grew up in and now lives near Toronto, and author Robertson Davies teaches at the University of Toronto. Media "guru" Marshall McLuhan, who made headlines around the world with his writings on the impact of communications media, was for years based at the university.

One of Canada's most important artists, Tom Thomson, lived in a little shack in the downtown Rosedale Ravine. Associated with Thomson were the Group of Seven, painters of Canada's national scene, who had their first show at the Art Gallery of Toronto on May 7, 1920.

Ethnic Diversity

Years ago, Toronto was overwhelmingly Anglo-Saxon in origin, but the population has grown increasingly diverse. Today, Metro boasts the largest Italian, Portuguese, and Jewish communities in Canada. There is also a large black population, strong Chinese and German communities, and many people of Indo-Pakistani, Greek, Ukrainian, Hispanic, Polish, Hungarian, Filipino, Baltic, Korean, Maltese, Yugoslav, and Arabic origin.

The city's newly cosmopolitan population has meant a jump in the number of restaurants and types of cuisine available. Twenty years ago, there were only a few French restaurants in Toronto. Today, there are hundreds. There is a bustling Chinatown, a Greek area, an Italian section, and a Jewish area, all offering traditional foods. Toronto celebrated its cultural and ethnic diversity this year with Caravan '84, held in late June, featuring pavilions around the city offering different types of food, drink, and entertainment. The West Indian community in late July and early August held Caribana '84, with a dance festival, a carnival, and a huge picnic.

Celebrating Sesqui

Some 20 million people visit Toronto each year, and the 1984 celebration, known as Sesqui, was expected to attract even more tourists. City Hall sported a giant birthday cake to welcome visitors—among them, Queen Elizabeth II of Britain and Pope John Paul II. But

Once almost exclusively Anglo-Saxon, Toronto's population has become increasingly diverse. Above, the city's thriving Chinatown.

45

Britain's Queen Elizabeth II helps celebrate Sesqui during her five-day stay in Toronto.

Toronto planned the party for its own people, as well as for tourists. The sesquicentennial turned into a 12-month-long history lesson for schoolchildren and for the hundreds of thousands of residents who weren't in Toronto ten years ago. Museums, art galleries, libraries, parks, and city buildings all mounted displays focusing on Toronto's heritage.

The major Sesqui events were scheduled to take place during the summer and early fall, starting in June with the Toronto International Festival. That month-long event featured more than 200 performances by world-famous musicians, singers, and dancers.

Several days at the end of June and the beginning of July were set aside to celebrate Canada's official birthday (July 1); special events included a birthday bash at Canada's Wonderland, a Disneyland-type theme park 8 miles north of Metro Toronto's boundaries. The province of Ontario hosted another birthday party on the lawns of Queen's Park, the historic old capitol building, with 5-cent hot dogs, soft drinks, and a full morning and afternoon of entertainment by local performers. Later in July, millions welcomed the historic sailing vessels called the Tall Ships at their rendezvous in Lake Ontario.

On August 15, the Canadian National Exhibition opened for its 105th season. Said to be the oldest and largest annual exhibition in the world, the CNE featured a huge midway, grandstand shows, and a special Sesqui program. The CNE ran through September 3, and 11 days later, on September 14, the pope arrived. During a three-day stay in the city, he said mass at Downsview Airport, before hundreds of thousands of people. On September 29, Queen Elizabeth and Prince Philip arrived in Toronto for a five-day visit.

A Haven for Visitors

Even when special events are not being held, Toronto is a city with attractions as varied as its population. The single largest tourist attraction is the downtown Eaton Centre, a huge, multilevel shopping mall—modeled after Milan's Galleria—in which live birds fly among the fountains, the trees, and the greenery. Next to the Eaton Centre in visitor appeal is the CN Tower, with its revolving restaurant, disco, and two observation levels. On a clear day, Rochester, N.Y.—a hundred miles away—is visible, plus Ontario's lake ports of Hamilton and St. Catharines.

Toronto's CNE Stadium is the home of the Toronto Blue Jays of baseball's American League, the Argonauts of the Canadian Football League, and the Blizzard of

Casa Loma, a 98-room castle built by a millionaire early in the century, is one of the many attractions heavily favored by tourists.

At one time considered a drab provincial backwater, Toronto is now a cultural mecca. Below, a Henry Moore sculpture adorns the grounds of the Art Gallery of Ontario, which houses the world's largest collection of Moore's works.

the North American Soccer League. Right across from the ballpark, sitting on struts on the lake, is Ontario Place, the province's futuristic entertainment complex, marked by a huge geodesic dome that houses the world's largest IMAX movie theater. In the fall and winter, the Toronto Maple Leafs of the National Hockey League skate at Maple Leaf Gardens.

Downtown King Street has become the city's cultural center, with the opening of the $40 million Roy Thomson Hall, the home of the Toronto Symphony Orchestra. The orchestra is generally considered Canada's finest. The country's leading dance and opera companies—the National Ballet of Canada and the Canadian Opera Company—are also based in Toronto.

The Metro Toronto Zoo, covering 710 rolling acres just northeast of the city, is one of the leading zoos in the world. There are also more than 50 miles of public beaches within Metro. In the summer, people may board one of three old ferries for the ten-minute trip across the harbor to the Toronto Islands, five islands with public beaches, parks, picnic areas, and a small amusement park. The parks all sport signs urging people to "Please walk on the grass." The welcome mat is out, as it is throughout Toronto.

The city's waterfront offers facilities for boating, dining, shopping, and entertainment.

1985 YEARBOOK
EVENTS OF 1984

CHRONOLOGY FOR 1984

January

3 • Syria freed a U.S. airman captured in Lebanon, after Democratic presidential aspirant Jesse Jackson traveled to Damascus to appeal for his release.

10 • The United States and the Vatican announced they were resuming diplomatic relations.

11 • A U.S. bipartisan commission on Central America, chaired by former Secretary of State Henry Kissinger, recommended greater economic aid to the area and conditional increased military aid to El Salvador.

FEB. 7

25 • In his State of the Union message, President Reagan cited "renewed energy and optimism throughout the land" and appealed for congressional cooperation in reducing the federal deficit.

29 • President Reagan formally announced his candidacy for a second term.

February

1 • A proposed $925.5 billion budget for fiscal 1985, including a $180.4 billion deficit, was sent to Congress by the president.

7 • President Reagan announced that the U.S. marine contingent of the multinational peace-keeping force in Lebanon would be withdrawn to ships offshore.

13 • Four days after the death of Soviet leader Yuri Andropov, Konstantin Chernenko was named to replace him as general secretary of the Soviet Communist Party.

19 • The Olympic winter games ended in Sarajevo, Yugoslavia.

28 • Gary Hart captured 37 percent of the vote in the New Hampshire Democratic primary, with favorite Walter Mondale taking only 28 percent.

29 • Canadian Prime Minister Pierre Elliott Trudeau announced he would resign as soon as a successor could be chosen.

March

5 • Under pressure from Syria, Lebanon's cabinet formally canceled the security and troop withdrawal agreement reached with Israel in May 1983.

20 • In the U.S. Senate, a proposed constitutional amendment to permit organized spoken prayer in public schools fell 11 votes short of the needed two-thirds majority.

24 • France announced that 1,250 French soldiers, the last contingent of the multinational peacekeeping force in Lebanon, would leave Beirut.

April

3 • The armed forces seized power in Guinea a week after the death of President Ahmed Sékou Touré, the nation's longtime leader.

10 • A week after a solid victory in the New York Democratic primary, Walter Mondale won the Pennsylvania primary, increasing his lead in the race for the party's presidential nomination.

17 • Gunfire from the Libyan embassy in London killed a British policewoman and wounded Libyans protesting the regime of Muammar al-Qaddafi.

26 • Former Premier Rashid Karami, a pro Syrian Sunni Muslim, was appointed prime minister of Lebanon, heading a government of national unity.

30 • During a six-day visit to China, President Reagan formalized accords providing for economic cooperation and scientific and cultural exchange.

May

6 • Moderate Christian Democrat José Napoléon Duarte was elected president of El Salvador, defeating right-wing leader Roberto d'Aubuisson in a runoff.

10 • The World Court issued a preliminary restraining order saying the United States should cease efforts to block or mine Nicaraguan ports.

14 • Jeanne Sauvé was installed as governor-general of Canada, becoming the first woman to hold the post.

24 • In El Salvador, five former national guardsmen were found guilty of the murder in 1980 of four U.S. churchwomen.

APRIL 17

June

5 • Hart triumphed in the California, New Mexico, and South Dakota primaries, but Mondale took New Jersey and West Virginia to finish the major primaries with a commanding lead in delegates.

6 • The Indian Army stormed the Sikhs' Golden Temple, which had become the headquarters of Sikh militants; hundreds died, including the Sikh extremist leader.

27 • As part of a "down payment" against expected huge federal budget deficits, the U.S. Congress voted to raise taxes by $50 billion over three years and cut spending by as much as $13 billion.

30 • Trudeau resigned as Canadian prime minister, and John Turner, chosen Liberal Party leader two weeks before, was sworn in as the new prime minister.

JULY 19

July

4 • Implementing a government peace plan, the Lebanese Army began moving in to take over militia strongholds and tear down the Green Line dividing Muslim West Beirut and Christian East Beirut.

14 • New Zealand's Labor Party, led by David Lange, won a decisive victory in parliamentary elections, defeating Prime Minister Robert Muldoon's National Party.

19 • At the Democratic National Convention in San Francisco, Walter Mondale accepted the nomination for president and Geraldine Ferraro was nominated as vice-president, the first woman to be nominated for that office by a major party.

21 • The Polish Parliament approved an amnesty authorizing release of most political prisoners.

23 • Neither major faction secured a majority in elections to Israel's 120-member Knesset; Labor won 44 seats, while the Likud bloc took 41.

28 • The summer Olympics opened in Los Angeles; despite a boycott by the Soviet bloc, a record 140 nations were represented.

August

12 • The summer Olympics ended, the United States having won a total of 174 medals (including a record 83 gold), West Germany 59, Romania 53, and Canada 44.

20 • In an effort to stem a growing controversy about their finances, Democratic vice-presidential nominee Geraldine Ferraro and her husband released financial records.

 • The UN Children's Fund issued a report saying that as a result of prolonged drought more than 7 million people in Ethiopia were facing starvation.

22 • In a single roll-call vote, the Republican National Convention nominated both President Reagan and Vice-President George Bush for a second term in office.

31 • In Israel, Likud leader Yitzhak Shamir and Labor leader Shimon Peres announced an agreement to form a "national unity" government, with first Peres and then Shamir to serve 25 months as prime minister.

September

4 • General elections in Canada saw the opposition Progressive Conservative Party, led by Brian Mulroney, score a sweeping victory over Prime Minister John Turner's Liberal Party.

9 • Pope John Paul II began a visit to Canada.

20 • A suicide truck bombing of the U.S. embassy annex outside East Beirut, Lebanon, left 14 dead, including two Americans.

26 • China and Great Britain initialed a draft agreement under which Hong Kong would revert to Chinese rule in 1997 but maintain its economic and social system for 50 years thereafter.

OCT. 1

October

1 • U.S. Labor Secretary Raymond Donovan confirmed he had been indicted by a New York grand jury, on charges involving his former company.

7 • The lagging presidential campaign of Walter Mondale received a boost when he appeared to outperform President Reagan in the first of two nationally televised debates.

12 • A bomb planted by the Irish Republican Army exploded at a Brighton, England, hotel where Prime Minister Margaret Thatcher and members of her cabinet were staying; four people, including a member of Parliament, were killed.

15 • El Salvador's President José Napoleón Duarte met with rebel leaders; the two sides agreed to set up a joint commission to study ways of ending the country's civil war.

23 • A Philippine commission investigating the 1983 assassination of opposition leader Be-

nigno Aquino said the killing was the result of a military plot.

30 • In Poland, the body of a priest who had been a supporter of the outlawed Solidarity labor movement was found in a reservoir 11 days after he had been abducted by officers of the state security police.

31 • Indian Prime Minister Indira Gandhi was assassinated by two Sikh members of her bodyguard; her son, Rajiv Gandhi, was sworn in as her successor.

November

4 • In Nicaragua, the ruling Sandinista National Liberation Front won an easy victory in presidential and legislative elections.

6 • President Reagan was reelected by a landslide, winning 525 electoral votes, the highest total in history, to Walter Mondale's 13; however, the Republicans lost ground in the U.S. Senate and made only modest gains in the Democratic-controlled House.

NOV. 6

DEC. 3

- Chilean President Augusto Pinochet Ugarte imposed a state of siege, for the first time in six years, in reaction to increasingly violent opposition.

16 • Six days after France and Libya announced completion of an agreed-upon troop withdrawal from Chad, French President François Mitterrand acknowledged that France knew Libyan troops remained there.

25 • In an operation at the Humana Heart Institute International in Louisville, Ky., William J. Schroeder became the second recipient of a permanent artificial heart.

29 • Argentina and Chile signed a Vatican-mediated treaty settling their longtime border dispute over the Beagle Channel.

December

1 • The Labor government of Australian Prime Minister Robert Hawke lost ground to a conservative coalition in national elections.

3 • A leak of poisonous gas from a Union Carbide insecticide plant in Bhopal, India, killed more than 2,000 people and severely affected tens of thousands others, in one of the worst industrial disasters in history.

9 • Iranian security agents gained entry to a hijacked Kuwaiti airliner, forced to land in Tehran five days earlier, and freed the last nine hostages; two American passengers had been murdered by the hijackers during the long siege.

26 • As part of a major offensive, Vietnamese troops overran the largest rebel camp in Vietnamese-occupied Cambodia.

29 • The Soviet Union and China signed major economic and technical accords, capping a nine-day visit to Peking by First Deputy Prime Minister Ivan Arkhipov.

31 • With his mandate overwhelmingly confirmed in general elections, Rajiv Gandhi was reinstalled as India's prime minister.

A

ACCIDENTS AND DISASTERS. The following were among the noteworthy accidents and disasters of 1984:

Jan. 14, South Korea: A hotel fire, touched off when a kerosene heater exploded in a sauna bath, killed 38 people in Pusan.

Jan.18, Japan: Fire broke out in an undersea coal mine off the southwest island of Kyushu, filling it with smoke and carbon monoxide; 83 miners lost their lives.

Jan. 22, Philippines: A ferry capsized in high seas between the southern islands of Tawi-tawi and Sibutu; at least 100 people were drowned.

Jan. 24, Great Britain: Sixteen crew members drowned when the Liberian freighter *Radiant Med* overturned during a gale in the English Channel near Guernsey.

Jan. 29, Africa: A hurricane bearing heavy rains struck southern Africa, causing more than 100 deaths from heavy flooding in Mozambique, Swaziland, and South Africa.

Feb. 10, India: A passenger train slammed into the rear of the Punjab Mail express near New Delhi after someone pulled the emergency cord; at least 43 were killed and 48 others injured.

Feb. 25, Brazil: Oil from a ruptured pipeline exploded near a shantytown on the outskirts of Cubatão; at least 500 people died in the tremendous blast and subsequent fire.

Mar. 28, Southern United States: Tornadoes cut a path more than 300 miles long through the Carolinas, killing 61 people and leaving over 1,200 injured.

Apr. 21, Mississippi: Tornadoes struck ten northern counties, leaving 15 people dead and more than 100 hurt.

Apr. 21, Yugoslavia: Nearly 40 miners perished when a methane gas explosion tore through the Vodna mine in the eastern part of the country.

Apr. 26–29, United States: Seventeen people were killed and scores injured when more than 100 tornadoes touched down from Oklahoma to Minnesota.

May 6–8, United States: Torrential rains swamped towns in the Deep South and Appalachia, and tornadoes added to the damage. Seventeen people died, ten of them drowning victims in the states of Kentucky and Tennessee.

May 13, Soviet Union: A massive explosion at an ammunition depot at the naval base of Severomorsk reportedly resulted in at least 200 deaths.

May 27, China: Torrential rains caused a landslide that buried buildings and inundated a copper mine in the city of Dongchuan; about 100 people lost their lives.

May 27, Oklahoma: Flash floods left 13 people dead in Tulsa; most of them drowned in cars swept off the roads by high waters.

May 28, Taiwan: Fire broke out in the second-floor restaurant of a downtown Taipei hotel, leaving 19 people dead and 53 injured.

June–Aug., Asia: Over 1,000 people perished and millions were left homeless in Bangladesh and northern India as a result of flooding and landslides during monsoon rains.

June 3, Bermuda: A sudden, fierce wind and huge waves quickly sank the 67-year-old square-rigger *Marques* near the start of a sailing race; 19 people were drowned, but nine crew members were rescued.

June 7–8, United States: A series of tornadoes battered the Plains states and the upper Midwest, killing at least 16 people.

June 9, Venezuela: Thirty-three military cadets were killed and eight injured in the state of Táchira, when their bus smashed into a railing and caught fire.

June 18, Angola: At least 50 people lost their lives when a speeding passenger train crashed southeast of Luanda.

June 20, Taiwan: A fire in a coal transport car sparked an explosion in the Hai-shan mine near Taipei, killing 74 miners.

June 30, South Africa: Near Jamestown, a bus plowed across a deep ditch and crashed into a tree, leaving 28 people dead.

July 4, Massachusetts: Fifteen people perished

when an arson fire engulfed a rooming house in Beverly, near Boston.

July 7, Alabama: Eleven people were drowned when a triple-deck paddlewheel excursion boat capsized in a storm in the Tennessee River.

July 7, Vermont: A Montreal-bound Amtrak train plunged into a ravine near Williston, Vt., after rains washed out a track bed; five people died and over 150 were hurt.

July 10, Taiwan: More than 100 miners lost their lives when a raging fire swept through the Mei-shan coal mine, northwest of Taipei.

July 14, Yugoslavia: More than 30 people were killed when a freight train crashed into the back of a passenger train temporarily halted on a siding in Divaca.

July 23, Illinois: Two fiery, earth-shaking explosions, felt up to 35 miles away, destroyed most of an oil refinery in Romeoville, near Chicago, leaving 17 people dead and over 20 injured.

July 30, Great Britain: A crowded express train traveling from Edinburgh to Glasgow derailed

after striking a cow on the tracks; 13 people were killed.

Aug. 5, Bangladesh: All 49 people on board a domestic flight from Chittagong died when the plane crashed into a marsh while trying to land at Dacca Airport in a storm.

Aug. 16, Brazil: After the fiery explosion of an offshore oil platform near Rio de Janeiro, 36 people drowned when their lifeboat capsized in rough seas.

Aug. 31–Sept. 2, South Korea: Torrential rains caused floods that left nearly 200 people dead and about 200,000 homeless.

Sept. 2–3, Philippines: Typhoon Ike ravaged the nation's seven major islands for two days; more than 2,000 people were reported dead, and about 200,000 homeless.

Sept. 18, Ecuador: An Ecuadoran DC-8 cargo jet crashed in a Quito residential neighborhood just after taking off; four crew members and 71 people on the ground were killed.

Sept. 23, India: A bus returning from a Himalayan shrine plummeted into a gorge near Srinagar; 34 Hindu pilgrims were killed.

Vermont Governor Richard Snelling (right foreground) coordinates rescue efforts near Williston, scene of a 13-car train wreck that killed five people and injured more than 150 others. Most of the 278 passengers aboard the northbound Amtrak Montrealer were asleep when it derailed early in the morning of July 7.

Oct. 26, Burundi: A bus plunged into a ravine near Bujumbura, leaving 43 dead and 18 seriously hurt.

Oct. 28, Philippines: Over 100 were drowned when a ferry carrying about 200 passengers sank in a storm off the island of Marinduque.

Oct. 31, Argentina: A train plowed into a commuter bus at a railroad crossing in a Buenos Aires suburb, killing more than 40 people.

Nov. 2–3, Egypt: Fire raced through the mud houses of the Nile delta village of Al Dahreya, killing more than 50 people and leaving an estimated 2,000 homeless.

Nov. 4–5, Philippines: Typhoon Agnes ripped across the Philippines, bringing heavy coastal seas and winds of up to 185 miles per hour. Over 500 people were reported dead, and hundreds of thousands were left homeless.

Nov. 7, India: A rope bridge across a swollen mountain stream in the state of Kerala collapsed, killing some 125 schoolchildren who had been on the bridge to watch a helicopter land.

Nov. 14, India: Hurricane-induced flooding caused more than 250 deaths in southern India and left about 200 villages seriously devastated by floodwaters.

Nov. 19, Mexico: A series of explosions at a government oil facility killed about 350 people and injured at least 500 others in the Mexico city suburb of Tlalnepantla.

Dec. 3, India: More than 2,000 people died as a result of a methyl isocyanate leak from a Union Carbide insecticide plant in Bhopal. Many others were seriously injured; up to 30 percent of the city's population, or 200,000 people, may have been affected. (See also INDIA.)

Dec. 5, Taiwan: At least 46 miners perished and 47 others were unaccounted for after an explosion at the Haishan Yikeng coal mine near Taipei.

Dec. 19, Utah: Fire broke out deep inside the Wilberg coal mine in Orangeville, leaving 27 workers dead, in the state's worst mining disaster since 1924.

Dec. 21, Soviet Union: Journalists reported that a gas explosion in an apartment building in Tbilisi, Soviet Georgia, had killed at least 100 people.   M.H.

ADVERTISING. The U.S. advertising industry showed substantial growth in 1984, as economic recovery reached most parts of the country. *Ad Week* predicted that total advertising expenditures would rise from $75.9 billion in 1983 to over $87 billion in 1984. All sectors of the industry prospered, with retail and cable advertising leading the way. The trend toward government deregulation continued during the year.

Regulation. The Bureau of Alcohol, Tobacco, and Firearms completed a review of alcoholic beverage advertising that it had begun in 1978. After studying the use of taste tests by advertisers with an eye toward establishing strict criteria for these tests, the BATF backed off and accepted the use of tests employing "any scientifically accepted procedure." The BATF, however, surprised alcoholic beverage advertisers by banning the use of subliminal advertising. The advertising industry, which generally denied using subliminal techniques, said that it saw no need for such a regulation.

The Federal Communications Commission lifted its 16-minutes-per-hour ceiling on television advertising. The current industry average was 12 minutes per hour. Industry experts did not expect this ruling to have as much effect on commercial clutter as the new "split 30" spot—two 15-second spots for products sold by the same advertiser. If this format should become popular, the number of spots per hour would increase dramatically and the number of total minutes of advertising probably would grow slowly.

A new Federal Trade Commission policy on "deception" in advertising stirred debate in 1984. The definition states that deception exists if there is a claim or failure to give information, concerning a material feature of the product or service advertised, that is likely to create a wrong impression in the minds of reasonable consumers. The term "reasonable consumer" is open to FTC interpretation on a case-by-case basis. The words "material feature" would clearly apply to such concrete product characteristics as the mileage of a tire, but probably not to more subjective attributes such as "luxury" or "comfort." Critics said the ambiguities in the regulation would weaken enforcement, as would a requirement that consumers show

Actress Clara Peller's face became almost as familiar to TV-watchers as those of the presidential candidates after she started demanding "Where's the beef?" Her much-quoted commercials spawned a seemingly endless volume of T-shirts, coffee mugs, and beach towels—and beefed up business for Wendy's, home of the square, allegedly meatier burger.

they suffered actual damage because of the deception.

Media. The big media news of the year had to be the summer Olympics. From an advertising standpoint, ABC was the real winner, as an estimated 180 million Americans watched that network's 180 hours of coverage, making the 1984 summer Olympics the most-watched televised event in the history of the medium. Ratings for the entire coverage by ABC exceeded the ratings over the same period for CBS and NBC combined. ABC reportedly made substantial profits.

ABC was also set to broadcast the January 1985 Super Bowl, at rates to advertisers of $1 million per commercial minute. Advertisers did not balk, however; Anheuser-Busch, Stroh's, IBM, and Nissan signed up promptly as soon as commercial time became available.

A study by A. C. Nielsen Company found that more than 12 percent of all homes with television sets also owned videocassette rec-

ords. More than 7 million VCRs were expected to be sold in the United States in 1984. Advertisers are concerned because the Nielsen study showed that more than half of those who record shows either edit commercials out of the program or speed past them when viewing the shows.

Advertisers. Miller Lite's camping trip spot, starring comedian Rodney Dangerfield as "The Creature," was expected to make the list of most frequently remembered television advertisements for 1984. Another candidate was Stroh's "Alex the Dog" spot, in which a dog retrieves Stroh's from the refrigerator for a group of men playing cards. (The spot ends with Alex drinking something in the kitchen. The Stroh's?) Most famous of all was the series of clever commercials for Wendy's hamburger restaurants, in which octogenarian actress Clara Peller angrily confronts a minuscule bit of meat being passed off as a hamburger by a rival chain. Her "where's the beef" query soon flared up everywhere, even on the Democratic primary campaign trail, with Walter Mondale using it to grill Democratic rival Gary Hart about the "meat" in Hart's vaunted "new ideas." Wendy's, lowliest of the Big Three U.S. burger restaurant chains, recorded a 32 percent sales increase for the first half of the year.

A new series of television spots for Pepsi created a furor before they were even broadcast, when the star, entertainer Michael Jackson, was injured in an explosion during the taping. The Jackson spots marked Pepsi's move away from the baby boom generation and toward teenagers.

Agencies. A. C. Nielsen Company, the world's largest marketing/advertising research company, was sold to Dun & Bradstreet Corporation in May for $1.08 billion of D&B stock. Later in the year, Arbitron Ratings Company, the fourth-largest U.S. research company, and Burke Marketing Services, the fifth-largest research firm, agreed to the biggest merger in the history of the marketing/advertising research industry.

B.G.V.

AFGHANISTAN. Fighting inside Afghanistan intensified in 1984, as both the resistance forces (Mujahedeen, or Holy Warriors) and the Soviet and Afghan government troops extended their operations and improved their tactics. As a result, casualties and economic devastation sharply increased.

The War. The Soviet military effort increased in size, operational capability, and tactical versatility. The estimated number of troops committed to Afghanistan increased from about 100,000 in 1983 to around 150,000 in 1984, according to some reports. This increase permitted a larger number of simultaneous operations. Greater effectiveness was also achieved in counterguerrilla tactics, including more precise and intensive ground/air assaults, the use of special ranger units to seize high ground or to surprise and ambush guerrillas, and the infiltration of trained agents into resistance bases to gather intelligence and create confusion. Soviet forces showed an increased ability to take the initiative in the fighting and inflict heavier casualties. However, for the most part the Soviet and Afghan armies appeared unable to extend control beyond the largest cities and provincial towns and the most vital facilities.

The Soviets, along with a small Afghan force, launched a major offensive in April. After days of heavy saturation bombing, thousands of troops pushed into the Panjshir Valley, a key guerrilla stronghold (north of the capital city of Kabul), where a truce between the central government and local guerrillas had expired early in the year. The attackers apparently suffered heavy casualties in the operation, many of them from land mines. There were reports that the Mujahedeen had received warning of the impending attack and had moved out in large numbers in advance.

Heavy fighting was also reported in the eastern provinces of Paktia and Nangarhar, around the cities of Ghazni and Herat, and in the Shomali region immediately north of Kabul. Soviet and Afghan Army assaults in these areas were accompanied by massive bombing intended to clear them of both civilians and resistance units. Deliberate efforts were made to destroy farms and domestic animals. These tactics generated a substantial increase in the number of Afghan refugees.

Resistance forces countered with more effective coordination between regional and local groups, better use of intelligence on impending attacks, alternative supply arrangements

requiring less dependence on stable civilian populations, and more deadly use of a widening variety of light weapons. The Soviet and Afghan armies were rarely able to destroy their opponents or hold ground they initially seized. In late August, Soviet helicopter gunships, searching for guerrillas in a Kabul suburb, reportedly suffered a devastating loss when they bombed their own troops by mistake, killing about 200.

The resistance groups also were said to be improving their offensive tactics, concentrating on ambushes of armed convoys, demolition of transportation and power facilities, hit-and-run assaults on government offices, and assassinations of officials.

Political Developments. Political unity continued to elude the resistance movement. A move to install ex-King Zahir Shar as the symbolic head of the resistance broke down early in the year, when no major military group would endorse him. Meanwhile, the government appeared to be achieving greater internal cohesion, largely as a result of a weakening of the Khalq faction of the ruling People's Democratic Party. The Parcham faction, led by President Babrak Karmal, reportedly increased its hold over key posts in the government. Erosion of their position within the government led some Khalq civilian and military officials to collaborate with the resistance.

In December it was announced that General Abdul Qadir, considered the number-two man in the government, had been replaced as defense minister by Lieutenant General Nazar Muhammad.

International Relations. UN Undersecretary-General Diego Cordóvez continued his attempts to bring together the governments of Afghanistan and Pakistan (the latter was said to be aiding the guerrillas) in negotiations aimed at a political agreement to end the war. Indirect talks involving the two governments resumed in the summer, but no progress was reported. Foreign military assistance to the resistance was believed on the increase. The U.S. commitment to the Mujahedeen was underlined by a joint congressional resolution, declaring support for the resistance struggle and authorizing $50 million to aid its cause.

See STATISTICS OF THE WORLD.   N.P.N.

Africa

Famine intensified in Africa during 1984, as drought in some areas moved into its third successive year. Negotiations raised hopes of reduced violence in the conflicts in southern Africa and in Chad, but in Western Sahara and the Horn of Africa even talks remained elusive.

The drought that assailed much of Africa in 1983 continued into 1984, although more rain was expected in southern Africa in the last months of the year. A report from the UN Food and Agriculture Organization in January said that as many as 150 million people were in danger of famine and malnutrition. By late in the year, 27 countries had been named as seriously affected.

In West Africa, the list included Benin, Cape Verde, Central African Republic, Chad, the Gambia, Ghana, Guinea, Guinea-Bissau, Mali, Mauritania, Morocco, São Tomé and Príncipe, Senegal, Togo, and Upper Volta (Burkina Faso). In the Horn of Africa, Ethiopia and Somalia were cited. In southern and eastern Africa, virtually all the countries were named: Angola, Botswana, Burundi, Kenya, Lesotho, Mozambique, Rwanda, Tanzania, Zambia, and Zimbabwe. Even South Africa, normally a food exporter, was suffering from the massive drought, with the maize (corn) industry reported to be virtually bankrupt and facing debts that had risen more than $500 million since 1980.

The effects of the drought were greatest in areas such as Chad, Ethiopia, and Mozambique, where relief efforts as well as farming were blocked by the disruption of war. In Mozambique, antigovernment guerrillas backed by South Africa even targeted international relief convoys for destruction. In other areas as well, the scale of the disaster far exceeded the capacity of African governments to cope, and international relief faced problems of transport and distribution even when it arrived in time. In October the famine in Ethiopia attracted more international attention, as reports reached American television screens, and increased aid was received from the United States

and other nations, as well as from international agencies. But relief officials still said that the lives of more than 7 million people in Ethiopia and hundreds of thousands elsewhere could be in danger.

Economic Developments. Famine was only the most visible part of Africa's economic crisis. A World Bank report released in September noted that, while the world economy had begun to recover from recession in 1983, "the recovery seem[ed] largely to have bypassed sub-Saharan Africa." For sub-Saharan Africa as a whole, per capita output in 1983 was 11 percent below the 1980 level, more than off-setting the modest gains of the 1970's. Low-income countries suffered a 0.3 percent decline from 1982 to 1983, while middle-income oil importers fell 3.4 percent and middle-income oil exporters dropped 7.3 percent. Even industrialized South Africa, hit by low gold prices as well as by drought, was suffering its worst recession in 50 years.

In addition, debt-servicing problems were expected to increase dramatically, from $4.1 billion payable in 1981 to an average of $11.6 billion a year in 1985–1987. International observers agreed that only the combined effects of internal reforms in African countries and increased international assistance could give the continent a chance to reverse the economic decline.

Organization of African Unity. The OAU held its 20th annual summit in Addis Ababa, Ethiopia, in November. The meeting was originally scheduled for May in Conakry, the capital of Guinea. But the death of Guinea's President Ahmed Sékou Touré in March forced a postponement. Disputes over Chad and Western Sahara, however, which had led to cancellation of the 1982 summit and delays in 1983, did not block the 1984 gathering.

Morocco did withdraw from the organization to protest the seating of the Saharan Arab Democratic Republic, a government-in-exile fighting for Western Sahara, a region claimed by Morocco. Zaire supported Morocco, and suspended its participation in the meeting. But in contrast to 1982 and 1983, Morocco failed to hold most other states to its position. Nigeria, Zimbabwe, and some other countries recognized the Saharan Republic, and even Morocco's allies had doubts about King Hassan's refusal to heed the OAU call for negotiations in the Saharan war.

The OAU chose Tanzanian President Julius Nyerere as chairman for 1985, replacing Ethiopian leader Mengistu Haile Mariam.

Southern Africa. A series of negotiations raised hopes for abatement of regional conflicts and for South African acceptance of independence for South West Africa (Namibia). But at year's end doubts remained about implementation of the Nkomati Accord between Mozambique and South Africa and about completion of the peace process in Angola and Namibia. Inside South Africa, moreover, conflict between the government and opponents of the system of white minority rule and racial discrimination reached new heights.

The Nkomati Accord, signed in March, pledged both Mozambique and South Africa to permit no action from their territories involving violence in the neighboring country. This implied that South Africa would cease support for the Mozambique National Resistance, the antigovernment guerrilla movement it had sponsored and that had wreaked havoc on Mozambique's economy. It also implied that Mozambique would deny transit or other facilities to guerrillas of the African National Congress, the nationalist movement which had carried out sabotage in South Africa. Mozambique quickly acted to restrict the ANC in Mozambique to a diplomatic presence, but it remained unclear to what extent South Africa was going to implement its side of the pact.

In February, Angola and South Africa agreed on a plan for withdrawal of South African troops from southern Angola. Withdrawal was originally slated to be complete within a month,

but it too was stalled, as U.S.-backed negotiations continued over independence of Namibia and withdrawal of Cuban troops from Angola. An additional obstacle was the antigovernment guerrilla movement Unita in Angola, which feared loss of South African support and sought to be included in negotiations.

The situation was complicated by the failure of constitutional changes in South Africa to keep the lid on black protest, which encompassed not only the ANC's sabotage attack but also mounting student boycotts, demonstrations, and even a general strike. Hundreds of

An Ethiopian, despair etched on his face, carries the body of a small starvation victim from the famine relief center in Korem. Despite massive outpourings of aid, tens of thousands starved to death in Africa's drought-induced famine.

Carrying pictures of Ahmed Sékou Touré, mourners attend the funeral of the 62-year-old Guinean president, who died on March 26. A charismatic but ironhanded leader, Touré had ruled Guinea for nearly 26 years.

people were reported killed and over 1,000 arrested.

Other Regions. Elsewhere on the continent, Nigeria's new military government, headed by Major General Mohammed Buhari, which had seized power in a coup on the last day of 1983, pledged to clean up the generally acknowledged rampant corruption. A number of civil servants were dismissed, and some former public officials were put on trial. However, there were charges of continuing corruption, and the government appeared unable to deal with the economic crisis precipitated by low prices for oil exports.

France and Libya agreed in late September to a simultaneous withdrawal of their troops from Chad; however, after France had brought back its troops, intelligence reports indicated that the bulk of the Libyan troops remained. Even with a withdrawal of foreign troops, it was expected that the country's civil war would continue. In Sudan, conflict persisted between President Jaafar al-Nimeiry's regime in Khartoum and southerners who objected to imposition of Islamic law and central government control. The Eritrean independence movement, as well as other opponents, remained at war with the Ethiopian government, which they accused of depriving rebel areas of famine relief supplies.

Elections held in Egypt in May and in Botswana in September returned the ruling parties to power with large majorities. On April 3, shortly after the death of Guinean President Sékou Touré, who had ruled Guinea since independence in 1958, the government was overthrown in a military coup. The new regime repudiated the policies of Sékou Touré and freed many political prisoners.

On December 12, the government of Mauritania was overthrown in a bloodless military coup, and Colonel Maouya Ould Sidi Ahmed Taya assumed power. The deposed president, Colonel Mohamed Khouna Ould Haidalla, was arrested the next day, on his return from a French-African meeting in Burundi. In Tanzania, Salim Ahmed Salim became the new prime minister, after Edward Sokoine died in an automobile accident. And Upper Volta, under the leadership of Thomas Sankara, adopted the new name Burkina Faso ("land of upright people") in August.

See also separate articles on many of the individual countries mentioned. W.M.

AGRICULTURE AND FOOD SUPPLIES. World food production increased about 5 percent in 1984, reflecting favorable growing conditions in most major producing areas. However, drought conditions plagued the Soviet Union and brought famine to parts of Africa.

World Output. Total world grain output was expected to hit just under 1.6 million tons, about 7 percent more than in 1983. (All ton figures are metric tons.) According to the U.S. Department of Agriculture (USDA), the wheat crop was a record 500 million tons. Coarse grain production of close to 800 million tons was up substantially from 1983. The rice harvest of well over 300 million tons (milled basis) was a record by a small margin. The soybean crop was forecast at well over 90 million tons, a substantial advance.

Combined output of red meats and poultry was up slightly over 1983. World centrifugal sugar production was forecast at just under 100 million tons (raw value), up more than 5 percent from a year earlier. The world coffee crop was put at 92 million bags (of 60 kilograms each), up slightly from revised estimates for 1983. Cotton was forecast at more than 76 million bales, well above the 1983 output.

United States. Despite hot dry weather across most of the Great Plains and into the Corn Belt, U.S. farmers harvested above-average crops. However, livestock producers cut back inventories in response to a squeeze on grain prices, and output of both beef and pork was well below the levels of 1983.

In September, the USDA's "all crop" production index was 110 (1977 = 100), as compared with 87 in 1983 and the revised record high of 118 in 1982. Food grain production (wheat, rye, and rice) was forecast at 77 million tons, 8 percent more than in 1983. The wheat forecast was 70 million tons (2.6 billion bushels), with a near-record yield of about 39 bushels per acre. Production of four feed grains (corn, sorghum grain, oats, and barley) was expected to total over 230 million tons, up more than 70 percent from 1983. Cotton was also up by over 70 percent.

The combined harvest of sugarcane and sugar beets, forecast at 49 million tons, was only slightly less than in 1983. Orange production dropped sharply from 9.5 million tons

G. Graham Davidson examines lettuce grown in midwinter at his Salisbury, Conn., agricultural factory, Agrownautics Inc. The loose-leaf lettuce, prized by gourmets, is grown hydroponically, using water-based nutrients instead of soil.

to an estimated 7.2 million, largely reflecting freeze damage to Florida Valencia oranges. California wine grape production, projected at 1.8 million tons, was off about 4 percent from 1983. Livestock breeding inventories were expected to be reduced because of a squeeze on producers' returns, while output of red meats declined about 2 percent to just over 38 billion pounds. This decrease was partially offset by an increase of 2 percent in production of broilers and turkeys, to nearly 16 billion pounds. These figures reflect a significant change in Americans' eating habits.

Egg production was steady at around 5.7 billion dozens. Milk output dropped 3 percent to 136 billion pounds. Milk cow numbers declined by more than 2 percent, and output per cow was down.

In mid-September, the USDA imposed a total quarantine on the shipment out of Florida of citrus plants and plant parts, including seeds,

63

and restrictions on the shipment of harvested fruit. The action was taken to halt the spread of citrus canker, an extremely contagious and destructive plant disease. Later in the month, the state government ordered citrus growers not to harvest fruit, even in groves that had previously been certified as canker-free.

Projected net cash farm income was estimated at $34–38 billion, down somewhat from the $40.1 billion reported for 1983. Despite the drop, the total income of the families of farm operators remained high. In 1983 the total was $24,092 per farm, the fifth highest on record, and it was expected to increase in 1984. Prices received by farmers for January–October 1984 averaged 3 percent higher than in the comparable period of 1983. Prices paid also moved up, but only by about 2 percent.

The commodity surplus situation improved in 1984. A payment-in-kind (PIK) program had pulled the bulk of government-owned grain and cotton out of storage, while drought further reduced commodity carryovers. However, despite donations to the needy and to other countries, surpluses continued to accumulate under the dairy price support program. The USDA supports milk prices by buying and storing carload lots of butter, cheese, and nonfat dry milk.

The average per-acre value of farm real estate declined 1 percent in the year ending April 1, 1984, in sharp contrast to a 6 percent drop in the previous 12 months. Nevertheless, it was the third straight year that farmland value had dropped.

U.S. agricultural exports rose 12 percent in the first nine months of fiscal 1984, to $29.8 billion. The increased value was the result of higher prices; export volume was 2 percent below the 1983 level. Increased grain exports to the Soviet Union accounted for part of the improved export situation.

Canada. For Canada, the year was neither particularly bad nor particularly good. The Canadian wheat crop, forecast at less than 21 million tons, was down more than 20 percent, the poorest in several years, a result of drought and a grasshopper infestation that hit southern parts of the grain belt. However, the expected coarse grain harvest of 22 million tons was up slightly. Expected output of beef and veal, at 1,025 thousand tons, was roughly in line with production in recent years.

Latin America and the Caribbean. Coffee production in the area was expected to total about 61 million bags (of 60 kilograms each), down about 3 percent from 1983. The harvest in Brazil, the world's largest producer, was forecast at 27 million bags, down some 3 million from 1983. Sugar production in the Latin American region totaled an estimated 29 million tons, up slightly from 1983.

A Florida worker torches young orange trees in Lake Alfred, using the only means known to ensure the eradication of citrus canker, a bacterial disease that defoliates and kills trees. Following the winter's devastating cold, the canker outbreak was the second calamity to strike the state's beleaguered citrus industry in 1984.

Western Europe. The wheat crop in the countries of the European Economic Community was forecast at 72 million tons, exceeding the previous record by over 20 percent. The projected coarse grain crop of 71 million tons was up about 13 percent. In early fall it was reported that EEC countries were increasing exports of feed grains to the Soviet Union and other countries, a step expected to hurt sales by American farmers.

Soviet Union and Eastern Europe. The Soviet Union had another poor crop year in 1984. Total grain production declined to an estimated 170 million tons, down about 10 percent from 1983. Annual requirements for all needs are almost 220 million tons. On that basis, it was estimated that Soviet grain imports in 1984–1985 would be over 40 million tons, much of which was expected to be supplied by the United States. The Soviet wheat crop was forecast at 78 million tons, the same as in 1983. The worst shortfall was in coarse grains, estimated at 86 million tons against 105 million in 1983. Grain production in Eastern Europe was forecast at over 100 million tons, up about 2 percent from 1983.

Africa. Africa suffered through its third year of drought and hunger. Millions were in danger of starving and were dependent on foreign food aid. In Mozambique, more than 100,000 people left their homes in the north to cross the border into Zimbabwe in search of food. Zimbabwe, however, also affected by the drought, had little to offer them. Ethiopia was in the grip of a particularly serious food crisis, with hundreds dying of starvation every day. Government mismanagement and corruption reportedly exacerbated the problem in Ethiopia and other affected countries. Western countries and international relief agencies provided hundreds of millions of dollars' worth of emergency aid.

Asia and Australia. Asia was fortunate in 1984: its food production was generally substantial enough to meet the needs of its large population. China had another good year. Total grain and cotton production, estimated at a record 400 million tons, was up about 3 percent. The projected rice harvest of 118 million tons (milled basis) set a record by a small margin, while the wheat crop of 84 million tons was

up about 3 percent. India expected to harvest a near-record grain crop of more than 130 million tons. Japan's projected rice harvest of 14 million tons (rough basis) dimmed hopes for U.S. rice exports to that country. Australia's 1983–1984 wheat harvest was close to 22 million tons, more than double the drought-ravaged 1982–1983 crop.   H.W.H.

ALABAMA. *See* STATISTICS OF THE WORLD.

ALASKA. *See* STATISTICS OF THE WORLD.

ALBANIA. After years of self-imposed isolation, Albania in 1984 moved tentatively toward better relations with the outside world. It established ties with Australia, continued to discuss normalization of relations with Greece, concluded air transport and other agreements with Turkey, and held talks with Italy and West Germany. In August, West German political leader Franz Josef Strauss visited Albania, becoming the first prominent Western European politician to do so since the end of World War II.

However, Albania took no perceptible steps to resume friendly ties with the Soviet Union, which it coupled with the United States as an "errant" superpower. Also, efforts to expand cultural links with Yugoslavia broke down in October; the barrier to better relations was what Albania called Yugoslavia's "policy of persecution" against the ethnic Albanian population in the Yugoslav province of Kosovo.

Party chief Enver Hoxha, who turned 76 in October, was believed ill and rarely appeared in public but the iron regime he had established remained firm. President Ramiz Alia, Hoxha's likely successor, and other loyal subordinates took care to laud Hoxha publicly as a "leader and teacher."

The Fifth Albanian National Games were held as part of festivities marking the 40th anniversary of Albania's liberation. There was no question of Albanian athletes competing in the summer Olympic Games, as the country has consistently refused to take part in any international gathering dominated by either of the "superpowers."

See STATISTICS OF THE WORLD.   R.A.P.

ALBERTA. *See* STATISTICS OF THE WORLD.

ALGERIA. In 1984, Algeria carried out a presidential election, passed significant social legislation, and launched a five-year plan.

The January 12 election of President Chadli Benjedid to a second five-year term highlighted the year in politics. Benjedid, the sole candidate, received over 95 percent of the popular vote. Three weeks earlier, he had been re-elected secretary-general of the ruling National Liberation Front (FLN) party at the FLN's fifth *congrès* (convention). In other political matters, the convention replaced 92 members of the party's Central Committee, principally with younger members who had no ties to the preceding regime of Houari Boumedienne.

On January 22, Benjedid named a new cabinet headed by Prime Minister Abdelhamid Brahimi. As minister of planning in the first Benjedid administration, Brahimi was viewed as the principal administrator of the president's economic policies, which emphasized decentralization, pragmatism, and efficiency. In addition to Brahimi, the cabinet contained six new ministers—most, like Brahimi, well-trained "technocrats"—as well as 14 vice-ministers.

In another major domestic development, the National Assembly passed the long-awaited Family Code in June, after lively debate. The controversial code, designed to strengthen women's legal rights in a traditionally patriarchal society, permits polygamy but sets conditions (equal treatment, the first wife's right to a divorce) that should limit the practice. Under the code, women also gained child custody rights and legal protection.

A steady stream of African leaders flowed through Algiers as Benjedid pursued support for his country's position in the ongoing conflict between Algerian-backed Polisario guerrillas and Morocco for control of Western Sahara. Among them were Tunisia's Habib Bourguiba and Thomas Sankara of Upper Volta (Burkina Faso). The Algerian government was pleased by Sankara's decision, announced in March, to recognize the Saharan Arab Democratic Republic (the Polisario government).

Figures released in 1984 documented a radical shift in foreign markets for Algerian energy exports during the period 1979–1983. Over that time span, the U.S. share of total Algerian energy exports fell from 50 percent to 17 percent, while that of the European Economic Community rose from 38 percent to 66 percent. Government forecasts for 1984 projected a 12 percent increase in overall energy export earnings, with over 80 percent of natural gas sales going to France and Italy. Meanwhile, in February, Algeria and the United States signed an agreement providing for U.S. aid to develop and improve agriculture. The government adopted the 1985–1989 five year plan in July; agriculture and water resources development were accorded top priority.

See STATISTICS OF THE WORLD.   R.A.M.

AMERICAN SAMOA. *See* STATISTICS OF THE WORLD.

ANGOLA. In January 1984, South Africa concluded a major offensive launched in Angola the month before, against the South West Africa People's Organization (Swapo), which has been waging a guerrilla campaign from bases in southern Angola, aimed at ending South African control of Namibia (South West Africa). The offensive, one of the largest since South Africa first occupied parts of Angola, followed a call by Pretoria for a cease-fire and a UN resolution demanding that South Africa withdraw from Angola. South African forces reportedly engaged Cuban and Angolan troops in intense fighting near Cuvelai. In all, 21 South African soldiers were killed in the campaign.

After the offensive, diplomatic efforts by the United States led to a meeting in February in Lusaka, Zambia, at which Angola and South Africa agreed to a cease-fire and to withdrawal of South African troops, with provision for monitoring by a joint commission. South Africa demanded that Swapo guerrillas be excluded from the zones evacuated by its troops so that there could be no infiltration into Namibia. The withdrawal was originally scheduled to be completed in one month, but it was still incomplete at year's end.

South Africa continued to link settlement of the Namibia issue to agreement on withdrawal of Cuban troops from Angola. The United States, which backed this linkage, was engaged in talks with Angola later in the year. In October, President José Eduardo dos Santos took a significant step when he dismissed his foreign minister, who took a hard line on conditions for withdrawing Cuban troops. Subsequently, U.S. officials said Angola had accepted the principle that a withdrawal of Cuban troops was a negotiable issue.

66

The guerrilla movement known as National Union for the Total Independence of Angola (Unita), which is supported by South Africa, stepped up its activity. In April, Unita took responsibility for a car bomb explosion that killed several Cubans and Angolans in Huambo. That same month, Unita released some 90 hostages, mainly Portuguese and Filipinos. The group also freed 16 British captives in May and in June, but warned that foreigners working in Angola would be considered targets of future attacks.

In April the Central Committee of the ruling Popular Movement for the Liberation of Angola–Workers' Party suspended two members for alleged involvement in diamond smuggling. The diamond industry was said to be losing as much as $150 million a year in revenue because of smuggling.

In March the state oil company, Sonangol, announced that production had reached 200,000 barrels per day, (up from 165,000 barrels per day in November 1983). The annual economic plan announced in April set a target of almost $2 billion in total export earnings, to come mostly from oil sales.

See STATISTICS OF THE WORLD.   W.M.

ANTHROPOLOGY. Indications that the orangutan could be humans' closest relatives attracted attention in anthropology during 1984, as did subsequent fossil finds in Kenya and the excavation of a Mayan tomb.

"First Cousin" Controversy. Paleoanthropologists were waging a spirited debate about the evolutionary relationship of the orangutan to *Homo sapiens*, the human species, basing their diverse views in part on the interpretation of 17-million-year-old teeth and jaw fragments of an ancient orangutan, classified in the genus *Sivapithecus*. The fragments had been discovered during late 1983 in Buluk, a remote northern part of Kenya, by a team of anthropologists led by Alan Walker, a paleoanthropologist at The Johns Hopkins University, and Richard Leakey, head of the National Museums of Kenya.

Previously discovered *Sivapithecus* fossils date back only 10–13 million years and had turned up only in Asia. Because humans and the great apes originated in Africa, anthropologists believed that *Sivapithecus* played no

significant role in their evolution—it was too young and in the wrong place. The age and location of this Kenya find, however, challenged that interpretation. According to Walker, the ancient *Sivapithecus* may be the common ancestor of both humans and the great apes. He said it was highly probable that *Sivapithecus* arose in Africa and then spread to Asia about 17 million years ago when the African and Asian continents were joined. The only living descendants of the Asian migrants are the orangutans of Borneo and Sumatra. The African group, however, probably evolved into three major lineages, which resulted in today's gorillas, chimpanzees, and humans.

At the May 1984 meeting of the American Association for the Advancement of Science, Jeffrey Schwartz, a physical anthropologist at the University of Pittsburgh, presented a theory somewhat similar to Walker's and disputed the current view concerning the orangutan's evolutionary relationship to humans. Schwartz maintained that the orangutan should be regarded as the *Homo sapiens'* closest living "cousin," because humans share many more important morphological traits with orangutans than with other great apes.

Other Fossil Discoveries. Two other recent fossil finds in Kenya by Leakey and Walker, made in mid-1984, provided new insights into the physical characteristics of our early ancestors. The first discovery, on Rusinga Island in Lake Victoria, was an exceptionally rich collection of 18-million-year-old bones of *Proconsul africanus*, a species thought to be a common ancestor of apes and humans. Previous *Proconsul* finds had been extremely fragmentary, and the new one was expected to contribute considerably to scientists' understanding of Proconsul's anatomy, growth patterns, and behavior.

The second discovery, made near Lake Turkana, was unusually complete remains—skull, collarbone, vertebrae, pelvis, ribs, limbs—of a "strapping" 12-year-old youth of the species *Homo erectus*. His estimated height of between 5 feet 4 inches and 5 feet 6 inches—which might have reached 6 feet in maturity—surprised scientists, who had generally considered the species to be much smaller. The similarity of the bones, about 1.6 million years old, to

Putting their heads together, a group of anthropologists at New York City's American Museum of Natural History confer over a massive assemblage of fossils representing several million years in the history of human evolution.

those of modern humans lent support to the belief of many researchers that *Homo erectus* was a direct ancestor of ours.

Family-of-Man Reunion. The American Museum of Natural History in New York City played host to a number of noteworthy individuals, both living and dead. Leading paleoanthropologists from around the world gathered to examine an unprecedented assembly of more than 40 fossils that collectively spanned the history of the human race. The exhibit, "Ancestors: Four Million Years of Humanity," which ran from mid-April to early September, was four years in the planning. Cocurator Ian Tat-

tersall called the fossils the "family portraits" of humanity. Specimens included the 2.25-million-year-old skull of the so-called Taung child, from South Africa; the Zinjanthropus skull, 1.75 million years old, found by Louis and Mary Leakey in Olduvai Gorge in Tanzania; and Java Man, found in Indonesia in 1890's, representing *Homo erectus*. Before the fossils went behind bulletproof glass for viewing by the general public, they were open to direct examination by the scientists.

Mayan Tomb Discovered. In May, a joint University of Texas and Guatemalan archaeological team discovered a well-preserved Mayan tomb from the fifth century A.D. The team came upon the tomb in the thick Petén jungle of northern Guatemala at a largely unexplored site containing four major temple complexes. Most previously discovered Mayan tombs had been ravaged by looters. This new find, fully intact, contained elaborate wall paintings, a male skeleton wrapped in a shroud, crafted pottery with hieroglyphics, and a screw-top jar. The artifacts are expected to tell scholars a great deal about Mayan life during the little understood Early Classic period. (*See also* ARCHAEOLOGY.)   P.J.M.

ANTIGUA AND BARBUDA. *See* STATISTICS OF THE WORLD.

ARAB LEAGUE. *See* INTERNATIONAL CONFERENCES.

ARCHAEOLOGY. In 1984 archaeologists discovered a rare intact tomb in Guatemala that may reveal much about the ancient Maya people. In Cyprus, evidence emerged of a first-century Roman city that could be as well preserved as Italy's Pompeii. A remarkable pair of Iron Age "chariot burials" were uncovered in Yorkshire, England. Off the coast of Turkey, the earliest shipwreck ever excavated yielded spectacular artifacts. In preparation since 1976, the first volume of a Sumerian dictionary made its appearance in May.

Intact Mayan Tomb. One of the most important archaeological events of the year occurred on May 15, when a team of archaeologists returned to the remote Petén jungle in northeastern Guatemala and uncovered an intact 1,500-year-old tomb among the ruins of a Mayan settlement near the Rio Azul (Blue River). The capstone had been detected in

1983 at the site, and the joint U.S.–Guatemalan expedition, financed by an emergency grant from the National Geographic Society, excavated the area as quickly as possible. Most Mayan tombs in Guatemala and elsewhere have been looted, so archaeologists were particularly excited to discover one that was untouched.

Inside they encountered three large wall paintings covered with Mayan symbols of authority. The expedition's director, Richard E. W. Adams of the University of Texas at San Antonio, believed that these and various artifacts that were found indicated that the occupant of the tomb, a male, was an administrator belonging to a ruling family of Tikal (a major Mayan city about 50 miles away). Adams dated the tomb to between A.D. 450 and A.D. 500, during the Early Classic Period. Fifteen pottery vessels and a number of carved jade beads helped in this determination.

Earthquake Victims on Cyprus. An initial five-week excavation at Curium, or Kourion, on Cyprus during the summer, under the direction of David Soren of the University of Arizona, turned up fascinating links to a disaster on the island that rivaled the volcanic eruption that buried Pompeii. According to preliminary reports, a late Roman community situated near the modern village of Episkopi was frozen in time when it was destroyed by an earthquake. The excavators' findings included the skeletons of a young girl and of a horse still tethered to a large feeding trough.

More than 350 Roman coins found in the excavated area all predate A.D. 365, which Soren hypothesized as a probable date for the earthquake. Soren argued that the earthquake was centered only 30 miles south of Curium and that the disaster might in fact have been the documented earthquake of July 21, A.D. 365, that shook the eastern Mediterranean.

A 1,500-year-old Mayan tomb, almost perfectly preserved, was uncovered by a National Geographic expedition deep in the jungle of Guatemala's northeastern Río Azul region. The elaborately painted burial chamber contained large wall paintings, rare pottery, and a shrouded male skeleton.

Chariot Burials in England. Two Iron Age chariot burials dating from the first to fourth centuries B.C. were uncovered in Yorkshire, England, this summer. Found at Wetwang Slack about 20 yards apart, they promised to be richer than any such graves discovered in Great Britain in the past hundred years. The chariots were expected to provide important information on prehistoric chariots, equipment, and weaponry, as well as on early Iron Age art styles. Ian Stead of the British Museum was in charge of the excavation.

One of the burials contained the body of a man (a warrior), and the other that of a woman. Each was buried with a side of pork, and each was surrounded by the parts of a dismantled chariot. The woman's grave contained richer bronze objects, including a mirror and a pin to hold her dress together. The most remarkable item, a find unprecedented for the Iron Age, was a bronze container with a small handle and a short length of chain. This may have been a "work box" that once held the woman's needle and thread. The decoration alone places it among the major early Celtic works of art in Britain.

The man's grave contained a particularly well preserved scabbard and hilt. Seven broken spearpoints had been destroyed intentionally and tossed into the grave. The sword, however, had been placed carefully over the body.

Bronze Age Shipwreck. A diving expedition led by anthropologist George F. Bass of Texas A & M University this summer began excavating the earliest shipwreck ever discovered. The ship, probably Greek, went down off the coast of Turkey in the 14th century B.C. with a cargo consisting largely of copper, tin, and glass ingots. Reportedly housing the most extensive collection of Bronze Age trade goods—including medallions, pottery, and gold objects—ever found beneath the sea, the wreck also yielded parts of the vessel's keel which, said Bass, "push back our knowledge of Mediterranean shipbuilding by nearly a millennium."

Sumerian Dictionary. A milestone in archaeological publishing was achieved in May with the appearance of the first volume of *The Sumerian Dictionary of the University Museum of the University of Pennsylvania*. The dictionary, under way since 1976, will revolutionize the study of the world's first great civilization, which flourished in the valleys of the Tigris and Euphrates rivers in what is now Iraq.

The Sumerians were prolific writers. Scratching wedge-shaped cuneiform symbols onto moist clay tablets, they described every aspect of their lives. Tens of thousands of these tablets have been unearthed by archaeologists during the past century. With the dictionary, the vocabulary of the tablets will for the first time have been collected and made available to all scholars in the field.   B.R.

ARCHITECTURE. The year 1984 may well be remembered for ephemeral architecture, which helped contain the costs of such events as the summer Olympics. Significant new buildings by Philip Johnson were among those completed, and the Museum of Modern Art reopened in New York City.

Ephemeral Designs. The privately funded Los Angeles summer Olympics was the year's most publicized design, as well as sports, event. The Los Angeles Olympic Organizing Committee decided not to build a large number of costly new facilities but, for the most part, to use existing ones scattered throughout the Los Angeles metropolitan area. The committee hired graphic designer Deborah Sussman of Sussman/Prejza and architect Jon Jerde of the Jerde Partnership to devise a design program tying together the disparate sites, spread over an area of about 450 square miles. Their solution—a canny concoction of stars and stripes, thousands of cardboard columns to remind viewers of ancient Greece, and snappy signs in bright Mediterranean colors such as deep pink and aqua—was intentionally geared to the television cameras. Splashy, pop—and inexpensive—this "Festive Federalism," as the graphics and architecture program was titled, may be a significant prototype for future Olympics.

Another city attempting to cut costs by substituting stage sets for architecture and reuse for new construction was New Orleans, host of the 1984 Louisiana World Exposition. Although failure at the box office led to a declaration of bankruptcy, this world's fair hoped to accomplish its aim of reviving a dilapidated waterfront warehouse district and turning it into a new tourist attraction. The Rouse Company, the power behind such successful urban

New York City's Museum of Modern Art unveiled its revamped quarters in May. Architect Cesar Pelli's glass-sheathed escalator bank, overlooking the museum's sculpture garden, was singled out for praise by many.

enterprises as Faneuil Hall in Boston, Harborplace in Baltimore, and South Street Seaport in New York City, was to convert part of the International Pavilion to a shopping center after the fair closed in November, and the collection of 19th-century warehouses renovated for the fair were to be converted to office and residential use. The two most memorable elements of the fair were to be torn down after the gates closed. One was Charles Moore's Wonderwall,

dubbed locally the "Great Wall of China as built by the Marx Brothers." It was a stationary Mardi Gras built of cardboard, wire mesh, and plaster of Paris. Los Angeles architect Frank Gehry's $5 million amphitheater, perched at the edge of the Mississippi River, was also to be dismantled after the festivities ended.

Museum of Modern Art. The much awaited reopening of the Museum of Modern Art in New York City earned mixed reviews. The

A fantasy made of cardboard, wire mesh, and plaster, Charles Moore's Wonderwall was an eye-catching sight at the 1984 Louisiana World Exposition; it was to be dismantled after the fair closed late in the year.

The Pittsburgh Plate Glass company's soaring Gothic headquarters, designed by architect Philip Johnson, was both criticized and applauded for its unusual medieval/modern look.

renovated and expanded museum, designed by Cesar Pelli & Associates of New Haven, was thought by some critics to be a functional but characterless essay in mainstream modernism. The MOMA condominium tower, completed months before the museum's May reopening, is a Pelli experiment in "decorating" the modernist glass box building, but the Mondrian-inspired facade, for all its shades of blue, gray, and white and elaborate mullion patterns, does not disguise the building's excessive bulk.

Philip Johnson. Architect Philip Johnson's much talked about tower for the American Telephone & Telegraph Company headquarters in New York City was completed at last in 1984. Even more outlandish to some critics, original to others, was the Pittsburgh Plate Glass Industries headquarters in Pittsburgh. Attributed

to the firm of John Burgee, Architect, with Philip Johnson, Consultant, the PPG headquarters, completed in late 1983 and formally dedicated in 1984, had a brilliant reflective glass tower crowned by Gothic spires and surrounded by low, cloister-like buildings. Almost as striking was Johnson's soaring art deco Transco Tower in Houston. Opened in 1984, the tower is a contemporary tribute to the monumental style of the Empire State Building.

Developments in Europe. In France there was a strong outcry over American architect I. M. Pei's scheme, unveiled in February, for a new entranceway for the Louvre, part of a major expansion of the museum. Pei, commissioned outright by President François Mitterrand without a competition, proposed a glass pyramid entrance pavilion at the center of the Louvre's main courtyard. Many considered the modernistic structure out of keeping with its surroundings, but Mitterrand was undeterred.

Elsewhere in Europe, several significant commissions were completed. British architect James Stirling's Stuttgart Museum, a witty and colorful structure that brings passersby into the museum with a curving sidewalk that cuts through the building itself, opened in March. Osward Matthias Ungers's architecture museum in Frankfurt, West Germany, is the first museum in the world dedicated solely to architecture. Its first show tackled the last 20 years of international architecture, examining all facets of the postmodern movement.

Awards. Richard Meier was honored this April as the sixth Pritzker Prize winner. Meier was awarded the $100,000 prize that accompanies "architecture's Nobel" for his "single-minded pursuit of new directions in contemporary architecture." What little surprise greeted the announcement stemmed not from Meier's obvious qualifications but from his nationality: Meier is the fourth American to win the international prize.

The same week that Meier won the Pritzker, New York *Times* architecture critic Paul Goldberger was awarded the Pulitzer Prize for criticism. The American Institute of Architects did not name a gold medalist this year but selected Kallmann, McKinnell & Wood as firm of the year; Ludwig Mies van der Rohe's Seagram Building in New York City won the

Twenty-five Year Award for distinguished and enduring architectural design. Ralph Erskine won the prestigious Wolf Foundation prize, Charles Correa the Royal Institute of British Architecture Gold Medal.

Revivals. Mies van der Rohe's last design before he died in 1969, for an office tower in the financial district of London, proved a source of controversy in 1984. Public hearings begain in May on an application by developer Peter Palumbo, owner of the architect's famous Farnsworth House in Plano, Ill., for a permit to build the tower. Preservationists and urbanists have objected to the project since the late 1960's, on the grounds that it would destroy or overshadow existing Victorian structures. Meanwhile, preparations for the 1986 celebration of the 100th anniversary of Mies's birth have begun in Chicago, and a group of Spanish architects completed a reconstruction, on the original site, of his innovative German pavilion for the 1929 International Exposition in Barcelona.

Another venerable architect, Frank Lloyd Wright, who died in 1959, was in the news. In June, even Wright experts were surprised when pieces of a house he designed for a New York City exhibition in 1953—the house was soon razed—turned up in a Westchester County, N.Y., basement. The pieces were sold at auction to Tom Monaghan, owner of the Detroit Tigers baseball team and a Wright buff, who planned to use them to reconstruct the house near Ann Arbor, Mich.

Obituary. Nathaniel A. Owings, 81, founding partner of the firm of Skidmore, Owings & Merrill, died on June 13. Although the firm that bears his name has come to symbolize corporate architecture in America, Owings in his later years became critical of mainstream modernism. As chairman of an advisory council on the redevelopment of Pennsylvania Avenue in Washington, D.C., and as a leader in the movement to protect California's Big Sur region, Owings castigated modernists and postmodernists alike for their failure to perceive and work for broader social goals.   D.D.B.

ARGENTINA. In 1984 the newly elected government of President Raúl Alfonsín had to grapple with serious domestic problems—among them, reform of the armed forces, justice for the relatives of those who had disappeared during the military's antiterrorist campaign, and revival of the national economy despite the burden of an enormous foreign debt of $45 billion.

Government and Politics. Alfonsín's Radical Party government, installed in December 1983, took definite steps in 1984 toward calling the armed forces to account. It repealed the military's amnesty decree of 1983 and carried forward proceedings against the nine military commanders who had composed Argentina's ruling juntas from 1976 to 1982—including ex-presidents General Jorge Rafael Videla, General Roberto Viola, and General Leopoldo Galtieri—charging them with "homicide, illegal privation of liberty, and torture of prisoners." In October, a federal court, citing "delays" by the military tribunal originally charged with trying those cases, transferred jurisdiction over them to civilian courts, although several other important cases remained under military jurisdiction. Evidence relating to atrocities under military rule was collected by the National Commission on the Disappearance of Persons, headed by novelist and social critic Ernesto Sabato. In a report issued on September 20, the commission said that at least 9,000 people had disappeared during the military's "dirty war" against dissidents (which began in 1976) and listed some 340 clandestine prisons that had been "run by high officials of the armed forces and security." As part of its program to curb the power of the armed forces, the government also cut the overall military budget by 40 percent, retired many high-ranking officers, phased down the conscript army from 100,000 to 80,000, and placed the country's large military-industrial complex directly under the Ministry of Defense's civilian control.

On June 7 the Radicals, Peronists, and more than a dozen smaller parties signed a pact that pledged them to defend Argentina's fledgling democracy and general goals. Despite the accord, conflict grew between the government and its Peronist opponents in Congress and the unions. Alfonsín's proposed reforms of union election rules were first defeated in the Senate and, as strike activity and labor protests over wage increases mounted, finally passed in a form favorable to the Peronist leadership of the General Confederation of Labor, the largest union grouping.

The end of censorship led to a cultural renewal, manifested in music festivals, art shows, and support for bookstores, cinemas, and the theater. University admissions were made open, and many of Argentina's 2 million exiles returned.

Economy. Alfonsín and his economic minister, Bernardo Grinspun, set three goals for the economy in 1984: to slow down skyrocketing inflation, to raise real wages, and to reactivate a stagnating economy. The year's budget, belatedly published in July, called for increases in spending on health, social welfare, and culture and education, accompanied by cuts in defense and national security. The principal problem was achieving all of this in the face of Argentina's foreign debt—the third-largest in the Third World.

By mid-1984 the economic plan was showing mixed results. The minimum wage was raised to 13,000 pesos a month in July (worth $220 at the then-current official rate of exchange), and real wages, which had dropped 30 percent from 1975 levels, had recovered some 20 percent in 1983 and another 4 percent by mid-1984. Still, the country was staggering under the weight of phenomenal inflation rates—an annual 433 percent in December 1983 and an estimated 648 percent as of September 1984. Exports did well, reaching $3.9 billion in the first five months of 1984 (against only $1.5 billion in imports), and the year's total was projected at $8 billion. A healthy trade surplus of $3.5 billion was projected for 1984. The trade figures represented a 50 percent increase over 1983 and were made possible largely by a successful wheat harvest.

Argentina played a major role in the emerging debtor nations' bloc, which saw 11 Latin American countries agree to coordinate information on regional debt negotiations. At a June meeting in Cartagena, Colombia, the group signed a declaration that the current debt crisis among many nations "could have grave political and social consequences" and that the debt issue was "not only a problem of the debtors but also of the creditors." At a second meeting in Mar del Plata, Argentina, Alfonsín urged that the region maintain a common front in dealing with its creditors.

Meanwhile, Argentina was struggling with its debt repayment problem. On March 31, Mexico, Venezuela, Brazil, and Colombia together lent $300 million to help Argentina pay overdue interest; another last-minute rescue operation on June 29 averted a second-quarter technical default. A further $900 million in interest payments was due at the end of September, at which time Argentina reached general agreement with the International Monetary Fund to institute austerity measures in exchange for new credit. U.S. and leading international banks subsequently reached a tentative accord with Argentina, calling for $4.2 billion in new loans, and in December the IMF approved a debt package with $1.4 billion in standby credits.

Foreign Affairs. A settlement was reached in the 100-year-old-conflict with Chile over the Beagle Channel. Vatican mediators secured an agreement from both sides to a compromise that would cede several islands to Chile but recognize the "bi-oceanic principle" south of Cape Horn (Argentinian sovereignty over Atlantic waters, Chilean sovereignty over Pacific waters). The terms were approved by the Argentine public in a November 25 referendum, by a margin of 77 percent to 21 percent, and the treaty was signed four days later in Rome.

In January a policy change toward the Central American conflict was announced, with Argentina halting sales of arms to the anti-Sandinista guerrillas and to Guatemala and joining in the call by the Contadora nations (Columbia, Mexico, Panama, and Venezuela) for a negotiated political settlement in the region. The shift was further indicated by a $49 million trade package with Nicaragua and a $600 million three-year credit line to Cuba for the purchase of Argentine goods.

See STATISTICS OF THE WORLD.   J.F.Jr.

ARIZONA. See STATISTICS OF THE WORLD.

ARKANSAS. See STATISTICS OF THE WORLD.

ART. The reopening of the Museum of Modern Art in New York City and the impressive prices paid for a variety of works were among developments in the art world during 1984.

Museum of Modern Art. Until its reopening in May, the Museum of Modern Art had been—

quite literally—in a mess since 1980. Over a four-year period, every piece in its collection was moved at least twice, as different portions of the old building were remodeled. The museum remained partially open for the first part of the renovation process, closing completely only during the final year of construction. Including both new construction and remodeled sections, the new MOMA doubled its available exhibition space.

An entirely new west wing, designed by Cesar Pelli, is contained in the first six floors of a 44-story condominium apartment tower. Meanwhile, some of the older spaces in the museum have been so significantly altered that they are hardly recognizable. Even the old sculpture garden has been modified by the addition of a bank of glass-enclosed escalators, a high-tech solution to the museum's internal traffic problems.

A major exhibition, " 'Primitivism' in 20th Century Art," assembled by William Rubin, the director of the museum's department of painting and sculpture, highlighted MOMA's fall season. Nearly 200 pieces of African, Oceanic, and North American Indian art—visually powerful, elemental, and often grotesque—were juxtaposed with paintings and sculpture of such artists as Picasso, Giacometti, and Miró in a demonstration of the roots of modernism. Many of the tribal pieces had actually been in the possession of the artists or known to have been seen by them; in other cases, similarities were "affinities," an emergence of artistic values startlingly related to the "primitive" as modern art evolved.

New Showplace. The Centre for the Fine Arts, Dade County's new museum, opened in Miami during the year. One of three buildings in the Metro-Dade Cultural Center, the South's newest museum will not form a collection of its own but will be a temporary home for touring works of art. The center's director, Jan van der Marck, hoped to be able to attract popular traveling exhibitions from other museums, as well as to originate traveling shows.

By adopting the role of temporary exhibitor, the center can make art of the highest quality available to its visitors. The opening exhibit was a good beginning. A fabulous show of more than 200 pieces ranging over the entire

Acrobats *is one of nine symbolic triptychs considered by many experts to be the crowning achievement of the German metaphysical painter Max Beckmann. (The center panel is shown here.) Rediscovered by the contemporary neoexpressionist movement, Beckmann was celebrated by a retrospective of his works that toured the United States in 1984, the 100th anniversary of his birth.*

history of art was put together through loans from 60 of the most distinguished museums.

Exhibitions. At the 41st Venice Biennale, American contributions, instead of being chosen by a member of the conservative "establishment," were selected by Marcia Tucker, who founded the New Museum in New York after she left the Whitney Museum several years ago. The exhibition, entitled *Paradise Lost/Paradise Regained: American Visions of the New Decade,* almost certainly gave European visitors a few works new to them. The show's intended theme was America, but that was about the only unifying element. Almost all of the artists represented in the exhibition were young. While most of the works were, in a sense, landscapes, the style and apparent content were varied, ranging from rather traditional pieces by April Gornick and George Green to the almost primitive, naive visions of Howard Finster and the sophisticated, totally of-the-moment work of Roger Brown and Eric Rischl.

The Metropolitan Museum's "Van Gogh in Arles" exhibition featured some of the French postimpressionist's most important work, including The Night Café, a masterpiece of emotional intensity.

A major retrospective of works by the French painter Pierre Bonnard (1867–1947) opened in February at the Centre Pompidou in Paris, later traveling to the Phillips Collection in Washington, D.C., and to the Dallas Museum of Art. The exhibition, which emphasized the artist's late works and included only a sampling of earlier paintings, was the first major reassessment of Bonnard in two decades. Jean-François Chevrier's catalog essay "Bonnard and Photography" attempted to link Bonnard's paintings to the large body of photographic negatives he is known to have made.

A highlight of the New York art year was *Van Gogh in Arles*, the first major exhibition ever of the 15-month period in 1888–1889 when Vincent Van Gogh made the bold explorations of subject, style, and color that marked the height of his career and a turning point in the development of 19th-century painting. Approximately 65 drawings and 75 paintings were arranged chronologically, taking the

viewer through the seasons, as Van Gogh encountered the town of Arles, its environs, and its people. The show opened at the Metropolitan Museum in October.

One of the hazards of a big solo exhibition is the difficulty of sustaining peak interest or excitement in a large number of similar works. The exhibition of paintings by the French artist Balthus, organized by the Centre Pompidou and the Metropolitan Museum of Art, faced just such a hazard. Balthus's personal style, when seen en masse, is diminished rather than enhanced. The real problem is not with the quality of his art, but with the fact that his works are so intimate and subtle. Although most critics seemed to agree that the exhibition was too much of a good thing, a few professed to have discovered that Balthus was overrated. The public disagreed, however, and prices for Balthus paintings rose dramatically. In 1984 two Balthus works sold for over half a million dollars each, including *La Sortie de Bain*, which established a new Balthus record at over $1.1 million.

Some critics reacted with diminished enthusiasm to a pair of retrospective exhibitions of work by Willem de Kooning, perhaps the last active first-rank master of the New York School. Separate but complementary exhibitions, of paintings and sculpture organized by Jörn Merkert and of drawings organized by Paul Cummings, were shown at three museums: the Centre Pompidou, the Whitney Museum of American Art in New York, and the Akademie der Kunst in West Berlin.

The Art Market. The duke of Devonshire offered to sell a small but select group of some 70 drawings by such artists as Raphael, Rembrandt, Lippi, Holbein, Mantegna, and Rubens to the British Museum for slightly less than $8 million. When the museum refused to buy at that price, the duke put them up for auction, where they sold in July for about $28 million. Most were purchased by the J. Paul Getty Museum in Malibu, Calif.

J. M. W. Turner's mid-19th-century oil painting *Seascape Folkestone,* which had been owned by Kenneth Clark, the late art historian, made art history itself. Bought from Lord Clark's estate for slightly over $10 million by a British dealer, it become the highest-priced painting ever sold at auction.

Thomas Hart Benton's ten-panel mural *America Today* was bought by the Equitable Life Assurance Society of the United States, to install in its new headquarters building in New York City. The mural was executed for the New School for Social Research at the height of the Depression, for virtually the price of its materials. Needing funds and reasoning that the mural was accessible to very few people, the school had sold it to a dealer with the stipulation that every effort be made to keep the panels together and in the United States. It was finally sold to Equitable for well over $3 million.

Forgeries. Two major museums, the Metropolitan Museum of Art in New York and the Kimbell Art Museum in Fort Worth, Texas, admitted that certain key works in their collections were not what they had been claimed to be.

At issue at the Metropolitan was the very heart of its collection of Renaissance decorative art: some 45 pieces were admitted in January to be 19th-century forgeries. Even the Rospigliosi Cup, attributed to Benvenuto Cellini and so often cited that it has, in fact, helped connoisseurs formulate a definition of Renaissance decorative art, was among the admitted forgeries. Two major factors made the discoveries possible. First, a collection of over a thousand drawings for Renaissance-style objets d'art, made by a 19th-century German gold-

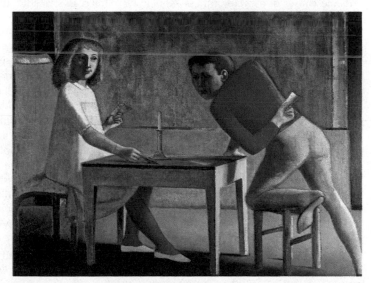

The Game of Cards, an oil painting by the French artist Balthus (Balthazar Klossowski de Rola), was one of the 112 works in a major retrospective at New York's Metropolitan Museum of Art. The exhibition, much of which was first seen at the Centre Pompidou in Paris, sparked interest from art lovers and critics.

smith and restorer named Reinhold Vasters, was discovered in the archives of the Victoria and Albert Museum in London, where they had gone unnoticed for more than 50 years. When it became apparent that these drawings were too detailed to be mere sketches of old pieces, museums all over the world began to examine their holdings closely. The second factor was a willingness by the museums to take the suspected objects apart to examine their materials and construction. The discovery of materials such as solder and of techniques for joining parts that were not used in the Renaissance made new dates absolutely essential. Some museums, like the Met and the Victoria and Albert itself, were able to trace many works in their collections to Vasters.

The probable forgery in Fort Worth was discovered through a somewhat different approach. When the Kimbell opened slightly over a decade ago, among its earliest and most acclaimed acquisitions was a series of frescoes purportedly salvaged from the apse of a French Romanesque church. Later, investigators noting stylistic similarities to the work of a known 20th-century forger conducted further technical, stylistic, and physical studies, which led them to conclude that the frescoes are most likely spurious.   E.S.R.

ASTRONOMY. Light "pollution" was a continuing problem for astronomers in 1984. Astronomers were also speculating as to the possible causes of a cycle of mass extinctions on our planet and analyzing the findings of the Infrared Astronomical Satellite.

City Lights. The biggest threat to optical astronomy is the glow in the sky at night caused by the lights of urban areas located near observatories. Particularly insidious sources of such "light pollution" are streetlamps that employ mercury or sodium vapor under high pressure. In February, astronomers at Palomar Observatory, whose 200-inch telescope is the largest in the United States, gained a major victory when the city council of nearby San Diego and the San Diego County Board of Supervisors agreed to use the only viable alternative, low-pressure sodium. In appreciation, the astronomers gave the name "San Diego" to a tiny asteroid discovered at Palomar in 1982. In December, the Board of Supervisors

also passed a law forbidding nonessential lighting after 11 P.M.

Palomar's sister observatory at Mount Wilson, northeast of Los Angeles, was less fortunate. Because of increasing light pollution, the Carnegie Institution of Washington, which operates the facility, decided to "mothball" its famous 100-inch telescope in 1985.

New Telescopes. The construction of two proposed monster telescopes moved closer to realization with the selection of final designs. One will be built by the University of California, thanks to a $36 million bequest. The main mirror will have a diameter of 10 meters (1 meter is 39.37 inches), twice that of the Palomar giant, and will comprise 36 2-meter nested hexagons. The other instrument, the National New Technology Telescope, is to be built for the National Optical Astronomy Observatories. It will have an effective diameter of 15 meters. The light-gathering surface will involve four mirrors, each 7½ meters in diameter.

Mass Extinctions. Evidence has been rapidly accumulating that, over a few hundred million years, the earth has suffered through at least 12 relatively brief periods in which families of living organisms died out in especially large numbers. Other mass extinctions can be identified yet farther back in the history of our planet. A study published in early 1984 found that these eras of death seem to occur at intervals spaced roughly 26 million years apart. If these conclusions are true, we are living halfway through such an interval—and the clock continues to run!

At least two explanations have been proposed. One hypothesizes that the sun has a companion star, dubbed Nemesis by one scientific team. Periodically, the star's gravitational influence would disrupt perhaps billions of the comets that are thought to exist in the far reaches of the solar system and send them earthward. The effect of the cometary bombardment on the earth would be to fling enormous quantities of debris into the atmosphere, thus dimming the sun's light, radically altering climate, and destroying many forms of life. A second explanation rests on the fact that the sun, as it moves in our Milky Way galaxy, periodically encounters huge clouds of interstellar dust and gas. One possible result is that the gravitational influence of such clouds could stir up the comet swarm.

See also LIFE SCIENCES: Biology.

Halley's Comet. Not expected to become widely visible until December 1985, Halley's Comet in 1984 remained a millionfold fainter than the naked eye can see. Good news for comet viewers, however, is that one study of the comet's appearances over the past 2,000 years indicates that when it becomes visible, Halley will be about five times brighter than previously anticipated. Thus, it will be more easily seen worldwide.

Infrared Astronomical Satellite. Many new findings were published stemming from the Infrared Astronomical Satellite, a U.S.-Dutch-British venture that operated for ten months in 1983. During its brief lifetime, IRAS discovered five comets—an unprecedented harvest for one instrument in so short a time. This success has been attributed to IRAS's extreme sensitivity to warmed dust and to the fact that many comets are much dustier than had been previously believed.

In 1983 it was reported that IRAS had detected around the bright star Vega a dust cloud that was warmer than the temperature of the surrounding space. At first, this observation was interpreted as indicating a planetary system in the process of forming. Now it appears, however, that a swarm of comets lying at a great distance from that star can also account for the data.

IRAS also gave astronomers new insights into the birth and old age of stars. The satellite's ability to see into dense clouds of dust revealed many sunlike stars just beginning to shine. One such object that was detected may be less than 24,000 years old, an eye blink in the history of the universe. Astronomers have for some time thought that stars cool as they approach old age, thereby permitting dust to form in their atmospheres. IRAS confirmed this idea, and it also found that many of these dying stars blow off interstellar dust bubbles during their waning years.

On a much grander scale, our Milky Way galaxy was found to contain vast clouds of very cold dust. Some of it forms long patches called infrared cirrus, a reference to a familiar cloud type in the earth's atmosphere. But much of it is found in a type of dust cloud that is more homogeneous and also more pervasive throughout the galaxy. The discovery of this material at least doubles the amount of non-luminous matter known to exist in the Milky Way. Thus it supplies some of the "missing" matter astronomers have long anticipated but could not detect. IRAS also looked at many distant galaxies and discovered that some of them emit over 1,000 times more infrared energy than a "normal" galaxy like the Milky Way. One such object, called Arp 220, emits 99 percent of its energy at infrared wavelengths. Extensive observations by ground-based astronomers indicate that this galaxy is probably undergoing an enormous burst of star formation at present.

Hub of the Milky Way. The nucleus of our Milky Way is hidden from sight by dust and gas, which can be penetrated only by infrared light and radio waves. Observations at these wavelengths have revealed such features as streams of high-velocity gas and a massive star cluster. A particularly unusual object, discovered in 1984, consists of an arc of parallel filaments, each some 130 light-years long and 3 light-years wide, that emit radio waves. These radio waves are highly polarized—a characteristic of radiation generated in a magnetic field. In this case the field is perpendicular to the plane of the galaxy. Rotation of the Milky Way carries gas across the magnetic-field lines, thereby converting mechanical energy into electricity. In other words, the hub of the Milky Way acts like a dynamo.

New Planet? University of Arizona astronomers announced in December the discovery of a huge gaseous object orbiting a faint star about 21 light-years from earth. Thought to be almost as large and 30 to 80 times as dense as Jupiter, it has an estimated surface temperature of 2,000°F. The discoverers considered the object as a new planet, the first direct evidence that other planetary systems exist; other researchers believed it might better be classified as a "brown dwarf," a failed star orbiting a true star. Further research was planned.   L.J.R.

AUSTRALIA. A generally optimistic tone prevailed in Australia during 1984 as the economy recovered from recession. Australians voted to

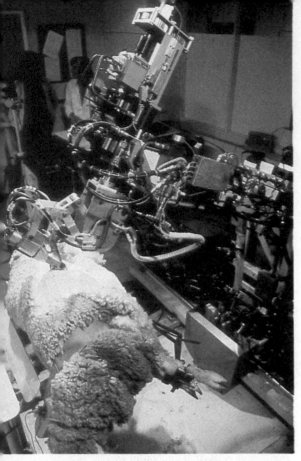

A sheepshearer shortage sparked the University of Western Australia's development of this robot shearer, which was expected to reduce the nation's $270 million annual wool-gathering costs. To guide its cutting operations, the robot's memory stores a map of a sheep's body.

cut from 25 to 16 seats in an enlarged 148-member House of Representatives. The Liberal and National parties that make up the conservative coalition gained 16 new seats. (In the enlarged Senate, the coalition won four new seats, Labor five; the small Democratic Party gained slightly, and a new antinuclear party won a seat.) The conservative gains confounded all pre-election polls, which had predicted a Labor landslide, and the results were seen as a personal setback for Hawke. The implications of a weakened Labor government for domestic and foreign policy were not clear.

Labor's lackluster showing may have resulted in part from disaffection on the part of leftists within the party, who opposed the more centrist policies of the Labor government. Among other things, the party's left wing had called for a ban on uranium mining and a prohibition against foreign military bases in Australia. Hawke sought to place much of the blame on complicated voting procedures, which had helped produce a large number of improperly marked, and therefore invalid, ballots. (Spoiled ballots amounted to about 7 percent of the total.)

Economic Developments. Australia's economy performed in a consistently encouraging fashion. It appeared that the recession had bottomed out in the second quarter of 1983. The financial year ending in June 1984 saw real economic growth of about 6.5 percent, and the rate of inflation had dropped to 7.5 percent. The number of people employed rose steadily, although this was not matched by an equivalent fall in unemployment.

A key economic decision, announced in December 1983, was to float the Australian dollar, whose value had for several years been fixed artificially by reference to a number of other currencies. The government also took steps in the direction of deregulating banks and moved to restructure Australian industry. Medicare, a health insurance system financed largely by a tax on incomes, was introduced in February, and tax cuts that reinforced the "accord" on prices and incomes between the Labor government and trade unions were introduced in August.

Crime and Corruption. A national furor erupted over allegations of corruption emanating from Labor-governed New South Wales. In February,

retain the Labor Party government, but by an unexpectedly narrow margin.

Elections. In October, Prime Minister Robert Hawke announced that a general election would be held on December 1, slightly more than halfway through his three-year term. During the seven-week campaign, Hawke's Labor Party stressed its "tremendous achievements in the economic and social fields and in the field of international relations." The opposition National-Liberal coalition, led by Andrew Peacock, focused its attack on Labor's taxation policies and on a new national health insurance plan, as well as on the issues of aborigine land rights, organized crime, and immigration policy. On election day, the Labor government was returned to power, but its majority was

a Melbourne newspaper began publishing a series of purported transcripts of telephone conversations illegally taped by members of the New South Wales police force since 1976. Some tapes suggested links between federal and state officials and organized crime figures, including drug traffickers. There also were taped conversations said to be between a Sydney solicitor, implicated in an alleged immigration racket, and Justice Lionel Murphy of the High Court of Australia, a radical jurist and a former Labor attorney general.

Initially, New South Wales Premier Neville Wran sought to minimize the scandal. After a month, however, he called an early election on the ground that his government had to demonstrate its credibility. On March 24 he was returned with a comfortable majority (although with fewer seats than he had had before the vote). Meanwhile, in the federal Senate, where Labor lacked a majority, the opposition established a select committee to investigate Justice Murphy's behavior. On August 22 the committee cleared Murphy of all charges suggested by the tapes, but it was split in its reaction to new allegations that the judge had attempted to improperly influence a state magistrate. A new Senate inquiry, completed in late October, found probable cause that he had exerted improper influence in the case, and

Judge Murphy then took a leave of absence from the court. In mid-December the director of public prosecutions announced that Murphy would be tried on criminal charges.

A moving incident was touched off when opposition leader Peacock accused Prime Minister Hawke of being soft on organized crime, including drug trafficking. Questioned about the charge during a television appearance, Hawke burst into tears. His wife, Hazel, subsequently revealed that the couple's 23-year-old daughter and her husband were under treatment for heroin addiction.

Foreign Affairs. In foreign affairs, Prime Minister Hawke followed a pragmatic policy. While seeking to maintain close ties with the United States, he set out early in the year on an 18-day, 17,000-mile visit to such neighbors of Australia as Hong Kong, Japan, South Korea, China, Singapore, and Malaysia. In each country Hawke talked principally about knocking down trade barriers. But he also stressed Australia's growing awareness of the need to play an active role in regional affairs rather than just being a European outpost on the rim of Asia.

Relations with neighboring Indonesia proved difficult. Visiting Jakarta in July, Foreign Minister Bill Hayden voiced Australia's reservations about Indonesia's annexation of East Timor,

Hawke Has His Wings Clipped

"Bob Hawke got a kick in the pants," gloated one opposition leader. Robert Hawke, head of Australia's Labor government, had risked his highly favorable image—he received a 70 percent approval rating in midyear opinion polls—by calling for early federal elections in December. The surprise result was a personal defeat for the ruggedly handsome prime minister who a year and a half earlier had engineered his party's most spectacular election triumph since World War II. Political pundits pondered the whys and wherefores of Labor's setback, with many pointing the finger at friction within Labor's own ranks. All agreed, however, that Hawke had been proved fallible and that he might find his freedom of action sharply limited in the future.

Robert Hawke

but he was rebuffed. Soon after, the Association of Southeast Asian Nations rejected Australian initiatives aimed at securing a dialogue with Vietnam and the withdrawal of Vietnamese forces from Cambodia.

The election of a fraternal Labor government in New Zealand in July presented problems for the Australian government. The New Zealanders were committed to prohibiting nuclear armed and nuclear powered vessels from entering their ports, a position Hawke had abandoned on his initial election in 1983. U.S. Secretary of State George Shultz, visiting the region in July for a meeting of Anzus Pact nations (Australia, New Zealand, and the United States), suggested that without port rights the alliance would be in jeopardy. Hawke was known to share his views. At a 14-nation meeting of the South Pacific Forum in Tuvalu in August, Hawke won agreement for the drafting of a treaty for a nuclear-free South Pacific; the terms would, however, still allow individual nations to decide whether to allow port rights to nuclear vessels of other nations.

Australian-Chinese relations proceeded smoothly. On a February visit to China, Hawke proposed that the two nations integrate their steel industries, with Australia providing raw materials and semifinished steel to Chinese mills. Later in the year, it was announced that Chinese and Australian interests would develop a new iron ore mine in Western Australia and that China had contracted to buy 2.5 million metric tons of Australian steam coal. The Australian government also announced it would grant a limited Australian banking license to the Chinese foreign trade bank, the Bank of China. In September, weekly flights between Australia and China were begun by the nations' international airlines.

See STATISTICS OF THE WORLD. B.J.

AUSTRIA. A sobering mood of pessimistic realism continued in Austria in 1984, the first full year of the coalition government of Chancellor Fred Sinowatz (Socialist Party) and Vice-Chancellor Norbert Steger (Freedom Party). This "hangover," following the heady years of spending under the Socialist government of the charismatic Bruno Kreisky, had significant economic symptoms. The iron and steel industries particularly required large-scale support in or-

der to remain competitive. The coalition government introduced tax increases, as well as an unpopular tax on interest on savings. Although by midyear the inflation rate was reported at about 5.5 percent—a figure lower than in many countries—a year earlier the rate had been less than 4 percent.

One of the bitterest public feuds was over the proposed construction of a hydroelectric plant in a nature reserve at Hainburg, on the Danube near the Czechoslovak border. This raised ecological and economic issues, with the unions favoring the project and conservationists opposing it. The Socialist Party, committed to full employment, backed the plant, and late in the year, the government announced that the project was officially approved.

In early September, Sinowatz reshuffled his cabinet. Among those departing were Finance Minister Herbert Salcher and Foreign Minister Erwin Lanc. Franz Vranitzky, director-general of Austria's second largest commercial bank, was named the new finance minister, and Leopold Gratz, the mayor of Vienna, was the new foreign minister. Some observers felt this reorganization was aimed partly at easing intraparty feuds involving Hannes Androsch, Salcher's predecessor as finance minister, who had been widely criticized for his personal financial dealings.

Austria's commitment to neutrality continued to present problems. Charges came from the United States that Austria had been shipping high technology to the Soviet Union. Austria protested sharply, but the matter was not settled without sour feelings both in Vienna and in Washington.

See STATISTICS OF THE WORLD. R.S.

AUTOMOBILE INDUSTRY. Sharply increased sales, healthy profits, and a swing toward midsize and luxury cars were key developments in the U.S. auto industry in 1984.

Sales. Passenger car sales in the United States during the 1984 model year totaled 10,322,417, an increase of 17.2 percent over 1983. Domestic producers sold 7,914,738 units, up 22.4 percent from 1983's total and their best showing since 1979. The Chevrolet Cavalier was the year's best-selling car. Midsize and large/luxury cars took almost one-half and one-fifth of the 1984 market, respectively.

A record 2,407,679 imported cars were sold in the United States during the 1984 model year, up 3.4 percent from 1983's total. Imports took 23 percent of the market, down from their all-time high of 27.8 percent in 1982. The top seller was Toyota, with 562,036 cars.

Truck sales surged to 3,919,594, an advance of 35 percent over 1983. Ford regained truck leadership from Chevrolet, selling 1,150,474 units, or 29 percent of the market.

Profits. The rise in sales, coupled with cost cutting, enabled the industry to earn record profits. GM netted $3.6 billion during the first nine months of 1984, compared to $2.4 billion in the first three-quarters of the previous year. Ford reported profits of $2.2 billion for the first nine months, up from $1 billion during the same period in 1983. Chrysler made $1.8 billion during the January–September period, an increase from $582 million over the first nine months of 1983. American Motors earned $12.3 million during the first nine months, after having lost $154 million during the same time span the previous year. The industry's full-year profits were expected to approach, if not exceed, $10 billion. Cash-rich GM spent $2.5 billion to buy Dallas-based Electronic Data Systems Corporation, the most expensive acquisition in the automaker's history.

New Models. Several aerodynamically styled replacements of fuel-sipping "econoboxes" were introduced. Quick to accelerate and easy to handle, some of the new cars are frank imitations of West Germany's prestigious Mercedes-Benz, BMW, and Porsche but are priced as much as $20,000 less than their foreign counterparts.

GM introduced three sporty front-wheel drive models—the Pontiac Grand Am, Oldsmobile Calais, and Buick Somerset Regal—as replacements for those companies' Grand Prix, Cutlass, and Regal models. The aerodynamically styled N body compacts were said to be keyed to the "yuppie" generation—young, urban professionals. Chevrolet unveiled the Sprint minicompact, the smallest car currently sold in the United States, in the summer and the subcompact Spectrum in the fall. Chevrolet's minivan, the rear-wheel-drive Astro, was introduced late in the year. In the spring, GM introduced new front-wheel-drive luxury cars—

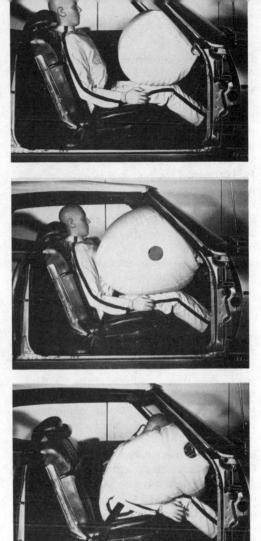

GREEN LIGHT FOR THE AIR BAG

Air bags or automatic seat belts may be mandatory in new cars by 1989. High-speed photographs above show how the air bag works: milliseconds after impact, the bag fills with nitrogen gas, cushioning the driver. It deflates almost immediately afterward.

the Buick Electra, Oldsmobile 98, and Cadillac de Ville/Fleetwood sedan.

Ford launched the luxurious West German–built Merkur (German for Mercury, the winged god), a sleek front-wheel-drive sedan sold throughout Europe as the Sierra. Chrysler unveiled three front-wheel-drive sports sedans—the LeBaron GTS, Plymouth Caravelle, and

83

Dodge Lancer—all derived from the firm's 600/ New Yorker sedans. American Motors introduced a convertible version of its Renault Alliance, the firm's first ragtop since the 1968 Rebel. Volkswagen's lagging Rabbit was replaced by the Golf (the name VW has used on the European version of the Rabbit) and its companion model, the Jetta.

Fuel Economy. For the second successive year, a gasoline-powered Honda achieved the best mileage among 1985 cars tested by the U.S. Environmental Protection Agency. Every top performer was powered by an imported engine, mostly diesels. Honda's Civic CRX hatchback led the mileage derby, achieving 49 miles per gallon in the city driving test, 54 mpg in highway testing.

General Motors and Ford, for the second successive year, failed to meet the U.S. government's required fleet mileage standard—set at 27 mpg on 1984 models. The companies avoided fines by applying credits gained from years when their cars bettered the standards. Not expecting to meet the 1985 model year standard of 27.5 mpg, the auto giants hoped the government would liberalize its requirements.

Labor. The United Automobile Workers and GM agreed on a three-year contract that provided some job security and modest wage hikes. The pact called for wage increases of 1 percent to 3.5 percent over the first year, based on job classification; productivity bonuses of 2.25 percent in each of the second and third years of the pact; improved pension benefits; and continuation of a modified cost-of-living allowance. The contract centerpiece was a six-year job security program calling for the company to establish a $1 billion fund to continue wages and benefits for workers laid off because of automation, other productivity gains, or foreign purchases in place of U.S. production. The fund was to be augmented by a $100 million job-protection plan designed to start new business ventures to employ some laid-off workers. The UAW-GM contract formed the basis for a UAW-Ford agreement that included a similar job security fund of $280 million, plus a moratorium on plant closings. That pact was ratified in October.

The Canadian branch of the UAW sought heftier wage hikes in lieu of job security in contract negotiations with GM in October. When GM offered instead a contract patterned on the U.S. agreement, some 36,000 workers struck GM's 13 Canadian plants. A settlement, ratified by the workers, ended the strike after almost two weeks.

Chrysler elected UAW President Owen Bieber to its board of directors, making the union leader only the second labor chief to sit on a major corporate board. Bieber's predecessor, Douglas Fraser, was the first.

Safety. The U.S. Department of Transportation ended a 15-year controversy over crash restraints by ordering that air bags or automatic seat belts be standard equipment in at least 10 percent of 1987 model cars. The percentage was to increase to 25 percent the following model year, 40 percent the year after, and 100 percent for 1990 models. The new regulation will not take effect, however, if states representing two-thirds of the total U.S. population pass mandatory seat-belt laws. Also, manufacturers will be exempt from compliance if they can equip cars with interiors capable of protecting passengers in a 30-mile-per-hour crash without the use of bags or belts.

Antilock brakes made their U.S. debut on 1985 models from two manufacturers. Ford installed a West German–made system on some Mark VII models, and Mercedes-Benz, which pioneered the advance in Europe, included antilock brakes on most of its models.

Recalls. On November 26, the U.S. Department of Transportation announced that General Motors Corporation was recalling 3.1 million of its 1978 to 1980 midsize cars for possible rear axle repairs—the largest recall of its kind since 1973. The callback followed reports of more than 1,000 rear-axle failures. The same day, Ford and Chrysler also announced recalls of various models to inspect and repair other potential safety defects. The General Motors recall was not formally ordered by the government and therefore not subject to federal supervision, a fact which drew criticism from safety advocates. A day earlier, in an unrelated action, GM refused a government request for a recall of 1.1 million 1980 X-cars, which the government contended had brake defects.

D.L.L

B

BAHAMAS. *See* STATISTICS OF THE WORLD. *See also* CARIBBEAN COUNTRIES.

BAHRAIN. *See* STATISTICS OF THE WORLD. *See also* PERSIAN GULF STATES.

BANGLADESH. In 1984, the military regime of President H. M. Ershad proceeded very slowly with its plans for reorganizing and decentralizing Bangladesh's governmental machinery and judiciary. The new system consisted of four levels: villages, grouped into unions; subdistricts, made up of a varying number of unions; municipal bodies; and the national Parliament.

On February 29, Ershad, under mounting political pressure, announced that elections for both the presidency and Parliament would be held simultaneously in May. But as relations between the government and the opposition failed to improve, he postponed the elections (just two weeks before they were to take place), until the end of the year. On October 11 he promised to begin rescinding martial law if opposition parties agreed to take part in the elections. Three days later, however, hundreds of thousands of people demonstrated in Dacca (Dhaka) to demand that a neutral caretaker government be installed to oversee the electoral process. Opposition parties did not file candidates, and the government announced yet another postponement, with no new date set. In late December, two people were killed when police fired on protesters during a 48-hour general strike. Hundreds were arrested.

On March 29, Ershad had appointed a new prime minister, 79-year-old Ataur Rahman Khan, ostensibly to help reach an accord with the political parties. In a further attempt to smooth the way for talks with the opposition, the government in early April had released over 200 political prisoners. The government had also instituted a land reform policy; it included a limitation on the acquisition of farmland, with families owning more than a set amount of land being prevented from acquiring any new land by way of inheritance, transfer, or gifts.

Of particular economic importance was the formal launching of the International Jute Organization in January, with Dacca as its headquarters. Its purpose was to examine ways and means for jute producers to improve their export levels.

Bangladesh's gross domestic product recorded a 3.7 percent growth rate in the 1983–1984 fiscal year. Although the agricultural sector's contribution to the GDP was the highest, it was lower than expected, in part because of heavy floods late in 1983. For the 1984–1985 fiscal year, government receipts were expected to amount to about $1.4 billion. The sector receiving the highest allocation was education.

Bangladesh's relations with India heated up when, in April, India began erecting a fence along the border between the two countries. India argued that the fence was necessary to prevent Bangladeshis from crossing illegally into its border state of Assam. The building of the fence led to clashes along the border.

See STATISTICS OF THE WORLD. S.-A.R.

BANKING AND FINANCE. Several large U.S. banks and savings institutions had serious problems in 1984. For most U.S. banking firms, however, the year saw earnings rise, a result of increased loan demand, relatively stable interest rates, and a decrease in the number of domestic nonperforming loans (in which the borrower, though still in business, cannot make payments). Foreign loans were another matter. Loans outstanding to Latin American debtors alone amounted to about 150 percent of the equity of major U.S. banks early in the year, and debtor nations struggled to deal with their debt problem and with austerity measures imposed on them by lending institutions.

Regulatory Changes. The problems with foreign loans pointed up U.S. bank weaknesses in two areas: the amount of primary capital maintained by many banks and the accounting techniques used for nonperforming loans. U.S. government regulators took steps to remedy these weaknesses.

85

Camping at the bank on Lexington Avenue in New York City, these hopeful homeowners were among thousands of prospective purchasers across the state who waited outside lending institutions to apply for a limited number of fixed-rate, reduced-interest mortgages, offered by the New York State Mortgage Agency on a first-come, first served basis.

In September, the Office of the Comptroller of the Currency issued a rule raising capital requirements for national banks. Under the new rule, all such banks, regardless of size, would be required to have total capital amounting to 6 percent of total assets. Of this, 5½ percent is to be in primary capital—those forms of capital that regulators consider most stable; one example of primary capital is capital surplus, income that remains after all financial commitments have been met. It was estimated that 151 national banks would have to raise $3.3 billion to meet the proposed new primary capital requirement.

In a June decision, both the Federal Reserve Board and the comptroller ruled that loans must be placed on nonaccrual status as soon as they become more than 90 days past due,

unless the loan is well secured and in the process of collection. Banks may not count as income unpaid interest on any loan in non-accrual status.

Step Toward Interstate Banking. In November the comptroller of the currency gave a number of bank holding companies permission to operate limited-service banking offices outside their home states. The Federal Reserve Board also had to approve the banks' applications. The comptroller's action was seen as a possible step on the way toward federal approval of interstate banking.

Troubled Banks. Nonperforming domestic loans almost caused the collapse of Chicago's Continental Illinois Corporation, the eighth-largest bank holding company in the United States as of the end of 1983. Continental had been hobbled by nonperformers, especially loans to energy-related companies. Some of these loans had been purchased from the Penn Square Bank of Oklahoma before it was closed down by federal regulators in 1982. In May 1984 rumors surfaced that Continental was on the verge of collapse. Its large certificates of deposit soon had to bear a higher interest rate in order to find buyers, and they were removed from the "run" of major banks—that is, they could no longer be traded interchangeably with the certificates of other major money-center banks. Continental obtained credit from the nation's largest banks and had access to the Federal Reserve's discount window for funding at a reduced interest rate. It was clear within a few weeks, however, that the firm would not be able to survive independently.

Help came on July 26, when the Federal Deposit Insurance Corporation announced an "assistance package" under which the FDIC would inject $1 billion in capital and acquire $4.5 billion in delinquent loans. The deal also included provisions for formation of a new holding company for the bank and replacement of Continental's two top officers. The controversial rescue constituted the largest package of federal support for any private enterprise in U.S. history. Some observers felt that the FDIC plan amounted to a "nationalizing" of the holding company, since the plan could ultimately leave the government with 80 percent of Continental's outstanding stock.

Another lender to the energy industry, InterFirst Corporation of Dallas, also faced serious problems. In January, the Securities and Exchange Commission ordered InterFirst to increase its reported third-quarter 1983 loss. The restatement was made necessary when the SEC challenged to the bank's tax-credit claim of over $50 million. The company wound up losing a total of $172 million in 1983, after posting $207 million in profits in 1982. As 1984 progressed, however, the outlook for the energy industry and its lender banks brightened. Most of the largest oil lenders, including InterFirst, were able to report profits through the first nine months of 1984.

The largest U.S. holding company of a thrift (savings) institution, Financial Corporation of America, ran into serious trouble when its management's aggressive financing style raised questions about the company's reliability. Among other things, Financial was criticized for its unconventional method of accounting for loans used to finance Government National Mortgage Association securities, or Ginnie Maes. The company's principal subsidiary, the American Savings and Loan Association, was facing a massive outflow of deposits, as major funding sources lost confidence in the firm, and there was talk of a federal bailout. On August 15, American Savings and Loan, under pressure from the SEC, reported a $78.9 million loss for the first half of the year, instead of the $75.3 million profit it had planned to report.

In August, the company, possibly under pressure from regulators, replaced its maverick chairman, Charles W. Knapp, with William J. Popejoy, formerly with Financial Federation Inc. Also, in order to gain increased liquidity, the company set up several swaps of some of its fixed-rate mortgages for securities, swaps made with the Federal Home Loan Mortgage Corporation and the Federal National Mortgage Association. These transactions brought $3 billion in funding to the ailing thrift. In September, Popejoy said Financial was seeking to raise $1 billion in new deposits through Wall Street brokerage houses and intended to shrink by $2 billion or $3 billion in assets by the end of the year; Financial later reported a third-quarter profit of $1.2 million, despite a heavy loss by American Savings and Loan.

Stock Market. During the first half of the year, the stock market retreated from the highs set in 1983, but the summer saw a strong recovery, based mainly on the perception that interest rates were going to ease, or at least stabilize at existing levels. The height of the stock market's summer rally came in early August, when new volume records were set on consecutive days. On August 2, a record 172.8 million shares were traded on the New York Stock Exchange. The following day, 236.6 million shares were traded. The burst helped lift the Dow Jones industrial average over 1200 and made the week the best ever for the stock market in both volume and price gains.

The stocks of financial services companies, including banks, thrifts, and brokerage firms, did not share completely in the stock market's summer turnaround. Bank stock investors were disillusioned by the impact of problem foreign loans and by the rising number of bank failures, which totaled 79 for the year. Thrift earnings were hurt by rising interest rates, and brokerage firms were still hurting from the poor markets of the first half of the year.

Later in the year, bond prices surged, and the stock market showed signs of rallying after weeks of sluggishness. On December 18, 169.1 million shares were traded and the Dow Jones went up by 34.78 points. The stock market rally proved to be short-lived, however, despite declining interest rates.

Interest Rates. The bank's prime lending rate, the base rate charged to business borrowers, stood at 13 percent in early September, up two percentage points from a year earlier. Other key interest rates had shown similar increases. Three-month commercial paper averaged 11.15 percent at the end of August, up from around 9 percent a year earlier; double-A-rated industrial bonds carried a 13.4 percent rate, up from 11.7 percent; and the federal funds rate, the rate of interest charged for overnight loans of excess reserves among commercial banks, was about 11.5 percent, up from less than 10 percent in 1983. By year's end, however, the prime rate and short-term interest rates had declined, with the prime rate back down to 10.75 percent. In late December the Fed cut its discount rate (for loans to financial institutions) to 8 percent, a six-year low.

Concluding a meeting of 11 Latin American nations in Colombia, Brazilian Foreign Minister Ramiro Saraiva Guerreiro is flanked by Venezuelan Foreign Minister Isidro Morales Paúl (left) and Argentine Economy Minister Bernardo Grinspun as he signs a joint statement calling for more help from lending nations.

The Dollar. Fueled by high U.S. interest rates, which drew investment funds to the United States, the value of the U.S. dollar relative to other major currencies soared. In September the dollar broke through what currency traders considered an important psychological barrier, becoming worth more than three West German marks for the first time since 1973. It also surged to all-time highs against the currencies of Britain, France, Italy, Denmark, Finland, Norway, and Sweden.

International Debt Crisis. Many of the world's developing nations, particularly those in Latin America, continued to grapple with the problem of repayment of foreign debts. Amid talk that default by the debtor nations could precipitate worldwide financial chaos, lender nations, such as the United States, began to recognize the need for long-range plans to deal with the debt crisis. Debtor nations, chafing under strict austerity measures imposed by lending institutions such as the International Monetary Fund (IMF), began to question the validity of such plans. This criticism became more pointed when debtors, expected to increase taxes and tighten government spending,

saw lender nations use deficit financing to pull themselves out of recession.

A major issue among the debtor nations was the large U.S. budget deficit, which was seen as keeping interest rates dangerously high and volatile. For these nations, interest payments on their foreign debt were already diverting large portions of export earnings from internal development. A sharp rise in interest rates would sabotage any progress toward solution of the debt problems. A new factor was the trend toward increased protectionism on the part of developed nations, which would hurt the export earnings of the debtors.

Agreements. A number of countries reached important agreements with creditors. Of particular note, Mexico, in September, reached a provisional agreement with its lender banks to restructure half of its $96 billion foreign debt. Under the terms of the agreement, $48.5 billion of principal falling due between 1982 and 1990 was rescheduled for payment over the next ten to 14 years. Another part of the agreement effectively lowered the interest rate Mexico was to pay on its debt. Mexico had to make no principal payments on the resched uled debt in 1985, $250 million in 1986, $500 million in 1987, and $1 billion in 1988. The agreement reflects a flexible approach urged by U.S. Federal Reserve Board Chairman Paul Volcker, who contended that Mexico should be "rewarded" for adopting stringent austerity measures.

Venezuela announced in late September that it had reached an agreement in principle with foreign banks to restructure $20.75 billion of its $27.5 billion in foreign debt. Payments on Venezuelan debt maturing between 1983 and 1988 were to be stretched out for 12½ years, beginning in mid-1985.

Brazil, the world's largest debtor nation, owing a total of about $98 billion, signed a loan pact with lenders in January that gave it $6.5 billion in new credit and rescheduled another $5.5 billion in debt.

Taking an aggressive stance, Argentina rebelled against sharply reducing economic growth in order to repay foreign debt. The new civilian government of President Raúl Alfonsín said it would reject standard austerity measures prescribed by the IMF, and it requested new loans on easier terms. Protracted negotiations followed between the Alfonsín government and the IMF, with the Fund pressing Argentina on the issues of wage control, growth of the money supply, and currency devaluation. A tentative accord was finally worked out under which Argentina agreed to institute some austerity measures, in return for $1.4 billion in fresh credits from the IMF, to be drawn over 15 months. Argentina then reached a tentative agreement in November with a group of major commercial banks that would result in a new $4.2 billion loan and the rescheduling of $13.4 billion in payments over a period of 12 years. Further negotiations led to a final agreement with the IMF on December 28.

An important debtor nation outside Latin America was the Philippines, which had a total debt burden of more than $25 billion in 1984. Under an agreement finalized in November, the Philippines government pledged to reduce its budget deficit, more tightly control the money supply, and curb inflation; in return, it received a $630 million standby credit from the IMF—and soon was able to obtain new credit from commercial banks.

Suspended Payments. Bolivia and Ecuador both rebelled at making payments on their foreign debt. On May 30, Bolivia announced that it was suspending payments to commercial banks on $1.05 billion in debt, and was also limiting repayment to international lending agencies to 25 percent of export earnings. The Bolivian government took this move after determining that payments on its total foreign debt would have amounted to about $977 million in 1984 and that it stood to earn only about $850 million from exports during the year. In June, Ecuador suspended payments on $247.5 million in debt falling due between then and the end of 1985. In December, the steering committee of Ecuador's creditor banks agreed to reschedule about $4.3 billion in public-sector debt and to provide over $1 billion in new financing.

Meetings of Debtor Nations. On June 21–22, ministers of 11 Latin American debtor nations met in the resort town of Cartagena, Colombia, to discuss ways of easing the burden of the region's foreign debt. Participants included the four largest debtors—Brazil, Mexico, Argentina, and Venezuela—as well as Bolivia, Chile, Colombia, the Dominican Republic, Ecuador, Peru, and Uruguay. The major concerns at the meeting were high U.S. interest rates and the protectionist trade policies of the developed nations. Rejecting the hard line taken earlier by Argentina in its dealings with the IMF, the conference gave assurances that Latin American nations did not plan to form a "debtor's cartel" but called on the industrialized nations to provide more help in shouldering the burden of world debt.

A second meeting was held in September, at Mar del Plata, Argentina. Stressing that a long-term solution to the debt crisis could not be worked out solely with foreign banks, the conference invited leading industrialized democracies to participate in a government-to-government dialogue some time in 1985.

J.P.F.

BARBADOS. *See* Statistics of the World.
BEHAVIORAL SCIENCES. *See* Health and Medicine *and* Life Sciences.
BELGIUM. The center-right coalition government of Premier Wilfried Martens showed continued stability during 1984; its main problem

was coping with the burden of heavy public expenditures. In March the government won a parliamentary confidence vote for a new program of spending cuts, aimed at reducing the net treasury borrowing requirement by 1987 to 7 percent of gross domestic product, compared with 12.5 percent in 1983. Among the new austerity measures, public and private sector employees were required to forgo a yearly 2 percent wage-indexation increase; these funds were to be allocated to the social security system. A comparable levy was imposed on the incomes of self-employed persons. Social security benefits were also reduced by 2 percent through 1986, although guaranteed minimum wages were to be increased by 2 percent in 1985 and 1986, and rent increases were to be restricted to the rate of wage indexation.

Belgium and Luxembourg signed a ten-year agreement to realign production, coordinate reductions in capacity, and restore profitability to their steel industries. Cockerill–Sambre, Belgium's financially troubled, state-controlled steel company; Arbed, the Luxembourg steel giant; and Sidmar, a jointly owned enterprise, agreed to continue financial, production, and marketing operations separately, while coordinating activities through a joint steering committee. The restructuring and reductions were expected to lead to eventual loss of 10,000 jobs in the two countries.

The Martens government succeeded in reducing the public net cash deficit from 14.4 percent of gross domestic product in 1983 to an estimated 13.3 percent in 1984. Nevertheless, the deficit remained one of the highest in Western Europe. Industrial output was forecast to increase in 1984 by about 4.5 percent and overall gross domestic product by 1.5 percent.

In October, a bomb seriously damaged the Brussels offices of Honeywell, a U.S. defense contractor that supplies missile components. Responsibility for the bombing, and for two other bombings of defense contractors in Brussels, was claimed by a group called the Communist Combatant Cells.

The Belgian government encountered opposition from the United States over a plan to sell a high-technology lathe to the Soviet Union. The U.S. government contended that the computerized machine would facilitate Soviet weapons production and was banned for export to the Soviet bloc under rules of the Coordinating Committee for Multilateral Export Controls, a Western group that screens exports to Communist countries. Belgium claimed the machine had been modified so that it did not violate COCOM rules. The controversy was resolved in August when the United States agreed to pay part of the purchase cost of the lathe, which was then to be bought by the Belgian Army.

In late November, the government announced it was delaying until 1985 a scheduled final decision on whether to allow deployment of 48 U.S. cruise missiles on Belgian soil.

See STATISTICS OF THE WORLD.   W.C.C.

BELIZE. In a general election on December 14, 1984, voters in Belize—a small, English-speaking democracy in Central America—turned out of office Prime Minister George Price, who had dominated Belizean politics for more than two decades, and his left-of-center People's United Party (PUP). Price, who had not lost an election in 30 years, was even denied his old seat in the 28-member lower house of the National Assembly. The conservative opposition United Democratic Party (UDP), headed by Manuel Esquivel—a former physics teacher and, since 1979, a member of the appointive Senate—won 21 Assembly seats, leaving the PUP with only seven. The results surprised many observers, who had expected a close election.

Economic issues played a major role in the campaign. Price, who had led the country to independence from Great Britain in 1981, was criticized by the opposition for excessive government control of the economy and for a failure to diversify the economy and attract foreign investment. A degree of disaffection with the Price administration was evidenced earlier, on January 13, when the UDP won all nine contested seats in municipal elections.

A major foreign-policy issue concerned Britain's continued military presence in Belize, which was strongly supported by the opposition—in part because the British presence contributes about 15 percent of Belize's gross national product.

See STATISTICS OF THE WORLD.   T.G.S

BENIN. See STATISTICS OF THE WORLD.
BHUTAN. See STATISTICS OF THE WORLD.
BLACKS IN THE UNITED STATES. The presidential candidacy of Jesse Jackson drew millions of blacks across the nation into the political process for the first time in 1984. Meanwhile, the more conservative political climate in Washington, D.C., was reflected in decisions by the Civil Rights Commission and the U.S. Supreme Court.

Civil Rights Commission. In January, Linda Chavez, appointed by President Ronald Reagan to be the new staff director of the Civil Rights Commission, recommended basic changes in the commission's agenda. The new program, she said, may reveal the adverse aspects of affirmative action, racial quotas, court-ordered busing, and bilingual education. Chavez declared that in the areas of housing, employment, and voting rights, numerical underrepresentation should not be presumed to imply discrimination. She noted a general decline in academic standards coinciding with affirmative action in college admissions and hiring. Chavez also urged a study of what she called the "radical" principle of equal pay for comparable jobs performed by men and women, which could "alter our existing marketplace economy." Chavez canceled a number of projects planned by the former CRC and placed controls on reports issued by state advisory groups. In other actions, on January 17 the commission officially renounced, by a 6–2 vote, the use of racial quotas for the promotion of blacks; this reversed the longstanding posture of previous CRC policy statements. In July, Clarence Pendleton, Jr., chairman of the CRC, protested President Reagan's hosting of a luncheon for black members of the administration; Pendleton said that such a luncheon was contrary to the policy of "working toward a race- and gender-neutral and color-blind society."

Supreme Court. The Reagan administration took a strong stand against the concept of affirmative action, which presumes a positive duty to remedy past discrimination against minorities. On June 12 the administration was given a major victory when the Supreme Court ruled in *Firefighters Local Union No. 1784* v. *Stotts* that an employer may not be compelled to override a valid seniority system in order to protect blacks against layoffs. The Reagan administration had vigorously supported the white firefighters of Memphis, Tenn., in their battle to preserve the seniority practice of "last hired—first fired," regardless of race. In its decision, the Court declared that remedies are available only to specific victims of discrimination and not to general classes of people. Assistant Attorney General William Bradford Reynolds, the Justice Department's civil rights chief, indicated his intention to use the decision to challenge several other pending cases relating to preferences in hiring and promotion on grounds of either race or sex. In July, Reynolds announced that federal fair housing laws do not require racial integration or "any particular balance in a neighborhood"; he said that the Justice Department was participating in suits to eliminate low-income housing quotas and race-conscious remedies.

National Politics. Black participation in politics reached a new peak in 1984, when the Reverend Jesse Jackson became the first black to make a serious bid for a major-party presidential nomination. He captured about one-sixth of the votes in the Democratic primaries. Although that total included few whites, blacks registered and turned out in record numbers to vote for him and boost him to a third-place finish at the national convention.

The long-term impact of the Jackson campaign could not be predicted. In the South, as whites shifted toward President Reagan and other Republican candidates, the Democratic Party in some states became increasingly populated by blacks—possibly hastening the day when the parties might be divided along racial lines. Nationwide, Walter Mondale won nine out of ten black votes on November 6. Blacks made no inroads in the U.S. Congress; the new U.S. House was slated to have ten black members, a decline of one.

See also PEOPLE IN THE NEWS: Jesse Jackson.

Self-Appraisals. Leaders of more than 100 organizations met at Fisk University in Nashville in May at a "Black Family Summit" to assess the problems and opportunities facing blacks. John Jacob, president of the National Urban League, warned that "we may have allowed our just anger at what America has done to

Participants in a voter registration drive, members of the National Association for the Advancement of Colored People carry "voter apathy" in a symbolic casket as they leave Richmond, Va., in August for a 350-mile march to New York City.

obscure our own need for self-discipline." He expressed concern that half of all black babies are born to unmarried women, that almost half of black families are headed by women, and that 70 percent of black single mothers live in poverty. Other statistics were equally distressing: unemployment among black men (16 percent) was nearly three times as high as among white men, and black family incomes averaged only 56 percent of white family incomes. Robert Hill of the Bureau of Social Science Research said blacks had relied too much on the government and needed to return to their basic institutions, such as the churches. Benjamin Hooks, executive director of the NAACP, said that blacks "must control our own destiny" by establishing and supporting black entrepreneurs, publishing the works of black authors, making venture capital available to black businesses, and joining the military to learn basic skills.

At a conference in Washington marking the 20th anniversary of the Civil Rights Act of 1964, black leaders concluded that this legislation had been a "modest achievement" which merely gave blacks what whites had already taken for granted. The civil rights leader Coretta Scott King said that although segre-

gationists no longer stood in schoolhouse doors, "segregated housing patterns and more subtle forms of racism prevent equal access to a quality public education." Louis Harris, the public opinion analyst, said that feelings of alienation and powerlessness among blacks had risen sharply over the past two decades.

M.Gr. & D.Y

BOLIVIA. On June 30, 1984, Bolivian President Hernán Siles Zuazo was kidnapped from the presidential palace and held prisoner for ten hours. Without backing from the armed forces, however, the apparent coup attempt collapsed. The president was released by his captors in ten hours, after he had arranged refuge for them in the Argentine embassy; they surrendered a few days later. Investigation revealed that the instigators were senior military officers, narcotics policemen, and civilian accomplices. Army Colonel Rolando Saravia Ortuño went into hiding when he was named as the leader. Some 100 people were arrested in the continuing probe, but most were released for lack of evidence.

In mid-August, the Bolivian government—in an operation financed by the United States—moved soldiers into the central Chaparé region the country's cocaine marketing and produc tion center. This action followed U.S. complaints that Bolivian authorities were not acting sufficiently to control drug traffic. However, the traffickers learned in advance that the soldiers were coming and fled from the area. Siles Zuazo subsequently announced he had decided to negotiate with drug traffickers, in an effort to end the drug trade. When the Bolivian legislature voted in October to censure that decision, the president staged a hunger strike in protest.

Siles Zuazo had some success in coping with disaffection within the military and the ruling coalition. In April, Jaime Paz Zamora, leader of the Revolutionary Left Movement (MIR), re-allied himself with the government, and Siles Zuazo appointed four MIR ministers to his cabinet. In July the president sought to placate military officers by replacing certain regional commanders.

In economic matters, the government announced in May that it was suspending payments on its burgeoning foreign debt until agreement could be reached with creditors. Late in the year, the powerful Bolivian Workers Central (COB), seeking wage increases and price controls, staged a series of nationwide strikes that paralyzed the country's economy. Amid the continuing protests, the government announced a 330 percent wage increase, which the union asserted was insufficient to offset new steep price increases and continuing high inflation, estimated at over 1,000 percent.

See STATISTICS OF THE WORLD.   L.L.P.

BOTSWANA. See STATISTICS OF THE WORLD.

BRAZIL. The prospect of elections for Brazil's first civilian president in two decades dominated the political scene in 1984. The government planned indirect elections, by a 686-member electoral college, to take place January 15, 1985. The opposition parties pressed unsuccessfully for a direct popular election instead.

Political Events. From January to late April 1984 the opposition, tapping enormous public support, organized demonstrations in every major city in favor of direct popular elections. The largest demonstrations took place on April 10 in Rio de Janeiro, where well over half a million people gathered, and on April 16 in São Paulo, where more than 1 million Brazil-

ians marched and rallied. In February the major opposition party, the Brazilian Democratic Party Movement (PMDB), introduced before Congress a proposed constitutional amendment to allow direct elections in November 1984.

On April 16, Brazil's incumbent president, General João Baptista Figueiredo, proposed a compromise amendment, retaining indirect elections in 1985 but calling for popular elections in 1988. Two days later, the government declared emergency measures in the capital city of Brasília and ten surrounding areas to curb unrest; the University of Brasília was closed, following student protests, and censorship was temporarily imposed on the media.

The PMDB proposal failed to win passage in Congress by the necessary two-thirds vote. The measure was, however, supported by 298 of the 479 deputies, and more than 50 members of the ruling Social Democratic Party (PDS) voted in favor of it. Opposition leaders then submitted another direct-vote proposal. After a lull in public activity, 10,000 people staged a protest against the government's voting laws on June 1 in Brasília. Later in June, Figueiredo withdrew his amendment, apparently for fear that opponents could force changes in it should it come to a vote.

Meanwhile, Figueiredo's control of his own party seemed to be slipping, as serious rifts occurred over the choice of a presidential candidate. There were four announced candidates: Vice-President Aureliano Chaves, former São Paulo Governor Paulo Salim Maluf, Interior Minister Mário Andreazza, and Senator Marcos Maciel. Before the party's August convention, however, Maciel and Chaves joined a dissident faction, the Liberal Front, which opposed Maluf's candidacy and allied itself with the opposition PMDB. The PMDB agreed to give the Front the vice-presidential slot on its ticket and several key ministries in exchange for its electoral college votes. Maluf, a wealthy conservative businessman well known for his assiduous courting of potential allies through favors and promises, defeated Vice-President Andreazza by 493 votes to 350 to win nomination at the PDS convention. As expected, the opposition PMDB, in alliance with the Liberal Front, gave the presidential nomination to Tancredo Neves, governor of Minas Gerais and a respected moderate. Toward the end of the year, Neves was attracting increasingly broad support.

Economy. Brazil continued to be plagued by falling demand, declining productivity, galloping inflation of over 200 percent, erosion of living standards, and high unemployment. The austerity program imposed by the government, to comply with the International Monetary Fund's guidelines in an attempt to pay off the huge foreign debt, brought no signs of recovery.

In order to finance its debt payments, the government cut imports by devaluing the cruzeiro and stimulated exports by seeking new markets. These policies resulted in a sizable trade surplus. Cutbacks in public spending also reduced import demand.

The political opposition and a large segment of the business community blamed Brazil's dismal economic conditions on the government's handling of the foreign debt. The debt was thought by many to reflect, in part, the legacy of decades of unrestricted state intervention in the economy. Others, however, advocated increased state intervention and abandonment of austerity measures.

Foreign Relations. After long negotiations, Brazil and the United States signed a military

Half a million Brazilians took to the streets of Rio de Janeiro in April to demand direct presidential elections. The massive rally climaxed months of political turmoil sparked by the military government's plan for selection of the new civilian president in 1985 by an electoral college.

cooperation agreement in February, restoring a relationship that was broken off in 1977 because of the military regime's anger over U.S. State Department criticism of human rights violations. In October, Brazil signed a military cooperation accord with Saudi Arabia, opening the way to arms sales to the most lucrative arms market in the Middle East.

See Statistics of the World. E.P.

BRITISH COLUMBIA. See Statistics of the World. See also Canada.

BRUNEI. On January 1, 1984, Brunei, the tiny, oil-rich sultanate on the island of Borneo, became fully independent, after 96 years of British rule. (The official name of the country is "Brunei Darussalam," meaning "Brunei, Abode of Peace.")

Formal celebration of independence was delayed until February 23, which was selected by religious officials as an auspicious date and designated as the first national day. Foreign guests included Britain's Prince Charles, the kings of Malaysia and Tonga, and the heads of government and other representatives of over 70 nations. Highlight of the four-day celebration was a banquet for more than 4,000 guests in the opulent new $250 million royal palace. The occasion received wide coverage from the international media, as much for the splendor of the palace, with its approximately 2,000 rooms and its air-conditioned stables, as for the festivities themselves.

The sultan, Sir Muda Hassanal Bolkiah, retained full authority, assuming the positions of head of state, prime minister, and minister of internal affairs and of finance. Most of the ministries were put in charge of members of the sultan's family: defense was given to his father, Haji Sir Oman Ali Saifuddin, who had abdicated in 1967 in favor of his son; foreign affairs to his brother Prince Muhammad; and culture, youth, and sports to his other brother, Prince Jefri, who was also named deputy finance minister.

Upon its independence, Brunei joined the British Commonwealth of Nations. On January 7, the nation also became the sixth member of the Association of Southeast Asian Nations (Asean). In September, Brunei became the 159th member of the United Nations.

See Statistics of the World. K.M.

Newly independent of Britain, the lilliputian sultanate of Brunei boasts a gargantuan home for its ruler, Sir Muda Hassanal Bolkiah (top). Said to be the largest royal residence in the world, the palace has two gold-leafed domes, 16 acres of marble floors, and an 800-car garage.

BULGARIA. Bulgarian Communist Party chief Todor Zhivkov completed his 30th year in power in March. By contrast to similar anniversaries in 1974 and 1979, the milestone was passed over in silence. The occasion found Zhivkov still fit at the age of 72. With the economy relatively sound, his position remained unchallenged. Ever a faithful ally of the Soviet Union in its years under Soviet leader

95

Leonid Brezhnev, he was not highly regarded by Brezhnev's successor, Yuri Andropov, but the accession of Konstantin Chernenko to power after Andropov's death in February restored Zhivkov's standing in the Kremlin.

A national party conference met March 22–23 after a year of planning. The largest Bulgarian party forum ever convened, it was attended by over 2,900 delegates. Its aim was to mobilize the entire party membership (823,000 people, almost 10 percent of the nation) to the task of improving quality of production.

In March, Zhivkov paid an official visit to Libya. Agreements were signed by Zhivkov and Libyan leader Muammar al-Qaddafi concerning the nearly 9,000 Bulgarians working in the country. In September, Zhivkov canceled a scheduled visit to West Germany. The action apparently resulted from pressure by the Soviet Union, which was worried by West German moves to improve relations with Eastern Europe.

In April, Bulgaria and Italy exchanged new ambassadors in a step toward resumption of normal diplomatic ties. Both countries had recalled their envoys in 1982 after the arrest in Rome of Bulgarian Airlines representative Sergei Antonov on suspicion of involvement in an assassination attempt on Pope John Paul II. Meanwhile, however, the case remained in the news. In October an Italian judge ordered Antonov (who remained in custody in Italy), two other Bulgarians formerly employed in the Bulgarian embassy in Rome, and four Turks to stand trial on charges of conspiring to kill the pope. Italy requested extradition of the former embassy employees, but, Italy has no extradition treaty with Bulgaria, and the two men remained in Bulgaria late in the year. In an open letter to the Italian prosecutor they protested that they were innocent.

See STATISTICS OF THE WORLD   R.A.P.

BURKINA FASO. See STATISTICS OF THE WORLD: Upper Volta. See also AFRICA.

BURMA. During 1984, Burmese government troops launched a heavy offensive against an estimated 5,000 Karen ethnic insurgents; it started in January and continued into the monsoon season in June, long past the time government offensives usually had concluded in the past. The effort was handicapped by a lack of an effective air-strike capability and by the nearly impregnable location of Karen strongholds. The Burmese army also struck strongly against former Nationalist Chinese irregulars, who were now engaged in the opium trade, as well as against insurgent Shan tribesmen, who were involved in drug production and traffic.

The Central Court of Justice in April rejected the appeal of Brigadier General Tin Oo, former head of Burmese intelligence, who had received five concurrent life sentences following his conviction on charges of corruption and misuse of office in 1983. Many felt that the conviction of Tin Oo reflected the fear of Burma's aging, iron-fisted leader, General Ne Win, that Tin Oo was amassing too strong a personal following.

Repercussions continued from the October 1983 bombing in the capital city of Rangoon, in which 17 Burmese and four visiting South Korean officials were killed. An appeal of the death sentences of the two surviving assassins, apparently North Korean terrorists, was rejected by the Burmese Supreme Court. Nonaligned Burma, which had broken relations with North Korea after the bombing, improved ties with South Korea, whose president had narrowly escaped assassination in the incident. Burma also improved relations with its neighbors. The Chinese foreign minister paid a visit to Rangoon in February, and Burma and India agreed in April on a delineation of the maritime boundary in the Andaman Sea, the Coco Channel, and the Bay of Bengal.

Burma's legal, socialist economy and its black market counterpart continued to function in tandem. Most medicines, car parts, shoe and plastic goods—up to 80 percent of the country's consumer goods in all—were probably being smuggled in. Illegally exported timber, precious stones, and other commoditie helped pay for the imports. The world's larges opium producer, Burma was expected to produce a record 1984 crop, despite government efforts in opium crop eradication. Japan, Burma's main source of foreign aid, extended a $18.5 million loan for airport, railroad, industrial, and medical projects.

See STATISTICS OF THE WORLD.   R.B

BURUNDI. See STATISTICS OF THE WORLD.

C

CABINET, UNITED STATES. See PRESIDENT OF THE UNITED STATES.

CALIFORNIA. See STATISTICS OF THE WORLD.

CAMBODIA. The war in Cambodia (Kampuchea) entered its sixth year in 1984, with no sign of an immediate solution. Vietnamese occupation forces, which had concluded a successful invasion of Cambodia early in 1979, controlled the capital city of Phnom Penh, all major towns, and most roadways. But the three major Cambodian resistance forces (the Communist Khmer Rouge led by Pol Pot; the non-Communist Khmer People's National Liberation Front, or KPNLF, led by Son Sann; and Prince Norodom Sihanouk's National United Front) made new inroads in western Cambodia, cutting off highways and transportation routes deep inside the country.

The Heng Samrin regime, installed and protected by the Vietnamese occupation troops, took new steps to enhance its claim as the legitimate government of Cambodia, signing major trade protocols with East Germany, Hungary, and the Soviet Union, as well as with Vietnam. The government also levied agricultural taxes, a tax based on land holdings in the provinces, and another tax on merchants.

The number of Vietnamese settlers rose for the second year, bringing the total in Cambodia to at least 300,000. Some became merchants in the capital; others fished or farmed.

The 1984 dry season was marked by greater fighting in the interior of Cambodia than any previous year, as Vietnamese forces clashed with resistance groups. The army of Phnom Penh, allied with the Vietnamese forces, continued to stay out of the main fighting. Early in the year, the Khmer Rouge claimed to have struck against major Vietnamese installations in northwest Cambodia, including an oil depot near the Vietnamese military headquarters at Siem Reap. The Vietnamese mounted a major offensive against the resistance in April. They successfully attacked a Khmer Rouge logistics base, a KPNLF camp at Sokh San, and a Khmer Rouge camp at Ban Scarat. Nearly 70,000 Cambodians fled the assaults, more than 40,000

taking refuge in Thailand. Vietnamese soldiers pursued their adversaries into Thailand, prompting a Thai complaint to the United Nations. Vietnam responded that Thailand had violated Cambodian airspace in its support of Cambodian antigovernment guerrillas.

Beginning in late November, the Vietnamese launched a new and well-prepared offensive against resistance bases in Cambodia, especially those of the KPNLF. Heavy casualties were reported, and over 60,000 people fled, many crossing the border to Thailand.

Son Sann's KPNLF appeared to gain ground in recruits, after having watched the Khmer Rouge win more recruits the previous year despite the record of atrocities during their rule in the late 1970's. Both groups appeared to benefit from renewed fears of Vietnamese plans to colonize Cambodia. China remained the chief source of military supplies for resistance forces. The Association of Southeast Asian Nations joined Son Sann in appealing to the United States to give arms to the non-Communist resistance, but the request was refused.

Foreign aid to the Cambodian government was diminishing amid pessimism about the prospects for internal peace. Factory output reportedly doubled in 1983, but the Cambodians were forced to trade precious rice and fish for manufactured goods from Vietnam. The 1984 estimated rice deficit was 177,000 tons, and one aid group warned that Cambodia could face a famine in 1985.

See STATISTICS OF THE WORLD. E.H.B.

CAMEROON. See STATISTICS OF THE WORLD.

CANADA. Canadian politics in 1984 underwent its greatest upheaval in a generation. Pierre Elliott Trudeau—since 1968 leader of the Liberal Party and, with a brief interruption, prime minister—retired in midyear. There followed a federal election that produced a Progressive Conservative Party government with the largest majority any party had ever won in the House of Commons. By the time Conservative leader Brian Mulroney (see biography in PEOPLE IN THE NEWS) was sworn into office as Canada's 18th prime minister on September

17, the Tory landslide appeared as nothing less than a seismic shift that had transformed the political landscape.

The Campaign. The chain of events began to unfold on February 29, when Trudeau ended months of speculation about his possible resignation by announcing his decision to leave politics. Within weeks, seven men were contesting the Liberal Party leadership, to be decided at a convention in mid-June: former Finance Minister John Turner (see biography in PEOPLE IN THE NEWS); Energy Minister Jean Chrétien, a powerful cabinet member and a long-standing ally of Trudeau; Economic Development Minister Donald Johnston; Employment Minister John Roberts; Justice Minister Mark MacGuigan; Indian Affairs Minister John Munro; and Agriculture Minister Eugene Whelan. However, the race was really between two main contenders—Chrétien and Turner.

Chrétien, the son of a mill worker from Shawinigan, Quebec, was a sentimental favorite. After growing up in a tar-paper house, he became a lawyer-politician in his 20's. He never lost the cheerful cockiness of a smart kid who had mastered street fighting early. Turner exuded the wealth and manner of his Toronto law practice and his corporate directorships. In 1968, as an ambitious young member of Parliament, Turner lost a party leadership race to Trudeau. He then held a series of senior portfolios under Trudeau before resigning from the cabinet in bitterness in 1975.

At the June convention, it took two ballots for Turner to gain a winning majority, receiving 1,862 votes to Chrétien's 1,368 and Johnston's 192. In the end, the delegates had decided that Turner was their best hope to beat Mulroney, an electrician's son who had become a rich and prominent Montreal lawyer (and president of the Iron Ore Company of Canada) before winning the Tory leadership in 1983. Many Liberals had concluded that, after Trudeau, English-speaking Canadians would not vote for another French-speaking Liberal leader. Also appealing was Turner's apparent position slightly to the right of both Chrétien and Trudeau.

Turner formally became prime minister on June 30. Although he had promised change during his campaign for the leadership, virtually all his cabinet appointees were Trudeau holdovers.

On July 9, after a flight to London to consult Queen Elizabeth and receive her agreement to postpone a scheduled summer visit to Canada, Turner announced that the nation would go to the polls September 4. Heartened by a Liberal

Goodbye to All That
Pierre Elliott Trudeau was a fixture in Canadian politics when he stepped down in 1984, after nearly 16 years as prime minister of Canada. He had been elected Liberal Party leader and then been swept into office on a wave of "Trudeaumania" in 1968, at the age of 48. From the first he communicated an aura of energy and joie de vivre. At home, he grappled untiringly with economic problems and vigorously supported the cause of national unity; opposing the separatist movement in his native Quebec, he led an ultimately successful drive to gain a new national constitution for Canada. He also sought to make Canada more independent of the United States, both by reducing U.S. ownership of Canadian business and by giving his country a distinctive voice in world affairs. A proud nationalist, Trudeau told an emotional audience just before his departure, "Our dreams for this beautiful country will never die."

Pierre Elliott Trudeau

"The Mighty Mulroney Machine," as the Canadian press dubbed Brian Mulroney's Progressive Conservative campaign organization, rolled to a stunning victory when Mulroney (pictured with his wife, Mila) was swept to power by a landslide vote in September elections.

surge in public opinion polls, Turner promised voters "a renewal of confidence and certainty." Mulroney urged Canadians to hold Turner and the Liberals to account for the Trudeau record. Mulroney said, "There is nothing wrong with Canada that a new government can't change." Edward Broadbent, leader of the New Democratic Party (NDP) (see biography in PEOPLE IN THE NEWS), scorned both Mulroney and Turner as spokesmen for corporations and the rich, referring to them as "the Bobbsey Twins of Bay Street." Mulroney chose to run in the Quebec district of Manicouagan, which included his hometown of Baie-Comeau, to bolster his party's struggle to win seats in traditionally Liberal Quebec. Turner ran in the district of Vancouver Quadra, to highlight his attempt to renew Liberal fortunes in the West.

From the start of the two-month campaign, Turner stumbled over matters of both style and substance. He never recovered from the sizable number of patronage appointments handed out immediately before and after he took office. A score of Liberal members of Parliament and dozens of other party supporters were rewarded with judgeships, positions on government boards, or ambassadorships—some by Trudeau, others by Turner under a written agreement with his predecessor. Mulroney ably exploited the episode as an abuse of power by a party too long in office. (Under Lester Pearson and Trudeau, the Liberals had held power since 1963 except for several months in 1979–1980.) Turner's speaking style never became comfortable or effective, his campaign organization was anything but organized, and he responded clumsily to an issue as bizarre as it was unexpected—his habit of patting women's bottoms in public. In a campaign in which women's votes carried considerable weight, Turner took a month to apologize.

Mulroney, meanwhile, ran an almost flawless campaign with a smooth organization. An

The Conservatives' Landslide

	PC	Lib.	NDP
Percentage of popular vote[1]	50	28	19
Seats In the House of Commons, by province and territory:			
Alberta	21	0	0
British Columbia	19	1	8
Manitoba	9	1	4
New Brunswick	9	1	0
Newfoundland and Labrador	4	3	0
Northwest Territories	2	0	0
Nova Scotia	9	2	0
Ontario[2]	67	14	13
Prince Edward Island	3	1	0
Quebec	58	17	0
Saskatchewan	9	0	5
Yukon Territory	1	0	0
Totals	211	40	30
1980 election results	103	147	32

[1] Minor parties and independent candidates won 3%
[2] An independent won one seat

Note: PC = Progressive Conservatives, Lib = Liberals, NDP = New Democratic Party

early bantering wisecrack about his own patronage plans embarrassed him, but he immediately apologized and turned the issue back on Turner, particularly in two nationally televised debates that left Turner looking nervous and defensive. Mulroney made a string of promises for economic revival but was vague about how they would be financed without enlarging the government deficit. As the weeks passed, the Liberals' early lead in the opinion polls vanished, and the Conservatives appeared on their way to a decisive majority.

Election Sweep. On election day, the forecasts proved right. Mulroney's Progressive Conservatives won an astonishing 211 seats in the 282-seat Commons, commanding majorities in all regions (see the accompanying table). The Liberals took just 40 seats, their worst showing since Confederation in 1867. The NDP, whom some observers had expected to be swept away in a Tory tide, won 30 seats—two fewer than they had in the previous Parliament. In Quebec, a Liberal stronghold for most of this century, the Conservatives won 58 of the province's 75 districts; they had obtained only one in the

1980 election. Turner did win his own Vancouver district, one of just two Liberal victories in the four western provinces. Of the 25 Turner cabinet members who ran for reelection, 15 fell to defeat. Said Turner on election night, "The people of Canada, coast to coast, have spoken, and the people are always right." Concluded Mulroney, in Baie-Comeau, "Our objective and our mandate is to create jobs and to get the economy of Canada moving again."

Mulroney's new cabinet included 11 more ministers than had served under Turner and boasted greater regional representation: a total of 13 posts were held by western Canadians. Eleven Quebecers were also named, as well as six women. In a Throne Speech read by Governor-General Jeanne Sauvé, Mulroney presented his agenda to Parliament on its opening November 5. His priorities included restoring a "true partnership" between Canada and the United States and dealing with the budget deficit.

Foreign Affairs. A major foreign-policy issue during the campaign was that of promoting a nuclear weapons freeze by the Soviet Union and the United States. The Trudeau cabinet had consistently opposed the freeze concept, but several Liberal parliamentary candidates (and the NDP) nonetheless endorsed the freeze proposal—among them, Liberal Party President Iona Campagnolo. She argued that Canada should press nuclear de-escalation on Washington. Turner and Mulroney, however, refused to endorse the freeze. Turner said he would continue the disarmament policy of Trudeau who had engaged in a round-the-world diplomatic mission to promote arms control negotiations between East and West.

During his last months in office, Trudeau was under attack for a five-year agreement with the United States, signed in February 1983, enabling U.S. cruise missiles to be tested in Canada. A coalition of peace groups and labor unions even took the cabinet decision to court, arguing that the tests would violate a constitutional right to "security of the person." Meanwhile, the first test occurred over northern Canada in March 1984. Such winter tests were intended to simulate air-launched cruise flights over snow-covered Siberia. While Trudeau described the decision to allow the testing as a contribution to the defense of the Western alliance, it was clearly also aimed at maintaining Canadian influence in Washington.

Economic Developments. The Canadian economy had emerged from a deep recession in 1983. But it was in the grip of two contrary forces: the stimulus of vigorous growth in the United States and the depressing impact of high domestic interest rates. A symptom of these conflicting pressures was the declining Canadian dollar, which fell about 6 U.S. cents in the first half of 1984, to a record low of 74.86 U.S. cents on July 11; as of late 1984, it had climbed back up to around 76 cents. In December, unemployment stood at nearly 11 percent. The gross national product was expanding moderately, but prospects for continued recovery were uncertain.

The falling Canadian dollar made Canadian goods cheaper in the United States, and exports across the border consequently soared. By midyear, the United States was taking more than 80 percent of all Canadian exports, compared to a normal share of about 65 percent. Clearly, the U.S. boom was fueling the Canadian recovery, and Canada showed a healthy trade surplus despite rising imports from Europe (where currencies declined against the Canadian dollar). But the higher value of the U.S. dollar meant higher prices for imports from the United States.

In response to high interest rates in the United States, the Bank of Canada maintained a policy of setting high central-bank rates—largely to prevent capital outflows that would cause sharp declines in the Canadian dollar. As a result, the Bank of Canada rate rose, peaking at 13.26 percent on July 12. (It later declined to less than 12 percent.)

Transitions. Jeanne Sauvé, a former cabinet minister and speaker of the House of Commons, succeeded Edward Schreyer as governor-general in May, becoming the first woman to serve in that post. Bora Laskin, chief justice of the Supreme Court of Canada, died on March 26, at 71. Named as his successor in mid-April was Brian Dickson, a Supreme Court justice since 1973. The following month, Gerald Le Dain was promoted to the Supreme Court from the Federal Court of Appeal.

Legislation. Two controversial bills became law during the first half of the year. The Canada Health Act, enacted in April, empowered the federal government to curtail medical insurance funding to provinces that permit doctors or hospitals to levy fees higher than those set under Canada's national medical insurance plan. Parliament also passed a bill in June setting up a civilian Canadian Security Intelligence Service to replace the scandal-plagued security service of the Royal Canadian Mounted Police. A royal commission previously found the RCMP Security Service had committed a

Canadian history was made in May when Jeanne Sauvé was invested as the nation's first woman governor-general. For Sauvé, 62 years old at the time, the honor capped an 11-year career in federal politics, following almost two decades as a prominent public affairs journalist.

variety of crimes, including thefts, break-ins, and illegal use of income tax returns.

Regional Review. Economic recovery was uneven in Canada's ten provinces and two territories. Industrial Ontario did relatively well; the unemployment rate was 8.5 percent in August, as against a national rate of 10.5 percent. In May the Conference Board of Canada forecast that Ontario would outstrip the other provinces in economic growth in 1984–1985, largely because of a projected 20 percent pickup in the automobile industry. The board predicted a 3 percent growth rate for Quebec, slightly above the national average; despite that province's steady recovery from the 1982 recession, however, unemployment was expected to continue at around 13 percent.

High unemployment, around 14 percent as of autumn, also afflicted the economies of British Columbia and New Brunswick. In both provinces the government instituted budget cuts in social programs, and New Brunswick reduced allocations for short-term job creation, from $15 million in 1983–1984 to $12 million in 1984–1985 (Canadian dollars used throughout).

In the prairie provinces of Alberta, Saskatchewan, and Manitoba, drought—in some areas the worst in 65 years—seriously affected grain production; adding to the problem were continuing low wheat prices, which in Saskatchewan, producer of 60 percent of Canada's wheat, accounted for a 35 percent decline in farm income in 1983. However, unemployment in Saskatchewan, as of August, was a moderate 7.2 percent; it was also relatively low in Manitoba, where the government nonetheless allotted $210 million in 1984–1985 for a provincial jobs fund.

Petroleum continued to be a bright spot in the economy. Because of higher prices for new oil discoveries, exploration was increased in Alberta. In Saskatchewan, the oil industry set records for drilling and sales of oil and gas exploration rights, and the federal and provincial government agreed on terms for a $3.2 billion heavy oil project. In the Northwest Territories, construction was under way on a $450 million, 545-mile underground pipeline intended to carry oil from the northern Mackenzie Valley to existing lines in Alberta.

A dispute between the federal government and the province of Newfoundland and Labrador, over rights to the rich Hibernia oil field on the Grand Banks of Newfoundland, was resolved in March when the Supreme Court of Canada unanimously confirmed a lower court's ruling that the federal government was the unchallenged owner of the continental shelf's mineral resources; the province, however, hoped to arrive at a favorable political settlement with Ottawa. A series of development agreements between Ottawa and Prince Edward Island were signed, totaling more than $120 million; they were aimed at funding programs in the province's main industries over a five-year period.

In Nova Scotia, Canada's largest fishing company, National Sea Products Ltd. of Halifax, was saved from bankruptcy when the federal government and a consortium of provincial businessmen invested a total of $30 million in the company. Depressed fish prices, however, continued to plague the industry, as did dwindling supplies of certain fish. In New Brunswick, commercial salmon fishermen accepted a federal government offer of $4,000 apiece not to fish, as part of an effort to conserve stock.

At Annapolis Royal, Nova Scotia, the first tide-powered hydroelectric plant in North America began operation. The $55 million plant had a capacity of about 20 megawatts of electricity.

In provincial elections in November, Premier John Buchanan of Nova Scotia led the Progressive Conservatives to their third consecutive victory, as they captured 42 of the provincial legislature's seats; the Liberals took six, the New Democratic Party three, and the Cape Breton Labor Party one.

Language issues continued to be important. In Manitoba, a local lawsuit that had wended its way to the Supreme Court of Canada threatened to invalidate all the province's 4,500 laws passed since 1890, when English was established as Manitoba's only official language, unless and until they were translated into French. In Quebec, a Supreme Court decision on July 26 declared unconstitutional sections of a French Language Charter that limited access to English-language schools to the chil-

What, Canadian beer drinkers wondered, will they think of next? The reactions of Andy Marcolini's customers at the Brunswick House in Toronto range from incredulity to amusement as the tavern manager serves their beer in newfangled, long-necked bottles, the first variation in 23 years from the short brown bottles traditionally used by Canadian brewers.

dren of those who had attended such schools in Quebec. In Ontario, legislation was enacted to make French an official language of the province's court system and allow all children the right to education in either French or English.

The official adoption, in May, of bilingualism in the Northwest Territories drew the opposition of local Inuit and Dene (Eskimo) groups, who feared their own native languages would be supplanted. Native claims were recognized in the Yukon Territory in March when the federal government granted land and hunting rights, as well as a multimillion-dollar cash settlement, to the Inuvialuit (MacKenzie Delta Eskimos).

Sporadic violence hit Quebec during the year. On May 8, a Canadian Armed Forces corporal, Denis Lortie, entered the National Assembly building in Quebec City and opened fire on bystanders with a submachine gun, killing three and wounding 13. On September 3, a 30-pound bomb exploded in Montreal's Central Station train terminal, killing three people and wounding more than 40 others. The bombing took place six days before the visit to Quebec of Pope John Paul II, and an anonymous note sent to station officials a few days before the bombing called for "the end of the unholy Vatican." On November 25, a predawn explosion in a 21-story apartment building in Montreal killed four men; police

believed they might have been making a dynamite bomb when the device exploded.

Papal Visit. Canada, whose population includes 11.9 million Catholics, warmly welcomed Pope John Paul II as he paid a historic 12-day visit in September. His itinerary encompassed the breadth of the nation, from St. John's, Newfoundland, to Vancouver, British Columbia, and included an unscheduled stop in Yellowknife, Northwest Territories, when fog prevented an airplane landing in Fort Simpson. During the visit, John Paul delivered strong statements in support of the right of self-determination for Canada's native Indian and Inuit peoples and condemned abortion.

Short Beer. One notable institutional change had nothing to do with politics. The stubby brown Canadian beer bottle, which every national brewery had used since 1961, suddenly lost its monopoly when several brewers introduced long-neck bottles for their own brands.

Royal Visit. Queen Elizabeth II, initially accompanied by Prince Philip, paid a 14-day visit to three Canadian provinces during September and October. The royal visit coincided with the 200th anniversary of the settlement in Canada of Loyalists who left the United States after the American Revolution, as well as with the bicentennial of New Brunswick and with Toronto's 150th anniversary.

See STATISTICS OF THE WORLD.   J.H.

CAPE VERDE. *See* Statistics of the World.

CARIBBEAN COUNTRIES. Economic realities returned to center stage in the Caribbean Basin in 1984 as excitement over the October 1983 U.S. invasion of Grenada began to fade into the background. With economic indicators generally negative for the region, the 13-member Caribbean Community (Caricom) agreed in July to give a higher priority to regionally made goods over products from abroad. President Ronald Reagan's Caribbean Basin Initiative (CBI), providing for duty-free access to U.S. markets for certain products, took effect January 1, but got off to a slow start. The U.S.-encouraged emphasis on security—some say "militarization"—was reflected in an infantry training program initiated by the United States in Jamaica and Barbados for military personnel from seven islands.

Haiti. Claude Duvalier, Haiti's official president-for-life, made fitful gestures toward complying with the provisions of a bill adopted by the U.S. Congress in late 1983 that set conditions for continued U.S. economic aid. The bill stipulated that Haiti must take steps to curb illegal immigration to the United States, cooperate with various relief programs, and implement political reforms. U.S. Secretary of State George Shultz certified to Congress in January that Haiti was making a concerted effort to correct political and social abuses and thus deserved continuing U.S. assistance. Duvalier called for parliamentary elections on February 12, the first since 1979. However, all but one of the 309 candidates competing for 59 assembly seats were members of Duvalier's party, and exiled opposition leaders were not allowed to return during the campaign. In March, Duvalier promised a free press and protection of human rights. But after opposition papers blossomed with criticism of the regime, Duvalier shut them down and banned all opposition political activity. In a follow-up report to Congress in May, Shultz requested continued aid for Haiti despite what he saw as critical lapses on its part.

Hungry people rioted in Cap-Haïtien and other northern towns in late May; in Gonaïves, mobs attacked a police barracks, military-owned shops, and food stores. Three persons were killed and dozens were injured in the riots. Duvalier sent in soldiers but sought to conciliate people by replacing local officials and distributing food and money. He fired five cabinet ministers, but the underlying problems of food shortages, police brutality, and corruption remained.

Low world prices reduced income for Haiti's principal exports, sugar and coffee, and production declined in the wake of the 1983 drought. Efforts to restock hog herds eradicated to prevent the spread of African swine fever proceeded slowly. Tourism continued to decline, in part because of concerns about a possible link between Haitians and the disease AIDS (acquired immune deficiency syndrome). However, Haiti's assembly industries, attracted by low wages, a productive labor force, and duty-free tariff preferences granted under the CBI, continued to expand. During the past decade, these industries have created 40,000 to 60,000 jobs.

Dominican Republic. Refinancing of the Dominican Republic's foreign debt, receipt of new U.S. aid, and restoration of investor confidence all depended on whether the nation would receive new assistance from the International Monetary Fund that had been arranged in 1983. The IMF had insisted on adoption of austerity measures, including large price increases on basic foodstuffs. Such increases adopted in April, proved intensely unpopular, strikes called in response by labor and business leaders got out of hand as slum dwellers rioted and looted. Some 4,000 people were arrested in a harsh crackdown by soldiers and police that left 50 dead and hundreds wounded. In August, the government bowed to IMF pressures and raised fuel prices. Other required measures were under discussion.

Declining world prices for sugar and bananas, a high rate of inflation, idle industrial capacity, and 30 percent unemployment continued to impair the economy. Pope John Paul II briefly visited the Dominican Republic, along with Puerto Rico, in October.

Suriname. Blaming Prime Minister Errol Alibux for the economic woes that had caused thousands of workers to strike and to call for free elections, Suriname's ruler, Lieutenant Colonel Dési Bouterse, dismissed Alibux and his cabinet in January. Wim Udenhout, a former English teacher, was named head of an "interim" cabinet in February. At a convention in May the February 25 Movement, formed by Bouterse in 1983 to institutionalize his revolution, chose its leaders and began efforts to revitalize fading support for the regime.

A five-week strike by bauxite workers that ended in late January cut production and depleted foreign currency reserves. The strike, joined by bank employees and electricity workers, had been triggered in part by an increase in income taxes, which the government rescinded. The settlement included the promise of a loan of approximately $200 to each worker and immunity from disciplinary measures for having gone on strike.

Trinidad and Tobago. Trinidad and Tobago experienced labor strife and other problems, as it continued to adjust to the aftermath of its recent oil boom. One bright spot was the fact that, after five years of decline, oil production stabilized during the first six months of 1984. Also, the government reached an agreement in principle with Texaco Inc. to buy for US$175 million the assets of its local subsidiary, including a refinery. After the visit of a Chinese delegation, the government announced an agreement on trade and economic cooperation with the People's Republic of China.

Jamaica. The economy received a lift as bauxite production rose sharply. In addition, during the first half of the year, tourist arrivals were running 3.6 percent above 1983's record pace. A loan of US$143.5 million from the IMF was expected to provide further economic relief. However, the cost of living rose by 20 percent in the first six months of 1984, and unemployment was above 20 percent. A food relief plan brought free milk, cornmeal, and rice to nearly half the population.

Guyana. High budget and trade deficits and a large foreign debt continued to threaten the economy. Following a sharp fall in production of Guyana's three main products—rice, sugar, and bauxite—President Forbes Burnham asked the Guyanese to make "attitudinal changes" and consume more local products. After the government devalued the dollar in January, the United States approved a $40 million loan from the Inter-American Development Bank. Later in the year, Burnham visited Bulgaria, North Korea, and China, where he reportedly reached major trade and aid agreements.

Bahamas. In December, a royal commission report to Parliament concluded that the smuggling of large amounts of drugs through the Bahamas had corrupted police officers and cabinet ministers and created large numbers of young addicts. Two cabinet members and a senator were specifically accused of taking bribes or of connections with organized crime. The report found no evidence linking Prime Minister Lynden Pindling to bribes from drug dealers, but two of the three commission members concluded that Pindling and his wife had spent substantial sums of money over and above Pindling's salary over the past few years. Opposition members of Parliament called for Pindling's resignation.

Elections. The ruling parties in St. Christopher and Nevis (St. Kitts–Nevis), Turks and Caicos, and Antigua and Barbuda retained power in elections held during the year. In St. Vincent and the Grenadines, however, the moderate opposition New Democratic Party won, and James Mitchell became the new prime minister.

See STATISTICS OF THE WORLD; CUBA; GRENADA; PUERTO RICO.   D.B., L.L.P., & P.W.
CENTRAL AFRICAN REPUBLIC. See STATISTICS OF THE WORLD.

CEYLON. See SRI LANKA.

CHAD. On September 17, 1984, after a two-day visit to Libya's capital by Claude Cheysson, then the French foreign minister, France announced an agreement with Libya for "total and simultaneous" withdrawal of French and Libyan troops from Chad. French forces had been dispatched to Chad in August 1983 to back the Chadian government of President Hissène Habré, while the Libyan forces were there to support the rebel army of former Chadian President Goukouni Oueddei. The presence of foreign troops had created a military stalemate, with neither France nor Libya in a position to win a victory. The French withdrawal was completed in early November, but reports indicated that large numbers of Libyan troops remained. The two Chadian factions continued to face each other across a 200-mile buffer zone that divided the country in two roughly above and below the 16th parallel. In October, as the French-Libyan withdrawal was supposedly proceeding, Chad's two opposing factions had held preliminary talks aimed at settlement to end the civil war, but the talks broke down.

French involvement in Chad had been unpopular at home, and the French had suffered their first battle casualty early in the year, when a French fighter-bomber was shot down in the buffer zone, and its pilot killed. The French retaliated by moving their defensive line and the buffer zone about 60 to 70 miles north to include the government stronghold of Oum Chalouba within the French defensive sphere. A Libyan-backed rebel column moved near Oum Chalouba to test French resolve but was defeated by government troops and French planes. French troops were then within easy striking distance from Libyan air bases, but Libya did not move to exploit the exposed French position. However, acts of terrorism added to the tension. In March a suitcase exploded in a French airliner refueling in the capital, and in April nine French soldiers were killed in a booby-trapped vehicle near Oum Chalouba.

In early November, Amnesty International charged that government troops in Chad had carried out hundreds of summary executions and random murders since September. The group put the number killed at more than 200 and alleged that, on one occasion, people were burned to death by government forces after they had taken refuge in a church.

In addition to civil war, Chad has been beset by chronic drought conditions. The 1983–1984 crop year was exceptionally dry, with rainfall only one-fifth of normal. As a result, in January, Chad was included in a list issued by the United Nations Food and Agriculture Organization of two dozen African nations facing an emergency food situation.

See STATISTICS OF THE WORLD.   G.L.

CHEMISTRY. Advances in chemistry being reported in 1984 ranged from a method to treat wood for making fine violins to new techniques for battling cockroaches. Scientists in West Germany reported the discovery of a new element.

Secrets of the Master Violin Makers. Joseph Nagyvary, a biochemist of Texas A&M University, believes he has rediscovered some of the secrets of the master violin makers who lived and worked near Cremona, Italy, over two centuries ago. These craftsmen, whose ranks include Antonio Stradivari, Giuseppe Guarnieri, and Nicolò Amati, produced stringed instruments whose tonal quality modern technicians have never been able to duplicate.

An amateur violin maker himself, Nagyvary analyzed pieces from two broken Guarnieri cellos being repaired and found a much higher mineral content than is present in the natural spruce or maple used in today's instruments. Wood cells are long, tubelike structures that have small holes, or caps, at each end, initially filled with pectin, a viscous component of sap. As untreated wood dries, the pectin hardens, sealing the caps and creating small sounding chambers that produce harsh, unpleasant overtones when the wood is made into an instrument. In the Guarnieri wood, however, Nagyvary found that more than 90 percent of the caps were unsealed. He also observed that the varnish on the Guarnieri wood was quite different from the oily and resinous varnishes used today.

Nagyvary devised a treatment that involved soaking the wood in various solutions of potassium tartrate and sand. This treatment not only makes the wood harder and stronger but it also removes the pectin before it can seal the caps. Nagyvary also developed a varnish based on chitin, an extremely strong compound, which he obtained from shrimp shells. He then began to build instruments that he hoped would rival those of the masters. Nagyvary's instruments have been highly praised by musicians, who say that their tonal quality is much closer to that of a Stradivari or Guarnieri than that of most modern instruments.

Cockroaches. Work conducted by Stuart Schreiber and colleagues at Yale University promises a new approach to the control of cockroaches. The group has developed a technique for producing large quantities of the cockroach sex pheromone, or chemical signal, known as periplanone-B. The pheromone, released by females, stimulates males to a mating frenzy so intense that they will mount other males if no females are present. More impor-

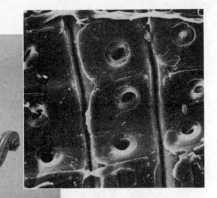

Biochemistry professor and amateur violin-maker Joseph Nagyvery displays an instrument he made from wood that was treated to prevent its cells from becoming sealed. Nagyvery believes that wood with open-ended cells (electronic microscope photograph, inset) is the secret of the pure-toned violins produced more than two centuries ago by the great masters.

tant, it impels the males to seek out the source of the chemical, which could thus be used both to disrupt normal mating and to lure the males into traps. The pheromone might eventually be used in conjunction with a new hormonelike chemical, manufactured by Zoecon Industries of Dallas, that produces sterility in immature roaches that come into contact with it.

Bitterest Substance. Investigators at the Atomergic Chemetals Corporation of Plainview, N.Y., have filed a patent application for what they claim is the bitterest substance known to date. Denatonium saccharide, a white, crystalline powder, has a lingering bitter taste even when diluted to one part in 100 million. The company speculates that it might be added to poisonous household products to deter ingestion by children.

Artificial Sweeteners. Several consumer groups have attempted, thus far unsuccessfully, to block the sale of aspartame, pending further tests. The popular low-calorie artificial sweetener is marketed as NutraSweet by G.D. Searle and Company and is used in diet soft drinks. The groups cited users' complaints of dizziness

and other ill effects. A report released by the Centers for Disease Control in November, however, found that the complaints were not clearcut and that there was no evidence of a link to aspartame. French scientists in Lyon, meanwhile, have synthesized a new compound related to aspartame that is 55,000 times sweeter than sugar. Such a compound might be preferable to aspartame, since it could be used in much smaller quantities, thus reducing both cost and risk.

Untested Chemicals. The vast majority of commercially important chemicals have not been adequately tested for safety, according to a report issued in March by the National Academy of Sciences. The report concluded that available data were insufficient to allow even a partial assessment of potential hazard for 64 percent of the ingredients in drugs, 66 percent of those in pesticides, 84 percent of those in cosmetics, 81 percent of food additives, and 90 percent of all other chemicals in commercial use. Over 53,000 chemicals are currently used in significant quantities, and most were put into commercial use before current rules on testing were adopted. The report does not

CHESS

Better Loving Through Chemistry

Requests for male subjects to test an experimental drug at Stanford University met with unusually overwhelming response. The drug is yohimbine hydrochloride, a chemical found in the bark of a West African tree, which had been used locally for centuries to treat high fevers and now is found to stimulate sexual behavior in male rats. Researchers would like to investigate the aphrodisiacal properties of the drug with humans in order to treat sexual dysfunction. But don't bother to contact Stanford, says Dr. Julian Davidson, a professor at the medical school. "We already have more volunteers than we can handle."

indicate that there is a health hazard from any of these substances, merely that their safety has not been demonstrated.

New Element. Scientists at a laboratory operated by the Society for Heavy Ion Research (GSI) in Darmstadt, West Germany, reported in April that they had created three atoms of a new element, bringing to 109 the total number of known elements. The scientists obtained the new element, called element 108, by firing a beam of iron-58 nuclei at a target of lead-208, creating atoms with 108 protons and 157 neutrons. The new atoms survived for about two-thousandths of a second, about 1,000 times longer than had been predicted, before undergoing radioactive disintegration.

See also ENVIRONMENT.   T.H.M.

CHESS. The world chess championship, between Anatoly Karpov and Gary Kasparov, got off to an explosive start in Moscow in the latter part of 1984. Karpov, the defending champion, playing subtle, positional, virtually flawless chess, jumped to a 4–0 lead in only nine games. But Karpov then gave up trying to attack and embarked on a cautious strategy. The match soon tapered off into a defensive marathon, less notable for its exciting play than for its tedious string of drawn games. By year's end, after nearly four months of play, Karpov led 5–1 (six wins were required for victory), and the match had set a new record for consecutive draws (17) as well as for total length and most draws in a title contest.

Kasparov, the Soviet wunderkind from Baku, had won the right to play for the world championship by capturing the final qualification match from his fellow countryman Vasily Smyslov, 8½–4½. Smyslov, a former world champion, did not win a single game in the match, which was played in Vilnius, Lithuania, in March and April. Kasparov gained his victory primarily by excelling in the endgame, his opponent's own specialty, with subtle, precise, forceful play.

In the semifinals, played in London in November and December 1983, Kasparov had used a different approach to defeat perennial contender Viktor Korchnoi, 7–4. Losing only the first game, he went on to beat Korchnoi, a former Soviet citizen living in Switzerland, with a careful, waiting strategy that eventually caused Korchnoi to overextend himself. The semifinal and final results moved Kasparov into first place in the world rankings. In the other semifinal, Smyslov defeated Zoltán Ribli of Hungary, 6½–4½.   J.T.S.

CHILE. General Augusto Pinochet, who in September 1984 celebrated the 11th anniversary of the military coup that brought him to power, dealt with increasing strong-arm methods against mounting domestic pressure for a transition back to democracy.

On March 23, the explosion of at least three bombs in Santiago brought to 130 the number of such attacks in major cities over the last few months, and on March 27, antigovernment groups, supported by large sectors of the business community, staged a massive national protest. Other major demonstrations followed, leading to two deaths, and in April college student boycotted classes to protest government policies.

Following the March 27 demonstrations, Pinochet acceded to demands of the business sector for change in economic policy by appointing new ministers of finance and the economy. This move appeared to mark the end of the influence in Chile of the free-market economists associated with the University of Chicago.

Interior Minister Sergio Onofre Jarpa Reyes, meanwhile, held talks with the Democratic Alliance, a coalition of opposition parties, but the dialogues proved fruitless. Jarpa indicated

A symbolically muzzled Chilean journalist calls for an end to press censorship during an October demonstration in Santiago; in two days of strikes and rallies protesting government repression, eight people were killed, 25 wounded, and hundreds arrested.

that the transition to democracy might be speeded up; but Pinochet later made it clear, in an August interview, that he had no intention of abandoning his twin posts of president and commander in chief of the army before the end of his term in 1989. His position led to growing opposition even among many on the right. The National Party, in particular, withdrew from a group of progovernment parties and adopted a critical posture toward the government.

In early September, widespread demonstrations led to nine deaths and hundreds of arrests. Pinochet extended his emergency powers, and the authorities briefly detained seven opposition leaders. The next month, more terrorist bombings preceded two days of protests, cul-

minating in a general strike. Eight people were killed. The government responded with mass arrests and began sending large numbers of suspects to internal exile in rural areas. On November 5, all cabinet members offered their resignations. Pinochet restored most members to their posts the next day; he also instituted a state of siege, under which the government broadened its powers to hold suspects without trial and imposed a curfew. In the weeks following the siege declaration, troops and police made repeated sweeps through the Santiago slums, rounding up citizens for mass questioning. Most were subsequently released, although an undisclosed number were reportedly detained as "subversives."

Efforts to reactivate the economy were stymied by Chile's massive foreign debt, as well as by stringent conditions imposed on Chile by the International Monetary Fund. In 1984, interest payments on the debt amounted to $2 billion, consuming half the nation's export earnings. Further aggravating the problem was an unprecedented drop in the world price of copper, a key export.

On November 29, Chile and Argentina signed a treaty worked out through Vatican mediation, resolving their long-standing territorial dispute over the Beagle Channel. It provided for Chilean ownership of three disputed islands in the channel and for Chilean sovereignty over Pacific Ocean waters south of Cape Horn, leaving Argentina with sovereignty over Atlantic waters south of Cape Horn.

See STATISTICS OF THE WORLD.   A.V.

CHINA. Politics and policy in the People's Republic of China were dominated in 1984, as for several years past, by the tough, pragmatic elder statesman Deng Xiaoping and his two most important lieutenants, Communist Party General Secretary Hu Yaobang and Premier Zhao Ziyang. This triumvirate was determined to promote the modernization of China by the year 2000, mainly through large-scale domestic and foreign investment and massive technology transfer from abroad, chiefly the West and Japan. This program was making significant progress.

Although pretending to a purely independent foreign policy of approximate equidistance between the superpowers, China actually con-

Peking poultry farmer Sun Guiying made history in April when he bought a Toyota and became the first peasant in the People's Republic to own a private car. Chinese shoppers spent a record $142 billion in 1983 on once-scorned consumer goods.

tinued to "tilt" noticeably toward the United States. However, Sino-Soviet relations appeared to improve markedly late in the year, with the visit of a high Soviet official and the signing of major agreements.

Politics and Government. Although the Cultural Revolution appeared to have burned out any interest in ideology for most Chinese, and although the top leadership under Deng Xiaoping was essentially pragmatic, Marxist-Leninist ideology was not dead as a factor in China's politics. The other senior leader, Chen Yun, was an aged economic planner with a more ideological outlook and was more disposed to follow the Soviet economic model than Deng. One of the signs of Chen's importance was the publication of a three-volume edition of his selected works in March. Most high-ranking Chinese leaders are protégés of either Deng or Chen.

A campaign of propaganda and police pressure against "spiritual pollution" from foreign influences, initiated by the Central Committee in late 1983, proved annoying and embarrass-

ing to Deng and Hu, inconvenienced Chinese who were involved in the modernization program or had legitimate contacts with foreigners, and raised serious doubts abroad about China's policies and the wisdom of investing there. Accordingly, beginning in January the campaign tended to evaporate, although it continued to be publicized as though it were both an ongoing reality and a great success. Deng Liqun, an ideologically oriented follower of Chen's, appears to have lost his post as Director of the Communist Party Central Committee's propaganda department at that time, although the Foreign Ministry officially denied this.

The Second Session of the Sixth National People's Congress, China's equivalent of a parliament, met May 15–30. The main report to which it listened, by Premier Zhao Ziyang, reaffirmed existing policies in all departments except in the economic and military fields. While the Congress was meeting, Deng Xiaoping gave a remarkable demonstration that he continued to be predominant among his colleagues. On May 25, in a session with People's

Congress delegates from Hong Kong and Macao, he publicly repudiated recent statements by former Foreign Minister Huang Hua and former Defense Minister Geng Biao that China would not send troops to Hong Kong after taking it over in 1997.

It was announced in December that 40 officers at the top ranks of the military had relinquished their "leading posts." Their retirement was regarded as a key victory for Deng in his drive to rid the officer corps of aging veterans resistant to modernizing changes.

Economy. In 1984, China, whose elite was fully committed to the so-called Four Modernizations (agriculture, industry, national defense, and science and technology), was near the end of its Sixth Five Year Plan (1981–1985). The goals of the plan represented a substantial "readjustment" (that is, a cutting back) of more ambitious ones set in early 1978, a time of temporary optimism before the second oil shock. In effect, the targets set in 1978 for attainment in 1985 were now scheduled for the year 2000.

The Sixth Five Year Plan envisaged the investment of around $100 billion in 890 projects, 120 of which were considered "key projects." Seventy of the key projects were under construction in 1984. Of these, 42 were related to energy (including nuclear power), transportation, and communications, areas in which the Chinese economy was notably weak; eight coal mines in various areas were being started or expanded, large hydroelectric projects were being built on the upper Yellow River and the middle Yangtze River, and eight ports, including Shanghai, were being modernized.

At a meeting of the Central Committee in late October, China's leadership approved a series of extensive reforms intended to make certain urban industries freer of state control and more competitive, both domestically and in foreign markets. The measures, to be introduced gradually, provided that plant managers would be able "to adopt flexible and diversified forms of operation," determining, for example, production and marketing in accordance with supply. The extensive consumer subsidies now in place would be phased out. Each affected enterprise, viewed as "a relatively independent economic entity," would have the right to set prices within "prescribed" limits, to fix wages, and to promote and otherwise reward its employees, especially younger, technically trained managers.

Trade. The first half of 1984 showed considerable increases in trade over the first half of the previous year. China's main partners—Japan, Hong Kong, and the United States—were the same as before. However, a new note of interest was the appearance on the list of South Korea.

Peking remained officially and deeply committed to an open policy toward the outside world; its main interest by far was the acquisition of foreign technology, especially high technology. Foreign firms were encouraged to invest, produce (mainly for export), and above all train Chinese workers in rapid rotation. For their part, foreign investors found the Chinese legal system vague and cumbersome, Chinese officials generally slow moving and not always competent, and Chinese workers hard to train and overpriced. Nevertheless, this form of meeting between East and West moved ahead. In April, for example, Peking reached agreement on a $600 million deal with Occidental Petroleum Corporation for a mammoth coal mine in Shanxi province.

China's economic relations with the United States progressed fairly satisfactorily, but there were problems. Peking protested complex new U.S. customs regulations that would make it more difficult for Chinese textiles to enter the United States, and there were fears that China would retaliate by curbing imports of U.S. grain. The most serious setback was the stalling of a potentially important agreement on nuclear power cooperation, initialed during President Ronald Reagan's April visit to China. Peking was apparently reluctant to give formal guarantees that it would not divert fissionable materials to military uses.

On the other hand, the United States and China signed agreements on scientific, technological, and industrial cooperation during an official visit Premier Zhao paid to Washington, D.C., in January. Overall U.S.–Chinese trade in 1983 amounted to $3.9 billion (down from $4.8 billion in 1982, according to revised official Chinese figures); China's exports to the United States amounted to $2.1 billion, its imports to $1.8 billion.

American sightseers Ronald and Nancy Reagan take in the view from the Great Wall at the close of their six-day visit to China in May. Seven hours of talks between Reagan and Chinese leaders produced agreements on cultural exchanges, corporate taxation, and nuclear cooperation.

Foreign Affairs. Peking appeared to have made an unpublished assessment that President Reagan was likely to be reelected and therefore decided to approve a presidential visit to China. The Reagan visit, in April, featured considerable presidential public relations aimed at the American voter. Some of the president's remarks went unreported by the Chinese media, and the Chinese rebuffed Reagan's overtures for explicit cooperation against the Soviet Union. Nevertheless, the visit on the whole appeared to have been a success.

At midsummer, in spite of essentially ritualistic Chinese protests at pro-Taiwan statements in the Democratic and Republican party platforms, U.S.–Chinese relations were reasonably good. One reason was the cordial reception given to Chinese athletes at the summer Olympic Games in Los Angeles, where they won the highly respectable total of 32 medals, including 15 gold.

Sino-Soviet relations received a boost with the nine-day visit of Soviet First Deputy Prime Minister Ivan Arkhipov, said to be the most important visit to Peking by a Soviet official in 15 years. At its conclusion on December 28, accords were signed providing for scientific, economic, and technological cooperation, including aid in modernizing industrial plants built decades ago by the Soviets. It was also announced that the two nations would greatly increase their bilateral trade. However, Soviet foreign policy, including the occupation of Afghanistan, remained an obstacle to further improvements in relations.

Sino-Japanese relations improved with the visit to China of Japan's prime minister, Yasuhiro Nakasone, in March. Nakasone offered the Chinese a loan of $2 billion for infrastructure projects.

Taiwan remained a source of frustration. Peking's conciliatory gestures toward the Nationalist leaders in Taipei were again spurned. Success, however, attended China's negotiations with Great Britain over the future of Hong Kong. On September 26 an agreement was initialed in Peking, conceding sovereignty to China in 1997 but preserving the colony's existing social and economic systems for at least 50 years thereafter. (*See* HONG KONG.)

See STATISTICS OF THE WORLD.   H.C.H.

CHINA, REPUBLIC OF. *See* TAIWAN.

CIVIL LIBERTIES AND CIVIL RIGHTS. In 1984, aided by an increasingly conservative Supreme Court, the Reagan administration frequently succeeded in modifying or reversing public policy in racial matters, church-state separation, and criminal procedure. In the area of women's rights the picture was mixed, but the overall theme in civil liberties was a shift toward the conservative point of view. (*See also* BLACKS IN THE UNITED STATES; WOMEN.)

Speech and Press. Two Supreme Court decisions reflected the current shift toward weakened First Amendment protection. In *Clark* v. *Community for Creative Non-Violence,* the Court upheld a ban on sleep-in protests in parks near the White House. According to the Court, the prohibition did not affect the content of speech and left ample alternatives, while protecting a legitimate government interest. In *Members of the City Council of Los Angeles* v. *Taxpayers for Vincent,* the justices upheld a ban on the posting of political posters on public property to avoid "visual clutter."

As a result of some Supreme Court rulings, the vulnerability of the press to libel suits was increased. In *Keeton* v. *Hustler Magazine* and *Calder* v. *Jones,* the Court ruled that libel suits may be brought in any state where a publication has substantial circulation, regardless of where the plaintiff lives. However, in *Bose Corp.* v. *Consumers Union of the United States,* the Court reinforced a 1964 decision limiting the right of public officials and public figures to sue for libel unless actual malice is demonstrated.

The decision of a jury in a federal district court in Roanoke, Va., on a libel suit brought by the Reverend Jerry Falwell against *Hustler* magazine publisher Larry Flynt was viewed by some observers as a setback to the media and a potentially chilling influence on free speech. Falwell had sued for libel because of a parody in Flynt's sexually explicit magazine suggesting that the Moral Majority leader was a drunkard who practiced incest. The jury said that, because the parody was too outrageous to be believed, no libel had occurred. Nevertheless, it ordered Flynt and the magazine's distributor to pay Falwell $100,000 in actual damages for emotional distress; Flynt himself was ordered

to pay another $100,000 in punitive damages. Defense lawyers said they would appeal.

The Minneapolis City Council twice passed legislation making pornography a form of discrimination against women and, therefore, liable to suit under the city's civil rights code, but both bills were vetoed by Mayor Donald Fraser, who doubted their constitutionality. A similar ordinance, adopted in Indianapolis, was overturned by a federal district court in November. The ruling was appealed. Opponents of such legislation maintain that it violates First Amendment guarantees of freedom of speech and press.

Church-State Issues. Tension increased between advocates of strict separation of church and state and those seeking a greater place for

Pornography as a violation of women's civil rights was a new concept that surfaced in a Minneapolis antipornography campaign. Legislation that would have classified pornography as discrimination against women, and thus actionable under the city's civil rights code, was twice passed by the Minneapolis city council and twice vetoed by the mayor.

Acquitted by a federal jury of drug conspiracy charges, John Z. DeLorean leaves the Los Angeles Federal Courthouse with his wife, Cristina Ferrare. Some jury members said they considered the former automobile magnate a victim of government entrapment. We wanted to send a message to the Department of Justice, said one juror, that it was wrong to "set up" citizens to commit crimes.

religious values in public policy. The presidential campaigns of Walter Mondale and Ronald Reagan were engulfed in arguments over issues like abortion and prayer in schools.

The issue of school prayer has been a source of controversy since 1962, when the Supreme Court barred organized prayer in public schools as inconsistent with the constitutional prohibition against the establishment of religion. The Senate on March 15 rejected, by an 81–15 vote, a proposed constitutional amendment to permit silent prayer in public schools; the overwhelming opposition was due in part to the fact that many senators prefer vocal prayer. On March 20, a constitutional amendment proposal sanctioning vocal prayer in public schools was defeated by a vote of 56 to 44—11 votes short of the two-thirds majority needed for passage. The measure had been strongly supported by President Reagan.

The administration fared better when Congress overwhelmingly approved a measure to permit students to hold religious (and political and philosophical) meetings in public high schools before or after school hours. The measure requires that meetings be voluntary, student-initiated, and free of sponsorship by a school or its teachers. On July 26, the House voted to require schools to permit "individuals in public schools the opportunity to participate in moments of silent prayer." The measure was then sent to the Senate, where it was rejected.

On March 5, the Supreme Court in *Lynch* v. *Donnelly* upheld a city's right to include a Nativity scene in its official Christmas display. In a major reversal that shifted the boundary between government and organized religion, the Court majority stressed that the Constitution does not require complete separation but "mandates accommodation" and that the crèche display in a Rhode Island city served a secular purpose. This marked the first time the Court has permitted the official display of an exclusively Christian symbol.

Following the Court's decision on the Rhode Island crèche case, the United States Park Service included a privately purchased manger scene in its annual Christmas Pageant of Peace on the Ellipse, a park area near the White House in Washington, D.C. The display was installed over objections raised by Jewish, Episcopal, Lutheran, and Unitarian groups, who had argued that another crèche case, this one involving a Nativity scene placed by a private group on public land in Scarsdale, N.Y., was still before the Supreme Court.

Draft. The Supreme Court upheld a law denying federal student aid to college students who fail to register for the draft. In *Selective Service System* v. *Minnesota Public Interest Research Group*, the Court denied that the law compelled self-incrimination or that it constituted legislative declaration of guilt without judicial trial.

Illegal Aliens. Some Court decisions unfavorably affected the status of aliens. In *Immigration and Naturalization Service* v. *Delgado*, the Supreme Court upheld the right of immigration officials to conduct "factory sweeps" to look for illegal aliens. In *INS* v. *Lopez-Mendoza*, the Court held that deportation of an alien is a civil proceeding and that criminal procedural protections—against illegal search and seizure, for example—do not apply. Finally, in *INS* v. *Stevic*, the Court ruled that aliens claiming political asylum must show "a clear probability" of being persecuted upon return to their native land.

Criminal Procedure. In an unusual display of dissension in April, three Supreme Court justices (John Paul Stevens, William J. Brennan, Jr., and Thurgood Marshall) accused the Court of forgetting its "primary role as the protector of the citizen and not the warden or the prosecutor." The attack came after the majority, in *Florida* v. *Myers*, voted without hearing arguments to reinstate a criminal conviction for sexual battery that had been voided because of a questionable police search. The dissenting justices noted that since 1981 the Court had issued 19 summary rulings involving rights of criminal defendants and had sided with the prosecution each time.

The most important development in criminal procedure was the Supreme Court's stand on the exclusionary rule, which excludes from a trial the use of illegally seized evidence. In *United States* v. *Leon* and *Massachusetts* v. *Sheppard*, the Court authorized an exception for evidence seized with a defective search warrant by police acting with "objective good faith." In *Nix* v. *Williams*, the Court held that illegally seized evidence may be used if it can be proved that the evidence would "inevitably" have been discovered by lawful means.

The Court generally took a narrow view of the rights of criminal suspects and prison inmates. The constitutional protection against unreasonable searches and seizures does not apply to prison cells, said the Court in *Hudson* v. *Palmer*. In *Block* v. *Rutherford*, the Court held that pretrial detainees have no right to "contact visits" with family or to observe searches of their cells.

For the first time since establishing it in 1966, the Supreme Court created an exception to the so-called Miranda rule, which requires police to warn suspects of their right to remain silent and have an attorney present during interrogation. *New York* v. *Quarles* involved the arrest of a rape suspect. Police, noting that he wore an empty gun holster, had questioned him about the location of the gun without first advising him of his rights. In the majority opinion, the Court cited the "immediate necessity" of locating a loaded gun in a public place which "outweighs the need for the [Miranda] rule protecting the Fifth Amendment's privilege against self-incrimination."

In *Pulley* v. *Harris*, the Court eliminated one of the few remaining obstacles to increased imposition of the death penalty, when it ruled that a state is not obliged to ensure that a death sentence in one case is consistent with the punishment imposed in similar cases.

The trial of former automobile manufacturer John Z. DeLorean ended August 16 when a federal jury found him not guilty of drug trafficking. DeLorean had been arrested following a government "sting" operation. The prosecution charged that he had conspired to obtain and distribute cocaine in an attempt to save his ailing automobile company. The case drew attention to the issue of entrapment, which involves the use of government agents posing as criminals to induce and expose criminal activity. Some jurors stated that they believed DeLorean had been entrapped by the government. To prove entrapment, it must be shown that the idea for the criminal act came from the government undercover agent, that the agent induced the defendant to commit the crime, and that the defendant was not ready or willing to commit the crime until induced to do so. Attorney General William French Smith said that the DeLorean verdict would not deter continued use of undercover sting operations.   M.Gr.

COINS AND COIN COLLECTING. The sale of three U.S. Mint–produced commemorative coins—two silver dollars and a $10 gold piece—had by the end of November reached its goal of netting $65 million to help underwrite the cost of hosting the summer Olympics in Los Angeles. The coins, which were legal tender in the United States, were sold at premiums far above face value. The Mint set aside $10 for each silver dollar sold and $50 for each gold piece, with the money to be shared equally by the United States Olympic Committee and the Los Angeles Olympic Organizing Committee. The 1983 silver dollar in the U.S. Olympic set depicted a classical discus thrower, while the 1984 dollar showed the "Gateway" sculpture outside the Los Angeles Coliseum, where the games were held. The $10 coin, also dated 1984, featured a pair of runners carrying the Olympic torch.

One problem facing the Olympic organizing committees was that of providing adequate mass transportation for thousands of athletes and many more thousands of spectators. With no government funds available, the Southern California Rapid Transit District (SCRTD) turned to coin collectors for revenues. Twenty-four different transportation tokens, depicting various Olympic sports, were produced. In addition to the tokens used for fares, tokens were boxed in deluxe sets and sold to collectors. The proceeds enabled SCRTD to deploy 550 buses for special Olympic service.

China's Olympic coin designs turned out to be prophetic. A 10-yuan silver piece featured the women's volleyball team, which went on to win a gold medal. A 5-yuan silver coin featured Chinese high-jumper Zhu Jianhua, who, just before the games, set a new world's record for the men's high jump at 7 feet, 10 inches.

In other areas of collecting, the U.S. Mint resumed the production of mint sets, a practice it had discontinued in 1981. The mint sets contained one coin each of the circulation issues from the Denver and Philadelphia mints, plus two small medals struck on cent blanks to signify the mint of issue. A cost reduction of $4 per set, from the previous $11 price, reflected the elimination from the sets of the Susan B. Anthony dollar.

The success of the commemorative coin program on behalf of the XXIII Olympiad generated a number of suggestions from members of the U.S. Congress and their constituents for more issues. Possibilities included coins to honor the diamond jubilee of the Boy Scouts of America in 1985 and an issue to help offset the costs of refurbishing the Statue of Liberty in time for its centennial in 1986.   E.C.R.

COLOMBIA. In March 1984, midterm elections were held at the municipal and departmental level, with the ruling Conservatives receiving less support than the Liberal opposition. Among the Liberal factions, the prospective presidential candidacy of Virgilio Barco Vargas was strengthened, while Luis Carlos Galán's new Liberals did not run as well as had been expected. Although the election results did not obligate President Belisario Betancur Cuartas to shuffle cabinet ministers, he did so in June. The new team retained a balance between Conservatives and Liberals. Conserva-

A Colombian police officer checks out some of the 13.8 tons of cocaine seized in a raid—the biggest in history—on a coca-processing plant deep in the jungle. The cocaine, valued at $1.2 billion, was later destroyed, and 40 people, one an American pilot, were arrested.

tive Augusto Ramírez Ocampo replaced Rodrigo Lloreda as foreign minister.

One of the policies on which President Bectancur worked the hardest was pacification; in 1982 he had supported a law offering amnesty to guerrilla groups. This year, a presidential commission signed a cease-fire agreement with the Colombian Revolutionary Armed Forces (FARC), the largest guerrilla organization. Agreements followed with the April 19 movement, or M-19, an urban group, and with the Popular Liberation Army, a Maoist-oriented group. Betancur's amnesty policies contributed to the resignations of four ranking officers, including General Fernando Landazábal Reyes, minister of defense.

On March 10, Colombian police carried out their biggest drug raid ever, seizing a record 13.8 tons of cocaine base and refined cocaine, with an estimated street value of $1.2 billion. The unprecedented raid was made on the Yari River, at a complex guarded by the FARC. Forty people, including a U.S. pilot, were arrested at the site. A few days later, police broke up a similar operation on the Meta River. Minister of Justice Rodrigo Lara Bonilla, who had led a crackdown on cocaine and marijuana rings, was machine-gunned to death in Bogotá on April 30. Following the assassination, President Betancur imposed a nationwide state of siege and agreed to extradite to the United States persons accused there of drug trafficking and other crimes.

Imports were severely restricted in April; 2,000 products were banned in an attempt to save jobs and protect foreign exchange holdings, which had dipped to about $960 million. Urban unemployment was placed at 13.4 percent in June. The peso was devalued through a series of mini-devaluations. Every effort was to be made to hold inflation below 20 percent. Coffee export income was aided by higher prices and a larger export quota.

A five-year economic accord was signed with the Soviet Union in May, providing for the renewal of an unlimited credit at 6 percent interest; the Soviets were to furnish jeeps, electric buses, capital goods, and spare parts, while Colombia would ship agricultural products, ferric chloride, and textiles.

See STATISTICS OF THE WORLD.   L.L.P.

COLORADO. See STATISTICS OF THE WORLD.

COMMONWEALTH OF NATIONS. In a regional conference in Port Moresby, Papua New Guinea, on August 8, 1984, 18 Asian and Pacific members of the Commonwealth of Nations condemned France for its continuing nuclear testing in the South Pacific and expressed opposition to the dumping of nuclear waste. The prime minister of Papua New Guinea, Michael Somare, praised the incoming Labor prime minister of New Zealand, David Lange, for his opposition to visits by nuclear-powered ships to New Zealand. At a later meeting of the South Pacific Forum in the state of Tuvalu, attended by nine Commonwealth countries and five others, a committee was set up to draft a treaty that would prohibit the acquisition, storage, and use of nuclear weapons in the South Pacific and bar the dumping of nuclear waste there.

In another matter, the finance ministers of 44 Commonwealth countries met in Toronto, Canada, on September 29 to address the global debt crisis. A report, presented to the foreign ministers, warned that "the world's financial safety is balanced on a knife edge" and recommended basic policy changes on the part of the International Monetary Fund (IMF) and other international agencies. It strongly criticized the IMF's policy of imposing stringent economic measures on debtor nations as a condition for obtaining loans, instead of encouraging the long-term economic expansion of developing countries.

On January 1, the newly independent nation of Brunei was admitted into the Commonwealth of Nations as the 49th member.   J.O.S.

COMMUNIST WORLD. Communist parties throughout the world comprised more than 80 million members in 1984. The Communist movement as a whole, however, continued to suffer from internal conflicts, exemplified by the Sino-Soviet split and the widening division between Moscow and most Western European Communist parties.

Soviet Transition. Yuri Andropov, who had assumed the leadership of the Communist Party of the Soviet Union (CPSU) after the death of Leonid Brezhnev in November 1982, died on February 9, after an extended illness. He was succeeded as party general secretary and as head of state by Konstantin Chernenko, 72, a longtime protégé of Brezhnev and, in 1982, Andropov's principal rival for the top post.

Chernenko, during his first year in power, reemphasized ideology in his efforts to stimulate the Soviet economy and deal with other Soviet problems. He did not move to replace the large number of party and governmental officials with backgrounds in the security police and intelligence service who were appointed during the short period of Andropov's preeminence. Chernenko's advanced age and poor health gave rise to speculation about his successor. The name that emerged most often was that of Mikhail Gorbachev, 53, a Central Committee member who was given major responsibilities and appeared to be in a position to succeed Chernenko.

U.S.–Soviet relations were generally poor. Late in the year, however, both sides appeared interested in improving relations, and it was agreed to hold high-level talks with the United States in early 1985 to devise a formula for the resumption of negotiations on arms control.

Eastern Europe. The political climate in Poland showed no sign of improvement despite a general amnesty granted by the government of General Wojciech Jaruzelski in July, during the 40th anniversary of the establishment of Communist rule in that country. The murder in October of Father Jerzy Popieluszko, an outspoken supporter of Solidarity, by state security officers resulted in a new outpouring of public support for the outlawed labor movement. The government responded with a new crackdown on human rights groups.

A significant political development in Eastern Europe was the open disagreement between the Soviets and their otherwise loyal East German allies concerning East-West relations. In August the East German leader, Erich Honecker, postponed a planned visit to Bonn under persistent Soviet pressure. For the East Germans—as well as for the other Eastern Europeans—maintaining good relations with West Germany, a source of high technology and easy loans, was essential. The Soviets, however, considered East Berlin's policy of détente with Bonn to be out of line with their own campaign against the West over the deployment by the North Atlantic Treaty Orga-

nization of new intermediate-range missiles in Western Europe. Following the postponement of Honecker's trip, Bulgaria's party chief, Todor Zhivkov, canceled his own scheduled visit to Bonn. Only Romania's leader, Nicolae Ceauşescu, the maverick in the Warsaw Pact, went ahead with his trip to West Germany, as planned, in October.

Comecon. At a summit meeting of the Eastern bloc's Council for Mutual Economic Assistance, or Comecon, held in Moscow in June, the member states laid stress on the need for joint efforts to develop high technology and improve food production. (Food shortages continued to be a problem in Poland and Romania.) That same month the Soviet government issued a decree, made public in early November, permitting the establishment of "direct links" between Soviet and other Eastern bloc (including Yugoslavian) factories. Observers noted that such links, intended to bypass the cumbersome bureaucracy of Comecon's structured economies, would facilitate Soviet access to the high-tech industries of East Germany and Poland, among others.

Warsaw Pact. The major concern facing the Soviet Union and its Warsaw Pact allies in the military area was the deployment of U.S. Pershing II and cruise missiles in Western Europe. In response, the Soviets expanded the number of SS-20 intermediate-range missiles in East Germany and Czechoslovakia. Although Eastern European leaders in general supported the Soviet decision to retaliate against what were seen as Western attempts to achieve nuclear superiority in Europe, several of them, notably Honecker and Zhivkov, expressed concern that their countries would be forced to shoulder an additional defense burden and would become targets for NATO missiles.

Asia. The ideological discord between China and the Soviet Union deepened in 1984, as China continued to adopt dramatic liberalizing reforms in its economic system and moved toward a closer trade and military relationship with the United States. In October the Chinese party's Central Committee announced that the government would introduce measured decentralization in the country's urban industries, modeled on that adopted, with favorable results, in agriculture.

Despite these and other signs of ideological differences, Sino-Soviet relations improved dramatically in December with the visit of a Soviet first deputy premier to Peking and the signing of accords calling for extensive cooperation between the two nations. Soviet activities in Asia remained an obstacle to further improvements in relations.

In Afghanistan, Soviet military tactics aimed at destroying the agricultural base and eliminating the civilian population from key valleys continued to encounter resistance from Mujahedeen rebels seeking to overthrow the Soviet-installed regime. By fall, the Soviets were reportedly increasing their troop strength through the use of crack airborne units that were stationed on the Soviet side of the border with Afghanistan.

Vietnam continued its efforts to pacify Cambodia (Kampuchea) and retained its dominion over that country and neighboring Laos. In a more encouraging development, North Korea, stirring out of its isolation, made overtures to South Korea, which expressed willingness to open discussions on a new relationship. After a shooting incident at the demilitarized zone on November 23, in which three North Korean border guards and one South Korean were killed, trade and development talks were suspended, but only temporarily.

Nonruling Parties. In July the French Communist Party (PCF) decided to withdraw from France's Socialist government, and in September the party formally announced it was ending its three-year cooperation with the Socialists, in what had become known as the "union of the left." The PCF's voting strength had been dropping steadily—from a high of about 20 percent in 1979 to about 16 percent in 1981 and to a low of a little over 11 percent in European Parliament elections in 1984. Georges Marchais, the secretary-general, announced that the party would develop a strategy of popular mobilization against the government's austerity program.

Italy's Communist Party, the largest in the West, lost its popular and widely respected leader, Enrico Berlinguer, who died on June 11 of a brain hemorrhage while campaigning for the European parliamentary elections. He was succeeded by Alessandro Natta, a close aide, who promised to continue the party's independent line.

In January, former members of the Spanish Communist Party (PCE) opposed to its advocacy of Eurocommunism announced the formation of a pro-Soviet Communist Party of the Peoples of Spain, headed by Ignacio Gallego, a veteran of the 1936–1939 Spanish Civil War. The PCE accused the splinter party of "sowing confusion" and "dividing the working class."

A continuing struggle between moderates and hard-liners also affected the leadership contest in the Finnish Communist Party. At its 20th congress in May, the party replaced its pro-Moscow chief, Jouko Kajanoja, with Arvo Aalto, a former general secretary strongly criticized by the Soviets.

See also articles on individual countries mentioned.   R.E.K.

COMOROS. See STATISTICS OF THE WORLD.

COMPUTERS. The year 1984 marked the end of the gold rush days in personal computers, as competition grew fiercer.

Hardware. In mid-January, Apple Computer Inc. unveiled its Macintosh computer, a machine that quickly captured the fancy of many computer enthusiasts. Apple designed the machine with the goal of making it easy to use, even for novices. Like the Lisa computer Apple introduced in 1983, it relies on concepts developed mainly at Xerox Corporation's Palo Alto Research Center. Instead of requiring conventional keyboard commands, the Macintosh uses tiny, easily understood graphic images, called icons, displayed on the computer's built-in, high-resolution, black-and-white screen. To enter a command, a Macintosh user simply points at the appropriate icon on the screen by using a "mouse"—a small device tethered to the computer. Apple's first version of the Macintosh had a rather limited memory—only 128 kilobytes (K) of random-access memory, or RAM. But Apple introduced a 512K version in September as well as a kit for upgrading the earlier model.

Besides the Macintosh, Apple released new versions of its larger Lisa computer, and in April the company brought out a new version of its Apple II. The lightweight Apple IIc is designed primarily for the home and student markets and has a built-in disk drive.

COMPUTERS

With innovations on the market such as a lightweight Apple IIc and a revamped PCjr, computer customers in 1984 often faced a mind-boggling array of choices.

'Do you have one that can help me decide which is the one for me?'

DRAWING BY MODELL: © 1980 THE NEW YORKER MAGAZINE, INC.

The Hewlett-Packard Company brought out the HP 110, a small, powerful, battery-powered portable computer with a 16-line liquid crystal display. The 110 had as much memory as many desktop computers—272K of RAM. Instead of using a disk drive, designers divided the internal memory so that part of it could be used in place of the disk-drive storage. Hewlett-Packard also built a word-processing program, a telecommunications program, and the popular electronic spreadsheet Lotus 1-2-3 (an accounting program) into the machine's large memory.

In the spring, Mindset Corporation, a new company in Sunnyvale, Calif., brought out a desktop computer specially designed for artists and others who wanted lush, colorful graphics. It attracted interest but had difficulty breaking into the market.

Taking on IBM, the American Telephone and Telegraph Company entered the mainstream computer business. AT&T brought out its 3B series minicomputers, as well as a personal computer, the 6300. The new 3B2 computer is not technically a minicomputer but a "supermicro" that can be used by as many as 18 persons at connected terminals. More powerful than an ordinary personal computer, it uses AT&T's popular Unix operating system software. The larger 3B5, a full-fledged minicomputer, can handle 60 users.

Soon after AT&T's debut, IBM turned the tables by introducing a more powerful personal computer, the PC AT, which outperforms both AT&T's 6300 and IBM's own PC. The PC AT, which got off to a strong start in sales, has a more powerful microprocessor than the other machines and thus a larger memory capacity. Intensifying its battle with AT&T, IBM also acquired the Rolm Corporation, a maker of telecommunications equipment, for approximately $1.25 billion.

In the chaotic market for home computers, IBM at first had difficulties selling its PCjr, a stripped-down version of the PC, with less memory, a single disk drive, and a controversial keyboard with hard rubber tablet keys. In mid-

Compute-a-Poem

Yes, computers can write poetry—of a sort. A software program recently devised by a senior at Hampshire College in Amherst, Mass., can churn out limericks at a rate of one per second. The limericks all have the correct number of syllables, they rhyme, and no two are alike—but they don't make a whole lot of sense. Example: "There once was a misfit from Stroghs/who build the byte over that rose/a byte lied a head/then switched on that shed/and dove off a leatherette nose."

120

summer IBM replaced the keyboard with a conventional design and added more memory, so that the PCjr could run software such as Lotus 1-2-3. Price cuts and rebates followed, and late in the year sales had increased dramatically. Coleco Industries, maker of the Adam home computer, also tried price-cutting, but sales continued to lag, and in early January 1985 the company announced it was pulling out of the home computer market.

Most firms making IBM-compatible computers faced brutal competition. One of the few that succeeded was the Compaq Computer Corporation of Houston. In 1983, its first year in business, Compaq's sales had topped $111 million. Compaq introduced a series of desktop models in 1984 that outperformed the IBM PC.

Software. Many smaller software firms withered away or sold out to larger companies. One market trend was the attempt to create large "integrated" software programs that tied together many separate functions. Lotus Development Corporation of Cambridge, Mass., for instance, brought out Symphony, a new program that incorporates word processing and other functions along with the 1-2-3 electronic spreadsheet.   W.D.M.

CONGO. See STATISTICS OF THE WORLD.

CONGRESS OF THE UNITED STATES. The second session of the 98th Congress, often overshadowed in public attention and made more partisan by the upcoming November elections, nevertheless managed to act on several important fiscal and foreign policy issues in 1984. Congress—especially the Democratic-controlled House—confronted President Ronald Reagan on national security issues, in some cases forcing changes in administration policies. Legislators continued to resist White House efforts to extend and enlarge the cuts in domestic social spending enacted during the first two years of Reagan's term. Congress rejected two constitutional amendments on school prayer, while authorizing voluntary religious meetings in public high schools (see CIVIL LIBERTIES AND CIVIL RIGHTS).

Budget. Reagan's proposed budget for fiscal year 1985 (beginning October 1, 1984) called for continued cuts in domestic spending together with major increases in military spending. The budget projected expenditures of $925.5 billion and revenues of $745.1 billion, leaving a deficit of $180.4 billion.

The administration's own economic advisers were concerned about the size of the deficits projected for 1985 and subsequent years, and Congress demanded more extensive measures to close the budget gap. The House adopted a budget resolution that called for a total reduction of $182 billion in the deficits projected by the administration for the next three years. The resolution called for military spending to rise 3.5 percent after inflation in fiscal 1985, as opposed to the 9.2 percent Reagan had requested. Republican Senate leaders joined the administration in developing a deficit reduction plan that became part of the budget resolution approved by the Senate on May 18. The Senate plan projected a reduction of $140.6 billion over three years. It called for a 7 percent rise in military spending in fiscal 1985, and for domestic cuts twice the size of those in the House resolution.

The two resolutions proved difficult to reconcile in a House-Senate conference committee. A compromise resolution was not approved until September, by which time some related appropriations and revenue legislation had already been enacted. Only four of 13 separate appropriations bills to fund government agencies for 1985 were approved by the beginning of the fiscal year on October 1. Congress had to enact a series of emergency bills to temporarily fund most government operations at existing levels. On October 11, both houses finally approved a $470 billion catchall appropriations bill covering the remaining agencies.

Taxation. As part of the deficit-reduction effort, both houses agreed on a compromise tax measure designed to raise about $50 billion in new revenues through 1987. The new law extended the 3 percent federal telephone excise tax, increased the excise tax on liquor, limited income averaging to reduce personal income taxes, restricted tax write-offs for real estate and business purchases, and tightened rules on tax shelters.

Defense. A September agreement ended a long Senate-House dispute over the defense budget. Reagan had proposed spending $313.4 billion in fiscal 1985 but then accepted the $299

121

billion figure in the Senate's deficit-reduction plan. The House, which had proposed a figure of $285.7 billion, offered to compromise, but the president and the Senate Republican leadership at first insisted on the higher figure. Senate Majority Leader Howard Baker (R, Tenn.) and House Speaker Thomas P. O'Neill, Jr. (D, Mass.) ultimately reached an agreement, which the White House accepted, providing for $292.9 billion, an inflation-adjusted increase of about 5 percent over fiscal 1984.

Congress dealt the administration a setback on the MX missile. Reagan had asked for 40 of the large, land-based intercontinental missiles, in addition to the 21 authorized in 1983, but he accepted the figure of 21 more MX missiles approved by the Senate. The House, however, voted money for only 15 missiles and required that production be approved by the new Congress in 1985. The agreement reached by Baker and O'Neill adopted the figure of 15 missiles and required two votes in

each house in 1985 on the question of continued production. Thus, MX opponents would need to win only one of four votes to stop production.

Central America. Three days after moderate José Napoleón Duarte defeated his right-wing opponent in El Salvador's runoff presidential election in May, the House authorized the full amount of military aid requested by Reagan for fiscal 1985. Congress eventually approved more military and economic aid than Reagan had originally sought. In August the House also reversed its previous opposition to supplementary military aid for El Salvador for fiscal 1984.

In April, Congress reacted strongly to the news that the Central Intelligence Agency had directed the mining of Nicaraguan harbors, causing damage to several ships. Several members of the Senate Select Committee on Intelligence said they had not been clearly informed of the operation, as required by law, and both houses passed nonbinding resolutions con-

President Reagan signed legislation on July 17 that promised withdrawal of federal highway funds from states that do not institute a 21-year-old drinking age. Among those present (front row, left to right), were Transportation Secretary Elizabeth Dole and Candy Lightner, founder of Mothers Against Drunk Driving.

Illegal immigrants from Mexico await deportation after their capture by the U.S. Border Patrol in Texas. The 98th Congress ended with the two houses unable to reconcile the differences between their respective versions of the Simpson–Mazzoli bill, which aimed at stemming the flow of "illegals" into the United States.

demning it. After the House rejected more aid for antigovernment guerrillas in Nicaragua, U.S. funding for them ran out. In the fall, both Houses banned aid to the guerrillas through February 1985; after that date, funding could be restored only by a presidential certification that the Sandinista government was undermining Nicaragua's neighbors and by an affirmative vote by Congress.

Anticrime Measures. A bipartisan package overhauling federal criminal laws easily passed both houses, after administration pressure forced the bill out of committee. Civil libertarians had strongly opposed provisions of the bill that gave federal judges wide authority to order preventive detention of allegedly dangerous defendants (rather than set bail) and that restricted use of the insanity defense and placed the burden of proving insanity on the defendant. The legislation also increased penalties for drug dealers, abolished parole for federal criminals, and established a commission to set a narrow range of possible sentences for various offenses.

Social Welfare. As part of a pension reform package signed by the president in August, Congress made changes intended to end discrimination against women in pension plans. The legislation required private employers to pay spouses the pensions of vested workers who die before retiring and gave state courts the authority to divide pension benefits as part of divorce settlements. The minimum age for participation in pension plans was lowered from 25 to 21.

A bill passed unanimously by both houses required states to set up systems for withholding child support payments from the wages and state tax refunds of persons who are delinquent in making such payments. Congress also required states to ensure adequate medical care for severely handicapped infants. Another measure liberalized eligibility standards for disability (*see* SOCIAL SECURITY).

Immigration Law. A conference committee was unable to reach a compromise between two versions of a measure to control illegal immigration, one passed in 1983 by the Senate and the other, on June 20, 1984, in a 216–211 vote, by the House. Both versions of the so-called Simpson-Mazzoli bill would have given amnesty to illegal aliens who could prove residence in the United States before a specified date, thereby making them legal U.S. residents; both also would have penalized employers who knowingly hired illegal aliens. The legislation was backed by the Reagan administration but was strongly opposed by powerful constituencies. Hispanics and civil libertarians opposed it on the grounds that employers would be led to discriminate against Hispanics in hiring, so as to avoid any problems as to their residency status.

Smoking and Drinking. Congress approved a bill providing for stronger and more specific

123

health warnings on cigarette packages and advertising. Responding to a nationwide campaign against drunken driving, Congress also voted to withhold some federal highway aid from states that did not raise their minimum drinking age to 21 within two years.

Ethics. On April 2, Representative George Hansen (R, Idaho) became the first person to be convicted of violating the 1978 Ethics in Government Act, which requires prominent federal officials to disclose their personal and family finances. A federal court jury in Washington, D.C., found Hansen guilty of four counts of filing incorrect financial statements. On June 25, Hansen was sentenced to five to 15 months in prison and fined $40,000. On July 31, the House voted, 354–42, to reprimand Hansen, its lightest punishment. Hansen, who remained free pending appeal, narrowly lost a reelection bid in November; he filed suit in an effort to have certain ballots invalidated which he claimed were illegal.

Senator Mark Hatfield (R, Ore.) came under scrutiny after disclosures that his wife, Antoinette, had accepted a fee from a Greek financier, Basil Tsakos, whose pipeline project her husband had promoted. Hatfield said it had been a mistake for his wife, a real-estate agent, to accept the $55,000, which the Hatfields said was for her services in helping Tsakos find an apartment. The senator denied any connection between the fee and his support of Tsakos's pipeline, which would carry Saudi Arabian oil across Africa. (Hatfield had arranged meetings for Tsakos and discussed the project with U.S. and African officials and an oil-company executive.) The Senate ethics committee voted unanimously to end its investigation, but the Justice Department continued its own inquiry. Hatfield was reelected in November.

New Lineup. After the November elections, the Republicans retained Senate control by a narrowed 53–47 margin, while the Democrats held a lessened majority in the House. Senate Republicans chose Robert Dole (Kan.) to replace the retiring Baker as majority leader. Other Republican senators gaining new prominence included Richard Lugar (Ind.) and Robert Packwood (Ore.), who became chairmen of the foreign relations and finance committees,

respectively. Senator Robert Byrd (West Va.) was reelected as Senate minority leader. In the House, Democrats again chose O'Neill as speaker.

See also ELECTION IN THE UNITED STATES; UNITED STATES OF AMERICA. J.E.S.

CONNECTICUT. *See* STATISTICS OF THE WORLD.

CONSTRUCTION. *See* HOUSING AND CONSTRUCTION.

COSTA RICA. In 1984, economic problems continued to place strains on the government of President Luis Alberto Monge and his National Liberation Party. Exports were declining, and the internal economy was expanding only slightly. After warnings from the International Monetary Fund, late in 1983, that Costa Rica's $220 million deficit must be cut by one-third, a series of agreements were drawn up providing for certain austerity measures. With future IMF loans of $100 million at stake, Costa Rica agreed that no foreign loans were to be used for current government operations, that a 15 percent tax be applied to business earnings and dividends, and that public employees be retired at the age of 61 and not be replaced.

Amid rumors of an impending coup, Monge in August asked for the resignations of his cabinet and of individuals holding upper-level administrative and ambassadorial posts. Observers saw this move as intended to silence critics on the right and to remove the more ineffectual of his earlier appointees. Among those not reappointed to the new government was Public Security Minister Angel Edmundo Solano.

Three leaders of the ruling National Liberation Party, Oscar Arias, Alberto Fait, and Carlos Manuel Castillo, declared their candidacies for the 1986 presidential election. Arias, a former party secretary-general, minister of planning, and legislative whip, was the favorite for the party nomination.

Relations with the United States were strained by a number of public observations by Ambassador Curtin Winsor, Jr., on Costa Rica's affairs; his outspokenness brought an unprecedented rebuke in January from the ruling party's political directorate. Relations with Nicaragua's Sandinista government remained tense and difficult. Border clashes early in May led to the fear of a possible full-scale war and to peace demonstrations in San José, the nation's capital.

A meeting of foreign ministers from 12 Western European and nine Latin American countries, held in San José in September, focused on the political and economic role of Western Europe in Central America.

See STATISTICS OF THE WORLD.   L.W.G.

COUNCIL FOR MUTUAL ECONOMIC ASSISTANCE. See COMMUNIST WORLD.

CRIME AND LAW ENFORCEMENT. A mass murder in a California town, acquittal of a well-known automobile manufacturer who had been taped discussing a cocaine deal, and charges of sexual molestation of children were a few of the crime stories that made headlines in 1984.

San Ysidro Mass Murder. On July 18, in a McDonald's restaurant in San Ysidro, Calif., a town south of San Diego near the Mexican border, James Oliver Huberty, 41, fatally shot 21 people and wounded 19 others. It was

believed to be the worst one-day mass murder by a single gunman in U.S. history.

Huberty, an unemployed security guard, had told his wife he was "going to hunt humans," and he left his San Ysidro home with a 12-gauge shotgun, a 9-millimeter Uzi semiautomatic rifle, and a 9-millimeter Browning semiautomatic pistol. He walked a half block to the restaurant with the weapons strapped around him, then apparently opened fire outside the restaurant and took refuge inside when police arrived. Victims were cut down by streams of gunfire; the dead included restaurant workers, customers, and passersby, many of them children. Huberty was killed by a police sharpshooter more than an hour after the shooting began. There was no clear motive for the murders, but Huberty had appeared despondent over the recent loss of his job.

Drugs and the Mafia. In what became known as the pizza connection case, 38 men were charged in April with operating an organized-

In what was said to be the worst one-day mass murder by a single killer in U.S. history, unemployed James Oliver Huberty, 41, killed 21 people, ranging in age from eight months to 74 years, at a McDonald's restaurant in San Ysidro, Calif., on July 18. Huberty was shot dead at the scene by a SWAT-team marksman.

Smiling serenely, 76-year-old Virginia McMartin poses in her Manhattan Beach, Calif., nursery school. In March, the white-haired, wheelchair-bound McMartin was charged, along with her daughter, two grandchildren, and three employees, with numerous counts of child molestation, including raping, sodomizing, and otherwise sexually abusing children in their care.

crime ring that, using a string of pizzerias as a cover, had brought approximately $650 million worth of heroin into the United States since 1979. The reputed leader of the ring, Gaetano Badalamenti, was arrested in Spain and later extradited to face charges in the United States. In November federal officials charged 14 more persons in the New York metropolitan area with using pizza parlors to camouflage a drug operation.

In Italy in September, authorities, using information from Tommaso Buscetta, a high-level Mafia member who had turned informer, staged a massive crackdown on organized crime in Sicily. Later in the year, Buscetta was brought to the United States, where he was secretly arraigned on drug trafficking charges and made available to federal authorities for questioning, under tight security. Meanwhile, it was revealed that U.S. law enforcement officials had learned of a previously unknown branch of the Sicilian Mafia in the United States, operating independently of American organized crime.

Child Molestation. In March, Virginia McMartin, 76, founder of a well regarded preschool in Manhattan Beach, Calif., was in-

dicted together with three family members and three employees, on numerous counts of child molestation. It was charged that, over a period of years, more than 40 children had been fondled, sodomized, raped, or otherwise abused at the school; it was also alleged that some children had been photographed for pornographic purposes. Authorities said that the children had been kept silent about the abuses by various means; in some instances, they said, defendants had mutilated small animals in front of the youngsters, threatening to harm their parents in a similar manner if they talked. In another case that attracted wide media attention, four employees at a Bronx, N.Y. day care center were accused of molesting at least ten children at the center. One was later cleared, but the others were indicted on more than 100 counts involving rape, sodomy, and sexual abuse.

Judicial Corruption. Seventeen men, including three sitting judges and a former judge, were indicted in a government sting operation after a federal probe of Cook County (Ill.) Circuit Court. The investigation, code-named Operation Greylord, involved wiretapping, bugging of a judge's chambers, enlistment of a judge as a microphone–carrying agent, and creation of false legal cases. More than 330 judges were investigated.

A court clerk was convicted in March, and two lawyers later pleaded guilty. Cook County Associate Circuit Court Judge John M. Murphy denied having ever taken bribes; nonetheless, a federal jury in June found him guilty of racketeering, mail fraud, and extortion. In August, Judge John G. Laurie was acquitted on charges that he accepted money from lawyers seeking to win favorable verdicts. In October, former Associate Circuit Judge John J. Devine was found guilty of extortion, mail fraud, and racketeering. Murphy was later sentenced to ten years in prison, and Devine to 15 years.

The first federal judge to be convicted of a crime committed while on the bench was Federal District Judge Harry E. Claiborne. The Las Vegas judge was convicted in August of filing tax returns in which he had underreported his income. He was sentenced in October to a two-year prison term and fined $10,000, but remained free pending appeal.

Brink's Robbery. The court case in the $1.6 million robbery of a Brink's armored truck came to a climax when Kathy Boudin reversed her previous plea and pleaded guilty to murder and robbery charges. A guard and two policemen had been killed during and after the 1981 robbery, in Rockland County, N.Y. Boudin, who contended she had not participated in the shootings, was sentenced to 20 years to life in prison. In June, Samuel Brown was sentenced to three consecutive terms of 25 years to life in prison for his part in the crime. Susan Rosenberg, who had been indicted in July 1982 for robbery and conspiracy in connection with the Brink's holdup, was arrested in November in Cherry Hill, N.J.

Von Bülow Case. The conviction of financier Claus von Bülow was overturned in April by the Rhode Island Supreme Court. In 1982 he had been found guilty of twice trying to murder his wealthy wife by injecting her with insulin. The court majority held that the evidence had justified a conviction if viewed in a light favorable to the prosecutor but that some evidence should not have been admitted because it was tainted by lack of a search warrant. The court also found that evidence possibly helpful to the defense had been improperly suppressed by the trial judge. In October the U.S. Supreme Court refused to overturn the Rhode Island court's ruling. Decision on a possible retrial was pending late in the year. Meanwhile, von Bülow's wife, Martha, remained in a coma with no perceptible brain function.

Klan Acquittal. In April, six Ku Klux Klansmen and three American Nazi Party members were acquitted of federal civil rights violations. The case grew out of the killing of five members of the Communist Workers Party and the wounding of seven others in a 1979 "Death to the Klan" rally in Greensboro, N.C. Five of the defendants were among six men acquitted in 1980 of state murder and rioting charges stemming from the same incident.

Mass Murder. Henry Lee Lucas was sentenced to death in April for the murder of an unidentified woman whose body was found along a Texas highway in 1979. Law enforcement officials said he was one of a new breed of "serial" murderers who prowl the country in search of victims. Lucas was also convicted

---

Crime Doesn't Pay

When four armed intruders burst into their Florida farmhouse, demanding $65,000 in cash and a supply of heroin, James and Ada Smith were dumbfounded. The only drugs the elderly couple had were nitroglycerin pills, which they gladly handed over. The gunmen angrily ripped what they thought was a new telephone off the wall, only to discover it was a can opener. They handcuffed the Smiths and jammed a gun against the neck of a friend who had dropped in, demanding the man's car keys. "You already dropped them," responded the friend. Eventually realizing they had the wrong house, the bandits fled with a few valuables, dropping a ring they had laboriously removed from Ada Smith's finger with soap. The four soon got lost looking for the Florida Turnpike; finally, they screeched past what they thought was a toll booth but which turned out to be the guardhouse to Homestead Air Force Base. Military police promptly accosted the hapless bandits and handed them over to Dade County police.

of six other Texas murders and faced at least 30 indictments in six states. He claimed to have killed up to 360 people.

Capital Punishment. The number of prisoners executed for crimes rose sharply in the United States in 1984. From 1976, when the U.S. Supreme Court ended a moratorium on executions, to 1983, only 11 persons were executed, but the total for 1984 came to 21, as more prisoners under sentence of death exhausted their appeals process. A decision by the Court in January 1984 was expected to be important in the long run in increasing the use of the death penalty; it held that a death sentence need not be reviewed to determine if it is comparable to punishments ordered in similar cases in the same state. As of late 1984, some 1,450 convicted murderers were on "death row" in the 38 states where capital punishment was permitted.

Velma Barfield, executed by lethal injection in North Carolina on November 2, was the first woman executed in the United States since 1962. She had been convicted of the poisoning death of her fiancé and also had admitted the fatal poisonings of three other persons, including her mother.

Spying. Government prosecutors elicited a deal from a California engineer caught in a scheme to sell U.S. defense secrets to Polish intelligence agents for $250,000. James Durward Harper, Jr. pleaded guilty in April to one of nine counts against him and agreed to testify for the prosecution in any related case.

In October, Richard W. Miller, who had just been dismissed from the FBI, and two Soviet émigrés were arrested in California on espionage charges. The émigrés were Svetlana Ogorodnikova and her estranged husband, Nikolay Ogorodnikov. Miller, the first FBI agent to be charged with espionage, allegedly gave classified FBI documents to the couple for $65,000 in gold and cash. He was indicted in November on additional charges involving bribery and theft of government property.

Legislation. On October 12, President Ronald Reagan signed an anticrime legislative package that overhauled federal criminal law. The legislation restricted the insanity defense in federal trials, abolished parole for federal prisoners, and gave federal judges the power to incarcerate certain allegedly dangerous defendants without bail before trial. Another act authorized funding for various child abuse and adoption programs, including a three-year $63 million project on family violence. In addition, the measure broadened the definition of child abuse to cover the withholding of appropriate medical treatment from severely handicapped babies.   L.S.G.

CUBA. In 1984, Cuba celebrated the 25th anniversary of the revolution that brought Fidel Castro to power. A report issued by the Organization of American States praised the Castro government for meeting the basic needs of its poorest citizens and for advances in nutrition, employment, medical care, and education, but it criticized Havana's restriction of political dissent and artistic freedom and condemned its violation of civil liberties and human rights.

Cubans enjoyed greater prosperity in 1984 than at any time since the first years of the revolution. The OAS declared Cuba to be the second best-fed nation in Latin America, after Argentina. Rationed goods, which in 1970 accounted for 97 percent of household expenditures, made up less than one-third by this year, as Cubans flocked to the "free markets"—introduced in 1980 to allow farmers and artisans to sell their surplus products—where they could purchase unrestricted supplies of both necessities and luxuries, albeit at much higher prices. The housing shortage, however, remained a serious problem.

An excellent tobacco harvest in 1983–1984 and increased nickel and citrus exports helped make up for a 1 million ton shortfall in sugar production and for plunging world sugar prices. Promising developments included the construction of Cuba's first nuclear energy plant (being built with the aid of the Soviet Union and Bulgaria) and of the largest oil refinery in the region. Cuba continued to purchase Soviet oil on favorable terms and to sell sugar to Moscow at a price far above the world market level. The low world price for sugar, however, reduced Cuba's hard currency earnings and, therefore, its capacity to import goods and technology from the West, increasing its dependence on the Soviet bloc. It also forced Havana early in the year to reschedule payments on $130 million in medium-term debt owed to 150 Western banks.

Relations with the United States continued to be Cuba's central foreign affairs concern, as Havana sought to thaw its cold war with Washington. There was, however, an escalating U.S.–Cuban war of words. The United States carried out war games (including a practice evacuation of military dependents) at its Guantánamo Bay naval base on Cuba, and the Reagan administration successfully argued before the U.S. Supreme Court that its 1982 ban on travel by Americans to Cuba should be upheld. Meanwhile, Cuba in May announced a doubling of its militia, to more than 1 million. In the second half of the year Cuba dramatically increased defense measures—conducting evacuation and combat drills, building bomb shelters, and digging trenches. Government officials claimed that Cuba was in imminent danger of a U.S. attack.

On the other hand, Havana signaled a readiness to assume a lower military profile abroad, reducing its military advisory group in Nicaragua, lowering its troop levels in Ethiopia, and agreeing in principle to withdraw its 25,000-man force from Angola as part of a regional settlement. Havana also continued to support a negotiated solution to the conflicts in Central America. The United States and Cuba did reach an important tentative accord late in the year, providing for the repatriation of some 2,500 Cuban convicts and mentally ill persons who had come to the United States in the Mariel boat lift in 1980 and were being detained in U.S. jails. Earlier in the year, the Reverend Jesse Jackson, then a candidate for the Democratic presidential nomination, visited Havana and gained the release of 26 Cuban political prisoners and 22 Americans being held in Cuban jails, most of them on drug charges.   P.W.

CYPRUS. The situation on divided Cyprus remained tense in 1984. Leaders of the newly proclaimed Turkish Republic of Northern Cyprus (TRNC) took further steps to create the trappings of an independent state in the northern third of the island, despite the absence of international recognition except from Turkey.

Early in the year, Rauf Denktash, acting president of the TRNC, announced a set of proposed solutions to the intercommunal dispute. They included the return of the Varosha section of Famagusta to the Greek Cypriots via the UN, the reopening of the international airport outside of Nicosia, and the establishment of bicommunal committees to discuss trade, tourism, water supply, and the environment. The Greek Cypriot government refused to discuss these proposals unless the Turkish Cypriot side accepted UN Security Council Resolution 541, which condemns the Turkish Cypriots' unilateral declaration of independence and calls for its reversal. Meanwhile, the Turkish Cypriots rejected a settlement plan presented to UN Secretary-General Javier Pérez de Cuéllar by Greek Cypriot President Spyros Kyprianou. It called for the withdrawal of all mainland Turkish troops from the island and creation of a strong federated government.

In April an exchange of ambassadors between the TRNC and Turkey drew a strong protest from Kyprianou and Greek Prime Minister Andreas Papandreou, his chief supporter. In August, however, Pérez de Cuéllar met

Presidential aspirant Jesse Jackson (left) takes leave of Cuban President Fidel Castro in Havana, as interpreter Juanita Vera looks on. Jackson succeeded in persuading Castro to free 22 Americans jailed in Cuba, most of them on drug charges, and 26 Cuban political prisoners.

separately in Vienna with TRNC and Greek Cypriot representatives, and he subsequently held separate meetings at UN headquarters in New York with Kyprianou and Denktash. The meetings led to an agreement for direct talks between the two sides, to be held in January.

In the TRNC a constitutional referendum, scheduled for late 1984 and to be followed by presidential and legislative elections, was postponed. The fledgling state did, however, adopt a new flag in March.

The Greek Cypriot economy continued to perform well. The inflation rate stabilized at just under 6 percent, and unemployment in early 1984 stood at 3.5 percent. Turkish Cyprus continued to rely heavily for loans and trade on Turkey, whose economy was also weak. By adopting the Turkish lira as its legal currency, it imported a high rate of inflation from the mainland.

See STATISTICS OF THE WORLD.   P.J.M.

CZECHOSLOVAKIA. The continued survival of the human rights movement Charter 77, along with a religious revival and the growth of clandestine publications, suggested that the Czechoslovak people in 1984 were emerging from the lethargy caused by stifled economic and intellectual growth. Political dissent took the form of practical criticism in some instances. In April a Charter 77 letter to Gustáv Husák, president and head of the Czechoslovak Communist Party, protested "protective supervision," under a law imposing restrictions on people who have been in prison. Those so restricted must report to the police at prescribed intervals, give advance notice when they travel, and submit to police entry and search of their homes.

In May, Czech playwright and dissident Václav Havel was awarded an honorary doctorate in absentia by France's University of Toulouse. Havel's acceptance speech, *Politics and Man's Conscience,* a philosophical discourse on the human predicament, was distributed clandestinely in Czechoslovakia. In October it was announced that Jaroslav Seifert, an admired Czech poet and signer of the original Charter 77 manifesto, had won the 1984 Nobel Prize for literature (*see* PRIZES AND AWARDS).

In May, Prime Minister Lubomír Štrougal visited Libyan leader Muammar al-Qaddafi. They agreed on a program of economic, scientific, and technical cooperation. Czechoslovakia was to supply Libya with industrial equipment, while Libya apparently was to step up oil exports, supplemented by cash payments. Czechoslovakia also was to provide arms, and reinforcements for the thousands of Czechoslovak "specialists" already in Libya, serving in economic, social, and military capacities.

The 1984 budget was 2 percent higher than 1983—an inadequate response to inflation. Industrial prices, reflecting higher energy costs, were expected to rise by 6.4 percent, wages by only 1.1 percent, and social subsidies by 7.9 percent. In February, as it has in past years, Czechoslovakia agreed to purchase a substantial amount of Soviet crude oil.

The Roman Catholic Church was attracting lay recruits to aid its survival underground and support its aboveground clergy. Clandestine publications chronicled government harassment, and priests in Slovakia protested against the pro-regime Pacem in Terris association.

See STATISTICS OF THE WORLD.   R.A.P.

D

DAHOMEY. *See* BENIN.

DANCE. Among other developments, 1984 was a bright year for Twyla Tharp. Her dance company received glowing reviews, and her commissions from the two largest U.S. ballet companies were among spring's biggest hits: *Bach Partita* and *Sinatra Suite* at the American Ballet Theatre (ABT) and *Brahms/Handel,* which she choreographed with New York City Ballet codirector Jerome Robbins, at the NYCB.

A big hit of the American Ballet Theatre's spring season was Twyla Tharp's elegantly classical Bach Partita, set to Bach's Partita No. 2 in D minor for unaccompanied violin. The 28-minute piece was danced by (from left) Robert La Fosse, Magali Messac, Cynthia Gregory, Fernando Bujones, Martine van Hamel, and Clark Tippet.

Tharp and Company. Tharp had several triumphs in addition to her hits at NYCB and ABT. In early July, her latest work, *Sorrow Floats*, had its world premiere at the annual American Dance Festival in Durham, N.C. Just a few days later, she and her troupe appeared on Broadway in a program made up of *Nine Sinatra Songs* and *Fait Accompli*, the two most popular works from her sold-out Winter season at the Brooklyn Academy of Music. The fall brought the September release of Milos Forman's film version of Peter Schaffer's *Amadeus*, for which Tharp choreographed the incidental dances and opera sequences, as well as a telecast on public television of the three ballets she created for ABT and its artistic director, Mikhail Baryshnikov—*The Little Ballet*, *Sinatra Suite*, and *Push Comes to Shove*. On November 13, Tharp's company performed at a state dinner honoring the Grand Duke of Luxembourg, the company's first appearance at the White House.

American Ballet Theatre. Artistic Director Mikhail Baryshnikov collaborated with fast-rising choreographer Peter Anastos in mounting a lavish *Cinderella* at the ABT. Although *Cinderella*, an evening-length work that is reputed

to have cost in excess of $1 million, got a generally hostile reception from the critics at its December 1983 premiere in Washington, D.C., as well as in the other cities, the ballet did astonishingly well at the box office and is said to have recouped ABT's entire investment in its first season. In fact, largely because of the success of *Cinderella* and the new Tharp ballets, attendance and grosses were up sharply for ABT over those of the 1982–1983 season. Artistically, however, the balance sheet looked less sanguine. Natalia Makarova's staging of Petipa's *Paquita* called for a unanimity of schooling and a level of technique that, despite marked improvement, the ABT corps did not yet command. The revival of Sir Kenneth MacMillan's *Triad*, originally created for the Royal Ballet in 1972, showed it still to be pretentiously dramatic.

MacMillan, however, promised to be an important presence around ABT in the immediate future. At Baryshnikov's instigation the former principal choreographer of the Royal Ballet was named artistic associate at ABT, in which capacity he will stage some of his ballets and assist with long-range planning. In a related move, John Taras was induced to leave the NYCB, where he had been a ballet master for 25 years, to become Baryshnikov's associate director.

New York City Ballet. Besides *Brahms/Handel,* its new Tharp/Robbins hit, the other major event at the NYCB was the revival, after more than a decade, of Balanchine's *Liebeslieder Walzer,* to Brahms's set of love songs. Under Karin von Aroldingen's scrupulous supervision and in David Mitchell's handsome new rococo decor, the production recaptured all of the work's freshness and originality. Robbins limited his additional contributions to an inconsequential Grecian idyll for eight women called *Antique Epitaphs* and a staging of *Moves,* his portentous 1959 "ballet in silence about relationships." Peter Martins, who shares the position of ballet master in chief with Robbins, created two ambitious works. *A Schubertiad* was an overextended ballet in which couples in a Viennese town house become romantically involved; the ballet bore superficial resemblances to *Liebeslieder* and invoked unflattering critical comparisons. *Réjouissance* was a more successful ceremonial piece, set to Bach orchestral suites, for three couples and their attendant ensembles.

NYCB's summer season in Saratoga Springs, N.Y., saw the premieres of works choreographed by two of its principal dancers, *Seven by Fire* by Bart Cook, and *Menuetto* by Helgi Tomasson, to Mozart's Divertimento in D, K.334.

Companies and Choreographers. NYCB's Martins, Tomasson, and Cook were beginning to supply repertory for other American companies as well as their own. Martins's *Mozart Violin Concerto* was offered by Philadelphia's Pennsylvania Ballet, and Tomasson's *Contradances,* to Beethoven, was staged by the Chamber Ballet U.S.A. An NYCB dancer-turned-choreographer, Jean-Pierre Bonnefous, produced *Three Overtures* (Berlioz) and *Schubert Symphony* for Pittsburgh Ballet Theatre. The San Francisco Ballet included new works of dancers from its own ranks—Kirk Peterson (*Cloudless Sulpher,* to an electronic score by Morton Subotnick) and Val Caniparoli (*Windows,* to Beethoven's "Moonlight" sonata).

The need for viable ballets has led some U.S. companies to look overseas for choreographers. Both the Joffrey and San Francisco ballets have sought out works by Jiři Kylián, the Czechborn director of the Netherlands Dance Theater. The Joffrey produced his *Dream Dances*

Artist for All Seasons
A major artistic force for two decades, the prolific modern dance choreographer Paul Taylor enjoyed wide acclaim for two important premieres in 1984— . . . *Byzantium,* a gripping, enigmatic study of moral decay, and *Equinox,* a plotless work set to the music of Brahms, described by one critic as "gnawingly beautiful." The 54-year-old Taylor achieves a harmonious synthesis of dance and music in works that in some cases are witty and joyful, in other cases seriously reflective and even somber. Taylor studied classical ballet with such performers as Antony Tudor and modern dance with Martha Graham; he performed with several modern dance companies, including Graham's, where he was a soloist for many years. In 1962, Taylor formed his own company and danced with that group until retiring as a performer in 1975.

Paul Taylor

in 1983–1984, and San Francisco added his *Forgotten Land* to its repertory.

Most companies found fresh stagings of the classics the safest bet for drawing large audiences. The Dance Theater of Harlem produced a unique *Giselle*. As designed by Carl Michel and staged by Frederic Franklin, the ballet is set in the Creole ambience of Louisiana in 1841, the year of *Giselle's* premiere at the Paris Opera. The first full-length ballet the Dance Theatre of Harlem ever tackled, *Giselle* served as a fitting climax to 15 years of the company's growth. The Boston Ballet marked its 20th year by staging a brand-new *Romeo and Juliet* by Washington Ballet choreographer Choo San Goh. Maurice Béjart's Belgian-based Ballet of the 20th Century commemorated its 25th year with an elaborate festival in Brussels.

Modern Dance. The American Dance Festival, currently held annually at Duke University in Durham, N.C., celebrated its 50th anniversary with a "First International Modern Dance Festival," which brought together the London Contemporary Dance Theatre from Britain, the Groupe Emile Dubois from France, the experimental Sankai Juku troupe from Japan, and other companies from India, the Philippines, and Indonesia. Martha Graham celebrated her 90th birthday by choreographing Stravinsky's formidable *Rite of Spring*. In July, the National Endowment for the Arts awarded her company a grant of $250,000 to make film records of her dances, part of a project that includes adding narration to existing films and developing an oral history of Graham's work through interviews. Paul Taylor offered two new works, *Equinox* and . . . *Byzantium*, during his company's April season in New York.

Visiting Companies. The most eagerly awaited of the foreign troupes to visit the United States was Pina Bausch's Wuppertaler Tanztheater from West Germany, which made its American debut at the Olympic Arts Festival in Los Angeles in June and was later seen at the Brooklyn Academy of Music and the Toronto International Festival. The Sankai Juku troupe also made its first U.S. appearance at the Olympic Arts Festival.

Transition. Rudolf Nureyev took command of the Paris Opera Ballet, succeeding Rosella Hightower, now the director of La Scala's ballet. Peter Schaufuss assumed direction of the London Festival Ballet, and William Forsyth became artistic director of the Frankfurt Ballet when Egon Madsen left to take over the Royal Swedish Ballet. The sudden death of the Boston Ballet's founder, E. Virginia Williams, led to the abrupt resignation of the company's artistic director, Violette Verdy, and the installation of Bruce Wells as interim director. Lew Christensen, the first leading male dancer in the United States for George Balanchine, died in October. He had been director and later codirector, with Michael Smuing of the San Francisco Ballet and was chief choreographer for many years. K.F.R.

DELAWARE. *See* STATISTICS OF THE WORLD.

DEMOCRATIC PARTY. In 1984, the Democrats restated the themes of compassion and equal opportunity for all—ideals that had carried them to many an electoral victory in years past. But against President Ronald Reagan the familiar old appeals, made this time by their presidential candidate, Walter Mondale, did not work, and the Democrats suffered a defeat in the presidential race of historic proportions. They won only Mondale's home state of Minnesota and the District of Columbia—13 out of 538 electoral votes. In congressional and local elections the Democrats did better, but it became apparent that—for the first time since 1932—they were no longer clearly the majority party across the United States.

The Nomination Battle. In the contest for the presidential nomination, the Democrats gave serious consideration—but not victory—to the candidate who said he had "new ideas," Senator Gary Hart (Col.). Nonetheless, the party known for being innovative since the era of President Franklin Roosevelt did come up with some new ideas. The Reverend Jesse Jackson was the first black to make a serious bid for a major-party presidential nomination. And U.S. Representative Geraldine Ferraro (N.Y.), the choice of Mondale, became the first woman to be nominated for the office of vice-president by a major party.

The race for the nomination had begun in 1983 with a clear front-runner—Mondale—and a number of challengers, mostly lesser known and underfinanced, hoping to bring him down. Mondale, once a U.S. senator and

Lined up for a February campaign debate in Boston were six contenders for the Democratic presidential nomination: (left to right) former Senator George McGovern, Senators John Glenn and Gary Hart, the Reverend Jesse Jackson, Senator Ernest Hollings, and former Vice-President Walter Mondale.

then the vice-president under President Jimmy Carter, lined up endorsements by the AFL–CIO, the National Organization for Women, and the National Education Association. He also gathered the lion's share of support from party officeholders and other leaders, many of whom, under a new rule, got convention seats as "super delegates."

Mondale also gained from the fact that Senator John Glenn (Ohio), the former astronaut, failed to get his candidacy off the ground, after a disastrous showing in the Iowa caucuses and a poor third place finish in the February New Hampshire primary. Despite strenuous efforts, four other aspirants—Senators Alan Cranston (Calif.) and Ernest Hollings (S.C.), former Senator George McGovern (S.D.), and former Governor Reuben Askew (Fla.)—never attracted wide support.

And yet, Mondale almost let the nomination slip away. For one thing, Jackson proved to be an almost messianic figure as he carried his heartfelt message of social justice to those he would describe in a convention speech as "the desperate, the damned, the disinherited, the disrespected, and the despised." Votes that went to Jackson in the primaries might otherwide have gone to Mondale, whose liberal credentials were well established. Also, Hart,

virtually unknown to the general public at first, struck a responsive chord with his warning that Mondale represented the policies of the unpopular Carter administration. Hart himself had a degree of charisma and a broad appeal to Democrats looking for change.

Mondale began by winning the Iowa caucuses in January but then stumbled in conservative, mischievous New Hampshire, where he came in second, with 28 percent of the vote; Hart scored an upset win with 37 percent. Other aspirants continued to fight on for varying lengths of time, but the contest soon settled into a grueling, often intemperate duel between Mondale and Hart, with Jackson as the wild card. Recalling other favorites who had been upset in the New Hampshire primary, political pundits speculated that Mondale might flounder, but the Minnesotan fought back against a mushrooming of support for Hart, winning two of five primaries on "Super Tuesday" (March 13), enough to keep his campaign going strong. Mondale encapsulated his counterattack in the question, borrowed from a fast-food commercial, "Where's the beef?" It implied that Hart's career and his "new ideas" were short on substance.

The former vice-president benefited from the base of labor and liberal support that Hart could not challenge overnight, even among his new-found "yuppie" supporters—young urban professionals. With all but three candidates out of the race, the contest may have been settled in Illinois on March 20, when Mondale defeated Hart by six percentage points in a state that often reveals the center of gravity in the Democratic Party. Mondale later won other key states as well, including New York on April 3 and Pennsylvania on April 10, as he continued to build delegate support.

Jackson's role, notably during candidate debates, was to urge unity against the Republican foe—while at the same time making demands on behalf of his supporters. For one thing, he asked the party to oppose runoff primaries in the South, which he believed discriminated against black candidates. Particularly in view of the fact that he had no real chance for the nomination, Jackson grabbed a surprising amount of attention—much of it negative, from the party's viewpoint. Jackson was slow to repudiate the views of a supporter, the Black Muslim preacher Louis Farrakhan, who often made remarks offensive to Jews. Jackson himself referred to New York City as "Hymietown" in a private conversation that became public.

Mondale stumbled at the end of the primary season, losing California and two other states to Hart on June 5, but he won big the same day in New Jersey and also took West Virginia. At noon the next day, Mondale claimed that he was over the top in delegate votes—but only after telephoning uncommitted delegates and soliciting their endorsements.

A Historic Convention. The politician who, someone had joked, "dared to be cautious" then conducted a widely publicized search for a vice-presidential nominee that included interviews with three women, two blacks, and a Hispanic. Mayors Tom Bradley of Los Angeles and Dianne Feinstein of San Francisco were said to be among those most favorably considered; in any event, on July 12, a few days before the party convention, Mondale named Ferraro as his choice. Her selection electrified a dispirited party that had felt headed for certain defeat in November, and it shifted attention from last-ditch bids by Hart and Jackson. Mondale's choice of Ferraro, an Italian Catholic, seemed a bid for votes from big cities, women,

and ethnic minorities and for the Catholic vote that Reagan had won from Carter in 1980.

Even a dustup over the party chairmanship—Mondale, just before the convention, sought to replace Charles Manatt with Bert Lance, the controversial former U.S. budget director from the Carter administration—failed to dampen the delegates' enthusiasm. Mondale did name Lance general chairman of his campaign, but the Georgian soon quit as displeasure persisted over his past.

Aside from the Ferraro nomination, made by acclamation, the convention in San Francisco from July 16 to 19 was memorable for its oratory. The keynoter, Governor Mario Cuomo of New York, spoke of the despair in Reagan's "shining city on a hill," which Cuomo likened to "a tale of two cities," rich and poor. Jackson, equally eloquent, apologized for things he had said, adding, "If . . . I have caused anyone discomfort, created pain, or revived someone's fears, that was not my truest self." Mondale's well-delivered acceptance speech was almost eclipsed by Ferraro's, in which she asserted, in reference to her nomination, "If we can do this, we can do anything."

Defeat. The fall campaign was an anticlimax for the Democrats. Mondale's "promise" to raise taxes dogged him thereafter as Reagan insisted that no new tax was needed to wipe out the huge federal deficits. Ferraro's undoubted effectiveness as a campaigner was undercut by persistent questions about her and her husband's finances. Hart's warning that Mondale represented the past gained credence on election day when young voters, usually a bastion of Democratic support, joined their elders in voting for Reagan. Blacks, Hispanics, Jews, and the poor (that is, those earning less than $10,000 a year) remained mostly in the Democratic column. Members of labor-union households supported Mondale by a modest margin. But other elements of the old "Roosevelt coalition," including blue-collar workers in general, white ethnics, and white southerners, supported Reagan.

The Future. The party's future was up for grabs. the highest-ranking elected Democrat, House Speaker Thomas P. O'Neill, Jr. (Mass.), planned to retire in 1986. There was no apparent front-runner for the 1988 presidential nomination;

Hart and Cuomo were being mentioned, as were Senators Bill Bradley (N.J.) and Joseph Biden (Del.), both of whom had won easy reelection on November 6.

See ELECTIONS IN THE UNITED STATES. See also biographies of Geraldine Ferraro, Gary Hart, Jesse Jackson, and Walter Mondale in PEOPLE IN THE NEWS.   D.Y.

DENMARK. Conservative Prime Minister Poul Schlüter called for new parliamentary elections in January 1984, when the Folketing (parliament) rejected his budget. Schlüter's hopes of winning greater legislative backing succeeded in part, since his Conservative-led four-party coalition—also including Liberals, Center Democrats, and members of the Christian People's Party—increased its combined number of seats from 65 to 77 (out of a total of 179). However, the coalition's gains occurred primarily at the expense of other nonsocialist parties, and Schlüter's coalition remained a minority government.

In the January 10 elections, three of the four coalition partners increased their representation, with the Conservatives' advance from 26 to 42 seats proving by far the most spectacular. The party that lost the most seats in the election was the opposition antitax Progressive Party led by the controversial Mogens Glistrup, who had campaigned for reelection from prison, where he was serving a three-year term for tax fraud. The Progressives' strength tumbled from 16 seats to six. The opposition Social Democratic Party lost three seats for a total of 56.

Prime Minister Schlüter presented a revised budget that reaffirmed his earlier determination to reduce public expenditures. He responded to Social Democratic concern about high un-employment by earmarking $50 million to employ younger workers, the group hardest hit by unemployment. The Folketing endorsed the budget, with the Social Democrats abstaining in the final vote.

Mogens Glistrup, who succeeded in his own bid for reelection, was temporarily released from jail. However, a legislative committee voted to lift his parliamentary immunity, and he returned to prison.

The European Economic Community agreed to allow Greenland, a Danish possession that has had home rule since 1979, to withdraw from the EEC on January 1, 1985. Greenland residents had voted in a 1982 referendum to quit the EEC. The accord allowed the territory to continue exporting certain items duty-free to EEC countries and provided for annual payments of $22 million to the Danish island for economic development. In return, Greenland agreed to permit EEC members to fish in its territorial waters.

At the initiative of the Social Democrats, the Folketing voted in May to halt further payment for the deployment of Pershing II and cruise missiles in Western Europe. Denmark thus became the first NATO country to disavow the 1979 decision providing for deployment of the missiles in five NATO countries, not including Denmark. Members of the governing coalition abstained during the vote.

See STATISTICS OF THE WORLD.   M.D.H.

DISTRICT OF COLUMBIA. See STATISTICS OF THE WORLD.

DJIBOUTI. See STATISTICS OF THE WORLD.

DOMINICA. See STATISTICS OF THE WORLD.

DOMINICAN REPUBLIC. See STATISTICS OF THE WORLD. See also CARIBBEAN COUNTRIES.

E

EARTH SCIENCES. Tornadoes and heavy rains ravaged parts of the United States in spring 1984, while drought affected the Southwest. Deep drilling on both land and sea held the attention of geologists and oceanographers.

CLIMATOLOGY

Destructive weather came early in the spring. A single massive coastal storm in late March, labeled by the U.S. National Weather Service as "one of the most severe general cyclonic storms in recent history," spawned 22 tornadoes in the Carolinas, 20-foot waves along the New Jersey shore, 80-mile-per-hour winds near Boston, and 2 feet of snow in the mountains of Pennsylvania. At least 61 persons were killed by the tornadoes. About a thousand persons were injured. Portions of the famed boardwalk in Atlantic City, N.J., were washed away by the huge waves, and some of the New Jersey coastal islands were isolated from the mainland for a time when roads became flooded. A stone lighthouse on Nantucket Island, Mass., was washed away by the storm.

Another severe storm, in early May, caused extensive flooding in the Deep South and Appalachia and produced more tornadoes in Mississippi, Alabama, Georgia, and Virginia. The flooding claimed a total of 17 lives. As the weather system approached the East Coast, damage was caused mainly by winds up to 85 mph that accompanied thunderstorms. In Baltimore, winds tore off a 30-foot section of the grandstand roof at Pimlico Race Track as a race was being run; 15 people were injured.

On the night of May 26–27, areas around the city of Tulsa, Okla., received between 9 and 13 inches of rain, the most ever received there during a 24-hour period. Thirteen people were killed. During the first week of June, another storm produced 49 tornadoes across the Plains states and the upper Midwest, killing at least 16 persons. Nine of the dead were from the town of Barneveld, Wis., which was demolished.

Hurricane Diana. On September 11 and 13, Hurricane Diana hit the North Carolina coast twice. Bringing 12-foot tides, winds of more than 115 mph, and torrential rains, it tore the roofs off buildings in coastal communities, demolished piers, and caused widespread power outages. In all Diana caused more than $65 million in damage, but no one was killed or injured.

Drought in the Southwest. For a large part of the year, rainfall in much of Texas and New Mexico was nearly nonexistent. Spring dust storms produced blizzard-like conditions. Dust from the Southwest was observed at altitudes as high as 6,000 feet and as far north as Ohio. In the High Plains and Big Bend areas of western

Upended trees, looking almost surreal as they lie neatly aligned around a roofless house in Bennettsville, S.C., mark the path of one of 22 killer tornadoes that ripped through the Carolinas in March.

In a spectacular display, Kilauea pours out a fiery river of molten lava, coinciding with a massive eruption from neighboring Mauna Loa, the world's largest active volcano. The simultaneous eruption of the two Hawaiian volcanoes was the first since 1868.

sions as to how lakes, streams, and soils became acidified by the air pollutants emitted by coal-fired power plants and other industrial facilities. Sulfur was said to be the primary offending pollutant. Recently obtained data were helping scientists to see the complex chemical role played by soils in determining the rate at which acid rain spoils lakes and streams—and the rate at which the lakes and streams can recover from the pollution.

In mid-June the National Acid Precipitation Assessment Program, a ten-year research effort mandated by Congress, issued its second annual report. It presented data indicating that acid rain may be contributing to major reductions in the growth and health of forests in Europe and the United States.   N.M.R.

GEOLOGY

Hawaii's Mauna Loa, the world's largest active volcano, began erupting on March 25, and the resulting outpouring of lava was its largest since 1950. The lava flowed to within 4 miles of the city of Hilo, which is approximately 35 miles northeast of the volcano's summit. Before the eruption there were several warning signs that Mauna Loa would become active. In September 1983 scientists of the U.S. Geological Survey's Hawaiian Volcano Observatory had noted earthquake activity on Mauna Loa and increased swelling of the summit dome, indications that an eruption was likely to occur within the next several years. Earthquake activity recommenced about an hour before the volcano actually erupted.

The main lava flow moved in a northeasterly direction, and a smaller flow branched away to the north. On March 30, this volcanic activity was augmented by the eruption of Kilauea, a volcano on the southeastern slope of Mauna Loa; Kilauea's molten lava moved toward Hawaii's southeastern coast. Kilauea ceased erupting on March 31, but Mauna Loa continued to spew out lava until mid-April. The total volume of lava that poured from Mauna Loa was estimated at over 200 million cubic yards.

Earthquake. On April 24, an earthquake measuring 6.2 on the Richter scale occurred on the Calaveras fault about 12 miles southeast of San Jose, Calif. The earthquake was felt throughout central California, and damage to private prop-

Texas, a substantial portion of the wheat crop was lost and the important cotton crop could not be planted because of the extreme dryness. In Texas alone, damage to crops and cattle was estimated at $1 billion.

Later in the year, heavy rains relieved the drought in Texas. Mid-October brought unseasonable snowstorms to the West, an early reminder for that region of the winter of 1983–1984, which had featured some of the most bitter cold on record.

Acid Rain. In early March a National Academy of Sciences panel reported the latest conclu-

erty and local government facilities was estimated at $10 million. Because of the concentration of damage near the town of Morgan Hill, the event was named the Morgan Hill earthquake. The epicenter (the point on the surface directly above the focus of the earthquake) was on the Calaveras fault zone about 3 miles west-southwest of Mount Hamilton and about 40 miles northwest of Hollister, Calif., which is near the junction of the Calaveras and San Andreas faults.

Deep Continental Drilling. On the Kola Peninsula, near the Barents Sea west of Murmansk, the Soviet Union made progress in reaching its target depth of 15 kilometers (about 9⅓ miles) for what will be the world's deepest hole. The well is part of an ambitious Soviet program of deep continental drilling to aid scientific research. There have already been a number of discoveries since drilling began, such as finding ore deposits and movements of gases and mineral-bearing waters at depths in the earth where it was previously thought impossible for them to exist. The Kola hole reached a depth of 12 kilometers late in 1983 and by mid-1984 approached 13 kilometers. Plans call for the target depth to be reached before 1990.

A second well, also with a target depth of 15 kilometers, was being drilled at Saatly, Azerbaijan, in the Kura River basin southwest of Baku. By midyear the Saatly well had reached 8½ kilometers.   R.L.K.

OCEANOGRAPHY

A new drilling ship was selected in March by the Texas A&M Research Foundation for the international Ocean Drilling Program, a continuation of the successful Deep Sea Drilling Project. The ship, the *SEDCO/BP-471*, once converted for scientific drilling operations, was equipped to retrieve cores of sediments and rocks from beneath the seafloor to help scientists investigating ancient oceanic climatic and current patterns and ocean-basin formation. *Glomar Challenger*, the vessel used since 1968 in the Deep Sea Drilling Project, had completed its operations in November 1983.

Testing and shakedown cruises for the new ship were scheduled to take place in late 1984 and early 1985. The *SEDCO/BP-471* was intended to accommodate 50 scientists and pro-

vide them with modern laboratory facilities. It was equipped to drill in waters as deep as 27,000 feet and could also handle a riser, a large-diameter pipe through which drilling takes place. Risers are necessary for drilling in the thick sediments near continents. Such deposits may contain oil, and the riser system prevents any possibility of their release into the ocean. Drilling in sediments near the continents is necessary for deciphering the early history of the formation of ocean basins. Riser drilling by the new ship is not anticipated before 1990. However, the first scientific drilling operations on the new ship were expected in early 1985, in the North Atlantic. The ship is specially designed for drilling in ice-infested waters in the high latitudes.

Satellite Mapping of the Ocean. Seasat, a satellite launched in 1978, provided the data for the most comprehensive map yet made of the ocean bottom. William Haxby of Columbia University's Lamont-Doherty Geological Observatory processed the satellite data to make the map, which shows many previously unknown extinct volcanoes on the seafloor. It also indicates more precisely the extent of the fracture zones (belts of mountainous seafloor terrain) that mark the movements of oceanic plates over the last 200 million years of earth history.

An altimeter on Seasat measured the distance between the satellite and the sea surface. If one knows the shape of the satellite orbit, it is possible to map the precise shape of the sea surface to within a few tens of centimeters. Such a map shows the deep depression in the sea surface that occurs over a trench, where the earth's gravity field has been disturbed by the movement of a crustal plate beneath an adjacent plate. The map also shows elevations of the sea surface above an undersea mountain, where the earth's gravity field has been disturbed by the presence of the large amount of volcanic rock making up the volcanic cone.

M.G.G.

ECONOMY AND BUSINESS. The U.S. economic recovery that had begun in 1983 turned into a boom in the first half of 1984. Despite high interest rates, business and consumer activity intensified, while inflation remained under control. However, analysts expressed fear that large federal budget deficits could eventually trigger an inflationary expansion of the money supply. The debt problems of developing countries continued to cause concern. Increased U.S. imports helped boost recovery in the industrial world, with Western Europe expecting real economic growth of about 3 percent for the year and Japan and Canada expected to do better than that.

U.S. Recovery. Final figures for 1983 showed an increase of 3.4 percent in the inflation-adjusted U.S. gross national product—surely not the weak recovery that some economists had forecast. Then, despite bad weather, GNP exploded at a 10.1 percent annual rate in the first quarter of 1984, and in the second quarter it rose by 7.1 percent. Growth slowed markedly in the third quarter, with the GNP rising by a 1.6 percent annual rate (revised figure); this slowdown was welcomed by many economists on the basis that more moderate growth could keep inflation low. At the same time, there were indications of higher growth in the fourth quarter.

Seeing their personal income rise at an annual rate of 10.3 percent in the January–June period, U.S. consumers spent vigorously, taking on more debt in the process. Personal consumption expenditures jumped 6 percent after inflation in the first half of the year. In the third quarter, personal income continued to rise, at a rate of 8.1 percent. Personal consumption spending remained stable in July and August, then increased overall in the next few months.

In December, the Commerce Department was estimating that sales of new cars and trucks would total 13.6 million units in 1984, 11.5 percent above the 1983 total. With quotas limiting the number of Japanese imports, many U.S. auto plants operated near full capacity. Spending for housing rose, despite high mortgage rates, then dropped off sharply. Home building proceeded at a seasonally adjusted annual rate of nearly 2 million units in the first half of the year but later declined somewhat.

Corporate profits advanced steadily throughout the year and in the third quarter were running 8 percent above the same period in 1983. However, businesses borrowed heavily, and the Federal Reserve warned that the business sector was "relatively vulnerable to adverse interest-rate developments," compared with previous recoveries.

In light of the mammoth U.S. budget deficit, some skeptics questioned President Reagan's ability to keep his promise not to raise taxes.

NOW, HERE'S MY PLAN. HE JUMPS DOWN ONTO THE OTHER SIDE OF THE PLANK. WHAT YOU DO IS YOU STAY RIGHT WHERE YOU ARE.

BUDGET DEFICIT

TAXES

Employment. Employment improved in the first half of 1984, with the civilian unemployment rate falling to 7.1 percent in June, the lowest level during Ronald Reagan's first term as president. Between July and October, civilian unemployment held steady at 7.4–7.5 percent; it then dipped back down to 7.1 percent in November. Wage increases remained moderate as workers, with the recession in mind, gave higher priority to job security than to large pay hikes.

Prices. The moderation of wage increases contributed to the low inflation, which ran only slightly above the 3.8 percent rate recorded in 1983. Other factors included falling energy prices, brought about by the continued oil glut, and the high value of the U.S. dollar in relation to other currencies, which had the effect of making imported goods less expensive for U.S. customers. As a result, U.S. firms competing against the cheaper imports were forced to forgo price hikes.

Balance of Trade. By making imports cheaper and U.S. exports more expensive abroad, the strong dollar helped produce a projected record-smashing $120 billion trade deficit for 1984. The adverse balance of trade was partially offset by the flow into the United States of $80 billion of foreign capital, lured by high interest rates. This influx fueled the U.S. recovery and helped fund the deficit. Economists worried about U.S. reliance on foreign capital for such purposes, contending that if the flow should diminish, a recession might result.

Interest Rates. According to many economists, if current economic trends remain unchanged, the United States could become a net debtor nation within a few years; that is, the value of U.S. debt to foreign countries would be greater than the value of U.S. overseas investments. Only a better-balanced value of the dollar in relation to other currencies would help arrest the trend, and most economists agree the only way for that to happen was to substantially reduce the interest rates that were drawing foreign capital to the United States.

With the economy growing rapidly in the first half of the year, the demand for credit by both businesses and consumers mounted. This development came on top of an already heavy demand on the available pool of credit by the

Trivial Phenomenon

Question: How did three Canadians—two ex-journalists and a retired hockey player—strike it rich with one bright idea and a bunch of reference books? Answer: They invented Trivial Pursuit, the most popular board game since Scrabble. By 1984, the question-and-answer game had become a hobby, even a compulsion, for growing numbers of born-again trivia buffs all over Canada and the United States. Question: As stores struggled to keep enough of the games in stock, along with supplies of tie-in items like Trivial Pursuit cartoon books and calendars, what were the three lucky inventors doing? Answer: Like millions of trivia addicts, they were sitting around for long hours immersed in trivial facts and figures—as they dreamed up more questions for a new edition of the game.

U.S. Treasury, which needed funds to service the deficit. In 1984 market-sensitive short-term interest rates rose but then dropped off late in the year. The federal-funds rate, which banks charge each other for overnight borrowing and which was a major influence on other market interest rates, rose from 9.5 percent in December 1983 to over 11.5 percent in August 1984; however, it then dropped back below 10 percent by December. The prime lending rate, the base rate that banks charge business borrowers, also rose and fell; it stood at around 11 percent in December. Long-term interest rates remained more stable.

As the economy boomed at midyear, there were fears in financial markets that the Federal Reserve Board would tighten the money supply to bring growth under control. However, in July the board decided against doing so, basically on three grounds. First, the growth of the money supply was within the Fed's target range for the year. Second, inflation showed no signs of accelerating. Third, the Fed did not want to further disturb the banking system, which had been shaken by the near-collapse of Continental Illinois. The Fed's decision, coupled with a modest slowing of economic growth and continued low inflation, led to a brief stock market rally in late July and early August. There was a very brief rally late in the year, as interest rates showed some improvement.

Federal Deficit. Most everyone who looked at the economy, except for the Reagan administration, agreed that the federal deficit was the culprit keeping interest rates too high. The deficit for fiscal year 1984 (ending September 30, 1984) was $175.3 billion. The Congressional Budget Office estimated that the deficit would rise to $263 billion by fiscal 1989 unless Congress cut spending or raised taxes. The CBO also argued that the huge deficits would cause higher interest rates. The Reagan administration, counting on lower interest rates, as well as a lower inflation rate and faster economic growth than projected by CBO, saw a 1989 deficit substantially below the CBO estimate. However, by mid-November, the administration had modified earlier predictions and projected that, with no spending cuts or tax hikes, the deficit would reach $200 billion by 1986.

In a report to Congress, the Federal Reserve Board noted that since 1979 federal debt had risen more than 80 percent, with interest payments on the debt jumping to an annual rate of $110 billion by 1984. The report said that the "policies of the federal government have provided an extraordinary stimulus to aggregate demand for goods and services, but they also have contributed to high interest rates, unsettled conditions in financial markets, and a startling deterioration of our balance of trade."

On February 1, President Ronald Reagan sent Congress a proposed budget for fiscal 1985 that called for spending of $925.5 billion and revenues of $745.1 billion. At the same time, to calm nervous financial markets, he proposed a deficit reduction "down payment" of $100 billion in tax increases and spending cuts over three years. Congress did not buy all of his deficit reduction proposals and instead approved a bill (signed by Reagan in July) that boosted taxes by about $50 billion over three years while calling for $13 billion in spending cuts. Several tax reductions scheduled to go into effect after 1984 were postponed or repealed, including those affecting "windfall" profits on newly discovered oil, estate and gift taxes, and telephone excise taxes. The legislation also limited allowable tax deductions for purchases of home computers and luxury cars.

The Future. During the third quarter of 1984, the government's index of lending economic indicators showed various declines. Many economists, buoyed by such figures as the lower 7.1 percent November unemployment rate, expected growth to pick up and remain brisk. Others believed that the economy would by and large slow down, but only gradually, and avoiding recession at least until 1986. Some economists saw more serious problems ahead. They argued that the Federal Reserve Board would be forced to expand the money supply to finance the government's debt. That would cause more inflation, they reasoned, and also cause a rapid decline in the value of the dollar.

Mergers and Acquisitions. A merger frenzy swept corporate America in 1984. In the first six months of the year alone, an unprecedented total of 15 billion-dollar deals were struck. Critics of the trend worried about the large sums of borrowed money involved, the diversion of capital from new goods and services, and the intimidating tactics sometimes used. Many target companies sought to evade their suitors, and in some cases paid "greenmail"— they bought out menacing investors at above-market prices. The $13.3 billion acquisition of Gulf Oil Corporation by Standard Oil Company of California (now the Chevron Corporation) was the largest merger ever. The three other biggest mergers also involved oil companies. Texaco Inc. paid $10.1 billion for Getty Oil Company, Mobil Corporation $5.7 billion for

Bean Curd for Dessert

It tastes like ice cream but has half the calories; it has lots of vitamins and no cholesterol. Made from tofu, or bean curd, the new product known as Tofutti is the gastronomic brainchild of former delicatessen owner David Mintz, who worked obsessively for years until he came up with the right formula for his dream dessert. People were skeptical at first— bean curd?—but the taste caught on, and Mintz's New York–based company, Tofu Time Inc., became a smashing success; in the hot summer days of 1984, Tofutti was a big seller at more than a thousand stores around the United States and Canada.

Leaders of the world's largest industrial democracies gathered in London for their tenth annual summit conference. Clockwise from left, U.S. President Ronald Reagan, British Prime Minister Margaret Thatcher, French President François Mitterrand, European Community executive commission President Gaston Thorn, Canadian Prime Minister Pierre Trudeau, and (back to camera) Japanese Prime Minister Yasuhiro Nakasone. Also attending the summit were Chancellor Helmut Kohl of West Germany and Premier Bettino Craxi of Italy.

The Superior Oil Company, and Royal Dutch Petroleum Company $5.5 billion for Shell Oil Company.

Other large mergers included the purchase of Carnation Company by Swiss-based Nestle S.A. for $3 billion, the largest non-oil merger in U.S. history; the purchase of St. Regis Paper Company by Champion International Corporation for $1.84 billion in cash and stock, which created the nation's largest paper producing company; and the $2.7 billion takeover of Esmark, Inc., by Beatrice Foods Company.

Debts of Developing Countries. The debt problems of developing countries remained acute. However, there was a major breakthrough with the negotiation of a long-term rescheduling of Mexico's foreign debt. The rescheduling agreement, involving some 550 commercial banks, was aimed at making Mexico's debt payments more manageable while providing financial room for further expansion of the Mexican economy. That economy had already given some cause for cautious optimism in 1984,

when it experienced the first real growth in output in three years, with more growth expected in 1985.

The debt-rescheduling package was approved by an advisory committee of the International Monetary Fund in September. For the first time since Mexico set off the world debt crisis in 1982 by announcing it could not service its foreign debt, international lenders had rejected a policy of short-term crisis management in favor of a long-term approach. The agreement spread out over 14 years the repayment of some $48.5 billion of Mexico's total of $96 billion in foreign debt. Another provision of the agreement effectively lowered the interest rate Mexico has to pay on the debt. Finally, the lending banks agreed to waive the commission normally charged for rescheduling.

Mexico's long-term restructuring proved to be the exception rather than the rule, however. Generally, the commercial banks continued to negotiate the rescheduling of debts, as they came due, for periods of a year or 18 months.

143

Another major debtor nation is Argentina, with $45 billion of foreign obligations. For months, Argentina's new civilian government, fearful of political repercussions at home, resisted IMF demands that it impose austerity in order to get its finances in better shape. Finally, in a tentative agreement reached in September, Argentina assented to an economic adjustment program in return for $1.4 billion in fresh IMF credits, to be drawn over 15 months. This paved the way for the start of negotiations between Argentina and leading commercial banks on restructuring Argentina's foreign debt. In November, Argentina and some of its leading creditor banks reached an agreement that provided for $4.2 billion in new loans and a rescheduling of $13.4 billion in payments, which would have come due in 1985, over a period of 12 years. Final agreement was reached with the IMF in December.

The United States, West Germany, and Great Britain blocked proposals by France and the developing countries for a $15 billion increase in special drawing rights (SDR's), a kind of international currency issued by the IMF. The poorer nations felt a fresh allocation of SDR's was needed to help them add to their reserves, pay off their debts, and finance imports. Many industrial nations contended that a new issue of SDR's might reignite global inflation.

Real interest rates, adjusted for inflation, remained very high. Many people blamed the high rates on the massive U.S. government budget deficits. The developing countries, who pay billions of dollars in higher interest on their debts for each one-point increase in the prime lending rate of U.S. commercial banks, complained loudly. At a meeting on June 21–22 of 11 Latin American debtor nations in Cartagena, Colombia, the delegates called for measures leading to drastic and immediate reduction of interest rates. They proposed creation of a "compensatory window" at the IMF, which would provide funds to debtor nations to offset the impact of interest rate hikes. In another proposal, they suggested that interest charges above a certain level should be converted into principal to be paid later.

London Economic Summit. At the annual economic summit, held in London on June 7–9, the leaders of the United States, Great Britain, West Germany, France, Canada, Italy, and Japan endorsed a ten-point program which British Prime Minister Margaret Thatcher characterized as a plan to "sustain the economic recovery, to create new jobs, and to spread our prosperity much more widely across the world." The leaders agreed to conduct a new round of trade negotiations and to increase the flow of resources to Third World countries (but no new money was visible). They spoke as well of the need to open their markets to the exports of developing countries.

Protectionism. Despite the London economic summit's statement of economically noble sentiments about free trade, protectionism continued to grow in the industrial nations. In the United States, the picture was mixed. President Reagan turned down industry requests for protection from imported tuna, stainless steel flatware, shoes, and copper. He also rejected a recommendation of the International Trade Commission (a U.S. government agency) for quotas or tariff relief for the steel industry. However, the United States did negotiate so-called voluntary quotas on steel imports with such nations as Brazil, Spain, and South Korea, which are not covered by previous agreements limiting steel imports. Other industrial nations also had mixed records in this area, although in general the swing toward increased protectionism was accelerating.

See also BANKING AND FINANCE and articles on individual countries mentioned.

W.N. & D.R.F.

ECUADOR. León Febres Cordero Rivadeneira was installed as Ecuador's 75th president on August 10, 1984. In his inaugural address, he referred to the economic convulsions Ecuador was experiencing and promised to resolve them with the help of a free market and more foreign investment. Febres Cordero said he would fight inflation, continue a negotiation of the country's massive foreign debt, and curtail land reform and other social programs. However, he faced a Congress controlled by opposition parties.

The conservative Febres Cordero had won the presidency by a margin of 130,000 votes in a runoff election on May 6 against liberal candidate Rodrigo Borja Cevallos, who had received a plurality among nine candidates in the first-round election in January. His winning campaign was based in part on promises of food, jobs, and housing to a population in want of all three. He won strong enough support in coastal areas to overcome an edge by Borja in Quito and most of the provinces.

Debt rescheduling continued to be a major economic priority. In May, the Central Bank reached agreement with foreign banks to reschedule, over eight years, $353 million in government debt owed in 1984. Rescheduling talks continued on $270 million owed overseas by the private sector. In June the outgoing government of Osvaldo Hurtado Larrea suspended payments on $241.5 million owed to foreign governments and banks before the end of 1985. As talks with the new government continued, opponents of austerity measures urged by the International Monetary Fund staged a 24-hour general strike in late October. In December, a steering committee of creditor banks agreed to new financing and rescheduling of $4.3 billion in debt.

While the economic outlook appeared gloomy, there were bright spots. The Inter-American Development Bank modified the provisions of nine loans to Ecuador, to ensure completion of pending development projects despite Ecuador's lack of funds. Shrimp exports were expected to bring in more than $1 billion, making this product the highest earner of foreign exchange, except for petroleum. New oil finds in the northeast, along the Colombian border, doubled earlier projections of reserves.

Ecuador figured prominently in hemispheric affairs by convening a meeting of Latin American and Caribbean governments in Quito in January to discuss an Ecuadoran position paper on the hemispheric debt issue. The resulting Declaration of Quito established a common Latin American position, calling for removal of trade barriers, lower lending rates and longer payback periods from banks, and additional commercial and financial credits.

Internal upheaval was caused by strikes of oil workers in Napo and Esmeraldas provinces begun in late February and early March. The strikes ended on March 17, a day after President Hurtado declared a nationwide state of emergency (lifted on March 27).

See STATISTICS OF THE WORLD.   L.L.P.

Working the crowd in a poor section of Guayaquil, León Febres Cordero Rivadeneira campaigns for Ecuador's presidency in January. A conservative, he ran second to his leftist opponent, Rodrigo Borja Cevallos, in a first round of voting, but defeated him in a May runoff election.

EDUCATION. Reform and renewal were the dominant themes in U.S. education in 1984, as legislators and school administrators responded to reports of serious deficits in the American public school system.

U.S. Secretary of Education Terrel H. Bell announced in November that he was leaving his cabinet post effective December 31, to return to private life. He said that during his term in office he had experienced the "beginning of a real renaissance of American education."

The Reform Issue. In a report titled *A Nation Responds,* submitted to President Ronald Reagan on May 11, Secretary Bell had heralded the coming of what he termed a "tidal wave of school reform which promises to renew American education." The need for such a national renewal was the chief subject of *A Nation at Risk,* a sharp critique of U.S. public schools compiled by the president's National Commission on Excellence in Education and issued in May 1983.

145

EDUCATION

After the 1983 commission report, Bell said, U.S. schools embarked on an "unprecedented" period of improvement, with most of the 50 states and the District of Columbia moving to enact reforms recommended in it. Forty-eight were considering tougher requirements for high school graduation, while 30 had already enacted measures requiring newly certified teachers to pass standardized basic-skills or "minimal competency" tests. Further, the secretary observed, 24 were considering some type of merit pay for teachers, typically in the form of higher pay for those designated as "master teachers." Six other states had already begun such programs. Secretary Bell also noted other signs of reform: among the 50 states and the District of Columbia, eight had decided to lengthen the school day or school year, 21 had taken steps to improve their textbooks, and 13 were considering higher academic requirements for students participating in sports and other extracurricular activities.

One state that embraced the reform movement with particular enthusiasm was Texas, where the state legislature passed one of the year's most sweeping education reform laws. The centerpiece of the bill was a $2.8 billion tax hike providing funds to raise teachers' salaries and pay for other improvements in the public schools. Spurred on by a state advisory panel that had lambasted Texas schools for being more interested in athletics than in academics, the state legislature mandated that, by 1986, both new and current school teachers and administrators would have to pass a "certification examination" to keep their jobs. Also, students at Texas colleges will have to pass one standardized test before being allowed to enter teacher-training programs, and another test upon graduation. Under the terms of the law, if a high percentage of students at a college fail the graduation exam, that school could lose its state accreditation.

Textbooks and SAT's. Earlier in the year, Secretary Bell called for action on the 1983

A curious child approaches "Turtle Tot," a robot with a vocabulary of 143 words. The electronic reptile was one of several such devices examined at a Columbia University Teachers College conference about computer-assisted instruction for the very young.

commission's recommendation that textbooks "should be upgraded . . . and made more rigorous." In a speech to the American Association of School Administrators in February, Bell charged that this recommendation had been "largely ignored" and that textbook publishers had continued to "dumb down" their books, emphasizing easier words and shorter sentences in an effort to ensure widespread acceptance. Publishers generally have replied that in developing textbooks they are guided by the wishes of school officials.

Regardless of who is at fault in the "dumbing down" controversy, some experts have contended that the use of simplified language in textbooks contributed to the year-by-year decline in Scholastic Aptitude Test (SAT) scores that started in the early 1960's and continued for almost two decades. Nevertheless, SAT scores began to improve slightly in 1982, and in June 1984 the scores of high school graduates increased by an average of one point in the verbal section and three points in the mathematical section, the biggest gain since scores first began to dip in 1963.

Attitudes Toward Education. "Americans are more favorably disposed toward the public schools today than at any time in the last decade," said George Gallup, Sr., in an analysis of the annual Gallup education poll written just three weeks before his death in July. About 42 percent of those surveyed in May gave their local public schools an "A" or "B" grade— up from 31 percent in 1983. The responses showed the highest level of public confidence in the public school system since 1976.

The significant increase in support apparently carried over to the public's perceptions of teachers and school officials. In the 1984 Gallup survey, 50 percent of those responding said teachers deserved an "A" or "B" rating— up from 39 percent in 1983. The survey found that the majority of the public favored a required national high school graduation test, but opposed a lengthening of the school day and school year. The respondents expressed mixed views on the interrelated questions of higher taxes and higher salaries for teachers. By a wide margin (66 percent to 22 percent), they favored candidates who were for increased federal spending for education. But

when asked if they were for or against an increase in taxes to support the public schools, more were "against" (47 percent) than were "for" (41 percent).

School Prayer. Another finding of the 1984 Gallup poll was that respondents favored, by 69 percent to 24 percent, passage of a constitutional amendment to allow prayer in public schools. Despite such apparently widespread support for a school prayer amendment, the U.S. Senate on March 20 narrowly rejected such a measure. The proposed amendment, backed strongly by the Reagan administration, would have removed any constitutional bar to "individual or group prayer in public schools" while prohibiting "the United States or any state" from composing words to such a prayer. In leading the fight against the proposed amendment, Senator Lowell Weicker (R, Conn.) argued that school-sanctioned prayer sessions would violate the rights of nonreligious students. The measure fell 11 votes short of winning the two-thirds majority needed.

Vocational Education. One of the key issues facing educational policymakers is the question of the kind of high school education needed by non–college-bound students. An answer to this question was supplied in a report issued in May by a special commission of educators and business leaders set up by the National Academy of Sciences. According to the report, employers of high school graduates tend to seek young people who display "an ability to learn" and who have an educational background "very nearly the same" as that of college-bound students. "Technical and vocational education can enhance a student's employability," the report said, "but it cannot substitute for education in the core competencies," among which were counted "the ability to read, write, reason and compute" and "sound work habits and a positive attitude." Pointing out that over the next half-century the job market will change considerably, the report declared that the employees who will survive in this market and move up the job ladder are those who can learn new skills. And a traditional academic education, rather than specialized training, appears to offer the best preparation for this rapidly changing workplace, the report concluded.

Hymnals in hand, advocates of a proposed constitutional amendment authorizing prayer in the public schools raise their voices at a rally on the steps of the U.S. Capitol. The amendment, despite a fervent campaign on its behalf, was defeated in the Senate.

The Teaching Profession. In a report on the "Coming Crisis in Teaching," released in August, the RAND Corporation pointed out that "the current highly educated and experienced teaching force is dwindling as older teachers retire in increasing numbers and many younger teachers leave for other professions." The report also concluded that the new recruits appeared to be less academically qualified than those who were leaving. To remedy this situation, RAND researcher Linda Darling-Hammond recommended several courses of action. In addition to establishing "competitive salaries for teachers," ranging from $20,000 to $50,000 a year, she proposed that school authorities offer recruitment incentives, such as scholarships or forgivable loans, for academically talented college students; improve teacher training, by making it more intellectually rigorous and by requiring internships supervised by senior teachers; improve working conditions, by allowing aides to assume many clerical and nonteaching tasks and by giving teachers more preparation time and decision-making authority; and, finally, allow experienced teachers to assume responsibility for supervising new teachers and developing new programs.

In a symbolic gesture of respect for teachers, President Reagan announced in August that he had directed the National Aeronautics and Space Administration to choose an elementary or secondary school teacher as the first "citizen passenger" to fly on the space shuttle, probably in late 1985 or early 1986.

Women's Rights. In a highly publicized decision handed down on February 28, the U.S. Supreme Court ruled, 6–3, that the federal government's ban on sex discrimination in education, mandated by Title IX of the Education Amendments of 1972, did not apply to school and college programs that received no federal aid. Title IX prohibits discrimination on the basis of sex in "any education program or activity receiving federal financial assistance." Federal officials had acted under the assumption that Title IX covered all programs, including athletic programs, at any school or college that received any funds from Washington, and even if federal funds came in so indirect a form as grants and loans to students. In *Grove City College* v. *Bell*, however, the Court overturned a federal appeals court ruling that Grove City College, a small private school in northwestern Pennsylvania, was subject to Title IX regulations. The college itself did not get any federal grants, although its students did, so the Court found that only Grove City's student aid office had to comply with the antidiscrimation provisions.

Some representatives of women's groups feared the Grove City ruling would lead to substantially increased discrimination against women in college athletic programs. Other observers, however, citing changing public attitudes and the already increased participation by women in college sports, believed the removal of federal requirements would not have a major impact on the policies of colleges and universities.

Enrollment and Spending. College enrollments appeared to be leveling out, and low-cost community colleges registered a sharp decline in enrollment in 1984. Many major universities, however, were not affected by a drop in available freshmen. Ivy League colleges and other highly prestigious private colleges and universities were flooded with applications, despite costs for tuition, room, and board that often topped $10,000 a year.

Nationwide, the cost of education continued to increase, rising by 6 percent in the 1983–1984 school year. During the 1984–1985 school year, $240 million will be spent on education in the United States, the U.S. Department of Education said in its annual forecast released in July. The DOE estimated that total enrollment in educational institutions would be down by 350,000, to about 56.3 million pupils, in fall 1984. When this total is added to the over 3 million Americans employed as teachers, the DOE noted, "education in the fall of 1984 would be . . . the primary activity of 59.7 million Americans," or more than one out of every four persons."   D.G.S.

EGYPT. In 1984, President Hosni Mubarak continued to move toward improving relations with Egypt's Arab brethren and with the Soviet Union. At home, the government took steps to allow the opposition a greater voice and role.

Foreign Affairs. Other Arab leaders began to edge closer toward restoring relations with Egypt in the wake of Mubarak's December 1983 meeting with Palestine Liberation Organization leader Yasir Arafat. In January, Egypt was readmitted to the Islamic Conference Organization by a vote of the heads of member states; only Syria, Libya, and Iran were opposed. In February, Mubarak met first with King Hassan of Morocco and then with King Hussein of Jordan. Relations with Iraq also improved as a result of Egypt's support in Iraq's war with Iran. No offer of readmission to the Arab League was made at the organization's March meeting. In late September, however, Jordan announced

Earning an Education

Administrators at Richmond High School in Indiana came up with an innovative way to bolster attendance. They proved to would-be stay-at-homes that education can pay—by promising a cash award of $100 to each student with perfect attendance in the 1983–1984 school year. The strategy worked almost too well. In all, 219 of the school's 1,600 students achieved perfect attendance, compared with only 37 the year before, and officials had to appeal to the public for donations to meet their obligations. The school was finally able to come up with the cash in time for summer vacation; however, administrators were said to be working on a different incentive plan for the future, with a less economic orientation.

it was resuming diplomatic ties with Egypt. Two weeks later, Mubarak traveled to Jordan for the first state visit by an Egyptian leader to an Arab country that had broken relations with Egypt after Camp David. In December, Hussein visited Cairo for three days of talks, and in a communiqué issued by the two leaders, Egypt officially endorsed Jordan's formula for a peaceful resolution of the Arab-Israeli conflict, based on return of occupied lands and "self-determination" for Palestinians.

Mubarak's efforts toward a rapprochement with the Soviet Union bore fruit when, on July 7, both countries formally announced the resumption of full diplomatic relations. This move apparently portended no fundamental shift in U.S.-Egyptian relations, since U.S. military and economic assistance to Egypt for 1984 was kept at the 1983 levels of $1.3 billion and $1 billion, respectively, maintaining Egypt's position as the second greatest recipient of American aid, after Israel. Mubarak and President Ronald Reagan met in February to discuss problems of mutual concern, with particular focus on means by which Egypt could meet interest payments on its $3.6 billion military debt.

Egypt did not alter the climate of "cold peace" in relations with Israel. Among the major irritants between the two nations were

149

the continuing expansion of Israeli settlements on the West Bank, Israel's occupation of South Lebanon, and Egypt's breaking off of relations with El Salvador and Costa Rica after those countries decided to move their embassies from Tel Aviv to Jerusalem.

During the summer attention was riveted on the mysterious mining of the Gulf of Suez and the Red Sea. By late September, at least 19 ships from diverse nations had been damaged by the mines, which threatened to disrupt traffic through the Suez Canal, traditionally one of Egypt's greatest earners of foreign exchange. Naval units from the United States, several European countries, and the Soviet Union conducted minesweeping operations to keep the canal open. Despite widespread speculation, and suspicion centering on Iran or Libya, there was no firm evidence as to what group or government was responsible for the minings.

In November the Egyptian government arrested four people hired by Libyan leader Muammar al-Qaddafi to assassinate a political opponent in Cairo. After foiling the assassination attempt, Egypt used faked photographs to trick Libya into announcing that the intended victim had been executed by Qaddafi's "suicide squads."

Domestic Politics. The parliamentary elections of May 27, the first in five years, were widely viewed as a test of Mubarak's pledge to bring democracy to Egypt. And although certain groups such as the Communists and radical Muslims were still banned from the political competition, five political parties did contest the elections. The ruling National Democratic Party captured 391 of the seats at stake in the People's Assembly, while the New Wafd party won the remaining 57 seats, the greatest number achieved by any opposition party since termination of the constitutional monarchy in 1952 and nearly twice the number of opposition seats held in the outgoing assembly.

Economy. The country's largest sources of foreign exchange—workers' remittances from abroad, Suez Canal revenues, oil revenues, and tourism—were expected to remain close to 1983 levels. In contrast to his predecessor's more liberal economic policies, Mubarak focused on a return to stricter economic planning and a reaffirmation of a faith in the public

sector, which accounted for about 75 percent of total investment. One trouble spot was the agricultural sector, where a 2 percent increase in output per year was failing to keep pace with a 2.8 percent annual increase in the population. As a result, the country once again had to import substantial amounts of food. Riots broke out in the city of Kafr ad Dawwar, near Alexandria, in September after the government raised food prices. A day after the protest—the first such episode since Mubarak came to power—food price rollbacks were announced.

See STATISTICS OF THE WORLD.   K.J.B.

ELECTIONS IN THE UNITED STATES. Ronald Reagan enjoyed a tidal-wave victory in the November 6, 1984, U.S. presidential election. In winning a second term as president, he carried 49 states and amassed a record total of 525 electoral votes. His Democratic opponent, former Vice-President Walter Mondale, carried only his home state of Minnesota (by a few thousand votes) and the District of Columbia, for a total of 13 electoral votes. In the popular vote, complete returns reported by the Associated Press showed Reagan, the Republican candidate, with 54,450,603 votes (59 percent) and Mondale with 37,573,671 votes (41 percent).

The 59 percent margin was close to, but still short of, the landslide margins achieved by Franklin D. Roosevelt in 1936, Lyndon Johnson in 1964, and Richard Nixon in 1972. Reagan took 70 percent or more of the vote in four states and 60 percent or more in 28 others and became the first president since Dwight Eisenhower to win back-to-back landslides.

Despite the Reagan landslide, the Democrats easily retained control of the U.S. House of Representatives, suffering only modest losses, and gained two seats in the Senate, reducing the Republican margin there to 53–47. The GOP gains in the House were too small to make up for its losses in the 1982 midterm elections and resurrect a majority coalition of Republicans and conservative Democrats there.

Presidential Campaign. The one dominant issue in the 1984 presidential campaign was Ronald Reagan himself. The central question for the voters on Election Day were whether they felt better off during his first term than

President Reagan shakes hands with Democratic candidate Walter Mondale at the beginning of their second presidential campaign debate, in Kansas City.

they had in the Carter years and whether Reagan had given the nation the kind of leadership it wanted.

The voters answered yes to both. With memories of a number of failed or flawed administrations in the recent past, Americans were looking most of all for strong and effective leadership. Reagan had hammered home this theme in 1980 against Jimmy Carter. He again made leadership a major issue in 1984.

In his first term, Reagan may have changed the direction of government in the United States more than any other president since Franklin D. Roosevelt. Reversing the latter's emphasis on economic intervention and government regulation, Reagan extolled the virtues of private enterprise and individual self-reliance and the economic efficacy of lower taxes and less government spending. He also promised to stand up to the Soviets and restore strength and decisiveness to U.S. foreign policy. His policies seemingly paid off in 1983 and 1984, as inflation fell and prosperity returned while the nation remained at peace. Reagan and his advisers presented the good news as a personal triumph by a strong leader. Their basic message was that Americans could once again be proud of their country and confident in their future. See also PRESIDENT OF THE UNITED STATES.

Reagan and Vice-President George Bush were renominated at the Republican National Convention in Dallas in August. The Democrats at their national convention the month before in San Francisco formally gave their presidential nomination to Mondale, who had piled up a decisive majority of delegate votes during a long and hard-fought primary campaign. Mondale made history by designating a woman, U.S. Representative Geraldine Ferraro of New York, as his choice for a running mate, and she was duly nominated for vice-president at the convention. See DEMOCRATIC PARTY; REPUBLICAN PARTY.

Labor Day, the traditional opening day of presidential campaigns, foreshadowed the outcome. From New York City to central Wisconsin to Long Beach, Calif., Labor Day failed to work for Mondale. Crowds did not materialize, his speeches did not reach beyond the obvious, his schedule slowly disintegrated, and his windup in California was so delayed that people in the audience were fainting from the heat as the sound system went on and off. At day's end, Mondale said, "We need a medic."

Reagan kicked off his campaign on Labor Day by going to the base of his support— Fountain Valley, in the heart of Orange County in California, his adopted home state. Speaking at a rally bedecked with multicolored balloons—a picture perfect for the nightly tele-

151

vision news—he derided his opponents as a "pack of pessimists" tied to special interest groups and to the failed policies of the past. For his part, he proclaimed, "Today we set out to achieve a victory for the future over the past, for opportunity over retreat, for hope over despair, and to move up to all that is possible and not down to that which we fear." Urging his listeners to help him "make America great again," he promised them, "You ain't seen nothin' yet!"

Meanwhile, Mondale, searching for a way to attack what one Democrat had called a "Teflon president" (whose popularity was such that no adverse charges would stick), asserted that Reagan had a "secret plan" to deal with soaring federal budget deficits by increasing taxes. Mondale made public his own plan and challenged the president to do the same. He proposed raising $85 billion in revenue over four years, principally by postponing the scheduled implementation of tax indexing (the linking of tax brackets to inflation) and by imposing a 10 percent tax surcharge on upper-income wage earners and a minimum 15 percent tax on corporations. But Reagan jumped on his opponent for seeking to raise taxes in the midst of an economic recovery, and Mondale's argument that Reagan would have to raise taxes to cure the deficit never took hold among the voters. Mondale was cast as the taxer and spender, Reagan as the architect of an economic recovery stimulated by tax cuts.

Another setback for Mondale was a controversy over the finances of his running mate, Representative Ferraro. Her historic nomination for vice-president had given him a temporary lift in the polls. A quick deflation followed, however, when it was discovered that Ferraro had failed to include, in the financial disclosure statements required of her as a House member, information on her husband, John Zaccaro, a New York City real estate developer. Income tax returns, along with other information about the couple's finances, eventually were released, but questions about some of Zaccaro's business practices and about Ferraro's use of her own and her husband's money in past political campaigns continued to plague the candidate. In a press conference on August 20, Ferraro stood up well to a 90-minute bombardment of queries on her finances. But

the damage had been done. (Ultimately, the Democratic ticket captured less than half of the women's vote—only 43 percent according to one survey.)

Mondale did benefit from a new surge in the polls after the first presidential debate with Reagan, in Louisville, Ky., on October 7. Reagan was placed on the defensive as he sought to explain his controversial positions on school prayer and abortion, the huge federal debt, and his alleged foot-dragging in the cleaning up of toxic waste dumps. The president did not do well. He did poorly on substance and also looked rusty at the start of the debate, hesitating in his delivery and fumbling in his presentation. By the end of the debate he seemed tired and was unable even to sustain a strong closing statement. The issue emerged that he had dismissed in the public mind with his own jokes—his age (at 73, he would be the oldest person ever to be elected president).

The second debate, held October 21 in Kansas City, was devoted to foreign policy. Mondale hammered away at the theme that Reagan was a decent individual with good intentions who simply did not know what was going on. Mondale cited events in Lebanon, spotlighting the October 1983 bombing of the Marine barracks in which 241 U.S. servicemen died. And he asserted that the president ought

to know where the weapons would be stationed in his proposed "Star Wars" antiballistic missile system—which the president said he did not know. Although Reagan had some rocky moments— giving wrong information, for example, on the CIA's role in Central America—he appeared much sharper and more confident than at Louisville. He regained the "age initiative" with a typical Reagan line, joking that he would not make age an issue in the campaign because "I am not going to exploit for political purposes my opponent's youth and inexperience." The damage done to him in the first debate had been mended in the second, and nothing Mondale said seemed to shake the people's confidence in his opponent. (Bush and Ferraro also debated, on October 11, in a spirited clash in which neither emerged as a clear winner.)

Reagan may have profited to some extent from the feeling of optimism generated by the summer Olympics, and even the Soviets in effect aided the Reagan cause. In an unusual interview with the Washington *Post* correspondent in Moscow just a few weeks before the election, Soviet leader Konstantin Chernenko showed flexibility in dealing with Reagan on nuclear arms control. It took the sting out of the Mondale charge that Reagan was the first president in 50 years not to meet with his

Walter Mondale was ebullient as he greeted voters after his first debate with Ronald Reagan in early October, but his campaign was no match for the magnificently orchestrated political show staged by the president, whose props included cascades of balloons, thunderous bands, and even the presidential railroad car Ferdinand Magellan (left) made famous by Harry Truman's triumphant 1948 "whistle-stop" campaign.

Hopeful smiles in place, Geraldine Ferraro and her husband, John Zaccaro, prepare to reveal personal financial data in August.

Soviet counterpart. A few weeks earlier Reagan had met with Soviet Foreign Minister Andrei Gromyko for private talks in the White House.

At the end, Mondale scarcely had a single issue that worked decisively in his favor, and the counting of the votes provided no surprises. Pollsters had predicted a Reagan win—by popular vote margins ranging from ten to 25 percentage points. Reagan actually won by 18 percentage points and among most groups of voters.

Congressional Elections. The Republican goal in the congressional campaign was clear from the outset: to capitalize on the expected Reagan landslide victory to retain a numerical majority in the Senate and to regain the "ideological majority" in the House of Representatives that the party had lost in the 1982 elections. However, Reagan's pulling power proved surprisingly limited. In the Senate the GOP did hold on to a slim majority, but the party suffered a net loss of two seats. In the House the power of incumbency kept the large Democratic majority substantially intact. The GOP gained 14 seats (with one undecided), much less than the 33-seat gain that accompanied the 1980 Reagan victory and well short of the 26 seats the Republicans dropped in 1982.

No congressional campaign drew more outside attention—or more out-of-state funding—than the one pitting Democratic challenger James B. Hunt, Jr., two-term governor of North Carolina, against ultraconservative Republican Senator Jesse Helms. Helms spent more than $14 million—$12 for each vote he received—to paint his opponent as the candidate of "the homosexuals, the labor union bosses, and the crooks." Hunt spent at least $8 million to tie Helms to the fundamentalist Moral Majority and to right-wing "death squads" in El Salvador. Buoyed by a strong turnout of Reagan supporters, Helms ended up winning, by a narrow 85,000-vote margin.

Reagan carried Illinois by more than 600,000 votes, but that was small consolation to another Republican, Senator Charles H. Percy, a one-time liberal who had wrapped himself in the Reagan mantle. Percy, chairman of the Senate

Foreign Relations Committee, lost narrowly to Representative Paul Simon, a five-term congressman. Simon was liberal enough to draw the Chicago vote, and as a representative of rural southern Illinois he cut into the Republicans' normally solid support downstate. Post-election analysts thought Percy just had too many enemies: farmers who felt he did not represent their interests, Jewish voters who faulted him for not tilting toward Israel, and conservatives who had never forgotten or forgiven his previous political leanings.

Two Republican senators departed by choice. Senate Majority Leader Howard H. Baker, Jr., of Tennessee, declined to seek reelection—in order, most observers believed, to prepare for a 1988 presidential run. Elected to Baker's Senate seat was U.S. Representative Albert Gore, Jr., a popular Democrat whose father had represented Tennessee in the Senate for nearly 20 years. Four-term Senator John Tower (R, Texas), chairman of the Armed Services Committee, also retired; his seat was won by a former Democrat, Representative Phil Gramm (R), a conservative who had been a leader of the pro-Reagan "boll weevil" Democratic faction in the House during the battles over tax and budget cuts in 1981. Another Republican, Roger W. Jepsen of Iowa, was sent into unplanned retirement by a liberal Democrat, Representative Tom Harkin, in a campaign that focused on the state's depressed economy and Jepsen's alleged moral lapses.

Leaving the Senate on the Democratic side were Paul Tsongas of Massachusetts, Jennings Randolph of West Virginia, and Walter Huddleston of Kentucky. Tsongas, a prominent liberal who retired because of illness, was replaced by Democratic Lieutenant Governor John F. Kerry, a former leader of Vietnam Veterans Against the War. Taking the seat of the retiring Randolph, a New Dealer who had served in the Senate since 1958, was Democratic Governor John D. ("Jay") Rockefeller IV, who spent over $9 million to eke out a victory over a little-known Republican businessman. The only upset was Huddleston's loss to a Republican county judge, Mitch McConnell, whose aggressive campaign effectively portrayed the senator as having lackluster voting and attendance records.

The Senators-Elect

Alabama—*Howell Heflin, D
Alaska—*Ted Stevens, R
Arkansas—*David Pryor, D
Colorado—*William Armstrong, R
Delaware—*Joseph R. Biden, Jr., D
Georgia—*Sam Nunn, D
Idaho—*James A. McClure, R
Illinois—*Paul Simon*, D
Iowa—*Tom Harkin*, D
Kansas—*Nancy Landon Kassebaum, R
Kentucky— *A. Mitchell McConnell*, R
Louisiana—*J. Bennett Johnston, D
Maine—*William S. Cohen, R
Massachusetts—John F. Kerry, D
Michigan—*Carl Levin, D
Minnesota—*Rudy Boschwitz, R
Mississippi—*Thad Cochran, R
Montana—*Max Baucus, D
Nebraska—*J. James Exon, D
New Hampshire—*Gordon J. Humphrey, R
New Jersey—*Bill Bradley, D
New Mexico—*Pete V. Domenici, R
North Carolina—*Jesse Helms, R
Oklahoma—*David L. Boren, D
Oregon—*Mark O. Hatfield, R
Rhode Island—*Claiborne Pell, D
South Carolina—*Strom Thurmond, R
South Dakota—*Larry Pressler, R
Tennessee—*Albert Gore, Jr.*, D
Texas—Phil Gramm, R
Virginia—*John W. Warner, R
West Virginia—John D. Rockefeller IV, D
Wyoming—*Alan K. Simpson, R

The Governors-Elect

Arkansas—*Bill Clinton, D
Delaware—*Michael N. Castle, R
Indiana—*Robert D. Orr, R
Missouri—John Ashcroft, R
Montana—*Ted Schwinden, D
New Hampshire—*John H. Sununu, R
North Carolina—*James G. Martin*, R
North Dakota—*George Sinner*, D
Rhode Island—*Edward D. DiPrete*, R
Utah—*Norman H. Bangerter*, R
Vermont—*Madeleine Kunin*, D
Washington—*Booth Gardner*, D
West Virginia—*Arch Moore*, R

*Denotes incumbent
R—Republican
D—Democrat

Name is in italics in cases where a seat changed parties

155

Victors in Senate races included (clockwise from upper left) Phil Gramm (R, Texas), here hugging his wife, Wendy, after a strenuous race; Albert Gore, Jr (D, Tenn.), who won retiring Majority Leader Howard Baker's seat; Alan Simpson (R, Wyo.), shown at a parade with his wife, Ann; incumbent Jesse Helms (R, N.C.), who defeated Governor James B. Hunt, Jr. in a bitterly fought contest; overwhelmingly reelected Democrat Bill Bradley of New Jersey; and Paul Simon (D, Ill.), who narrowly defeated incumbent Charles H. Percy.

In the House, about 95 percent of those incumbents who chose to run again were reelected. No Democratic committee chairman lost; the closest call came in Oklahoma, where James Jones, chairman of the House Budget Committee and a prime target for the Republicans, raised a $1 million war chest and barely held back the Reagan tide. The costliest House race took place in Manhattan's "Silk Stocking" district, where the brash Democratic challenger, Andrew Stein, and the moderate Republican incumbent, S. William ("Bill") Green, spent a combined total of nearly $? million in a race that gave Green a fourth term.

Several House contests hinged on questions of character. Censured by the House and convicted for filing false financial disclosure forms with Congress, George Hansen (R, Idaho) failed by a tiny margin (170 votes) to win reelection. (He filed suit in an attempt to overturn the result.) In Illinois, Daniel Crane (R), censured for having had sexual relations with a young female page, also lost his seat to a Democratic challenger. In Massachusetts, on the other hand, Gerry Studds (D), censured by the House for having had homosexual relations with a teenage page, won reelection after turning the scandal into a gay rights issue.

The election held little cheer for female and minority candidates. In the Senate, incumbent Republican Nancy Landon Kassebaum of Kansas won reelection easily, but all nine women who challenged incumbents went down to defeat. Similarly, the 20 female incumbents in the House who sought reelection held their districts, but of 45 other female candidates for House seats, only two won. The number of Hispanics in the House rose by one, to ten; the number of blacks declined by one, to 19. The strongest black challenger, Robert Clark, failed to unseat a white incumbent, Webb Franklin (R, Miss.), despite redistricting that gave blacks a demographic majority.

Governors and Legislators. Only 13 states elected governors in 1984. The Republicans won eight of the contests, a net gain of one, but the Democrats still reigned supreme in the nation's statehouses by a lopsided margin of 34–16. In the closest race, in Vermont, Madeleine Kunin, a Democrat, won after contending that the state needed a full-time governor, not the caretaker she suggested her opponent would be. The Democrats picked up two more statehouses in North Dakota and Washington, where George Sinner and Booth Gardner, respectively, defeated the incumbents. Republicans picked up four governorships in states where incumbent Democrats did not seek reelection. In West Virginia, former Governor Arch Moore regained the office he had held

157

before; other Republican gains were in North Carolina (James Martin), Rhode Island (Edward DiPrete), and Utah (Norman Bangerter).

Nationwide, the Republicans gained about 300 seats in the 50 state legislatures, but Democrats still controlled the legislatures in a majority of the states.

Exit Polls. One sidelight of the election was the debate over the ethics and consequences of exit polling—the interviewing of voters as they leave voting places. Ever since the 1980 presidential election, when the television networks, with the help of such polling, predicted Reagan's triumph while voting was still going on in many states, critics of the practice have decried its allegedly antidemocratic effects. Fearful that early projections could discourage voters from casting ballots in states where polls were still open, Congress in 1984 passed nonbinding resolutions deploring such prognostications. The networks, however, contended that exit polling yielded legitimate news which they had the right and obligation to report as promptly as possible. On Election Day all three networks refrained from forecasting the results of state races before balloting had ended in the states involved. But the presidential election remained fair game: all three had predicted the outcome by 8:31 P.M. Eastern standard time, while polls were still open throughout the West and in many Eastern states.

See also biographies of George Bush, Geraldine Ferraro, and Walter Mondale in PEOPLE IN THE NEWS.   R.H. & G.M.H.

ELECTRONICS. In consumer electronics, 1984 was another boom year. Sales for products like videocassette recorders, or VCR's, soared. The industry saw several important advances in technology.

In March, the Federal Communications Commission authorized U.S. television stations to broadcast in stereo. Each TV channel is allowed three audio channels—two channels to create stereo sound, the third for other purposes. It was expected many broadcasters would use the third for simultaneous foreign-language broadcasts. To pick up stereo signals, viewers with newer "stereo-ready" sets can buy decoders.

In 1983, the Sony Corporation introduced stereo capability for its Beta-format VCR's.

Vermont Democrat Madeleine Kunin signals victory in the nation's closest gubernatorial race. Her defeat of John Easton (R) made her Vermont's first woman governor.

Manufacturers of the rival VHS format responded in 1984, as several companies, including Japan's Matsushita Electric Industrial Company, introduced VHS Hi-Fi. In a conventional VHS recorder, a single fixed audio head records at relatively slow speed. In VHS Hi-Fi, two rotary audio heads record at higher speeds. The result is full stereo sound with a dynamic range of more than 80 decibels.

Another major innovation in the VCR field in 1984 was the "camcorder," a compact, hand-held, battery-powered camera/recorder combination. Weighing about 6 pounds, the new camcorders are much easier to use than the earlier two-piece camera/recorders, which required users to shoulder the camera and carry a separate video recorder.

In VCR technology, there have been two mutually incompatible recorder systems—Beta and VHS. In the fall, the Eastman Kodak Company began to market a third system, using smaller, 8-millimeter tapes instead of the half inch tapes used by both Beta and VHS cassettes. Kodak's cassette is roughly the size of a standard audio cassette and this allows for a more compact VCR.

In June, Matsushita brought out the first digital TV set, designed so that two images can be displayed at once; one takes up most of the viewing area, while the second is in a corner of the screen. Viewers can watch one show while monitoring a second. Digital technology also makes it possible to freeze a frame or zoom in for a close-up. The NEC Corporation of Japan introduced a set that allows viewers to store an image in the set's memory and then print it out. In a digital set, much of the conventional electronic circuitry is replaced by semiconductor chips. Five tiny chips developed by the ITT Corporation can replace over 350 components—meaning that digital sets should need less service.

Matsushita introduced a slender AM/FM stereo radio. About the size of a credit card, it weighs just 1.34 ounces, including a battery.

See also TELEVISION AND RADIO BROAD-CASTING.   W.D.M.

EL SALVADOR. El Salvador implemented its new constitution in 1984, most notably by electing a political moderate, José Napoleón Duarte, as president; he replaced provisional President Alvaro Magaña. Duarte, encountering stiff domestic opposition from both left and right, had difficulty making concrete progress at home; he was more successful in improving relations with other countries, including the United States, on whom he leaned heavily for military and economic aid. The civil war against left-wing guerrillas continued, amid hopes for some rapprochement.

Presidential Election. After a bitter campaign of harsh personal denunciations, Christian Democrat José Napoleón Duarte, 58, won a five-year term as president in a runoff election on May 6 (see biography in PEOPLE IN THE NEWS). His margin of victory was 54 percent, to 46 percent for Roberto d'Aubuisson of the ultra-rightist Nationalist Republican Alliance (Arena). Although d'Aubuisson carried eight of 14 departments in El Salvador, Duarte won in the capital by some 130,000 votes. D'Aubuisson charged that the election was fraudulent, citing irregularities at the ballot boxes and CIA support for Arena opponents. D'Aubuisson himself was accused of having organized the infamous right-wing death squads that accounted for a large share of the violence since 1979.

The May 6 runoff was necessitated by the failure of any of the eight candidates to win a majority in the March 25 presidential balloting.

Government and Politics. On June 1, Duarte took office as the first popularly elected pres-ident of El Salvador in over 50 years. He called on all Salvadorans to unite in a social pact to achieve peace, and promised to terminate death-squad activity, seek to end the civil war by negotiation, revive land reform, modify his earlier nationalization of foreign trade, and offer amnesty to rebels.

Despite several early legislative defeats, the Duarte government's initial accomplishments included the disbanding in June of a notorious 100-man intelligence unit of the treasury police that had been linked to the death squads. Moderates were appointed to head the national and treasury police.

In August the president announced the formation of a special commission to investigate a series of apparently politically motivated crimes, including the murder of Archbishop Oscar Arnulfo Romero in March 1980 and the killing of two U.S. labor-union aides and a Salvadoran land reform official in January 1981. In November the Salvadoran Supreme Court cleared an army officer accused of ordering the 1981 slayings, but Duarte ordered the officer discharged from the army without pension. Earlier, in May, the long-delayed trial of five former national guardsmen for the December 1980 slayings of four American church-women was concluded; the five were convicted of the crime and received 30-year jail sentences. But Duarte still faced criticism from human rights activists, who charged among other things that he had reneged on his promise to end arbitrary detentions, abuse of office by public authorities, and aerial bombardments of civilians.

Initially, Duarte appeared to retreat on another campaign promise, to open a dialogue with the leftist opposition. Then, during a speech on October 8 before the UN General Assembly, he extended a surprise invitation to guerrilla leaders to meet with him a week later. The invitation was accepted. The results of the October 15 meeting were politically inconclusive, mainly because the rebels did not feel that Duarte's offer to let them participate in 1985 elections constituted the direct sharing of broadly based government powers they wanted. Although the two sides did agree to establish a joint commission to continue negotiations, by year's end talks between the government and the rebels seemed to be stalemated. The two sides did agree, however, to a cease-fire for the Christmas and New Year's holiday.

Guerrilla Activity. The war of attrition featured some daring maneuvers by the rebel units. The guerrilla forces on January 1 blew up the Cuscatlán suspension bridge 67 miles east of San Salvador. The loss of that bridge was a serious blow to morale as it interrupted the major road link with the eastern part of the country. In June the insurgents captured and briefly held the Cerrón Grande hydroelectric dam, largest in the country; that operation claimed the lives of 60 soldiers.

When Colonel Joseph Stringham, commander of U.S. advisers (offically 55 in number) in El Salvador, ended his tour of duty in June, he claimed that the Salvadoran military forces had taken the initiative from guerrillas because commanders whose tactics were considered outdated were being replaced. In a new offensive initiated in late August, government forces started a sweep of rebel areas in a central department. Throughout the conflict, massacres of civilians were reported.

The Salvadoran army suffered a severe setback on October 23 when its most effective combat commander, Lieutenant Colonel Domingo Monterrosa, was killed in a helicopter crash in rebel-held territory. Thirteen others on the craft, including three senior combat officers were also reportedly killed. Guerrillas claimed to have shot the helicopter down.

Economic Conditions. The declining output (since 1979) of coffee, El Salvador's leading export crop, was attributed to poor weather, plant disease, guerrilla attacks, and landowners' unwillingness to invest in production, but surpluses from previous years were to be sold to maintain export revenues. Outside assistance continued with loans of $45 million from

Villagers in San Miguel, El Salvador, line up to vote in the first round of a bitterly fought presidential campaign. When none of the eight contenders received a majority, the three front-runners competed in a May runoff, which was won handily by José Napoleón Duarte.

the World Bank and $40 million from the Inter-American Development Bank, along with $10 million from the United Nations Development Program.

Labor restiveness increased. No wage increases had been granted in four years, prices of basic commodities had soared, and labor leaders continued to disappear. Although strikes were illegal, postal workers won higher pay in June after a 45-day work stoppage.

Foreign Relations. The question of U.S. financial aid to El Salvador, particularly military aid, was hotly debated in Congress and throughout the United States in 1984. Critics of Reagan administration policy expressed misgivings because of continuing human rights abuses in El Salvador and fear that the United States might be becoming too deeply involved in Central America. Ultimately, Congress became more responsive to President Ronald Reagan's appeals for more aid. In 1984, Congress approved $64.8 million in military aid and $131.8 million in supplemental military aid. In economic assistance, $195.5 million was approved for fiscal 1984, with $134.8 million in supplemental aid following. For the 1985 fiscal year, Congress approved $180 million in military aid and $360 million in economic assistance.

Support for El Salvador on Capitol Hill increased substantially after Duarte was elected president in May and then visited Washington twice to lobby personally for military aid. Duarte also visited five European countries in July to seek help, and in Bonn he achieved a major success when Chancellor Helmut Kohl agreed to the resumption of West German economic aid to El Salvador.

See STATISTICS OF THE WORLD.　　　L.L.P.

ENERGY. Economic recovery pushed total U.S. energy consumption during the first seven months of 1984 about 8 percent above the level of a year earlier. However, lagging coal exports caused declines in U.S. coal production. The Great Plains coal gasification plant began production of natural gas.

Coal. Data for the first half of 1984 indicated that strong economic recovery had boosted U.S. coal consumption about 14 percent above year-earlier levels. Coal consumption in 1983 had increased a modest 4.2 percent over 1982 consumption, largely because of increased coal use by electrical utilities in response to greater electrical energy consumption.

Nevertheless, the U.S. coal industry faced an uncertain future. Producers can mine about 200 million tons a year more than they can sell. Electrical utilities account for almost 85 percent of U.S. coal consumption, and electrical energy use was increasing at a much slower rate than it did in the 1960's and early 1970's. The steel industry substantially reduced its coal use in recent years. In addition, lower oil prices and the possibility of federal legislation to control acid rain produced by coal-burning plants slowed conversions from oil to coal by electrical utilities and industrial users.

From 106 million tons in 1982, U.S. coal exports plunged to 78 million tons in 1983. The causes of the decline included stable or declining world oil prices, the worldwide economic recession, the high value of the dollar in international currency markets, and sharply increased coal exports from Poland. U.S. exports of coal during the first half of 1984 were approximately 10 percent above year-earlier levels, but large increases in coal exports appear unlikely for the remainder of the 1980's. Because of the sharp drop in export sales, U.S. coal production decreased about 7 percent in 1983. A record 29 percent of coal production came from Western states, and surface mining accounted for 62 percent of the total.

Coal versus Nuclear Power. In September the Electric Power Research Institute, which is funded by investor owned utilities, released preliminary results of a study showing that electricity produced from nuclear plants has become much more expensive than electricity from new coal-fired plants. Power from some of the nuclear units coming on line between 1983 and the early 1990's may cost 50 percent more than power from comparable coal-fired plants, the study found. This is the first time in the history of commercial nuclear power that power from nuclear units has become much more expensive than power from coal plants, and it marks a dramatic reversal from the early 1970's, when electricity from nuclear plants was much cheaper. Construction costs of nuclear plants have generally risen much more rapidly than costs of coal plants, and high

161

interest rates and regulatory delays have increased financing costs.

Another report, released in February by the Congressional Office of Technology Assessment (OTA), concluded that "without significant changes in the technology, management, and level of public acceptance, nuclear power in the United States is unlikely to be expanded in this century beyond the reactors already under construction. Currently, nuclear power plants present too many financial risks as a result of uncertainties in electric demand growth, very high capital costs, operating problems, increasing regulatory requirements, and growing public opposition."

Synthetic Fuels. The first synthetic natural gas produced at the Great Plains coal gasification plant near Beulah, N.D., flowed into the U.S. natural gas pipeline system on July 28. The plant was expected to cost $2.1 billion but started up under budget and ahead of construction schedule. When fully operational, the plant is designed to produce an average of 125 million cubic feet (Mcf) per day of synthetic natural gas from lignite.

The plant still faces financial difficulties, however. The Great Plains project began selling gas to pipeline companies for $6.15/Mcf, a price pegged to the price of No. 2 fuel oil, but the price fell along with fuel prices later in the year. Production cost is expected to be $8–$10/Mcf when the plant becomes fully operational. The five partners in the project (American Natural Resources Company, Tenneco Inc., Transco Energy Company, Midcon Corporation, and Pacific Lighting Corporation) are seeking price guarantees for the gas from the U.S. Synthetic Fuels Corporation. The companies told the SFC they would be forced to abandon it if they did not receive solid financial support.

The SFC itself remained mired in controversy and its future clouded with uncertainty. The corporation has been crippled by allegations of financial scandal and mismanagement, resignations from the board of directors, an exodus of senior officials, and disputes between Congress and the White House over the program's future. Nominations for vacant seats on the board were stalled by the administration's insistence that Congress cut back the corpora-

tion's funding. Since the board lacked a quorum, it was unable to conduct even routine business.

The administration originally proposed cutting the SFC's $13.28 billion authorization to $5 billion but eventually accepted a compromise that left the corporation with $7.9 billion. In August, the House voted to ban further funding of the Cathedral Bluffs and Parachute Creek oil shale projects in Colorado, but this provision was deleted from the funding legislation approved by both houses in October.

See also NUCLEAR POWER; ORGANIZATION OF PETROLEUM EXPORTING COUNTRIES; PETROLEUM AND NATURAL GAS.   D.F.A.

ENVIRONMENT. In 1984, the Reagan administration again came under fire for its environmental policies. A series of restrictions and bans were imposed on a pesticide, EDB, that has been shown to cause cancer in animals. And a federal judge held the U.S. government responsible for several cases of cancer apparently resulting from radiation fallout.

Environmental Law. A study released in mid-July documented what was described as an "extraordinary failure" of the U.S. government to implement federal environment laws. The report, *America's Toxic Protection Gap*, prepared for Environmental Safety, a nonpartisan association of professionals in the environmental and public health fields, was based largely on data from recent reports and documents produced by the government. It found that just six of the 546 abandoned toxic waste dumps regarded as of highest priority had been cleaned up since the "superfund" law to finance such projects had been enacted in 1980. The report also charged that because the EPA chronically lacked the staff and funds to police polluters, many industrial firms were routinely breaking environmental laws in the expectation that they would never be caught.

In July the U.S. General Accounting Office issued two reports on the EPA's performance in identifying, assessing, and controlling an unreasonable health risks posed by the 60,000 existing chemicals and 1,000 new ones introduced annually. The GAO said that the agency had moved to control only four chemicals and was doing "priority" reviews of only two others. One of the reports found that the agency

Fenced by barbed wire and ominous words (Danger; Radiation; Keep Out), a compound near Juárez, Mexico, holds the truck used by Vincente Sotelo (above, with his family) to transport a steel canister he sold to a local junkyard for $10. Unknown to Sotelo, the canister contained 6,000 pellets of highly radioactive cobalt; these were later mixed with scrap metal and used to make furniture and building materials. By eventually exposing large numbers of people to radiation, Sotelo's unwitting act triggered what may have been North America's worst nuclear accident.

assessments tended to focus on the first use proposed for a chemical rather than on all possible uses.

Faced with pending legal action, the EPA agreed in September to reinvestigate possible dangers to health posed by 13 pesticides it had licensed in the first two years of the Reagan administration after closed meetings with the manufacturers of the chemicals. The agency also promised to make no regulatory decisions on the basis of such closed meetings.

In December, the EPA and its administrator, William D. Ruckelshaus, were held in contempt of court by a federal district court judge for failing to issue standards for emissions of radioactive particles as required by the Clean Air Act. The Sierra Club had brought suit against EPA over the issue in 1982.

In November, President Ronald Reagan surprised some environmentalists when he signed an important piece of environmental legislation; the measure tightened federal restrictions

163

on toxic waste disposal and also extended regulations to small companies that had previously been exempt.

Ruckelshaus Resignation. Despite continuing criticism of the Reagan administration's environment policies, Ruckelshaus was widely considered to have improved both the workings and the public image of the EPA since returning as administrator in May 1983. Stating that he had accomplished what he had been brought back to do, Ruckelshaus announced in November that he was resigning, effective January 5, 1985. Lee M. Thomas, head of the agency's toxic waste program, was named to succeed him, subject to Senate confirmation.

EDB. Before the fall of 1983, few Americans had heard of ethylene dibromide (EDB). By mid-1984, the compound was virtually a household word. Although EDB had long been used as an additive in leaded gasoline to control engine knock, it was the chemical's role as a pesticide that was responsible for its sudden notoriety. Now believed by some scientists to be capable of causing gene mutations and cancer in humans, EDB was a major ingredient in 122 pesticide products.

In the fall of 1983, citing animal studies that showed exposure to the chemical (through the skin, by ingestion, and by inhalation) caused cancer, the EPA had imposed an emergency ban on its use as a soil fumigant and proposed phasing out the pesticide's other major uses. In February 1984 the EPA announced an emergency move to expedite EDB's removal from the U.S. diet. The use of EDB on stored grain and on grain-milling machinery was prohibited, and voluntary guidelines were issued for permissible levels of the pesticide in already

One-third of West Germany's splendid forests—like this one, near the Ruhr River—are dead or dying, as are millions of trees in other European countries, the United States, and Canada. Acid rain is believed to be a major contributor to the destruction.

contaminated grain-based foods. These limits were later made mandatory. Studies conducted by the EPA had shown that 1 percent of grain-based processed foods appeared to contain residues of EDB, at levels higher than the agency now proposed as being temporarily acceptable. In March the EPA announced restrictions on the use of EDB on citrus fruits and papayas, while imposing a total ban on use of the chemical on these fruits effective in September. In November the EPA proposed rules that would tighten restraints on the disposal of EDB wastes from production of gasoline additives and other chemicals.

Lead in Gasoline. In July, the EPA proposed new rules that would reduce the amount of lead allowed in gasoline 91 percent by January 1, 1986. Current standards, established in 1982, allow 1.1 grams of lead per gallon of gas; the new rules would allow only 0.1 gram. High concentrations of lead in the blood have long been known to cause many illnesses; newer studies indicate that even at very low concentrations, lead can cause mental impairment. Studies have also shown a strong correspondence between the average level of lead in human blood and the amount of lead in gasoline. The EPA estimates that some 97,000 children, mostly in cities, now require medical attention because of lead in the bloodstream. The new rules were expected to reduce this figure by more than 50 percent.

Wood Preservatives. In July, the EPA banned the sale to consumers of wood preservatives containing creosote, pentachlorophenol, and arsenic compounds. All three types of materials have been shown to cause cancer and birth defects in animals. The regulations, which take effect in February 1985, will allow use of the chemicals only by specially trained and certified workers. Consumers will still be allowed to purchase treated wood, however. About 1 billion pounds of the chemicals are used in the United States each year to protect lumber and products like lawn furniture.

Nuclear Bomb Tests and Cancer. Debate continued in 1984 over whether radioactive fallout from tests of nuclear weapons during the 1950's and 1960's contributed to the development of leukemia among some residents living downwind from the Nevada Test Site. Research

reported in January by a trio of U.S. National Cancer Institute scientists, headed by Charles Land, failed to confirm the fallout-leukemia link that had been reported five years earlier in a study by Joseph Lyon and colleagues at the University of Utah. It also challenged the statistical techniques used by Lyon. Lyon stood by his methods and his findings, however, and said that follow-up studies conducted by his team only strengthened the fallout-leukemia tie.

The NCI criticism didn't deter U.S. District Court Judge Bruce Jenkins from ruling on May 10 that the U.S. government was negligent in protecting the public from excessive exposure to test-caused radiation. Since the government had failed to warn the people who lived downwind from the tests about the dangers of fallout, and had failed to inform the public of ways to lessen contamination, it was therefore responsible for the subsequent development of cancer in ten civilians. Eight of the ten had contracted types of leukemia associated with radiation exposure; one, breast cancer; and one (the only victim still alive), thyroid cancer. The government was ordered to pay compensation of $2.66 million in nine of the cases, with the sum for the tenth case to be determined later. Fourteen other claims of radiation-related cancers were dismissed.

Agent Orange. In May an out-of-court settlement was reached in a suit brought by Vietnam veterans against seven manufacturers of Agent Orange, a herbicide used as a defoliant by the U.S. military in Vietnam. The veterans claimed that exposure to the herbicide and its contaminants—particularly dioxin—had produced various health problems in themselves and their families. Under the settlement, which was tentatively approved by the federal judge overseeing the case, the veterans agreed to drop the suit if the manufacturers established a $180 million fund for the relief of veterans and their families. Meanwhile, a government study released in August concluded that Vietnam veterans overall appear to have no increased risk of having children with birth defects. The report did indicate, however, that veterans most likely to have been exposed to Agent Orange seemed to have a greater risk of fathering children with specific rare, crippling defects.

In an effort to increase knowledge of the effects of exposure to Agent Orange, the federal government launched a broad $100 million research project, involving some 50 studies, that could take more than a decade to complete. Also, a measure was enacted providing compensation for certain Vietnam veterans exposed to the herbicide and establishing a commission to review the basis of other veterans' claims.

Acid Rain. Controversy over the abnormally acidic precipitation known as acid rain continued. The main cause of acid rain is widely believed to be emissions of sulfur dioxide and other acid-forming compounds from the smoke-stacks of fossil-fuel power plants and factories. The Reagan administration maintained that costly action to remedy the problem would be premature, since more research was needed; others believed action should be taken promptly. In March, several northeastern states sued the EPA to force a ruling on petitions by New York, Pennsylvania, and Maine, calling on the EPA to bring about reductions in sulfur dioxide emissions in midwestern and border states, which the suing states contended were causing acid rain in the northeast. In October a federal district court judge ruled that the EPA had to rule on the petition, and in December the agency issued a ruling rejecting it. An appeal was filed.

On the international front, representatives of nine European countries and Canada met in Ottawa to seek ways to reduce sulfur dioxide emissions. The countries attending pledged to reduce their own emissions by at least 30 percent during the next ten years, but several nations responsible for significant quantities of emissions were not represented.

Arctic Haze. The first scientific references to arctic haze appeared in the March 1914 field notes of an expedition on Beitstad Glacier in the Arctic Ocean. Observed periodically ever since, this atmospheric phenomenon baffled scientists, who were unable to explain why the pristine arctic should be host to dingy clouds reminiscent of industrial London or smog-choked Los Angeles. In May 1984, however, an answer was at last suggested, in a collection of 28 research papers contained in a special edition of the scientific journal *Geophysical Research Letters*. The reports were based on air and ground measurements of arctic haze made by at least 12 different research groups from four countries.

The research confirmed that the substances released into the air when fossil fuels are burned can travel long distances, reaching even the arctic. It proved arctic haze to be exactly what it had always looked like: industrial smog. The minute, airborne particles of "black carbon" identified by researchers from the Lawrence Berkeley Laboratory in California, for instance, have only one possible source—combustion. The scientists characterized as "remarkable" the immense quantities of these carbon particles found floating above the arctic. In one cloud band about 1,600 feet up, particles were measured at a concentration that not only was five times greater than that day's arctic ground-level average, but also was greater than the annual average concentration just outside San Francisco. Peak concentrations measured at 3,300 feet up were only 2½ times lower than those for heavily polluted New York City.

Because the tiny carbon-rich particles in this haze are black, they effectively absorb the sun's energy. This means they could lead to a substantial warming of the earth's atmosphere. Scientists from the National Aeronautics and Space Administration's Ames Research Center in California estimated that such atmospheric heating could melt enough polar ice to "move the arctic ice cap boundaries northward." This, in turn, could promote additional global warming, seriously altering climate patterns and surface temperatures throughout the world.

Norwegian researchers studying levels of nickel, lead, and zinc in the arctic haze reported that these industrial pollutants appeared to emanate from copper and nickel smelters on the Kola Peninsula in northwest Russia and steel mills in the southern Soviet Urals. But a team of American and Australian scientists studying movements of air masses into the arctic found that Asia and the eastern United States may also be contributing to the haze.

Asbestos. A class action suit on behalf of U.S. primary and secondary schools against 55 manufacturers of asbestos was allowed to go forward by a federal district judge in September

Asbestos, the fibers of which can cause cancer and the lung disease asbestosis if inhaled in sufficient quantities, has been used—for example, in ceiling tiles—in thousands of school buildings across the United States. The EPA estimates that approximately 15 million students attend school in buildings containing asbestos; the cost of removing the material has been put at $1.4 billion. By joining the suit, schools can seek not only compensation of removal costs but also punitive damages.

Strip-mining. A 1979 lawsuit filed by environmentalists and charging the U.S. Interior Department with failure to collect fines for violations of a federal strip-mining law was settled out of court in October. Under the settlement, the Interior Department is required to attempt retroactive collection, with interest, of up to $150 million in unpaid fines assessed under the 1977 Surface Mining Control and Reclamation Act.

Lavelle Case. In January, former EPA official Rita M. Lavelle, who had been convicted in December 1983 of perjury and obstructing a congressional investigation of the EPA's handling of its toxic waste cleanup program, was fined $10,000, sentenced to a six-months' prison term, and assigned to an additional five years on probation doing community service.

J.R. & T.H.M.

EQUATORIAL GUINEA. See STATISTICS OF THE WORLD.

ETHIOPIA. In September 1984, a Communist party was officially created as the sole legal party in Ethiopia. Meanwhile, conflicts with guerrilla groups continued, and the country was in the grip of its worst famine in a decade.

A five-day national congress in Ethiopia's capital city of Addis Ababa formally created the Worker's Party of Ethiopia, the country's first Communist party. The nation's ruler, Lieutenant Colonel Mengistu Haile Mariam, was named secretary-general. The seven members of the Provisional Military Administrative Council, previously the ruling body in the country, were named to an 11-member party Politburo, headed by Mengistu. The party convention also elected a 136-member Central Committee and approved a ten-year economic plan.

In May, Eritrean rebels launched a series of attacks against the government, including one in which the Eritrean People's Liberation Front reported the destruction of 30 aircraft at Asmara Air Force Base. The regime also encountered serious disagreements with its putative allies, including the Somali rebel coalition known as the Somali Democratic Salvation Front, which resulted in open fighting between the Ethiopians and SDSF. In June, three of the four major Eritrean rebel groups announced a unification of their efforts against the Addis Ababa government; Sudan and Saudi Arabia were said to have sponsored this effort in order to undermine Ethiopia's Marxist regime. The principal immediate result was stepped-up attacks on Ethiopian garrison towns in Eritrea. Meanwhile, Ethiopia and Sudan frequently exchanged warnings over alleged border violations by aircraft.

A horrendous drought and serious pest infestation decimated food crops, and more than 7 million Ethiopians were said to be at risk of starvation; by autumn, more than 100 people a day were dying of hunger. The U.S. government committed itself to providing more than $300 million in emergency food aid to Ethiopia and other famine-struck sub-Saharan nations; additional aid was received from the European Economic Community, other countries, and private relief agencies. Relief efforts were seriously hindered by the guerrilla warfare in the northern provinces and by a lack of roads in the area. The Ethiopian government was blamed for failing to distribute food in areas whose residents were sympathetic to the rebels and for having allegedly spend lavish sums on the party congress. There were also criticisms in the United States that the U.S. government had not moved promptly enough in providing needed assistance.

The Ethiopian government meanwhile announced plans to resettle 1.5 million peasants from the famine-ravaged north to the more fertile south. The relocation scheme was strongly criticized by some observers, who felt that it was inhumane, that it could overtax the currently fertile south's environment, and that it was being used by the government to disperse rebel supporters. By mid-December, 70,000 farmers had been resettled.

Three men, one a Somali military officer,

hijacked a Somali jet on November 24; the plane and its 108 passengers were held under threat of death at the Addis Ababa airport for four days. After negotiating a pledge from Somalia that it would not execute seven condemned political prisoners, the hijackers released the passengers unharmed.

See STATISTICS OF THE WORLD.   R.B.

EUROPEAN COMMUNITIES, a supranational organization comprising the European Economic Community (EEC), the European Atomic Energy Community, and the European Coal and Steel Community. These communities are frequently referred to jointly as the European Community (EC), or Common Market. In 1984 the ten member countries were Belgium, Denmark, France, Great Britain, Greece, Ireland, Italy, Luxembourg, the Netherlands, and West Germany.

Controversy over the EC budget dominated the attention of member countries in 1984. Great Britain had complained for some time that it had been paying more into the budget than it received back in benefits. (Two-thirds of the EC's budget consists of agricultural subsidies; since agriculture makes up only a small proportion of the British economy, the Thatcher government argued that it was entitled to substantial rebates.) While the other members agreed that some annual rebate should be granted to Britain, they maintained that the amount requested—$850 million for 1984 and $1 billion for 1985—was too large. A two-day meeting in March adjourned with acrimony on both sides and no agreement. Premier Bettino Craxi of Italy blamed Britain for what he called the "paralysis of Europe."

Efforts to remove the impasse finally succeeded at a June summit meeting at Fontainebleau, France. Under the terms of a compromise agreement, Britain was to receive rebates amounting to $600 million for 1983, $800 milion for 1984, and in subsequent years 66 percent of the difference between its value-added tax contribution to the EC and what it receives in benefits.

An impasse also developed at a December summit meeting, held in Dublin, when Greece threatened to block Spain and Portugal's admission into the Common Market—tentatively set for January 1, 1986—unless the EC provided

some $5 billion over a five-year period to protect Greek and Italian farmers from agricultural competition. Other members balked at Greece's demand. Irish Prime Minister Garret FitzGerald warned that economic differences "could have profound political consequences" for the Community.

In March, after months of stalemated meetings, the agricultural ministers of the EC reached agreement on a reform of the Common Agricultural Policy. The agreement provided for a reduction in EC dairy production quotas and an end to a complex system of monetary compensation amounts designed to counteract differing currency strengths. EC milk production was to be reduced from 105 million to 98 million metric tons by 1985.

Another problem faced by the Community was the decreasing demand for European steel. Production quotas were extended through 1985, designed to distribute orders fairly among members, and Belgium and Luxembourg agreed to a major steel industry restructuring.

In February the Community approved a five-year technology research program, called the European Strategic Program for Research and Development in Information Technology, or "Esprit," to help the EC obtain larger shares of the world information technology market, currently dominated by the United States and Japan. The EC would contribute almost $640 million to the program, with private industry providing matching funds.

Elections to the 434-member European Parliament were held in June. Turnout among the 200 million eligible voters was considerably lower than in 1979, reflecting diminished interest and confidence in the body. Governing parties of both left and right generally did badly, with the vote for extremist parties often up from that received in previous elections to the European Parliament.

In July, Jacques Delors, former finance minister in the Socialist government of France, was chosen as the new head of the European Commission, the EC's executive arm, replacing Gaston Thorn of Luxembourg. Delors's four-year term was scheduled to begin in January 1985.

See also articles on individual countries mentioned.   J.O.S.

F

FASHION. Women's fashions of spring 1984 emphasized clean, uncluttered lines, freedom of movement, and elimination of heavy construction, tailoring, and superfluous details. There was an impressive array of choices in hemlines, waistlines, and silhouettes. Fall saw an androgynous trend, as menswear influenced women's styles. Men's clothes were classic but comfortable.

Soft Spring. During the spring, suits were in evidence, many of them softer in feeling than they had been. Jackets were loose and flowing, often of printed silk; blouses had the look of lingerie. Other suits sported square-cut, double-breasted jackets over long, lean skirts. Dresses most often hung, chemise-style, straight from shoulder to calf or even ankle, although many designers defined waistlines with pretty sashes and stopped hemlines at the knee.

American sportswear designers produced racy, free-form separates united by a sense of flexibility and minimalism. Calvin Klein offered a wheat-colored linen dress with elbow-length kimono sleeves and a center placket of small buttons to the calf. The dress could be worn loose or with a narrow leather or lizard belt. Perry Ellis's clothes epitomized the season's bare simplicity. One calf-length chemise of dark-blue pleated linen sported a front-and-back sailor collar of pure white. Ralph Lauren was typically romantic and outdoorsy. Full-cut jodhpur-style pants were teamed with high-throated Victorian blouses; big white silk shirts topped pleated, cuffed trousers.

European designers tended to emphasize gray, brown, and navy and generally used more tailoring than their U.S. counterparts. Yves Saint Laurent's clothes ranged from elegant and sophisticated to witty. His crisply tailored separates had a safari feeling, and flirtatious evening clothes were often worn with sequin-studded veils. Giorgio Armani continued his man-tailored looks, while Japanese designer Issey Miyake used unusual fabrics wrapped and draped into even more unusual shapes. Karl Lagerfeld produced a ladylike

collection of classic, Chanel-like dresses and suits.

Tailored Fall. In fall, women's wear showed surprising similarity to menswear, with over-scaled coats, perfectly tailored jackets, double-pleated pants topped by shirts and ties or sweaters, and flat, oxford-like shoes. Clothing remained feminine, while transmitting a real sense of power and assertiveness.

Alexander Julian layered a brown-on-taupe plaid slouchy jacket over a teal V-neck sweater and white button-down–collar shirt, shown with a tie and brown trousers. Calvin Klein

Overnight fashion superstar Stephen Sprouse became the darling of the under-30 crowd with such glittery, punk-inspired ensembles as this psychedelic alphabet dress and pile coat in Day-Glo red.

Among the best of the year's popular androgynous clothes—neither male nor female in emphasis—were Giorgio Armani's elegantly overscaled coats (above), worn with shirts and pleated, perfectly tailored pants.

Hot colors were big news, as Karl Lagerfeld demonstrated with a pair of sophisticated but sexy dresses in rich purple (left), worn with hats in the same shade.

offered an oversized black-and-white herringbone coat over a glen plaid jacket, worn with a tan crewneck sweater and wide-cuffed trousers. An Anne Klein patterned-wool polo coat topped a matching blazer, worn with a cashmere turtleneck sweater and white flannel pants. Tailored dresses conformed to the menswear trend, with lots of haberdashery pinstripes and such fabrics as worsted and gabardine.

Other trends included the bright, hot colors which surfaced in the coats and dresses of Ellis, Oscar de la Renta, Adam Beall, and Adele Simpson. Stephen Sprouse's Day-Glo-colored minidresses and fake fur coats caused a special stir. "Jersey-dressing," using supple,

knitted fabrics to create soft, comfortable, body-conscious clothing, contrasted with the menswear look.

Evening clothes for fall were simple and narrow in shape, relying for glamour on luxurious fabrics, ornate beading and embroidery, or bright jewel tones. Gold and silver lamé and Lurex were important fabrics. Brightly colored satins were featured by de la Renta, Simpson, Halston, Norma Kamali, and Bill Blass.

Classic Menswear. Menswear for spring featured pared-down elegance and lack of restrictions in fit. Cool blues, tan, seersucker, and new pales such as celery and sand were popular. Armani offered a single-breasted linen suit in pale gray, while Alan Flusser showed a double-breasted, black-and-white checked wool model. Calvin Klein produced a double-breasted black-and-white glen plaid linen suit with peak lapels.

Sportswear harkened back to an era of Hawaiian print shirts and surfer and Bermuda shorts. White linen slacks were topped with black linen cardigan vests or blazers, and darkest navy showed up in dress shirts as well as cabled sweaters. Color, bright and hot, was often played against black or used as in Gianfranco Ruffini's bold painter-striped sweater and Sprouse's surprising graffiti-printed shorts.

Fall menswear showed a true respect for comfort as well as styling, with soft-shouldered suits sporting a more generous cut. While traditional blues and grays continued to dominate, subtle, dark, jewel tones cropped up in sport coats. Casual clothes and sportswear were more rugged than usual, with lots of distressed leather, shearling, tweedy cable-stitched sweaters, and thick plaid jackets.

F.J.G.

FIJI. *See* STATISTICS OF THE WORLD.

FINLAND. Stimulated by increased exports to Western Europe and the United States, Finnish economic performance gradually improved in 1984. Preliminary figures showed that the annual growth rate of the Finnish economy had risen to about 4 percent, while the unemployment rate had fallen slightly, from 7 percent in 1983 to about 6 percent. Finnish trade with the West rose a projected 32 percent, while exports to the Soviet Union (which are financed primarily through the import of Soviet oil) declined about 20 percent. Finland's largest business firms achieved significantly higher profits.

Contributing to the improved economy was an agreement in March between employers and the Federation of Labor Unions on a two-year wage pact. The accord, which narrowly averted a threatened general strike, provided for a 3.2 percent wage hike in 1984 and a 3.6 percent increase the following year.

An important political factor helping to stimulate economic growth was the stability of the Finnish government, a coalition (in office since spring 1983) of Prime Minister Kalevi Sorsa's Social Democratic Party, the agrarian-based

Center Party, the Swedish People's Party, and the Rural Party.

Karl-August Fagerholm died on May 22 at the age of 82. Known as a man of conciliation, he served three times as prime minister and was a member of Parliament for 36 years.

See STATISTICS OF THE WORLD. M.D.H.

FISHERIES. The International Whaling Commission (IWC) continued efforts to restrict whaling, and the World Court arbitrated a U.S.–Canadian fisheries dispute.

In June the IWC lowered by about one-third the global commercial whaling quota for the 1984–1985 season, the last year of whale hunting before a five-year moratorium on all commercial whaling was to take effect. By denying a Japanese request to catch 400 sperm whales, the IWC also closed the last loophole in its 1981 ban on the commercial killing of sperm whales. The United States threatened to restrict U.S. fishing rights of countries not complying with IWC decisions but, later in the year, excluded a limited Japanese catch of sperm whales in 1984–1985 from such sanctions. In return, Japan withdrew its protest against the IWC ban on sperm whaling. (The United States claimed, but Japan denied, that Japan had also agreed to end all commercial whaling by 1988.)

The World Court, in October, ended a two-decade-old boundary dispute between the United States and Canada. At issue was jurisdiction over 30,000 square nautical miles of open sea including the Gulf of Maine and the Georges Bank, a vital fishing area. The court laid down a boundary that granted the United States about three-fourths of the Georges Bank.

In July the U.S. State Department announced it would relax a ban on Soviet commercial fishing in U.S. waters, imposed in response to the Soviet invasion of Afghanistan. The new policy allowed the Soviets rights to harvest about 50,000 metric tons of fish annually, as compared to the 40,000 tons a year the Soviet Union had landed in U.S. waters before the sanction was imposed. D.R.W.

FLORIDA. *See* STATISTICS OF THE WORLD.

FORMOSA. *See* TAIWAN.

FRANCE. In 1984, French Prime Minister Pierre Mauroy resigned, and the Communist Party subsequently withdrew from the governing coalition. President François Mitterrand suffered electoral, economic, and foreign-policy setbacks during the year.

New Cabinet. In mid-July, Mitterrand accepted the resignation of Mauroy and his government and named Minister of Industry Laurent Fabius to replace Mauroy as prime minister. The Fabius appointment underlined Mitterrand's determination to carry on with an economic program stressing modernization and elimination of inefficient industrial sectors. Mauroy had advocated the traditional Socialist program of expanded government intervention in the economy and protection of working-class interests, and he was on good terms with the Communists. Fabius, on the other hand, represented the middle-class intellectual tradition in French socialism.

As director of the budget in 1981 and 1982, Fabius had sought to extract greater revenues from the wealthy. Named minister of industry in March 1983, just as government policy shifted toward austerity, he had then announced plans to cut back or eliminate subsidies to unprofitable industries in steel, coal mining, and shipbuilding. At 37, Fabius became the youngest French prime minister in a century. By appointing him, Mitterrand attempted to bring an image of freshness and vigor to his government, in addition to emphasizing continued economic austerity.

Because Mitterrand's program had led to high unemployment and because it stressed greater reliance on private capital, it was opposed by the French Communist Party (PCF), a partner in the governing coalition. When Fabius was appointed, PCF leaders sought unsuccessfully to wring concessions from him on employment and industrial policy. After heated discussions, the PCF Central Committee decided not to accept any positions in the new cabinet but to selectively support the government in the National Assembly.

The new cabinet was made up of Socialists and two smaller left-wing groups. Pierre Bérégovoy, a Mitterrand loyalist, was appointed finance minister. Claude Cheysson continued at this time as foreign minister and Roland Dumas as minister for European affairs and government spokesman.

European Parliament. In elections to the European Parliament—the legislative body of the

Determined nuns march with nearly a million other demonstrators who, displaying such slogans as "Freedom Means Choice," converged on Paris in June to protest a proposed law they saw as a threat to France's predominantly Roman Catholic private school system.

European Community—in June, the Communists took the hardest blow, winning only 11 percent of the popular vote. The Socialists also lost ground, though not so heavily. The center-right opposition made substantial gains, which it interpreted as a repudiation of the Mitterrand government. The most dramatic result of the election was the 2.2 million votes cast for the extreme-right National Front, which took its first seats in the European Parliament.

Private Schools. During the spring and early summer, hundreds of thousands rallied in Versailles and Paris to protest the government's education reform bill. The target of these protests was that part of the legislation—known as the *loi Savary* after Alain Savary, the minister of education who proposed them—which would tighten state control over private (mostly Roman Catholic) schools. The government pays the salaries and benefits of private school teachers. The legislation would have placed private school budgets under the control of regional governments, limited the number of teachers, and encouraged them to hold civil service status; its effect, according to the protesters, would have been to abridge the freedoms of the private schools.

The protests, backed by many conservative politicians, led the government to speak of possible compromise. The week before the cabinet shake-up, Mitterrand finally withdrew the legislation and said that he would seek a constitutional amendment to permit national referenda on issues involving "public liberties."

Labor Troubles. Around the beginning of 1984, violence erupted at the Talbot plant in Poissy, west of Paris. Militants at the plant, which belongs to Peugeot, France's largest automaker, had been on strike since early December 1983 over planned layoffs of nearly 3,000 employees. The government offered Peugeot a $144 million subsidy for reducing the layoffs by 1,000, and the company agreed. The plant opened for work on January 3, but workers opposed to the layoffs moved in and stopped production. The next day, workers demanding access to their jobs confronted strikers, and two days of serious violence ensued. More than 80 persons were hurt before police separated the two groups.

In February, thousands of truckers blockaded roads in half the country's departments. The blockade was precipitated when French and Italian customs officials staged a work slow-down and trucks backed up at the Mont Blanc tunnel. The truckers demanded reimbursement for lost time as well as other concessions on insurance and taxes. The blockade spread, the army was called out, and some trucks were removed by cranes. Meanwhile, thousands of industrial workers were laid off because of a lack of supplies as a result of the blockade, and urban food markets were running out of stocks. Nearly 100,000 winter vacationers were trapped on the roads.

The blockade represented an explosion of frustrations that had been pent up for years. Most French truckers are either independent owner-operators or employees of small companies. Their grievances included high taxes and fuel costs, lack of benefits, uncertain employment, and the necessity of working long hours. The minister of transport at the time, Charles Fiterman, a Communist, denounced the blockade and announced his refusal to submit to "ultimatums." Government representatives and leaders of the owner-operators' association agreed to talk and to consider grievances, and truckers slowly and reluctantly moved their vehicles. No concessions were immediately forthcoming, however.

1985 Budget. The 1985 budget—the first to be presented by the Fabius government—was announced in September. Featuring across-the-board income tax cuts, it also held public spending to an increase of just 6 percent, roughly the same as the expected inflation rate. Finance Minister Bérégovoy said the tax cuts would encourage consumer spending and stimulate the economy.

Basque Guerrillas. Ever since the Fascist victory in the Spanish Civil War, France has provided asylum to Spanish political exiles, including Basque nationalists. But in August a French court ruled that a group of Basque separatists accused of various crimes, including murder, could be extradited to Spain. As the defendants continued a hunger strike, claiming the right to be treated as political refugees, Basque violence broke out in Spain, with a series of attacks on French offices and factories there. The French Basque country

173

Remembering D-Day, American veterans, many of them accompanied by their wives, listen to military bands performing at Utah Beach, site of one of the 1944 Allied landings in Normandy that changed the course of World War II.

also experienced sporadic violence both from ETA (Basque) guerrillas and from rightist groups. Ultimately, after all appeals failed, three Basque defendants were extradited to Spain, while four others, accused of lesser crimes, were flown into exile in Togo.

Foreign Policy. On September 17, France and Libya announced agreement to a "total and simultaneous" withdrawal of their forces from Chad, beginning September 25. In early November, France and Libya jointly announced that the withdrawal was complete. Subsequent reports, however, indicated that substantial numbers of Libyan troops had not been withdrawn. The French government at first insisted that the Libyan withdrawal was complete but ultimately conceded that many Libyans remained. The confusions and contradictions surrounding the episode were regarded as a major policy blunder. In early December, Claude Cheysson was replaced as foreign minister by Roland Dumas.

The French occupation had in effect produced a stalemate in the conflict, dividing Chad into two parts—one controlled by Libyan-backed rebels, the other by French-government troops. There had, however, been some French casualties. In January, a French reconnaissance jet was shot down over rebel territory and its pilot killed, and in April, nine French soldiers died when their vehicle was booby-trapped.

Mitterrand met with President Ronald Reagan and U.S. business leaders during his first state visit to the United States in March. He urged Reagan to work for mutual arms reductions and dialogue with Moscow, and he offered support for the basic U.S. posture in negotiations. Addressing Congress, Mitterrand warned of the dangers of poverty, underdevelopment, and revolution in the Third World. He differed with the U.S. administration in stressing the role of internal factors in breeding revolution.

During a state visit to the Soviet Union in June, the French president sought to balance

France's close relationship with the United States and its support of U.S. missile deployment in Western Europe with maintaining in some degree the special Franco-Soviet relationship fostered by his predecessors. However, the two sides did no more than to disagree on major questions. Mitterrand reiterated France's refusal to allow French nuclear weapons to be included in any superpower arms-reduction negotiations. At a dinner hosted by Soviet leader Konstantin Chernenko, the French president addressed the issue of human rights, making specific references to the Helsinki accords, to Soviet treatment of dissident Andrei Sakharov, and to the suppression of the Solidarity movement in Poland.

In January, France announced the sale to Saudi Arabia of a $4.5 billion system of anti-aircraft weaponry to protect oil fields and other strategic installations. The sale was the largest arms contract ever secured by the French.

French troops sent to Lebanon as part of a multinational peacekeeping contingent were withdrawn in March. American, British, and Italian forces had left in February. The French had proposed a new multinational force under UN auspices, but the Soviet Union vetoed this plan in the Security Council; the French foreign minister said French troops could not stay in Lebanon on their own, and the last French members of the force left in March.

See STATISTICS OF THE WORLD.　　　S.E.

G

GABON. See STATISTICS OF THE WORLD.
GAMBIA, THE. See STATISTICS OF THE WORLD.
GEORGIA. See STATISTICS OF THE WORLD.
GERMAN DEMOCRATIC REPUBLIC, *or* **EAST GERMANY.** In a dramatic reversal of customary practice, the German Democratic Republic (GDR) took a moderate stance in international affairs in 1984, pursuing closer relations with West Germany despite pressure from Soviet hard-liners to intensify the cold war in response to the placing of new U.S. missiles in Western Europe.

Inter-German Relations. In March, Erich Honecker, party chief and president of the GDR, accepted an invitation to pay a visit in the fall to West Germany, the first such trip ever of an East German party leader. The scheduling of the trip symbolized East and West German determination to keep alive the idea of détente. In September, however, the visit was postponed (but not canceled) as a result of pressure from the Soviet Union.

The East German push toward cooperation with West Germany was based primarily on economic considerations. The GDR owed over $9 billion to Western banks, and its best opportunity to improve its economic position lay in expanding trade and other relationships with West Germany. For various services rendered to the West Germans, such as maintaining road and rail transit through the GDR to West Berlin, and from gifts from West Germans to friends and relatives in the GDR, the East Germans gained an estimated $700 million in hard currency in 1984.

In July the West German government approved a new credit to East Germany of approximately $330 million. The West Germans received in return an easing of restrictions on travel in the GDR.

Political Emigrants. In two incidents in January, groups of East Germans sought asylum in foreign diplomatic missions in the GDR as a means of leaving the country. After negotiations in East Berlin, six people gained permission to emigrate from the U.S. embassy there, with another dozen or so leaving from the West German mission. In February a group of 12 to 20 East Germans attempted the same tactic at the West German embassy in Prague. Among the successful emigrants was a family of five that included a niece of GDR Prime Minister Willi Stoph. During February and March the regime allowed some 13,000 East Germans to emigrate, but emigration levels were subsequently cut back.

In June it was discovered that 55 people had taken refuge in the West German mission in

On strike for a 35-hour week, members of I.G. Metall, a huge West German union of metalworkers, picket in Stuttgart. In the biggest work stoppage in the Federal Republic's history, 440,000 workers in automotive and allied trades stayed off their jobs for several weeks. They returned in July, after compromising on a 38.5-hour week.

East Berlin. GDR authorities allowed the 55 to leave the country on the condition that the mission accept no new refugees. In early October more than 150 East Germans sought asylum in the West German embassy in Prague. Soon after, smaller numbers sought asylum in West German embassies in Budapest, Warsaw, and Bucharest. By early November some 40 of them had decided to quit the embassy after receiving assurances that they would not be punished if they returned to East Germany and sought to emigrate through legal channels.

Olympic Games. East Germany won nine gold medals at the winter Olympics in Sarajevo, Yugoslavia, compared with six for the Soviet Union and four for the United States. In August, having boycotted the summer Olympics in Los Angeles, the East Germans attended the counterpart Soviet-bloc Friendship '84 Games in Moscow, where East German athletes broke a number of world records and, in many instances, bettered times that had won gold medals in Los Angeles.

See STATISTICS OF THE WORLD.   R.J.W.

GERMANY, FEDERAL REPUBLIC OF, or WEST GERMANY. A growing domestic political scandal, the postponement of a historic East German visit, and the weak showing of the Free Democratic Party in elections were major stories in West Germany in 1984.

Politics. The ascent of the Greens—an environmental, antinuclear, antiestablishment party that is especially popular among young, well educated people—continued in 1984. They outpolled the Free Democratic Party (FDP) in March in municipal elections in Bavaria and in the state election in Baden-Württemberg, as well as in municipal elections in Rhineland-Palatinate and the Saar in June, North Rhine-Westphalia in September, and Baden-Württemberg in October. Also in June, the nationwide elections to the European Parliament, considered a barometer of domestic politics, saw the FDP suffer its greatest defeat. With 4.8 percent of the vote, it failed to gain the minimum 5 percent required to receive any seats at all. The Greens took 8.2 percent of the vote and picked up seven seats.

The two Christian Democratic parties—the Christian Democratic Union (CDU) of Chancellor Helmut Kohl and the Christian Social Union (CSU) in Bavaria—and the opposition Social Democratic Party (SPD) received more than three percentage points less of the vote than they had in the last European Parliament elections, in 1979. In the face of the defeat, Hans-Dietrich Genscher, FDP leader for ten years, announced he would give up that position by February 1985, but would remain as foreign minister and deputy chancellor in the Kohl government.

Some of the FDP's troubles could be traced back to 1982, when the party overthrew the coalition government of SPD Chancellor Helmut Schmidt by abandoning the coalition and forming a new government with the CDU/CSU. It was also hurt by a scandal concerning Economics Minister Otto Lambsdorff, an FDP member, who had been indicted in 1983 by a state prosecutor on charges of corruption. Allegedly, the holding company Friedrich Flick Industrieverwaltung gave his party 135,000 marks (approximately $50,000) in campaign contributions in return for tax breaks. The first incumbent minister of the Federal Republic ever to be indicted, Lambsdorff resigned from the ministry in June. (Free Democrat Martin Bangemann was named his successor.) In October it was further alleged that Flick had paid half a million dollars to Rainer Barzel, the speaker of the Bundestag (lower house of parliament), in the 1970's to persuade him to relinquish the Christian Democratic leadership to Kohl. Both Barzel and Kohl denied the charges, but Barzel resigned in late October and was replaced by Philipp Jenninger. In November, Kohl admitted he had personally accepted over $50,000 in campaign contributions from Flick for the CDU in the 1970's. He denied having been influenced by the money but admitted having violated campaign finance laws.

In a related event, the Kohl government received its first major defeat in May, when it withdrew from consideration a draft law to grant amnesty to businessmen and politicians involved in illegally deducting campaign contributions from income taxes. Government leaders argued that existing legislation simply made no provision for the enormous funding needed by today's parties, and that members of all major parties had been involved in such transactions. The bill was withdrawn, however, after the proposal provoked a press and public opinion uproar, followed by a rebellion on the part of rank-and-file FDP Bundestag deputies that made it unlikely it could be passed.

Inter-German Relations. The last-minute postponement by East German party chief Erich Honecker of his trip to West Germany, scheduled for late September, drew expressions of regret from Bonn. Earlier, however, in late August, a CDU leader in the Bundestag, responding to speculation that the East Germans would yield to Soviet pressure and cancel the trip, remarked that the Federal Republic's future did not "depend on whether Mr. Honecker pays us the honor of a visit." The remark was condemned by the East Germans as "unworthy" and "detrimental." The Kohl government, for its part, affirmed its intention not to let the postponement impede developing ties between the two German states (see EAST GERMANY).

U.S. Relations. West Germany continued to act as a broker between East and West. In

Wild West Germany

One weekend in June, about 3,000 closet cowboys and Indians set up tents, tepees, and makeshift saloons outside Munich, near the Austrian border, and whooped it up in costume, toting six-shooters, slugging whiskey, and swapping yarns around the campfire. It was the 35th annual opening to the West, staged at a temporary "No Name City" by members of West Germany's thriving Wild West clubs. The Wall Street Journal has reported that there may be as many as 100,000 German aficionados of the American ride 'em cowboy days, who spend much of their spare time reading up on Western lore or watching B-movies. After a few days' powwow every spring, the residents of No Name City break camp and return to a more mundane existence as bankers, lawyers, computer programmers, and the like. Their town melts into the landscape, to reappear somewhere else in the German countryside a year later.

GERMANY

February, at the funeral of Soviet leader Yuri Andropov in Moscow, Chancellor Kohl asked the new party chief, Konstantin Chernenko, to get together with U.S. President Ronald Reagan for a summit conference. On a visit to Washington in March, Kohl placed greatest emphasis on the need to revive an East-West dialogue.

A major issue between West Germany and the United States was West Germany's contribution to the North Atlantic Treaty Organization (NATO). The United States, claiming that it contributed more to European defense than all 15 other NATO partners combined, won a pledge for members to increase their defense budgets by 3 percent in real terms each year. Given a difficult economic climate, however, West Germany budgeted a 1985 defense increase of less than 1 percent in real terms.

New President. Richard von Weizsäcker, a Christian Democrat and former mayor of West Berlin, was elected to West Germany's highest (but largely ceremonial) office by the Federal Assembly in May. The Assembly, which includes the 520 Bundestag deputies and an equal number of representatives elected by state parliaments, gave von Weizsäcker 832 votes.

Economic Developments. The cautious recovery of the West German economy from a growth rate of only 1.3 percent in 1983 peaked in the first half of 1984. Economists in August scaled down their estimated rate for the year from 3.5 to 2.5 percent and projected an even lower rate for 1985 of 2.0 percent. The recovery was in part a victim of a too successful fight against inflation. In July, for the first time in the history of the Federal Republic, there was no upward movement in overall price levels.

Deflationary pressures were provided by steadily shrinking budget deficits. In addition, high interest rates in the United States brought about the export of funds that might have increased domestic demand and investment.

The strong U.S. dollar in 1984 made West German exports somewhat cheaper, and the foreign trade balance for the first half of the year showed a surplus of about $6.5 billion, a near record.

Economic recovery was hurt by a seven-week strike beginning in May of some 440,000 workers in the automobile industry and allied trades. This was reflected in a drop in industrial production in June of 8.7 percent compared

Arriving in the West German city of Giessen, an East German family adds to the unprecedented flow of emigration permitted by the German Democratic Republic early in the year. Tight controls over would-be émigrés were later reimposed by East Germany, but there were other signs of improving relations.

with June 1983. The workers demanded a reduction in the work week from 40 to 35 hours without any cuts in pay. Management fought to prevent a breach of the time-honored 40-hour week, and the result was one of the longest and hardest strikes since the founding of the Federal Republic. In July the workers settled for a 38.5-hour week and a small increase in wages.

In July the unemployment rate stood at 8.9 percent, the same as in July 1983. The government was attempting to lure foreign workers back to their homes by refunding their social security contributions and in some cases by making large cash relocation payments.

Hitler Diaries Trial. The trial of three persons accused of being responsible for the 1983 sale of forged diaries of Adolf Hitler began in August in Hamburg. Gerd Heidemann, a former reporter for the West German magazine *Stern*, and Konrad Kujau, a dealer in Nazi documents and other memorabilia, were both charged with fraud in connection with the forgery of the diaries and their sale to *Stern* for more than $3 million, none of which had been recovered.

See STATISTICS OF THE WORLD.   R.J.W.

GHANA. *See* STATISTICS OF THE WORLD.

GREAT BRITAIN. British society was exposed to political violence on a large scale in 1984. The Irish Republican Army made a nearly successful attempt on the lives of Prime Minister Margaret Thatcher (see biography in PEOPLE IN THE NEWS) and members of her cabinet. In the coalfields, a bitter labor dispute was marked by violence greater than anything witnessed in Britain for half a century.

IRA Attack. Just before 3 A.M. on October 12, a bomb planted by the IRA exploded in the Grand Hotel in the south coast resort of Brighton, where the Conservative Party was having its annual conference. The bomb, 20 pounds of gelignite according to the police, caused the collapse of an entire section of the building, where the prime minister and most of the cabinet were staying. Four people were killed. More than 30 were seriously injured, among them John Wakeham, the government chief whip in the House of Commons, and Norman Tebbit, the secretary of state for trade and industry and considered a possible successor to Thatcher. Thatcher, who narrowly escaped

injury, insisted that business continue as usual, and that afternoon she delivered a scheduled address to the conference, to tumultuous applause.

Coal Strike. The coal miners' strike began in March. It seemed to have little effect on the public power supply or on other industries, but it had a far-reaching impact on the country politically and socially. Critics charged that the strikers had a political motivation: to bring down a Conservative government that was determined to curb what it regarded as the overweening power of the trade unions.

The protagonists in the dispute were, on the miners' side, Arthur Scargill and, on the government's side, Ian MacGregor. They were a study in contrasts. Scargill, a man in his 40's who had been elected president of the National Union of Mineworkers (NUM) for life in 1981, was an avowed Marxist, with a stated ambition to mobilize the industrial working class for political ends. MacGregor, a man in his 70's, was chairman of the state-owned National Coal Board. A Scottish-born American businessman, he had been hired by the British government from the investment firm of Lazard Frères, in New York, first to sort out the nationalized steel industry and then to revamp, and make more competitive, the nationalized coal industry.

When MacGregor took over the coal industry, it was operating at a loss, offset by government subsidies. The coal board therefore announced proposals for closing down 20 pits and reducing the work force by 20,000. Severance terms were offered that were better than almost any other in both the public and private sectors, and a guarantee was later given that work would be found in the industry for all who wished to stay in it. Scargill asserted that the proposals masked more drastic plans to close 70 pits and eliminate 70,000 jobs. The coal board played into his hands. Cortonwood colliery, in the Yorkshire coalfield, had just received an infusion of miners from pits that had been closed. They were led to believe that they had at least five years of work there ahead of them. Within weeks of their arrival, however, the imminent closure of Cortonwood was being discussed. To the miners, it appeared to be proof that the board was not to be trusted.

A gaping hole reveals mangled rooms in the Grand Hotel in Brighton, England, where Prime Minister Margaret Thatcher narrowly escaped death from an Irish Republican Army bomb. Four people died and more than 30 others were injured by the explosion, but the IRA failed in its apparent objective: the killing of Thatcher and members of her cabinet, gathered at the hotel for the annual Conservative Party conference.

The men at Cortonwood struck on March 5, and the NUM executive endorsed the action three days later. The strike spread rapidly through the coalfields of Yorkshire, Scotland, and southern Wales. By March 12, half the pits in the country were idle; by March 21, three-quarters. But a national strike failed to materialize. The union insisted that no pit should be closed that could still be safely mined.

When mass picketing began at the striking coal mines, the police were in place in massive force. Thus, pits were kept open, and miners who were determined to work were allowed to do so; but violent clashes between pickets and police could not be avoided. On one occasion, on June 18, some 6,000 miners gathered at Orgreave coking plant in Yorkshire, to be confronted by about 3,000 policemen. Something like a battle ensued. Some 80 people

were injured, including Scargill (slightly), and 93 were arrested. Altogether, after six months of the strike, there were 6,400 arrests; 670 policemen suffered injuries. Scenes like those at Orgreave, relayed on television, shocked the public, most of whom had not known industrial violence on that scale before.

The coal board at the very beginning went to the High Court and was granted an injunction to restrain the Yorkshire strikers of the NUM from picketing in other parts of the country. (Such "secondary" picketing was illegal under legislation passed by the Thatcher government.) The miners ignored the injunction, and the coal board decided against taking further steps.

On September 28, however, a London judge, ruling on a suit by two working miners who complained of union intimidation, found that the strike was not "official" under the union's constitution and so the union could not threaten nonstrikers with disciplinary measures. Saying he could not allow the union to ignore his ruling, the judge on October 10 fined the NUM £200,000 (close to $300,000) and Scargill £1,000 (over $1,000) for contempt of court. The union was given two weeks to pay the fine. It refused to pay, and the judge ordered that all its physical and financial assets be sequestered, or seized.

By the end of October there had been ten negotiating sessions between the coal board and the union. On October 31 what were described as "last chance" talks between the board and the union broke down. The following month, the strike appeared to be weakening, as many miners, enticed by substantial Christmas bonuses, returned to work.

The Economy. With more than 3 million Britons out of work, representing over 13 percent of the labor force, the Thatcher government continued to face a grave challenge in 1984. In the speech from the throne on November 6, however, the government offered no programs to alleviate unemployment, saying only that it remained "deeply concerned." In the speech, the government pledged continuing efforts to return state companies to private hands and to control public spending.

Earlier, on March 13, Chancellor of the Exchequer Nigel Lawson, in introducing the 1984–1985 budget, noted that inflation had been brought down from a peak of 20 percent, in 1980, to 4.5 percent, the lowest figure since the 1960's. At the same time, output was expected to grow 3 percent in the year ahead. Productivity in manufacturing industries had risen by 6 percent.

The budget was broadly neutral in fiscal terms. But it included certain tax reforms, such as the withdrawal of tax relief on life insurance premiums and a reduction of stamp duty on the purchase of shares and houses. Investment allowances were to be phased out in return for a lower rate of corporation tax. The proposed fiscal and tax reforms proved immediately stimulating to the financial markets.

Late in the year, the pound dropped below $1.20, the lowest it had ever been. Since January its value had fallen by close to 20 percent against the dollar.

The government favored a policy of privatizing state-owned corporations, usually by flotation on the stock market, both to raise revenue and to promote competition and efficiency. In 1984, for example, it disposed of Enterprise Oil (formerly the British Gas Corporation's North Sea oil interests), Jaguar Motors, and Sealink (formerly the railway's sea ferries). The government put slightly over half of British Telecom, the national telephone system, on the market late in the year, hoping to raise more than $4 billion over two years.

Politics. At its annual conference, at Blackpool in October, the Labor Party condemned the police for whatever violence had occurred during the coal miners' strike, leading party leader Neil Kinnock to denounce violence from all sides (many Britons blamed the union for the violence). Earlier, the party, reflecting the tug-of-war between the militants and the increasingly outvoted moderates in its ranks, had issued a statement on defense policy that combined a firm commitment to the North Atlantic Treaty Organization with a demand that all U.S. bases in Britain be closed.

Tony Benn, the left's standard-bearer in the parliamentary Labor Party, was returned to Parliament in a by-election at Chesterfield on March 1; he had lost his Bristol seat in 1983. The Social Democratic Party gained its seventh member in Parliament in a June by-election.

European Community. The wrangle over Britain's contribution to the budget of the European Community came to a head in 1984. The

The Ha'penny Is History

On March 29, Britain's Royal Mint stopped coining the halfpenny, after more than 700 years, and the venerable coin, once silver but then bronze, ceased being legal tender at the end of the year. Introduced by King Edward I in 1280 to avoid cutting up pennies for small change, the halfpenny could still buy a bit of children's candy as late as the 1960's. But by the early 1980's it had been shrunk by inflation to very small change and cost more than its face value to mint. A halfpenny dropped on the floor was often more likely to get swept away than saved, though some Britons still prized its virtues as a makeshift screwdriver.

Thatcher government had repeatedly complained that existing financial arrangements left Britain paying a disproportionately heavy net contribution to the Community, which then wasted its substance on open-ended agricultural subsidies consuming three-quarters of its revenues. A meeting of Community heads of government, at Brussels in March, concluded without result, but another meeting, at Fontainebleau on June 25–26, reached an agreement that amounted to considerably less than what Thatcher had been holding out for. It did not provide for basic reforms such as reductions of trade barriers and overhaul of the agricultural support system. It provided limited rebates partly compensating for Britain's heavy net contribution to the Community.

Northern Ireland. James Prior, secretary of state for Northern Ireland since 1981, stepped down on September 10. He was succeeded by Douglas Hurd, a former diplomat and a novelist.

In November, Prime Minister Thatcher, after meeting with Irish Prime Minister Garret FitzGerald in London, told reporters that she categorically rejected all three proposals for Northern Ireland put forth by the New Ireland Forum, in its report issued May 2, and conveyed by FitzGerald: a unified Ireland (the preferred option), a confederation between Ulster and Ireland, and joint British-Irish administration of the north. The British government's reaction to the proposals caused a furor in Ireland.

Northern Ireland's economy showed signs of recovery in 1984, as some of its prominent manufacturing firms appeared to be getting in better shape. For example, Short Brothers, aircraft manufacturers, rolled out the first of 18 Sherpa airplanes for the U.S. Air Force, with options for 48 more.

Hong Kong. As Britain's lease over the New Territories, which account for 92 percent of the area of Hong Kong, was due to expire in 1997, the Thatcher government continued holding talks with Chinese representatives over the colony's future. Negotiations were concluded in September, and on December 19, Thatcher and Chinese leader Deng Xiaoping formally signed an agreement, in Peking, under which Hong Kong would become an autonomous "special administrative region" of China (see HONG KONG).

Superpower Relations. On her return from Peking, Thatcher stopped over in the United States, where she met with President Ronald Reagan. She publicly expressed approval of administration efforts to conduct research into a "star wars" space defense system and said she and Reagan were in agreement on basic arms control issues. A few days earlier, while playing host to Mikhail Gorbachev, a leading

"Victory to the NUM" was the battle cry of striking members of Britain's National Union of Mineworkers who took over the London headquarters of the National Coal Board. The miners left the building peacefully, but their sometimes violent strike proved to be one of the longest in Britain's history.

member of the Soviet Politburo, in London, Thatcher had voiced uneasiness about a space arms race not limited by treaty.

Libyan Embassy Incident. On April 17 a gunman inside the Libyan embassy in London fired at Libyan demonstrators outside who were protesting the regime of Muammar al-Qaddafi. A British policewoman was killed, and several demonstrators were wounded. A few days later, Britain broke diplomatic relations with Libya.

Royal Family. On September 15 a second child was born to the Prince and Princess of Wales: a son, named Henry Charles Albert David, who stood third in line of succession to the throne.

Queen Elizabeth II made several trips in 1984: in March to Jordan; in June to Normandy, France (to commemmorate the 40th anniversary of the June 6, 1944, Allied landing); in September–October to Canada; and in October to the United States (especially for private visits to several horse farms in Kentucky).

See STATISTICS OF THE WORLD. See also COMMONWEALTH OF NATIONS. T.J.O.H.

GREECE. In 1984, the Socialist government of Prime Minister Andreas Papandreou experienced lingering tensions in its relations with Turkey and the United States. The Cyprus issue and rivalry over U.S. military aid were major sources of contention between Greece and Turkey. In April, Turkey formally exchanged ambassadors with the self-proclaimed Turkish Republic of Northern Cyprus, drawing strong protests from Greece. Greece also protested a proposal by the Reagan administration to increase U.S. military aid to Turkey from $715 million in fiscal year 1984 to $755 million in fiscal 1985, while keeping aid to Greece at $500 million. Moved by Greek objections, Congress ultimately approved only $700 million for Turkey.

On March 30, U.S. Secretary of Defense Caspar Weinberger arrived in Athens for a two-day visit, during which he met privately with Papandreou. The two focused on the discord between Greece and Turkey. Papandreou persisted in refusing to allow Greek participation in North Atlantic Treaty Organization exercises in the Aegean area so long as some of Greece's Aegean islands, at Turkey's insistence, were excluded. In July the United States threatened

to block the sale by Norway of 16 used F-5 interceptor aircraft to Greece. (Norway had received the warplanes as a gift but could not sell them without U.S. approval.) Washington was showing its displeasure with the release by Greece, earlier in the year, of an alleged Arab terrorist accused of plotting to transport explosives on commercial flights from Athens to Tel Aviv. Greece countered by threatening to close down two Voice of America relay stations on Greek soil. The matter was soon resolved by negotiation, and both threats were withdrawn. However, U.S.–Greek relations were strained again in September when Papandreou visited Libya and signed an extensive trade agreement with the government of Muammar al-Qaddafi.

As part of its efforts to bolster Greece's defenses, the Papandreou government announced in November that it would purchase 40 U.S. F-16G jet fighter planes and 40 French Mirage-2000's over the next decade; it reserved the option of ordering 20 more aircraft within the next three years. The total purchase of 100 planes would cost close to $3 billion, including spare parts and training.

With a three-year record behind him and the prospect of parliamentary elections no later than the fall of 1985, Papandreou had to deal with tension in his own party, the Panhellenic Socialist Movement. He tried to hold his centrist base without alienating his left-wing supporters; critics on the left had charged him with designing policies that were contradictory and more moderate than his radical public rhetoric. Papandreou sought to appease the right wing by placing George Mavros, a centrist oriented toward Western Europe, at the head of his party's ticket in the elections for the European Parliament.

In the European elections, held on June 17, the Socialists, with 42 percent of the popular vote, captured ten of the 24 seats allocated to Greece. New Democracy, the main opposition party, with 38 percent, secured nine seats. The Moscow-oriented Communist Party of Greece gained 12 percent of the vote and a total of three seats.

New Democracy's aging leader, Evangelos Averoff, subsequently stepped down. He was succeeded by Constantine Mitsotakis, a former foreign minister, considered a match for Papandreou in charisma.

A new five-year plan (1983–1987) for economic and social development, approved by Parliament at the end of 1983, set a growth rate target of 3.5–4 percent for the period, to be achieved by an average investment expansion of 8.5 percent. Forecasts by the European Economic Community, made public in the spring, provided a mixed picture of how the Greek economy was expected to perform in 1984. The gross domestic product was expected to increase by 1.6 percent, in contrast to 0.3 percent in 1983. Unemployment was projected to rise from 7.8 percent in 1983 to 8.6 percent.

See STATISTICS OF THE WORLD. J.A.P.

GRENADA. The Caribbean nation of Grenada, scene of a U.S.-led invasion in 1983, returned to parliamentary democracy in 1984. In the December 3 election a centrist coalition led by Herbert Blaize won 14 of the 15 seats in Parliament. Blaize's New National Party had been created in August by the merger of three parties. Their objective was to present a united front against the right-of-center party led by Sir Eric Gairy, a former prime minister overthrown by a leftist coup in 1979. Gairy's Grenada United Labor Party won only one seat in Parliament in the December election, while the leftists, with only 5 percent of the popular vote, were completely shut out. Blaize, the new prime minister, was a soft-spoken 66-year-old lawyer and former civil servant.

On August 8, 19 former army and government officials accused of murdering Prime Minister Maurice Bishop and seven others in the October 1983 party schism that led to the invasion were ordered to stand trial. Those to be tried included former Deputy Prime Minister Bernard Coard; his wife, Phyllis; and former army commander Hudson Austin. Commencement of the actual trial was repeatedly delayed.

Late in the year, a 400-member Caribbean peacekeeping force, supported by 240 U.S. troops, remained on the island. Compensation paid by the United States to Grenadians for damages resulting from the invasion amounted to about $1.6 million as of December, when the U.S. claims office was completing its task. The United States also planned aid for Grenada

of about $57 million, including $19 million for completion of the international airport at Point Salines. The airport, begun in 1980 with help from Cuba, opened in October, but with work remaining to be done. St. George's University Medical School reopened in January; President Ronald Reagan had cited the "rescue" of its 600 American students as a major motive for the invasion.

See STATISTICS OF THE WORLD. D.B.

GUAM. *See* STATISTICS OF THE WORLD.

GUATEMALA. The regime of General Oscar Humberto Mejía Víctores remained in power in 1984, as preparations were made for a gradual transition to civilian rule. Voting for an 88-seat constituent assembly that would draw up a new constitution for Guatemala was held on July 1. The moderate Christian Democrats, with about 17.2 percent, were the top vote getters, but close behind was a newly registered party, the center-right National Union of the Center. Each received 22 seats in the assembly, which convened in September.

Mejía Víctores, head of state since an August 1983 military coup, stated explicitly that the constituent assembly's jurisdiction would cover only the drafting of a constitution and an electoral law. The body would not be empowered to name a provisional president for the country. Mejía Víctores said that general elections would be held in 1985 and that he would not be a candidate for the presidency. He insisted, however, that he would remain in office until he transferred the executive power to a civilian president elected by the people under a new consititution. His personal influence seemed somewhat limited; real policy making power appeared to remain in the hands of zonal commanders and other officers.

Under the Mejía Víctores regime, paramilitary death-squad activity continued; during his first year as head of state, it was estimated 1,300 Guatemalans were murdered and more than 400 were abducted. Meanwhile, guerrilla activity was largely confined to the northern border region. The army's antiguerrilla campaign enjoyed some success, which was attributed to the proliferation of the civil self-defense patrols started in 1981. Large numbers of Guatemalan refugees still were living in camps in Mexico.

The overall outlook for the economy remained gloomy. Unable to sell manufactured products to either El Salvador or Nicaragua in the amounts of past years, Guatemala looked toward the development of its nearly untouched energy resources. The $800 million Chixoy hydroelectric plant, which had opened in 1983, was shut down in April 1984 because of a major problem that would add at least $30 million to its cost. Disbursement of remaining funds from a $120 million International Monetary Fund standby arrangement was suspended because the Mejía Víctores government refused to implement measures to cut the budget deficit.

An agreement was announced in June between the Coca-Cola Company and its union at a franchise in Guatemala City, where the work force had been laid off in February. It was hoped that the plant would reopen with new owners who would recognize the union and negotiate a new labor contract. The strike had global ramifications, with a worldwide coalition of food industry unions organizing a boycott against Coca-Cola products.

The newly appointed U.S. ambassador, Alberto Piedra, announced in August that his government would supply $20 million in economic assistance. (The amount was later reduced to $17.8 million when family-planning funds were eliminated.) Guatemala was not receiving military aid from the United States and declined an invitation to participate in U.S.-Honduran-Salvadoran military exercises during the spring.

In September it was announced that Guatemala and Spain were reestablishing diplomatic relations, broken off in 1980 after Guatemalan troops stormed the Spanish embassy following its occupation by Guatemalan Indian peasants.

See Statistics of the World.   L.L.P.

GUINEA. Ahmed Sékou Touré, president of Guinea for 26 years and an active political figure among emerging African nations, died during heart surgery in the United States, at Cleveland Clinic Hospital, on March 26, 1984. A week later, the Guinean government was taken over by a group of middle-ranking officers, who dissolved the ruling Guinean Democratic Party and suspended the constitution, while stating an intention to move toward restoration of democratic rule. The new Military Committee for National Recovery (CMRN) pledged to avoid any personal dictatorship in the future. This group included Colonel Lansana Conté as head of state and Colonel Diarra Traoré as prime minister. The regime freed more than 1,000 political prisoners, who told of torture and inhumane conditions.

The CMRN's takeover and repudiation of the Touré legacy was greeted with satisfaction by France, and other Western or Western-oriented nations, although it was conceded that Touré had in recent years sought to modify his leftist orientation and tilt Guinea's foreign policy back toward the West. France agreed to help with several long-pending development projects. The upsurge of interest by Western countries came at an opportune time for the weak Guinean economy, additionally burdened by drought and the aftermath of two earthquakes in late 1983. At the same time, a chill in Soviet-Guinean relations that had begun in 1975 seemed to have ended in September 1984, when the Soviet Union and Guinea signed a $102 million loan agreement. The Soviets gained a share in Guinea's rich bauxite mines through the agreement, which provided for mine refurbishing.

See Statistics of the World.   E.B.

GUINEA-BISSAU. See Statistics of the World.
GUYANA. See Statistics of the World. See also Caribbean Countries.

H

HAITI. See Statistics of the World. See also Caribbean Countries.

HAWAII. See Statistics of the World. See also State Government Review.

Health and Medicine

In 1984, William Schroeder became the second person ever to receive an artificial heart. In another pioneering procedure, surgeons implanted a baboon heart in a critically ill newborn infant, known to the public as "Baby Fae."

MEDICINE

Among the major medical events of 1984 were the implanting of an artificial heart in a new human patient and the transplant of an animal heart into a human infant. Important advances were made in reproductive medicine, AIDS research, and the development of new vaccines.

Artificial Heart. On November 25, at the Humana Heart Institute International in Louisville, Ky., 52-year-old William Schroeder of Jasper, Ind., became the second recipient of a permanently implanted artificial heart. The plastic-and-aluminum device, labeled the Jarvik 7, was designed by Dr. Robert K. Jarvik, and was similar to the Jarvik model implanted in December 1982 in the first recipient, Dr. Barney Clark. Clark had died on March 23, 1983, after surviving 112 days.

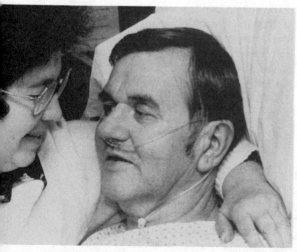

William Schroeder, 52, talks to his wife, Margaret, before the November 25 operation at Humana Heart Institute International in Louisville, Ky., that made him the world's second recipient of a permanent artificial heart.

Schroeder, a retired federal worker, was a heavy smoker who suffered from diabetes and cardiomyopathy—an ailment that weakens heart muscle—and had been given only days to live without surgery. His early postoperative progress was remarkable: after two days he was breathing without mechanical assistance and was asking for a beer, and within two weeks was exuberantly telling reporters that he felt "super." Doctors stated that his new heart was working faultlessly. On December 13, however, Schroeder apparently suffered a series of strokes, which left his memory impaired. He was also said to be suffering from depression. Doctors later said the strokes appeared unrelated to any problem with the artificial heart, and they remained optimistic about his prognosis. Schroeder would, however, remain attached by two hoses to the device's 323-pound power system (except for brief respites permitted by a second, portable system), and he remained vulnerable to life-threatening complications that could arise at any time.

Schroeder's case brought renewed publicity to the surgeon for both implants, William C DeVries, and to his new employer, Humana Inc., third-largest private hospital chain in the United States. DeVries had moved to Humana from the University of Utah, where he had operated on Clark, partly because of Humana's offer to fund up to 100 implant procedures Humana was willing to expend large sums on such a program as a possible source of favorable publicity and prestige; some critics, however believed that research of this type should no be performed at profit-making institutions.

Baboon Heart Transplant. On October 26, in a highly experimental surgical procedure, the heart of a young female baboon was transplanted to a 12-day-old baby girl, identified as "Baby Fae," who was suffering from a fatal congenital heart defect. Previous attempts a an animal heart transplant had met with quick rejection of the donated organ by the immune system, but increased knowledge of transplant techniques and improved drugs to combat rejection contributed to the initial success of the procedure, performed at the Loma Linda (Calif.) University Medical Center by a team headed by Dr. Leonard L. Bailey.

By October 30, Baby Fae, who was receiving the new drug cyclosporine and steroid drugs to prevent organ rejection, had already become the longest surviving recipient of a transplanted animal heart. Hopes that she would achieve longer-term survival were based in part on the fact that a newborn's immune system is immature and thus apparently less likely to reject a transplanted organ. However, about two weeks after surgery a serious rejection episode ensued, leading to kidney failure. Despite attempts to save her with stronger anti-rejection drugs and kidney therapy, Baby Fae died on November 15, having lived for 20 days with the transplanted heart. Her doctors claimed that she had lived more comfortably after the transplant than do untreated infants and that much had been learned that might help future patients. Others, however, criticized the procedure and, especially, what was considered to be insufficient public information. It was questioned whether Baby Fae's parents had been given full information about other options before they granted their permission. There was also some debate over whether surgeons should have made more efforts to seek a human donor, although the likelihood of finding one was said to be slight.

Embryo Transfers. The techniques were different but the results were the same: Australian and American researchers both announced the birth of babies as a result of embryo transfer procedures, in which the egg is produced by one woman but carried to term by another.

The Australian birth, announced by Dr. Carl Wood in January, used essentially the same technique developed in the so-called test-tube baby programs (in vitro fertilization). In this technique, eggs are removed from the ovaries of a woman unable to become pregnant naturally because her fallopian tubes are blocked. The eggs are then fertilized in the laboratory with her husband's sperm, and one is implanted

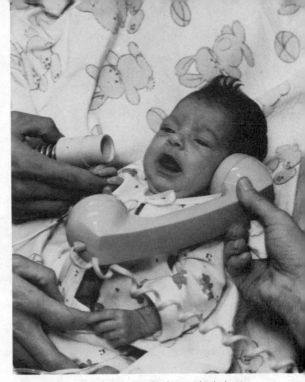

Thirteen days after receiving the heart of a baboon, 3½-week-old Baby Fae (so called to protect her parents' anonymity) listens to the voice of her mother, who had a cold and was temporarily barred from personal contact with her daughter. Baby Fae, who survived for 20 days after the historic surgery, was the longest living human recipient of an animal heart.

in the woman's womb. If the implant takes, the woman becomes pregnant. In the embryo transfer variant that produced this year's birth, physicians took an extra egg from one woman and, with the donor's permission, used it in an attempt to achieve pregnancy in a recipient woman who was unable to produce viable eggs. The egg from the donor, who was matched with the recipient according to appearance and other factors, was placed in a glass dish with sperm from the husband of the recipient. After fertilization had occurred, the embryo was implanted in the recipient, and the resulting pregnancy produced a healthy baby boy.

The American researchers, who announced their first successful birth in February, used a different, somewhat more controversial technique. Instead of fertilizing the donor egg in the laboratory, the researchers artificially inseminated the donor woman with sperm from

The birth of a normal baby after the implantation of an embryo that had been frozen and then thawed is announced by Doctors Carl Wood and Linda Mohr, key members of the Melbourne in vitro fertilization team responsible for the project's success. Baby Zoe (pictured at center) weighed in at 5 pounds, 13 ounces.

the recipient's husband. Then, after five days, the embryo was flushed from the donor, using a method called lavage, and was implanted in the woman who carried the child to term. This technique is more controversial because the lavage may not always remove the embryo from the donor; if it does not, the donor is left with a possible unwanted pregnancy.

Dr. Wood reported another breakthrough in the treatment of infertility in April, as he and his colleagues announced the birth of the first baby born from an embryo that had been frozen and then thawed. The technique will allow infertile women to try repeatedly to achieve pregnancy in the in vitro program, while being subjected only once to the procedure used to remove eggs for fertilization.

The 1983 deaths of a husband and wife from California being treated for infertility at a Melbourne, Australia, hospital, left the fate of two frozen embryos—created from the woman's ova and sperm from an anonymous donor—in doubt. A scholarly committee recommended in September 1984 that the embryos be destroyed, but the Victoria parliament subsequently passed a measure calling for the embryos to be implanted in a surrogate mother and, when delivered, put up for adoption.

AIDS Virus. In almost simultaneous announcements, scientists in the United States and France reported that they had identified a virus that is the likely cause of AIDS (acquired immune deficiency syndrome), the mysterious disorder that has struck some 7,000 victims in the United States alone since it was first identified in 1981. Meanwhile, the number of new cases reported each quarter continued to rise. Europe was also reporting an increasing number of AIDS cases, although the incidence was still less than 10 percent of that in the United States. As in the United States, male homosexuals and bisexuals accounted for most of the European cases. The as-yet incurable disorder destroys the body's immune system, thereby rendering its victims vulnerable to many disease-causing agents. AIDS generally strikes certain groups: intravenous drug abusers, hemophiliacs, and Haitians, as well as homosexual males.

In the United States, Dr. Robert Gallo and colleagues at the National Cancer Institute announced in May that a virus called human T-cell lymphotropic virus III (HTLV-III) is probably the agent responsible for AIDS. At the same time, scientists at the Pasteur Institute in Paris announced that they had isolated a similar—probably identical—virus that they named lymphadenopathy-associated virus, or LAV. The French scientists said they had isolated LAV antibodies (substances produced in the body to combat particular disease agents) in patients with AIDS or patients with pre-AIDS syndrome and in healthy homosexual men. The probable identification of an AIDS virus meant that scientists could begin work toward a vaccine, and before that on a test to screen blood for the virus before the blood is used in transfusions, thus preventing further transmission of AIDS by that route.

Other advances in AIDS research included the finding of direct evidence for the transmission of the virus through blood and confirmation by British workers that the lymphadenopathy, or disease of the lymphatic system, noted in some members of high-risk groups is indeed a precursor of AIDS. The results of the same study suggest that lymphadenopathy does not always develop into AIDS, since the condition of some subjects having that disease remained stable or improved.

In the first large review of autopsy findings of AIDS victims, Dr. Kevin Welch and colleagues at the University of California School of Medicine in San Francisco found that AIDS victims suffer far more widespread and dramatic organ damage than previously suspected, with virtually every organ of the body commonly affected.

Recombinant DNA Technology. There were further advances in developing medical applications for recombinant DNA technology, or genetic engineering, whereby DNA is manipulated in the laboratory to change the genetic makeup of cells and enable them to produce large quantities of particular biological substances. The first vaccine prepared by recombinant DNA technology, developed to provide immunity against a form of hepatitis, was tested in humans, and a genetically engineered blood-clotting protein known as Factor VIII, used to treat hemophilia, was produced by Genentech Inc. (neither was expected to be generally available for at least several years). Both advances were of particular interest because human blood is used in current methods for producing the two substances, which poses a theoretical risk of contamination by the agent that causes AIDS.

Recombinant DNA technology was also used to identify and reproduce, in the laboratory, a protein responsible for stimulating immunity in humans to the "sporozoite" form of the malaria-causing parasite. Some scientists estimated that a malaria vaccine based on this achievement could be ready for testing in one two years. The worldwide battle against malaria has been growing more difficult because of an increasing resistance to insecticides by the *Anopheles* mosquito responsible for spreading malaria-causing parasites, and also because of an increasing resistance by the parasites themselves to the primary antimalarial drug, chloroquine.

Hepatitis Research. Significant progress was made in combating a major public health problem when two groups of researchers, working separately, announced that they had identified a virus (or viruses) responsible for non-A non-B hepatitis, a liver ailment that is the form of hepatitis most often transmitted through blood transfusions. In October, workers from the Food and Drug Administration and National Institutes of Health announced that they had detected a retrovirus or family of retroviruses in blood samples of 18 patients suffering from the disease. A month later, scientists from the New York Blood Center reported finding the discovery of a virus, apparently belonging to a previously undescribed class, in chimpanzees inoculated with blood serum from cases of non-A non-B hepatitis. It was not yet known whether the two groups had actually discovered the same or different viruses.

Chicken Pox Vaccine. Chicken pox, one of the last childhood diseases for which there has been no vaccine, may soon be a thing of the past if new findings are confirmed by further

---

Yes, . . . Uh-huh . . .

Now for only $7.50, you can have a light-weight therapy session anytime, anywhere, with Walk-A-Shrink, a 45-minute cassette designed for use with headphones. As you stroll or jog along, a comforting male voice asks, "What are you thinking?" and at one-minute intervals encourages, approves, and probes with remarks such as "Yes, go on," and "Why do you think that is?" The mindless "shrink" is actually a New York City cabinetmaker, one Stanley Mulfield, who thought up the idea as a joke. The tape is available at some New York City retail outlets and by mail order through Regression Productions.

research. In a study of 914 children, scientists at the University of Pennsylvania found that a vaccine developed from a live but weakened strain of the varicella (chicken pox) virus is both safe and effective in preventing the highly contagious ailment, which, in a very small number of children, may lead to pneumonia or encephalitis.

Drug Approval. Revised regulations that would enable the Food and Drug Administration to cut as much as six months, or 20 percent, from the time required to approve a new drug for marketing were announced in December. Under strictly defined conditions, the new rules would allow the approval of new drugs entirely on the basis of clinical testing outside the United States. Moreover, the amount of paperwork required of drug companies would be substantially reduced. The new rules, expected to go into effect in 1985, would also strengthen requirements for manufacturers to report adverse drug reactions, so as to permit more rapid withdrawal of harmful medications.

Dr. Robert Gallo checks a test tube in a National Cancer Institute laboratory, where he and a research team identified a virus that probably causes AIDS (acquired immune deficiency syndrome). The discovery was hailed as a first step toward conquering the usually fatal disease.

Implant for the Totally Deaf. In November the Food and Drug Administration approved use of the cochlear implant, or "electronic inner ear." The device could aid many severely deaf people—those having a malfunction of the minute hair cells in the cochlea, a structure in the inner ear. These patients would, with the implant, be able to hear such sounds as car horns and doorbells and detect changes in inflection or volume in conversation. The cochlear implant was developed by Dr. William House, of the House Ear Institute in Los Angeles, and was being manufactured by the 3M Company of St. Paul, Minn.

Cholesterol and Heart Disease. Dramatic results from a ten-year U.S. government–sponsored study of heart disease in 3,806 men (ages 35–59) with high cholesterol levels appeared to confirm that reducing the level of cholesterol in the blood does lower the risk of coronary heart disease. Previous research had linked high cholesterol levels with an increased risk of heart disease, but this study, reported in January, was the first to show that the danger can be lowered for high-risk populations by decreasing their cholesterol levels.

Half the men in the study received the drug cholestyramine, which lowers levels of low-density lipoprotein cholesterol, believed to be the type of cholesterol most involved in the development of coronary heart disease. The other half of the sample received a placebo. Both groups followed a restricted-cholesterol diet, and all of the men were monitored for seven to ten years. The men who had taken the drug showed a marked decrease in cholesterol levels and equally significant declines in the rates of heart disease and death; they suffered 19 percent fewer nonfatal and 24 percent fewer fatal heart attacks than those in the placebo group. The researchers cautioned that the study's findings do not necessarily apply to other cholesterol-lowering drugs.

Understanding Alzheimer's Disease. Scientists moved several steps closer to an understanding of Alzheimer's disease, the progressive neurological disorder that destroys brain tissue and afflicts more than 1.5 million Americans. At Harvard Medical School, Drs. Elizabeth M. Sajdel-Sulkowska and Charles A. Marotta studied tissue from the brains of six patients who had died of Alzheimer's disease, and made molecular comparisons with tissue taken from four normal brains. In the tissue from the Alzheimer's patients, they found a consistent biochemical defect that results in a decrease in the production of protein in the brain. Meanwhile, scientists at the University of Iowa identified the areas of the brain where damage resulting in memory loss occurs. According to their study, based on analysis of the brains of deceased Alzheimer's patients, the damage is confined to highly specific areas of the hippocampus, the part of the brain responsible for memory. This finding contradicts the earlier belief that the tangled nerve fibers that characterize the disease were widely and randomly distributed.

Vasectomy and Health. Vasectomy, the severing and tying off of the tube that releases sperm, is the most effective form of birth control available to men, but questions have been raised about its possible effects on other aspects of health, particularly the immune system. A study of 10,590 men conducted by researchers at 12 institutions found, surprisingly, that vasectomized men are actually healthier in some respects than their counterparts who have not undergone this procedure. No damage to the immune system was found, and with the exception of one disease, an inflammation of the scrotum called epididymitis-orchitis, the incidence of cancer and other diseases for vasectomized men was similar to or lower than for their counterparts.

Herpes. Herpes simplex, the sexually transmitted disease that reached epidemic levels several years ago, continued to be a major public health problem. The disease is characterized by clusters of small, painful blisters in the genital area; some victims have very frequent outbreaks, while others seldom have problems. No cure has yet been discovered, but two new studies, one from Middlesex Hospital Medical School in London and the other from the U.S. National Institute of Allergy and Infectious Diseases, found that acyclovir, the only drug used to treat the recurring ailment, also helped suppress outbreaks.

Exercise and Health. Two studies that were published in July, both based on statistical surveys, added new fuel to the continuing

Dr. Howard Green of Harvard Medical School (right) uses Dr. G. Gregory Gallico as a prop to help explain the technique he developed for artificially producing real human skin. In Green's treatment, small sections of a burn patient's undamaged skin are removed and placed in a growth-stimulating solution; after they have expanded in area, they are grafted onto the victim. The new technique helped save the lives of two Caspar, Wyo., brothers who had suffered burns over 95 percent of their bodies.

debate over the role of exercise, particularly jogging, in promoting health and longevity. One study, by researchers at Harvard and Stanford universities and the Marathon Oil Company, indicated that even moderate exercise by middle-aged and older men can help prolong life. The second study, conducted in Dallas, found that men and women who exercised were less likely to develop high blood pressure than those who did not.

Shortly before release of the two studies, James Fixx, author of *The Complete Book of Running* (1977), which helped start a national exercise trend, died suddenly while jogging in Vermont. As a young man Fixx had been overweight and smoked heavily, and his father had died at 43 of a heart attack. Autopsy revealed that the 52-year-old Fixx had severe atherosclerosis. The question was asked: did his years of dedicated jogging prolong or shorten his life?

191

HEALTH REPORT CARD

How Americans Are Doing in Following Good Health Practices

Practice	Percentage
Moderate alcohol use	88%
Checking blood pressure	82%
Not smoking	70%
Getting 7–8 hours of sleep	64%
Getting enough vitamins and minerals	63%
Obeying speed limits	61%
Consuming fiber	59%
Restricting sodium	53%
Restricting cholesterol	42%
Exercising strenuously	34%
Maintaining ideal weight	23%
Wearing seat belts	19%

Note: Scores reflect percentage of compliance, based on a survey of 1,254 adults.

Most doctors believe that exercise, particularly regular, prudent exercise, usually does help to reduce death rates but in some cases can hasten sudden death from a heart attack. This view received support from a study published in October by researchers at the universities of North Carolina and Washington. The findings suggested that men who engage in strenuous exercise run a lower overall risk of a heart attack but that their chances of suffering an attack are greater while exercising than at other times.

Smoking. In the spring the U.S. surgeon general released another report on smoking and health, which asserted that approximately 50,000 deaths from chronic respiratory diseases (such as bronchitis and emphysema) in 1983 were directly attributable to smoking. One chapter in the report emphasized the growing evidence of health dangers from passive smoking (inhaling smoke from other people's cigarettes). This has become a matter of growing public concern, particularly as homes and offices are made more airtight to keep down energy costs.

Later in the year, federal legislation was enacted requiring cigarette companies to provide new health warnings on cigarette packages and in advertisements. Unlike the existing warning, the new warnings—a series of four designed to appear in rotation—was to state specific hazards attributable to smoking.

Prevention Index. The Prevention Research Center, funded by *Prevention* magazine, released the first data from a project to measure progress made in the United States in improving health-related behavior and the public health environment. The project, conducted in cooperation with the survey research firm of Louis Harris and Associates Inc., in its initial phase, surveyed 1,254 adults with respect to 21 health-related practices.

This first "report card" concluded that the health-related behavior of the adult U.S. population was roughly 62 percent as good as it could be. Americans were found to be doing well in using alcohol moderately (88 percent of those surveyed complied), socializing regularly (83 percent), and having their blood pressure checked (82 percent). They were doing less well in having their teeth examined (71 percent), not smoking (70 percent), and controling stress (68 percent). And they were doing rather poorly in restricting fat in their diet (55 percent), exercising strenuously (34 percent), and wearing seat belts (19 percent). Additional ratings were included on practices particularly affecting women's and children's health.

MENTAL HEALTH

During 1984 findings were reported giving clues to the cause of manic-depressive illness, and the initial results of a comprehensive survey of the mental health of Americans were released.

Manic-depression. Investigators at the National Institute of Mental Health in Bethesda, Md., and Wayne State University in Detroit, reported in July that they had discovered a genetic disorder that apparently helps trigger episodes of manic-depression, a mental illness characterized by sharp mood swings. The finding was strong evidence that many cases of mental illness may be biochemical in origin.

The research team cultured skin cells from victims of severe manic-depression and compared them to skin cells cultured from healthy individuals. The scientists found that the cells from the manic-depressives had a much greater sensitivity to acetylcholine, a neurotransmitter, or substance that carries message in the brain. The existence of this biochemical abnormality, which was found to be genetically transmitted, indicates that drug therapy or a combination of drugs and psychotherapy may be the most effective treatment for the illness.

Mental Health of Americans. The first results of the most comprehensive survey ever made of psychiatric problems among Americans indicated that 18.7 percent of the adult population, or almost one in five, suffered from at least one mental health disorder. These findings, released in October, were based on nationwide projection of data collected in interviews with about 10,000 people, according to study director Dr. Darrel A. Regier of the National Institute of Mental Health.

Anxiety disorders were found to be the most common, affecting about 8.3 percent of adults; substance abuse disorders (including alcohol abuse) were next at 6.4 percent. About 1 percent suffered from schizophrenia. Also included in the data were depressive illness, serious antisocial behavior, and severe impairment of mental function.

S.W. & J.F.J.

HONDURAS. The unexpected occurred in Honduras in 1984 when military strongman Gustavo Alvarez Martínez was removed from power and sent into exile by dissident elements within his own military establishment. The general's ouster as armed forces commander, in late March, left the civilian president, Roberto Suazo Córdova, as undisputed leader of his country.

Alvarez's ouster was the most significant political event since the Liberal Party took power early in 1982 after democratic elections. He had come to dominate the making of both foreign and domestic policies, and his influence had far outstripped that of President Suazo. Alvarez was the country's leading supporter of the anti-Sandinista guerrillas, and he helped the United States turn Honduras into a major base for anti-Communist efforts in the region. However, Alvarez's autocratic style of leadership created antipathy within the armed forces, particularly at the intermediate command level. U.S. plans to continue training Salvadorans on Honduran soil, popular dissatisfaction with human rights abuses, and Alvarez's obvious intervention in civilian political issues set the stage for his ouster. Several other top generals, including the armed forces chief of staff, were forced to resign. General Walter López Reyes succeeded Alvarez as commander of the armed forces.

In November, the FBI in Miami arrested eight people—including one of the ousted generals—for allegedly plotting to assassinate Suazo. The plotters were allegedly intending to sell a large cache of cocaine to finance the operation. The Honduran government sought extradition of the conspirators to face charges of high treason.

Honduras appeared to solidify its role as a

Jeanetic Medicine

Wearing skin-tight jeans may be more than a fashion statement—it could save your life. According to an article in the *British Medical Journal*, tight jeans can help prevent an accident victim with below-the-waist injuries from going into shock, by controlling hemorrhaging. (Doctors are advised to replace body fluids at such times before removing the jeans; otherwise, as happened in one case, the patient's blood pressure may drop to a dangerously low level.)

major actor in the Central American conflict by virtue of two significant U.S. military maneuvers conducted in Honduras, known, respectively, as Big Pine II and Grenadier I. These maneuvers were designed to make clear the U.S. commitment to Nicaraguan antigovernment guerrillas and to the democratic elections conducted in neighboring El Salvador. They also provided an opportunity for the United States to construct airfields and other facilities throughout Honduras.

However, the alliance between Honduras and the United States also showed strains. While there had previously been only muted internal criticism in Honduras of the U.S. military presence, growing public dissatisfaction surfaced in 1984, particularly after General Alvarez's ouster. Late in the year, Honduras reportedly was seeking increased U.S. aid and other concessions as a condition of continued military cooperation with the United States.

The economy remained a serious problem. Unemployment reached an estimated 20 percent of the work force, with another 60 percent reportedly underemployed. In late August, the president announced a cabinet shakeup aimed chiefly at producing improvements in the economic situation. New ministers were appointed for finance and economy, and new heads were appointed to two other cabinet-level economic posts.

To diffuse continuing pressure for agrarian reform, Suazo gave legal recognition to the militant National Union of Peasants, which led a number of efforts to occupy land. The government pointed out that it had already provided land titles to more than 1,500 small-scale and medium-scale coffee growers in the department of Santa Barbara. Discontent with Suazo's rule was also linked to alleged continuing human rights abuses.

See STATISTICS OF THE WORLD. M.B.R.

HONG KONG. After 143 years of colonial rule, Great Britain on December 19, 1984, signed an agreement with China providing for China's resumption of sovereignty over Hong Kong on July 1, 1997, when Britain's lease over 92 percent of the territory's land area expires. A "joint declaration" stipulated that Hong Kong would enjoy a "high degree of autonomy" in all areas except foreign affairs and defense, as a "special administrative region" of China after 1997. Under the accord, to which China committed itself for a period of 50 years, the government of Hong Kong would consist of local inhabitants, with an elected legislature, an independent judiciary, and a chief executive appointed by Peking.

The future of Hong Kong is determined by Chinese and British diplomatic teams negotiating the return of the British colony to China in 1997. The British side, led by Foreign Secretary Sir Geoffrey Howe (second from right), held 22 sessions with its Chinese counterpart before an agreement was reached.

The current social and economic system in Hong Kong would remain unchanged for the 50 years. China hoped that this "one country, two systems" formula could also be applied to Macao and to Taiwan.

In annexes to the agreement, China stipulated, among other things, that the rights and freedoms of Hong Kong citizens would be maintained, that private property and the present system of land ownership would be preserved, that Hong Kong would continue as a free port and separate customs area, and that Peking would not levy taxes on Hong Kong. Hong Kong's legal system, including the use of English common law, would also be maintained. Although China reserved the right to station troops in Hong Kong, it would grant the local government responsibility for law and order. China's position would be codified in a basic law that would govern Peking's future relations with Hong Kong. A Sino-British joint liaison group would be set up in 1985 and continue in existence to the year 2000, to aid implementation of the agreement.

The agreement, which was initialed on September 26, was formally endorsed by the territory's Legislative Council on October 18.

In a "Green Paper on Representative Government," issued in July, Hong Kong officials proposed the gradual introduction of elections to fill seats on the Legislative Council. These councilors would elect members to the Executive Council. The governor "in due course" would cease to preside over the legislature, but for the time being he would exercise the same powers and continue to derive authority from the British Crown.   J.P.B.

HOUSING AND CONSTRUCTION. Although high interest rates slowed construction and housing sales at times during 1984, both industries continued the recovery that began in 1983. Data for October showed spending for new construction was running at an annual rate of about $315 billion; the value of construction put in place for all of 1983 was $263 billion.

Housing Starts. Home builders enjoyed their second year of the housing recovery, starting a total of 1.74 million new homes. That was an improvement over the 1.71 million homes started in 1983 and considerably better than the 1.07 million started in 1982. The Commerce Department had surprised the industry by reporting that housing starts for February were at a seasonally adjusted annual rate of 2.26 million; the prospect of a year's total exceeding 2 million housing starts—a total not attained since 1978—holds a mystical appeal for the industry. That goal, however, proved unattainable in 1984.

Improvement in the housing industry was uneven geographically. The big winners (as measured by increases in housing starts) were California, Florida, and Arizona. The big losers were Texas, Oklahoma, Alaska, and Nevada. The top ten housing markets, in terms of new housing starts, were Dallas/Ft. Worth; Phoenix; Atlanta; Houston; Washington, D.C.; Tampa/St. Petersburg, Fla.; Los Angeles/Long Beach; West Palm Beach/Boca Raton,Fla.; Riverside/San Bernardino, Calif.; and Orlando, Fla. Although Dallas/Ft. Worth still ranked first, its total fell about 19 percent from 1983 levels.

Home Prices and Sales. Home prices inched up slightly. In October, the median price of an existing home was about $72,300, up 4 percent from 1983. The median new home price was put at $79,700, up 5 percent. Housing affordability declined according to one basic measure: in 1984, a family earning the median income had only 83 percent of the income needed to qualify for a mortgage on a median-priced existing home.

Sales of existing single-family homes held fairly steady. Expectations were for a slight increase over the 2.7 million resales recorded in 1983. New home sales were 6 percent ahead of the 1983 pace through September. For all of 1984, they were projected to increase about 3 percent from the 623,000 units sold in the previous year.

Mortgage Loans. The interest rate for a 25-year fixed-rate loan with a 25 percent down payment peaked at over 15 percent in July. With interest rates extremely high, adjustable-rate mortgage loans for both new and existing home sales helped make home ownership available to many who could not afford a fixed-rate mortgage loan. By late in the year, as interest rates declined, fixed rates became more popular, but ARM's continued to dominate the marketplace.

What Homes Cost in Selected Cities

Atlanta	$63,900
Baltimore	67,700
Boston	95,600
Chicago	80,300
Dallas–Fort Worth	86,500
Detroit	49,600
Houston	77,600
Los Angeles	117,000
Miami	81,500
New York	105,400
Orlando	87,600[1]
Philadelphia	61,800
San Diego	98,900
San Francisco	135,000
Washington, D.C.	95,500

Note: Median sales prices in metropolitan areas for existing single-family homes, second quarter of 1984.
[1] January–July 1984.
Source: National Association of Realtors

What $100,000 would buy in 1984 depended on where it was spent. In a rundown San Francisco exurb, it bought the three-bedroom house above ($112,000). In Ramsey, N.J., outside New York City, it paid for a modest 13-year-old dwelling (below right, $100,000), and in Orlando, Fla., for a new, airconditioned home with a swimming pool (above right, $105,605).

Early in the year, when ARM's were adjusted upward, some homeowners were hit with "payment shock"—their mortgage had increased more than anticipated and thus they were strapped to make the new payments. Congress held hearings on ARM's and warned lenders to regulate themselves adequately or else face congressional regulation.

The Federal Housing Administration, a New Deal agency that insures home loans, marked its 50th year in 1984. It celebrated in June in Pompton Plains, N.J., site of the first home built with FHA financing; it was built in 1934 and bought with a $4,800 mortgage.

Overall Construction Activity. *Dodge Reports* found that the total value of new construction contracts in the residential, commercial, industrial, utility, and public works sectors amounted to $162 billion for the first nine months of the year, up 9 percent from the same period in 1983. Office and commercial building construction hit an all-time high in June.

Real value of new office construction was up substantially for the first half of the year, and during the summer it held at a seasonally adjusted annual rate of $26 billion. About one-third of all nonresidential construction was additions and alterations to existing structures, according to estimates by Chicago Title and Trust Company.

Labor and Materials. In the construction industry overall, employment grew to 4.66 million persons in September. The unemployment rate lingered at about 14 percent, well below the peak of 22.8 percent in October 1982. The average hourly wage for contract construction dropped slightly, to $12.15 as of September. Observers noted that wage stability contributed to the containment of construction costs, a major reason for the strength of the recovery in the industry.

As for materials, steel prices held steady, increasing by less than 1 percent. Ready-mix concrete prices rose, showing an increase of

sociologist and dissident publisher Gabor Demszky. On being stopped in his car by two policemen, Demszky had protested the examination of his correspondence and had been beaten. Found guilty of assault, he received a six-month suspended prison sentence and was placed on probation for three years, with restrictions that would hamper his independent AB Publishing Company, involved in the clandestine circulation of government-suppressed literature. The trial drew protests both within Hungary and in the West.

Reflecting the balanced course it tries to maintain, Hungary received a succession of official visitors from both East and West. Western guests included British Prime Minister Margaret Thatcher in February, Italian Premier Bettino Craxi in April, and West German Chancellor Helmut Kohl in June. Meanwhile, in March, Czechoslovak Premier Lubomír Štrougal came to Budapest to discuss economic and trade matters. In October, party leader János Kádár met with French President François Mitterrand in Paris, in the first visit by a Soviet-bloc leader to France since Mitterrand took office in 1981.

A joint Hungarian-Czechoslovak hydroelectric project on the Danube River between Bratislava and Budapest provoked strong environmental opposition. It was reported in midyear that 50,000 people, led by 4,000 scientists and intellectuals, had signed a petition, protesting irreparable damage to the landscape and environment, obstruction to navigation, destruction of the aquifer that is Hungary's main source of water, and exorbitant costs.

See STATISTICS OF THE WORLD. R.A.P.

about 4 percent for the year; lumber prices, on the other hand, tumbled 25 percent from February to September. J.C.

HUNGARY. During 1984 the Hungarian government continued to deal with dissent while cultivating relations with both East and West.

In May the Budapest metropolitan court upheld a sentence given by a lower court to

I

ICELAND. After no other candidates filed to seek the presidency, Vigdís Finnbogadóttir in June was declared to have been elected to her second straight four-year term as Iceland's chief executive. She was solemnly sworn in at a ceremony in August.

Icelandic representatives attended a session of the North Atlantic Treaty Organization's Military Committee in Brussels, Belgium, in May. It was the first time in over 30 years that observers from Iceland had been present during the committee's deliberations. Iceland had sent the observers to the session because the agenda included discussion of the extension of the NATO radar network in the country. Although Iceland has no armed forces, it is a member of NATO. Its sending of observers was an indication of its desire to take an active part in planning Iceland-related NATO defense policies.

Iceland's Statistical Bureau estimated that export earnings could drop in 1984 by as much as 11 percent because of the decline in the cod catch; layoffs and unemployment were also forecast for the fishing sector, the nation's largest employer. The situation was partially alleviated, however, by increases reported in the scallop, shrimp, and capelin catches.

The inflation rate, which was running at about 100 percent in mid-1983, was rolled back to 12–14 percent by June 1984, although public dissatisfaction with anti-inflation measures taken by the government, including a wage freeze, was widespread.

See STATISTICS OF THE WORLD.   E.J.F.

IDAHO. See STATISTICS OF THE WORLD.

ILLINOIS. See STATISTICS OF THE WORLD.

INDIA. Prime Minister Indira Gandhi, leader of the world's most populous democracy for 15 years, was assassinated in October 1984 by Sikh bodyguards. Her son Rajiv was named her successor as Congress Party leader and prime minister and won an overwhelming mandate in December general elections. The assassination, climaxing a year of unrest and violence, sparked new waves of violence in which masses of people were killed. In an unrelated disaster, over 2,000 persons perished in December following a leak of poisonous gas from an insecticide plant in Bhopal.

Gandhi Assassination. Prime Minister Gandhi was assassinated on the morning of October 31 in New Delhi, as she walked from her house across a garden to her office. She died from gunshot wounds inflicted by two trusted Sikh bodyguards, in apparent revenge for the government siege earlier in the year of a Sikh shrine that had become a refuge for armed Sikh separatists. One of the guards was later killed, reportedly during an escape attempt after being captured. The other, who was wounded, later reportedly confessed and named others as involved in the conspiracy. By the

end of the year, five Sikhs were in custody in connection with the assassination, and police and Supreme Court inquiries were continuing.

Bloody reprisals against Sikhs followed the assassination; more than 1,000 persons were killed in violence that was finally controlled by the army. Curfews were ordered in dozens of cities, and soldiers reportedly had orders to shoot rioters on sight. Widespread looting and destruction of property occurred, and some 20,000 Sikhs fled to refugee camps for safety. Meanwhile, an estimated 80,000 persons, including almost 100 foreign dignitaries, attended Indira Gandhi's funeral in New Delhi on November 3. Rajiv Gandhi lit the Hindu funeral pyre bearing his mother's body.

For millions, Indira Gandhi had personified India itself for almost 20 years. Her father, Jawaharlal Nehru, was India's first prime minister. Working closely with him, Gandhi had served a long political apprenticeship before she was elected president of the Congress Party in 1959. Nehru died in 1964; two years later, Gandhi became prime minister. Under her, India became the dominant power in the region, supporting East Pakistan (now Bangladesh) in its civil war against West Pakistan. A nuclear power since 1964, India acted as a leader of the so-called nonaligned bloc, while maintaining closer ties with the Soviet Union than with the United States.

In 1975 a court ruled that Gandhi's previous election had been illegal. In response to rising opposition, she imposed a de facto dictatorship, imprisoning political opponents and instituting press censorship. The voters turned her out of office in 1977, then brought her back to power in 1980. After her younger son and political heir, Sanjay, died in a plane crash in 1980, Gandhi turned to her older son, Rajiv, who had previously showed little interest in politics, and groomed him for a political career.

General Elections. The Congress-I Party, under the leadership of Rajiv Gandhi, captured at least 396 of the 508 seats at stake in late December general elections. (Voting in turbulent Punjab and Assam was postponed indefinitely, and several other seats were to be decided in elections scheduled for 1985.) The margin of close to 80 percent was the largest ever achieved by the Congress Party. Although five cabinet or subcabinet members lost seats and the party lost ground in Andhra Pradesh, nearly every important opposition leader was defeated, including Atal Bihari Vajpayee, head of the National People's Party and a particularly prominent opposition spokesman. Gandhi himself easily won reelection from his constituency, defeating his estranged sister-in-law, Menaka Gandhi, by 300,000 votes. The strong mandate helped give him breathing space to establish himself and shape a course for the country's future. Rajiv Gandhi indicated after the elections that foreign policy would remain basically the same but that there would be changes in domestic policy. He was reinstalled as prime minister on December 31, along with a 39-member cabinet retaining only half of those in the previous one.

Punjab Violence. The assassination of Indira Gandhi was seen as stemming from a series of violent confrontations in the northern state of Punjab, where the conflicts were religious and economic as well as political in nature. Most of the world's 14 million Sikhs, a distinct religious community, live in Punjab. Best known for their military prowess, they have also suc-

ceeded in business, agriculture, and the professions. The Akali Dal, a moderate Sikh party, had ruled Punjab until the Congress-I party took control of the state in 1980; the latter sought to undermine the Akali Dal by boosting rival Sikh leaders. One of these, Jarnail Singh Bhindranwale, turned against his central-government sponsors and demanded a separate Sikh nation.

Early in 1984, Bhindranwale occupied the holiest Sikh shrine, the Golden Temple in Amritsar. Several hundred militant young followers joined him and turned the temple into an armed base for outside terrorist acts. By June, officials estimated that nearly 300 Hindus, moderate Sikhs, and others had been killed by the militants. On June 2 the Indian army took command of security in Punjab, and on June 6 it launched a tank attack on the temple compound. An estimated 1,000 Sikhs were killed (among them, Bhindranwale himself); thousands were wounded, and 4,000 were captured. About 100 Indian government soldiers were killed.

After that incident, thousands of Sikh soldiers mutinied; in one regiment Sikhs killed their commander before being killed by other troops.

Heir to Leadership

Rajiv Gandhi, who suddenly became prime minister of India at the age of 40 after his mother's assassination, might have preferred private life to the awesome responsibility of guiding a troubled nation of 746 million people. The dutiful son and grandson of prime ministers, he had remained in the shadow of his fiery younger brother, Sanjay, until Sanjay's death in 1980 in a plane accident. Rajiv had earned a degree in mechanical engineering from Cambridge University and then seemed content in his job as a pilot for Indian Airlines. But, with his mother's encouragement, he agreed to run for his late brother's seat in Parliament in 1981 and was elected. He was subsequently chosen as one of the general secretaries of the Congress-I party and became known as a strong foe of political corruption. His overwhelming mandate in December 1984 elections helped give him the credibility to shape a decisive course for India's future.

Rajiv Gandhi

Overnight, Sikhs around the world began to view India's government and its Hindu majority as enemies of their faith. Inevitably, the focus of attention for those seeking revenge would be Indira Gandhi.

Conflicts. Before the assassination, unrest plagued several other states. Violent protests erupted in Kashmir and Andhra Pradesh after governors appointed by Indira Gandhi ousted popular locally elected leaders, using debatable legal authority. However, after a wave of violence and a general strike, the governor of Andhra Pradesh was forced to resign and the locally-elected leader, N. T. Rama Rao, was restored as chief minister. Violence also occurred in northeastern India after Muslim immigrants from Bangladesh settled on fertile land. Angry local residents destroyed their property and drove them away. In Tamil Nadu, Tamil separatists agitated for their own nation, to be carved out of a portion of Sri Lanka, to the south. Some Tamil leaders urged an invasion of Sri Lanka to save their Tamil brothers, who were facing an unequal struggle against that nation's Sinhalese majority. Finally, in May, Bombay and its environs saw fighting between Hindus and Muslims that left more than 250 people dead.

Union Carbide Tragedy. Disaster in a different form struck in Bhopal in central India early on the morning of December 3. Highly toxic gas leaked from one of three underground storage tanks at a Union Carbide pesticide plant and spread as a white cloud through a crowded slum area. More than 2,000 persons died from contact with the gas, some immediately in their beds, others as they sought to flee or received emergency care in nearby hospitals. It was estimated that tens of thousands would suffer permanent disabilities, in what was said to be history's worst industrial accident. The gas, methyl isocyanate, caused blindness in many victims, and it was feared that other effects could include sterility, kidney and liver

A Nation Mourns

The funeral pyre of Indira Gandhi, assassinated Indian leader (above), is flanked by members of her family; her son Rajiv (in white hat) was named to his mother's post of prime minister.

nfections, tuberculosis, and brain damage. Officials of the U.S.-based Union Carbide Corporation declined to speculate about what had caused the gas leak, pending an investigation. Safety problems had been reported at the plant in 1982, but the company said they had been largely corrected since then. Warren Anderson, chairman of the company, was detained briefly by authorities during a visit to India to discuss relief assistance. The plant reopened about two weeks after the accident to neutralize the remaining methyl isocyanate; tens of thousands fled the city during that operation but began returning as it was reportedly concluded.

Foreign Affairs. India claimed that arms and funds found inside the Golden Temple after the bloody June raid had been smuggled across its western border. Pakistan denied any such support to the Sikh militants of the Punjab. In Kashmir, however, prolonged exchanges of fire across the UN cease-fire line raised some fear of renewed fighting between India and Pakistan. It was also feared that China might be shipping nuclear fuel or equipment to Pakistan. According to officials in the Reagan administration, some advisers to Prime Minister Indira Gandhi had recommended that India attack a Pakistani atomic installation to prevent the development of nuclear weapons.

U.S.–Indian relations were generally cordial, although India voiced concern over U.S. military aid to Pakistan. The declassification of secret materials by Rockwell International Corporation, allowing India to buy advanced weapons systems, strengthened U.S.–Indian ties.

Defense Minister Dmitri Ustinov led a Soviet delegation in a visit to India in March. An agreement was concluded for India to buy arms, including MiG fighters, from the Soviet Union. In April, Indian air force pilot Rakesh Sharma became India's first man in space, as he took part in an eight-day Soviet space mission.

See STATISTICS OF THE WORLD. S.A.W.

INDIANA. *See* STATISTICS OF THE WORLD.

INDIANS, AMERICAN. For many Indians, 1984 was a difficult year. Tribes were struggling with economic problems. There was a revival of opposition, from various organizations, to hunting and fishing treaty rights and other special status for Indian tribes. In this context, a presidential commission released a report on Indian economic development, and a federal Indian health care bill was vetoed by the president.

Government and Economic Development. On October 11, after holding hearings throughout Indian country, a nine-member Presidential Commission on Indian Reservation Economies delivered to the White House a progress report in which a number of obstacles to Indian economic development, many involving the federal government, were named. The report said that the federal trust responsibility for Indians conflicted with the government's recently enunciated policy of Indian self-determination. It asserted that federal education and employment training programs had failed to produce suitably skilled labor pools on reservations and that the federal contract and procurement system had not effectively used the Buy Indian Act and Small Business Administration programs to improve Indian market opportunities. Further problems cited were the instability of many tribal governments and the fact that some were more concerned about the social and political issues involved in the operation of tribal businesses than about efficiency and profits.

Indian Health Care Bill. On October 19, President Ronald Reagan vetoed legislation that would have extended and amended the Indian Health Care Improvement Act of 1976. The measure had been supported by Indians throughout the United States, as well as by such senators as Barry Goldwater of Arizona, Paul Laxalt of Nevada, and Mark Andrews of North Dakota, chairman of the Senate Select Committee on Indian Affairs. In addition to providing funds to eliminate backlogs in Indian health care services, the bill would have provided scholarships and grants to Indians who wished to acquire training in the health professions in order to enter the Indian Health Service (IHS). It would also have extended IHS services to urban Indians.

In his veto statement, Reagan said he supported the intent and objectives of the legislation but that it contained "troublesome" flaws: It required the federal government to assume responsibility for the health care of Montana Indians who live on reservations and do not pay local taxes, which the president said would set an undesirable precedent, and it would have elevated the IHS from a bureau of the Department of Health and Human Services to an agency, directed by an assistant secretary for Indian affairs, a move Reagan called "unconstitutional."

Water Rights. Interior Secretary William Clark renegotiated a 1978 water settlement act with the Ak-Chin Indian community of Arizona. The 1978 act had never been funded or implemented, in part because its delivery system would have cost $100 million, more than double the amount authorized by the act. The tribe agreed to reduce its entitlement from 85,000 to 75,000 acre-feet of water annually, and the Yuma-Mesa Division of the Gila Reclamation Project agreed to reallocate 50,000 acre-feet to Ak-Chin for a yearly fee of $11.7 million. The rest of the Ak-Chin entitlement was to be fulfilled through allocation of water

from the Central Arizona Project. When President Reagan signed the amended Ak-Chin settlement bill, Clark observed: "It isn't often we get a chance to fulfill a long-standing obligation to an Indian tribe, save the taxpayers tens of millions of dollars, foster water conservation, and add to the benefits of other water users in a state."

AIM Leader Sentenced. Dennis Banks, cofounder of the activist American Indian Movement, ended a nine-year flight from South Dakota authorities September 13, when he returned to the state and surrendered to local law enforcement officials in Rapid City. Banks, a Chippewa Indian from Minnesota, was sentenced October 8 to three years in prison by Circuit Court Judge Marshall Young. He had been convicted of assault and rioting in connection with a 1973 demonstration at the Custer County Courthouse but had fled before sentencing.   V.L.

INDONESIA. Murders of known criminals by unidentified death squads continued in 1984. A border dispute with Papua New Guinea placed further strain on Indonesia's relations with Australia.

Domestic Violence. By August it was estimated that from 3,000 to 5,000 persons—nearly al of them known criminals, gang members, o other social malefactors—had been executed by death squads, although, based on published reports of the number of bodies found, the incidence of such killings appeared to be abating. The government denied having sanctioned the killings. Violent crime has reportedly decreased markedly since the summary executions reached their height in 1983. There has been concern, however, that some people may have been killed for political or financial reasons, or by mistake. Such fears were len some support by the shooting death of a campus activist in Jakarta.

In September, a mob of about 1,500 Muslim youths rampaged through a slum section o Jakarta and clashed with government troops. The violence was sparked by the arrest of fou youths accused of beating a security guar who had entered a mosque and blacked ou antigovernment posters. After being urged b militant Muslim preachers to take revenge fo the arrests, the mob attacked a local army po and set fire to shops, stores, and cars. The riot reportedly left at least 18 dead and more than 50 wounded.

Foreign Affairs. The Indonesian province of Irian Jaya (also known as West Irian) occupies the western half of the island of New Guinea; the eastern half of the island is the independent country of Papua New Guinea, once a possession of Australia. Reports of disturbances near the province's capital in February prompted an influx of refugees to Papua New Guinea. Papua New Guinea subsequently charged that Indonesian jets had violated its airspace and, in response, expelled an Indonesian military attaché from its capital, Port Moresby.

The border problem with Papua New Guinea further strained relations with Australia, which had also been critical of Indonesia's 1976 annexation of the former Portuguese colony of East Timor. It was reported early in the year that full-scale fighting had resumed between East Timorese insurgents and Indonesian forces, and accounts of famine and human rights violations continued to come from the area.

Development Plan. After last-minute austerity cuts to reduce project budget deficits—from $5 billion a year to $3 billion—Indonesia's fourth five-year development plan (Repelita IV) was launched on April 1. Industrial growth was targeted at 9.5 percent a year.

See STATISTICS OF THE WORLD.   K.M.

INTERNATIONAL CONFERENCES. A variety of international conferences were held in 1984. For some not covered below, see AFRICA; COMMONWEALTH OF NATIONS; NORTH ATLANTIC TREATY ORGANIZATION; ORGANIZATION OF AMERICAN STATES; ORGANIZATION OF PETROLEUM EXPORTING COUNTRIES; UNITED NATIONS.

European Security Conference. The 35 member nations of the Conference on Confidence-and Security-Building Measures and Disarmament in Europe convened in Stockholm in January for the opening session of a special disarmament conference intended to hammer out a resolution on the reduction of nuclear arsenals in Europe. The meetings were held in three separate phases in 1984 and were scheduled to continue through November 1986, when it was expected that the resolution would be ready for presentation to a session of the full conference. The 1984 Sessions were oc-

cupied mainly in seeking to agree on an order of business.

Islamic Conference Organization. The fourth summit of the Islamic Conference Organization (ICO), held in Casablanca, Morocco, in mid-January, was attended by representatives of 40 member nations. Not represented were Afghanistan and Egypt, both of which had been suspended, and Iran, which boycotted the meeting because of the presence of an Iraqi delegation. After two days of closed debate, during which the delegates voted to readmit Egypt to membership, the conference ended with the adoption of the "Casablanca Charter," which emphasized the necessity of strengthened ties between members, and established committees to deal with inter-member conflicts. Syria and Libya had walked out of the January meeting, but were present in December, along with Iran, at the annual foreign ministers meeting, held in Sana, Yemen Arab Republic, at which Egypt was seated for the first time.

Arab League. Meeting at an emergency session in Tunis in May, foreign ministers of the Arab League departed from their traditional stance of public unanimity and overrode Syria and Libya to accuse Iran of aggression in its war with Iraq. The ministers also specifically denounced Iran for its attacks on Arab shipping in the Persian Gulf. Officials later said Iraq was not similarly blamed because its attacks on shipping had been confined to a specified war zone.

Asean Conference. The foreign ministers of nations comprising the Association of Southeast Asian Nations—Brunei, Thailand, Indonesia, Malaysia, Singapore, and the Philippines—held their 17th annual meeting in Jakarta in mid-July. The Asean ministers once again called on Vietnam to remove its troops from Cambodia and to support a reconciliation of Cambodia's opposing factions. Following two days of closed talks, the ministers were joined by representatives of Australia, Japan, New Zealand, and the United States; the combined group announced an agreement on a Pacific economic development plan in which wealthier nations would offer technical training to the region's less developed countries.

M.W.T.

IOWA. *See* STATISTICS OF THE WORLD.

IRAN. The costly and inconclusive war with Iraq continued to dominate events in Iran in 1984. The Islamic regime headed by the Ayatollah Khomeini celebrated the fifth anniversary of its coming to power and held parliamentary elections.

War With Iraq. Having achieved a limited success near Basra in February and March with a series of "human-wave" assaults, Iran launched no major ground offensive in the summer, despite repeated threats to do so. Iran's failure to strike puzzled many observers, some of whom attributed it to fear of devastating retaliation by Iraq. On May 31, Iraq had declared that it would respond to any new Iranian offensive by destroying the Kharg Island oil facilities, through which more than 80 percent of Iranian oil exports flow.

On the night of October 17–18 Iranian forces launched "limited attacks" against Iraqi positions north of Baghdad. An Iranian claim that its forces had won a "spectacular victory" was disputed by Iraq. Later in the month, a series of Iranian raids dislodged Iraqi troops from entrenched positions inside the Iranian border.

In response to continuing Iraqi attacks against Iranian shipping and oil facilities, Iran consistently threatened to block the Strait of Hormuz, through which all ships must pass to exit the Persian Gulf. From May onward, Iranian planes carried out intermittent attacks against neutral shipping in the Gulf. On June 5, two Iranian fighters were shot down by Saudi Arabian aircraft patrolling the shipping lanes.

With the Gulf a virtual war zone and Iranian oil exports threatened, Tehran in June proposed that a UN-sponsored agreement between the belligerents to suspend attacks against civilian centers, which took effect on June 12, be extended to cover all Gulf shipping. When Baghdad responded by demanding an Iranian guarantee of safety for all Iraqi shipping, ports, and waterways, the overture was withdrawn.

Foreign Relations. In January the Reagan administration reiterated that the United States would not tolerate Iranian closure of the Strait of Hormuz, and the following month a U.S. destroyer operating in the strait fired warning shots at an Iranian patrol plane and frigate that approached it too closely. In November the United States resumed diplomatic relations with Iraq, though maintaining official neutrality in the war. U.S.–Iranian relations remained severed.

Iran's already strained relationship with France worsened after four Iranian officers hijacked a military aircraft on June 15 and eventually reached France, where they remained despite Iranian demands that they be returned. Six

The faces of these Iranian soldiers, photographed in Iraqi internment, demonstrate the toll taken by the protracted conflict; as the war dragged on, Iran increased its recruitment of the very young and the old.

weeks later, it was the French government's turn to protest, when three pro-Khomeini hijackers seized an Air France airliner and forced it to fly to Tehran. The hijackers demanded the release of five Iranians jailed in France, and they threatened to kill the French passengers one by one if the demand was not met. After France refused, the hijackers released the passengers and crew, blew up the jet, and surrendered to Iranian authorities.

In the Arab world, Iran's two staunchest friends, Syria and Libya, failed in efforts to sidetrack an Arab League condemnation of Iran. On May 20, the foreign ministers of the League issued a resolution accusing Iran of aggression in the war with Iraq and specifically denouncing Iranian air attacks against Arab shipping in the Persian Gulf.

Hijackings. Following the Air France hijacking in late July, there was a series of air piracy incidents. On August 7, two teenagers claiming to be foes of the Islamic regime seized an Iran Air Airbus with approximately 300 persons on board shortly after it took off from Tehran. The hijackers eventually directed the jet to Rome, where they released their hostages and surrendered. Three weeks later, another Iran Air Airbus was hijacked, by a young couple who forced the plane to fly to Baghdad. After setting free their 204 hostages there, they were granted asylum by Iraqi authorities, who announced that any dissident Iranian skyjackers would be welcomed. That offer was quickly taken up by five Iranian citizens, who on September 8, took over an Iran Air Boeing 707 with 118 others on board and ordered it flown to Baghdad. Once again, all hostages were released unharmed. The biggest air piracy story of the year, however, came when a Kuwaiti jet carrying 161 passengers was hijacked on December 4 and forced to fly to Tehran. Two U.S. passengers were eventually slain before the plane was taken over by Iranian security forces five days later. SEE MIDDLE EAST.

Politics. Iranian opposition groups outside the country called for a boycott of the April 15 elections to the Majlis (parliament), and inside Iran the Freedom Movement of former Prime Minister Mehdi Bazargan refused to take part, citing the fact that all candidates had to be screened by the Pasdaran (Revolutionary

Guards), the prosecutor general's office, and other agencies. About half of those elected were new to the Majlis, but the body once again was dominated by members of Khomeini's Islamic Republican Party and allied groups.

When the new Majlis held its first session on May 28, Hojatolislam Hashemi Rafsanjani was reelected as speaker. Although Mir Hussein Moussavi continued as prime minister, five members of the 23-person cabinet (including Defense Minister Muhammad Salimi) were rejected in a show of strength by militant Majlis members.

Bombing in Tehran. On August 23, a terrorist bomb exploded in a Tehran street, killing 18 people and injuring about 300 others. Two anti-Khomeini groups claimed responsibility for the incident.

See STATISTICS OF THE WORLD.   J.S.I.

IRAQ. The protracted war with Iran affected all developments in Iraq in 1984. The heavy economic, social, and political burdens of the war led the Iraqi government to intensify efforts to press Iran into seeking a negotiated settlement to the conflict. Iran, however, did not appear to be interested.

War With Iran. In February, the Iraqi army faced one of its major challenges in the "Khybar" offensive launched by Iranian forces, which overran the artificial islands and oil fields of Majnoon (in the marshes north of Basra) and penetrated to within a few miles of the key Basra-Baghdad highway. In repeated clashes over the next several weeks, Iraqi forces managed to halt the offensive, although attempts to retake Majnoon were unsuccessful. In the aftermath of the fighting, Iran accused Iraq of resorting to chemical weapons to halt the offensive; similar charges were also made by the U.S. State Department. Iraq denied having used such weapons. A United Nations investigatory team confirmed that chemical weapons had been used in fighting and that Iranian soldiers had been exposed to them, but the report did not specifically accuse Iraq of responsibility.

In the course of the Khybar offensive, Iraqi forces also initiated major air, rocket, and artillery attacks against nearby Iranian civilian centers, which in turn led to Iranian retaliation in kind. An undertaking to refrain from attacks

Casualties in the long conflict between Iraq and Iran, two Iranian soldiers lie dead in their foxhole, with the Iraqi village of Beida ablaze in the background.

of this type that was made by both parties in mid-February soon collapsed, but a more effective UN-mediated agreement to forego attacks on civilian targets took effect in June.

By that time, the focus of the war had shifted to the Persian Gulf. On February 27, Iraq declared a blockade against Iran's Kharg Island oil facility. In seeking to enforce that blockade, the Iraqi air force carried out dozens of attacks during the year against both Iranian and neutral vessels in the Gulf. In these attacks, Iraq's Super Etendard aircraft, recently acquired from France, saw action for the first time. In May, Iraq threatened to totally destroy Kharg Island if Iran launched a threatened general offensive against the Iraqi lines. To the surprise of many observers, no such offensive was undertaken during the summer. Iranian forces did launch limited attacks north of Baghdad in mid-October; Iraq claimed the attacks had been contained but conceded the loss of some ground. By the end of October, Iranian raids had dislodged Iraqi troops from positions inside

Iran. Iran claimed to have killed 2,000 Iraqi soldiers in these actions.

Foreign Relations. Iraq continued to receive diplomatic support from most Arab states, with the exception of Algeria, Syria, and Libya. An Arab League conference in March criticized Iran for refusing to enter negotiations aimed at ending the war and called for curbs on exports of strategic materials to Iran. In May the League condemned Iranian attacks on Gulf shipping.

Iraq and the United States announced in November that they were resuming diplomatic relations, broken since Israel's victory in the 1967 Arab-Israeli war. Meanwhile, the Soviet Union agreed to do preliminary work on a new nuclear power plant in Iraq (a previous French-built facility was destroyed by Israeli bombers in 1981). It was announced in May that recent petrochemical and power generation agreements with the Soviet Union, financed through Soviet loans, were worth some $1 billion.

Economy. Despite massive subsidies and loans, especially from other Arab states, Iraq was suffering from severely depleted foreign exchange reserves, mainly because of drastically reduced oil exports as a result of the war. The government negotiated a $500 million loan from France early in the year and also was concluding agreements with friendly neighboring states for the construction of oil pipelines through those countries to expand its oil export capabilities.

Kurdish Pact. In January, Baghdad announced that an agreement had been signed with one of the two main Kurdish nationalist groups, Jalal Talabani's Patriotic Union of Kurdistan. The pact provided for a cease-fire between the Iraqi army and PUK, a broadening of Kurdish autonomy and an extension of the autonomous region to a wider area of Northern Iraq, and the creation of a 40,000-strong Kurdish army.

See STATISTICS OF THE WORLD.   J.S.I.

IRELAND, NORTHERN. *See* GREAT BRITAIN.

IRELAND, REPUBLIC OF. In 1984, a forum of Irish political leaders sought to give new impetus to the search for a settlement of the "national question" of Irish unity, and Ireland welcomed a visiting "favorite son," U.S. President Ronald Reagan.

The mission of the New Ireland Forum was to consider how a united Ireland might be established through peaceful means. All nonviolent political parties from both parts of Ireland had been invited by Irish Prime Minister Garret FitzGerald, but from the North came only the moderate, predominantly Catholic Social Democratic and Labor Party, led by John Hume. The Dublin parliament was represented by the Fine Gael, Fianna Fáil, and Labor parties. The forum's final report, issued in May, was highly critical of Britain's role in Ireland, but it emphasized the need for consent. A new Ireland, the report asserted, should preferably be a "unitary state, achieved by agreement and consent, embracing the whole island of Ireland and providing irrevocable guarantees for the protection and preservation of both the unionist and nationalist identities."

After the report was released, FitzGerald described the unitary state model as only a preferred option and stressed that other options, involving confederation or joint authority, might also be discussed. FitzGerald met with British Prime Minister Margaret Thatcher in Novem-

ber; after the talks, she publicly ruled out all three options. FitzGerald characterized her statement as "gratuitously offensive."

In June, President Reagan visited the tiny village of Ballyporeen in County Tipperary, where genealogists had traced his ancestry. Reagan also received an honorary doctorate of law from the University College at Galway, dined in Dublin Castle, addressed a joint session of the Irish parliament, and encountered—at a distance—scattered public demonstrations protesting U.S. nuclear policies and U.S. policy in Central America. In public remarks, the president denounced Americans who contribute money that funds political violence in Northern Ireland.

The Irish coalition government was strained by division over how to put the public finances in order and reduce government debt. The budget in January increased taxes markedly without substantially reducing borrowing needs. As rising interest rates increased the costs of debt service, the government introduced new economies in August, including a halving of food subsidies on milk, butter, and bread.

In mid-October the Irish fishery patrol boat *Aisling* discovered the Spanish trawler *Sonia* fishing illegally in Irish waters and, together with another patrol boat, gave chase. The Irish boats fired on the trawler when, according to Irish sources, it tried to ram the *Aisling*. The *Sonia* reached British waters but, amid heavy seas and gale-force winds, was taking on water. The crew was rescued, and the trawler, according to Spanish sources, sank.

See STATISTICS OF THE WORLD.   T.J.O.H.

ISRAEL. The general election campaign in Israel and the subsequent struggle to form a new government consumed much of 1984 and delayed efforts to surmount the economic crisis and launch new foreign-policy initiatives.

Election. As the economic crisis worsened early in the year, calls for new elections were heard, even from within the ruling Likud bloc. In March the defection of the small Sephardic Tami party left Likud without a majority in the Knesset (parliament), and Likud reluctantly agreed to elections on July 23. The opposition Labor Party entered the campaign united, after potential rivals chose not to challenge party leader Shimon Peres (see biography in PEOPLE

After protracted efforts to form a new government, Likud leader Yitzhak Shamir (left) and Labor's Shimon Peres raise their glasses to toast a unique partnership: Peres was to be prime minister and Shamir foreign minister for the first half of Israel's new administration; the two would then switch roles.

IN THE NEWS). Labor conducted a low-key—even lackluster and uninspiring—campaign. Likud was vulnerable on the economy, with inflation running at an annual rate of 400 percent and with foreign reserves tumbling, and it also bore responsibility for the protracted ordeal in Lebanon, where Israeli troops were still suffering casualties in terrorist attacks. Yet Labor did not deal with the Lebanese war in the campaign, and it revealed its plans for the economy only in generalities. Labor also erred by including only one Israeli Arab and one person under age 40 on its list of candidates for safe seats in the Knesset.

Likud entered the campaign in some disarray, because Yitzhak Shamir, who had been prime minister only since October 1983 (see biography in PEOPLE IN THE NEWS), had to fend off a challenge to his leadership by former Foreign Minister Ariel Sharon. Nonetheless, Likud waged a hard-hitting populist campaign, emphasizing all that it had done for the "common man" and asserting that Israel's economic problems were relatively insignificant compared to the achievements of Likud rule. Sephardic Israelis of Afro-Asian descent, who still resented their perceived second-class status when Labor was in power, strongly supported Likud.

Needing 61 seats to command a majority in the 120-seat Knesset, both Likud and Labor fell far short. Labor captured 44 seats and Likud 41, both fewer than their totals in the 1981 election. As in 1981, smaller parties were a significant factor. The 15 parties that captured one to five seats each ranged across the political spectrum. They were led by such diverse personalities as the moderate former Defense Minister Ezer Weizman, who favored a Lebanon pullout and better relations with Egypt and the Soviet Union, and ultranationalist Rabbi Meir Kahane, who is from Brooklyn, N.Y. The National Religious Party, previously the country's third largest party, was beset by divisions and won only four seats.

The Unity Government. Neither Peres nor Shamir was able to form a majority coalition, and, after a great deal of haggling, the two men agreed to form a national unity government. Under their agreement Peres and then Shamir would serve as prime minister for 25 months each. Each would serve as deputy prime minister and as foreign minister under the other. The cabinet ministries were to be shared by the two parties, though each could assign some posts to minor parties. Despite criticism within both the major and minor parties, the Knesset, voting 89–18, approved the national unity government on September 14.

Economy. In February the Knesset passed the Shamir government's austerity budget for the fiscal year beginning April 1; it included spending cuts for each government department, cuts in food and fuel subsidies, and higher health insurance rates. In September, with the inflation rate soaring further and with the foreign debt at $23 billion, the new national unity government devalued the shekel, cut the budget slightly, cut food and fuel subsidies sharply, approved a one-time property tax, and closed tax loopholes. Importation of some luxury items was banned for six months in October, and in November wages and prices were frozen for three months.

Prime Minister Peres visited Washington, D.C., in October, and met with President Ronald Reagan, seeking new U.S. aid. Reagan indicated that $1.2 billion in economic aid authorized by Congress would be paid immediately rather than in quarterly installments; action on other aid was deferred.

Foreign Relations. Plans by the United States to sell arms to Arab countries troubled Israel in 1984. A similar difference of opinion existed with West Germany. During a visit to Israel in January, German Chancellor Helmut Kohl noted that West Germany bore a "special responsibility" for Israel's security, but he also said he was willing to sell defensive weapons to Saudi Arabia.

Egyptian-Israeli relations grew cooler, as Egypt refused to send its ambassador, withdrawn in 1982, back to Israel. A leading problem was Israel's continued occupation of South Lebanon. Prospects for a withdrawal were dimmed in March when Lebanese President Amin Gemayel abrogated the Israeli-Lebanese peace agreement of May 1983. That accord had called for simultaneous withdrawal from Lebanon of Israeli and Syrian forces, but Syria had refused to go along. Troop withdrawal talks between Lebanon and Israel began November 7 under United Nations auspices; they recessed on December 20 with the two sides seemingly far apart.

Tensions between Syria and Israel remained high. On June 28, however, a prisoner-of-war exchange took place, with 291 Syrian captives of the 1982 fighting, 20 Golan Druze, and 72 Syrian dead exchanged for six Israelis and the bodies of five Israelis. Jordan refused to enter formal peace talks with Israel, though informal talks continued on mutual problems. In an important gesture toward Israel, King Hassan of Morocco attended a conference held in May by the Moroccan Jewish community.

Terrorism. Acts of terrorism by Israelis—apparently right-wing zealots—against Arabs became more frequent. In the spring police cracked a ring of suspected terrorists believed responsible for many incidents. Charges were brought against 25 Jewish West Bank settlers and two Army officers. Two were soon found guilty, but most were being tried together late in the year.

On April 12, four Arab guerrillas hijacked a bus and forced the driver to take it to the Gaza Strip. After Israeli soldiers shot out the tires, the guerrillas—holding 35 passengers hostage—demanded safe passage to Egypt and release of 500 Palestinians in Israeli prisons. Soldiers stormed the bus and freed the passengers, although one passenger was killed and seven wounded in the assault. Two guerrillas were killed outright, and it was later determined by a commission appointed by the Defense Ministry that the other two were killed by security forces after being taken into custody. Other terrorist attacks on Israelis took several lives and injured many persons.

See STATISTICS OF THE WORLD. R.O.F.

ITALY. By the end of 1984 the coalition government under Italy's first Socialist premier, Bettino Craxi, had been in power for almost a year and a half—quite a long tenure by Italian standards. Besides the Socialists, the coalition included the Christian Democrats, still numerically the largest party, and three smaller lay parties—the Social Democrats, Liberals, and Republicans.

Domestic Politics. Early in the year, Craxi and Cardinal Agostino Casaroli, the Vatican secretary of state, signed a concordat on officially separating church and state in Italy. Under the February 18 concordat, among other things, Roman Catholicism ceased to be the state religion, Rome lost its official designation as a "sacred city," and religious instruction in state schools was no longer mandatory.

The wartime fascist regime of Benito Mussolini passed a law requiring government employees to be at least 5 feet, 3 inches tall; still on the books, it caused the dismissal of Justice Ministry secretary Antonella Crielesi, 5 feet, 1 inch tall. Public outrage over Crielesi's case was expected to result in the law's repeal.

Craxi's coalition, while generally stable, foundered early in May, following an allegation that Budget Minister Pietro Longo appeared on a membership list of the secret Propaganda Two (P-2) Masonic lodge, banned in 1982 as a subversive organization. Longo strenuously denied the allegation, but he resigned July 12 after an investigatory commission found the list of P-2 members to be "authentic."

Disaster befell the opposition Communist Party with the death, on June 11, of its general secretary, Enrico Berlinguer, at age 62. Berlinguer, a Sardinian, had been leader of the Italian Communist Party since 1972 and was the virtual inventor of what is called Eurocommunism, which is typified by commitment to democracy and independence from Moscow. Alessandro Natta, 66, president of the Communist Party's central control commission, was elected as Berlinguer's successor on June 26.

The June 17 elections to the European Parliament, considered a first test for the Craxi government, brought disappointment to the Socialists, who won only 11 percent of the vote. The Communist vote, perhaps reflecting a wave of sympathy for Berlinguer, went up from 30 percent to 33 percent and, for the first time in a nationwide election, surpassed that of the Christian Democrats, who at 33 percent improved slightly on their 1983 position. Still, the Socialist-led coalition was holding firm.

Leaders of the five parties in the coalition, taking advantage of an improving economic situation, signed a cooperation agreement on July 26 designed to keep the Craxi government in office for at least several more months. The agreement seemed to hold in late November, when the Communists tried to bring a motion in Parliament against Foreign Minister Giulio Andreotti, a Christian Democrat and five times prime minister, charging him with abuse of office in an oil tax scandal in 1974. The motion was defeated by a vote of 484 to 421; if it had passed, it might have led to the collapse of the Craxi coalition.

Terrorism. After a period of relative quiet, political terrorism struck again. On December 23 a bomb exploded on a Naples-to-Milan express train, which was carrying at least 700 holiday travelers, while it was inside the Apennine Tunnel between Bologna and Florence. Authorities reported that 15 people had been killed and 180 injured. Both right-wing and left-wing organizations, including the Red Brigades, took responsibility for the attack. In angry reaction to the new outbreak of violence, thousands of Italians demonstrated in Milan, Rome, Bologna, Florence, and other cities. The government promised to fight terrorism with "maximum energy."

On December 6 a Milan court had sentenced 19 members of the Red Brigades to life imprisonment for murder and other crimes; nearly a hundred others on trial were given lesser sentences. Earlier, a number of captured terrorists, including all but 14 of some 70 Autonomists (members of the extreme leftist group Workers'

Autonomy), had received long prison sentences.

Economy. Much of Craxi's energy was aimed at seeking to reduce the rate of inflation, running at 12.5 percent in January, to 10 percent by limiting the wage increases set by the *scala mobile* system, which automatically indexed increases to match the rate of inflation. In mid-February, the government decreed that 1984 wage hikes would be limited to three percentage points less than the projected inflation rate. The decree went into effect immediately, but would lapse if parliamentary approval were not obtained within 60 days. Despite strenuous opposition from the Communists, who objected to compulsory wage controls, the decree got through the Senate on March 23, but approval from the Chamber of Deputies, delayed by numerous speeches and amendments introduced by the Communists, did not come until just after the April 16 deadline. The cabinet therefore, on April 17, approved a new anti-inflation decree similar to the previous one, except that its effect was to be limited to the first six months of the year. This measure was approved by the Chamber of Deputies on May 24 and passed the Senate on June 8, with the Communists walking out in protest. The decree's progress through Parliament was long and complicated but apparently successful: the rate of inflation did come down to 10 percent.

Despite a large public sector deficit (estimated in 1983 to be nearly 17 percent of the gross domestic product), Italy's economy showed signs of a slight upturn. There was some industrial revival in the private sector, and a number of trade agreements were concluded with foreign companies. Although Italy's labor costs remained high, the *scala mobile* modification was expected to help bring them down. By midyear, however, there was a record trade deficit, largely attributed to increased energy imports and a strong U.S. dollar.

Military Affairs. The installation of U.S. cruise missiles at Comiso, Sicily, in late 1983 sparked a series of demonstrations, culminating on May 3, 1984, when Italian police dismantled three "peace camps," on the outskirts of Comiso, making 13 arrests. In another development, the Italian contingent of the multinational peacekeeping force in Lebanon was withdrawn February 20.

Mafia Crackdown. A new extradition treaty between the United States and Italy was expected to aid efforts of Italian and U.S. law enforcement officials against organized crime. Acting on information supplied by Tommaso Buscetta, a high-level member of the Sicilian Mafia, Italian authorities in late September arrested 70 suspected Mafia members and served 200 warrants on individuals already in prison. Soon thereafter, U.S. authorities, at the request of Italian officials, arrested suspects linked to the Sicilian organization, for possible extradition; in turn, Italy agreed to extradite Buscetta to the United States. In December,

Arrested in the biggest anti-Mafia raid since World War II, Andrea DiGirolamo is escorted by police to a chartered plane waiting in Palermo, Sicily, to fly him and other suspected Mafia leaders to a northern Italian prison. In a predawn sweep on September 29, the Italian police methodically rounded up suspected members of the criminal organization whose names had been revealed by imprisoned Mafia boss Tommaso Buscetta.

Italian police arrested 97 more Mafia suspects, issued new warrants against 103 people already in jail, and sought 170 others in a widening investigation.

The Banco Ambrosiano Affair. Repercussions of the collapse, in June 1982, of the Milan-based Banco Ambrosiano continued. Italian authorities were still attempting to pinpoint the involvement of the Vatican bank, the Istituto per le Opere di Religione (IOR), which had holdings in the Banco Ambrosiano. The IOR management, including its chairman, Archbishop Paul Marcinkus, were under investigation by Milan magistrates for fraud in connection with the bankruptcy of the Ambrosiano group. On May 25, in Geneva, the IOR agreed to pay the Banco Ambrosiano's creditors up to $250 million of the final settlement against the bank, with the understanding that the creditors would make no further claims against the IOR or the Banco Ambrosiano's successor, the Nuovo Banco Ambrosiano.

Papal Assassination Plot. The complicated story of the possible Bulgarian connection with the attempt to assassinate the pope in Rome in May 1981 saw new developments. In October, Judge Ilario Martella decided there was sufficient evidence to order three Bulgarian officials, along with four Turks, to stand trial on conspiracy charges. The judge also decided to order Mehmet Ali Agca, a Turk convicted of carrying out the assassination attempt, to stand trial on new charges. Of the seven new defendants, only one of the Bulgarians and two of the Turks were actually in Italian custody. Judge Martella also stated that one of the Turks still at large, right-wing terrorist Oral Celik, had fired at the pope along with Agca.

See STATISTICS OF THE WORLD.   M.G.

IVORY COAST. See STATISTICS OF THE WORLD.

J

JAMAICA. See STATISTICS OF THE WORLD. See also CARIBBEAN COUNTRIES.

JAPAN. On October 31, 1984, Yasuhiro Nakasone was reelected to the presidency of Japan's ruling Liberal Democratic Party (LDP), which enabled him to remain as prime minister. Earlier in the year, concern over Japanese education prompted the Diet (parliament) to appoint a special committee to study possible reforms.

Politics and Government. Nakasone became the first Japanese prime minister since 1972 to serve more than two years in office. The support of controversial former Prime Minister Kakuei Tanaka, who had been convicted in 1983 of bribe-taking, had helped him maintain political strength; his potential rivals dropped out of contention, and his nomination by the party was unopposed.

Hours after his renomination, Nakasone announced a new cabinet, the previous one having resigned, as is the custom. Shintaro Abe was again named foreign minister, and Noboru Takeshita was again appointed finance minister. Shigeru Ishimoto, the first woman named to the cabinet in more than two decades, became director general of the Environment Agency. Other cabinet and party posts were distributed among all five major LDP factions.

Earlier in the year, cooperation among the opposition parties in boycotting the Diet was effective in bringing about important LDP concessions. A March boycott forced concessions on the fiscal year 1985 budget in May and led to a three-month extension of the spring Diet session, which was also boycotted. The opposition was objecting primarily to a government plan to reduce the national health insurance system's funding of salaried workers' benefits by 10 percent. To ensure passage of important budgetary programs in the extended Diet session, Nakasone was forced to return early from a London summit meeting of leaders of major industrial democracies in June and to cancel planned July trips to Australia and New Zealand.

U.S. Relations. Government officials of Japan and the United States were in close contact throughout the year. In one week in May, Vice-President George Bush, Secretary of State George Shultz, and Secretary of Defense Caspar Weinberger were all in Tokyo, each for separate reasons. Japan began to supply advanced technology to the U.S. military, and in June Japanese forces participated in the RimPac joint naval exercises in the Pacific.

A few economic issues that had caused considerable problems in the past were settled. For example, U.S. demands for reduced restrictions on high-technology markets where American firms are highly competitive were met without much argument. A Japanese bill to reduce copyright protection on foreign computer software—a proposal that had alarmed American companies—was shelved. A trade liberalization package announced on April 27 included new reductions of tariffs and simplification of import and certification procedures. Finally, after months of debate, the Japanese government agreed to increase foreign participation in the influential advisory councils that help shape Japan's industrial policy.

A more contentious issue was the liberalization of Japanese financial markets, which the United States began arguing for in 1983. Despite deep divisions between the two sides, a compromise agreement was finally reached in May. The agreement permitted more dealing in the yen outside Japan in the so-called Euroyen market. It made domestic Japanese financial markets more open to foreign financial companies—in particular, it allowed them to manage Japanese pension funds, which in 1984 were over $50 billion. It also promoted slow deregulation of domestic capital markets, starting with the removal of restrictions on interest rates for large deposits over the following two to three years.

With Japanese exports of steel to the United States rising, the Reagan administration late in the year requested that they be held back. Japanese officials said the request could hurt trade relations between the two countries, since the exports were conducted in an "orderly"

Working on a "fifth-generation" computer that Japanese scientists hope will be able to reason much like a human being, researchers test a robot's ability to follow voice commands. Long successful in the duplication of Western inventions, Japan was increasing its emphasis on original techology; in 1984, the nation spent $25 billion on research and development.

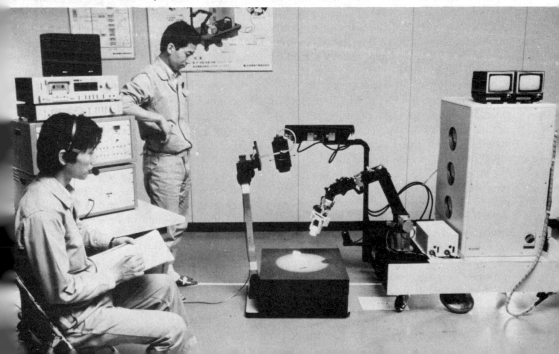

Their book bags ever present, uniformed junior high school students take a lunch break in Tokyo. A government commission was established to study critics' charges that the Japanese school system is overly zealous in training its students, resulting in a lack of spontaneity and creativity.

fashion and were low compared with the peak year of 1976. The government nevertheless agreed to a one-year limitation.

Defense. Japan's defense policies did not lead to as much bilateral friction as in the preceding few years. This was despite the fact that the relatively small defense budget was increased only 6.55 percent for fiscal year 1984, just slightly more than the 6.5 percent increase in 1983. The smallness of the increase reflected the political realities of Japan's tightest budget of the postwar period, and also the unpopularity of defense spending with the Japanese public. For fiscal 1985, government leaders agreed on a slightly larger, 6.9 percent increase.

A five-year plan to strengthen the Japanese military from April 1983 to March 1988 had been drawn up under U.S. pressure, but weapons purchases have fallen considerably behind schedule. With the budget restrictions and Japan's defense policy limiting military spending to less than 1 percent of the gross national product, it became clear that the five-year-plan levels would not be achieved, and in May the timetable was extended to 1991.

Education. In August the Diet approved a three-year study of Japanese education—an area that has always been one of the highest social priorities in Japan. Japanese youngsters spend much more time in school and in doing homework than do young Americans, and there have been increasing concerns in recent years that pressures on Japanese youth may be too intense. The importance of the series of examinations students must pass to get into good schools and eventually into a university leads many youngsters to attend private "cram schools" outside regular school hours to compete more effectively with their peers. Another concern is that the strong emphasis on acquiring specific skills—factoring quadratic equations in ninth grade, say—leaves students with an inability to do the kind of creative thinking needed for basic (as opposed to applied) research in an age of high technology.

A committee was created to weigh these problems—the Ad Hoc Advisory Council on Educational Reform, with 25 members appointed by the prime minister and approved by the Diet. But opposition parties, particularly those on the left, were suspicious of Nakasone's motives. Japan Socialist Party leader Masashi Ishibashi said the prime minister was really seeking to reintroduce, under the guise of tradition, an element of nationalism into the nation's schools.

Foreign Affairs. During a visit to China, beginning on March 23, Nakasone received a warm welcome and the first Chinese 19-gun salute in 18 years. Nakasone announced a seven-year, $2 billion credit as a down payment on a new era of economic cooperation, and the Chinese promised to solve problems of patent and investor rights that had kept Japanese investments to a small fraction of all foreign investment in China.

On June 7–9, Nakasone conferred with leaders of other major industrial democracies at a London summit meeting. Japan, along with the United States and Canada, was able to gain European agreement for new multilateral talks on trade restrictions.

The Man with 21 Faces. By late October a fifth of Japan's policemen were guarding candy shelves or checking leads in an extortion plot against Morinaga, a candy manufacturer. A gang, calling itself the Man with 21 Faces after a popular Japanese crime story series, had threatened to place cyanide-laced candy in stores if the company did not hand over 100 million yen (about $400,000). At least 15 boxes of poison candy, bearing the warning "eat and die," were found on retail shelves, and the extortionists promised to begin distributing poison candy with no warnings if the money was not forthcoming. The group was believed responsible for the March kidnapping of the president of another candy-maker, Ezaki Glico, and for making similar extortion demands after he escaped. No poison candy was found at that time, and in June the gang had announced

Chopsticks

Could it be true? According to a survey by the Japanese Ministry of Education, nearly half the nation's elementary school children say they do not know how to properly wield chopsticks—or *hashi*, as the Japanese call them. Observers say faulty chopstick technique is a common failing among Japanese under 30; Western eating habits, the education system, and parents' own loss of the skill have been blamed. Since adherence to traditional forms is an essential element of the Japanese way of life, the decline is a cause of wide concern, whatever the explanation. Trainer chopsticks have sold well, and courses in proper *hashi* use are now being offered to help avert cultural disaster at the dining table.

that it had "become bored with this affair" and was calling it off.

See STATISTICS OF THE WORLD.   M.S.B.

JORDAN. In a surprise move early in 1984, King Hussein convened the Jordanian parliament for the first time in ten years. The parliament, whose lower house consists of 30 representatives of the West Bank, populated largely by Palestinians, and 30 of the East Bank, had been dissolved in 1974 after an Arab League summit conference had recognized the Palestinian Liberation Organization (PLO) as the sole representative of the Palestinian people. In 1984 delegates were appointed to fill West Bank vacancies, and by-elections were held for vacant East Bank seats.

On January 10, the cabinet of Prime Minister Badran resigned and was replaced by a new cabinet under Ahmad Obaidat, minister of the interior at the time of his appointment. The new cabinet included a larger number of West Bank representatives.

PLO Chairman Yasir Arafat arrived in Amman on February 26 for renewed talks with Hussein on the status of a future Palestinian "entity" on the West Bank. In August, Arafat said an agreement in principle had been reached with Jordan on some form of Palestinian-Jordanian confederation, but the details of such a confederation had not been worked out.

Deteriorating relations with neighboring Syria and with Libya were exacerbated by a September announcement that diplomatic ties with Egypt, severed by Jordan in 1979, would be resumed. Egyptian President Husni Mubarak visited Jordan in October, and Hussein visited Egypt in December. After the latter visit, the two governments issued a communiqué agreeing on the principles of United Nations Resolution 242 as a basis for Arab-Israeli peace. Jordan also continued to give strong support to Iraq. Iraq's inability, because of its war with Iran, to export oil via the Persian Gulf led to a Jordanian-Iraqi agreement to build a $1 billion pipeline linking Iraqi oil fields with the Jordanian port of Aqaba.

On March 1 the administration of U.S. President Ronald Reagan informed Congress that it planned to sell Jordan more than 1,600 Stinger antiaircraft missiles, worth over $130 million. Congressional opposition, fueled by supporters of Israel who feared the missiles might someday be used against Israel, was strong, and Hussein reacted to the opposition by severely criticizing American Middle East policy. When the Reagan administration withdrew the Stinger proposal later in March, Hussein reiterated earlier statements that Jordan would purchase weapons from whatever source available.

The 1984 budget estimated expenditures of $2.08 billion, down from 1983, and revenues of $2.06 billion, also down from the preceding year. Principal expenditures were for defense and for development. Severe drought conditions caused shortages of food and animal feed that necessitated increased imports and hindered economic recovery.

See STATISTICS OF THE WORLD.   C.H.A.

K

KAMPUCHEA. See CAMBODIA.
KANSAS. See STATISTICS OF THE WORLD.
KENTUCKY. See STATISTICS OF THE WORLD.
KENYA. Kenya's President Daniel arap Moi continued efforts in 1984 to assert the government's authority and bolster its security, while normalizing the political climate, two years after a coup attempt that had seriously shaken the regime. Trials of military personnel involved in the August 1982 coup attempt were completed, as the last of more than 1,000 servicemen accused of participation in the coup or of failure to act against it were convicted and sentenced by the courts. The two alleged leaders of the coup attempt, Air Force Private H. Ochuka and Sergeant Pancras Okumu, were sentenced to death for high treason, bringing the total number of death sentences to 14.

In mid-1984, President Moi announced an amnesty for Kenyan exiles abroad, and several former members of Parliament who had fled to Tanzania in 1981 and 1982 returned to Kenya without being prosecuted. In December, he released four political detainees, two of them former members of Parliament, and freed 5,000 jailed criminals.

Charles Njonjo, a powerful figure in the Moi government until his ouster from the cabinet in June 1983, was officially expelled from the ruling Kenya African National Union party in September 1984, along with 14 others. In addition, a judicial commission found him guilty of involvement in the 1982 coup attempt in Kenya and in a 1981 coup attempt in the

Seychelles Islands, but cleared him of charges of having embezzled money. Moi confirmed Njono's expulsion from Kanu, and hence from political life, but granted him a pardon for his alleged crimes.

Kenya continued to maintain good relations with the United States, a major contributor of aid, and the United States made use of Kenya's port of Mombasa for resupply of ships in the Indian Ocean.

Agriculture had improved significantly in 1983, as had the trade balance. However, the economic picture began to darken as the expected March to May rains failed to materialize in 1984. Serious food shortages developed, and food prices rose. The government waited until mid-June to request outside aid in paying for 1.5 million tons of needed grain imports, and the necessity of diverting foreign exchange reserves into importing basic foods severely threatened prospects for recovery.

See STATISTICS OF THE WORLD.   J.K.

KHMER REPUBLIC. See CAMBODIA.
KIRIBATI. See STATISTICS OF THE WORLD.
KOREA, DEMOCRATIC PEOPLE'S REPUBLIC OF, or **NORTH KOREA.** The year 1984 was highlighted by President Kim Il Sung's extended six-week trip at midyear to Moscow, every Eastern European capital, and China. However, the trip's only tangible result seemed to be ratification of a friendship treaty with East Germany in June.

Domestically, the position of the president's son, Kim Chong Il, as heir apparent was strengthened by his growing public recognition as second in power and leader of the Korean Workers' (Communist) Party. There were indications of underlying economic difficulties, despite claims of new heights in industrial and agricultural production. A desire to hasten economic progress may have prompted the regime's policy statement in January declaring its readiness to trade with capitalist countries. A treaty to undertake joint economic projects with China was signed in August.

North Korea conducted a massive propaganda campaign on behalf of its proposal for tripartite reunification talks with the South and the United States but continued to refuse South Korea's demands for direct North–South talks. Talks aimed at the formation of joint North-South athletic teams for international competition broke down. However, North Korea's surprising offer of humanitarian aid to the South, after heavy September floods left 200,000 homeless, was accepted and carried out. Economic talks were later begun but were temporarily broken off after an incident at the demilitarized zone (see KOREA, REPUBLIC OF).

See STATISTICS OF THE WORLD.   D.S.M.

KOREA, REPUBLIC OF, or SOUTH KOREA.
South Korea remained generally stable in 1984, as the nation prepared for parliamentary elections in early 1985.

Politics and Government. Continuing to ease the government's restrictions on its opponents, President Chun Doo Hwan in February lifted a ban on political activity by 202 people who had been blacklisted in 1980. In May, 1,203 prisoners were paroled, and amnesty was granted in August to 1,730 persons. Opposition parties focused on such issues as election reform, press freedom, establishing elected local governments, and restoring the rights of the remaining proscribed politicians. Although the authorities continued the liberalization, begun in 1983, of controls on university students and faculty, the government's willingness still to use force on campuses was shown in late October, when more than 5,000 riot policemen broke up antigovernment demonstrations at Seoul National University. There also was a surge of student protests late in the year.

Economic Developments. U.S. concerns about its trade deficit with South Korea and about

South Korean President Chun Doo Hwan and his wife, Lee Sun Ja, are all smiles as they are greeted by Japanese Emperor Hirohito (right) during an unprecedented visit to Tokyo in September. The emperor made a roundabout, but clear, apology for Japan's treatment of Korea before and during World War II.

South Korean restrictions on U.S. trade and investment were conveyed by a special presidential trade delegation in January and by Treasury Secretary Donald Regan, who visited in March. In the same month U.S. benefits to South Korean exports under the Generalized System of Preferences (for developing countries) were cut on 15 items that earned $600 million for the republic in 1983. This action was followed by U.S. decisions that South Korea had been dumping color television sets and some steel products at prices cheaper than those charged in Korea.

The South Koreans, with a large if diminishing global payments deficit that exceeded $1 billion by June, were anxious to reduce their deficit and also preserve their American market. The purchase of $3.3 billion in U.S. goods was arranged, and voluntary limits were placed by producers on certain steel and television exports to the United States.

International Relations and Security. The annual Team Spirit exercise in February and March, involving nearly 200,000 South Korean and 60,000 U.S. troops, was marred by the collision of the U.S. aircraft carrier *Kitty Hawk* with a Soviet nuclear submarine and by the crash of a U.S. helicopter that killed 29 South Korean and U.S. servicemen. In May, at the annual joint security consultations, Defense Secretary Caspar Weinberger pledged U.S. support to strengthen air and artillery forces in South Korea.

September saw the first visit ever by a South Korean chief of state to Japan. President Chun's trip was climaxed by a low-key acknowledgment by Emperor Hirohito that Korea had suffered at Japan's hands.

On November 15, representatives of South and North Korea met at P'anmunjŏm, in the demilitarized zone (DMZ) between the two countries, and agreed to hold normal talks on trade and economic development. On November 27, however, North Korea called off the talks. The day before, North Korean troops and soldiers of the United Nations Command in South Korea had exchanged gunfire in the DMZ, when a Soviet citizen, visiting North Korea as part of a Soviet delegation, ran across the DMZ in an attempt to defect. Three North Korean and one South Korean border guards were killed; six other troops, including an American soldier, were wounded. The Soviet defector escaped unhurt. In mid-December, Seoul and P'yŏngyang, putting the incident aside, agreed to resume their talks in early 1985.

In May, South Korea was visited by Pope John Paul II, who celebrated outdoor masses in Seoul, Kwangju, and Pusan that were attended by more than a million people. International attention began to focus increasingly on South Korea as site of the 1988 Olympic Games, and Olympic officials were in attendance for the dedication of a new sports stadium constructed for the games.

See STATISTICS OF THE WORLD.   D.S.M.

KUWAIT. Kuwait's support for Iraq in the latter's war with Iran brought Iranian retaliation in 1984. Beginning in late May, Iranian warplanes made a series of attacks on Kuwaiti oil tankers in the Persian Gulf. Alarmed by this development, Kuwait joined with the other members of the Gulf Cooperation Council (Saudi Arabia, Oman, Bahrain, the United Arab Emirates, and Qatar) in condemning what the council called Iranian aggression and appealing to the United Nations to take diplomatic action against Iran. In response, the UN Security Council on June 1 voted to condemn all attacks on neutral shipping in the gulf but failed to single out Iran as the sole responsible party.

Iran's escalation of the war also led Kuwait to seek U.S. permission to purchase Stinger antiaircraft missiles, which Washington had supplied to Saudi Arabia in May. In late June, however, the Reagan administration turned down the Kuwaiti request, citing congressional opposition to the proposed sale. The Kuwaiti government turned to the Soviet Union and on August 15 concluded an arms deal worth an estimated $327 million with Moscow. Included in the deal were tanks and antiaircraft and antiship missiles.

Domestically, March saw the conclusion of the trial of 25 men for terrorist bombings in Kuwait City in 1983, with five of the men acquitted, six sentenced to death (three in absentia), and 14 sentenced to prison terms. The government blamed the bombings on al-Dawa, a militant Shiite Muslim organization that was opposed to the largely Sunni Muslim regime.

Kuwait's economic scene showed recovery of crude oil production from a low of 650,000 barrels per day at one point in 1983 to close to million b/d by mid-1984. (Kuwait's output was, however, cut to 900,000 b/d at a late October meeting of the Organization of Petroleum Exporting Countries.) The Kuwait Petroleum Company continued aggressive expansion of its refining and marketing operations in Western Europe, in order to provide greater market stability for Kuwait crude oil and petroleum products.

See STATISTICS OF THE WORLD. *See also* MIDDLE EAST.   L.A.K.

L

LABOR UNIONS. The improvement in the U.S. economy in 1984 helped reverse an actual decline in wages negotiated in collective bargaining settlements in early 1983. The year's negotiated wage hikes were fairly modest, however. Major collective bargaining contracts settled in U.S. private industry in the first nine months of 1984 resulted in average wage increases of 2.5 percent in the first contract year and 2.8 percent annually over the life of the contracts, according to the U.S. Bureau of Labor Statistics. The last time the same parties bargained (two to three years previously in most cases), average wage hikes were 8.6 percent in the first year and 7.2 percent annually over the contract life. The overall level of wage settlements in 1984 was dampened by construction industry wage increases that averaged less than 0.9 percent the first year and 1.2 percent annually over the life of the contracts—the lowest averages for the industry for

any period since the Bureau of Labor Statistics began keeping such data in 1968.

Bumpy Flights. The airline industry remained at the forefront of labor news. Continental Air Lines pilots and flight attendants continued to protest the company's unilateral abrogation of its labor agreements (as a result of filing for reorganization under Chapter 11 of the federal bankruptcy law) by picketing at airports around the United States. The dispute intensified in February when the U.S. Supreme Court ruled in *NLRB* v. *Bildisco & Bildisco* that employers filing for Chapter 11 reorganization may temporarily terminate or alter collective bargaining agreements, even before a judge has heard the case. Continental Air Lines subsequently proceeded to expand its operations, and by midyear was declaring a modest operating profit. Nevertheless, the *Bildisco* decision provoked such outrage from organized labor that Congress, in June, passed bankruptcy legislation

Disneyland is picketed by striking members of the Teamsters Union, who in September rejected a wage freeze offered by the giant amusement park in Anaheim, Calif. More than one-third of the 5,000 people employed at "the happiest place on earth" walked out—but they accepted a freeze and returned to their jobs the next month.

aimed at exempting labor agreements from the provisions of Chapter 11 except under carefully controlled circumstances.

On April 24 the shareholders of Eastern Airlines elected two union officers to the company's board of directors, joining Pan American World Airways and Western Airlines in a trend that may ultimately change U.S. labor-management relationships. Eastern employees, as a result of bargaining accords, increased their ownership of company stock to 25 percent.

The Hyatt Corporation, which had acquired and was struggling to restart bankrupt Braniff International, obtained concessionary five-year agreements with the unions, providing for significant increases in productivity, wage concessions averaging 30–40 percent, and cross-utilization of employees within various classifications. The airline resumed service under the new agreements on March 1.

Bargaining in Autos. Master agreements between the United Automobile Workers and the two largest U.S. automobile manufacturers, General Motors and Ford, expired on September 14, presenting first-term UAW President Owen F. Bieber with a serious dilemma. With thousands of UAW members still on layoff, job security was the union's top priority in new contract negotiations. The expiring agreements, however, were hammered out in 1982 to provide relief to a financially troubled industry. Concessions granted by the UAW that year froze wages and raised productivity, which—coupled with the subsequent rise in demand for automobiles—helped GM and Ford achieve combined earnings of $5 billion in the first half of 1984. Workers received some of this money in the form of profit sharing, but company executives received bonuses and stock amounting to thousands of dollars, with some high-ranking executives receiving bonuses in seven figures. These developments placed pressure on Bieber and his associates to seek substantial wage and benefit increases as well as improvements in job security. Shortly before midnight on September 14, with no new agreement yet reached, the UAW initiated selective strikes against GM plants employing about 110,000 workers, and more than half of GM's automotive production was shut down as a result.

On September 21, UAW bargainers reached a tentative agreement with GM on a three-year contract that addressed the problem of job loss caused by the introduction of new manufacturing technologies. The union did not win any guarantees on numbers of jobs to be preserved despite automation, but GM agreed to set up a $1 billion six-year fund for compensating workers left jobless or for retraining them. In return, the UAW settled for modest wage increases, averaging about 2.5 percent the first year. The pact was subsequently ratified by 57 percent of the rank and file. At Ford, a contract providing a similar pay hike and a $280 million job-security fund won approval in October.

Coal Mining. Richard Trumka, facing his first round of collective bargaining as president of the United Mine Workers, obtained changes that gave him more control of the union and its bargaining procedures. One of the changes permitted him to call selective strikes against coal operators, a major departure from the union's tradition of striking all operators simultaneously under a policy of "no contract, no work."

In contract negotiations, early success was achieved with several bituminous coal mining operations in the West, and in September agreement was reached with the Bituminous Coal Operators Association on a new 40-month contract. The pact called for wage hikes of $1.40 an hour (approximately 10 percent) over the life of the contract and provided some new job-security clauses.

Postal Workers. Some 650,000 postal workers engaged in long and sometimes acrimonious bargaining with the U.S Postal Service. Management, insisting that postal workers received wages and benefits that were much higher than those in related industries, pressed for a three-year wage freeze on existing workers' pay and a plan to create a two-tier wage scale, in which new employees would be paid an average of $5,300 a year less than veterans in the same jobs. Postmaster General William F. Bolger threatened to fire strikers and allow private companies to deliver the mail if postal employees went out on strike, an illegal move for federal government workers. After existing contracts expired in July, the National Association of Letter Carriers and the American Postal

Workers Union, together representing over 500,000 workers, voted at their separate conventions to submit their contract dispute to binding arbitration. On December 24, the arbitrators announced terms for the settlement, providing a 5 percent wage increase per year for the most senior employees, while new employees will receive about 25 percent less than the old $19,562 starting pay.

Ma Bell Breakup. The Communications Workers of America lost members in the wake of the January 1, 1984, breakup of the American Telephone & Telegraph Company, even though the reorganized AT&T and the seven regional companies it spun off had not yet met targets for cuts in the work force as they struggled to compete in a new nonregulated telecommunications market. As a result of deregulation, consumers can decide whether to use AT&T's long-distance service or switch to less expensive nonunion alternatives. To discourage customer defections, the CWA launched a $4 million advertising campaign aimed at convincing people that cheaper is not necessarily better.

Other Industries. A bitter and violent strike involved primarily the Arizona operations of the Phelps Dodge Corporation, a major copper producer, and 2,250 members of the United Steelworkers and 12 other unions. The walkout began July 1, 1983, after the unions refused to accept a three-year wage freeze without cost of living adjustments (COLA's). Frequent incidents of property damage and violence occurred after replacement workers were hired by the company and some former strikers crossed picket lines to return to work. After continuing to operate with nonunion workers or nearly a year, the company temporarily closed its New Cornelia mine near Ajo, Ariz., because of low worldwide copper prices. In December, the company announced the closing of its Morenci, Ariz., smelter, which had been manned by nonunion workers. Strikers hailed the decision, predicting that the whole mine would close and that the company would soon agree to a contract. Smelter workers protested the decision and complained of harassment by strikers.

Pressure to hold down health care costs resulted in hard bargaining in the hospital and health care industry. Approximately 50,000 members of District 1199 of the Retail, Wholesale, and Department Store Union struck hospitals and nursing homes in New York City and on Long Island in July and August. The strike ended with overwhelming ratification of a two-year contract providing for annual 5 percent pay raises and alternate weekends off.

In California, Disneyland suffered its third and largest strike since the amusement park opened in 1955. Approximately 1,800 ride operators, sales clerks, and janitors rejected a wage freeze when their contract expired in September. The three-week strike ended in October, when the unions did accept a new contract with a two-year wage freeze—but some improved job security.

Politics. After giving Walter Mondale its formal endorsement in 1983, the AFL-CIO was active during 1984 in its support of his successful bid for the Democratic presidential nomination. When the Democratic National Convention met in San Francisco in July, AFL-CIO President Lane Kirkland and other labor leaders were in attendance. Union leaders also backed the nomination of Geraldine Ferraro as Mondale's running mate and worked for the Democratic ticket in the fall campaign. About the only dissenter was Jackie Presser, president of the Teamsters, who publicly voiced his disapproval of the Mondale-Ferraro ticket and was a notable visitor at the Republican National Convention in Dallas in August.

The rank and file was less strong in its support for the Mondale-Ferraro ticket. Mondale won just 53 percent of the vote from members of union households, as against 45 percent for Reagan, according to a New York Times/CBS News poll taken among voters leaving polling places. Among blue-collar workers as a whole, Mondale actually lost to Reagan, by 46 percent to 53 percent, according to the same poll.

G.H.

LAOS. In 1984 the Lao People's Democratic Republic (LPDR) remained under the tutelage of its more powerful neighbor, Vietnam, and continued its economic reliance and close political association with the Soviet Union, which still supplied approximately 60 percent of Laos's foreign aid. The interaction between Laos and Vietnam was symbolized by an agreement reached early in the year calling for Vietnamese assistance in political affairs, agriculture, and trade.

Laos's links with Vietnam and the Soviet Union, and its mistrust of China, largely defined the LPDR's foreign policy posture. Laos gave strong public support to the Vietnamese position on the critical Cambodian issue, rejecting an Asean (Association of Southeast Asian Nations) proposal for the withdrawal of Vietnamese troops and the holding of free elections. The LPDR maintained that Vietnamese troops could be withdrawn from Cambodia only when China ended its threat to the three Indochinese countries.

The gradual improvement of relations between Laos and Thailand was marred by border incidents. In particular, a dispute erupted in June involving three small border villages over which each country claimed sovereignty. Talks regarding the disputed territory proved unfruitful, and border clashes resumed during the late summer.

Relations between Laos and the United States continued their modest improvement. The cooperation provided by the LPDR in 1983 in the search for American servicemen missing in action (MIA) was maintained during 1984, with the LPDR granting permission to the U.S Joint Casualty Resolution Center to excavate a site in southern Laos in the search for the remains of 13 American servicemen whose plane crashed there in 1972.

According to estimates, the flow of refugees from Laos into Thailand was increasing, in part because of Thai policies expediting refugee resettlement in third countries. Conversely, there was a continuing population flow back into Laos, aided by a voluntary repatriation program initiated by the UN High Commissioner for Refugees.

See STATISTICS OF THE WORLD.   J.J.Z.

LEBANON. Violence and instability continued to haunt Lebanon in 1984 during its tenth year of political chaos. Despite creation of a national unity government, the nation's prospects for emerging intact as a unified, independent sovereign state seemed cloudy. The western multinational force withdrew, and Syria's influence grew accordingly. Israeli forces remained in southern Lebanon.

Sectarian Fighting. Fighting that broke out in Beirut in January pitted Druze Muslim militias against the Lebanese Army and Christian Phalangists. In early February, after the army shelled Shiite Muslim slums, the cabinet of Sunni Muslim Prime Minister Shafiq al-Wazzan resigned and Lebanese President Amin Gemayel denounced Druze and Shiite leaders as Syrian surrogates.

Thereafter, the fighting spread and became more destructive. By February 7, the Druze and Shiites had seized full control of west Beirut, which is largely Muslim. Nearly half of the army refused to fight or deserted to the Muslim militia forces. At this point, the United States announced in effect that it would withdraw its contingent in the multinational peacekeeping force; Great Britain, Italy, and finally France soon made the same decision. All of the Western forces were out of Lebanon by March 31.

Gemayel announced February 16 that he had accepted a Saudi Arabian peace plan that called for renunciation of the 1983 peace accord with Israel. The accord had called for simultaneous withdrawal of Syrian and Israeli forces from Lebanon, but Syria had not accepted it. The Saudi plan, which also called for withdrawal of foreign forces, was not accepted either by Israel or by Syria. On March 5, Lebanon formally abrogated the 1983 peace accord.

The New Government. Leaders of various Lebanese factions met in Lausanne, Switzerland, in March, to discuss "national reconciliation." Gemayel's proposals for political reform were rejected by the Muslims on the ground that they did not ensure that the Christians in general, and the Maronites in particular, would let power be shared equally with the other religious communities. The ultimate failure of the Lausanne talks could also be attributed to feuds within each faction.

In Damascus in April, Gemayel and Syrian officials formulated a plan for disengaging the warring factions. On April 26, Gemayel named Rashid Karami, a leading opposition politician, as prime minister, and, after a month of negotiation, a government of national unity under Karami was chosen. On June 23 the new government approved a security plan that in cluded a cease-fire and abolition of the so-called Green Line, a string of barricades and fortifications that separated the Muslim and Christian sections of Beirut. The army itself was reorganized with authority distributed more equitably among Christians and Muslims.

By the end of July the Green Line was down and the army had taken up positions through Beirut. In response to widespread popular demonstrations protesting the disappearance of 3,000 abducted persons in recent years, the government on September 18 called on all factions to release their hostages. Meanwhile, opposition by Druze leader Walid Jumblatt, who viewed the army as still under the domination of militant Phalangists, prevented it from extending state control to the mountains outside Beirut.

On November 26, new Lebanese Army troops were deployed in Beirut in an effort to stem continuing factional fighting there and form the basis for new efforts to extend government control to the north and south. Subsequently, on December 20, the army took control of the northern port city of Tripoli. The move followed an accord reached by rival factions there, with Syrian cooperation.

Two principal Lebanese figures died in August. The highest-ranking Druze army officer was killed in a helicopter crash. Also, Pierre Gemayel, the president's father and a founder of the Phalangist party, died just as it appeared that he was exerting a moderating influence in the Christian community.

Foreign Relations. Israel's army remained in southern Lebanon, while Syria continued to exercise control in northern and eastern Lebanon. Syria's growing influence was reflected anew in October in the election of a pro-Syrian Shiite leader as speaker of Parliament. Israel's declining influence was represented by the closing in July of its "liaison office" (actually, quasi-embassy) in east Beirut. Meanwhile, armed resistance to the Israeli occupation was growing in southern Lebanon. Lebanese and Israeli military officers opened talks in November under UN auspices, to work out conditions for an Israeli withdrawal. The question of who would maintain security in southern Lebanon was the major stumbling block to an agreement. The talks recessed on December 20.

Cleanup activities start at the bomb-scarred American Embassy annex outside Christian East Beirut, after the building was struck in a new act of terrorism on September 20.

Debate on the American role in Lebanon continued early in the year in the United States, and was aggravated by further acts of violence including the assassination of Malcolm Kerr, president of the American University in Beirut, on January 18. Later in the year, on September 20, a truck bomb exploded at the U.S. embassy annex in a suburb of east Beirut; at least 14 persons, including two U.S. servicemen, were killed. A militant Muslim group called the Islamic Holy War claimed responsibility. In October, the United States began to reduce the size of its embassy staff, as threats against the embassy continued.

223

The Economy. Amid the strife, Lebanon's gross national product declined. The value of the Lebanese pound had been halved since 1982, and industrial production and exports also fell sharply. The agricultural and industrial sectors were virtually stagnant; the government also faced a deficit of around $1.5 billion. Industrial plants had been heavily damaged during the fighting, and the Beirut International Airport remained closed between February and July.

See STATISTICS OF THE WORLD.   M.C.H.

LESOTHO. See STATISTICS OF THE WORLD.

LIBERIA. See STATISTICS OF THE WORLD.

LIBRARIES. In 1984 the Library of Congress was making plans to rehabilitate its deteriorating books, the New York Public Library completed the first phase of an ambitious renovation program, and libraries were opening up in other parts of the United States. The nonprofit Library of America was expanding its program

Its walls adorned with murals depicting New York's major publishing houses, the DeWitt Wallace Periodical Room of the New York Public Library gleams richly in the aftermath of its $2 million restoration, part of a continuing $45 million project to repair and renovate the 73-year-old, Renaissance-style building.

to make American classics more available to the public.

Library of Congress. A project aimed at giving new life to old books, utilizing a process patented by Library of Congress chemists, could add 400 to 600 years to the life of books made from wood-pulp paper. According to the librarian of Congress, Daniel Boorstin, one of the greatest problems facing libraries today is "the rapid deterioration of their collections because of the unstable quality of paper produced since around 1850." A survey of the Library of Congress collection, about 80 million items, indicated that 75 percent would benefit from the new process, which neutralizes acid-induced loss of strength in paper used in books. The rest of the collection must be transferred to another format, such as microfilm, which is a much more costly process.

An $11.5 million facility was to be built for the Library of Congress at Fort Detrick, a military installation in Frederick, Md., in which about 500,000 items a year could be put through the acid-neutralization process. Scholars, librarians, and archivists were concerned that, unless efficient action is taken, much of the library's collection could soon deteriorate to a point where it could not be saved. The life for unneutralized acid-paper books ranges from about 50 to 100 years.

New Libraries and Renovations. The new $39 million, eight-story main library building of the Broward County, Fla., Library System in Fort Lauderdale was dedicated April 29; the building will also serve three higher education institutions in the area. A large central atrium links the interior areas of the building. The new $22 million Walter Royal Davis Library at the University of North Carolina at Chapel Hill provides shelving for 1.8 million volumes and seating for 3,013.

Plans to locate the Ronald Reagan presidential library on the campus of Stanford University, in Palo Alto, Calif., were approved by White House representatives and officials of the university. A museum also was to be built on the site.

The first phase of the restoration of the New York Public Library's handsome main building (constructed in 1911) was completed in 1984. At a cost of $19 million, the Beaux-Arts façade was cleaned, the grand entrance hall, with its vaulted ceiling and great staircases, was restored, and an exhibition hall was restored and reopened, among other improvements. Work on the building and an upgrading of its research facilities was to continue for 14 years.

Library of America. The Library of America, a nonprofit project created to "publish the central writings of America's literature, and to keep the published volumes permanently in print and available to the public" added the works of Stephen Crane, Thomas Jefferson, and Edgar Allan Poe. The LOA volumes are printed on extremely thin, acid-free paper, which saves shelf space in libraries, reduces production costs, and extends the life of the paper. The Helena Rubenstein Foundation made a $25,000 grant to fund the purchase of LOA volumes by New York public libraries. Additional aid was being sought from corporations and foundations to obtain volumes for public libraries in other areas that were unable to afford the series.

Besides keeping classics in print, the project maintains full, well-edited texts in computer database. Commercial publishers who wish to issue their own editions can rent the LOA tapes and present the text in any format they choose, while avoiding the expense of editing the texts anew.

Fund-raising. The entertainer Johnny Carson spearheaded a fund-raising effort to buy books for the Hollywood, Calif., Regional Library, which had been destroyed by fire. More than $1 million was obtained, including a National Endowment for the Humanities challenge grant of $500,000. The library building was being replaced by a new structure made possible by a $3 million gift from the Samuel Goldwyn Foundation.

The St. Paul, Minn., Public Library, aided by the St. Paul Foundation, earned $2 million from a successful fund-raising drive. The funds were earmarked to purchase a theft detection system and an automated circulation system, and for other projects designed to cut operating costs.

Library Events. "Knowledge Is Power" was the theme of National Library Week, held April 8–14. Banned Books Week, September 8–15, was observed in support of the hundreds of books, such as *The Catcher in the Rye, Slaugh-*terhouse Five, and *Of Mice and Men,* that have been challenged across the United States; the observance was cosponsored by the American Booksellers Association, the American Library Association, the National Association of College Stores, the Association of American Publishers, and the American Society of Journalists and Authors.

The International Federation of Library Associations and Institutions' 50th general conference was held in Nairobi, Kenya, August 19–25. The 39th annual conference of the Canadian Library Association was held in Toronto, from June 7 to June 12. The 103rd annual conference of the American Library Association was held in Dallas, June 23–28; its theme was "Paths to Power."   R.J.S.

LIBYA. In 1984, Libya agreed to pull out of Chad but then apparently failed to do so. Relations with Egypt, Sudan, and Great Britain deteriorated, but Libya signed a treaty of friendship with Morocco.

Involvement in Chad. On September 17, Libya and France announced an agreement to withdraw their respective forces from Chad. An estimated 5,000 Libyan troops were in northern Chad, supporting the rebel forces of former Chadian President Goukouni Oueddei; to the south, on the other side of a 200-mile-wide buffer zone, were some 3,000 French troops deployed in support of the government forces of President Hissène Habré. In early November the French and Libyan governments announced completion of the withdrawal. According to U.S. intelligence reports, however, large numbers of Libyan troops remained, as the French government ultimately acknowledged.

Earlier, on January 25, a French Jaguar jet was shot down as it flew in the buffer zone. France blamed Libya for the attack, and on January 27, French troops were ordered to advance 60–70 miles northward into the buffer zone. The threat of a serious confrontation was defused after French-Libyan talks.

Relations With Sudan and Egypt. Accusing Libya of backing a separatist rebellion in southern Sudan, Sudanese President Jaafar al-Nimeiry charged Tripoli with having staged an air raid on Omdurman on March 14 in which five people were killed.

Egypt accused Libya of laying mines in the

Red Sea that damaged at least 19 vessels during the summer. Egyptian suspicions focused specifically on a Libyan vessel, the *Ghat,* that had entered the Suez Canal on July 6, bound for the Ethiopian port of Aseb on the Red Sea, and returned through the canal 15 days later. Normally such a trip would have taken less time.

Violence in Britain. On April 17, in London, 11 of about 70 Libyans conducting a protest against the Qaddafi regime were wounded and a British policewoman was killed by machine-gun fire from inside the Libyan embassy. The Libyan government ascribed the incident to provocation by the demonstrators and British police and, invoking diplomatic immunity, refused to allow British investigators to enter the embassy or question possible suspects. The British government on April 22 severed diplomatic relations with Libya and ordered all those who were inside the embassy to leave Britain.

Mending Fences. Qaddafi and King Hassan of Morocco announced in mid-August that they had agreed to unite their two countries, even though they are 1,500 miles apart and have profound political differences. The plan was seen by some as a response to a recently concluded treaty of friendship, from which Libya was excluded, linking Tunisia, Algeria, and Mauritania.

Qaddafi also sought to improve relations with several European countries, as he met with the leaders of France, Greece, and Spain late in the year.

Domestic Affairs. On May 8, approximately 15 gunmen attacked the barracks in Tripoli where Qaddafi normally resides. All of the rebels reportedly were killed in a five-hour gun battle. The National Front for the Salvation of Libya took responsibility for the attack. Qaddafi blamed the Muslim Brotherhood, which he claimed had been helped by anti-Libyan governments.

On August 28, Qaddafi inaugurated a scheme to bring almost 300 million cubic feet of water daily to the populated coastal region around Tripoli and Benghazi. The project will involve the laying of over 1,200 miles of steel and concrete pipes, at a cost of at least $11 billion.

See STATISTICS OF THE WORLD. A.D.

LIECHTENSTEIN. See STATISTICS OF THE WORLD.

LIFE SCIENCES. Evidence of periodic mass extinctions down through the ages attracted interest in 1984. Scientists learned more about how plants defend themselves from attack and about how males contribute to the food reserves of insect eggs.

BIOLOGY

Indications of a cyclical pattern in mass species extinctions helped to suggest that evolution was not as gradual and steady as had once been thought. The biotechnology boom brought new breakthroughs and also raised legal issues. Detailed knowledge of the cellular life cycle of a tiny roundworm promised to give biologists a wider insight into cellular processes.

Spaced-out Extinctions. Classical evolutionary theory pictures a process of slow and steady adaptation and change, in which the rate of appearance of new species approximately balances the rate of extinction of old ones. Evidence has been rapidly accumulating, however, that the evolutionary process may have been frequently interrupted by large-scale environmental disturbances, causing the extinction of groups of organisms and the development of new ones.

It has long been recognized that abrupt major changes are reflected in the fossil record, the best-known being at the boundary between the Cretaceous and Tertiary periods, 65 million years ago, when approximately three out of four animal species became extinct. That event marked the end of the dinosaurs and the beginning of recognizably modern communities of land and sea animals. In 1980, Luis Alvarez and several colleagues at the Lawrence Berkeley Laboratory of the University of California at Berkeley had reported evidence for an extraterrestrial cause—possibly the impact of an asteroid or other heavenly body hitting the earth—of the Cretaceous-Tertiary extinction event. This theory provoked much active research, and during a scientific meeting held in early 1984 at the Lawrence Berkeley Laboratory (and at an earlier meeting at Northern Arizona University), new ideas were presented that attracted wide attention.

This recent flurry of excitement stemmed from a study by David Raup and John Sepkosk of the University of Chicago, eventually published in February. The study analyzed the extinction record of 567 families of fossil marine organisms and found evidence that particularly large numbers of extinctions took place on 12 separate occasions. There were strong indications that these mass extinctions tended to occur in cycles, at intervals of roughly 26 million years. Meanwhile, Walter Alvarez and Richard Muller of the University of California at Berkeley have detected a similar cycle in the ages of large (greater than 10 kilometers, or 6⅕ miles, in diameter) meteor craters on the earth's surface.

These observations could have profound implications for evolutionary biologists, since many scientists have rejected the slow evolutionary changes of the Darwinian model as inadequate to explain life's diversity. The new evidence shows that, even assuming a background of steady evolution, major bursts of rapid evolution are to be expected after each catastrophe, as new opportunities open up for the few survivors.

Speculation abounds as to what might account for the regular interval of about 26 million years. Raup and Sepkoski were cautious, suggesting simply that the cause was extraterrestrial, perhaps involving meteor impacts on earth. Other theories have been advanced by astronomers. On one point all scientists are agreed, however. We are in the middle of the cycle at present and should be safe from another extinction crisis for about 13 million years—if we do not produce our own in the next few decades.

See also ASTRONOMY.

Ancient Human DNA. Archaeologists in December found two human skulls approximately 7,000 years old, with their brains largely intact, buried in peat at the bottom of a lake near Titusville, Fla. They were the oldest intact human brains ever found. A chemical analysis reportedly showed that the brain tissue still retained much of its DNA, or deoxyribonucleic acid, the spiral-like material that determines heredity. The skulls were believed to be those of a young man about 25 and a woman about 45. By studying the brains' DNA content, scientists hoped to further their understanding of human genetic evolution.

Biotechnology Boom. Because much of the emphasis in the biotechnology industry has

The sudden disappearance of the dinosaurs, 65 million years ago, is the subject of several new theories; one suggests that a companion star to the sun may have caused meteors to plunge to earth over a long period, producing mass extinctions.

switched from basic research to marketing, analysts called 1984 the year of the product. The once startling techniques of genetic engineering—isolating a particular gene from one living thing and inserting it into a microorganism, whereby the organism would be given the specific traits governed by the gene—have become routine. The challenge now lies in identifying a product that can be genetically engineered and for which there is a market, adjusting laboratory techniques for large-scale production, and then shepherding it through premarket testing. Over $2 billion has been invested by private companies in research and development, and some predict that annual sales of biotechnology-related products will reach the billion-dollar level in the next few years.

New Products. A number of genetically engineered products were tested in humans. These included several forms of interferon, a naturally

227

occurring antiviral substance thought to have potential as an anticancer agent; human growth hormone, for use in treating certain growth disorders; interleukin-2, an infection-fighting compound normally produced by human white blood cells that may be useful in treating diseases believed to be caused by malfunctioning of the immune system; and tissue-type plasminogen activator, an enzyme that may dissolve blood clots in a heart attack victim.

Major breakthroughs were made recently in the development of products used to detect disease and to test for the presence of viruses and other materials; one approach involves the use of DNA probes. The DNA found in living cells carries all of the cell's genetic information. A DNA molecule normally consists of the well-known double helix—two chemical strands held together by a phenomenon known as complementary base pairing. If the double helix is separated into two strands, each will

Steven Lindow, a professor of plant pathology at the University of California at Berkeley, examines a vessel containing bacteria genetically modified to reduce the formation of ice crystals. A federal judge's injunction thwarted Lindow's plan to release a crop of the modified organisms in a potato field, thereby testing their ability to reduce frost damage to crops.

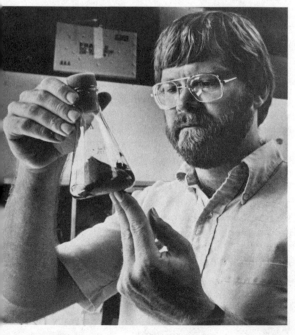

seek to unite with other strands that have complementary base units.

In developing DNA probes as a diagnostic tool, biochemists have synthesized specific DNA molecules by taking advantage of the propensity of DNA strands to unite. The probe is a single strand of DNA complementary to the DNA of a specific virus. This probe can be placed in a test tube along with a sample of blood from an individual suspected of being infected with the virus. If the virus is present in the blood, its DNA (separated into single strands by heat or chemical treatment) will combine with the probe to form a characteristic double helix whose presence can be monitored. This provides a very specific and sensitive test for the presence of the virus. A number of DNA probes—including probes for hepatitis B virus, for a virus that has been linked to acquired immune deficiency syndrome, and for herpes simplex types I and II—were already being sold to research scientists.

Genetic Engineering and the Law. On May 16, federal Judge John J. Sirica issued an injunction halting an experiment that would have involved the first release of a genetically engineered organism into the environment. Sirica ruled that the U.S National Institutes of Health (NIH) had approved the experiment without sufficiently evaluating its potential environmental impact. The case involved a modified strain of *Pseudomonas syringae*, a bacterium that normally promotes the formation of ice crystals. Steven Lindow of the University of California at Berkeley had found that if certain genes are deleted from the bacterium, it loses this frost-producing ability. In the proposed experiment, Lindow planned to release the modified bacteria in a field of potato plants in northern California. He hoped to demonstrate that the altered bacteria would displace the naturally occurring bacteria and would thereby reduce frost damage to the plants.

Both NIH and the University of California filed appeals of Sirica's ruling. In the meantime, however, the ruling applied only to researchers who receive federal funding. In June one private company received permission from NIH to conduct an experiment virtually identical to that proposed by Lindow.

On October 1 the Humane Society of the

United States and genetic engineering critic Jeremy Rifkin filed suit against the U.S. Agriculture Department in an effort to halt certain experiments conducted by the department. The experiments, involving the transfer of human growth genes into the genetic material of pigs and sheep to make them grow larger, were alleged to violate "the moral and ethical canons of civilization."

Cellular Secrets of a Tiny Worm. A tiny nematode worm called *Caenorhabditis elegans* now has the distinction of being the first multicellular organism for which the entire developmental sequence of cell division, growth, and differentiation is known. Studies on the development of *C. elegans* began two decades ago in Great Britain under the direction of Sydney Brenner of the Medical Research Council's Laboratory of Molecular Biology in Cambridge. The tiny (1-millimeter, or about four-hundredths of an inch) worm has unique advantages for scientists studying cell division and embryology. It reproduces rapidly and is transparent, allowing cell division to be watched in the undisturbed living embryo. Above all, only 671 cells are generated during embryonic growth. A human, by contrast, has about a million million cells. Study of the development process of nematodes, despite certain peculiarities of the group, sheds light on processes in all multicellular animals.

The full developmental sequence of *C. elegans* from fertilized egg to newly hatched larva was described by a research team led by J.E. Sulston, of the Cambridge MRC Laboratory; these and earlier findings were reviewed in depth in the June 22 and July 6 issues of *Science* magazine. A number of surprises have been revealed. As the embryo forms and develops, about one-sixth of the cells produced die and are engulfed by other cells. This may prove to be an evolutionary mechanism, since the loss of one cell at an early stage results in the loss of all its "offspring" and in major changes in the adult. The fate of each cell in the worm is defined exactly by its position in the developmental sequence. Sulston and his colleagues showed that experimental killing of single cells by laser pulses resulted in completely predictable losses of regions of the larval body.

Another surprise was the discovery of a simple form of segmentation (repetition of parts along the body, as in earthworms or insects) as a transient developmental feature in what is normally considered a completely nonsegmented group of worms. Also, the animal "breaks the rules" by making nerve tissue from what should become muscle tissue, and vice versa.

The new findings on nematode development were expected to reveal, with further analysis, a great deal about the processes of cell division and development. Even more important discoveries will come when scientists' rapidly growing knowledge of the genetics of the animal is applied to the newly described developmental sequence, giving at last some understanding of how genetic differences are expressed during the process of development of organisms.

The Mad March Hare? Lewis Carroll made the world familiar with the strange "madness" of the brown hare. During the month of March, males competing for mates are supposed to indulge in crazy chasing episodes and boxing contests. Alas, like so many attractive legends, this one now appears to have no foundation in fact. In a report published in June, two British researchers, Anthony Holley of Sommerset and Paul Greenwood of the University of Durham, told of their six years of observation of a hare population with an astronomical telescope. Chasing and boxing were observed throughout the long breeding season from January to August, but only 14 percent of these incidents occurred in March. All of the boxing episodes in which the sex of the participants was known actually took place between a female and a male. In fact, the "boxer" was nearly always the female, and the "boxed" was the smaller, lighter male. Holley and Greenwood suggested that the female boxes to discourage overly amorous suitors—hardly mad behavior at all!

A Fast Sting Operation. Cnidarians, a group of primitive animals including sea anemones, jellyfish, and hydroids, contain stinging structures called nematocysts. When triggered, these shoot out a long pointed filament, through which poison is injected into prey or predator. Nematocyst discharge is very fast when watched under a microscope, and a study by T. Holstein and P. Tardent of the University of Zürich-Irchel in Switzerland showed it to be the fastest form of cell movement known. Using high-speed cinematography (40,000 frames per second), and triggering nematocyst discharge electrically, the biologists found that in the early stages the nematocyst tip moves 0.02 millimeter in ten-millionths of a second, an average speed of 2 meters a second. To achieve this speed from a standing start, the tip must experience an acceleration of 40,000G (that is, 40,000 times more than that produced on an object by the earth's gravity). This is greater than the acceleration undergone by a bullet in a rifle.

BOTANY

In 1984, botanists reported interesting findings on how plants defend themselves from animals and disease and described fossil flowers more than 90 million years old.

Plant Defense Mechanisms. Plants have a poorly understood immunological system to protect them against attacks by plant-eating animals and disease-causing organisms. Several recent studies are beginning to reveal how subtle and complex the plants' systems can be. The most general plant defense seems to be the incorporation of toxic or distasteful chemicals, such as phenols or tannins, within the leaves. Manufacturing these chemicals costs energy and resources that could otherwise be used for growth or reproduction; however, the chemicals have an obvious value to the plant.

Studies by Peter Steinberg of the University of California at Santa Cruz suggest that in the marine intertidal kelp *Alaria marginata* the cost of making the chemicals is significant. Steinberg found that the kelp had different levels of tannins in its two types of fronds. Reproductive (sporophyll) fronds had about five times the tannin levels of vegetative fronds. Data showed that the sporophylls suffered significantly less damage from plant-eating sea snails than did the vegetative fronds. Reproduction is of paramount importance to all living things, and so the sporophylls were granted the maximum protective investment. The cost of the defense must be fairly high, because little could be spared to defend the less vital vegetative parts.

If defense is expensive, it is logical to delay

A prehistoric flower that bloomed more than 90 million years ago was one of the striking fossils found in the Dakota formation and described recently by Indiana University scientists. The blossom's showy petals and pollen type indicate that it was insect pollinated.

investment until the plant is actually under attack, but this may be too late unless the response is very fast. Richard Karban and James R. Carey of the University of California at Davis found evidence that early exposure to disease-causing agents can immunize plants against later attacks. The scientists briefly exposed cotton seedlings to mites at an early stage when the seed leaves were just unfolding. The mites were removed, and the plants continued growing for 12 days. When young plants were re-exposed to mite infestation, those that had previously been exposed suffered significantly less damage than did other (control) plants never exposed to attack. By this stage the original seed leaves had dropped off, so the effects of early immunization had been distributed around the plant and "remembered" in a way reminiscent of defense mechanisms in mammals.

Blossoms in the Rocks. Modern flowering plants, or angiosperms, evolved during the Cretaceous period, but their earliest forms are poorly known because of the scarcity of their distinctive flowers in fossil deposits. James Basinger and David Dilcher of Indiana University at Bloomington described a remarkable series of fossils from the Dakota formation, dated at about 94 million years ago. The fossil flowers have attractive fivefold symmetry and look quite modern, with well-developed sepals, petals, and anthers still containing pollen. The showy petals and pollen type show that, even at this early stage of angiosperm evolution, the plants were already insect pollinated. Although not classifiable within any single modern plant group, the flowers resembled today's roses, saxifrages, and buckthorns.

ZOOLOGY

Zoologists reported several studies of the male role in nutritionally enriching insect eggs and described an insect with a unique capacity to tolerate cold.

Male Investment in Insect Egg Production. It is commonly assumed in zoology that males contribute less than females to their offspring. At the most fundamental level, eggs are always far larger and contain much greater food reserves than individual sperm cells. Egg production represents a substantial investment of food and energy by females, although males may help in other ways, such as in territorial defense. It may come as some surprise, then, to discover cases where males contribute to the food reserves of their partners' eggs. In most insects, during mating males transfer sperm "gift wrapped" in packages called spermatophores, from which the sperm is later emptied into the female genital tract. In crickets and katydids, the spermatophore usually consists of two parts, the sperm-filled ampulla and a large gelatinous mass called the spermatophylax, which is eaten by the female after mating.

B. J. Bowen, C. G. Codd, and D. T. Gwynne of the University of Western Australia studied the katydid Requena verticalis, in which the males produce a very large spermatophylax rich in protein. The scientists raised the male katydids on diets containing radioactively labeled protein, so that a radioactive tracer was present in the spermatophylax material. After females ate the labeled material, the radioac-

tivity concentrated mainly in their developing eggs. This showed that the male contributes substantially to the nourishment of the eggs that his sperm, stored in the female, will eventually fertilize.

Not all male contributions are as generous. Scott K. Sakaluk of Erindale College, University of Toronto, studied the decorated cricket *Gryllodes supplicans*, which, like the Australian katydid, makes a substantial spermatophylax that is eaten by the female after mating. The

Unconcerned about her baby's stripes, Kelly, a Kentucky quarterhorse, nuzzles her new foal, a full-blooded zebra, at the Louisville Zoo. Kelly was the surrogate mother in the first successful transplant of a zebra embryo into a horse's womb; the experiment gave hope to zoologists for increasing the populations of vanishing equine breeds.

meal—begun as soon as mating is completed—usually takes the female an average of 40 minutes. Twelve minutes later, about 52 minutes after mating, she removes and eats the sperm ampulla. If the female loses the spermatophylax prematurely, before she has finished eating it, she eats the sperm ampulla before the sperm has been fully transferred, thus frustrating the objectives of the male. Sakaluk found that complete sperm discharge from the ampulla took about 50 minutes. After this, its removal by the female would not jeopardize the success of the mating. The system is remarkably well balanced. The female gains a useful food supply, but the male provides only enough food to delay the female the necessary 50 minutes to guarantee complete transfer of the sperm.

Therese Markow and Paul Ankney of Arizona State University at Tempe have discovered that male fruit flies contribute in a similar way to egg resources. *Drosophila mojavensis* females mate daily before laying eggs, even if they already contain viable sperm. Again, radioactive labeling was used to trace the movement within the female of the male-derived material. As expected, after mating, all the tracer was concentrated at first within the female reproductive tract, but after 24 hours a significant amount was within the developing eggs. In this species, material gained from males by repeated matings contributes substantially to egg production. Markow and Ankney found no such male investment in the closely related *Drosophila melanogaster*. The scientists reasoned that *D. melanogaster* is a cosmopolitan and opportunistic species that feeds on a wide range of materials and that seldom experiences a shortage of food. *D. mojavensis,* on the other hand, feeds only on rotting organ-pipe cactus, which is a limited resource. In this species, therefore, the male contribution to egg formation would apparently be of much greater value.

Nautilus Research. The class Cephalopoda includes the octopus, squid, and cuttlefish. These invertebrate animals are largely shell-less swimmers, very successful in modern seas, but their ancestors had elegant external coiled shells, which they used as containers for gas that provided buoyancy. The sole survivor of this ancient stock is the lovely pearly nautilus of tropical seas. Nautiluses live in deep water and are only rarely seen alive by biologists, but they are of great interest for the light they may shed on the ecology of their once-common fossil relatives.

Recently it has become possible to trap and mark nautiluses and return them undamaged to their deep-sea habitats. Two fascinating studies have appeared, both based on the *Nautilus* populations on the steep submarine cliffs of the Pacific island of Palau. Peter Ward, of the University of California at Davis, led a group that equipped individuals of the free-swimming *N. belauensis* with electronic transducers, which transmitted accurate depth measurements to scientists on the surface. The mollusks revealed surprisingly large-scale migrations, achieving a daily vertical average of 650 feet, sometimes swimming as deep as 1,600 ft. in daytime and rising to as high as 300 ft. at night. They sustained daily pressure changes as great as 500 pounds per square inch. In the second study, W. Bruce Saunders of Bryn Mawr College was able to recapture some of the 2,000 animals (of the same species) that he had previously marked and released. He found that, unlike most other modern cephalopods, these grow very slowly and may live for more than 20 years.

Coldest Insect. Shiro Kohshima of Japan's Kyoto University described the only insects known to spend their entire life in snow. The insect, a midge called *Diamesa,* lives above 15,000 ft. altitude on a glacier in Nepal. Larvae feed on bacteria and algae in subsurface melt channels. The flightless adults do not feed; they can remain active at temperatures as low as 3° Fahrenheit but become paralyzed at the temperature of the human palm. These cold tolerant insects inhabit what may be the simplest ecosystem yet described.

S.M.H. & T.H.M.

LITERATURE. Among the major literary developments of 1984 were:

AMERICAN

In a somewhat lackluster year for literature the watchword seems to have been "epic." The American public favored long, massive books. Prominent fiction came from old masters and lesser known lights as well.

Fiction. Novels conceived on this grand scale included Gore Vidal's *Lincoln: A Novel,* Joyce Carol Oates's *Mysteries of Winterthurn,* and George Garrett's *The Succession.* Vidal's novel, as usual, divided the critics. Some reviewers attacked this panoramic Civil War novel as overly speculative, padded, and wooden. Others felt that it was a splendid portrayal of a man too long viewed as a secular saint. Oates's *Mysteries of Winterthurn* continued her cycle of novels that parody, or pay homage to, classic Victorian fiction. *Winterthurn* is a kind of Victorian detective novel à la Wilkie Collins, laced with impossible crimes and starring a Holmesian investigator. Throughout, Oates reproduces to perfection the winding sentences of her penny-dreadful predecessors—perhaps too much so for many readers. So, too, George Garrett's *The Succession,* set in the Elizabethan world of his much admired *Death of the Fox,* struck many readers as cloyingly rich in its plum-pudding virtuosity.

For pure linguistic virtuosity, no one writing today matches John Updike. His novel *The Witches of Eastwick* focuses on three attractive women, with particularly rich sexual lives, who happen to practice sorcery. The trio becomes involved with a mysterious stranger, who plays the women off against each other and gradually destroys their sisterhood. What starts off as a comic novel about a small New England town darkens into a somber meditation on the need for sexual and personal responsibility.

Three other old masters of the novel also made appearances. Saul Bellow's *Him With His Foot in His Mouth and Other Stories* reveals a more mellow and relaxed writer than much of his recent work (such as *The Dean's December*). William Burroughs, by contrast, continues unregenerately down the garden path with his wild boys, gun and drug worship, and strangely fascinating storytelling in *The Place of Dead Roads.* Norman Mailer's *Tough Guys Don't Dance* adopted the format of the detective story but none of its charm.

Two epic family sagas, both set in the Midwest, fared well. Helen Hooven Santmyer's *. . . And Ladies of the Club''* was first published by Ohio State University Press to little notice. But serendipitously, this novel—the

Eudora Welty leaves her Jackson, Miss., house to attend a three day "Southern literary festival" celebrating both her 75th birthday and the surprise bestsellerdom of her slim autobiographical sketch, One Writer's Beginnings.

life's work of a woman in her late 80's from Xenia, Ohio—came to the attention of a New York publisher. In a flurry there followed book-club rights, a major advertising budget, and a place at the top of the best-seller lists. The novel recounts in minuscule detail the life of a small town, as reflected in the trials, tribulations, and occasional triumphs of the members of a ladies' literary circle. The other saga—Jayne Anne Phillips's *Machine Dreams*—follows the fortunes of a working-class West Virginia family after World War II. The book established Phillips, who is in her early 30's, as a figure to be watched. In like fashion, Robb Forman Dew confirmed the promise of the witty *Dale Loves Sophie to Death* in the much more somber but equally accomplished *The Time of Her Life,* which shows how two childish parents destroy their sensitive daughter.

Other notable novels included Joseph Heller's *God Knows,* a comic retelling of the biblical story of King David that drew both praise and groans from reviewers. *Foreign*

Affairs by Alison Lurie explores the social and sexual entanglements of a group of Americans abroad, and Paula Fox gives a graceful, sensitive account of a girl's lonely odyssey from a small Caribbean island to the maids' quarters of New York City in *A Servant's Tale.*

Big dominated other categories of fiction as well. T. E. D. Klein's *The Ceremonies* announced a major talent in the field of supernatural fiction; his novel—a blend of H. P. Lovecraft and Arthur Machen—features ancient evil biding its time, a New Jersey cult, and two innocents from New York. Lauded for its style and characterization, the book was, however, generally felt to be overlong. More popular was *The Talisman,* a fantasy by Stephen King and Peter Straub, about a boy's quest to find the talisman that will save his mother's life and heal an alternate world. Frank Herbert continued his science-fiction cycle about the planet Arrakis, more familiarly known as Dune. *Heretics of Dune,* despite its overt philosophizing, was probably Herbert's best book since the original *Dune.*

Literary Nonfiction. The epic sensibility also appeared in literary nonfiction. Alfred Kazin's *An American Procession* attempts to sum up 100 years of literature in the United States, from Emerson to Fitzgerald and Hemingway. Critical opinion varied: Some reviewers saw the book as the crowning achievement in Kazin's distinguished career; others sadly asserted that the book was prolix, sloppy, unscholarly, and without original thought.

Laurence Bergreen's biography, *James Agee: A Life,* drew raves from its readers but sharp criticism from the legendary writer's friends and family. Bergreen's use of Agee's fiction to illuminate his life was especially criticized. Many felt, though, that the Agee clan simply did not want their idol to be shown with feet of clay. Other important biographies, all of them long, were Scott Donaldson's *E. B. White,* Jackson J. Benson's *The True Adventures of John Steinbeck, Writer,* and Virginia Spencer Carr's *Dos Passos.* Slender and elegant, like the author herself, was *One Writer's Beginnings,* by Eudora Welty, a surprise best-seller for Harvard University Press. Of similar elegance and wit was *The Collected Prose of Elizabeth Bishop.*

Literary essayists flourished. Gilbert Sorrentino, the highly regarded author of *Mulligan Stew* and other engagingly bawdy and linguistically inventive novels, collected his criticism in *Something Said.* Another popular experimentalist, John Barth, also collected his pieces in *The Friday Book.* William Gass came out with *Habitats of the Word: Essays,* another volume to set beside *Fiction and the Figures of Life* and *The World Within the Word.*

The year also saw the appearance of important collections of literary letters penned by poet-critics Delmore Schwartz, John Crowe Ransom, and Randall Jarrell, as well as of the fourth volume of The *Letters of Henry James,* edited by Leon Edel.

History and Current Events. The presidential election year witnessed an outpouring of books on politics and current events. New York City's Edward Koch produced *Mayor,* and that state's chief executive offered *Diaries of Mario M. Cuomo: The Campaign for Governor.* Among those who looked back on their roles in public life were former Secretary of State Alexander M. Haig, Jr., with *Caveat: Realism, Reagan, and Foreign Policy;* former White House Press Secretary Jody Powell in *The Other Side of the Story;* and Rosalynn Carter with *First Lady from Plains.* Former President Richard Nixon called for a return to "hard-headed détente" in his book *Real Peace. Time* magazine diplomatic correspondent Strobe Talbott's *Deadly Gambits: The Reagan Administration and the Stalemate in Nuclear Arms Control* critically assessed the superpowers' disarmament deadlock and the continued existence of want amid plenty was the subject of Michael Harrington's *The New American Poverty.*

The year also saw the publication of an admiring biography of former Vice-President Hubert Humphrey, by Carl Solberg, and of the second volume in Stephen E. Ambrose's even handed biography of former President Dwight Eisenhower. *Churchill and Roosevelt: The Complete Correspondence,* edited by Warren F. Kimball, offered a revealing look at the special relationship between the United States and Britain and their respective leaders in a period of crisis.

War and its aftermath continued to engross both writers and readers. An English-language edition of Lucjan Dubroszycki's documentary history of wartime Poland, *The Chronicles of the Lodz Ghetto, 1941–1944*, was brought out, as were *"The Good Years": An Oral History of World War II*, by Studs Terkel, and, in fitting commemoration of the 40th anniversary of the Normandy invasion, Max Hastings's *Overlord: D-Day and the Battle for Normandy*.

Poetry. Although several newer poets—including William Matthews, Charles Wright, and Molly Peacock—published important collections, the major books were from established masters. In *A Wave*, John Ashbery let up on his clotted, overpacked verse for a more straightforward account of love lost and remembered. Philip Levine's *Selected Poems* brought together the cream of this somber poet and social activist. Allen Ginsberg was enshrined in a massive *Collected Poems*, from "Howl," the anthem of the beat generation, to his latest experiments with Eastern philosophy, pansexualism, and social commentary. M.D.

AUSTRALIAN

Several fine novels were published in Australia in 1984, as well as some provocative critical works and complete editions of older classics.

Fiction and Poetry. Three noteworthy novels explored interesting themes. John Hooker's *The Bush Soldiers* was "a rattling good yarn" about Australia between the wars and a generation seeking its political and social identity. David Malouf's *Harland's Half Acre* told the story of a self-taught artist, against the backdrop of changing Australian culture over the past half century. David Ireland's hero in his latest novel, *Archimedes and the Seagle*, was a dog. Unlike his other books, this was a happy story, pervaded with optimism about humanity.

Following its outstanding success with *The Complete Works of A.B. Paterson*, Lansdowne Press published a companion two-volume set, *The Complete Works of Henry Lawson*. Lawson, the archetypal "bush" writer, is Australia's most popular author and a must for newcomers to Australian literature.

In poetry, the year saw the publication, 116 years after his death, of *The Poetical Works of Charles Harpur*, Australia's first true poet.

Nonfiction. Three observers explored different facets of the country's literature and literary scene. Poet, novelist, publisher, editor, and essayist Geoffrey Dutton discussed nationalism in Australian literature on a highly personal level in *Snow on the Saltbush: The Australian Literary Experience*. John Docker, himself an academic, mounted an attack against academic literary criticism in his book *In a Critical Condition: Reading Australian Literature*. He dubbed English department incumbents "elitist" and "formalist" and argued that they do not like live authors around to contradict their views—"The death of the author is the birth of the critic." Lynne Strahan traced the development of the literary journal *Meanjin* through its first 25 years and examined its role in Australia's cultural history in *Just City and the Mirrors: Meanjin Quarterly and the Intellectual Front 1940–1965*.

Another notable contribution was Dorothy Green's *The Music of Love: Critical Essays on Literature and Life*, which established her as one of the country's finest literary critics.

Australian poet David Malouf won wide critical praise for Harland's Half Acre, a novel that explored the lives of a painter and his agent, Australia's European roots, and the country's own native culture.

LITERATURE

Awards. The National Book Council announced its nominees for Ten Best Books of the Decade. The three fiction titles were *The Twybourne Affair* by Patrick White, *An Imaginary Life* by David Malouf, and *Flying Home* by Moris Lurie. Three were biographies: Patrick White's *Flaws in the Glass*, A.B. Facey's *A Fortunate Life*, and Geoffrey Serle's *John Monash*. The remainder were three histories—Manning Clark's *A History of Australia*, Geoffrey Blainey's *Triumph of the Nomads*, and Eric Rolls's *A Million Wild Acres*—and one book of poetry, Bruce Dawe's *Sometimes Gladness*. The New South Wales premier's literary awards went to Beverley Farmer for *Milk* (fiction), Sylvia Lawson for *The Archibald Paradox* (nonfiction), and Les Murray for *The People's Otherworld* (poetry).

Murray's book also won the Australian Literary Society's Gold Medal, while Lawson's book won the Walter McRae Russell Award. Kate Grenville took the Australian-Vogel $10,000 literary award, which guarantees publication, for the manuscript of a comic novel, *Bea's Story*, about a girl growing up to be an eccentric.

Obituary. Xavier Herbert, the passionate idealist and portrayer of social evils in his novels *Capricornia, Soldiers' Women,* and *Poor Fellow My Country*, died at the age of 83.   I.K.

CANADIAN

English-language fiction continued to dominate the literary scene in 1984. Several provocative novels were published; short-story collections garnered critical acclaim and large audiences.

Fiction. Four volumes in a new series of short-story collections were published: W. P. Kinsella's *The Thrill of the Grass;* Norman Levine's *Champagne Barn;* Spider Robinson's science fiction collection, *Melancholy Elephants;* and, the finest of the quartet, Timothy Findley's retrospective *Dinner Along The Amazon.* Among other collections, Isabel Huggan's *The Elizabeth Stories* vividly depicts the fear, pain, and defiance marking a young girl's uneasy childhood and adolescence. Also appearing were Sandra Birdsell's second collection of stories, *Ladies of the House,* and Leon Rooke's *A Bolt of White Cloth.*

The most interesting English-language novels were characterized by ambition and daring.

Mordecai Richler, whose novel, The Apprenticeship of Duddy Kravitz, *became a hit Hollywood movie, published* Home Sweet Home, *a collection of sharp-eyed essays and articles on subjects ranging from death to ice hockey to ballet.*

Timothy Findley's *Not Wanted on the Voyage* retold the Noah's flood myth as an apocalyptic fable for our time. Guy Vanderhaeghe, who won the 1982 Governor-General's Award for Fiction with his collection *Man Descending,* developed a character from that book into the protagonist of his first novel, *My Present Age.* Audrey Thomas's *Intertidal Life* gave a woman's account of a marital breakup that does not spare the protagonist from criticism, and Sylvia Fraser's *Berlin Solstice* described the rise of fascism as experienced by those on the Axis side.

French-language works included Miche Tremblay's *Des nouvelles d'Edouard* ("Edward's Journal"), the fourth volume in his chronicles of Plateau Mont-Royale. Roch Carrier, Quebec's most prolific and powerful short story writer, published *De l'amour dans le ferraille* ("Love in the scrap heap").

Poetry. Novelist, poet, songwriter, and singe Leonard Cohen published *Book of Mercy*, poetic meditations on mercy as the route to personal peace. In *Interlunar*, Margaret Atwood displays a sharp eye and clear wit. Roo Borson, Ralph Gustafson, and Al Purdy also brought out new collections.

Nicole Brossard's *Double impression: poèmes et textes 1967–1984* ("Double impression: poems and texts") offers a full perspective on the career of one of Quebec's finest poets. The earthy, explicit sensuality of André Roy's poetry dominated his new volume. There were interesting new collections from Jacques Brault, Gilbert Langevin, and Denis Vanier.

Nonfiction. Mordecai Richler's *Home Sweet Home: My Canadian Album* mingles poignant autobiography and cogent journalism in essays suffused with wit and irony. Playwright Erika Ritter excels at topical humor in *Urban Scrawl*. More serious is novelist Victory-Lévy Beaulieu's collection of critical writings, *Entre la sainteté et le terrorisme* ("Between sanctity and terrorism").

The highlight of the fall literary season in Quebec was *La détresse et l'enchantment* ("The distress and the enchantment"), the first volume of Gabrielle Roy's autobiography, which is being edited posthumously. In her novels, Roy, who died in 1983, ushered in a new era of realism in Quebec fiction.

English Canada continued to examine and celebrate its literary history. Lorraine McMullen's *An Odd Attempt in a Woman: The Literary Life of Frances Brooke* explores the life and literary milieu of the writer of the first Canadian novel, *The History of Emily Montague* (written in 1769). *E. J. Pratt: The Truant Years 1882–1927* is the first volume of David G. Pitt's biography of the poet. *The Anthology Anthology*, edited by Robert Weaver, includes short stories and poetry that first appeared on the CBC-Radio program *Anthology*, which celebrated its 30th anniversary in 1984. The special 100th issue of *Canadian Literature*, marking the journal's 25th anniversary, contained essays and poems by 97 writers.

Awards. The Governor-General's Awards for 1983 went to Leon Rooke for *Shakespeare's Dog* and Suzanne Jacob for *Laura Laur* (fiction); to Suzanne Paradis for *Un goût de sel* ("A taste of salt") and David Donnell for *Settlements* (poetry); to René Gingras for *Syncope* ("Syncopation") and Anne Chislett for *Quiet in the Land* (drama), and to Maurice Cusson for *Le contrôle social du crime* ("The societal control of crime") and Jeffery Williams for *Byng of Vimy* (nonfiction). D.S.

ENGLISH

Work by both established and lesser-known writers captured attention in 1984.

Fiction. Inevitably, much was expected in 1984 from William Golding, winner of the 1983 Nobel Prize for literature. But critics were puzzled and disconcerted by his new novel, *The Paper Men*, a pessimistic, black-comic saga of flight and pursuit through half of Europe. The protagonists were an aging English literary lion and an obnoxious American academic determined to become the other's authorized biographer; the characters seemed to be two sides of one unwholesome personality, locked in a conflict for dominance.

Kingsley Amis's first novel in four years, *Stanley and the Women*, was a provocative companion piece for his earlier misogynistic comedy, *Jake's Thing*. Also uncompromising in dealing with the war between the sexes was Fay Weldon's Gothic fable *The Life and Loves of a She-Devil*, which charted the remorseless course of a plain wife's monstrously efficient revenge. Relief from rancor was provided by the exhilarating satirical comedy of *Small World*, by David Lodge. Two haunting short novels memorably evoked some of the "horrors of our time," in a phrase from Elaine Feinstein's *The Border*. The struggles of her Jewish intellectuals, Austrian refugees in Paris in the late 1930's, to come to terms with their heritage and their relationships were vividly recreated in diary extracts, letters, and a handful of poems. In *The Pork Butcher*, David Hughes depicted an elderly German compulsively driven by memories of an episode in wartime France to return to the scene of his guilt.

Belfast was the setting for Bernard Mac Laverty's *Secrets*, a volume of evocative short stories by one of Northern Ireland's best younger writers. *The Last Romantic out of Belfast*, by Sam Keery, was a promising first novel of an Irish boyhood. *Cold Heaven*, by Irish novelist Brian Moore, portrayed the supernatural influences on the life of a woman who continues to rebel against God though her husband has apparently risen from the dead.

LITERATURE

After a ten-year professional career as a leading steeplechase jockey, Dick Francis has become a best-selling author, acclaimed by critics as a master of action narrative, careful characterization, and authentically detailed settings. Francis's new adventure tale The Danger was—like his previous 23 books—set in the world of horse racing.

Against a background of the woolen trade in the north of England, John Braine's The Two of Us followed the vicissitudes of a family business at odds with the new technology. In Present Times, by David Storey, a middle-aged ex-rugby star was reduced to writing sports reports for the local paper, eventually laid off, and victimized by everyone around him. Equally patient and put-upon, the headmaster-hero of Stanley Middleton's excellent The Daysman proved somewhat more successful at coping. The protagonist of Muriel Spark's The Only Problem, a scholarly writing about the Book of Job, had to deal with his own suffering, the increasing messiness of his life, and the comforters and persecutors who come to talk about his wife-turned-terrorist. Dick Francis's adventure story, The Danger, published in the United States in the spring, quickly became a bestseller. The former steeplechaser, whose two dozen works of fiction all have a racing background, was named an Officer of the British Empire when Queen Elizabeth included his name on her 1984 New Year's Honors List.

Biography. In A Cup of News, by Charles Nicholl, the 16th-century satirist Thomas Nashe sprang to exuberant life. Brian Fothergill's The Strawberry Hill Set studied Horace Walpole and his circle. Hazlitt: The Mind of a Critic, by David Bromwich, gave a comprehensive account of the essayist's ideas and fierce radicalism. In Thomas Carlyle, Fred Kaplan concentrated on the life and character of the cantankerous sage of Chelsea.

Drama. Hugh Whitemore's Pack of Lies was the year's most successful straight play. Based on the story of a London couple discovered to be Soviet spies, it compassionately portrayed their agonized conflicts of loyalty. Tom and Viv, by Michael Hastings, depicted the gradual disintegration of T. S. Eliot's first marriage and implicitly linked the poet's private grief with his religious faith and with the despair voiced in his poetry.

Several plays by established dramatists shared a common theme: the discrepancy between human aspiration and its fulfillment. True purpose eluded the weary hero of television writer Dennis Potter's first play for the stage, Sufficient Carbohydrate, amid the drunken and amorous antics of two business executives and their wives on holiday on a Greek island. The Common Pursuit, by Simon Gray, wryly followed the failure over 15 years of five Cambridge schoolmates to fulfill early promise and scholarly aims. The disappointed protagonist of Michael Frayn's Benefactors was an architect whose idealistic liberal intentions were constantly thwarted.

David Pownall's portrait of Stalin in Master Class, set in the Kremlin during the cultural crackdown of 1948, explored the psychology of dictatorship and the repression of artistic freedom in a Communist state. Terry Johnson, in his bizarre and chilling Cries From the Mammal House, used allegory to convey his cynical view of Britain today. Alan Ayckbourn in Intimate Exchanges, offered no less than eight full-length alternative versions of the unpredictable adventures of a regal but sprightly headmaster's wife. His other new play, A Chorus of Disapproval, concerned the disil lusioning education of a stagestruck innocent enmeshed in the schemes of an amateur dramatic society.

Poet Laureate. Britain's poet laureate since 1972, Sir John Betjeman, died in May at the age of 77. Philip Larkin was widely expected to replace him; the choice instead, named by Queen Elizabeth in December, was Ted Hughes, a prolific, fiery poet whose first book of verse, *Hawk of Rain,* appeared in 1957. Hughes is perhaps most famous to the general public as the husband of the late American poet Sylvia Plath.   M.W.

WORLD

New and newly translated literary works from Europe and Latin America gained a favorable response from readers and critics in 1984.

French. Among works of French fiction to appear in translation were Michel Tournier's *The Fetishist,* with grim stories that hover between reality and the grotesque, and *The Poet Assassinated and Other Stories* by Guillaume Apollinaire (1880–1918), which combines fantasy with commentary on the hostile reception of a conventional world to offbeat thinking. Also appearing in English were the short works of Marcel Schwob (1867–1905), in *The King in the Golden Mask,* and those of Paul Morand (1888–1976) in *Fancy Goods.* The latter represented the first publication of translations of Morand's work by Ezra Pound, which had been turned down in the 1920's by a conservative British publisher.

Among new novels published in France were Claude Mauriac's *Zabé,* which explores the deranged mind of a murderer retracing his life, and Pascal Quignard's clever and informative historical novel *Les Tablettes de buis d'Apronenia Avitia* ("The boxwood tablets of Apronenia"), in which a fairly ordinary woman records her impressions of everyday life in imperial Rome. In the newly translated novel *Salad Days,* Françoise Sagan adroitly tells the story of a lover who wishes to impress people by taking "credit" for a crime he did not commit.

Two memoirs that had made news in France appeared in translation. George Simenon's *Intimate Memoirs: Including Marie-Jo's Book* revealed the craft behind his hundreds of popular psychological novels, but also the dark side of his personal life. Simone de Beauvoir's *Adieux: A Farewell to Sartre* adds to our knowledge of contemporary philosophers whose ideas helped to shape modern intellectual perspectives. With the newly translated *The Conquest of America,* the noted Bulgarian linguistic theorist Tzvetan Todorov, now living in Paris, goes beyond the documented history of the destruction of Aztec civilization to examine the interaction of vastly different cultures.

In the spring, Senegalese poet and statesman Léopold Sédar Senghor, who writes in French, English, and an African language, became the first black to be elected to the French Academy.

German. Among the most ambitious publication projects of the year was the appearance in German, in five volumes, of the works of Paul Celan (1920–1970), encompassing nearly all the author's prose and poetry. Celan was born in Romania but since 1948 had lived in self-imposed exile in France. Another major compilation was the three-volume *Das grosse Brecht Liederbuch,* an extensive collection of song texts and performance scores for Bertolt Brecht's plays.

Beat Sterchi's *Blösch,* an untranslated, parodistic novel published in Switzerland, was strongly reminiscent of George Orwell's *Animal Farm,* although *Blösch* focuses less on politics and more on the social disasters that stem from the excessive mechanization of agriculture. From Austrian writer Peter Handke came the novel, certain to be translated soon, *Der Chinese des Schmerzens* ("The mandarin of pain"), in which a scholar explores the idea of "threshold awareness" between past and present, society and nature, and action and inaction. In Gert Hofmann's translated novel *The Spectacle at the Tower,* a troubled German husband and wife on tour in Sicily stray into a forsaken and primitive village. Nobel Prize–winner Heinrich Böll offers a candid reconstruction of German social and political attitudes in the memoir *What's to Become of the Boy?*

Italian. In *Postscript to the Name of the Rose,* Umberto Eco tells how he came to write his international best-seller and provides welcome clues to its meanings. The late Dino Buzzati is well represented in a second anthology entitled *The Siren,* which encompasses his earliest novella, *Barnabo of the Mountains (Barnabo della montagne,* 1933), and his journalistic pieces of the 1960's. New and old translations of Italo Calvino's short stories written between 1940 and 1960 have been assembled under the title *Difficult Loves;* these stories portray the extraordinarily well-articulated experiences of ordinary people caught in embarrassing dilemmas. *Marcovaldo* is a companion volume in which Calvino's psychological stories explore the idea that events in the lives of city dwellers occur in tandem with the seasons.

Two nonfiction works were translated after receiving wide discussion in Italy. Francesco Alberoni's *Falling in Love* is a deep and wide-ranging sociological study of a universal phenomenon and its social effects. In Marcello Conati's *Encounters with Verdi,* the life and times of the biographically elusive opera composer are brought to life through the writings of journalists, acquaintances, and musicians who were his contemporaries.

Portuguese and Spanish. Readers of Latin American fiction and poetry were treated to many new works in translation. Written in Portuguese, Autran Dourado's Brazilian novel *Orisco do bordado,* translated as *Pattern for a Tapestry,* is a fine portrayal of adolescence and manhood in a changing culture. José Donoso's *A House in the Country* is a haunting allegorical novel about modern life, although its setting is a hundred years old. Julio Cortázar died in February, but his works continue to appear in translation; his stories in *A Certain Lucas* have a surreal quality, as the characters thumb their noses at a mechanical universe and pursue their own fancies.

Merce Rodoreda, who died in 1983, was a Catalan novelist of rare stylistic distinction; in a newly translated collection, *My Christina and Other Stories,* she gives poignant voice to women's emotional experiences. Also appearing were Heberto Padilla's high-spirited, semiautobiographical *Heroes Are Grazing in My Garden,* written in exile from Castro's Cuba, and *Selected Poems* by the Mexican diplomat and man of letters Octavio Paz, translated by noted American poets.

Russian. Works of Yuri Trifonov, who died in 1981, continued to appear in translation. His novel *The Old Man,* evokes with candor and realism the days of civil warfare after World War I and the social and political life of the modern Soviet Union. In another absorbing work, the great soprano Galina Vishnevskaya, now an émigré, tells of her experiences in *Galina: A Russian Story.*

Czech. Like his other translated fiction, *The Unbearable Lightness of Being* features Milan Kundera's black philosophical humor in picturing the restrictiveness of everyday life in Prague. Another writer living in exile, Jose Skvorecky, richly describes the resettling of Czech immigrants in Canada in his long novel *The Engineer of Human Souls;* the author's seventh work of fiction to be translated into English, it has the qualities of a modern masterpiece. A highlight of the year was the award of the Nobel Prize for literature to Jaroslav Seifert, an 83-year-old Czech poet, patriot, and

The Engineer of Human Souls, *a semiautobiographical novel by Josef Skvorecky, a 15-year resident of Toronto who was born in Czechoslovakia, was hailed as "extraordinary" and "a masterpiece" by Canadian and U.S. critics. The 1984 English translation of* Engineer *was widely celebrated in the North American literary world but ignored in Czechoslovakia, where Skvorecky's books are banned.*

Joining the Ranks of the "Immortals"
The March induction of Léopold Sédar Senghor, 77, into the 350-year-old Académie Francaise was notable for more than one reason. Known for his poetry in French, English and an African language, Senghor was the first black ever named to the Academy. He also had enjoyed a long career as statesman, having served from 1960 to 1980 as first president of his native Senegal. Senghor was educated primarily in France, where he taught for many years. His first volume of poetry, *Chants d'ombre* (Songs of Shadow, 1945) was an early literary expression of *négritude*, an influential concept of African cultural identity developed by Senghor and others in Paris in the 1930's. He continued to follow this inspiration in the poems and prose works over a long writing career, at the same time forming his own political party in Senegal and leading his country during and after independence.

Léopold Sédar Senghor

champion of human rights. Seifert was the first Czech ever to win the literary prize (*see* PRIZES AND AWARDS).

Yiddish. *In the Storm,* by Sholom Aleichem, was first published in 1907 at a time when the persecution of Jews sparked their emigration from Russia. The novel—rediscovered and translated for the first time—has all the features of his better known work. S.M.

BOOKS FOR CHILDREN

While juvenile hardcover books were declining in popularity in the United States during 1984, paperback sales rose dramatically. Publishers expanded softcover offerings in all categories—picture books, middle readers, and young adult novels—to attract thrifty customers.

Trends. There was a phenomenal increase in paperback series for teenagers, especially romances; U.S. publishers launched at least eight new romance series. Another category that attracted many young readers was the multiple-ending story in paperback. Fiction series for middle readers and older readers based on the occult, ESP, and supernatural forces also proved popular, as did adventure stories and space exploits. There was a new series of solve-it-yourself computer mysteries starring two young sleuths, the Byte Brothers, who figure out various crimes with the aid of their home computer. Also, on the upswing during the

year were tie-ins and spin-offs from television shows, films, and comics, featuring such characters as Smurfs, Care Bears, the Muppets, Garfield, and Indiana Jones.

Books were offered to the youngest readers—children aged two months to five years—that float, pop up, fold out, play a song, tell a simple story, or show basic concepts. A few of the standouts in "baby lit" were Little Toy Board Books by Rodney Peppé, Colin Mc-Naughton's *Seasons,* Little Animal Books by the Dutch artist Peter Spier, and *The Goodnight Moon Room,* a delightful pop-up adaptation of Margaret Wise Brown's perennial favorite, *Goodnight Moon,* featuring Clement Hurd's enchanting pictures.

Firsts and favorites. Edith Kunhardt devised a companion volume to the classic, *Pat the Bunny,* written by her mother, Dorothy Kunhardt, in 1940. Edith's *Pat the Cat* uses her mother's innovative approach, in which children can move objects, sniff, stroke, and squeeze a teddy bear, and, of course, pat a cat. William Steig's 1969 picture book, *The Bad Island,* was revised and retitled *Rotten Island.* The art, drawn in fluorescent dyes, was reshot for vibrant color. In the story, animals who live on Rotten Island rejoice in its rottenness. When a flower appears, they rage at its beauty and fight until they all become extinct.

He kisses Alceste, Charmaine, Suzette, Jeannot, Gabrielle, and Mama Blériot.
Papa climbs into the cockpit. His friend Alfred Le Blanc spins the propeller.
It is 4:35 a.m.

Winner of the 1984 Caldecott Medal for best illustrated children's book, Alice and Martin Provensen's The Glorious Flight: Across the Channel with Louis Blériot *tells the story of the French aviation pioneer's epic flight from Calais to Dover on July 25, 1909.*

New and beautiful editions of timeless favorites were well represented. Prizewinning artist Anita Lobel lent her paintings to Clement C. Moore's yuletide poem *The Night Before Christmas;* in Lobel's version, full-color pictures restore the verse to its original urban, Victorian setting. More than 50 nursery rhymes were gathered in a new edition of *Mother Goose,* compiled and illustrated by Michael Hague. Classics issued in gift editions included: *The Story of the Champions of the Round Table* by Howard Pyle, with his drawings, and Paul Creswick's 1957 version of *Robin Hood,* featuring N. C. Wyeth's illustrations. Another best bet for Christmas gift giving was *The Larousse Book of Nursery Rhymes,* edited by Robert Owen; the verses were brought to life with photographs of stunning Royal Doulton tile pictures. *Hansel and Gretel* was turned into a

knockout volume through the collaboration of Rika Lesser, who retold the tale, and Paul O. Zelinsky, who furnished colorful paintings.

Prizes. Two publishers held contests for teenagers, with publication as the prize for the best novel. The winner of the Avon/Flare Young Adult Novel Competition was 17-year-old Lee J. Hindle, whose *Dragon Fall* centered on a boy able to bring toy dragons to life. Joyce Sweeney's *Center Line* garnered her the Delacorte Press Prize; Sweeney told a compelling tale about five brothers who leave home together after they grow tired of being abused by their alcoholic father.

The American Library Association's Newbery Medal was awarded to Beverly Cleary for *Dear Mr. Henshaw,* a collection of a boy's letters to his favorite author, illustrated by Paul O. Zelinsky. The Caldecott Medal, given for the best

American picture book, was presented to Alice and Martin Provensen for *The Glorious Flight: Across the Channel With Louis Blériot*. The husband-and-wife team supplied both text and paintings in their tale of the Frenchman who made aviation history.

Mitsumasa Anno and Christine Nöstlinger won the prestigious Hans Christian Andersen Medals, awarded biennially by the International Board on Books for Young People to one author and one illustrator for an entire body of work. Japanese artist Anno has been universally praised for his wordless volumes of intricate watercolors, such as *Anno's Journey* and *Anno's U.S.A.* Nöstlinger, an Austrian author, has written more than 12 novels for young people, including *Konrad, Luke and Angela*, and *Marrying Off Mother*.

The Association of American Publishers eliminated its prizes for children's books as part of a decrease in categories for the American Book Awards. Among the reasons given were the excessive cost and the diluted value of each award.   D.R.

LOUISIANA. *See* STATISTICS OF THE WORLD.

LUXEMBOURG. General elections, held on June 17, 1984, substantially changed the composition of Luxembourg's center-right coalition government. The new coalition consisted of the Social Christians (25 seats) and the Socialists (21 seats), while the Liberals (14 seats) moved into opposition for the first time in five years. Jacques Santer (Social Christian) became the new premier, and Jacques Poos, the Socialist Party leader, became the country's vice-president.

On January 13, Luxembourg and Belgium reached agreement on the future cooperation of their major steel companies. Luxembourg's Arbed will coordinate operations with Cockerill-Sambre of Belgium and Sidmar, a jointly owned company. Luxembourg steel workers staged a peaceful protest over the plan, expected to eliminate about 10,000 jobs in both countries.

In May the government announced plans to put in orbit, by 1986, two U.S.-made satellites that would transmit up to 16 commercial television channels throughout Europe. The project, named Coronet, was designed to establish a strong position for Luxembourg in Europe's commercial television market.

In November, Luxembourg's head of state, Grand Duke Jean, made his first official visit to the United States.

See STATISTICS OF THE WORLD.   W.C.C.

Dr. Seuss Is Not a Moose

Theodor Seuss Geisel, the writer and illustrator known as Dr. Seuss, turned 80 in 1984 and won a special Pulitzer citation for a parade of books featuring unforgettable characters and whimsical verse, liberally sprinkled with nonsense words, that have entertained children for decades. His first book, *And to Think That I Saw It on Mulberry Street,* was an immediate hit in 1937. Other Seuss treasures have included *Horton Hears a Who, How the Grinch Stole Christmas, Yertle the Turtle,* and, in 1984, *The Butter Battle Book.* Many Dr. Seuss books, beginning with the enormously successful *The Cat in the Hat,* are specially designed to encourage young children to read by themselves. Geisel's work has been translated into 20 languages. More than 100 million copies of his books have been sold worldwide, and he has also created award-winning television and movie cartoons.

Dr. Seuss

M

MADAGASCAR. *See* STATISTICS OF THE WORLD.
MAINE. *See* STATISTICS OF THE WORLD.
MALAWI. *See* STATISTICS OF THE WORLD.
MALAYSIA. The year 1984 started with a resolution of the lengthy constitutional dispute between Malaysia's elected government and its royal rulers. The government had proposed constitutional amendments denying the king the power to declare a state of emergency and providing that a bill would automatically become law 15 days after being passed by Parliament, thus depriving the king of the right to veto legislation. Both amendments were strongly opposed by the country's nine hereditary sultans, who rule nine of Malaysia's 13 states and who choose the king every five years from among themselves.

In the compromise that was eventually reached, the amendment regarding state-of-emergency powers was dropped, and it was agreed that if a bill does not receive the king's approval within 30 days after being passed by Parliament, it goes back to Parliament for revision or a second vote; if Parliament passes the bill a second time, it automatically becomes law one month later.

The sultan of Johor, Mahmood Iskander, widely regarded as independent and strong-willed, was chosen king in February. He was the senior surviving sultan after the death in January of Idris Shah of Perak.

Elections held on May 25 for posts in the powerful United Malays National Organization (UMNO), the dominant party in the ruling National Front coalition, were considered a vindication of the policies of Prime Minister Mahathir Mohamed, who had precipitated the constitutional crisis by proposing the controversial amendments. Most of Mahathir's choices won their contests. In a key election, UMNO deputy president Musa Hitam was reelected, defeating Minister of Finance Tengku Razaleigh Hamzah, a political opponent of the prime minister.

The Malaysian Chinese Association, second largest member of the ruling National Front coalition, was rocked by scandal when various party officials charged that "phantom members" were entered on the roster of party membership, presumably so that the acting MCA president, Neo Yee Pan, and his supporters could increase the number of their delegates at party elections. The MCA vice-president, Tan Koon Swan, demanded an investigation of membership lists; in response, Neo Yee Pan expelled Tan and many of his key supporters from the party. Tan called for a special party meeting in May, which demonstrated broad membership approval of his position, but party leaders refused to recognize it. MCA elections scheduled for July were postponed pending the outcome of a court decision regarding the validity of the voting lists.

Concerns about freedom of the press heightened as the official national news service, Bernama, assumed sole distributorship for all foreign news agencies. A law passed in March made journalists and publishers liable for prosecution for a variety of offenses, including printing items disapproved of by the government. Individuals could be prosecuted for possessing a single issue of a banned periodical.

Economic recovery continued, with real growth during 1984 expected to be about 6 percent. In other economic news, the troubled government-backed Bank Bumiputra had its capital accounts restocked when the national oil company, Petronas, agreed to a $1 billion bailout in September. Petronas took control of the bank and covered the debts accumulated by the bank's subsidiary, Bumiputra Malaysia Finance.

See STATISTICS OF THE WORLD. K.M

MALDIVES. *See* STATISTICS OF THE WORLD.
MALI. *See* STATISTICS OF THE WORLD.
MALTA. On December 22, 1984, the prime minister of Malta, Dom Mintoff, resigned his office, and the deputy leader of the ruling Socialist Labor Party, Carmelo Mifsud-Bonnici was sworn in as his successor. He was to serve as prime minister until the next general election, scheduled for 1986.

Mintoff, who was 68 years old, had been

prime minister since 1971. An architect and civil engineer who served as the leader of his party for 35 years, Mintoff pursued a pronouncedly nonaligned foreign policy as prime minister.

Mifsud-Bonnici, a lawyer who had become deputy party leader in 1980 and party leader–designate two years later, also had been Malta's education minister. In this capacity he was a driving force behind legislation enacted earlier in 1984, requiring that all private Roman Catholic secondary schools cease charging tuition or else be closed down by the state. The controversial legislation led to a delay in the opening of the Catholic schools in the fall, but they eventually opened under Church auspices after the archbishop agreed to end tuition charges.

Early in the year, Mintoff and his designated successor, Mifsud-Bonnici, visited Libya to discuss future employment of Maltese workers there. In February, Malta and the Soviet Union signed a three-year agreement calling for more trade, the repair of Soviet ships in Malta's dry docks, and the building of a factory to produce surgical equipment.

An existing wage and price freeze was extended into 1984. Early in the year, unemployment was around 9 percent, and tourism was declining.

See STATISTICS OF THE WORLD.   P.J.M.

MANITOBA. See STATISTICS OF THE WORLD. See also CANADA.

MANUFACTURING INDUSTRIES. The U.S. industrial recovery continued during 1984. The Commerce Department reported that businesses planned to increase their capital spending by 14 percent during the year as a whole, and industrial output rose through most of the year.

Recovery was vigorous early in the year but then began to lag somewhat. Figures for industrial production edged downward in September for the first time in 22 months, and declined again in October. At the same time, orders for durable goods continued a zigzag decline begun in the spring, retreating to under $100 billion in September. Use of the nation's factories, mines, and utilities also fell in September, for the second consecutive month, to 82 percent of capacity.

Late in the year, however, there were signs of a renewed pickup in the economy. In November, industrial production at U.S. factories, mines, and utilities rose by 0.4 percent, and orders to factories for durable goods surged by 8.3 percent, the biggest gain in over four years. Military orders accounted for over half of the gain, but nonmilitary orders still went up by a healthy 3.3 percent. Nevertheless, there still were deep-seated problems in some manufacturing industries. Cheap foreign imports remained a major focus of concern, perhaps most notably in the steel industry.

Steel. The decline of the U.S. steel industry in recent years has become apparent, in distressing statistics that run counter to trends in other industries. Employment in the industry, which averaged around 450,000 from 1975 to 1979, fell to 243,000 in 1983. Industry losses in 1982 and 1983 exceeded $6 billion. By mid-1984, plants were operating at only 57 percent of capacity. Outdated plants and equipment, high labor costs, and a falling world demand for steel contributed to the weakness, but the companies and their workers placed most of the blame on a fourth problem—unfair competition because of cheap imports, mostly from Third World countries. In the first six months of 1984, imports claimed 24 percent of the U.S. steel market, and figures for later months were slightly higher.

Companies were already taking drastic steps to avert disaster. David M. Roderick, chairman of U.S. Steel, closed down operations that were losing money and diversified into other areas, including petroleum. After a disastrous year in 1983, U.S. Steel moved into the profit column, where it remained for at least the first three quarters of 1984. Its hefty third-quarter profit was mostly a result of operations outside the steel sector, but even its steel operations made a slight profit. However, the industry as a whole appeared to be having a generally weak year, with many steel producers reporting losses.

Companies looked to the U.S. government for help. Support began to form in the U.S. House of Representatives for a "Fair Trade in Steel Act" that would roll back imports to 15 percent of the U.S. market. Meanwhile, in response to a petition by Bethlehem Steel

MANUFACTURING INDUSTRIES

Corporation and the United Steel Workers union, the U.S. International Trade Commission ruled that foreign imports were seriously hurting a large part of the U.S. steel industry. On July 11, the ITC recommended, by a 3–2 vote, that President Ronald Reagan impose import quotas on five major types of imported steel to remedy the problem.

A national debate ensued, with opponents of quotas warning that they were a step toward protectionism, responsible for worldwide economic slumps in the past. It was also argued that quotas would drive up prices, reduce demand for automobiles and durable goods, and give the industry less incentive to modernize. On September 18, in the midst of election-year pressures, Reagan announced a compromise plan. He directed William Brock, his special trade representative, to negotiate "voluntary" import restrictions within 90 days. Brazil, Spain, and South Korea were said to be among the prime targets. Brock said that, with

the help of the plan, foreign steel would drop to roughly an 18.5 percent share of the U.S. market.

The president's action fell short of industry hopes for strict quotas and higher tariffs on imported steel, while other observers regarded the plan as protectionism in disguise. In any event, on December 19, the U.S. government announced it had concluded pacts with seven leading steel exporting nations to reduce their 1985 shipments to the United States by 30 percent. The seven countries were Japan, South Korea, Brazil, Mexico, Spain, Australia, and South Africa. All except Japan agreed to continue reduced levels over a five-year period. U.S. steel producers also stood to gain from an accord being negotiated with the European Economic Community in December, limiting EEC exports of steel pipe and tubes to 7.6 percent of the U.S. market.

The administration's action on steel imports contrasted with its response to a similar petition

Made in Brazil, a shipment of steel pipes is unloaded at the port of Houston. Protectionism became a hot U.S. political issue, as increasing numbers of industries asked the government for import quotas to shield them against foreign competition.

from copper producers; in September, Reagan had refused to grant tariffs, quotas, or other forms of protection for copper. (Most of the president's advisers had argued that any form of protection would mean unacceptably higher prices for products made with copper and would cost more jobs in the fabricating sector of the industry than it would save in the mining sector.)

Textiles. The textile industry also looked to the U.S. government for relief from cheap imports. The American Textile Manufacturers Institute, Inc., said in July that imports of textiles and apparel had more than doubled in four years. The Reagan administration responded in August, saying it would tighten the so-called "country of origin" labeling requirements. This step was aimed at preventing a country from evading its quota by transshipping products through a third nation so that, when delivered to the United States, they would be charged against the quota of that nation. The new rules would provide that only products wholly manufactured or "substantially transformed" in a nation could count toward that nation's quota.

Announcement of the new rules, which applied to quotas established under the Multi-Fiber Arrangement of the General Agreement on Tariffs and Trade (GATT), brought complaints from importers and from some importing countries. Retailers said that implementing the rules would disrupt shipment of clothing ordered for the Christmas buying season. Although the new rules were to go into effect September 7, their implementation was postponed. GATT subsequently urged the United States not to impose the rules, and China threatened to retaliate against American grain imports. In a compromise, the new rules were not imposed on imports ordered before August 3 and scheduled for delivery before October 31. U.S. clothing and textile manufacturers hoped to gain from a new law being implemented in 1985, which required labeling to identify all U.S.-made garments and household fabrics, and thus promote their sale.

Data released during 1984 suggested an industry in equilibrium. Some 744,000 workers were employed in September, and mills were operating at 84 percent of capacity as of August—indicators which were virtually un-

changed from 1983. Total fiber consumption increased slightly in the first six months of 1984, as compared with January–June 1983. Textile industry exports declined slightly over the same period.

Machine Tools. In the machine-tool industry, the debate over imports was tinged with the national security issue. Manufacturers, who turn out the high-precision metal-cutting tools used in the production of a variety of parts for airplanes and other vehicles and machines, argued that trade disruptions during a national emergency could prevent importers from supplying tools to the United States. In June 1983, the industry had petitioned the administration to limit imports to 17.5 percent of the domestic market, at a time when imports were running at about 39 percent. West Germany, the world's leading exporter of machine tools, was among the nations concerned by the petition. The Commerce Department reportedly urged the president to impose quotas; critics of the industry continued to argue that companies should make more efforts to modernize and compete.

Orders received by the U.S. machine-tool industry continued to fluctuate widely. From $5.6 billion in orders received in 1979, requests from customers had fallen to $1.5 billion in 1982 and improved only to $1.7 billion in 1983; increasing national prosperity brought about a projected rebound to about $3 billion for 1984. The industry was still operating at only about 60 percent of capacity, and employment—at 67,000 workers—remained about 30 percent below 1979.

Paper Industry. The economic surge in 1984 carried the paper industry to high levels of profitability. During the first six months of the year, 34 companies manufacturing paper and allied products reported a 20 percent increase in sales and a 79 percent gain in net profits after taxes. Production within the industry during the first six months stood at 35 million tons, 9 percent above the same period in 1983, which had been a record.

Business paper sales, as expected, led the way, with "computer fodder" in especially strong demand. Newsprint did well as the recovery generated a sharp increase in newspaper advertising and circulation. The demand for boxes in which to ship goods pushed

247

manufacturers of linerboard to the limits of their capacity.

Electrical Machinery. According to the National Electrical Manufacturers Association, electrical product sales were expected to increase 9.9 percent (after inflation) during 1984, returning the industry to prerecession levels. Sales for 1985 were expected to increase a modest additional amount, about 4 percent after inflation. The biggest projected sales gains in 1984 were in wire and cable and in industrial equipment (such as electric motors and generators, arc welding equipment, and general-purpose mechanical, electromechanical, and solid state industrial controls and control systems). Sales in these two main categories increased 14 percent.   L.R.H. & D.Y.

MARYLAND. See Statistics of the World.

MASSACHUSETTS. See Statistics of the World.

MAURITANIA. See Statistics of the World. See also Africa.

MAURITIUS. See Statistics of the World.

MEXICO. Mired in an economic depression from which they appeared slowly to be emerging, Mexicans concerned themselves mostly with surviving in 1984. Much attention was concentrated on foreign affairs and campaigns against official corruption.

Economic Developments. Indications were that the gross domestic product grew slightly in 1984, possibly by 1 percent, following two years of decline. Inflation fell from 1983's 80 percent to about 55 percent according to official estimates, indicating that it was being brought under control, although not as rapidly as had been hoped for. On the darker side, the Labor Congress, a grouping of trade unions, declared that half the workers in Mexico were unemployed or underemployed.

The depression was blamed on the country's $96 billion foreign debt, largely contracted during the oil boom of the 1970's. With little credit now available, public spending has been slashed. Factories were working at a fraction of their capacity, as few dollars were available for the purchase of raw materials. While the official austerity won warm praise from world bankers and the International Monetary Fund, in Mexico fears of impending social upheaval frequently were voiced. As a result, money continued to flow out of the country. On the positive side, the government was successful in September in rescheduling some $48.5 billion of its debt, stretching out payments over 14 years and getting a lower interest rate.

A proposed 1985 budget, introduced in December, called for a 54 percent spending increase. The government proposed to increase economic growth to 3–4 percent and cut inflation to 35 percent.

Foreign Affairs. Washington, according to some circles, had indicated it would support Mexico's request for easier debt terms, but only if Mexico in turn would cease opposing U.S. policies in Central America. Under former President José López Portillo (1976–1982), Mexico had actively supported the Sandinista regime in Nicaragua and given tacit recognition to the guerrillas in El Salvador. These policies did appear to be modified in 1984, but probably not as a result of U.S. pressure. President Miguel de la Madrid Hurtado, during a spring tour of Argentina, Brazil, Colombia, Panama, and Venezuela, reportedly was warned by several of his colleagues about the dangers of Soviet and Cuban infiltration in Central America. Shortly afterward, he met with U.S. President Ronald Reagan in Washington. Within weeks the U.S. secretary of state was in Nicaragua for talks, and Mexico sent its foreign minister to San Salvador to attend the inauguration of President José Napoleón Duarte, thus demonstrating its support for that government. In the months that followed, American and Nicaraguan representatives held a series of negotiating sessions in Mexico.

Some 46,000 Guatemalan refugees have sought haven in Mexico as a result of turmoil in that country. On April 30 a military force, apparently Guatemalan Army troops, raided a refugee camp on the Mexican side of the border, killing several people. In secret talks that followed, the Guatemalan government apparently complained that some refugee camps were being used as guerrilla bases. Mexico agreed to move the refugees hundreds of miles into the interior. Efforts also were begun to persuade the refugees to accept repatriation.

Population Problems. The problems of a soaring population were underscored at a UN population conference held in Mexico City during August. While few conclusions were

A Red Cross worker carries two badly burned children to safety in the aftermath of a November gas explosion near Mexico City that killed about 350 people, severely injured 500 others, and caused the evacuation of 100,000 residents of the working-class district of Tlalnepantla.

reached at the gathering, it was reported that Mexico had trimmed its population growth rate from 3.2 percent annually in the mid-1970's to 2.4 percent. Nevertheless, it was also noted that some 18 million people lived in metropolitan Mexico City, making it one of the largest cities on earth.

Politics and Government. During 1984 the government put up for sale stock in about 340 companies, stock acquired as a result of the 1982 nationalization of the country's banks. By offering to return many of the banks' holdings to the private sector, the administration reaffirmed its commitment to a mixed economy, allaying the anxiety of many.

Its image tarnished by widespread corruption during the López Portillo administration, the Institutional Revolutionary Party (PRI) reaffirmed its commitment to honesty in government, a program known in Mexico as Moral Renovation. Following the jailing for embezzlement of Jorge Diaz Serrano, former head of the government oil company, the public learned that Arturo Durazo Moreno, the Mexico City police chief appointed by López Portillo, apparently was the worst criminal in the country. He was accused of mass murder, dealing in

narcotics, extortion, and more. By then Durazo had gone abroad, but on May 29 he was seized by the FBI in Puerto Rico and was then transported to Los Angeles to await extradition hearings.

There was considerable speculation that López Portillo knew about Durazo's activities and shared his ill-gotten wealth, but when asked whether charges would be brought against the former president, de la Madrid declared he was not interested in witch hunts.

Mexico City Tragedy. About 350 people were killed when the explosion of a gas truck on November 19 ignited four tanks of liquefied gas at a government-operated oil facility. The nearby working-class neighborhood of Tlalnepantla, turned into an inferno by a seven-hour storm of flaming debris, was sealed off by government troops as rescue workers brought out victims and organized the evacuation of 100,000 residents. Government spokesmen, who called the $1 million facility a total loss, said the plant would be rebuilt in a nonpopulated area.

See STATISTICS OF THE WORLD   J.H.B.

MICHIGAN. *See* STATISTICS OF THE WORLD.

MICRONESIA. *See* STATISTICS OF THE WORLD.

Middle East

Tensions remained high in the Middle East in 1984. In Lebanon, a new government of national unity could not mask deep conflicts among sectarian factions. In Israel, an inconclusive election produced a national government that faced serious challenges. The war between Iran and Iraq dragged on.

Lebanon continued to dominate events in the Middle East during 1984. Repercussions of the Lebanese civil war were felt in the U.S. presidential election and in the election for Israel's Knesset. Despite attempts at reconciliation, fighting between diverse factions within Lebanon continued. By the end of the year, both the United States and Israel had suffered major political setbacks as a result of the Lebanese situation; Syria had risen in influence through its backing for a new coalition government in the country. Western peacekeeping forces had withdrawn, and Israel was negotiating a withdrawal. Yasir Arafat's "moderate" wing of the Palestine Liberation Organization (PLO) sought to recover from the defeat it had sustained in Lebanon during 1983 at the hands of the Syrians and their Palestinian allies.

Multinational Force. International attempts at peacekeeping and mediation in Lebanon all but terminated with the retreat of the multinational force comprising U.S., French, Italian, and British units. Although President Ronald Reagan asserted in January that the United States could not withdraw its troops without calling into question Washington's commitment to "moderation and negotiation" in the Middle East, continued attacks by militant Lebanese Muslims on the American Marines stationed at the Beirut International Airport led to their withdrawal during February. The Marines were replaced by Lebanese Shiite militiamen and the Lebanese army. Soon after the U.S. troops were evacuated to American warships off the coast, the fleet was also withdrawn. On March 30, Reagan wrote to Congress that U.S. participation in the multinational force was ended even though "the United States has not abandoned Lebanon."

The U.S. withdrawal set the pace for evacuation of other members of the international force. After the Italians and British also left, France announced that it could not alone bear the responsibility of the international community toward Lebanon and completed its troop withdrawal by March 31.

The Israeli Occupation. Israel's continued occupation of the southern third of Lebanon and the continuing casualties, including more than 600 dead since the 1982 invasion, were the focus of attack by the Labor opposition during the campaign leading to the July Knesset election. Although Israel had withdrawn its forces from Beirut to the Awali River during 1983, attacks on its troops by Shiite zealots in the south increased. Some of those who had welcomed Israel's defeat of the PLO forces in southern Lebanon during 1982 turned against the Israeli occupation, often with guerrilla tactics. Israeli public opinion polls indicated a desire to end the occupation; even the governing Likud coalition early in the year was divided over continuing it.

Israel's position was further undermined by deterioration in relations with the formerly friendly regime of Lebanese President Amin Gemayel. Under increasing pressure from Syria and its Lebanese allies, Gemayel began to criticize the May 17, 1983, peace agreement with Israel, and on March 5, the Lebanese cabinet declared it void. Syria approved that decision, but the United States and Israel denounced it as a setback for peace in the region.

Following the election in Israel and formation of a new national unity government there in September, Lebanese-Israeli negotiations were begun on an Israeli withdrawal from Lebanon. Although Lebanon resisted direct peace ne-

250

gotiations at the diplomatic level, arrangements were made for talks between Israeli and Lebanese military officers under auspices of the United Nations Interim Force in Lebanon (Unifil). Syria approved the new meetings, although it refused to give guarantees, demanded by Israel, to prevent Palestinians from reentering the south or to refrain from sending Syrian troops into the zone. When the talks recessed in late December they appeared stalemated, with Lebanon resisting Israeli demands for UN forces and the Israeli-backed South Lebanon Army to have major security responsibilities along the border. The Party of God, a fundamentalist Shiite faction loyal to the Iranian leader, Ayatollah Ruhollah Khomeini, condemned the talks with Israel as a "sacrilege" and called for additional resistance to the occupation.

Lebanese in Conflict. Hopes for ending factional conflict within Lebanon rose and fell. During March, Lebanese leaders met in Lausanne, Switzerland, at a "reconciliation" conference intended to work out new power-sharing arrangements among the different religious sects. But the conference broke up within two weeks without any agreement, and fighting broke out again in Beirut. Within the capital, antigovernment Druze and Shiite militias had already seized west Beirut from the army during February. The Druze also strength-ened their positions in the Shouf mountains south of Beirut and gained control of parts of the coastal road from Beirut to the south.

By March the Druze and a Sunni Muslim militia were engaged in heavy combat for control of west Beirut. Druze and Shiite militias also fought for ascendency in the city. While the various Muslim forces fought each other, shooting continued across the Green Line separating Beirut into Maronite and non-Maronite sectors. Fighting also raged in Tripoli, Lebanon's second largest city, among Muslim factions and between pro- and anti-Syrian militias.

Extension of Syrian influence was evident in President Gemayel's appointment of Rashid Karami as prime minister in April. The new Lebanese national unity government, formed in still another effort to halt the civil war and devise new constitutional arrangements, included leaders of Syrian-allied factions that had been combating the government since Gemayel became president in 1982. New appointments included Walid Jumblatt, leader of the largely Druze Progressive Socialist Party, as minister of tourism and public works and his Shiite ally, Nabih Berri, leader of Amal, as minister for southern Lebanon. Berri insisted on the post because most of the area's Shiite Muslim majority are members of his political-ethnic constituency.

The new unity government was to develop

Shiite Muslim militiamen ride through the center of West Beirut in a captured armored personnel carrier during February battles for control of the city.

a scheme for reallocating political power among the various religious factions to reflect demographic changes in recent years. The Maronites, once the largest religious group, now ranked third; Shiites Muslims were first and Sunni Muslims second. Plans also called for restructuring the army, placing it under greater civilian control and giving Muslims a larger share in its management. To demonstrate Arab nationalist orientation, the new government closed all remaining Israeli offices in Beirut and issued sharp demands for evacuation of all Israeli troops, although it made no mention of a Syrian withdrawal.

In July the Karami government was able to reopen the Beirut airport and to end division of the city by the Green Line. The Lebanese army replaced the militias, which voluntarily

President Hosni Mubarak of Egypt (right) reviews troops at Amman's military airport with his host, King Hussein of Jordan (left). Mubarak's October visit was the first by an Egyptian head of state to an Arab country since Egypt made peace with Israel in 1979.

disarmed in most parts of the capital. Still, the government and army seemed unable to eliminate factional fighting in Beirut or to extend their writ much beyond the capital. In November, Syria and Lebanon agreed on a new deployment plan, and more Lebanese troops were moved into the capital. The following month, the Lebanese army assumed control of Tripoli from private militias and sought to end civil strife in that city. The proposed Lebanese constituent assembly, which was to have drawn up new governmental arrangements, seemed unable to make progress; it was hampered by continuing factional disagreements within the cabinet.

Israel's New Government. Breakup of the Likud multiparty coalition during March led to the July 23 election for Israel's 11th Knesset. The 1984 campaign was relatively quiet compared to the elections in 1981. Results of the balloting were a surprise because public opinion polls had predicted a much greater lead over Likud for the opposition Labor Alignment. The parties were separated by only three seats; Labor won 44 and Likud 41. Because no party won a majority (61 seats), and because neither Labor nor Likud alone could create a majority coalition, it was necessary to form a new Labor/Likud government. Seven other parties also participated in the coalition government, formed in September. Labor leader Shimon Peres became prime minister for 25 months; then he was to change places with Foreign Minister Yitzhak Shamir, the Likud leader. Twenty-six parties in all had run for the Knesset, but only 15 gained the minimum 1 percent required to obtain seats.

The most critical issue facing the new government, aside from Lebanon, was Israel's economic crisis. Late in the year it appeared that inflation for 1984 would reach 600 percent. (Most Israelis, however, were protected against inflation by a scheme of salary indexing which increased pay rates as prices rose. Interest rates rose to more than 20 percent a month by September. Foreign debt, which was the world's highest on a per capita basis, totaled $23 billion, although most of it was not owed to private banks but to the U.S. government.

The Peres government initiated austerity measures soon after taking office in September

A Saudi Arabian oil tanker, one of the casualties of the long-drawn-out war between Iraq and Iran, burns in the Persian Gulf after being struck by airborne Iraqi missiles.

making cuts in the national budget, in subsidies for basic food items and in social services, and imposing levies and fees on services such as education that had been free or heavily subsidized. By November the government made a package deal with the country's powerful trade union federation, the Histadrut, and with leading industrialists to freeze wages and prices for three months. The deal also included agreement by the unions to waive much of the benefit derived from indexing, so that real wages would decline.

Shortly after becoming prime minister, Peres visited Washington, D.C., to discuss increases in the $2.6 billion in US economic and military aid promised for the 1985 fiscal year. However, no specific commitments for additional assistance were made. The U.S. Congress did approve negotiations for creation of free trade zone to facilitate the sale of Israeli products in the American market.

Elections and Diplomacy in Egypt. Egypt held elections for its parliament in May, the first free elections since the 1952 Egyptian revolution. President Hosni Mubarak's National Democratic Party won 391 of the 448 elected seats; the opposition center-right New Wafd party took the remaining 57. In addition, the president appointed ten more members, making a total of 458. The other opposition parties fell short of the 8 percent of the popular vote required for representation.

During 1984, Egypt's isolation brought about by the 1979 peace treaty with Israel was diminished. In January the 45-member Islamic Conference voted to readmit Egypt. In September, Jordan announced it was resuming diplomatic relations with Egypt, broken since 1979. Of 17 Arab nations that had severed ties with Egypt in 1979, Jordan was the first to reverse this step. Subsequently, Mubarak visited Jordan, and Jordan's King Hussein visited Egypt, where both leaders called on the PLO to accept a peace settlement based on Palestinian "self-determination" and a return of occupied Arab lands.

The Gulf War. The stalemate in the war between Iraq and Iran continued as the war entered its fifth year. A major attack by Iran, anticipated during the summer, failed to materialize, although Iran did succeed in penetrating Iraqi territory. Fighting extended into the Persian Gulf, as Iraq intensified air attacks on oil tankers entering or leaving Iran's southern ports. Iran accused Iraq of using chemical warfare early in the year, an issue that led the United States to enforce stricter regulations on sales of chemical compounds to both countries. On the political level, the war continued to divide the Arab world between Syria and Libya, backing Iran, and Jordan, Saudi Arabia, and Egypt, all of whom gave military and economic assistance to Iraq. Although proclaiming neutrality in the war, both the super-

253

powers assisted Iraq, the United States with a loan guarantee for an oil pipeline between Iraq and Jordan, the Soviet Union with increased military supplies. The United States also acted to resume relations with Iraq.

Hijacking Drama in Tehran. A bloody hijacking riveted world attention on the Middle East late in 1984. On December 4, four Arab-speaking men seized control of a Kuwaiti jetliner flying from Kuwait to Pakistan with 161 people aboard and forced the pilot to land in Tehran. The gunmen demanded the release of 17 convicted terrorists held in Kuwait and threatened to blow up the plane. Kuwait rejected the demand. Two American men, both employed by the U.S. Agency for International Development, were shot to death by the hijackers, and two others were tortured and abused. All but nine of the hostages had been released by December 9 when Iranian security forces gained entrance to the plane, allegedly disguised as a doctor and a cleanup crew, and captured the gunmen. The U.S. government charged that Iran had encouraged the hijackers, and some officials believed there was collusion. The Iranian government refused U.S. and Kuwaiti demands for extradition of the hijackers but said it would put them on trial in Iran.

See MILTARY AND NAVAL AFFAIRS; PALESTINE LIBERATION ORGANIZATION; and articles on individual countries mentioned and other Middle Eastern countries.   D.P.

MILITARY AND NAVAL AFFAIRS. The Middle East and Central America continued to be racked by armed conflict in 1984. Local governments and militias—with direct and indirect help from the superpowers—battled in half a dozen countries in the two regions. The warfare took a toll of civilian targets as well, as a truck bomb ripped into the U.S. embassy annex near Beirut and mines and air attacks damaged civilian vessels on the high seas. The United States and Soviet Union held no nuclear arms control talks during 1984, and both powers continued military buildups.

Lebanon. Local militias allied with Syria and Iran helped drive U.S. and European peacekeeping forces out of Lebanon early in the year. By year-end, Israel also was negotiating a withdrawal of its troops, having suffered large numbers of casualties there.

The U.S. military position in Lebanon had continued to deteriorate early in the year, despite White House efforts to carry on in the wake of the October 23, 1983, terrorist truck-bombing that killed 241 U.S. servicemen, mostly Marines, near Beirut. The 1,400-member U.S. Marine force repeatedly came under fire from the country's warring militias. In return, from mid-December 1983 through January 1984, the U.S. battleship *New Jersey* fired from time to time on Syrian positions east of Beirut. But, despite the awesome size of the ship's 16-inch guns and two-ton shells, the militia forces

A hijacker, one of four who seized a Kuwaiti jetliner, negotiates with an Iranian official at the Tehran airport. The plane was seized December 4, en route to Pakistan; two American passengers were killed by the hijackers before Iranian security forces freed the remaining passengers.

French troops begin a pull-out from Chad, following an agreement between Libya and France that called for the simultaneous withdrawal of both countries' forces. In violation of its pledge, however, Libya reportedly continued to maintain a sizable military contingent in the central African nation.

seemed unimpaired. In the United States, meanwhile, bipartisan support for the Marine mission in Lebanon (part of a multinational Western peacekeeping force) was unraveling, as fears of further terrorist attacks mounted. To prevent similar suicide bombings in the Washington area, huge concrete barriers were erected at some entrances to the White House, the Pentagon, and the State Department.

The administration at first resisted congressional demands for a U.S. withdrawal from Lebanon. In January the president informed the Marine Corps that it might have to keep troops in Lebanon for another year, until the Lebanese government could consolidate itself and the United States could train the Lebanese Army to take on and defeat the militias. In an interview published in the Wall Street Journal on February 3, President Reagan accused House Speaker Thomas P. O'Neill, Jr. (D, Mass.), of having advocated "surrender" by calling for withdrawal. The president said that a U.S. pullout would be "pretty disastrous" both for Lebanon and for the United States.

Just four days later, however, the president ordered the Marines in Beirut removed to ships offshore. The White House declined to call the move a withdrawal, labeling it instead a "redeployment." But the move signaled the end of the Western peacekeeping mission, as other nations prepared to pull out their contingents. In late March, France became the last member of the peacekeeping force to indicate was leaving Beirut. Syria, a Soviet ally, was

left as the most influential force in Lebanon. In the months that followed, Lebanon's pro-U.S. government was forced to accept Syrian terms for internal changes and to renounce its budding, U.S.–fostered ties with Israel.

On September 20, a new U.S. embassy annex outside Beirut was ripped apart by a truck bomb similar to the one used against the Marines in 1983. At least 14 people died, including two American servicemen. The U.S. ambassador, Reginald Bartholemew, was among the dozens of wounded. Security arrangements had not been completed at the time of the bombing, and no U.S. personnel were guarding the building, despite the fact that threats of an attack on a U.S. installation had just been made. U.S. intelligence agencies attributed the September suicide bombing to pro-Iranian Muslim terrorists; there was evidence that a militant group called Party of God, which might at times use the name Islamic Holy War, was responsible. (In an effort to prevent further such terrorist acts in the Mideast and elsewhere, the U.S. Congress approved an administration request to fund security improvements at U.S. embassies around the world.)

In Southern Lebanon, meanwhile, the Israeli troops who had freed the area from Palestinian guerrilla control in 1982 were sustaining steady losses in Shiite militia attacks. Late in the year, Israel, anxious to end the casualties and shed the huge cost of its occupation, was seeking to negotiate a withdrawal, even though Syria's occupying troops would remain in place. Israel

255

Sleek and deadly, the first production model of the Air Force's new B1-B bomber awaits its test flight at the Rockwell International Corporation's Palmdale, Calif., airfield. Ninety-nine more of the $200 million aircraft were scheduled to be built.

was, however, demanding that UN forces and the Israeli-backed South Lebanon Army have the major role in maintaining security along the border.

Persian Gulf and Red Sea. The war between Iran and Iraq took a turn that military analysts had long feared: the two nations initiated air attacks on oil tankers in the Persian Gulf. Iraq began the attacks in February, and Iran joined in soon after. Some tankers were sunk and many others damaged, and insurance rates for tankers in the gulf rose. But, contrary to expectations, the bombings did not significantly affect the flow of oil to the West.

The United States and allied Arab nations nevertheless acted to protect against possible damage to their oil trade. In May, President Reagan authorized the emergency sale to Saudi Arabia of hundreds of shoulder-fired Stinger antiaircraft missiles, to guard against air attacks from Iran across the gulf. On June 5, Iran attempted a raid on ships near Saudi Arabia, but two Iranian aircraft were shot down by American-built F-15 fighters flown by Saudis. Around the same time, the U.S. Navy began providing warships to escort tankers in the gulf which it had chartered to provide fuel for the American fleet in the nearby Arabian Sea.

On the ground, the Iran-Iraq war remained stalemated, as Iran continued to threaten, but not carry out, a massive drive deep into Iraq. Both nations appeared badly damaged by the war's human and economic toll, but mediation efforts were unsuccessful.

The Persian Gulf attacks spurred greater use

of the Red Sea, between Egypt and Saudi Arabia, for shipments of oil and other cargoes. But in July and August a number of cargo ships were hit and damaged by mines in the Red Sea. The United States, Great Britain, France, and even the Soviet Union sent minesweeping forces to the Red Sea to remove the devices, but few were found. It was believed that the mines had been sown in one operation, for the purpose of disrupting Egyptian shipping. Iran applauded the mine explosions at first, then denied responsibility for them. Egyptian officials suspected Libya, especially after British minesweepers found an unusual mine off Egypt that had apparently been built in the Soviet Union, Libya's military benefactor.

Central America. U.S. military forces did not intervene directly in the civil wars in El Salvador and Nicaragua, but U.S. training, funding, and intelligence agents were heavily involved, as illustrated by various incidents during the year.

A U.S. Army helicopter pilot, part of a large U.S. training mission based in Honduras, was killed by gunfire, apparently from Nicaragua, after his helicopter was forced down in Honduras near the Nicaraguan border on January 11. In October, four employees of the Central Intelligence Agency were killed when their unarmed plane crashed during a surveillance mission over El Salvador.

In Nicaragua itself, U.S.–backed rebels fighting the leftist Sandinista government mined key harbors early in the year. The mines, which according to later reports were actually laid by Latin American commandos, damaged some foreign cargo ships, including a Soviet vessel. The United States initially said that those who did the mining had acted alone, and the Reagan administration informed the International Court of Justice that the United States would ignore any ruling it made in a Nicaraguan lawsuit charging the United States with responsibility for the mining. However, it was soon revealed that the rebel mining operation had been directed by U.S. intelligence agents aboard an offshore "mother ship" owned by the CIA. The revelation caused an uproar in Congress, which had not been informed of the CIA involvement. Congress subsequently passed nonbinding resolutions stating that the United States should refrain from directly participating in further mining operations in Nicaragua. Congress also failed to renew funding for the rebels after it ran out in the summer.

Despite restrictions on U.S. government aid to anti-Sandinista rebels, unofficial American assistance apparently was growing. The "contras" opposing the Nicaraguan regime reportedly raised money from individuals and corporations in the United States, and American mercenaries traveled to Nicaragua to join the rebels forces. On September 1, two mercenaries died in combat when their helicopter was shot down on the Nicaragua-Honduras border.

U.S. military aid for El Salvador fared much better in the U.S. Congress, especially after that country elected a moderate, José Napoleón Duarte, as president. Duarte, who had pledged to negotiate with leftist rebels and to halt the activity of right-wing "death squads," campaigned actively for U.S. support, and in August, Congress more than doubled the level of military aid to El Salvador.

Meanwhile, in November, the International Court of Justice, rebuffing the U.S. position on Nicaragua's case, ruled that it did have jurisdiction over the dispute and that Nicaragua deserved a hearing.

The Pentagon continued to stage huge military maneuvers in the Caribbean and off the shores of Central America that involved up to 30,000 U.S. troops at times. The war games were seen both as training for operations like the 1983 U.S. invasion of Grenada and as warnings to Cuba and Nicaragua. At the same time, however, the U.S. Army's School of the

Americas, a facility in Panama where the United States had trained Latin Americans since the 1940's, was closed at the request of Panama's government.

North Africa. The United States continued to assist pro-Western North African nations apparently threatened by attacks from Libya. In March, after the bombing of a Sudanese city, apparently by Libya, two U.S. Awacs planes were sent by request to Egypt, to deter Libyan leader Muammar al-Qaddafi from any further hostile actions. The planes were withdrawn the next month. In July, U.S. Navy warplanes flew missions off Libya over the Gulf of Sidra, which Libya continued to consider as within its territory.

France and Libya, which had taken opposite sides in Chad's civil war, agreed in September to simultaneously withdraw their forces from Chad, and France implemented its side of the agreement. However, intelligence reports indicated that Libya still retained a sizable force in support of antigovernment forces in that country.

Soviet Developments. In April the Soviet Navy held its most ambitious war games ever, attracting much U.S. and other Western interest. The maneuvers centered in the North Atlantic, where U.S. naval planners also focus much attention. But Soviet fleets elsewhere also participated, including a unit in the Caribbean.

In May, Moscow announced it had deployed additional missile-carrying submarines off American coasts, in retaliation for the U.S. deployment of new nuclear missiles in Europe during late 1983. Disaster struck the Soviet Navy during the same month, when a mysterious explosion at a naval arms depot near Murmansk was said by U.S. intelligence to have destroyed much of the missile inventory of the powerful northern fleet, in addition to causing at least 200 deaths.

The Soviet Union was also embarrassed by several incidents at sea involving its submarines. In the most notable incident, a Soviet nuclear submarine tried to surface beneath a U.S. aircraft carrier it had been shadowing near Japan. The collision did minor damage to the carrier and severe damage to the submarine.

Moscow continued its long-running nuclear

weapons buildup, according to U.S. intelligence estimates. In June the Pentagon said that, for the first time, the Soviet Union had surpassed the United States in number of nuclear warheads, with 36,000 warheads in all. The Soviets had already reportedly attained the lead in number and size of missiles. And in August, the Soviet Union announced that it had successfully tested long-range, ground-launched cruise missiles, a response to U.S. deployment of similar weapons.

Soviet troops, now numbering up to 150,000, remained bogged down in mountainous Afghanistan, five years after the Red Army had swept into the primitive nation to shore up a Marxist government there. The Soviets and their local allies continued to control the main cities, but Muslim guerrillas, supplied from camps in Pakistan, still were able to hold their ground in mountain areas. Using helicopter gunships, the Soviets scored victories over the rebels but failed to snuff out their resistance.

Arms Control. U.S.–Soviet talks on the control of nuclear arms remained suspended during 1984. In late 1983, following the deployment in Western Europe of U.S. cruise and Pershing II missiles, the Soviet Union had walked out of the two principal negotiations, the strategic arms reduction talks (START) and the intermediate nuclear force (INF) talks. The only military-related agreement reached between the United States and the Soviet Union during Reagan's entire first term was a relatively minor measure, signed in July 1984, to make technical improvements in the Washington-Moscow communications "hot line."

During the same month, following U.S. announcements of space weapons tests, Moscow proposed arms control talks on limiting or banning space-based weapons, to be held in September. Some experts suspected the proposal was a ploy to stop the United States from catching up to or surpassing the Soviets in space weaponry. But the White House, under fire in an election year for lack of progress in arms control, immediately accepted. The talks were not held, however, because Moscow and Washington, in a series of angry public statements, disagreed on an agenda. The United States generally wanted to include missiles and the other arms that had been covered by the

talks Moscow had quit in 1983, but the Soviets refused.

By year's end, however, the two powers appeared to be moving toward an all-encompassing "umbrella" negotiation that would cover nuclear, conventional, and space weapons. Reagan met with Soviet Foreign Minister Andrei Gromyko in September to discuss resuming talks. After Reagan's reelection, Moscow indicated a willingness in principle for umbrella talks, and Gromyko agreed to meet with Secretary of State George Shultz in January 1985 to pursue plans for negotiations.

U. S. Developments. The United States tested its first antisatellite missile in late January, bringing it closer to matching the long-standing Soviet capability for destroying enemy reconnaissance and communication satellites. Another such test was announced in November. And, in a dramatic demonstration on June 11, a dummy ballistic missile warhead was destroyed in space by a new U.S. experimental weapon. The Pentagon hailed it as proof of the potential effectiveness of the "star wars" space-based antimissile defense proposed by Reagan in 1983.

All three U.S. military services fielded new combat equipment of many types, as a $1.6 trillion U.S. arms buildup began to bear fruit. Especially notable was the installation, in June, of the first long-range cruise missiles on U.S. nuclear attack submarines, the smaller sister ships of the giant Trident missile submarines. The new cruise missiles give these swift and stealthy craft the ability for the first time to attack the Soviet land mass.

In September, Rockwell International Corporation rolled out the first production model of the new version of the B-1 bomber, the nuclear-armed aircraft canceled by President Jimmy Carter and resurrected by Reagan. Plans called for building 100 of the B-1B bombers at a cost of about $200 million each. But the program received a setback a few days before the rollout ceremony, when an older B-1 prototype crashed during flight tests.

Defense Budget. President Reagan in February proposed a huge 18 percent boost in Defense Department budget authority for the 1985 fiscal year beginning October 1. He requested $313 billion in spending authority for the military,

13 percent increase after adjusting for inflation, and more than double the spending authority received by the Pentagon in 1980, the year he was elected.

But Congress, facing annual budget deficits of around $200 billion, reacted as it had in 1983, forcing the White House to scale back its request and winding up by approving less than $300 billion in spending authority. The final appropriation for the Pentagon, contained in a catchall "continuing resolution" bill covering most of the government, was still lower, providing for a 5 percent inflation-adjusted increase over 1983.

Congress also cut the president's request for additional MX missiles. He had asked for 40 more missiles for fiscal year 1985, but Congress approved only 15. It later froze funds even for these 15, pending further votes for authorization and appropriation in 1985. However, 21 missiles funded in 1983 were unaffected.

Pentagon Scandals. Revelations of overpricing and poor quality of weapons continued, despite a flurry of new regulations issued by Defense Secretary Caspar Weinberger in an effort to reform buying practices. National Semiconductor Corporation pleaded guilty to improperly testing computer microchips for the military and paid a penalty of $1.75 million. Texas

Instruments and Signetics corporations were also criticized for their microchips.

Charging defective workmanship, the military temporarily suspended payments to Hughes Aircraft Company for several important types of conventional combat missiles it supplied. The firm's shipments of major radar systems for the Air Force and Navy also were suspended because of poor quality control. In November, however, partial payment to Hughes recommenced when the Air Force concluded that the company was making progress in correcting missile defects. Ford Motor Company's Divad air defense gun, for which the Army planned to pay billions, performed poorly in tests, and funding for it was cancelled. The Navy's new, costly F-18 fighter, built by the McDonnell Douglas and Northrop corporations, developed cracks in its tail.

A grand jury investigating the General Dynamics Corporation received information from a former corporation vice-president that General Dynamics had defrauded the government of hundreds of millions of dollars in false claims for cost overruns on a nuclear attack submarine. Retired Admiral Hyman Rickover admitted that he had accepted gifts worth thousands of dollars from the company while head of the Navy's nuclear submarine program.

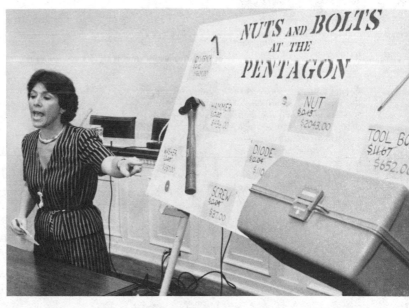

A $2,043 nut (store price 13¢) is among the items pointed out by Representative Barbara Boxer (D, Calif.) during a press conference that dramatized wasteful purchasing policies at the Pentagon. Boxer also called attention to a $3 washer for which the government paid $387, and the $652 price tag on a toolbox that cost $11.67 at a hardware store.

The Pentagon conceded that it was still overpaying for spare parts and that many unused spares, still new in boxes, were being thrown out. Congress considered measures to cut weapons costs and improve quality. One measure to win passage was a provision in the defense authorization bill requiring that spare parts be bought competitively and directly from manufacturers.

Military Readiness. In March, the Washington *Post* obtained an internal Pentagon report saying that, over three years, the number of combat-ready Army units had slipped 25 percent and the number of combat-ready Air Force units 15 percent; the readiness of naval air squadrons also was reported to have dropped. In July, the New York *Times* disclosed that an 18-month House committee study had found that none of the three services could sustain themselves in conventional combat with the Soviet Union for more than a brief period.

The Reagan administration called the leaks politically motivated and timed to embarrass the president during an election year. The White House said the internal Pentagon report had been misinterpreted and overblown by the press, and Defense Secretary Caspar Weinberger called the congressional study erroneous and "dangerously wrong." Democrats, recalling that Reagan had used similar leaks during his 1980 campaign against Carter, charged that the huge Reagan defense buildup was misdi-

New attention is being paid to the veterans of America's most unpopular war. Above, the Joint Services Honor Guard carries the casket of the Vietnam war's unknown serviceman down the steps of the Capitol en route to the Arlington National Cemetery. At right, an ex-soldier inspects the new section of the Vietnam veterans' memorial unveiled in Washington, D.C., this year.

rected, focusing on big-ticket nuclear and conventional weapons instead of on such mundane items as spare parts and ammunition, which are vital to combat readiness.

Vietnam Remembered. In May, nine years after the Vietnam war ended, an unknown U.S. soldier from that conflict was interred at Arlington National Cemetery with unknown servicemen from World War I, World War II, and the Korean war. President Reagan awarded the soldier a posthumous Congressional Medal of Honor. Later in the year, on Veterans Day, Reagan formally accepted the Vietnam veterans' memorial in Washington, D.C. The first part of the monument—two black granite walls engraved with the names of the dead and missing—had been completed in 1982. The second part, a statue of three servicemen, was unveiled in 1984.

See NORTH ATLANTIC TREATY ORGANIZATION and articles on individual countries mentioned
W.S.M.

MINERAL AND METAL INDUSTRY. See ENERGY; LABOR UNIONS; MANUFACTURING INDUSTRIES; PETROLEUM AND NATURAL GAS.

MINNESOTA. See STATISTICS OF THE WORLD.

MISSISSIPPI. See STATISTICS OF THE WORLD.

MISSOURI. See STATISTICS OF THE WORLD.

MONACO. See STATISTICS OF THE WORLD.

MONGOLIAN PEOPLE'S REPUBLIC. See STATISTICS OF THE WORLD.

MONTANA. See STATISTICS OF THE WORLD.

MOROCCO. In the ninth year of its struggle with Polisario Front guerrillas over the Western Sahara, the former Spanish colony which it had annexed, Morocco in 1984 consolidated its control over important areas in the disputed territory. Army engineer units constructed two new sections of a defensive sand-and-dirt wall that protects most of the Western Sahara's major population centers as well as valuable phosphate deposits at Bukraa. The defenses proved successful during the year. A major attack was launched by Polisario against the Bukraa sector, in late December 1983, but it was repulsed the following month.

On November 12, however, at the opening of a summit meeting of the Organization of African Unity in Ethiopia, Polisario's government-in-exile, the Saharan Arab Democratic Republic, scored a diplomatic victory, when it was seated as the organization's 51st member. Morocco reacted by withdrawing from the OAU. Zaire supported Morocco by suspending its own membership.

On August 13, Morocco's moderate government disturbed its Western allies by signing a unity agreement with the radical, anti-Western regime of Muammar al-Qaddafi of Libya. The agreement established an "Arab–African Union" in which each state retained its sovereignty; it was to be administered by a permanent secretariat headed, for alternating two-year periods, by each national leader. The treaty also called for common approaches in foreign policy and close cooperation in economic, social, and political matters. The agreement was overwhelmingly endorsed by Moroccan voters in an August 31 referendum. To allay U.S. concern, King Hassan dispatched his top adviser to meet with U.S. officials in Washington in early September.

In the first parliamentary elections since 1977, 67 percent of Morocco's 7.4 million registered voters cast ballots for 199 members of the Chamber of Deputies. (The remaining members are chosen by an electoral college.) The largest vote-getter of the nine political parties, with 25 percent of the vote and 55 seats, was the progovernment Constitutional Union.

The nation was rocked in January by an outbreak of urban unrest. When army and security forces moved in to quell the disturbances, bloody clashes ensued, leaving as many as 200 people dead. The violence ended when King Hassan cancelled recently imposed price increases on bread, sugar, and cooking oil.

See STATISTICS OF THE WORLD. J.D.

MOTION PICTURES. A change in the system for rating motion pictures was approved in 1984. The hyperkinetic influence of MTV (Music Television) was apparent on the big screen, and many other films aimed at the youth market continued to unreel.

Ratings Change. For years there had been pressure to alter the system of rating movies, so as to better serve the needs of parents in guiding children's movie selections. But the Motion Picture Association of America (MPAA), the trade association consisting of nine major movie companies, had resisted tampering with

Darryl Hannah charmed audiences in director Ron Howard's Splash, *an unexpectedly successful love story about a man and a mermaid.*

what it considered an effective operation by its Classification and Ratings Administration. A groundswell of criticism against assigning a PG (parental guidance suggested) to two particularly violent summer blockbusters, *Indiana Jones and the Temple of Doom* and *Gremlins,* finally tipped the balance. The new category of PG-13 was adopted, signifying to parents that special care was advised before permitting children under 13 to see a movie so labeled.

The new rating created an intermediate cat- egory between a plain PG and R (no one under 17 admitted unless accompanied by a parent or guardian). These three were now the major categories, since G (general audience) was rarely used anymore, while X, the most stringent rating (no one under 17 allowed), was used only occasionally when R was thought to be not strict enough. The rating change recognized that some films might be suitable for teenagers but not for younger children. The new rating posed the likelihood that many films

A Soldier's Story *was transplanted to the screen from a Pulitzer Prize–winning play by Charles Fuller, staged in 1981 by the Negro Ensemble Company. A number of NEC cast members, including Larry Riley (playing the guitar), appeared in the film, which starred Howard E. Rollins, Jr., and Adolph Caesar.*

that would previously have been tagged R would now be labeled PG-13—a possibility that drew criticism from religious groups and others.

Jack Valenti, president of the MPAA, made certain that the organization's revised ratings were affixed to videocassettes of movies. To forestall the passage of laws regulating the sale of cassettes, the MPAA made an agreement with the major cassette distributors to include on the package the rating used when the film played in theaters. The pact is nonenforceable, but the effect is to offer advice to parents on the suitability for children of what is brought into the home.

New Influence. The immense popularity of music videos among the MTV (Music Television) generation was being reflected in cinema, as producers and directors rushed to cash in on the trend. Many movies that showed strength at the box office were designed in the music video mold. *Flashdance*, a big hit in the summer of 1983, was a pacesetter; others in its wake included *Footloose*, *Electric Dreams*, and the phenomenally successful *Purple Rain*, starring the charismatic rock musician Prince. The flashy use of fast editing in these films,

coupled with hectic song and dance movement, catered to the diminished attention spans of many viewers.

Audience Division. The proliferation of youth-oriented films in the summer left grownups with a diminished range of choice. Summer months are traditionally the time when companies release films they judge most likely to attract the young; the fact that these films were successful in 1984 led the theaters to hold them for long runs. Among the biggest hits were *Ghostbusters*, *Indiana Jones and the Temple of Doom*, *Gremlins*, *The Karate Kid*, *Purple Rain*, *Bachelor Party*, and *Revenge of the Nerds*.

Splash, a surprise hit earlier in the year, directed by Ron Howard, had a somewhat broader appeal, with its lighthearted fantasy of love between man and mermaid.

By fall, the releases included films of more mature bent. Among them were numerous dramas dealing with the economic struggles of Americans, past and present. There was also an accent on films depicting life in different regions of the country. Robert Benton (*Kramer vs. Kramer*) wrote and directed *Places in the Heart*, set in his hometown of Waxahachie, Texas, during the Great Depression and starring

A standout among several American regional films, Places in the Heart *starred* Sally Field *as the widowed mother of Yankton Hatten (left) and Gennie James.*

Sally Field in a stirring performance as a widow battling to retain her farm. *Country*, teaming Jessica Lange and Sam Shepard, depicted hard times suffered by today's farmers in the Midwest. In *The River*, set in Tennessee, Sissy Spacek and Mel Gibson played farmers also subjected to hard times.

West German director Wim Wenders found material in the American Southwest for *Paris, Texas*, the tale of a man's search for his wife, who deserted him, and his son's love in the midst of an odd assortment of characters; the movie won the top award at the Cannes Film Festival. Conflict between real estate developers and environmentalists in Florida was the subject of Victor Nuñez's *A Flash of Green*, which stars Ed Harris.

Quality Movies. In addition to some of those mentioned above, 1984 yielded many films of exceptional quality, including Norman Jewison's *A Soldier's Story*, based on Charles Fuller's Pulitzer Prize–winning play about the solution and implications of the mysterious murder of a black sergeant at a Southern army base during World War II; John Huston's *Under the Volcano*, adapted from Malcolm Lowry's cult classic and starring Albert Finney; and James Ivory's *The Bostonians*, from the Henry James novel, with Vanessa Redgrave and Christopher Reeve. Other fine films included Paul Mazursky's *Moscow on the Hudson*, starring Robin Williams as a Russian saxophone player who defects in Bloomingdale's department store while visiting New York City; Richard Benjamin's bittersweet *Racing With the Moon*, a look at growing up during World War II; Gregory Nava's *El Norte*, a moving film about a refugee brother and sister from Guatemala trying to make a new life in Los Angeles; John Cassavetes's demanding *Love Streams*, an examination of relationships, seen in the emotional clash of a brother and sister played by Cassavetes and his wife, Gena Rowlands; and Barry Levinson's screen adaptation of Bernard Malamud's novel *The Natural*, starring Robert Redford as an aging baseball hero. *Amadeus*, Milos Forman's adoptation of Peter Shaffer's hit play, won plaudits from many critics.

Director John Sayles, lauded for his earlier *The Return of the Secaucus Seven* and other low-budget films, was back with one of the year's offbeat treats, *The Brother From Another Planet*, in which a black visitor from space lands in New York City. An impressive directorial debut was made by Marisa Silver, whose *Old Enough* contemplated the relationship between two very different New York City teenagers. *This Is Spinal Tap*, directed by Rob Reiner, was an inventive documentary-style satire of the rock-and-roll scene. Woody Allen's comedy *Broadway Danny Rose*, an affectionate look at characters on the fringe of show business, featured Mia Farrow as Tina, the tough woman Allen's Danny Rose falls for.

Foreign Films. Daniel Petrie's memories of growing up in Nova Scotia are part of his movie, *Bay Boy*, which was filmed there and introduced Kiefer Sutherland, the son of actor Donald Sutherland, as costar with Liv Ullman. *The Gods Must Be Crazy*, made in Botswana by Jamie Uys, commented hilariously on the perils of civilization. The potential of Australian cinema was indicated anew by *Careful, He Might Hear You*, an engrossing story seen largely from the viewpoint of an orphaned boy whose aunts battle for his custody. *Sugar Cane Alley*, in French with English subtitles, proved to be a striking drama about life in Martinique among sugarcane workers in 1931.

Ingmar Bergman continued to make films for television that also play in theaters. *After the Rehearsal*, his latest tour de force, dealt with the musings of a theater director about his work and life. Federico Fellini's *And the Ship Sails On* was a meditation on society as symbolized by an assortment of passengers sailing on a mission to scatter the ashes of a great opera diva. Lina Wertmuller's *A Joke of Destiny* spoofed political chaos in Italy and, by inference, in the world at large. French director Diane Kurys's *Entre Nous* celebrated the friendship of two married women. Bertrand Tavernier's *A Sunday in the Country*, a gentle reflection on art, family ties, and aging, was reminiscent of Jean Renoir's work and won Tavernier the best director award at Cannes. *The Basileus Quartet*, a well-reviewed film directed by Fabio Carpi, recounted what happens to the surviving members of a quartet after a handsome and unruly young musician replaces the violinist who died.

Japanese film, long in the doldrums as a

Too violent, in the opinion of many critics, for their PG ratings, Indiana Jones and the Temple of Doom (right), starring Harrison Ford (far right), and Gremlins (below), starring Zach Galligan, led to the establishment of a new rating: PG-13, which signaled parents of under-13's to think carefully before sending susceptible children to such films.

result of television and cassettes, has been getting a lift from a generation of new directors. The infusion was illustrated by *The Family Game,* in which writer-director Yoshimitsu Morita satirized middle-class life. A more traditional story came from veteran director Shohei Imamura, whose *The Ballad of Narayama* pictured struggles and rituals among peasants of a mountain village in Japan 100 years ago.

Late Entries. Among eagerly awaited films released toward the end of the year were David Lean's version of E. M. Forster's *A Passage to India; Falling In Love,* pairing Robert De Niro and Meryl Streep; and the elaborate science fiction saga *Dune,* directed by David Lynch with a $40 million budget, a project based on the 1965 novel by Frank Herbert. *A Passage to India,* starring Victor Banerjee, Judy Davis, and Peggy Ashcroft, easily made critics' ten-best lists for the year. Also well received was *The Killing Fields,* the harrowing and poignant true story of the friendship between a newspaper reporter and his Cambodian assistant during a barbaric period in Cambodian history.

On the Lighter Side. Some legendary characters refuse to die. Add to the long list of Tarzan movies *Greystoke: The Legend of Tarzan, Lord of the Apes,* a lavish, sometimes somber version of the adventures of Tarzan, played this time by Christopher Lambert, with the late Sir Ralph Richardson as Tarzan's crusty grandfather. *Sheena, Queen of the Jungle* featured Tanya Roberts as the blond jungle queen in an insipid, tongue-in-cheek adventure. The most ridiculed film of the year was *Bolero,* starring Bo Derek and containing soft core sex scenes that were more ludicrous than erotic. One of the most successful was *Beverly Hills Cop,* starring Eddie Murphy, which opened in early December and dominated the holiday season at box offices all over the United States. A likable offering late in the year was *The Flamingo Kid*, a Garry Marshall film starring Matt Dillon.

Oscars. *Terms of Endearment,* garnered the Oscar for best picture, and yielded other awards to James L. Brooks as best director and for best screeplay adaptation, Shirley MacLaine as best actress, and Jack Nicholson as best supporting actor. Robert Duvall won as best actor for *Tender Mercies,* and the best original screenplay award went to Horton Foote, also for *Tender Mercies.* Linda Hunt took the best supporting actress award for playing a male dwarf in *The Year of Living Dangerously.* The best foreign-language film was judged to be Ingmar Bergman's *Fanny and Alexander.* (*See also* PEOPLE IN THE NEWS: Shirley MacLaine.)

Behind the Scenes. On the business side, the biggest stir in 1984 occurred with the resignation of Barry Diller, chairman and chief executive officer of Paramount Pictures Corporation, and his move to the same positions at 20th Century-Fox Film Corporation on October 1. Ever-insecure Hollywood executives braced for a round of musical chairs. Diller's appointment to Fox raised expectations that he could strengthen the company, beset with a string of unsuccessful movies.

Hollywood had come to look upon the feature-film videocassette trade as a major source of revenue. But questions remained about how the creative forces (directors, writers, actors) could be guaranteed a share in the profits and how the movie companies could avoid losses through piracy and through the use of home recording equipment to tape movies—whether from borrowed cassettes or from showings of the films on television. The film industry was dealt a blow when, in a long-awaited ruling, the Supreme Court decided that home videotaping of films shown on television does not violate copyright laws if the copies are for personal use only. The ruling meant that film companies would not be entitled to royalty payments from manufacturers and users of the videotape machines.   W.W.

MOZAMBIQUE. On March 16, 1984, after months of negotiations, Mozambique concluded a "nonaggression and good neighborliness" pact with South Africa. Under the terms of the Nkomati accord, as it was called, each state undertook to "forbid and prevent" in its territory "the organization of irregular forces or armed bands, including mercenaries," that intend to attack the other. Mozambique's President Samora Machel hoped the accord would provide relief from attacks of the South African–backed Mozambique National Resistance (MNR), a guerrilla movement opposed to Mozambique's Marxist regime. South Africa, for its part, was suffering a severe recession and hoped to win a respite from the mounting costs of the guerrilla campaign of the African National Congress (ANC), a black nationalist organization which, according to South Africa, had been using Mozambique as a base.

As a result of the accord, South Africa no longer retaliated against Mozambique for guerrilla attacks in South Africa by the ANC; however, MNR attacks in Mozambique persisted. In October, it was announced that Mozambique and the MNR had agreed in principle to pursue negotiations leading to a genuine cease-fire, but talks proved inconclusive.

Mozambique improved relations with Western countries, especially the United States, which had played a behind-the-scenes role in facilitating negotiations that led to the Nkomati accord. At the same time, Mozambique maintained close ties with the Soviet Union and other Communist countries.

Economically, war and drought continued to exact a heavy toll, with as many as 100,000–150,000 Mozambicans fleeing to neighboring Zimbabwe in search of food. As food shortages worsened during the year, international food aid was lagging, partly because famine in Ethiopia was diverting attention away from Mozambique. UN relief officials predicted that, with food reseves low, a serious famine was developing. On the brighter side, negotiations for a rescheduling of Mozambique's estimated $1.4 billion debt to Western creditors were successfully concluded in October. The month before, the country joined the World Bank and the International Monetary Fund.

See STATISTICS OF THE WORLD.   W.M.

MUSIC. The following were among developments of interest in popular and classical music during 1984:

POPULAR MUSIC

The world of American popular music was

dominated in 1984 by Michael Jackson's phenomenal conquest of the charts and his national tour with his brothers (see biography in PEOPLE IN THE NEWS) and by the funk-rock star Prince, who gave him a run for his money on the movie screens with his semiautobiographical *Purple Rain*. Rock 'n' roll continued to exploit video for all it was worth. Jazz lost Count Basie, one of its brightest stars (see OBITUARIES), but a new generation of traditionalists joined with a mellowed avant–garde to reassert basic values.

Rock. Outlets for videos kept increasing; both Ted Turner and the MTV network announced additional all-music-video channels for cable television, and numerous other network and cable organizations were producing their own video-based shows. Ironically, these developments resulted in freezing out innovative bands that had started the video trend in the first place. MTV no longer had to take any videos it could get but could pick and choose, and even change its own rules. Frank Sinatra—certainly not a rock singer—made it onto MTV, despite the network's past insistence, when turning down black artists' videos, that it broadcast only rock 'n' roll.

The assertion that black people do not play rock 'n' roll was again disproved when Prince (Prince Rogers Nelson), a part-black singer and songwriter who fronts a multiracial, multisexual band called the Revolution, debuted his film *Purple Rain*. This film is a quasiautobiographical look at a Minneapolis-based musician whose band's music is too difficult for some of his audience to handle. The negligible plot did not prevent it from becoming one of the year's top grossers, probably because of stunning concert sequences featuring Prince, Morris Day and the Time, Dez Dickerson, and Apollonia Kotero and Apollonia 6, all of whom were Prince's associates from early days in Minneapolis. Called by some a $7 million rock video, it destroyed all barriers between rock and funk on the charts and swept any racially based arguments aside. Indeed, movies that were primarily strings of rock videos definitely marked a trend. The immensely successful *Footloose* soundtrack spawned a half dozen hit singles.

Broadway and pop, meanwhile, dipped cau-

The rock music phenomenon known as Prince made a blockbuster movie called Purple Rain; a smash hit, it destroyed once and for all the myth that rock 'n' roll has only white fans.

tious toes in the video waters, the former with "Rum Tum Tugger," a number from Andrew Lloyd Weber's musical *Cats* reorchestrated for a five-piece rock band. Barbra Streisand fans were treated to the star's first video ever—"Left in the Dark," from her latest album, *Emotion*.

Offscreen, the year's biggest rock news was heavy metal, a genre characterized by ear-splitting volume, ponderous rhythms, hyperkinetic guitar work, screaming vocals, and, usually, an overlay of pseudosatanism. Critics and radio station programmers alike were dismayed, but like punk, heavy metal proved to be a very popular genre despite a lack of airplay and a generally disapproving press. Many of the bands (Accept, U.F.O., Scorpions) were German; others (Marillion, Black Sabbath, Dio) were British. Some of the most overtly satanic (Queensryche, Mötley Crüe,

Michael Jackson, arguably the most popular musician in the world, performs for adoring fans during his midsummer tour, one of the flashiest, most lucrative spectacles in rock music history.

Belting out his latest hit, "Dancing in the Dark," Bruce Springsteen makes a surprise appearance at a Lancaster, Pa., nightclub before embarking on his first world tour in three years.

Twisted Sister) were American. Since the market was flooded with albums by metal bands, and since metal's audience is fairly narrow—overwhelmingly white, teenaged, and male—each band had limited prospects.

In general, traditional rock of the nonmetal variety took a beating. A notable exception was Bruce Springsteen, who released his best album in some time, *Born in the U.S.A.,* had a hit single ("Dancing in the Dark") from the album, and launched another of his marathon world tours at summer's end.

British rock seemed to be at the end of its creative tether. Teen idols Duran Duran sold plenty of records, thanks to expensive videos, and synthesizer duo the Eurythmics also made quite an impression on U.S. rock fans, but both had fading stars back home. The one band Americans and Britons agreed upon was Culture Club, with its heavily made-up lead singer and media idol, Boy George. George's U.S. counterpart in outrageousness was Cyndi Lauper, a veteran rock 'n' roller who got new clothes and a new haircut, did an album's worth of fine songs, and exploited her image (a wrestling fan sporting thrift-shop dresses) for all it was worth, making some feminist statements along the way.

Probably the biggest success story in Britain was a homosexual disco act from Liverpool called Frankie Goes to Hollywood. After gaining notoriety when their first video and single, "Relax," was banned by the BBC for sexual overtones, they released an antiwar song, "Two Tribes," featuring the voice of an actor playing Ronald Reagan. Canny marketing led them to remix both songs several different ways, making it possible for the British fan to buy no fewer than 17 different versions of the two songs.

Soul. The Jacksons, formerly the "Jackson Five," decided to regroup for a last album and tour, since several of them (most notably Michael, whose hot *Thriller* album became the biggest-selling album in record history) had embarked on solo careers as performers or producers. The group album, *Victory,* was a mélange of styles and approaches; the tour that followed threatened to swamp the album in controversy. After a last-minute change in promoters—New England Patriots boss Chuck Sullivan took over in June—there was much dissatisfaction and frustration over ticket policy: a minimum of four tickets at $30 each had to be applied for, and orders were filled by lottery. The day before the tour opened in Kansas City, the Jacksons announced that they were returning to the traditional means of ticket sales, although the price remained the same. In Knoxville, Michael received death threats, but the show went on.

Middle America discovered break dancing. This form of street-corner dancing originated in New York City, where youths would put down a piece of cardboard for traction and engage in jerky motions that included spinning on the back and the head. The music that accompanied break dancing was usually the heavily electronic "hip-hop" style favored in big cities. New break-dancing movies included *Breakin'*, a quickie filmed in Los Angeles, and *Beat Street,* a high-dollar production done in New York, coproduced by Harry Belafonte and record producer Arthur Baker. Before long, instruction books, records, and videocassettes were everywhere, as were break dancers themselves.

The break-dancing fad served to introduce electronic percussion and sequenced synthesizer patterns to even the most mainstream black pop, as artists realized that this sound appealed to the young black audience they had lost to Michael Jackson, Prince, and the host of hip-hop artists. Probably the most extreme example was the collaboration of James Brown, with 30 years of soul hits behind him, and Afrika Bambaataa, one of hip-hop's most inventive producers, to do the single "Unity."

Country. Country music limped through 1984 in desultory fashion, still searching for an identity outside of mainstream pop music and still failing to find it. A symptom of this identity crisis could be seen in patriarch Willie Nelson's unlikely pairing with Spanish crooner Julio Iglesias to record a duet, "For All the Girls I've Loved." The record sold well but struck many people as being as apt a mixture as oil and water. There was also the duo act Moe (Bandy) and Joe (Stampley), who dressed like Boy George for a song called "Where's the Dress?"

To try to remedy the poor sales situation, country turned to video, with at least two cable stations now devoted to country music: the Nashville Network, a hodgepodge of game shows, talk shows, performances, and videos, and CMTV (no relation to MTV), which ran 24 hours of country videos. Neither network proved a raging success.

Oh Boy!

While social commentators tried to explain the wild enthusiasm among diverse audiences for androgynous pop singers, Boy George, lead singer of the British band Culture Club, continued to enrapture fans as he appeared in dyed and braided hair, painted eyebrows, heavy mascara and lipstick, and baggy clothes. George Alan O'Dowd, born in 1961 in a working class London suburb, decided early on that the way out of a mundane existence was to dress bizarrely and hang out at hip clubs. His smooth voice, middle-of-the-road music, and songwriting talent also helped propel him to stardom. The Culture Club's first single, "Do You Really Want to Hurt Me," was a 1982 hit in Britain and the United States; 1984 became a banner year, as the group won the Grammy Award for Best New Artist and then played to ecstatic audiences on sold-out tours of North America.

Boy George

Jazz. Jazz was quietly expanding its audience, with more people taking an interest in "serious," non–pop-oriented jazz. Such former avantgardists as Archie Shepp and the younger saxophonist-composer David Murray reminded listeners that their music did not exist in a traditionless vacuum, and the remarkable Marsalis family of New Orleans continued to win acclaim. Branford, the saxophonist and younger brother of Wynton, managed to expand the hard-bop tradition without recourse to the "free" language of the 1960's. Wynton, for his part, won two Grammies, one in the field of jazz and the other for his superb reading of trumpet concerti by Haydn, Hummel, and Leopold Mozart. Wynton also played a few dates with Sonny Rollins, and critics said the saxophone giant hadn't sounded so good in years.

Another Grammy winner was Herbie Hancock, although he won for a 1983 hip-hop instrumental, "Rockit" (also made into a video). Hancock continued to run the gamut from more pop-oriented commercial music to straight-ahead jazz.

Play It Again and Again, Sammy

Seated behind the keyboard with his half-finished manhattan, a dirty ashtray, and a jar for tips, Sammy Sands has become a familiar fixture to patrons of a restaurant-lounge in the Atlanta suburb of Tucker, Ga. Night after night, clad in a silver lamé jacket and open-necked shirt, he sings, plays, and winks at the audience, in routines featuring country music and supper club patter. ("You remember World War II," muses Sammy. "It was in all the newspapers.") Actually, Sammy is more of a fixture than you might think: he's an animated robot. The music and jokes are on tapes, and the sound comes from a speaker behind his molded fiberglass head. Warner Communications, Sammy's creator, operates a chain of family-type restaurants, featuring cartoon character robots like Bugs Bunny and Daffy Duck. Gadget Cafe in Tucker was the first to make use of "talent" geared to an adult crowd—though Sammy's detractors dismiss him as a glorified jukebox who can't really mix with his audience.

Although jazz hasn't matched rock's earnings power, two major record-industry moves relevant to jazz were announced. Orrin Keepnews, a longtime owner of the Riverside and Milestone labels, announced that he was leaving Fantasy Records, which distributes those labels, to form another all-jazz label, to be distributed by a major record company. And Bruce Lundvall, who as an executive at Elektra Records started the critically acclaimed Elektra/Musician label, left to join Capitol Records. He announced that he not only would bring the Musician roster with him but also, thanks to Capitol's ownership by Thorn EMI, would resurrect the long-dormant Blue Note label (which produced much of the classic jazz in the 1950's and 1960's), both for reissues and for contemporary talent. Lundvall made good on the Blue Note promise (first releases were slated for early 1985). E.W.

CLASSICAL MUSIC

The most visible focal point of serious music in the United States in 1984 was Los Angeles, where the Olympic Arts Festival took place (in conjunction with the XXIII Olympiad) from June 1 to August 12. The arts festival offered a generous display of music, highlighted by the first U.S. appearance of the Royal Opera of Covent Garden. The Royal Opera, breaking its long-held tradition of unveiling new productions only at home, presented a new *Turandot*—an electric, not very satisfying endeavor, in which Romanian producer Andrei Serban employed Kabuki actors and converted Ping, Pang, and Pong into a commedia dell'arte troupe. Also untraditional was August Everding's production of *Die Zauberflöte*, which dressed Sarastro and his court in the costumes of 18th-century gentlemen. The third presentation, Britten's *Peter Grimes*, fulfilled all expectations, with Jon Vickers overwhelmingly effective in one of his greatest roles. Sir Colin Davis conducted all 11 performances of the three operas.

The instrumental side of the Olympic Arts Festival received mixed responses, with the warmest clearly reserved for the most conservative fare. The contemporary series explored the marriage of high technology and acoustical instruments, with Morton Subotnick's *The Double Life of Amphibians*—a 70-minute "stage-

concert" for acoustical instruments, computer-generated sounds, three voices, and a dancer—emerging as the most substantial offering. Karlheinz Stockhausen was represented by his *Stern-klang,* designed for five ensembles scattered in a wooded setting on the northern fringes of the San Fernando Valley; listeners were invited to wander at will for the piece's three hours.

Opera. Elsewhere in the United States, musical life displayed its customary vigor. The Metropolitan Opera in New York City brought in the reigning Wagnerian soprano Hildegard Behrens to sing Isolde, an assignment she fulfilled with radiance of sound, clarity of enunciation, and a wide spectrum of emotional expression. The Met also presented its first-ever Handel opera, *Rinaldo,* with Marilyn Horne in the title role and bass Samuel Ramey as the Saracen general Argante. As the 1984–1985 season began, Placido Domingo tackled the heldentenor role of Lohengrin for the first time, displaying not only the requisite stamina but also lyricism and a legato singing too seldom heard in Wagner; as Ortrud, soprano Eva Marton was nothing less than thrilling.

The San Francisco Opera continued its Wagner *Ring* cycle with a powerful *Siegfried,* in which René Kollo sang the title role and Eva Marton was Brünnhilde; Edo de Waart con-

Audiences applauded the New York City Opera's *Carmen,* set in the Spanish Civil War; in the rousing scene above, mezzo-soprano Victoria Vergara, an anti-Franco Carmen, tempts her "fascist" admirers with oranges. The English National Opera's modernized production of Rigoletto, with Dennis O'Neill as the unfaithful Duke (below), was a hit with London audiences but met opposition from Italian-American groups in New York because of its setting—the Little Italy Mafioso world of the 1950's.

ducted. The performance was enhanced by the use of supertitles (simultaneous English translations projected over the proscenium arch).

The Santa Fe Opera, as is its custom, ventured off the beaten path, presenting the U.S. premiere of Hans Werner Henze's *We Come to the River*—a gigantic opus (three orchestras, 111 characters) seeking to depict the despotism of the ruling classes over the poor of the world. In the view of some critics, however, the work failed to make its characters seem real. Another composer having trouble convincing audiences was Leonard Bernstein, whose reworking of his *A Quiet Place* was given at Washington's Kennedy Center (presented as a sequel to *Trouble in Tahiti*); the new version still failed to arouse sympathy for a cast of characters whose sufferings were said to "repel rather than move."

Philip Glass, on the other hand, stirred widespread enthusiasm for his new opera *Akhnaten,* given its world premiere in Stuttgart in March. A so-called minimalist, Glass refined the use of the typical repeated chordal patterns in this genre to reveal a fine awareness of texture and timbre, creating a work of power and beauty. *Akhnaten* made its U.S. debut at the Houston Opera in October. Another Glass work, *Einstein on the Beach,* was presented at the Brooklyn Academy of Music.

The Boston Shakespeare Company, late in the 1983–1984 season, gave the first American performance of *The Lighthouse,* by Peter Maxwell Davies, an eerie story based on a true incident involving the disappearance of three lighthouse keepers off the coast of Scotland. Peter Sellars directed. Boston's Musica Viva ventured into space-age opera with *Icarus—A Sky Opera,* by Paul Earls. The production employed lasers, television, synthesizers, cosmic projectors, and a Day-Glo balloon, with, however, little personal impact.

The English National Opera enlivened the American scene with a successful summer tour. It included an imaginative but somewhat controversial *Rigoletto,* in which Jonathan Miller set the action in New York City's Mafia underworld during the 1950's.

Instrumental Music. John Harbison had his ballet *Ulysses' Bow* premiered by the Pittsburgh

Symphony under André Previn and his First Symphony unveiled by the Boston Symphony under Seiji Ozawa. To one critic, the former work was "voluptuous" and "sophisticated"; the latter, a paean to "simple, life-enhancing joy." Charles Wuorinen garnered praise for his Third Piano Concerto, a 12-tone work written for Garrick Ohlsson and played by him with the Albany Symphony. Gunther Schuller's new Saxophone Concerto, in its premiere by Kenneth Radnofsky and the Pittsburgh Symphony, was deemed a well-crafted piece respecting "a traditional classic style."

Ralph Shapey's Double Concerto for Violin and Cello, conducted by the composer with the Juilliard Symphony, was short on melodic invention but made an impact through its vitality. Donald Erb's *Prismatic Variations* prompted enthusiasm at its premiere in St. Louis by virtue of its use of some 80 young musicians stationed around the auditorium, who joined in with sounds produced from soda bottles, harmonicas, telephone bells, and the like.

William Bolcom's three-hour song cycle based on texts by William Blake, *Songs of Innocence and Experience,* was given its premiere by the University of Michigan at Ann Arbor. Bolcom demonstrated his abilities as a melodist by creating songs that frequently echo popular style but remain personal. The late Roy Harris's 34-year-old violin concerto was given a delayed premiere by Gregory Fulkerson and the North Carolina Symphony; it was harmonically conservative and somewhat discursive.

At least one U.S. premiere of a European work stirred more than usual interest. The Boston Symphony under Colin Davis presented Michael Tippett's *The Mask of Time,* a massive two-hour work for solo voices, chorus, and an orchestra with expanded percussion section. Some criticized it as episodic and diffuse.

Appointments and Awards. Herbert Blomstedt was slated to succeed Edo de Waart as music director of the San Francisco Symphony in 1985. Joseph Silverstein, for many years associate conductor and concertmaster of the Boston Symphony, took over the Utah Symphony. André Previn announced he would leave Pittsburgh to become music director of the Los Angeles Philharmonic in 1985.

The 1984 Pulitzer Prize in music went to the English composer Bernard Rands for *Canti del Sole,* a cycle based on "sun poems" in French, Italian, German, and English. The work had received its premiere by the New York Philharmonic with tenor Paul Sperry during the June 1983 New Horizons Festival.

Europe. U.S. composer Henry Brant embraced the entire city of Amsterdam during the Holland Festival, in the course of a week devoted to his music. In *Bran(d)t aan de Amstel* (*Fire on the Amstel*), he utilized the city's canals, employing four barges carrying 26 musicians each (25 flutists and one percussionist); as the barges made their way along various routes, they passed land-based ensembles that added their own sounds to that of the ensembles floating by. In the grand finale, the barges were joined by a youth jazz band, two choruses, two brass bands, and four street organs, in addition to crowd noises and automobile horns.

In England, Oliver Knussen's fantasy opera *The Wild Things* was granted a resoundingly successful premiere by the Glyndebourne company with the London Sinfonietta. Based on the children's book *Where the Wild Things Are,* by the American author Maurice Sendak (who wrote the libretto and designed the sets), Knussen's score was colorful and vigorous. The English National Opera gave the first professional staging in Britain in 70 years of Wagner's *Rienzi,* updating it to depict a 1930's totalitarian state. Pulling out all the stops, the production rained propaganda leaflets down on the audience and aimed the glaring headlights of an approaching tank out into the auditorium.

The Glyndebourne Festival celebrated its 50th anniversary with *Marriage of Figaro* to begin the season, commemorating the 1934 festival opener of the same opera by the now-legendary team of conductor Fritz Busch and producer Carl Ebert. This time around, Bernard Haitink conducted, with zest, his first-ever *Figaro.*   S.F.

RECORDINGS

The compact disc (CD) consolidated its hold on the international record market in 1984, and on the U.S. classical music market in particular. By August the American CD catalog boasted 1,000 titles—expected to double by the end of the year—most of them classical.

The rapid acceptance of the CD and the early realization of its remarkable potential were shown by the release of a complete digital recording of Wagner's *Ring* cycle, conducted by Marek Janowski on the East German Eurodisc label. Meanwhile, the first recorded *Ring*—conducted by Sir Georg Solti for London Records—was being released on CD, opera by opera, starting in the fall.

The first CD to make the most of the new format's available playing time, about 75 minutes, was a Beethoven Ninth, on the Denon label; performed by the Berlin State Orchestra and conducted by Otmar Suitner, it played 71 minutes and sold for $19.95. The first label to sell below $15 was the independent classical (and jazz) label Sine Qua Non, which offered its very first CD's at $14.98 list.

Classical cassettes remained popular, with continually growing sales. Deutsche Grammophon even introduced a "Walkman" line of classical reissues on tape, at a suggested list price of $6.98. Some of the midprice cassette lines brought recordings to the United States for the first time. RCA in August put out the first part of Erato's Presence series, at $5.98 list for either long-playing record (LP) or cassette, drawn from the company's early catalog and featuring such artists as Montserrat Caballé, Raymond Leppard, and Maurice André. Meanwhile, Angel Records, acknowledging the increased interest in the cassette format, reached back into its vaults for a golden-age series of operatic and choral reissues. Included were the Gobbi-Schwarzkopf-Karajan recording of Verdi's *Falstaff,* the Callas-Serafin *Norma,* Giulini's Verdi *Requiem,* and Handel's *Messiah* conducted by Klemperer.

Celebrations. Two eminent pianists were honored with recordings. Observing Claudio Arrau's 80th birthday, Philips completed its vast *Arrau Edition* with multirecord sets devoted to the music of Debussy and Liszt. The entire collection came to eight volumes, with a total of 58 LP's. Both RCA and Angel memorialized the late Artur Rubinstein. RCA launched a series of five multirecord albums titled *Rubinstein: The Chopin Collection,* drawing upon the enormous catalog the late pianist built up over his 42 years with the company, and Angel released a set of four albums on its Seraphim label called *The Young Rubinstein,* covering the period when he was signed to EMI.

New Stars. A number of young artists were particularly, prominent, notably two 23-year-olds: violinist Cho-Liang Lin and trumpeter Wynton Marsalis, both CBS Masterworks recording artists. Another young artist, Murray Perahia, finished his Mozart piano concerto recording project and set out on a Beethoven cycle, with Bernard Haitink and the Concertgebouw Orchestra. Vladimir Ashkenazy seemed to turn up with a new London release every other month, either as a pianist, conductor, or both—even as an orchestrator/conductor in his own rendering of Mussorgsky's *Pictures at an Exhibition.* Daniel Barenboim displayed his versatility in two Deutsche Grammophon releases devoted to Wagner, in one as a solo pianist playing a collection of Liszt transcriptions and in the other as conductor of the Orchestre de Paris in a program of preludes and overtures. Alfred Brendel and James Levine collaborated on a much-admired Philips set of the five Beethoven piano concertos, recorded live with the Chicago Symphony. The Bulgarian soprano Ghena Dimitrova emerged as the opera world's brightest new star, a decision reached by her fans well before Angel released her first aria album in August.

Opera. The general slowdown in opera recordings noted in 1983 continued, though Angel maintained a fairly busy schedule. The company fired a double-barreled salute to the Glyndebourne Festival on its 50th anniversary with the release of a three-record set, a compilation of EMI archive recordings dating from the historic *Figaro* of 1934, and a new recording of *Don Giovanni* conducted by Haitink, with Thomas Allen in the title role—a studio recreation of the Glyndebourne revival of 1982. Angel also released Massenet's *Manon* (Ileana Cotrubas, Michel Plasson) and Verdi's *Ernani* (Placido Domingo, Riccardo Muti), as well as an English-language *Rigoletto* derived from the English National Opera production seen in the United States during the summer.

London Records produced the first digital recording of Boito's *Mefistofele* (Nicolai Ghiaurov, Oliviero de Fabritiis), and Erato released a new *Carmen* (Julia Migenes-Johnson, Placido Domingo, Lorin Maazel) from the soundtrack of the Francesco Rosi film. Peter Brook's *Carmen* was recorded by Pathé Marconi in France, tying in nicely with its successful run in New York.   C.B.

NETHERLANDS, THE. In 1984, the center-right coalition government of Christian Democratic Prime Minister Ruud Lubbers continued to implement austerity measures, aimed at reducing the deficit. The government also won approval of a controversial compromise measure covering deployment of cruise missiles.

The 1984 budget, approved by the Netherlands Parliament in late 1983, had provided for a controversial 3 percent reduction in salaries of public service employees and in social security benefits. In September 1984 the government submitted to Parliament its 1985 budget, which called for further austerity measures intended to reduce the country's deficit from 10.6 percent of the gross national product in 1984 to a projected 9.7 percent in 1985. Approved in October, the budget cut social security, civil servants' salaries, and health insurance by nearly $3 billion.

The modest economic recovery that began in 1983 was expected to continue, producing a 1.5 percent real increase in gross domestic product in 1984. Export growth, forecast at around 4.5 percent for the year, was strengthened by increased industrial productivity, low inflation, and increased foreign demand. A trade surplus of $3.5 billion in 1984 and $6 billion in 1985 was projected. On the darker side, the unemployment rate, at 18 percent of the work force in March, was one of the highest in Western Europe.

On June 14, Parliament narrowly approved a cabinet decision to postpone, until no later than 1988, the possible deployment of U.S. cruise missiles in the Netherlands. The NATO decision of December 1979 had envisioned stationing 48 missiles in the Netherlands beginning in 1986. The June 14 decision marked the first time the government had formally agreed to any deployment of missiles on Dutch soil, but it delayed acceptance of missiles and made the final decision dependent on arms control talks between the United States and Soviet Union. If the United States and the Soviet Union were to agree by November 1, 1985, to cut back on missile deployment, the Netherlands would deploy a reduced number. Also, if the Soviets were to freeze the number of their SS-20 warheads at the June 1984 level, the Netherlands would accept no missiles.

On February 1, it was announced that China had agreed to restore full diplomatic relations with the Netherlands, having received a promise that the Netherlands would not sell any further military equipment to Taiwan. China had downgraded relations with the Netherlands in 1981, following the Netherlands' sale of two conventional submarines to Taiwan.

See STATISTICS OF THE WORLD. W.C.C.

NEVADA. See STATISTICS OF THE WORLD.

NEW BRUNSWICK. See STATISTICS OF THE WORLD. See also CANADA.

NEW CALEDONIA. See PACIFIC ISLANDS.

NEWFOUNDLAND. See STATISTICS OF THE WORLD. See also CANADA.

NEW HAMPSHIRE. See STATISTICS OF THE WORLD.

NEW JERSEY. See STATISTICS OF THE WORLD.

NEW MEXICO. See STATISTICS OF THE WORLD.

NEW YORK. See STATISTICS OF THE WORLD.

NEW ZEALAND. In general elections on July 14, 1984, New Zealand's opposition Labor Party, led by David Lange, ousted Sir Robert Muldoon, head of the National Party government. Muldoon had called elections in the hope of retrieving a solid majority in Parliament, but soon after his announcement he was falling behind in the polls. Lange in his campaign focused on the government's economic performance and projected an image of consensus-style leadership. Accused of divisiveness during his nine years in office, Muldoon claimed success for his anti-inflationary program and defended his policy of economic interventionism, but to no avail. By capturing 43 percent of the popular vote, Lange's Labor

New Zealand's New Prime Minister
On July 26, David Lange (pronounced LONG-ee), 41, was sworn in as New Zealand's prime minister, the youngest to hold that office in this century. He had led the Labor Party to victory, defeating incumbent Robert Muldoon and the conservative National Party government in office since 1975. An idealist with strong sympathies for the poor, Lange had ignored lucrative job offers after law school to work as a public defender. He won a parliamentary seat in 1977 and was elected party leader in 1983. Lange's earnestness and fervent rhetorical style (he is a Methodist lay preacher) facilitated his rapid political ascent, as did the surgery he underwent to reduce his weight to around 245 pounds, from a high of 381. He pledged to attack New Zealand's economic woes and showed a particular interest in foreign affairs, taking the post of foreign minister for himself.
David Lange

Maori warrior Jerry Rautangata (left), flanked by Archbishop Paul Reeves of New Zealand and tribal elder Sony Waru (in ceremonial cape), assists in the opening of a rare exhibition of sacred Maori sculpture at New York's Metropolitan Museum of Art. The show included a 16-foot-tall carved wooden gateway (below) that had once guarded a New Zealand village.

Party won 56 seats, for an absolute majority in the 95-member Parliament.

On July 24, Lange appointed a cabinet, composed of members selected by a Labor Party caucus. Lange himself assumed the foreign affairs portfolio. Geoffrey Palmer was appointed deputy prime minister, attorney general, and minister of justice; Roger Douglas was named finance minister. On November 29, Muldoon was voted out as leader of the National Party; he was replaced by Jim McLay, the deputy party leader.

Earlier in the year, there was extensive labor unrest. In March, the Muldoon government ordered a US$4-a-week increase in pay, the first increase in more than 18 months. The unions, angry that the government planned to retain wage controls while freezing prices, demanded at least twice the increase and held joint meetings in protest. A bomb explosion in the Trades Hall in Wellington, where a number of unions are headquartered, exacerbated the tense situation; one man was killed in the blast. On June 13, emergency legislation forced 2,000 strikers to resume work at the Marsden Point oil refinery project.

In June, Muldoon's government ordered banks and insurance companies to limit interest rates to 15 percent. Subsequently after the announcement of the election, Muldoon stemmed a run on the New Zealand dollar, triggered by rumors of possible devaluation, by restricting foreign exchange dealings. As caretaker prime minister after the election, Muldoon tried to avoid devaluing the dollar, but had to follow the wishes of the incoming government, which ordered it devalued by 20 percent.

Following the election, Lange expressed a desire to avoid confrontation with the United States but repeated his party's pledge to ban nuclear-armed and nuclear-powered ships from New Zealand waters, a move that would bar U.S. ships. Meanwhile, U.S. Secretary of State George Shultz conferred with New Zealand leaders on a visit there. To avert a crisis within the Anzus military alliance (consisting of Australia, New Zealand, and the United States), the United States agreed not to send any warships to New Zealand waters before mid-1985.

See STATISTICS OF THE WORLD.   F.D.S.

NICARAGUA. In 1984 the ruling Sandinistas won an electoral mandate in the first national election held in Nicaragua since they seized power in 1979; however, the main opposition coalition did not participate. The United States continued to oppose the leftist regime.

Internal Politics. In March, Nicaragua's Council of State approved an electoral law that lifted emergency restrictions on demonstrations and rallies. Parties agreeing to participate in elections were guaranteed state campaign financing and equal access to the media. The Sandinista National Liberation Front (FSLN) nominated junta members Daniel Ortega Saavedra and Sergio Ramírez for president and vice-president. The principal opposition coalition, the Ramiro Sacasa Nicaraguan Democratic Coordinate, refused to participate, claiming harassment by Sandinista supporters and a lack of satisfactory conditions for open and free elections. The Independent Liberal Party left the ruling coalition to field its own candidate, but also later withdrew, leaving seven presidential candidates in all. Ortega and Ramírez were elected on November 4, as the FSLN won 63 percent of the vote. The

Sandinistas also won 61 of the 90 directly elected National Assembly seats.

During the year the regime feuded with the Roman Catholic Church hierarchy, which opposed the military draft. Archbishop Miguel Obando y Bravo went to the United States to raise funds privately for an anti-Sandinista political organizing effort. In July he led a march of 200 people in Managua to protest the arrest of a priest accused of sabotage. The government then expelled ten antigovernment foreign priests. Four priests in the government were under Vatican pressure to resign, and after the education minister, Reverend Fernando Cardenal, refused to do so he was dismissed from the Jesuit order.

Rebel Activity. Rebel groups, or contras, claimed responsibility for the mining of Nicaraguan harbors between March and May, but it later became known that non-Nicaraguans supervised by the U.S. Central Intelligence Agency had actually planted the mines. The U.S. Congress condemned the mining and ended military aid to the rebels.

The United States sought to unify the two major insurgent groups. Eden Pastora Gomez, leader of the Revolutionary Democratic Alliance (ARDE), refused to join with the Nicaraguan Democratic Force (FDN), which he regarded as tainted by former national guardsmen who had served under the dictator Anastasio Somoza Debayle, and he led a breakaway from ARDE when that group allied itself with the FDN. On May 30, Pastora was injured and five persons were killed when a bomb exploded at a press conference he was conducting just inside the Nicaraguan border.

In September, Nicaragua agreed to sign a draft peace treaty worked out by the so-called Contadora group—Colombia, Mexico, Panama, and Venezuela—that would commit Nicaragua to talk with opposing groups. After U.S. and other objections were raised to the draft, a revision was undertaken.

Foreign Relations. U.S. efforts to destabilize the Nicaraguan government met growing international criticism. The General Agreement on Tariffs and Trade held that the United States had violated its rules by cutting Nicaragua's sugar quota. In April the United States vetoed a UN Security Council resolution condemning the mining of Nicaraguan harbors. After the United States excluded itself from the jurisdiction of the International Court of Justice on Central American cases, the Court, in response to a request by Nicaragua, issued a preliminary restraining order against the blockading or mining of Nicaraguan ports.

After Nicaragua confirmed that it was building a military airport, the United States warned it not to acquire advanced combat aircraft. Nicaragua nevertheless said it would acquire Soviet MIG jets. In November U.S. intelligence services reported—apparently inaccurately— that the Soviet Union had already delivered MIG's to Nicaragua. Nicaragua put its forces on combat alert to guard against what it considered to be a possible U.S. invasion.

See also UNITED STATES.

Economy. The mining of Nicaragua's harbors and the destruction of oil-storage facilities in late 1983 (another CIA operation) set back the economy. Exxon refused to transport Mexican oil to Nicaragua. The government shifted to a defense economy, featuring tighter centralized planning.

See STATISTICS OF THE WORLD.   R.S.-S.

NIGER. *See* STATISTICS OF THE WORLD.

NIGERIA. Nigeria experienced political, economic, and social upheaval in 1984, in the wake of an efficiently executed military coup, which deposed the civilian government on December 31, 1983. The new Federal Military Government was apparently dominated by moderate and pragmatic senior military officers. Major General Mohammed Buhari assumed the posts of head of state and commander in chief of the armed forces. While the state governors under the new regime were military or police officers, the 18-member cabinet, appointed in mid-January, included 11 civilians.

The new government took office pledging to eliminate corruption, punish previous wrongdoing, and prune public expenditures. It acted to dismiss large numbers of civil servants, to prosecute former public officials suspected of corruption, to dissolve political parties, and to curb freedom of the press. The first official of the deposed government to be convicted of corruption was former Finance Minister Victor Masi, who was sentenced to a 23-year jail term in October.

Daniel Ortega Saavedra, presidential candidate of Nicaragua's Sandinista National Liberation Front, casts his ballot in Managua on Nov. 4. He was elected with 63 percent of the vote.

Part of the Nigerian government's campaign to reduce national inefficiency, a billboard in Lagos questions workers about their efforts on the job, and a poster (inset) urges citizens to report "environmental nuisances."

On October 1, Nigeria's independence day, the regime took a conciliatory step by releasing 250 prisoners, and another 2,551 prisoners were reportedly released on December 31, the coup anniversary. However, an alleged plot to assassinate Buhari and his ministers at independence day ceremonies led to the arrest and execution of more than 40 soldiers.

The nation was stunned late in February by an outbreak of rioting in Yola by a banned extremist Islamic sect, the Maitatsine sect. The army had to be called in to quell the rioting, which left at least 1,000 dead and 30,000 homeless.

Hardship persisted as new state and federal governments imposed austerity measures. Subsidies to government-controlled corporations were sharply curtailed, and many schools, colleges, and universities were closed. Con-

sumers chafed at continuing inflation and scarcity of basic commodities, while trade unions protested the government's freeze on wages. Drought reduced the harvest in a number of northern states, pushing up food prices still further.

The Buhari government won an important concession when OPEC agreed in July to raise the Nigerian oil production quota to 1.4 million barrels per day in August and to 1.45 million b/d in September. In mid-October, however, weak demand and price cuts by others induced Nigeria to cut the price of principal grades of oil unilaterally by $2 a barrel, to $28.

Nigeria's relations with Britain plunged into crisis on July 5, when British customs agents foiled an attempted kidnapping of former Transport Minister Umaru Dikko (who had been living in London), shortly before a crate car-

279

rying his drugged and unconscious body was to be placed on a Lagos-bound plane as diplomatic baggage. Three Israelis and a Nigerian were arrested. The Buhari government disavowed any connection with the incident but, in a popular move, said it would seek to extradite Dikko, whose vows to overthrow the military regime and rumored ill-gotten wealth had made him a most-wanted fugitive.

See STATISTICS OF THE WORLD.   L.D.

NORTH ATLANTIC TREATY ORGANIZATION. The relationship of NATO to the Soviet Union and the Warsaw Pact was among major issues within the alliance during 1984, in the wake of the Soviet decision in late 1983 to break off arms talks with the United States.

Missiles in Europe. After the Soviets broke off the arms talks on limiting medium-range missiles in Europe, according to NATO sources, they proceeded to deploy nine new triple-warhead SS-20 missiles in the Western part of the Soviet Union. Meanwhile, although massive popular demonstrations in late 1983 failed to seriously interfere with initial deployment of U.S. Pershing II and cruise missiles in Europe, there was still cause for concern over full implementation of the plan. In May the Danish Parliament voted to halt further payments of Denmark's share of the cost of the missiles' installation. The next month, the Dutch cabinet, in a decision backed by the parliament, voted to postpone until November 1985 a final decision on how many cruise missiles would be deployed on Dutch soil, pending possible U.S.-Soviet negotiations on reductions. It was decided to deploy all 48 missiles, as originally planned, if no U.S.-Soviet agreement on missile limitation was reached, but the deployment deadline was extended from 1986 to 1988. (Public opinion polls had shown that 63 percent of the Dutch people favored rejection of the missiles.)

NATO Policy. NATO leaders also were concerned by public remarks of government leaders and others. In January, at a symposium of government and business leaders in Switzerland, Canadian Prime Minister Pierre Elliott Trudeau created a stir when he said he did not believe that the United States would launch a missile attack if Western Europe were overrun from the east. Other NATO leaders were said

to be unhappy over these negative remarks. However, the new conservative government of Prime Minister Brian Mulroney clearly affirmed a desire for warm relations with the United States and a close commitment to NATO in its existing structure.

In March, in a *Time* magazine article, former U.S. Secretary of State Henry Kissinger praised the decision of Western European governments to go ahead with the deployment of Pershing II and cruise missiles despite popular opposition. However, he went on to criticize NATO's seeming inability to develop an "agreed, credible" overall strategy; in particular, he cited the serious inferiority of NATO conventional forces in comparison with those of the Warsaw Pact. Kissinger argued that this strategic weakness, combined with popular opposition to the deployment of U.S. missiles, seemed to weaken the arms negotiating position of the United States. Soviet intransigence, he bluntly asserted, was a consequence of a Western European atmosphere of "appeasement." In his five-page article, entitled "A Plan to Reshape NATO," Kissinger proposed giving the office of NATO supreme commander, previously always filled by an American, to a European, with an American deputy. In addition, he suggested that arms control delegations in Europe should be led by Europeans and that their countries should concentrate on a buildup of conventional forces. The Kissinger article drew criticism from both sides of the Atlantic and defenses of NATO's present structure.

Ministerial Meetings. In late October, defense and foreign ministers from seven leading NATO countries did indeed meet together without the United States. They agreed to follow up on earlier plans and reorganize a little known intergovernmental agency, the Western Europe Union, to coordinate defense programs as part of an effort to create a "European identity" on arms policy. However, the tone of the meeting was said to be strongly pro-American, and interest in keeping the United States at arms length was said to be on the wane.

In the light of some reported disagreements within the alliance, it had seemed critical to make a show of unity at the spring NATO foreign ministers conference, held in Washington at the end of May. This was the aim of the final communiqué, entitled "Washington Statement on East-West Relations," which appeared to be a compromise between the two factions in the alliance. One, led by the United States, emphasized firmness toward the Soviet Union, while the other, led by West Germany, espoused the revival of détente. The document called for "genuine détente" but criticized the Soviet military buildup and the Soviets' "relentless" attempt to split NATO over the issue of missile deployment.

At a subsequent NATO foreign ministers conference, held in Brussels in December, Lord Carrington, the NATO secretary-general, reaffirmed the organization's "unity and resolve" to back the U.S. approach to arms reduction talks, which Secretary of State George Shultz was to outline to Soviet Foreign Minister Andrei Gromyko during their scheduled meeting in Geneva in early January 1985. The final communiqué, while emphasizing hope for progress in such talks, stressed the importance of "adequate forces to guarantee . . . collective security."

NATO defense ministers, also meeting in Brussels in December, approved a fund of nearly $8 billion, to be used over the next six years to improve NATO communications centers, command posts, and aircraft shelters. Equipment dumps would also be upgraded and critical ammunition replenished.

East-West Talks. The 35-nation Conference on Confidence- and Security-Building Measures was convened in Stockholm early in the year; its goal was to develop measures to reduce the risk of war in Europe. French Foreign Minister Claude Cheysson and U.S. Secretary of State George Shultz addressed the conference on behalf of NATO, presenting a six-point program that included a call for exchange of information on military units stationed from the Atlantic to the Urals and for the admission of military observers from opposing sides to all significant military exercises. No substantive progress was reported.

In March the Mutual and Balanced Force Reduction Talks reconvened in Vienna, with the presentation of a new NATO proposal. The talks had been stalemated over the method by which current troop levels in Central Europe would be assured and verified. The NATO

proposal dropped the earlier Western requirement that the two sides agree on the number of opposing troops stationed in the region. Instead, NATO agreed to accept Warsaw Pact estimates if they fell within an acceptable range (5–10 percent) of Western estimates. The new plan also called for an initial reduction of 13,000 NATO troops and 30,000 Warsaw Pact troops as part of a five-year plan of phased withdrawal. The Warsaw Pact had previously agreed to reduce its strength by only 20,000. On May 24 it formally rejected the NATO proposal.

Kiessling Dismissal. In January, West German General Gunther Kiessling was dismissed from his post as NATO deputy supreme commander. There were rumors that Kiessling was removed because it had been discovered that he was a homosexual. Kiessling denied the contention; official spokesmen would say only that the dismissal had been for "national security reasons" and that the general had been vulnerable to blackmail.

See also COMMUNIST WORLD; MILITARY AND NAVAL AFFAIRS; and articles on NATO member nations.   J.O.S.

NORTH CAROLINA. See STATISTICS OF THE WORLD.

NORTH DAKOTA. See STATISTICS OF THE WORLD.

NORTHWEST TERRITORIES. See STATISTICS OF THE WORLD. See also CANADA.

NORWAY. In 1984, Prime Minister Kaare Willoch and his Conservative Party were cheered by generally positive economic indicators but had to contend with a major spy scandal. After several sluggish years, the economy improved marginally; government officials projected that the annual growth rate would increase to 2.5 percent by year's end. Oil revenues were up. Inflation was somewhat high; in mid-August prices were 6.2 percent higher than a year earlier. However, unemployment as of October 1 was only 3.7 percent.

Some labor troubles did afflict the government, which had urged the trade unions to restrict wage demands to a maximum increase of 5 percent in an effort to reduce domestic inflation. The powerful Union of Iron and Metal Workers sought a 6.6 percent increase, while the Union of Municipal Employees demanded 7 percent. When negotiations with the latter broke down in May, some 10,000 public officials briefly went on strike. The final overall wage agreements for 1984–1985 averaged 5.9 percent.

Oil production increased significantly at the Stratfjord field in the North Sea. Norway's oil production for the first eight months of 1984 was up 12 percent over 1983. The minister of finance announced in May that increasing revenue from oil and gas would enable the government to pay off the national debt by early 1985. The picture, however, became less clear later in the year. Norway, reacting to a world oil glut, on October 15 cut the price of its oil by $1.25–1.60 a barrel (dropping the price to $28.50–28.85).

The Conservative-led four-party coalition government sponsored legislation during the spring to facilitate drilling in offshore waters by multinational corporations. The government also released a large number of drilling blocks in the North Sea and for the first time permitted foreign firms to drill above the arctic circle. In October it was disclosed that the state-owned Statoil Corporation had discovered a huge gas field in the Barents Sea near northern Norway. The field, dubbed Snow White, was thought to be almost double the size of the country's biggest previously known field.

In January, Arne Treholt, head of the press section in the Information Department at the Foreign Ministry, was arrested for espionage. For 15 years, Trehold had allegedly provided the KGB (the Soviet Union's security and foreign intelligence agency) with information concerning Norwegian security and foreign policies. The career diplomat had served, among other posts, as a member of the Norwegian delegation to the United Nations. After Treholt's arrest, the government expelled five officials from the Soviet embassy and trade mission for espionage.

Talks concerning the boundary between Norway and the Soviet Union in the Barents Sea ended in January in Moscow with no signs of progress. At stake were 60,000 square miles of territory believed to contain rich oil and gas deposits.

See STATISTICS OF THE WORLD.   M.D.H.

NOVA SCOTIA. See STATISTICS OF THE WORLD. See also CANADA.

NUCLEAR POWER. The U.S. nuclear power industry continued to be hit with plant cancellations, construction suspensions, and other setbacks in 1984. Internationally, a group of Western countries that supply nuclear technology reportedly reached an agreement on export controls.

Nuclear Power Plants. In January, Philadelphia Electric Company announced it was suspending work on its Limerick No. 2 reactor for 18 months. Although $3.3 billion had already been spent on the project, the estimated cost of completion exceeded $6.4 billion. In July, Consumers Power Company canceled its Midland nuclear plant at Midland, Mich. The utility chose to scrap the project, on which it had already spent $4 billion, because of escalating costs and failure to get approval for a rate increase needed to attract additional investment. In August the Tennessee Valley Authority board of directors decided to abandon four partially completed nuclear units in which $2.7 billion had already been invested. In November, Public Service Company of Indiana officially canceled its Marble Hill plant at Madison, Ind., on which $2.8 billion had already been spent; the projected cost of completing the project had soared to more than $7 billion.

Three Ohio utilities announced in August that they would convert the nearly complete Zimmer nuclear power plant at Moscow, Ohio to a coal-burning unit, the first time such a conversion has been attempted by a utility in the United States. Although the Zimmer plant was 97 percent completed, it had experienced continuing management, safety, and financial problems, and the federal Nuclear Regulatory Commission (NRC) had ordered the suspension of work on the plant in 1982. The utilities said the conversion would cost $3.4 billion; $1.2 billion had already been spent on construction of the original nuclear facility.

In the West, full-power testing began on Washington Public Power Supply System Unit No. 2 in May, 12 years after construction had been started. Commercial operation began in December. The unit is the only one of five originally planned by WPPSS that was certain to be completed. Meanwhile, the Pacific Gas and Electric Company began testing one unit at its controversial Diablo Canyon, Calif., plant, intending to bring it to full operation in early 1985, despite continuing legal challenges.

Several other utilities were experiencing difficulties in obtaining operating licenses for nearly completed nuclear plants. In January, an NRC licensing board ruled that the Commonwealth Edison Company could not begin operation of the Byron Nuclear Power Station near Rockford, Ill., because quality controls during the plant's construction had been inadequate. In October, however, the board overturned its decision, allowing the loading of fuel and the conducting of tests. The Long Island Lighting Company's plant at Shoreham, N.Y., also had problems. Authorities in Suffolk County, where the plant is located, refused to develop an emergency evacuation plan for the surrounding area, arguing that no such plan would be realistic; such a plan is required before license for full operation can be issued. However, in late November the NRC gave partial approval for low-power testing at Shoreham.

Nuclear Waste. In April the Department of Energy released its draft plan for the civilian radioactive waste management program, as required by the 1983 Nuclear Waste Policy Act (NWPA). The plan reported that the department had signed contracts with 56 organizations, including 46 utilities, for disposal of spent nuclear fuel or high-level waste beginning in 1998, when the nation's first permanent underground repository for nuclear waste is supposed to open. In November the department reached tentative agreement with the state of Washington for possible use of the Hanford Nuclear Reservation there as depository. Yucca Mountain, Nev., and Deaf Smith County, Texas, were named in December as two other possible nuclear disposal sites, but the governors of those states immediately voiced opposition.

The 1983 law also requires the president to evaluate by January 1985 the feasibility of using one or more commercial nuclear waste repositories for the disposal of high-level defense waste. In a draft report issued in August, the Department of Energy recommended disposal of high-level defense wastes in a combined commercial and defense repository because of the cost advantage which this option offers.

Parading protesters demonstrate their hostility to the Long Island Lighting Company's nuclear power plant at Shoreham, N.Y. Shoreham was one of several U.S. nuclear facilities, representing the investment of billions of dollars, that remained uncompleted or out of operation because of skyrocketing costs, environmentalists' opposition, or public and government doubts about their safety.

High-level defense waste is now generated and stored at three Department of Energy facilities, in South Carolina, Idaho, and Washington.

Nuclear Suppliers' Meeting. In July, representatives of 12 Western nations that are exporters of nuclear technology met privately in Luxembourg to discuss ways of stopping the spread of nuclear weapons. According to reports, the 12 countries agreed on the need for expanded safeguards on existing nuclear facilities and for tighter controls over nuclear transfers. Among the concerns that had led to the meeting—the first involving most members of the so-called London Suppliers' Club since 1977—was the increase in the number of suppliers, which now included China and Brazil, and in countries approaching a nuclear weapons capability, such as Pakistan. Western members did not invite the Soviet Union and the other Eastern European members to participate.

See also ENERGY.   D.F.A.

283

O

OBITUARIES. Each entry below contains the name of a notable person who died in 1984. It also contains a brief description of the accomplishments and events that contributed to making each person notable.

Adams, Ansel, 82, influential American photographer whose majestic, consummately crafted landscape photographs of the nation's West earned him a worldwide reputation. Over a long and distinguished career, Adams was a fervent champion of photography as art and was an ardent environmentalist. April 22 in Monterey, Calif.

Aiken, George D., 92, former Vermont governor and longtime Republican senator (1941–1975) who was a critic of the Vietnam war, an early advocate of food stamps, and an activist in farm legislation. November 19 in Montpelier, Vt.

Aleixandre y Merlo, Vicente, 86, influential Spanish poet who won the 1977 Nobel Prize for literature; an antifascist and one of the

Walter Alston led the Dodgers to four World Series championships in his 23 years as manager.

Generation of 1927 poets, he used often striking images to deal with such themes as love and death. December 13 in Madrid.

Alston, Walter, 72, American baseball figure; as manager of the Brooklyn and Los Angeles Dodgers for 23 years, the third-longest managerial tenure in baseball history, he led the team to seven National League pennants and four World Series championships. October 1 in Oxford, Ohio.

Andropov, Yuri Vladimirovich, 69, general secretary of the Soviet Communist Party since November 1982. A former longtime head of the Soviet KGB, he quickly consolidated his power during his short time as Soviet party chief, acquiring additional roles as titular president of the Soviet Union and chairman of the National Defense Council. He appeared to wield considerable influence, despite illness that kept him from public view for six months. His tenure was marked by efforts to curb corruption and promote economic efficiency at home and by East-West tensions over nuclear missile deployment in Europe, over continued Soviet involvement in Afghanistan, and over the Soviet downing of a South Korean airliner in September 1983. February 9 in Moscow.

Ariès, Philippe, 69, French historian whose study *Centuries of Childhood* (published in the United States in 1962) analyzed changes in education and attitudes toward children from the end of the Middle Ages to the 18th century. February 8 in southern France.

Ashton-Warner, Sylvia, 75, New Zealand teacher and author whose novel *Spinster* (1959) became an international best-seller. April 28 in Tauranga, New Zealand.

Atkinson, (Justin) Brooks, 89, American drama critic; his more than 30 years as the erudite theater critic for the *New York Times* coincided with the rise of serious American drama by such figures as Eugene O'Neill and Tennessee Williams. During World War II he served as a foreign correspondent, winning a Pulitzer Prize for reporting. January 13 in Huntsville, Ala.

Barry, Jack, 66, American television game show producer and host; virtually banned from

Count Basie's orchestra was the epitome of swing. It was a top group in the Big Band era and enjoyed renewed popularity starting in the 1950's.

flowing sound of swing, had a major influence on modern jazz. April 26 in Hollywood, Fla.

Bergeron, Victor Jules, 81, American restaurateur who served his interpretation of Polynesian food in 21 Trader Vic's restaurants in six nations. October 11 in Hillsborough, Calif.

Berlinguer, Enrico, 62, general secretary of the Italian Communist Party since 1972; under his pragmatic leadership the party distanced itself from Moscow and achieved significantly greater popularity and political influence in Italy, but not what Berlinguer called the historic compromise—Communist participation in a coalition government. June 11 in Padua, Italy.

Betjeman, Sir John, 77, Britain's poet laureate since 1972; his witty, often nostalgic verse, decribed by W. H. Auden as "slick but not streamlined," appealed to a wide audience. May 19 in Trebetherick, England.

Brassaï (Gyula Halász), 84, pioneering Hungarian-born French photographer who chronicled the nightlife of the seamier side of Paris, most notably in the well-known photographic collection *Paris de Nuit* (1933). July 8 on the Côte d'Azur near Nice, France.

Bratteli, Trygve, 74, prime minister of Norway from 1971 to 1972 and again from 1973

broadcasting in the late 1950's, amid revelations that contestants on his quiz show *21* had been coached, he made a comeback in the 1970's with *The Joker's Wild*. May 2 in New York City.

Barzini, Luigi, 75, urbane Italian author, journalist, and member of Parliament; his book *The Italians*, a wry analysis of Italian character, culture, and history, was an international bestseller but offended many of his compatriots. March 30 in Rome.

Basehart, Richard, 70, sonorous-voiced American actor of stage and screen who was best known for his role as Admiral Nelson in the television series *Voyage to the Bottom of the Sea*. September 17 in Los Angeles.

Basie, William ("Count"), 79, American jazz pianist and bandleader who led one of the great orchestras during the Big Band era and enjoyed renewed popularity in the 1950's; Basie classics like *One O'Clock Jump and Jumpin' at the Woodside*, which typified the

Brassaï, one of the century's major European photographers, was famed for his authentic portraits of the Paris demimonde.

Richard Burton, the flamboyant son of a Welsh coal miner, scored a Broadway triumph as King Arthur in Camelot *and shone in many classic films—though he also accepted roles in many second-rate ones.*

to 1976; a lifelong Labor Party member, he spent World War II in a German concentration camp because of his anti-Nazi resistance. November 20 in Oslo.

Brautigan, Richard, 49, American avantgarde author who wrote *Trout Fishing in America* and other offbeat favorites of the "counterculture" of the 1960's. Found dead October 25 in Bolinas, Calif., an apparent suicide

Bricktop (Ada Beatrice Queen Victoria Louise Virginia Smith), 89, American-born singer and nightclub owner whose sparkling personality helped make her cabarets in Paris, Rome, and Mexico City popular with the literati and the fashionable. January 31 in New York City.

Buckler, Ernest, 75, Canadian novelist, shortstory writer, and essayist whose fiction, set in the Nova Scotian world of the Annapolis Valley, celebrated the power of the human heart to transcend a senseless world; one of his best known works was his first novel, *The Mountain and the Valley,* written in 1952. March 4 in Bridgetown, Nova Scotia.

Bull, Peter, 72, veteran British actor known for his glowering character roles in the films *Dr. Strangelove* and *The African Queen;* he

was also a versatile author and a world-famous collector of teddy bears. May 21 in London.

Bunker, Ellsworth, 90, imperturbable patrician American diplomat; after over 30 years as a business executive, he served as ambassador to Argentina, Italy, India, and South Vietnam and as chief U.S. negotiator of the Panama Canal treaties. September 27 in Brattleboro, Vt.

Burton, Richard (Richard Jenkins, Jr.), 58, Welsh-born British actor whose tempestuous personal life gained him as much fame as his stage and screen performances. With his magnetic presence and resonant voice, he commanded the stage in *Hamlet, Camelot,* and *Equus,* and he appeared in such classic motion pictures as *Becket* (1964), *The Spy Who Came in From the Cold* (1965), and *Who's Afraid of Virginia Woolf?* (1966). But a long list of second-rate films and his well-publicized drinking problem and extravagant life-style led many to believe he never lived up to his promise. He was married five times, twice to actress Elizabeth Taylor; their relationship caused a huge scandal when it began in 1961 on the set of the movie *Cleopatra.* August 5 in Geneva.

Truman Capote's writings ranged from his brilliant first novel of a boy's self-discovery, Other Voices, Other Rooms, *to the unfinished* Answered Prayers, *an often-scandalous roman à clef.*

Campbell, Clarence Sutherland, 78, stately Canadian lawyer who was president of the National Hockey League for 31 years, until his retirement in 1977. June 24 in Montreal.

Capote, Truman, 59, celebrated, eccentric American novelist and short-story writer who used clear, skillfully crafted prose to explore a world often bizarre and sometimes brutal. His first novel, *Other Voices, Other Rooms* (1948), the story of a boy's self-discovery in a decaying Southern mansion, won him literary fame at the age of 23; later works included *Breakfast at Tiffany's* (1958) and the "nonfiction novel" *In Cold Blood* (1966), a factual account, using novelistic techniques, of the murder of a Kansas farm family and the arrest and execution of the killers. Capote avidly pursued celebrity, on televison talk shows and in high society, and had freely acknowledged drinking and drug problems. August 25 in Bel Air, Calif.

Christensen, Lew, 75, one of the first great U.S.–born ballet dancers and a prominent choreographer and teacher of ballet. October 9 in Burlingame, Calif.

Church, Frank, 59, U.S. senator from Idaho for 24 years (1957–1981) and one-time chairman of the Senate's Foreign Relations Committee. An eloquent champion of liberal causes and an early critic of U.S. involvement in Vietnam, he chaired the Senate Select Committee on Intelligence in 1975–1976, and, in 1976, waged an energetic but unsuccessful campaign for the Democratic presidential nomination. April 7 in Bethesda, Md.

Clark, Mark Wayne, 87, American general who commanded the U.S. Fifth Army during the hard-fought Italian campaign of World War II that led to the capture of Rome in June 1944; he came to prominence for his role in the planning and execution of the 1942 North African invasion, and he served as supreme commander of UN troops in the last year of the Korean war (1952–1953). April 17 in Charleston, S.C.

Coogan, Jackie (John Leslie Coogan, Jr.), 69, American actor who was Hollywood's first major child movie star. Selected at age four to star with Charlie Chaplin in *The Kid* (1919), he went on to make a fortune as a child actor but got to keep little of it; among his adult roles was that of Uncle Fester in *The Addams*

General Mark W. Clark led the U.S. Fifth Army during World War II in the Italian campaign that led to the capture of Rome; he also served as UN supreme commander in the Korean war.

Family television series. March 1 in Santa Monica, Calif.

Cori, Carl F., 87, Czechoslovakian-American biochemist who, with his late wife, Gerty Radnitz, shared the 1947 Nobel Prize in medicine for research on the starch glycogen. October 20 in Cambridge, Mass.

Cortázar, Julio, 69, Argentine writer whose sharply original short stories and novels, often exploring existential themes, are rich in imagery and subtle humor. An anti-Peronist who supported the Cuban and Nicaraguan revolutions, he had lived abroad since 1951. February 12 in Paris.

Cronin, Joe, 77, American baseball player. An All-Star shortstop and outstanding clutch hitter, with a lifetime average of .301, he played in the majors from 1926 to 1945, mainly with the Washington Senators and Boston Red Sox; he began 14 years as president of the American League in 1959. September 7 in Osterville, Mass.

De Filippo, Eduardo, 84, prominent Italian playwright and actor; his comedies about Neapolitan life, including *Filumena Marturano* (adapted for the screen as *Marriage Italian Style*), were widely performed in Italy and abroad. November 1 in Rome.

Dirac, Paul Adrien Maurice, 82, British physicist who reconciled quantum theory with Einstein's relativity theory; he was a co-winner of the Nobel Prize in physics in 1933. October 20 in Tallahassee, Fla.

Dors, Diana, 52, platinum-blond British actress hailed in the 1950's as that nation's answer to Marilyn Monroe; she appeared in such lightweight films as *Good Time Girls* and *I Married a Woman*. May 4 in Windsor, England.

Eckstein, Otto, 56, German-born American economist, Harvard professor, and former White House adviser under Lyndon Johnson; he co-founded Data Resources Inc., a phenomenally successful economic forecasting company. March 22 in Boston.

Egan, William A., 69, American politician. An energetic leader of Alaska's drive for statehood and its first governor after statehood was achieved in 1959, he served three terms in office. May 6 in Anchorage, Alaska.

Empson, Sir William, 77, influential British man of letters and teacher, known for his abstruse, strikingly original poetry and for his penetrating critical works, most notably *Seven Types of Ambiguity* (1930). April 15 in London.

Fixx, James Fuller, 52, American runner and author whose 1977 best-seller, *The Complete Book of Running,* did much to popularize running as a way to physical fitness and long life. July 20 in Hardwick, Vt., of a heart attack while jogging.

Foreman, Carl, 69, American screenwriter, producer, and director who wrote scripts for *High Noon* and *The Guns of Navarone;* blacklisted in the 1950's, he moved to London where he anonymously coauthored the Oscar-winning screenplay for *The Bridge on the River Kwai* (1957). June 26 in Beverly Hills, Calif.

Foucault, Michel, 57, French philosopher and teacher; in *Madness and Civilization* and other works he analyzed such concepts as insanity, sexuality, and crime as instruments of social control. June 25 in Paris.

Gallup, George Horace, 82, pioneer American pollster who helped make public opinion polls a standard tool in politics, marketing, and academic research; his Gallup Poll, which introduced new sampling methods to measure public opinion in a diverse population, had its first big success when it correctly predicted the election victory of Franklin D. Roosevelt in 1936. July 26 in Tschingel, Switzerland.

Gandhi, Indira, 66, charismatic prime minister of India for much of the past two decades. She took a pragmatic, often authoritarian approach to her country's economic problems and its ethnic and religious divisions, and became a leader of the Third World movement. The daughter of Jawaharlal Nehru, she first became prime minister in 1966. Nine years later, facing an economic crisis and sharp political criticism, she declared a state of emergency and jailed most of her major opponents. In a backlash against her dictatorial emergency rule, she was voted out of office in 1977, only to be returned to power three years later. Assassinated outside her home in New Delhi on October 31.

Jim Fixx, whose best-selling books helped make running a national pastime, died of a heart attack while jogging in Vermont.

Gaye, Marvin, Jr., 44, American soul singer who rose to fame in the 1960's with such Motown hits as "Hitch Hike" and "I Heard It Through the Grapevine." He later produced and composed his own albums, grappling with social issues in *What's Going On* (1971), and recently turned to sexually explicit themes in hits like "Sexual Healing." Shot and killed April 1 in Los Angeles, after a dispute with his father.

Gaynor, Janet, 77, American actress who in 1928 won the first Oscar for best actress; her projection of innocence and vulnerability made her one of the movies' most popular leading ladies through the 1930's. September 14, of complications from a 1982 auto accident, in Palm Springs, Calif.

Gemayel, Pierre, 78, Lebanese politician. A founder and leader since 1937 of the Maronite Christian Phalange Party, he had been a member of Parliament since 1960 and was a cabinet member at the time of his death; he was the father of Lebanese President Amin Gemayel. August 29 in Bikfeiya, Lebanon.

Gobbi, Tito, 68, Italian baritone whose singing talent was more than matched by his spellbinding acting ability; he was best known for his portrayal of the sinister Scarpia in Puccini's *Tosca*. March 5 in Rome.

Guillén, Jorge, 91, prizewinning Spanish poet whose book *Cántico,* published and painstakingly revised in four editions, was a celebration of life and an effort to achieve "pure poetry." February 6 in Málaga, Spain.

Haddad, Saad, 47, Lebanese Army major who in 1976 formed his own militia. The group, trained and armed by Israel, operated in southern Lebanon, often fighting Palestinian forces. January 14 in Marj 'Uyun, Lebanon.

Harris, Sir Arthur Travers, 91, single-minded marshal of Britain's Royal Air Force who directed the controversial saturation bombing of German cities between 1942 and 1945. April 5 at Goring-on-Thames, England.

Hauser, Gayelord, 89, German-born American health food advocate; a popular society figure, he wrote widely on the virtues of such "wonder foods" as brewer's yeast and yogurt, besides broadcasting his views on radio and television for many years. December 26 in North Hollywood, Calif.

Lillian Hellman, the eminent dramatist who wrote The Little Foxes *and* Watch on the Rhine, *also penned three books of controversial memoirs.*

Hellman, Lillian, 79(?), eminent American dramatist, screenwriter, and memoirist. In popular and critically successful plays such as *The Children's Hour* (1934), *The Little Foxes* (1939), and the anti-Nazi *Watch on the Rhine* (1941), she explored powerful human emotions like malice, greed, and heroism. She was blacklisted in the early 1950's for refusing to testify about associates, and she did not have another original play staged until the award-winning *Toys in the Attic* in 1960. Subsequently, her three books of memoirs—*An Unfinished Woman* (1969), *Pentimento* (1974), and *Scoundrel Time* (1976)—won critical accaim, while drawing criticism from some for alleged inaccuracies June 30 in Martha's Vineyard, Mass.

Hexum, Jon-Erik, 26, American actor starring in the television series *Cover Up.* In a bizarre tragedy, he jokingly shot himself in the head with a gun loaded with blanks; the explosion proved fatal. October 18 in Los Angeles.

Hill, Lister, 89, U.S. senator from Alabama who in three decades in the Senate (1938–1968) sponsored major health and education measures. December 20 in Montgomery, Ala.

OBITUARIES

Himes, Chester, 75, American expatriate author of novels on racial themes and of detective fiction, including *Cotton Comes to Harlem.* November 12 in Moraira, Spain.

Hoyt, Waite Charles, 84, American baseball player who was a Hall of Fame pitcher for the mighty New York Yankees of the 1920's and other teams. In a 21-year major-league career, he had 237 victories and an earned-run average of 3.59. August 25 in Cincinnati.

Hughes, Richard, 77, Australian-born foreign and war correspondent for British and Australian publications; his vivid personality was a model for fictional characters created by John le Carré and Ian Fleming. January 4 in Hong Kong.

Hunsaker, Jerome Clarke, 98, American engineer and aviation pioneer who designed the first plane to cross the Atlantic. September 10 in Boston.

Hunter, Alberta, 89, mellow-voiced American blues singer who gave up her career to become a nurse in 1954; after her retirement from nursing in 1977, she began a new singing career. October 17 in New York City.

Hurd, Peter, 80, American artist whose paintings and lithographs of the American Southwest won wide acclaim; he gained his greatest notoriety, however, when his commissioned portrait of President Lyndon Johnson was rejected by the president as "the ugliest thing I ever saw." July 9 in Roswell, N.M.

Jaffe, Sam, 93, veteran American character actor whose parts ranged from that of High Lama in the film *Lost Horizon* (1937) and Indian water boy in *Gunga Din* (1939) to the role of Dr. Zorba in the *Ben Casey* television series of the 1960's. March 24 in Beverly Hills, Calif.

Jenkins, Gordon, 73, American composer, conductor, and arranger who gained fame with his 1945 composition "Manhattan Tower"; he won a 1965 Grammy for his arrangement of Frank Sinatra's recording of "It Was a Very Good Year." May 1 in Malibu, Calif.

Jóhannesson, Ólafur, 71, Icelandic statesman and head of the nation's Progressive Party who served as prime minister from 1971 to 1974 and from 1978 to 1979. May 20 in Reykjavík.

Johnson, Uwe, 49, German novelist who moved from East Germany to the West in 1959 to publish his first major work, *Speculations About Jakob;* with Günter Grass and Heinrich Böll, he was lauded as a major creative voice in postwar German literature. Death in Shearness, England, announced March 13.

Kapitza, Peter Leonidovich, 89, Soviet physicist and 1978 Nobel laureate who made major discoveries in magnetism and low-temperature physics. After spending much of his early career in England, in 1934 he became head of the Soviet Union's Institute of Physical Problems; he was dismissed in 1946, reportedly for refusing to work on the atomic bomb, but was later reinstated. April 8 in Moscow.

Kastler, Alfred, 81, French physicist who won a 1966 Nobel Prize for devising a technique that led to the development of lasers. January 7 in Bandol, France.

Kaufman, Andy, 35, versatile offbeat American comedian who played the immigrant mechanic Latka Gravas on the television comedy *Taxi* and enjoyed a love-hate relationship with television audiences for his bizarre impersonations on *Saturday Night Live.* May 16 in Los Angeles.

Kennedy, David Anthony, 28, troubled son of the late U.S. Senator Robert F. Kennedy; he unsuccessfully battled a drug addiction problem. Found dead April 25 of an accidental drug overdose in Palm Beach, Fla.

Khrushchev, Nina Petrovna, 84, widow of former Soviet leader Nikita S. Khrushchev; unlike wives of other high Soviet officials, she often appeared in public with her husband and drew attention as a personality on trips abroad. August 8 in Moscow.

King, Martin Luther, Sr., 84, Baptist minister and pioneering American civil rights leader; father of the Reverend Martin Luther King, Jr. Beginning in the 1930's, he struggled to win rights for blacks in Atlanta; he continued his activism as his son rose to national fame. November 11 in Atlanta.

Knopf, Alfred A., 91, American publisher known for his commitment to literary excellence. In 1915 he founded the firm (now a division of Random House) that still bears his name, and he ran it until the age of 80. Over the years, he published such American writers as Willa Cather, John Hersey, Dashiell Hammett, and John Updike. He also introduced

U.S. readers to major foreign authors, including Thomas Mann, Albert Camus, Sigrid Undset, and Gabriel García Márquez. August 11 in Purchase, N.Y.

Krasner, Lee (Lee Krasner Pollock), 75, powerful American Abstract Expressionist painter; long overshadowed by her late husband and creative partner, Jackson Pollock, she won recognition in recent years as a major artist in her own right. June 19 in New York City.

Kroc, Ray Albert, 81, American entrepreneur; a former salesman of paper cups and milk shake machines, he built McDonald's into the largest chain of fast-food restaurants in the world; he was also owner of the San Diego Padres baseball team. January 14 in San Diego.

Kubik, Gail Thompson, 69, American composer of vividly lyrical and original works, ranging from symphonies and chamber music pieces to motion picture scores; he received a Pulitzer Prize in 1952 for *Symphony Concertante*. July 20 in Claremont, Calif.

Laskin, Bora, 71, chief justice of the Supreme Court of Canada since 1973. Known for his brilliant legal mind and compassion for minorities, he generally took the progressive side in controversial issues. He was the first Jew to be named to the court. March 26 in Ottawa.

Lattimore, Richmond, 77, distinguished American poet, translator, and classical scholar, best known for his fine verse translations of Homer's *Iliad* and *Odyssey*. February 26 in Rosemont, Pa.

Lawford, Peter, 61, suave British born American actor whose films included *Easter Parade* (1948), *The White Cliffs of Dover* (1944), and *Ocean's Eleven* (1960); married for 12 years to Patricia Kennedy, sister of the former president, he also was a member of the Hollywood clique centered around Frank Sinatra, known as the "Rat Pack." December 24 in Los Angeles.

Lonergan, Bernard J. F., 79, Canadian Jesuit philosopher and theologian whose writings had a major influence on Roman Catholic thought throughout the world. November 26 in Pickering, Ontario.

Losey, Joseph, 75, American film director noted for his opulent portrayals of moral decadence; blacklisted in the United States during the 1950's, he made a series of acclaimed films in Europe, including *The Servant* (1963), *Accident* (1966), and *The Go-Between* (1970). June 22 in London.

Lowenstein-Wertheim-Freudenberg, Prince Hubertus zu, 78, German historian, author, member of parliament, active Roman Catholic layman, and early opponent of Adolf Hitler who, as a refugee, from the early 1930's to the end of the war, aided in mobilizing American opinion in opposition to Nazism. November 28 in Bonn, West Germany.

Machito (Frank Raul Grillo), 75(?), Cuban bandleader and vocalist who helped bring an Afro-Cuban rhythm to jazz and dance music beginning in the 1940's. April 15 in London.

Malik, Adam, 67, Indonesian statesman, serving as foreign minister from 1966 to 1977 and vice-president from 1978 to 1983; he was president of the United Nations General Assembly in 1971. September 5 in Bandung, Indonesia.

Mason, James, 75, suave, sophisticated British-born film star. Among a wide variety of roles over his long career, the best-known

In his 50-year acting career, British actor James Mason played the swashbuckling hero or the romantic villain in many of his more than 100 films.

Ethel Merman's stint as Annie Oakley, in Annie Get Your Gun, was one of her many brilliant performances in a long string of brassy musical comedy hits.

include those of Svengali in *The Seventh Veil* (1945), General Erwin Rommel in *The Desert Fox* (1951), an alcoholic actor in the 1954 remake of *A Star Is Born*, Humbert Humbert in *Lolita* (1962), and an unscrupulous lawyer in *The Verdict* (1982). July 27 in Lausanne, Switzerland.

Mercer, Mabel, 84, American cabaret singer who influenced a generation of vocalists from Billie Holiday to Johnny Mathis; she was greatly admired for her timing and ability to convey the emotional nuances of a song. April 20 in Pittsfield, Mass.

Merman, Ethel (Ethel Agnes Zimmermann), 75(?), American musical comedy superstar whose booming voice and brassy style enthralled theater and film audiences for 50 years. Merman made her Broadway debut in the 1930 George Gershwin hit *Girl Crazy,* bringing down the house with "I Got Rhythm"; later Broadway successes included Cole Porter's *Anything Goes* and *Dubarry Was a Lady,* Irving Berlin's *Annie Get Your Gun,* and the Jule Styne–Stephen Sondheim musical *Gypsy,* which she considered her best performance. She also made more than a dozen films, including *Alexander's Ragtime Band* and *There's No Business Like Show Business.* February 15 in New York City.

Mitchell, Clarence M., Jr., 73, American civil rights figure; a longtime chief lobbyist for the National Association for the Advancement of Colored People, he was especially influential in winning passage of the Fair Housing Act of 1968. March 18 in Baltimore.

Mohieddin, Fuad, 58, prime minister of Egypt under President Hosni Mubarak and secretary-general of the ruling National Democratic Party; he aided Mubarak in forming a government after President Anwar al-Sadat's assassination in 1981. June 5 in Cairo.

Naguib, Muhammad, 83, Egyptian general who became president of Egypt after the July 1952 coup that forced King Farouk to abdicate and ended the monarchy; two years later, Naguib was deposed and put under house arrest by Gamal Abdel Nasser, and he was not freed until 1971, after Nasser's death. August 28 in Cairo.

Niemöller, (Freidrich Gustav Emil) Martin, 92, German Protestant preacher and church leader; imprisoned in concentration camps during World War II for his outspoken criticisms of Hitler, he later became a prominent pacifist and a critic of nuclear arms. March 6 in Wiesbaden, West Germany.

O'Flaherty, Liam, 88, Irish novelist and short-story writer whose unsentimental works portrayed the struggle for economic self-sufficiency and freedom in Ireland; his best-known books included *The Informer* (1925), later made into a well-known film, and *Famine* (1937). September 7 in Dublin.

Oppen, George, 76, Pulitzer Prize–winning American poet associated with the spare, unembellished style known as Objectivism; he was also politically active in left-wing circles. July 7 in Albany, Calif.

Owings, Nathaniel A., 81, award-winning American architect; as co-founder of the architectural firm Skidmore, Owings & Merrill, he presided over more than $3 billion in construction projects, including such skyscrapers as New York City's trend-setting Lever House. June 13 in Jacona, N.M.

Peckinpah, Sam, 59, maverick Hollywood film director; first known for a string of successful, often graphically violent westerns, including *The Wild Bunch,* he made similar use of violence in such non-western films as *Straw Dogs* and *The Getaway.* December 28 in Inglewood, Calif.

Peerce, Jan (Jacob Pincus Perelmuth), 80, American operatic tenor; he sang with the Metropolitan Opera for 27 years, appearing in over 200 performances, and remained highly active after his 1968 retirement, going on concert tours, making films, and shining in the Broadway musical *Fiddler on the Roof.* December 15 in New York City.

Perkins, Carl D., 71, liberal Democratic congressman from Kentucky since 1949; as chairman of the House Education and Labor Committee, he was a powerful champion of the poor and guided passage of major social legislation, including measures on child nutrition, coal-mine safety, and federal aid to schools. August 3 in Lexington, Ky.

Petrosian, Tigran Vartanovich, 55, Soviet chess grandmaster and world champion from 1963 to 1969, he was known for his vigilant defensive play and caution in attack. Death announced August 14 in Moscow.

Phillips, Esther, 48, versatile, gruff-voiced American blues singer, famous from the age of 13 as "Little Esther" and later acknowledged by the Beatles as a major influence on rock music. August 7 in Torrance, Calif.

British man of letters J. B. Priestley, who was also a broadcaster and commentator, wrote more than 130 books and plays in his long career.

Canadian-born actor William Powell played the dapper, sophisticated Nick Charles in the classic Thin Man detective films.

Pidgeon, Walter, 87, Canadian-born actor whose gentlemanly charm graced more than 100 films over nearly half a century; among the most notable were several—including *Mrs. Miniver* (1942) and *Madame Curie* (1943)—in which he starred with Greer Garson. September 25 in Santa Monica, Calif.

Powell, William, 91, American actor; a suave Hollywood leading man of the 1930's and 1940's who played detective Nick Charles in films based on Dashiell Hammett's *Thin Man* stories, Powell also won acclaim for roles as Florenz Ziegfeld, as the title character in *Life With Father,* and as the ship's doctor in *Mister Roberts.* March 5 in Palm Springs, Calif.

Priestley, J(ohn) B(oynton), 89, prolific British novelist, playwright, and essayist. Priestley's portrayal of English life often had a satirical edge, as in the vivid, frequently humorous characterizations in the novel *The Good Companions* (1929), a sprawling international bestseller that helped make long novels popular. Another thematic concern, a fascination with the human experience of time, was most evident in his plays, such as the highly popular *Dangerous Corner* (1932). His political writings, such as those for the weekly *New Statesman,* reflected generally leftist sympathies. August 14 in Stratford-on-Avon, England.

Rahner, Karl, 80, German Jesuit theologian; one of the world's leading Roman Catholic theologians, he combined insights from existentialism and modern biblical criticism with a devotion to Catholic tradition. March 30 in Innsbruck, Austria.

Raskin, Judith, 56, American lyric soprano. As a leading singer with the New York Opera and then (1962–1972) the Metropolitan Opera, she was especially noted for her roles in Mozart operas and her purity of sound. December 21 in New York City.

Renault, Gilbert, 79, much decorated hero of the French Resistance; under the name of Colonel Rémy, he organized the Free French intelligence network in German-occupied France and later wrote of his exploits. July 29 in Guingamp, France.

Robson, Dame Flora, 82, powerful British actress of stage and screen; she won plaudits for a variety of roles, including that of Queen Elizabeth in the 1936 film *Fire Over England.* July 7 in Brighton, England.

Rock, John, 94, American physician; a co-developer of the birth control pill and a pioneer in the study of human fertility, he was the first scientist to fertilize a human egg in a test tube. December 5 in Peterborough, N.H.

Rowe, James H., Jr., 75, American political figure; a lawyer and special adviser to President Franklin D. Roosevelt; one of the original New Dealers, he was a power in Democratic politics for 40 years. June 17 in Washington, D.C.

Ryle, Martin, 66, British astronomer who shared the 1974 Nobel Prize in physics for his development of radio-astronomy techniques that made possible the mapping of enormous, distant objects in space. October 14 in Cambridge, England.

Salan, Raoul, 85, much-decorated French general who in 1961 led an abortive military revolt in Algeria aimed at maintaining French control and averting independence; he was captured and imprisoned in 1962 but later pardoned. July 3 in Paris.

Sands, Billy, 73, American stage and television actor best known as Private Dino Paparelli on the *Phil Silvers Show* and as Seaman Harrison ("Tinker") Bell in *McHale's Navy.* August 27 in Los Angeles.

Schwartz, Arthur, 83, American composer of songs for the Broadway stage and for movies; with lyricist Howard Dietz he wrote such standards as "Dancing in the Dark" and "That's Entertainment." September 4 in Kintnersville, Pa.

Shaw, Irwin, 71, prolific American author of novels, short stories, and plays; he was best known for his 1948 novel of World War II, *The Young Lions,* which drew wide critical acclaim, and for *Rich Man, Poor Man* (1970), a popular novel made into a television miniseries. May 16 in Davos, Switzerland.

Shehan, Lawrence Cardinal, 86, American religious leader who had served as Roman Catholic archbishop of Baltimore; a cardinal since 1965, he was a leading advocate of religious ecumenism and racial integration. August 26 in Baltimore.

Sheppard, Eugenia, 85 (?), American society and fashion reporter whose breezy, gossipy

Irwin Shaw's best-known novels include The Young Lions *and* Rich Man, Poor Man.

"Inside Fashion" column, appearing in close to 100 newspapers in the 1950's and 1960's, showed a careful eye for fashion trends and a new concern for those who created and wore trend-setting clothes. November 11 in New York City.

Sholokhov, Mikhail Alexandrovich, 78, acclaimed Soviet author whose multivolume epic novel of Cossack life, translated into English as *And Quiet Flows the Don* (1934) and *The Don Flows Home to the Sea* (1940), helped bring him a 1965 Nobel Prize. A longtime Communist Party member, he increasingly adhered to party guidelines in his work and harshly denounced dissident authors such as Boris Pasternak and Aleksandr Solzhenitsyn. February 21 in Veshenskaya, Soviet Union.

Sinclair, Gordon, 83, veteran Canadian journalist and broadcaster who delighted audiences with his colorful dress, feisty style, and outspoken observations. May 17 in Toronto.

Slipyj, Josyf Cardinal, 92, major archbishop of the Ukrainian Catholic Church; named metropolitan of Lvov in 1944, he spent 18 years in imprisonment and exile in the Soviet Union, until the Vatican obtained his release in 1963. September 7 in Vatican City.

Sokoine, Edward, 46, prime minister of Tanzania since February 1983, and previously from 1977 to 1980; he was considered the most probable successor to President Julius K. Nyerere. April 12 in a car accident near Morogoro, Tanzania.

Souvanna Phouma, 82, Laotian prince and former prime minister; prior to his ouster by the Communist Pathet Lao in 1975, he had sought to guide his country along a neutralist course but was unable to overcome deep-seated divisions. January 10 in Vientiane, Laos.

Speidel, Hans, 87, German general who served as commander of NATO land forces in Central Europe from 1957 to 1963; he was a key conspirator in the abortive 1944 plot to assassinate Adolf Hitler. November 28 in Bad Honnef, West Germany.

Thornton, Willie Mae ("Big Mama"), 57, influential American blues singer whose classic renditions of "Hound Dog" and "Ball and Chain" inspired such performers as Elvis Presley, Janis Joplin, and Aretha Franklin. July 25 in Los Angeles.

Canadian newsman Gordon Sinclair was known for his colorful style and for his candid, often surprising observations.

Touré, Ahmed Sékou, 62, president of Guinea since independence in 1958 and black Africa's longest-serving head of state at the time of his death. A spellbinding orator and ardent black nationalist, he successfully campaigned for a severance of all ties with France in a 1958 referendum and at first led his country on a strongly leftist course, also gaining a reputation for harshly repressive rule. In the 1970's he moved toward closer ties with the West. March 26 at a hospital in Cleveland.

Truffaut, François, 52, French film director noted for his sentimental style and his depictions of children and of the obsessions of love; his movies included *The 400 Blows* (1959), *Jules and Jim* (1961), *Soft Skin* (1964), *Stolen Kisses* (1968), and the Academy Award–win-

New Wave film director François Truffaut, one of the most important filmmakers of the century, had his first big success with The 400 Blows.

ning *Day for Night* (1973). He was a leading member of the New Wave group of filmmakers and wrote extensively on the cinema. October 21 in Neuilly-sur-Seine, France.

Tubb, Ernest, 70, American country music performer; influential pioneer of country music's honky-tonk sound, he was a star of radio's "Grand Ole Opry" for 40 years and one of Nashville's most consistent hit-makers. September 6 in Nashville, Tenn.

Ulam, Stanislaw Marcin, 75, Polish-born American mathematician who with Edward Teller played a key role in developing the hydrogen bomb. May 13 in Santa Fe, N.M.

Ustinov, Dmitri Fedorovich, 76, Soviet marshal and defense minister since 1976. An engineer and former armaments minister, he played a major role in mobilizing the arms industry during World War II and guiding the postwar Soviet military buildup; also named a full member of the Politburo in 1976, he became a key Soviet power, regarded as a backer of hard-line foreign policy combined with economic reform at home. Death on December 20 announced the next day.

Voorhis, Jerry, 83, five-term Democratic congressman from California; he was best known for his 1946 defeat by political newcomer Richard M. Nixon, which marked the beginning of Nixon's road to the White House. September 11 in Claremont, Calif.

Wallace, Lila Acheson, 94, American publisher and philanthropist; a cofounder of the *Reader's Digest* with her husband, DeWitt Wallace, she donated more than $60 million of the Wallace fortune to the arts and to various charities. May 8 in Mount Kisco, N.Y.

Former Olympic swimming champion Johnny Weissmuller was well known to movie audiences as the monosyllabic Tarzan of the Apes.

Waring, Fred M., 84, American conductor and composer whose softly melodic vocal and instrumental group, the Pennsylvanians, was a fixture of American popular music for more than half a century, performing on radio and television, on concert tours, and at the White House. He also invented the Waring Blendor. July 29 in Danville, Pa.

Weissmuller, Johnny, 79, American swimmer and movie star; winner of five Olympic gold medals in swimming during the 1920's, he later became the most famous screen Tarzan. January 20 in Acapulco, Mexico.

Werner, Oskar, 61, Austrian actor best known for his roles in such films as *Jules and Jim* and *Ship of Fools* and for his classic interpretation of Hamlet on the German stage. October 23 in Marburg, West Germany.

West, Jessamyn (Mary Jessamyn West), 81, American author whose collection of stories about Quaker farmers of the Civil War era, entitled *The Friendly Persuasion* (1945), became an immediate success and was made into a popular film. February 23 in Napa, Calif.

Willson, Meredith, 82, American composer, librettist, and lyricist of *The Music Man,* one of the outstanding musical comedies of the 1950's; an accomplished flutist, he also composed extensively for radio and films. June 15 in Santa Monica, Calif.

Wilson, Jackie, 49, American Golden Gloves boxer turned rock-and-roll singer; his 1959 hit "Lonely Teardrops" earned him his first gold record and launched him on the road to success. January 21 in Mt. Holly, N.J.

Wilson, Peter Cecil, 71, British auctioneer who as chairman of Sotheby's from 1958 to 1980 transformed the small London art-auction house into a global enterprise operating in 21 countries. June 3 in Paris.

Winogrand, Garry, 56, pioneering American photographer celebrated for "the snapshot aesthetic"—street scenes and public events shot with a wide-angle lens and a seemingly artless spontaneity. March 19 in Tijuana, Mexico.

Winwood, Estelle, 101, durable British-born actress who played the Fairy Godmother in the film *The Glass Slipper* (1955); she had hundreds of other roles on stage, screen, and television since her theatrical debut in 1888. June 20 in Los Angeles.

Jessamyn West wrote movingly about Quaker farmers of the Civil War era in The Friendly Persuasion.

Wrather, John Devereaux (Jack), 66, American oil, real estate, TV-radio-film entrepreneur and charter member of Ronald Reagan's original "kitchen cabinet"; his TV productions included *The Lone Ranger* and *Lassie.* November 12 in Santa Monica, Calif.

Yadin, Yigael, 67, Israeli military figure, statesman, and archaeologist; a hero-strategist in the 1948 Arab-Israeli war and later Israel's foremost archaeologist, noted for his excavation of the fortress of Masada and other archaeological discoveries in the Holy Lands. From 1977 to 1981, Yadin served in government as deputy prime minister. June 28 in Hadera, Israel.

Young, Stephen M., 95, often cantankerous Ohio Democrat who served 20 years in the U.S. House and Senate prior to his retirement at the age of 81. December 1 in Washington, D.C.   P.H.

OHIO. See STATISTICS OF THE WORLD.

OKLAHOMA. See STATISTICS OF THE WORLD.

OMAN. See STATISTICS OF THE WORLD. See also PERSIAN GULF STATES.

ONTARIO. See STATISTICS OF THE WORLD. See also CANADA.

OREGON. See STATISTICS OF THE WORLD.

ORGANIZATION OF AMERICAN STATES. Jaõa Clemente Baena Soares, of Brazil, was elected secretary-general of the Organization of American States at a special General Assembly held in Washington, D.C., in March. His election was unanimous, but it followed the withdrawal of another candidate, Val T. McComie of Barbados, the assistant secretary-general. McComie's candidacy had represented an apparent bid by the organization's English-speaking Caribbean members to increase their influence. It pointed up tensions between the relatively new Caribbean members, many of them tiny nations, and the older Spanish-speaking members.

At the same March meeting, the Caribbean island nation of St. Kitts–Nevis (St. Christopher and Nevis) was admitted as the 32nd member of the organization.

In April, the retiring secretary-general of the OAS, Alejandro Orfila of Argentina, who was resigning a year before the end of his term, was formally chastised by the Permanent Council for dual employment. In addition to his more than $7,000 monthly salary from the OAS, Orfila had violated OAS rules by accepting $25,000 per month from a second employer, a Washington public relations firm, during his final three months in office.

The 14th annual OAS General Assembly, held in Brasília in November, was dominated by public addresses and behind-the-scenes meetings concerning the nearly two-year-old effort of the so-called Contadora group (Mexico, Columbia, Venezuela, and Panama) to mediate hostilities among the countries of Central America. In speeches at the conference, most of the Latin American foreign ministers endorsed the Contadora effort, as did U.S. Secretary of State George Shultz. However, there was disagreement over the Contadora group's latest draft regional peace treaty. The draft, produced in September and accepted by Nicaragua, was rejected by Honduras, El Salvador, and Costa Rica, which proposed amendments. These amendments were said to go beyond a U.S. insistence that any demilitarization in the region be verifiable and to provide leeway for continuing U.S. military maneuvers in Central America.

At the November meeting, the OAS voted to censure the departed secretary-general for his dual employment earlier in the year, but a move to rescind Orfila's pension did not succeed. Many speakers lamented the OAS's lack of effectiveness and called for it to take a more active role in such areas as peace negotiations (currently being handled outside the framework of the OAS by the Contadora group) and debt problems (being discussed by the group of 11 debtor nations known as the Cartagena group). A special plenary session of the organization was set for 1985 to discuss revisions of the OAS charter.   L.L.P

ORGANIZATION OF PETROLEUM EXPORTING COUNTRIES. Throughout 1984 the Organization of Petroleum Exporting Countries (OPEC) was plagued by factional tensions and diminished credibility, with some of its 13 members discounting prices and others selling more than their allocated quotas. The major rift was between large OPEC producers with small populations, like Saudi Arabia, Kuwait, and the United Arab Emirates, and the more financially pressed OPEC producers with large populations and expansive development requirements, such as Nigeria and Indonesia. International supplies were not affected when Iraq and Iran began staging attacks on oil tankers in the Persian Gulf early in the year; prices did not rise and anticipated shortages failed to appear.

Efforts by OPEC watchdog and monitoring committees to hold the line on prices and production quotas were frustrated in October, when Nigeria unilaterally cut prices by $2 a barrel, following the lead of two non-OPEC countries, Great Britain and Norway, which cut oil prices by over $1 a barrel. (Canada later cut oil prices as well.)

The cuts precipitated an emergency OPEC meeting in Geneva from October 29 to October 31. Following the meeting, OPEC ministers announced that, beginning November 1, OPEC would cut its overall oil production ceiling from 17.5 million barrels a day, established in 1983, to 16 million barrels. Theoretically, the agreement provided production cuts of 8.57 percent for all members, but in practice the poorer nations were able to exceed their maximum allocations so long as some other member accepted an equivalent reduction. The cuts were to be distributed among 11 members only, with neither Nigeria nor Iraq included. Saudi Arabia agreed to the largest cut—647,000 barrels a day—lowering its quota to 4,353,000 barrels, far below its one-time production of 7 million barrels a day. Other members agreeing to cutbacks of 100,000 barrels a day or more were Indonesia, Iran, Kuwait, Libya, United Arab Emirates, and Venezuela. To reinforce OPEC's position, Sheikh Ahmed Zaki Yamani, Saudi Arabia's oil minister, obtained agreement from Mexico and Egypt, neither of them OPEC members, to accept a temporary combined production cut of 130,000 barrels a day.

OPEC also was facing growing problems in its pricing structure. One difficulty was the $3-a-barrel differential between heavy and the more expensive light crude oil. New technology has made it possible to extract nearly as much energy from heavy oil as from light, and increasing pressure of competition from heavy crude threatened to undermine the price for Saudi Arabian light, used as OPEC's benchmark for sales in the world markets. At a meeting in December, OPEC ministers agreed to an interim pricing arrangement increasing the price of heavy crude by 50 cents a barrel while reducing the light crude price by 25 cents, but Nigeria and Algeria broke ranks and refused to go along. Nigeria complained that the plan was not bold enough to solve the problem. Ministers also approved an auditing plan that would place observers in OPEC countries to monitor oil production and pricing to determine whether the organization's guidelines are observed. However, Algeria promptly balked at part of the plan, by indicating it would not allow its petroleum condensates to be audited.   D.P.

P

PACIFIC ISLANDS. French nuclear weapons tests at Mururoa, port calls by U.S. warships, and proposed dumping of nuclear waste in the Pacific Ocean were matters of concern in the Pacific Islands during 1984. Governmental protests culminated in denunciation of the testing by 14 members of the South Pacific Forum, meeting on Tuvalu in late August. The Forum also appointed a committee to draw up a draft treaty to declare the region a nuclear-free zone. Signatories of the treaty would agree not to store or test nuclear weapons and to oppose the dumping of nuclear wastes. The question of banning visits by nuclear-powered warships would be left up to individual states.

In September, Palau residents voted by a two-to-one margin in favor of a new proposed compact of free association with the United States, which would make Palau an independent nation but leave the United States responsible for its defense. Discussions continued in Palau after the vote, however, because of an antinuclear clause in Palau's constitution, which conflicted with the defense program of the United States.

In the French territory of New Caledonia, the Republican Party, backed by French settlers

---

A Bird in the Head

MacGillivray's petrel, a small black and brown bird that had been officially sighted only one time, 129 years ago, recently put an emphatic end to rumors of its extinction by crashing into an ornithologist's head. British naturalist Dick Watling had made several trips to the island of Gau in Fiji to look for the bird; he finally proved it still existed when he lured a specimen in from the sea one night with lights and recordings. Watling examined the dazed bird after it struck his head, then let it go, unwilling to take a specimen until he knew how many more there might be.

opposed to independence, won a majority of seats in November elections to a territorial assembly. (French settlers are in the majority in the territory.) The elections were, however, boycotted by native Melanesian separatists associated with the leading independence group, the Kanaka Socialist National Liberation Front, which staged a series of violent acts to dramatize its demands for immediate independence. France sought to calm the violence by indicating it would speed up the timetable for possible independence; the original plan called for a referendum on self-determination to be held in 1989. In early December the French government sent a special emissary to the island to negotiate an interim political settlement between the Melanesians, or Kanaks, and the settlers. The day after he arrived, however, ten Melanesian separatists were ambushed and massacred in the continuing unrest.

A U.S. tuna boat violated the Solomon Islands' 200-mile economic zone and was seized. The United States does not recognize coastal rights within that zone to migratory species such as tuna. The crew were fined and then released; meanwhile, the United States embargoed tuna products from the Solomons.

In May, Pope John Paul II paid a brief visit to the island of Guadalcanal, where he prayed for those killed in the World War II Battle of Guadalcanal.

See STATISTICS OF THE WORLD. R.A.S.

PAKISTAN. Muhammad Zia ul-Haq continued to govern Pakistan as president and chief martial law administrator in 1984, encountering sporadic widespread protests.

Politics and Government. By January, order had been restored to Sind Province, torn by criminal and politically motivated violence since August 1983. The violence was provoked in part by Zia's announced plan to hold partyless national and provincial elections in 1985, with separate indirect elections for a strong chief executive. The most violent protests were attributed to the Pakistan People's Party (PPP) of Zulfikar Ali Bhutto (Zia's predecessor, hanged in 1979), which continued to have a wide following.

Concerned about the violence, Zia met with opposition leaders and, in the course of the year, released many politicians who had been detained. Among them were Benazir Bhutto, Ali Bhutto's daughter and leader of the PPP, who was freed from house arrest in January

Pope John Paul II extends a hand to a Roman Catholic tribesman in Mount Hagen, Papua New Guinea, where 180,000 people gathered for a mass celebrated by the pontiff in pidgin English.

and permitted to leave the country for medical treatment, and Asghar Khan, leader of the party Tehrik-i-Istiqlal.

In April, Zia considered holding a referendum instead of elections, sparking new protests, especially among students who opposed the government for having banned their unions. More than a thousand students were arrested, and universities in Karachi, Lahore, and Peshawar were closed. In early December he announced that a referendum would be held on December 19; at the same time, he issued a decree making it a crime for anyone to call for its boycott. The referendum question was whether Zia should seek a five-year extension of his presidency in 1985 elections and whether Islamic law should continue to be applied strictly; according to the government, about 98 percent of the voters responded favorably.

In September, Zia announced that 56 members of the armed forces would be tried for plotting with Indian and Libyan agents to overthrow the government. Two of Bhutto's sons, leaders of the terrorist group Al-Zulfiqar, and believed to be in Libya, were to be tried in absentia.

Foreign Affairs. Relations with India continued to be shadowed by the issue of alleged Pakistani aid to Sikh dissidents in the Indian state of Punjab. On July 5, Sikh militants hijacked an Indian Airlines jet and forced it to fly to Pakistan, where they demanded release of Sikhs jailed in India and compensation for damages in the Indian army's raid on the Sikh's Golden Temple in June. After the militants surrendered on July 6, Pakistan refused Indian requests for their extradition. In October there were reports of increased Indian-Pakistan skirmishes in Kashmir. Following the assassination of Indian Prime Minister Indira Gandhi on October 31, Zia declared a three-day period of mourning and pledged to support her son and successor, Rajiv, in building "a relationship of trust and confidence" between the two countries.

U.S. Vice-President George Bush visited Pakistan in May. He lauded the government for its assistance to Afghan refugees and met with refugees at a camp near the Kyber Pass, where he promised continued U.S. support.

Pakistan played a major role early in the year in reviving the pact known as the Regional Cooperation for Development, established to encourage cooperation among Pakistan, Iran, and Turkey in socioeconomic and cultural matters.

Economy. Pakistan continued to depend on foreign aid to offset its trade deficits. For the fiscal year beginning July 1, Pakistan received $1.8 billion in long-term, low-interest loans. The 1984–1985 budget aimed at a growth of 8.5 percent in the gross domestic product and an effective 14 percent increase in development expenditures.

See STATISTICS OF THE WORLD. L.Z.

PALAU. See PACIFIC ISLANDS.

PALESTINE LIBERATION ORGANIZATION. The year 1984 found the Palestine Liberation Organization still seeking to recover from blows dealt it by the Israeli invasion of Lebanon in 1982 and by a Syrian-backed rebellion in its most important constituent group, al-Fatah, in 1983. PLO chairman Yasir Arafat tried, with limited success, to surmount the organization's internal divisions and revive its momentum.

Early in the year, many observers felt that Arafat was finished as leader of the PLO, but the chairman held onto his authority and managed to reduce the Syrian-backed Abu Musa faction to an isolated minority in Palestinian politics. He did so despite dissatisfaction among many with what was seen as his indecisive leadership, his military errors during the Israeli onslaught in Lebanon, and his failure to choose between a military stance and a diplomatic approach. In fact, Arafat remained popular among rank-and-file Palestinians, and many, concerned that PLO unity should be preserved, were bitter toward the Syrian-backed Palestinian fighters who had taken up arms against Arafat and forced his contingent to flee from Lebanon in late 1983.

Arafat attempted throughout the year to reunify PLO ranks and reassert his authority. In January the al-Fatah Central Council, meeting in Tunis, expelled Abu Musa and four other rebel leaders. In February, Arafat met with Jordan's King Hussein in Amman, despite Syria's antipathy for any form of Jordanian-PLO cooperation. Four Damascus-based Palestinian organizations—the Democratic Alliance—attended a reconciliation meeting with Fatah loyalists in South Yemen in March. Feelings

301

PLO leader Yasir Arafat (center) confers with other PLO officials at the organization's council meeting in November, during which Arafat sought to firm up his shaky control over the Palestinian movement.

ran so high after the meeting that al-Fatah threatened to call its own general conference that would exclude the Alliance groups. However, some progress was made at a second meeting in Algiers in April, and a consensus on at least some points emerged in Aden in June. The resulting agreement, later formalized in Algiers, called for intensified resistance to Israeli rule in the West Bank and the Gaza Strip, while criticizing Arafat's visit to Egypt in late 1983 and insisting that relations with Jordan not detract from the PLO's status as sole representative of the Palestinians. The pact also condemned the use of arms to settle internal disputes. Two new vice-chairmen representing left-wing factions were named to act as a check on Arafat.

At a meeting of the Palestine National Council, held under tight security in Amman, Jordan, in November, Arafat offered to resign as PLO leader, but he consented to stay on at the insistence of the council, which functions as government-in-exile. Syrian-backed rebels did not attend the meeting. The council supported a call by King Hussein for a Middle East peace conference and elected a new speaker of the parliament, replacing a Syrian-backed incumbent. The meeting provoked an increase in violence among PLO factions. Among later incidents that may have been related was the murder of a PLO executive committee member and former mayor of Hebron, Fahad Kawasmeh, in Amman on December 29. Arafat blamed Syria for the killing.

Throughout the year, sporadic acts of terrorism were carried out by Palestinians within Israel and in the Israeli-occupied West Bank and Gaza Strip. It was unclear to what extent the PLO was responsible. M.C.H.

PANAMA. In May 1984, Panama had its first popular presidential elections in 16 years, with the military-backed candidate winning a narrow victory according to disputed official results.

In January the ruling Democratic Revolutionary Party named its presidential candidate for the election—the country's first direct election since 1968, when General Omar Torrijos came to power. The party nominee, backed by the powerful National Defense Force and its commander, General Manuel Antonio Noriega, was Nicolás Ardito Barletta Vallarina, a 45-year-old economist who had served as ministry of planning under Torrijos. Incumbent

President Ricardo de la Espriella resigned in February, reportedly under pressure, after having refused to shuffle the cabinet as desired by the military. Vice-President Jorge Illueca temporarily succeeded de la Espriella as president, pending the election and inauguration of a successor.

The May 6 election further destabilized the political scene, which had been in flux since the death of Torrijos in 1981. Many people believed that Barletta's principal opponent, Arnulfo Arias Madrid, an 83-year-old physician and three-time former president overthrown by the military in 1968, had actually won the election and that he was then robbed of his victory by the military and the official party. The official final results, announced ten days after the voting, showed Barletta to have defeated Arias by only 1,713 votes out of some 600,000 cast. Barletta said he would head a "unity government" and concentrate on attacking the country's economic problems. He was sworn in on October 11.

The economy continued to stagnate with the deterioration of public financing and private sector investment, coupled with a public debt of about $3.5 billion, the highest per capita debt in Latin America. Unemployment was said to be as high as 50 percent in some areas. On the positive side, inflation was low, and because of the relative importance of the service sector, the economy was not overly affected by falling commodity prices on world markets. As a member of the Contadora Group, Panama, in its official position toward the Central American crisis, continued to emphasize the principles of dialogue, negotiation, democratic coexistence, economic development, and separation of regional issues from the global East-West conflict. Some government initiatives seemed to suggest Panamanian support for the United States, but others indicated neutrality or even opposition. Panama declined to participate in joint military exercises with the United States in Honduras and closed the U.S. Army's School of the Americas, which had trained thousands of Central American military personnel since the 1940's.

See STATISTICS OF THE WORLD. S.R.

APUA NEW GUINEA. See STATISTICS OF THE WORLD.

PARAGUAY. In 1984, mixed signals emanated from President Alfredo Stroessner, the army general who has ruled Paraguay continuously since the 1954 coup. A "political opening," seemed to occur in January and February. Exiled political leaders of the Mopoco Party (a breakaway faction of the ruling Colorado Party) were allowed to return. The opposition Febrerista Party was able to hold a rally on February 17 in the capital, attended by 2,000 people. However, in March, Aldo Zucolillo, publisher of ABC Color, Paraguay's largest newspaper, was arrested, and the paper closed by the Interior Ministry. ABC Color was accused of political agitation and subversion for publishing statements by Mopoco leader Miguel Angel González Casablanca, who had returned in 1983 from a 25-year exile. Zucolillo was later released. In April, the government detained four U.S. lawyers on a human rights tour, finally deporting them to Brazil. In June, a politically oriented sports magazine, written largely by former ABC Color journalists, was closed down after one issue.

Newspaper articles maintained that high-ranking Paraguayan military officials continued to be involved with the smuggling of liquor, cigarettes, and narcotics. This official corruption was reportedly encouraged by the Stroessner regime but, at the same time, strongly resented by many junior officers.

With industry, construction, and tourism in decline, much hope was placed on the 1984 cotton and soybean crops, which together generate 60 percent of the country's export earnings. In June, the World Bank guaranteed a $15 million loan to farmers by a commercial bank. The loan featured fixed installment payments on principal and interest throughout the period of the loan. Additional debt incurred through increased interest rates would be paid at the end of the loan period, which would be extended for this purpose.

Brazil unilaterally decided to withhold payments accruing to Paraguay from the output of the jointly operated hydroelectric installation at Itaipú (which began operating in October), to compensate for money owed by Paraguay for Brazilian exports.

See STATISTICS OF THE WORLD. J.F.

PENNSYLVANIA. See STATISTICS OF THE WORLD.

303

People in the News

The parade of new and familiar celebrities continued in 1984, as crowned heads, first families, the lucky, the talented, and the fleet attracted media attention.

The lives of the rich and famous furnished the occasion for amusement, diversion, and sometimes sympathy in 1984, a year dominated in large party by politics. In an age of media supremacy, politicians had to hone their communication skills or suffer the consequences. Presidential and royal families, Olympic champions and film stars, beauty pageant queens, lottery winners, and even one intrepid balloonist found themselves thrust under the bright, sometimes harsh light of public scrutiny.

As the U.S. first family, the Reagans conducted their lives and campaign appearances partly in a media-wise series of photo oppor-

tunities and appealing images. In August, at the Republican National Convention in Dallas, an evocative 18-minute film celebrating the presidency of **Ronald Reagan** preceded the appearance of the man himself to accept the party's nomination. Earlier in the proceedings, the image of the president, waving from a giant-screen television to a diminutive, real-life **Nancy Reagan** at the podium, showed the Great Communicator in firm command of the medium.

In contrast to convention politics, the marriage of the Reagans' daughter **Patti Davis** to yoga instructor **Paul Grilley**, 25, during the

Former President Jimmy Carter (right) discusses carpentry work needed in a Manhattan tenement with the manager of the Habitat for Humanity project. Carter and 40 fellow Georgians traveled to New York by bus to help restore the burned-out building.

same month, was a quiet affair. The 31-year-old actress, known for her mildly countercultural views, tied the knot in a private ceremony at the Hotel Bel-Air in California—3,000 miles from the spotlight of the White House Rose Garden. Asked if she had cried during her daughter's wedding, Nancy Reagan replied, "That's like asking me if I breathe."

The tranquil family image was shattered later in the year, however, when the press reported a flare-up revolving around **Michael Reagan**, 38, the president's adopted son by his first marriage to actress **Jane Wyman** and the father of his only two grandchildren. Nancy Reagan asserted in an interview that Michael had been estranged from his father for the past three years; Michael replied that it was more a matter of jealousy on the part of the first lady toward the family of another marriage, and he said that she should apologize for the public remark. **Maureen Reagan,** the president's oldest daughter, joined the fray on her father's side. The quarrel appeared to have been patched up in late December, when Michael and his family held a three-hour reunion with the president and his wife in a Los Angeles hotel where the first family was staying. The meeting marked the first time President Reagan had ever seen Michael's daughter, 20-month-old **Ashley**.

After the tiring election campaign was over, defeated candidate **Walter Mondale** offered a brief analysis, saying that he had never "warmed" to television, or vice versa. Most observers believed that Mondale's discomfort on that score had played at least some role in his landslide loss. One Mondale speechwriter, when asked who else could have beaten Reagan, theorized, "Robert Redford. Maybe Walter Cronkite."

But being down does not mean being out. Former President **Richard M. Nixon** kept making his way into the headlines. Early in the year, he had set his sights on purchasing a $1.8 million co-op apartment on New York's elegant Park Avenue. His intention was reportedly to sell his suburban New Jersey estate and move to Manhattan, where his ailing wife, **Pat**, would be more comfortable. Controversy, as always, pursued them. A 92-year-old liberal philanthropist, charging that the Nixons' ten-

ancy would turn the building into a "tourist attraction," led a brief opposition to the co-op sale. Nixon easily won acceptance from the co-op board, but later decided to cancel the move. The former president resurfaced in April, when a series of television interviews with former aide **Frank Gannon** were broadcast. The exposure probably helped Nixon in his tireless effort to put the Watergate scandal behind him and emerge as something of an elder statesman in the GOP.

Another former occupant of the White House, **Jimmy Carter**, traveled by bus from Georgia to New York City for a brief stint as a construction worker. As part of an effort organized by Habitat for Humanity, a nonprofit group, home carpenter Carter spent five days of a vacation with like-minded volunteers renovating a burned-out New York City apartment building. A little hard labor didn't faze the former chief executive. "I've been doing this sort of work all my life," he observed.

The family of former President John F. Kennedy suffered a new tragedy when **David Kennedy**, 28, son of the late Senator Robert F. Kennedy, died of an apparent drug overdose in April. His body was found in a $250-a-night hotel room in Palm Beach, Fla., near the home of the ailing matriarch **Rose Kennedy,** whom family members were visiting. David's drug abuse problems were well-known; in 1979 he made headlines when he was mugged in a Harlem hotel known as a meeting place for drug dealers and addicts. He had tried unsuccessfully to beat his addiction; observers said that he was never able to recover from the trauma, at age 13, of seeing his father assassinated on television.

On a brighter note, David's older brother **Robert F. Kennedy, Jr.**, celebrated the birth of a son in September. He and his wife, **Emily**, named the boy Robert F. Kennedy III. JFK's daughter **Caroline**, 26, television coordinator for New York's Museum of Modern Art, went to Boston to raise funds for the John F. Kennedy Library Foundation, which encourages young people to work for constructive change through political action. Her mother, **Jacqueline Kennedy Onassis**, editor for a New York publishing firm, appeared before the New York State legislature to lobby for granting landmark status to architecturally noteworthy places of worship. During the year, the former first lady also won a court action barring model **Barbara Reynolds** from appearing in advertisements as a Jackie lookalike and halting further use of a Christian Dior ad that showed a wedding scene with Jackie O. seemingly one of the guests.

The daughter of another former head of state, **Svetlana Alliluyeva**, startled the Western world by returning in October to the country once ruled by her father, Joseph Stalin, and resuming Soviet citizenship. Alliluyeva had emigrated to the West 17 years earlier, living for 15 years in the United States and for two in Great Britain. In a prepared statement issued in Moscow, Alliluyeva claimed she had not felt free in the West "a single day." However, she indicated that her strongest reason for returning had been a desire to be nearer to her physician son, and her geophysicist daughter. Alliluyeva's American-born daughter, **Olga Peters**, 13, the child of a former marriage to architect William Wesley Peters, went with her to Moscow—not eagerly, according to some reports. By late December, Svetlana Alliluyeva had reportedly moved to her father's native Georgia.

The British royal family were newsmakers as

Svetlana Alliluyeva, daughter of former Soviet dictator Joseph Stalin, explains at a news conference in Moscow why she decided to return to her homeland after 17 years in the United States and Britain.

always. **Charles** and **Diana**, the Prince and Princess of Wales, had a second son on September 15, whom they named **Prince Henry Charles Albert David.** But headlines proclaimed simply that everyone was "Wild About Harry." Older brother **William**, 2, charmed reporters at his own press conference in the summer, peeking through a cameraman's viewfinder and uttering his first on-the-record remarks. (He said, "Who's that?")

Diana, at age 23, showed no signs of settling into matronly ways, however. For the opening of Parliament in autumn, she appeared with her hair rolled into a classic coiffure topped off by a diamond tiara. Before the dailies were through debating the switch from her famous shorter, breezy style, she bobbed up at a London community center with yet another new style.

Prince Charles stirred a small tempest on his own when, as honored speaker at a banquet of the Royal Institute of British Architects in May, he invidiously compared modern architectural design to traditional buildings that he claimed were more to the taste of the average Briton. His younger brother, **Prince Andrew**, found a new amour: model and dancer **Katie Rabett**. She was less controversial than her predecessor, sometime–porn actress **Koo Stark**, who by now had apparently recovered from her breakup with the prince; she married the heir to a trading stamp fortune in August. Scandalous headlines erupted when a Fleet Street tabloid published what it said were photos of Andrew's new girlfriend in the nude, but they were later declared to be fakes. The prince himself remained irrepressible. Visiting the set of the MGM film *2010* in Hollywood, he accidentally-on-purpose splattered accompanying journalists with paint from a spray gun, declaring "I enjoyed that." (One of the newspapers later sent the prince a bill for damaged cameras.)

Queen Elizabeth II set a busy pace for herself with a number of trips. In late September she began a two-week visit to Canada, accompanied for most of the tour by **Prince Philip**. She took part in ceremonies observing the 200th anniversary of the settlement of New Brunswick and Ontario and the 150th birthday of Toronto. Following her Canadian trip, the queen made a private visit to the bluegrass

Twenty-day-old Prince Henry Charles Albert David poses with his parents, the Prince and Princess of Wales, and his older brother, Prince William, at Kensington Palace. Prince Harry, third in line for the British throne, was born on September 15.

area of Kentucky, where she placidly enjoyed viewing the local thoroughbred stock, and she also made a visit to Wyoming. On an earlier state visit to Jordan, however, the queen attracted some controversy when she made public comments that seemed to express sympathy for the Palestinian cause and disapproval of Israeli settlements on the West Bank.

Meanwhile, in Monaco, **Princess Caroline,** 27, and husband **Stefano Casiraghi,** 24, announced the birth of a son, **Andréa Albert Grace,** in June, to the delight of first-time grandfather **Prince Ranier** III. Although the birth took place less than six months after Caroline's marriage, there was little scandal, confirming once again that times have changed. Younger sister **Princess Stephanie** drew her share of attention after the French magazine *Paris-Match* published photos of the princess on the Riviera, in a barely-there swimsuit, with **Anthony De-on.** The shots raised questions about where her boyfriend of two years, **Paul Belmondo,** stood in Stephanie's affections. Both of her friends are sons of French movie stars.

The Olympic games put their own royalty into the limelight. Newborn **Alexander Ryan Mahre** demonstrated a promising sense of timing by entering the world just half an hour before his dad, U.S. skier **Phil Mahre,** finished first in the men's slalom event at the winter Olympics in Sarajevo, Yugoslavia. The world's newest gymnastic darling, 16-year-old **Mary Lou Retton** of West Virginia, ensured that her winning smile and lithe figure would remain highly visible by signing contracts with Vidal Sassoon, McDonald's, and that all-American breakfast standby, Wheaties. Retton and women's marathon winner **Joan Benoit,** of Maine, were named amateur sportswomen of the year by the Women's Sport Foundation.

One of the world's best-known sports celebrities, **Muhammad Ali,** entered the Neurological Institute of New York for evaluation of symptoms that included slurred speech, slowed movement, and tremor. Doctors diagnosed the ailment as Parkinson's syndrome (less serious than the better known Parkinson's disease), with the blows to the head received during

307

Princess Caroline of Monaco leaves the hospital in June with her newborn son, Andréa Albert Grace. She was accompanied by her father, Prince Rainier (left), and her husband, Stefano Casiraghi.

Ali's boxing career cited as a probable cause. With medication, Ali's prognosis was considered good. Tributes to the boxer poured in, and his flair for making friends and news was evident despite his illness. Before being discharged, he received Democratic politician **Jesse Jackson,** with reporters and photographers crowding the scene.

Another sad story involved **Vanessa Williams,** 21, the first black woman to wear the Miss America crown. She was forced to relinquish her title in July, after it was disclosed that *Penthouse* magazine was publishing nude photographs showing her in lesbian-style embraces with another woman. Williams admitted having posed for the photos in 1982, for a freelance photographer, who eventually sold them to *Penthouse* publisher **Bob Guccione.** (Late in the year, the magazine published a second set of compromising pictures as well.) The crown was turned over to first runner-up **Suzette Charles,** 21, of New Jersey, also a black. She was succeeded in September by the new winner, 20-year-old **Sharlene Wells** of Utah. The daughter of a Mormon missionary, Wells seemed a conspicuously conservative choice; she does not smoke, drink, or take drugs and does not condone premarital sex.

Elizabeth Taylor went through a difficult year. In January she completed a seven-week stay at the Betty Ford Center in Rancho Mirage, Calif., for treatment of dependence on painkillers and sleeping pills. (**Liza Minnelli** and **Mary Tyler Moore** were among other patients at the center during the year, as was **Peter Lawford,** the debonair British-born film star and onetime Kennedy family in-law who died in December at the age of 61.) Taylor also had to face a personal tragedy when former husband **Richard Burton,** 58, died suddenly in August from a cerebral hemorrhage. The flamboyant Welshman was widely mourned as one of the great actors of all time, but Taylor was unable to attend the funeral in Europe because of the crush of the press. The 52-year-old actress later announced that her long-standing engagement to Mexican lawyer **Victor Gonzalez Luna** was off, but by the end of the year she was engaged to **Dennis Stein,** a New York City entrepreneur whom she reportedly had met on a blind date.

British actress **Vanessa Redgrave** enjoyed a legal triumph. In November a federal jury in Boston awarded her $100,000 in damages because the Boston Symphony Orchestra had canceled her scheduled performances as a narrator in six concerts during 1982. The jurors deemed the cancellations a breach of contract, although they rejected Redgrave's claim that the action had been a political one, motivated by her outspoken support of the Palestinian Liberation Organization.

On the other hand, **Stacy Keach,** the film actor starring in television's *Mickey Spillane's Mike Hammer,* pleaded guilty to having imported 1.3 ounces of cocaine into Great Britain in the spring. He was sentenced late in the year to nine months in a British prison, which he began serving immediately. Production of the series was suspended.

Famous couples continued to get together in 1984. In February, **Elton John,** 36, married German sound engineer **Renate Blauel,** 30. Another singer, rocker **Jerry Lee Lewis,** 48, was married for a sixth time, to budding country singer **Kerrie Macarver,** 22, in an April ceremony in Memphis. Lewis's last wife died in 1983 of a suspected drug overdose. In September, television and screen comedy stars **Gilda Radner,** 37, and **Gene Wilder,** 49, opted for a quiet civil ceremony in a small village in the south of France. To avoid publicity, they had neatly sidetracked the press by announcing they would wed in October in Connecticut. Sprightly **Sally Field,** 38, married movie producer **Alan Greisman,** 37, later in the year. **Jamie Lee Curtis,** 26, and **Christopher Guest,** 36, of the movie *This Is Spinal Tap,* tied the knot in December, as did singer **Olivia Newton-John,** 36, wed to **Matt Lattanzi,** 25, in an elaborate setting at her Malibu Canyon, Calif., estate. The most talked-about marriage, however, was undoubtedly that of veteran bachelor **Joe Namath** to actress **Deborah Lynn Mays,** 22, in November. The 41-year-old quarterback-turned-actor-turned-businessman was also in the news for launching yet another new venture: a line of men's underwear bearing his name.

Rolling Stone **Mick Jagger,** 40, and his long-time girlfriend, model **Jerry Hall,** 27, did not get married, but they did welcome a child,

Elizabeth Scarlett Jagger, in March. "Mick's a great father," said Hall on the *Today* show. But she hired a nanny to help out anyway.

John DeLorean remained in the news even after his acquittal in August on charges that he had conspired to sell $24 million worth of cocaine in an effort to save his ailing company. DeLorean's wife, actress-model **Cristina Ferrare,** had been a faithful companion during the grueling trial, but in October the couple announced that, after 11 years of marriage, they were filing for divorce. Meanwhile, DeLorean ran a full-page ad in a Los Angeles newspaper

Vanessa Williams, the first black Miss America, surrendered her crown in July, two months ahead of schedule, when it was disclosed that she had posed in the nude for a photographer in 1982. Penthouse magazine subsequently published the photographs.

Ex-quarterback Joe Namath completed a pass for the heart of actress Deborah Lynn Mays, whom he married in Fort Lauderdale, Fla., in November.

asking for public donations to help defray his legal expenses, estimated at over $1 million. According to a spokesman, contributions were plentiful.

Best-selling author **James Michener** proved the envy of many alumni societies when he donated $2 million to his alma mater, Swarthmore College. The Pulitzer Prize winner, orphaned from infancy, had received a $2,000 scholarship from the Quaker institution as an entering freshman in 1925; without it, he avows, he could not have attended college. Michener called his donation the repayment of a 59-year-old "loan"—with $1,998,000 in interest. Another college graduate was spotlighted when **Kristine Holderied** became the first woman to rank at the top of a U.S. Naval Academy graduating class. Holderied, an oceanography major, achieved a grade point average of 3.88 (out of 4.0), while also singing in the choir, playing softball and basketball, and serving as deputy commander of the midshipman brigade.

Persistence, daring, and skill marked another notable "first." After almost 84 hours in the air, American **Joe W. Kittinger,** 56, en route from Caribou, Me., triumphantly crash-landed near Savona, Italy, on September 18, becoming the first person ever to cross the Atlantic alone in a balloon. Kittinger had traveled some 3,535 miles in his helium-filled, ten-story-high balloon, dubbed *Rosie O'Grady's*.

The year confirmed still another expression of the American dream: that anyone can strike it rich. In September a Chicago printer won the largest lottery prize ever awarded to one individual—$40 million. **Michael Wittkowski,** 28, told the press that spending the bonanza would be a family affair, since he planned to share the winnings equally with his father, brother, and sister who had been buying tickets with him as a team. Like many other lottery winners he claimed that all that money would not really change his ways. His immediate plans included an engagement ring for his girlfriend, **Frances Pappas,** and Cubs baseball tickets. P.L.W.

Michael Wittkowski, a Chicago printer, and his fiancée, Frances Pappas, celebrate after he won the largest lottery prize ever awarded one individual—$40 million, in the Illinois state lottery.

BROADBENT, (JOHN) EDWARD

Leader of Canada's New Democratic Party, born March 21, 1936, in Oshawa, Ontario. Early in 1984, the small New Democratic Party appeared to be headed toward eclipse as the third force in Canadian politics. A Gallup poll in March indicated that only 11 percent of those questioned would vote for the NDP; four months later, the party's standing in the polls—its lowest in 24 years—remained unchanged. In the election on September 4, however, the NDP stood up strongly to the Conservative tidal wave, holding on to 30 of its 32 seats in Parliament. The credit was given largely to Ed Broadbent, who, in the opinion of many, proved the most impressive campaigner of the three major party leaders.

Born into a Conservative family, Broadbent studied at the University of Toronto and the London School of Economics and Political Science. Between 1955 and 1958 he served in the Royal Canadian Air Force. In 1965 he became professor of political science at York University, in Ontario.

Broadbent entered politics "because of a conscious choice . . . to build a different kind of Canada." Regarding himself as a fighter for "ordinary people," he joined the NDP—a left-of-center political party—and in 1968 ran successfully for a seat in Parliament. In 1974 he became parliamentary chief of the NDP, and the following year he was elected the party's national leader. A member of the Socialist International, he was named its vice-president in 1976.

BUSH, GEORGE H(ERBERT) W(ALKER)

U.S. vice-president, born June 12, 1924, in Milton, Mass. To many, George Bush remained a paradox. During Reagan's first term he was a model vice-president: hard-working, self-effacing, and loyal. Yet there lingered the memory that he had been the hope of Republican Party moderates against Ronald Reagan in the 1980 primary campaign, when he labeled Reagan's fiscal policies as "voodoo economics."

Bush's loyalty in the vice-presidency earned him Reagan's confidence. When some Republican conservatives mounted a "dump Bush" campaign in 1983, Reagan stopped them. On August 23, 1984, George Bush stood next to

Edward Broadbent, leader of Canada's New Democratic Party, predicted that his party would be the "real opposition" to the victorious Progressive Conservatives after the NDP finished not far behind the Liberals in the September general elections.

George Bush, who was reelected vice-president on the Republican ticket headed by President Ronald Reagan, became an early favorite to win the GOP presidential nomination in 1988.

Reagan at the Republican National Convention in Dallas to accept his party's renomination as vice-president, and he went on with Reagan to win reelection in November.

The son of Wall Street financier and U.S. Senator Prescott Bush, George Bush grew up near Greenwich, Conn. He served as a Navy combat pilot in World War II. After graduating from Yale University, he moved to Texas with his wife, Barbara, made a fortune in oil-drilling, and became active in politics. His résumé includes stints as a congressman, UN ambassador, Republican national chairman, envoy to China, and CIA director. During his first term as vice-president, Bush logged over 500,000 air miles representing the administration throughout the world. He also chaired the government's crisis management team, handling such delicate matters as the U.S. Marine withdrawal from Lebanon.

During the 1984 campaign, Bush visited more than 90 cities. At every stop he assailed the Democrats, contrasting their policies of "gloom and doom" with Reagan's optimistic message of pride and prosperity. There were Republican red faces during the controversy over whether Bush would release his federal income tax returns (he did). His overheard remark that he had tried "to kick a little ass" in his debate with Geraldine Ferraro also caused some embarrassment. But on balance, his performance appeared to give a healthy boost to the Republican campaign.

Konstantin Chernenko was named general secretary of the Communist Party of the Soviet Union in February, four days after the death of his predecessor, Yuri Andropov. Chernenko thus became the country's third leader in 15 months.

CHERNENKO, KONSTANTIN USTINOVICH

General secretary of the Soviet Communist Party, born September 24, 1911, in a village in Siberia. An aging member of the old guard who had been passed over for Yuri Andropov after the death of Leonid Brezhnev, Chernenko was chosen leader of the Soviet Union on February 13 after Andropov himself died in office. Within two months Chernenko was also elected chairman of the Presidium of the Supreme Soviet (making him head of state) and chairman of the Defense Council, completing the triumvirate of offices held by his predecessors. Nevertheless, party and government decision-making appeared to be more collegial under Chernenko than in the past.

During Chernenko's tenure in 1984, relations with China showed strong improvement, while signals toward the United States were mixed. There was the usual criticism of U.S. defense and other policies and the Soviet-led boycott of the Los Angeles Olympics, but Chernenko also called for a "drastic change" in U.S.–Soviet relations. On November 22 the two countries announced that Gromyko and Secretary of State George Shultz would meet in Geneva in January to negotiate an agenda for arms control talks; this was soon followed by relatively conciliatory remarks by the Soviet leader.

Born to a peasant family, Chernenko left school at the age of 12 to become a farm worker, later joining the Communist Youth League and eventually the Communist Party. In the early 1950's he met and became the trusted friend and "political valet" of Leonid Brezhnev, moving to Moscow with Brezhnev and joining the Politburo in 1978 under Brezhnev's aegis.

Chernenko showed occasional difficulty when speaking in public and was often absent from major public occasions, including the funeral of Defense Minister Dmitri Ustinov in December. (In that case, it was believed that the cold weather would have aggravated his emphysema.) His age and doubts about his health led many to regard him as an interim leader, but at least for the present, he appeared firmly entrenched.

DUARTE, JOSÉ NAPOLÉON

President of El Salvador, born November 23, 1926, in San Salvador. In a runoff election on May 6, Duarte, leader of the centrist Christian Democratic Party, took 54 percent of the vote to defeat ultraright candidate Roberto d'Aubuisson, becoming the first freely elected civilian president of the country in more than 50 years.

To many observers the elections, conducted in the midst of civil war, were a triumph for Duarte and democracy. The U.S. government had spent some $7 million to make the polling process fraud-resistant, and, more controversially, had funneled covert funds to the Duarte campaign to counter his heavily funded opponent.

Despite Duarte's electoral mandate, he remained an anathema to many Salvadorans. Those on the far right saw him as an unwitting ally of the Communists and feared his history of support for land reform and industrial nationalization. Many leftists believed him to be a tool of the United States, naïve in thinking he could curb the power of the landowners and military. During his first months in office, he appeared to be walking a fine line between trying to ease the worst human rights abuses, and not treading so heavily as to incur too strong a backlash from the right. On trips to the United States and Western European capitals he won strong support for his approach.

Remembered by old friends as a confident and headstrong youth, Duarte earned a civil engineering degree in the United States at the University of Notre Dame and then returned home in 1948 to enter politics. An ardent populist, he helped found the Christian Democratic Party and served three terms as mayor of San Salvador. In 1972 he narrowly lost his bid for presidency to a promilitary candidate

in a rigged election; he was later arrested and severely beaten for supporting a failed coup against the winner. After seven years of exile in Venezuela he returned, and in alliance with former adversaries in the military, served as president from 1980 to 1982.

FERRARO, GERALDINE A(NNE)

U.S. representative, born August 26, 1935, in Newburgh, N.Y. Ferraro was the first woman, and the first Italian-American, to be nominated for the vice-presidency by a major party. Although her candidacy did not stave off a Reagan landslide, or win the wide support from women that Democrats had hoped it would, it gained national recognition for the hitherto little-known congresswoman from New York City's borough of Queens. And it marked a major breakthrough for women. "My candidacy," Ferraro asserted when she conceded defeat in November, "has said the days of discrimination are numbered. American women will never again be second-class citizens."

Campaigning across the country, Ferraro drew huge crowds, which responded enthusiastically to her natural, forthright manner

The election of José Napoleón Duarte as president of El Salvador in May brought with it the promise that democratic institutions might flourish in the strife-torn Central American nation.

Representative Geraldine Ferraro (D, N.Y), shown here as she conceded defeat on November 6, was the first woman to be nominated for the office of vice-president on a major-party ticket.

dren were born—and to local politics, and in 1974, Ferraro became an assistant district attorney.

In 1978, despite her generally liberal views, Ferraro was elected to the U.S. House from New York's traditionally conservative 9th Congressional District. She easily won reelection in 1980 and 1982 and rose quickly in House Democratic ranks, with Speaker Thomas P. ("Tip") O'Neill, Jr., as her mentor. Twice elected secretary of the Democratic caucus, she was appointed by O'Neill to the influential Budget Committee in 1983 and chaired the 1984 Democratic platform committee.

GOODEN, DWIGHT (EUGENE)

Pitcher for the New York Mets, born November 16, 1964, in Tampa, Fla. The Mets' astonishing rise from National League doormat in 1983 to pennant contender in 1984 was spearheaded by the equally astounding talents of Dwight Gooden, the league's Rookie of the Year. The

with chants of "Gerry, Gerry." Her aplomb served her well; in a masterful press conference performance, she did much to quell controversy over delayed disclosure of her family finances. A Catholic with a pro-choice stand on abortion, she met the issue head-on, defending her position against criticism by anti-abortion forces.

After the election, the House Ethics Committee found that Ferraro actually had violated provisions of the Ethics in Government Act, by failing to report details of her husband's finances. But the panel ruled that the violations had not been intentional and recommended no formal congressional action against her, citing lack of time. In an unrelated matter, the Federal Election Commission cleared Ferraro and her husband of charges that they had violated federal election laws in her 1978 congressional campaign.

The daughter of Dominick Ferraro, an Italian immigrant, and Antonetta Ferraro, Ferraro graduated from Marymount Manhattan College, taught elementary school in Queens, and attended Fordham University Law School at night, earning her law degree in 1960. Soon afterward, she married John Zaccaro, a real estate developer. During the next 14 years she devoted her energies to her family—three chil-

Dwight Gooden, a 19-year-old pitcher for the New York Mets, finished the season with 276 strikeouts, a record for a major league rookie, and was named National League Rookie of the Year.

19-year-old right-hander struck out opposing batters at a record-setting rate on the way to a 17–9 won-lost record and a meager 2.60 earned run average. Relying mainly on a blazing fastball, clocked at over 95 miles per hour, as well as excellent control (especially for a young pitcher), Gooden finished the season with 276 strikeouts. That total—a record 11.44 per nine-inning game—was the most ever by a major league rookie.

Gooden, the youngest of Daniel and Ella Gooden's six children, was a stellar Little League performer as a third baseman. Once he began pitching at 12, it became obvious that he had found his vocation. The Mets made Gooden their first choice in the June 1982 free-agent draft, right after his senior year at Tampa's Hillsborough High School. The following year, on the Mets' Class A team in Lynchburg, Va., he struck out an amazing 300 batters in 191 innings; on the strength of his performance, he was invited to the parent club's 1984 spring training camp.

Gooden burst onto the national scene in the July 10 All-Star game, during which he struck out the side in the first inning he pitched. Later, on September 7, he struck out 11 batters in a winning effort over the division-leading Chicago Cubs, thereby surpassing Grover Cleveland Alexander's 73-year-old National League record of 227 strikeouts by a rookie pitcher. Five days later, striking out 16 Pittsburgh Pirates in a 2–0 Mets win, he eclipsed Herb Score's 1955 major league rookie record of 245 strikeouts. With another 16-strikeout performance against the Philadelphia Phillies on September 17, Gooden broke the National League record of 31 strikeouts in two consecutive starts (set by Hall-of-Famer Sandy Koufax in 1959) and tied the major league record of 32 (set by Luis Tiant in 1968 and equaled by Nolan Ryan in 1974).

HART, GARRY W(ARREN)

U.S. senator, born November 28, 1936, in Ottawa, Kan. "I love New Hampshire," Gary Hart said happily on the night of February 28. Colorado's Democrat senator was savoring his spectacular upset victory over the front-runner, former Vice-President Walter Mondale, in the state's presidential primary. Emerging from nowhere, he had made himself a force to be

Basing his campaign on "new ideas," Senator Gary Hart (Colo.) offered a strong challenge to front-runner Walter Mondale in the race for the Democratic presidential nomination.

reckoned with among the small army of Democrats seeking to gain the party's 1984 presidential nomination. But Hart could not convert an early string of primary victories into enough delegates to seriously erode Mondale's position and capture the nomination away from him.

In the Senate, Hart was regarded as a serious and independent thinker, particularly on national security issues, and he based his presidential campaign on a forceful appeal to the theme of "new ideas." However, his ideas on most issues differed only slightly from those of Mondale, who began charging that Hart's "new ideas" lacked definition—a contention he drove home by repeating the advertising slogan,

An effective orator with a flair for capturing public attention, the Reverend Jesse Jackson, a Democrat, became the first black leader to make a serious bid for a major-party presidential nomination.

"Where's the beef?" While losing key primaries, including those in Illinois and New York, Hart stayed in the fight all the way to California, which he won, but it was clear when the convention opened that Mondale was assured of the nomination. Nonetheless, Hart spoke to the convention in a last bid for support, warning that Reagan could be defeated only if the party offered "a new generation of ideas to a new generation of voters." Hart ended up with 1,200.5 votes to 2,191 for Mondale.

Born Gary Hartpence, he changed his surname after his graduation from Bethany Nazarene College; he went on at first to study for the ministry, at Yale Divinity School, but later turned to law, winning a degree from Yale Law School in 1964. Hart subsequently worked in the U.S. departments of Justice and Interior, joined a Denver law firm, and became involved in politics. In 1970 he met George McGovern, a long-shot Democratic presidential candidate,

and managed his successful bid for the 1972 nomination. Hart himself was elected to the U.S. Senate in 1974 and reelected in 1980.

JACKSON, JESSE L(OUIS)

Baptist minister and civil rights leader, born October 8, 1941, in Greenville, S.C. At the Democratic National Convention, Walter Mondale's nomination for president was assured. But no one could forget the dramatic speech by the first serious black candidate for president. "God is not finished with me yet," said Jesse Jackson as he ran through his familiar themes of poverty and oppression. He ended with the soulful burst of emotion that was his trademark: "Our time has come! Our time has come!"

With little money, Jackson carried more than 40 congressional districts and three-fourths of the black vote in the primaries. If he never created a "rainbow coalition" among the poor and rejected, as he had envisioned, he did capture the public's imagination. He also captured negative headlines at times. Early in the year, it was learned through black reporter Milton Coleman that Jackson had used the words "Hymie" and "Hymietown" in private conversation to refer to Jews and New York City. The incident haunted him until he finally apologized. Next, a Jackson supporter, Louis Farrakhan, the fiery black preacher who headed a group called the Nation of Islam, branded Coleman a traitor to his race. Jackson eventually denounced Farrakhan's comments but still did not condemn him personally.

After the primaries, Jackson pointed out that he had received 17 percent of the total primary vote but only 7 percent of the delegates—evidence, he believed, that the party rules were unfair. He also assailed Mondale for refusing to consider him for vice-president. Jackson's leverage was, however, limited by this time; one poll showed that most blacks now backed Mondale; it appeared that they viewed Jackson with pride but saw him more as their spokesman than as a potential president. Having visited Syria and won the release of a captured U.S. flier early in the year, he visited Cuba in June, met with Fidel Castro, and arranged the release of many Americans and Cuban prisoners. It was a typical Jackson gesture, both bold and controversial.

JACKSON, MICHAEL (JOE)

Popular singer and entertainer, born August 29, 1958, in Gary, Ind. At age 26, Michael Jackson has amassed a fortune few performers ever can claim. His face is one of the most familiar in the world. His *Thriller* album has sold over 35 million copies worldwide, more than any other record in history. And his personal idiosyncrasies, including the ever-present spangled single glove, have prompted a continuing fascination with this elflike entertainer with the high voice and razor-sharp dance moves.

Jackson's offstage manner is vulnerable and shy, his life-style reclusive and somewhat ascetic. A Jehovah's Witness and a vegetarian, Michael lives a quiet existence with his parents,

A hyperkinetic dancer with a soft, high-pitched singing voice, 26-year-old Michael Jackson ruled the world of pop music. He won eight Grammy awards, saw his Thriller *album sell 35 million copies, and conducted a tumultuous nationwide concert tour.*

two sisters, and a small menagerie on an Encino, Calif. estate. He began his career at age 5, as lead singer of the Jackson Five, a group formed with his four older brothers and coached by his father, a construction worker and guitarist. In the early 1970's the group appeared on Motown Records and sold millions of copies. Later, four Jackson brothers, including Michael, left Motown to sign with Epic Records as the Jacksons; the group, also including youngest brother Randy, continued their string of hits and were allowed to be their own producers.

In 1978, Michael made his movie debut, appearing as the Scarecrow with longtime mentor Diana Ross in *The Wiz.* In 1979 he released a solo album, *Off the Wall,* which sold 8 million copies. The subsequent Jacksons album, *Triumph,* did very well too. Michael's *Thriller* was the most successful of all, partly because of the videos produced for "Billie Jean" and "Beat It," featuring his eccentric, stylized dancing.

In January, Michael was burned on his scalp during the filming of a pyrotechnical Pepsi commercial. He recovered well and went on in March to garner an unprecedented eight Grammy awards. Then came a musical reunion with his brothers for another album, *Victory,* and a celebratory nationwide tour, complete with laser beams, clouds of smoke, and magic effects. Despite initial controversy over the sale of tickets by lottery (the system was soon scrapped), the tour ended up as another Jackson success.

LEWIS, CARL (FREDERICK CARLTON)

Olympic track and field star, born July 1, 1961, in Montgomery, Ala. In the 1984 summer Olympics, Carl Lewis was expected not only to win, but also to set records in all four events in which he competed, as he tried to duplicate the 1936 feat of the legendary Jesse Owens. Despite such pressure, the quietly self-confident athlete held to his own strategy, won his four golds, and entered the ranks of the world's great all-time sports figures.

Athletics was almost preordained for the son of Bill and Evelyn Lewis. Both parents had excelled in track and field. Both became high school track coaches, and encouraged athletic accomplishment in Carl, his two older brothers,

Striving to live up to the high expectations of the public and the media, Carl Lewis won four gold medals in track and field at the summer Olympics, equaling the achievement of Jesse Owens in 1936.

Shirley MacLaine celebrated her 50th birthday in style in a year which saw her star on Broadway, win an Oscar as best actress, and become a best-selling author.

and his younger sister Carol, a top U.S. women's long jumper. Lewis was a star jumper at his Willingboro, N.J., high school and at the University of Houston, until he was declared ineligible to compete in 1982 because of poor grades. Subsequently, as a member of the Santa Monica (Calif.) Track Club, he emerged as the nation's premier sprinter and long jumper.

Talent and training led to brilliance in Los Angeles. His first two victories, in the 100 meter and the long jump, were achieved with such ease that they left many fans disappointed that no world records had been set; during the long jump event, after he had sewed up the

gold medal with a 28'¼" jump, he decided to pass up his last four jumps and not challenge the world record—thereby attracting scattered boos. There were no complaints, however, about his victory on August 8 in the 200 m, when he ran the third fastest time ever, nor about his running of the anchor leg three days later for the U.S. 400-m relay team that set another record.

Lewis lives in an elegant Victorian home in Houston, takes acting lessons, and with his manager has developed a "marketing strategy" to guide his future. In answer to the inevitable charges that he is aloof and money-minded, friends say he is a reserved, even shy person who has worked hard and deserves to enjoy his hard-earned financial success.

MACLAINE, SHIRLEY

Actress and entertainer, born April 24, 1934, in Richmond, Va. Shirley MacLaine's achievements as she approached her 50th birthday would satisfy most people for a lifetime. For her success in the challenging role of Aurora Greenway, the mother in the tragicomic film *Terms of Endearment*, MacLaine won a long-elusive first Oscar, after four previous nominations. She dazzled New York in a revamped version of her Las Vegas nightclub act, *Shirley MacLaine on Broadway*. Her latest book, *Out on a Limb*, in which she discusses her belief in spiritualism and reincarnation and her love affair with an unidentified British politician, was a best-seller. Capping it all was a glowing cover story in *Time* magazine that celebrated her milestone birthday, and her recent achievements, with gusto.

Born Shirley MacLean Beaty, older sister to actor Warren Beatty (who added his own second "t" to the name), MacLaine decided at an early age to become a dancer. Her big break came in Hollywood storybook fashion when, one day in 1954, she went on as a substitute for the star in the Broadway musical *Pajama Game*; in the audience was producer Hal Wallis, who was so impressed that he signed her to a multiyear movie contract. Starring roles in a wide variety of popular films followed—including *Some Came Running* (1958), *The Apartment* (1960), *Irma La Douce*, and *The Turning Point* (1977), for all of which she received Oscar nominations.

Offscreen, MacLaine has a reputation as a "lovable kook," who has been known to take off on the spur of the moment to seek her identity on a mountaintop in Bhutan or with the Indians of Peru. Also a feminist and political activist, she has worked energetically for liberal causes, joining in Vietnam war protests, marching for civil rights, and campaigning for Democratic presidential aspirants Robert Kennedy and George McGovern. In 1954 she married producer-businessman Steve Parker, with whom she had a daughter, Stephanie Sachiko ("Sachi"), born in 1956. She was divorced in 1982.

MONDALE, WALTER F(REDERICK)

U.S. presidential candidate, born January 5, 1928, in Ceylon, Minn. "I did my best and I worked my heart out," said Walter ("Fritz") Mondale after it was all over. That he did. Although his pursuit of the presidency was ultimately unsuccessful, it drew from him reserves of energy and intensity unexpected by many.

At the beginning of the year, Mondale was widely perceived as an earnest yet somewhat colorless politician, a firm advocate of mainstream liberalism but an uninspiring campaigner, who virtually had a lock on the democratic nomination thanks to lengthy, painstaking preparation and an efficient organization. Early primary defeats by Senator Gary Hart, however, seemed to bring out the fighter in him, somewhat enhancing his popular appeal among Democrats.

After he did lock up the nomination, Mondale made a bold attempt to capture the imagination of the electorate by choosing a woman

Walter Mondale knew both triumph and heartbreak in 1984, winning an unusually intense battle for the Democratic presidential nomination and then losing to President Ronald Reagan in November in a coast-to-coast landslide.

(Geraldine Ferraro) as his running mate on the Democratic ticket. But his campaign seemed plagued by poor staff work and by controversy, such as a damaging flap over the personal finances of Ferraro and her husband. Mondale himself was unable to captivate the public in the ways that Ronald Reagan—or Ferraro—could. He did, however, make a strong impression in the two nationally televised debates (especially the first) with Reagan.

After the election, Mondale analyzed his defeat. Pitted against a well-liked incumbent at a time of seeming economic prosperity, he had failed, he said, to get his message across. Noting that politics required a mastery of television—a strong point of Reagan's—Mondale put much of the blame on his own failure to master that medium during the course of the campaign.

The son of a Methodist minister, Fritz Mondale rose to prominence in Minnesota as a protégé of former Senator Humbert Humphrey. When Humphrey went on to become vice-president, Mondale succeeded him in the Sen-

Burdened by the worst recession in five decades, Canadians turned away from the ruling Liberals and voted overwhelmingly for candidates of the Progressive Conservative Party headed by Brian Mulroney, who became prime minister at the age of 45.

ate, serving until his own vice-presidency under Jimmy Carter (1977–1981). Shortly after his loss to Reagan, Mondale indicated he did not plan to seek elective office again and would return to Washington to work as a lawyer. "I think the time has come to pursue certain economic necessities, among other things," he said. He also hoped and believed that history would look back fondly on a creditable and honorable campaign.

MULRONEY, (MARTIN) BRIAN

Prime minister of Canada, born March 20, 1939, in Baie-Comeau, Quebec. Canada approached its first general election in nearly five years on September 4 with feelings of uncertainty. The economy was a major issue. Beyond that, Canadians, after 21 years of almost continuous Liberal Party rule, were beginning to be restless.

As leader of the opposition Progressive Conservative Party, Mulroney, running for a seat in Parliament from a Quebec electoral district, promised a "new beginning" and a "new spirit." The newness tactic and Mulroney's confident bearing in television debates and on the hustings clicked with the voters. The polls had scarcely closed election night than the tallies began to show the Conservatives winning a landslide. Out of 282 seats in the House of Commons, they took 211 (another seat was won by a pro-Tory independent). The Liberals, under John Turner, took a meager 40 seats, and the New Democratic Party, headed by Edward Broadbent, claimed the remaining 30 seats. In a country frequently racked by regional and ethnic factionalism, the Conservatives won a majority in all ten provinces. In Quebec, traditionally a liberal stronghold, they managed to capture 58 out of 75 seats.

As the 18th prime minister of Canada, Mulroney moved into his official residence at 24 Sussex Drive, Ottawa, with his wife, Mila, and their three children and began tackling the country's problems. The Throne Speech, delivered by the governor-general in November, and representing the government's policies, promised to promote growth energetically and deal with the budget deficit, in part by calling a national economic summit involving diverse groups of people. The speech promised to restore "true partnership between Canada and the United States" and to place emphasis on Canada's role in the North Atlantic Treaty Organization. In a later policy announcement, his government proposed to abolish many existing curbs on U.S. and other foreign investment that had been imposed under the Liberal government of Pierre Elliott Trudeau.

PERES, SHIMON

Prime minister of Israel, born 1923 in Wolozyn, Poland. Shimon Peres's assumption of office as prime minister following the July elections was a bittersweet occasion for the Israeli politician. In his 40-odd years as a member of Israel's Labor Party, Peres had achieved a reputation as a skillful infighter, but as a perennial also-ran as well. As defense minister in the 1970's, he had twice tried and failed to unseat archrival Yitzhak Rabin for the party chairmanship (and thus prime ministership). Eventually gaining the chairmanship when Rabin resigned in 1977, he promptly lost in general elections to fiery Menachem Begin's right-wing Likud bloc.

Peres's 1984 ascent to leadership was not the triumph he had sought. Peres had been projected as clear winner in the July elections. Instead, neither party won enough votes to put together a ruling coalition without the other. The two parties eventually negotiated an arrangement whereby the office of prime minister would be shared, with Peres taking the first turn since Labor had won a larger popular vote. Despite this unpromising compromise, Peres appeared to be gaining rapidly in popularity during his first 100 days in office.

The arrangement was an ambiguous climax to a long and varied career. Peres had emigrated to Palestine around 1934, where he was raised on a kibbutz. He turned to political activity at 18 by joining the Labor youth movement. Soon he became a protégé of David Ben Gurion, who named him director general of the Defense Ministry when Peres was only 29. Unlike most other leaders of his generation, Peres had no combat experience in Israel's wars. But, sent abroad on arms-purchasing missions, he is credited with having significantly helped develop Israel's formidable military force; in fact, few other politicians in Israel are as knowledgeable about weaponry and military affairs.

Shimon Peres tackled a tough job, becoming prime minister of Israel during a period of economic crisis. He was chosen to lead a national-unity government after an inconclusive election.

SHAMIR, YITZHAK

Deputy premier and foreign minister of Israel, born October 15, 1915, in Ruzinoy in eastern Poland. When Menachem Begin was forced, for health reasons, to resign as leader of the right-wing Likud parliamentary bloc and as prime minister of Israel in 1983, he handed over the reins of power to longtime friend and political ally Yitzhak Shamir, who took office in October 1983. However, Shamir inherited neither Begin's popularity among conservative voters nor the strong loyalty of members of the Likud coalition. With a scant eight-vote majority in the Knesset (parliament), Shamir was also beset by urgent economic problems. He survived a no-confidence vote in January, but as a result of continuing economic problems, he lost his parliamentary majority in March, and general elections were scheduled for July.

The outcome of the balloting was the strangest in modern Israel's history. With neither the Labor nor the Likud party able to form a majority coalition, long weeks of negotiations finally produced a national unity government in which Labor's Shimon Peres would be prime minister for the first 25 months; the Likud leader would then take office for the second half of the new

321

British Prime Minister Margaret Thatcher survived an assassination attempt when a bomb demolished part of a hotel in which she was staying.

government's scheduled 50-month life. Prior to that time, Shamir, as party leader, was to serve as deputy premier and foreign minister in the unwieldy new 25-member cabinet.

Skeptics doubted whether such a government could accomplish very much or last its full term. Meanwhile Shamir, while awaiting his anticipated return to leadership, had to contemplate the presence in the cabinet of Ariel Sharon, as minister of trade and industry. The former Likud defense minister still sought the prime ministership, and he was considered a possible formidable competitor who might topple Shamir.

THATCHER, MARGARET (HILDA ROBERTS)

Prime minister of Great Britain, born October 13, 1925, in Grantham, England. The year brought economic troubles, difficult negotiations, and then, in mid-October, a terrorist bombing that nearly killed Thatcher and key members of her government.

The bomb, apparently set by Irish Republican Army terrorists, went off early in the morning at a Brighton hotel, where the Conservative Party had gathered for its annual conference. Four people were killed. Thatcher was not hurt, but the bathroom of her suite, which she had just left, was destroyed. She characterized the attack as "the work of a few evil men" and insisted that the party conference continue as planned. A few days later, explaining why she had wept on leaving church services, she said, "It just occurred to me that this is a day I was not meant to see."

Thatcher also had to deal with a protracted and violent strike by members of the militant National Union of Mineworkers over a proposal to close down unprofitable coal mines. Exacerbating the economic situation were Britain's severe unemployment—the number of jobless reached a post–World War II high of more than 3 million—and high interest rates, as well as a sharply declining pound.

In foreign affairs, Thatcher encountered unexpected violence in April, when a gunman inside the Libyan embassy in London fired at a group of demonstrators, killing a woman constable and igniting a diplomatic dispute between Britain and Libya. With typical resoluteness, she responded by breaking diplomatic relations. During the year, the Thatcher government worked out an agreement with China over the future of Hong Kong, where British dominion was due to expire in 1997, and with the European Economic Community over Britain's contribution, which London judged unfairly disproportionate to what it got in return. Thatcher herself hosted an economic summit conference of major Western industrial nations in June and went to China late in the year to sign the Hong Kong accord.

TURNER, JOHN N(APIER)

Leader of Canada's Liberal Party, born June 9, 1929, in Richmond, England. On June 16, cheering delegates at a convention of the ruling Liberal Party chose John Turner—a silver-haired patrician described as "prime ministerial"—to succeed retiring Liberal Prime Minister Pierre Elliott Trudeau as party leader and thus as head of the government. Two weeks later, Turner was sworn in as Canada's 17th prime minister. Ahead in the polls and overconfident, he called elections quickly to secure his standing. However, his popularity ratings soon began to slip, and in the September 4 elections the Liberals were swept out of office in a landslide. Turner, barely keeping his British Columbia electoral district, was out of power after only 80 days.

his battered party was left holding only 40 of 282 seats in the new Parliament, compared with 147 after Trudeau's last electoral victory in 1980.

The Liberals' loss was attributed in part to mistakes made by their standard-bearer. One of Turner's first acts in office, for example, was to make a series of patronage appointments that Trudeau had asked for to reward old friends. During the campaign itself, in contrast to his earlier image, Turner appeared wooden, nervous, and prone to surprising inaccuracies in public statements. In his worst gaffe, he was twice spotted patting the bottoms of women colleagues; in answer to criticisms that his actions were sexist and patronizing, he lamely explained that he was a "tactile" politician.

Turner had pursued a traditional path to politics. After his father died when John was two, his mother, a Canadian, moved the family to Ottawa and later to Vancouver. Turner attended the University of British Columbia, where he was a track star, and then went on to obtain a law degree before joining a Quebec law firm.

John Turner, a Liberal, had the dubious distinction of serving as Canada's prime minister for only two months before his party was voted out of power in September's parliamentary election.

In 1962 he won a seat in Parliament from a Montreal district, and in 1965 he joined the cabinet of Prime Minister Lester Pearson. Named finance minister by Trudeau in 1972, he held the powerful post for three years but resigned after a political dispute with the prime minister. Subsequently, as a corporate lawyer, Turner continued to be touted as a likely successor to Trudeau as party leader and prime minister.

S.L.D., J.A.

PERSIAN GULF STATES. For the small Persian Gulf states, as for their larger neighbors, tensions generated by the Iran–Iraq war dominated events in 1984. Qatar, the United Arab Emirates (U.A.E.), Oman, and Bahrain generally supported announcements by the United States that it would not sit by if Iran carried out threats to block the Strait of Hormuz and cut off the flow of oil through the Persian Gulf. In Oman, where U.S. forces have base rights, U.S. Marines practiced amphibious landings.

During the year, more than 60 vessels were hit by Iranian or Iraqi air attacks in the Gulf. In May, in response to such attacks against neutral shipping, the Gulf Cooperation Council (comprising Bahrain, Oman, Qatar, the U.A.E., Kuwait, and Saudi Arabia) specifically condemned "Iranian aggression" and called for an emergency UN Security Council session. The session produced a compromise resolution generally deploring any such attacks.

In late November, the Gulf Cooperation Council, meeting in Kuwait, agreed to establish a rapid deployment force to defend member nations against external military threats. The force would reportedly consist of 10,000 or more troops, drawn from member nations, to be activated only for joint military training exercises and in the event of an actual military threat.

On February 8 the U.A.E. ambassador to France was killed by gunmen in Paris. The Arab Revolutionary Brigades claimed responsibility, citing the expulsion of Palestinians from the U.A.E. and "imperialist" links between the emirates and the United States.

See STATISTICS OF THE WORLD. See also KUWAIT; ORGANIZATION OF PETROLEUM EXPORTING COUNTRIES; SAUDI ARABIA; YEMEN, PEOPLE'S DEMOCRATIC REPUBLIC OF; YEMEN ARAB REPUBLIC.

L.A.K.

PERU. In 1984, President Fernando Belaúnde Terry faced a moribund economy, a bloody guerrilla war, and mounting popular discontent. Unemployment was high, and inflation was expected to remain at an annual rate of close to 100 percent. Exports fetched low prices in weak markets, and these earnings were needed to service the foreign debt.

Refinancing of the foreign debt was a problem, since Peru had not met earlier agreements with the International Monetary Fund. In February, a new agreement with the IMF called for austerity measures. The program evoked protest: a million peasants blocked roads on March 1–3, and the major labor federations called a 24-hour general strike for March 22. Belaúnde declared a state of emergency and promised not to implement the austerity measures. The change of policy led to the resignation of the prime minister and the finance minister but did not avert a strike. On April 26, a slightly more lenient pact was signed with the IMF; widespread strikes and protest demonstrations ensued.

Belaúnde shuffled his cabinet in mid-October. Luis Percovich was named prime minister and foreign minister, replacing Sandro Mariátegui, who had been appointed prior to the March 22 general strike. On November 29, a new 24-hour general strike was staged in major cities to protest government economic policies; about 300 people were reportedly arrested.

The regime intensified its four-year campaign against the Sendero Luminoso (Shining Path) guerrillas. But, while security personnel made massive sweeps through the Sendero stronghold in the south, the guerrillas opened a new front to the north. Here, the government's U.S.–supported program to eradicate the cocaine industry had angered local residents, who sought an alliance with the revolutionaries. In November, the guerrillas or drug traffickers allied to them attacked workers hired to destroy coca plants (the main ingredient in cocaine). Nineteen people were killed, and the project was suspended.

See STATISTICS OF THE WORLD. D.W.

PETROLEUM AND NATURAL GAS. World crude oil and condensate production rose slightly during the first seven months of 1984.

In October, oil price cuts by four countries led to an agreement by members of the Organization of Petroleum Exporting Countries to reduce production.

Oil. World oil production in the first seven months of 1984 was about 2.3 million barrels per day higher than in the comparable period of 1983, and OPEC production rose by 1.6 million b/d. Saudi Arabia's production increased from 4.45 million b/d in January–July 1983 to about 5.1 million b/d a year later. Although world oil production of 54.11 million b/d in the first seven months was 6 percent higher than year-earlier production, demand rose more slowly, and oil prices dropped on the spot market. By the end of August, the price of OPEC oil on the spot market had fallen to about $27 a barrel. Although this had risen by mid-November to about $28 a barrel, it was still below OPEC's benchmark price of $29 a barrel for Arabian light crude.

Stung by sagging oil prices and announcements of cuts by individual countries, OPEC members held an emergency meeting in Geneva at the end of October. They agreed to cut oil production by 1.5 million b/d from their agreed-upon ceiling of 17.5 million b/d. Discussion of problems in OPEC's oil pricing structure was delayed until a scheduled meeting in December, at which time an effort was made to resolve that problem. (See ORGANIZATION OF PETROLEUM EXPORTING COUNTRIES.)

In the United States, colder than normal weather and robust economic growth helped push consumption of petroleum in the first three quarters up approximately 5 percent over levels a year earlier. This increase in demand, together with essentially stable domestic crude production, caused imports to jump sharply. The 1983 U.S. consumption figure of 5.56 billion barrels was 19 percent below the peak of 6.88 billion barrels consumed in 1978 and was essentially equal to 1971 consumption.

Natural Gas. Marketed production of natural gas declined from 18.52 trillion cubic feet in 1982 to 16.66 trillion cubic feet in 1983, a drop of 10 percent. Net imports of natural gas and consumption of dry natural gas also decreased in 1983. Despite the drops in production and consumption, natural gas prices continued to rise as a result of the 1978 Natural

Gas Policy Act (NGPA). Both producers and pipeline companies sought in 1984 to have Congress revise the NGPA. Producers wanted more rapid decontrol of prices, and pipeline companies wanted relief from the contracts they had signed when supplies were tight and oil prices were high. However, Congress could not find a compromise and did not act.

D.F.A.

PETS. American Kennel Club registration figures released early in 1984 showed that the cocker spaniel had become the most popular breed of dog in the United States, pushing the poodle into second place after a 23-year reign as top dog. Among the 128 breeds recognized by the AKC, the third spot fell to the Labrador retriever, which displaced the Doberman pinscher to the number-four position. The other top ten breeds were: German shepherd, golden retriever, beagle, miniature schnauzer, dachshund, and Shetland sheepdog. Increasing the most in relative popularity was the Rottweiler; representatives of this large black-and-tan working-dog breed entered the select group of the 25 most popular breeds, scoring a 43 percent increase in registrations.

The AKC's Centennial Show, held in Philadelphia in November, was only the second show staged by the AKC since its founding in September 1884. The winner was a German shepherd, Ch. Covy Tucker Hills Manhattan, a black-and-tan five-year-old. With more than 8,000 dogs representing 128 recognized pure breeds, the event was by far the largest dog show ever held in the United States. Several weeks prior to the show, the U.S. Postal Service saluted the AKC by issuing four stamps featuring eight different dog breeds; it was the first time a pedigreed dog had appeared on a U.S. postage stamp.

Best in Show at the 108th Westminster Kennel Club show in February was a Newfoundland, Ch. Seaward's Blackbeard. Weighing 155 pounds, the dog was the top-winning Newfoundland in the history of the breed. Newfoundlands fared less well in their AKC popularity ranking; the breed placed 52nd, down one position from the previous year, despite an increase in their total registration.

Shorthaired cat breeds, such as the Abyssinian and Burmese, gained in popularity, but not

Ch. Seward's Blackbeard, a Newfoundland weighing 155 pounds, poses with its handler and a judge, after being named Best in Show at the Westminster Kennel Club show in February in New York City.

Chin Up, Chow Down

Dogs living or traveling in the south of France can now take advantage of a new restaurant in Nice just for them, where they can enjoy gourmet food in relaxed surroundings, free from human prejudice against beasts at table. The Beach Regency Hotel's Resto-Chien, overlooking the Mediterranean, serves a full-course menu; a typical meal might include a soupish gravy appetizer, fresh pasta tossed with chunks of turkey, and crème caramel for dessert, all whipped up by the same kitchen that services the hotel's other, strictly-for-humans restaurant. Prices run from $5 to $10 for a complete dinner, excluding drinks. Seating is limited, so reserve ahead.

at the same rate as the more recently recognized Tonkinese or the longhaired Maine coon cat. Poll results showed that more than 28 percent of all U.S. households surveyed owned at least one cat—which helped to account for the fact that Americans spent almost $1 billion during the year on veterinary care for their feline pets.

Late in the year, tropical fish fanciers had an opportunity to purchase the limited available supplies of half-black discus, a new color variety of *Symphysodon aequifasciata,* one of the most expensive of freshwater aquarium species. European breeders developed a long-finned variety of the popular cardinal tetra, but the new variety was not yet in good supply.

N.P.

PHILIPPINES. The investigation into the assassination of Benigno Aquino continued to rivet attention in 1984. Aquino, leader of the non-Communist opposition to President Ferdinand

Anthony Melton is embraced by his mother, as they follow the swimming pig that saved the boy's life when he narrowly escaped drowning in a Houston lake. The pig, named Priscilla, won the Stillman Award, given by the American Humane Society.

Marcos, was shot dead in August 1983 at Manila International Airport on his return from de facto exile in the United States. The government claimed that Rolando Galman, killed by the military at the scene, had been hired by Communists, penetrated airport security, and killed Aquino. A board headed by former court of appeals justice Corazón Agrava, named by Marcos to investigate the slayings, released different conclusions in October 1984. All members contended that Aquino had died as a result of a military plot; they disagreed only on how high up the chain of command the conspiracy went. Agrava issued her own report, accusing an air force general and six soldiers. The other four members named 26 members of the military, including General Fabian Ver, the armed forces chief of staff and a cousin and close associate of Marcos. Ver took a leave of absence, and subpoenas were issued to the accused by a newly appointed government tribunal.

Anger among opposition groups remained high, and some boycotted the May 14 National Assembly elections. Despite the boycott, opposition parties and independents did well, winning nearly 40 percent of the seats. In December, 12 major opposition leaders, signed a declaration of unity calling for a new constitution, legalization of the Communist Party, and the removal of foreign military bases.

The government announced on November 6 that Marcos would run again when his term expired in 1987. Later that month, Marcos receded from public view, and rumors circulated that he was seriously ill and had undergone major surgery. However, he reemerged after 25 days, at a cabinet meeting, appearing by then to be in good health.

Among insurgent groups, the Communist-led New People's Army grew in strength and, as of late 1984, was said to control 20 percent of all villages. The Moro National Liberation Front, composed of Islamic separatists, showed signs of cooperating with the NPA.

To stimulate exports, boost tourism, and curb imports, the peso was sharply devalued. Even so, output in most sectors continued to drop. Bank lending rates exceeded 50 percent by September. The director of the scandal-rocked central bank resigned; officials had overstated the country's financial reserves and understated its foreign debt in order to get international aid. Later in the year, however, the government announced a $10 billion International Monetary Fund plan that included restructuring of debt owed to foreign banks, along with new loans, trade financing, and standby credit.

Marcos was criticized for a "shoot to disable" policy toward alleged criminals, implemented for a time as part of a crackdown on crime. The policy was carried out by undercover agents riding the capital's buses to protect passengers; more than 30 people were reportedly killed in the crackdown.

See STATISTICS OF THE WORLD.   L.R.

PHOTOGRAPHY. The announcement by the J. Paul Getty Museum in Malibu, Calif., that it had purchased nine major European and American collections of photographs was a major development of 1984. The depth and breadth of the Getty collection promised to permit the extensive critical and historical examination the field has lacked. Among figures in the world of photography who died during the year were Ansel Adams, Garry Winogrand, and Brassaï (see OBITUARIES).

The Getty Museum. Collections acquired by the Getty included the two most prestigious holdings in the United States, those of Arnold Crane of Chicago and Samuel Wagstaff, Jr., of New York City. Smaller but vital collections were also acquired, giving the Getty a starting collection of 20,000 photographs. Only the International Museum of Photography at the George Eastman House in Rochester, N.Y., was thought to have a collection of greater importance. The acquisitions brought together significant holdings of daguerrotypes, early European photography, and major groupings of German and Czech artists from the 1920's and 1930's. They also contained the largest and most important holdings of August Sander's work and the photographs by the 19th-century American painter Thomas Eakins.

Other Institutions. The Los Angeles County Museum of Art received a $1 million grant to establish a photography department. In San Diego, the Museum of Photographic Art opened its doors. At the University of Arizona, in Tucson, the Center for Creative Photography was completing a multimillion dollar state-of-

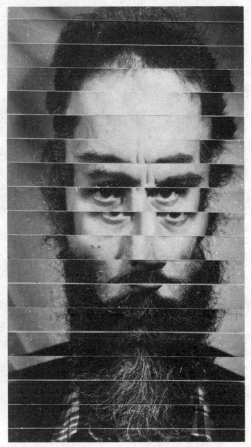

The artist's complex personality is conveyed in this self-portrait, part of a show called "Lucas Samaras: Polaroid Photographs, 1969–1983," which originated at the Pompidou Center in Paris and toured the United States in 1984. Samaras, a Greek-born painter and sculptor, formed the portrait by cutting strips from a large photograph and intermingling them to make a continuous but distorted image.

the-art building to house, preserve, and exhibit its archives.

The Art Market. Dealers agreed that the 1983–1984 season was the best for the photography market since 1979–1980. Several successful new galleries opened in New York City. West Coast dealers reported growing public interest in the collecting of photographs. Auction houses enjoyed their best season since 1979–1980, with salesrooms packed and vigorous competition for important works. For the first time, photography had survived a depression in the

327

art market and continued as an established force in that market. Its recognition as a significant art form now seemed secure.

Exhibitions. The growing vitality of the West Coast scene was demonstrated by the number of shows originating there. From the San Francisco Museum of Modern Art came an exhibit of rare photographs by the Russian Constructivist artist Alexander Rodchenko, which traveled to seven other institutions. Also traveling from the San Francisco museum was "Photography in California: 1945–1980."

In the East, the George Eastman House museum presented 200 prints from its archives covering the history of photography. Hillwood Art Gallery at Long Island University/CW Post Campus in Greenvale, N.Y., assembled the first U.S. exhibit of rare work by Italian Futurist photographers of the early 20th century. New York City's Museum of Modern Art staged a 200-print retrospective of the stylish work of Irving Penn; the exhibit was to travel to five U.S. cities in all.

William Eggleston's color photos of Graceland, the late singer Elvis Presley's home, received favorable attention when they appeared in different parts of the United States. Other contemporary shows included exhibits of Mark Klett's Western landscapes, the conceptual work of Joel Peter Witkin, photographs by painters Lucas Samaras and David Hockney, and the work of legendary fashion photographer Horst.

Technology. Fuji renewed its challenge to Kodak for the first place among high-speed color negative films. Fujicolor HR 1600 is two-thirds of a stop faster than Improved Kodacolor VR 1000. Both films provide fine-grain resolution at a high-speed or limited-light exposures. The 3M Company introduced high-resolution (HR) color print films at ISO 100, 200, and 400.

Ansel Adams (above) died at 82 as the world's most widely exhibited photographer. Exemplifying his majestic black-and-white landscapes is a portrait of Mount Williamson in the Sierra Nevada (left).

Further flexibility in color film was offered by Kodak's new Professional Ektachrome P800/1600, a fast slide film designed to be pushed from ISO 400 to ISO 1600, while keeping excellent color quality. For black and white photographers, Kodak released Polyfiber paper, a variable-contrast fiber-based paper designed to give brilliant whites, deep blacks, and a long range of tones in between. It replaces Polycontrast Rapid and Polycontrast papers.

New cameras included the compact Pentax 645, a medium-format full-system camera with built-in motor drive, interchangeable film inserts, and multimode exposure automation, and the Canon F-1 High Speed Motor Drive camera, which can shoot up to 14 frames per second, approaching the 16 fps of motion-picture photography.   B.B.S.

PHYSICS. Progress in physics in 1984 included discovery of the top quark, a particle whose existence had been predicted, and the tentative finding of an entirely unanticipated particle, the zeta.

The Top Quark. The avidly sought elementary particle known as the top quark was discovered in June in Switzerland at the European Laboratory for Particle Physics (CERN), by a 151-member international group. Heading the group was Carlo Rubbia, a CERN physicist and co-winner of the 1984 Nobel Prize in physics (*see* PRIZES AND AWARDS).

The top quark joins the five previously known species of quarks: up, down, strange, charm, and bottom. Quarks are the constituents of the constituents of atomic nuclei. Protons, for example, comprise three quarks—two ups and a down—while neutrons consist of two downs and an up. Quarks interact with one another in three ways. The so-called strong nuclear force binds them together so strongly that they appear in nature only as composites, in the form of elementary particles such as the proton, the neutron, and the various mesons. The so-called weak force, which is responsible for processes like radioactive beta decay (the decay of a radioactive atomic nucleus through the emission of a beta particle—an electron or positron—and of a neutrino), allows quarks to be transformed from one species to another. And because quarks have an electric charge, they repulse and attract one another by means of the familiar electromagnetic force, as do all charged particles.

The quantum theory that describes the weak and electromagnetic forces (electroweak theory) requires that quarks come in pairs, although it does not say how many pairs there must be. (In theories of this type, known as quantum field theories, forces are transmitted between interacting particles by other particles, known as field quanta.) Hence, physicists had been expecting the top quark to pop up. They were not sure where, however, because the theory also does not predict the mass of the particle. It now turns out that the top quark's mass (still only approximately fixed, at between 30 and 50 times that of the proton) is so large that just one accelerator in the world has enough energy to produce it.

That accelerator is CERN's proton-antiproton collider. Beams of protons and antiprotons collide head-on in this machine. Occasionally, quarks and antiquarks within the protons and antiprotons will annihilate one another, generating a fireball of pure energy that materializes into other particles. Among the possible products of the collisions are so-called W particles—the weak-force equivalent of the quantum of the electromagnetic field, the photon. The W quickly decays, sometimes into a top and bottom quark pair. The presence of these particles is detected from their decay products.

Zeta Particle. In July, a team of 79 U.S. and European physicists reported the tentative discovery of a totally unexpected particle, called the zeta. The work was done using the DORIS machine at the German Electron Synchrotron (DESY) laboratory at Hamburg. DORIS accelerates beams of electrons and positrons to an energy of just over 5 billion electron volts, which then collide head-on. When an electron and positron collide and are annihilated, the resulting energy can go directly to the creation of a quark and the corresponding antiquark. In DORIS, a bottom quark and antiquark are created. Until the top quark came along, the bottom, with a mass just five times that of the proton, was the heaviest known. The bottom quark and antiquark are bound together to make a particle called the upsilon, which decays almost instantaneously. About one time in 200 the decay is to the particle now known as the zeta, which is about eight times as heavy as the proton. There is, however, no place for the zeta in the standard theories of elementary particles. Theorists have conjectured the possible existence of many types of particles, but none have properties matching those of the zeta. If further experiments confirm the zeta's existence, physicists will have to revise their thinking.

Energy-Free Computing. Attention focused once again on a recurring question in computer development: What is the minimum energy needed to do computation? Although the weight of scientific opinion supports the proposition that, at least in principle, no net energy need be expended, the issue is theoretical; at present real computers based on the switching action of semiconductor transistors soak up 100 million times more energy than the minimum value fixed by those who argue against energy-free computing.

The issue involves the thermodynamic notion of reversibility. The laws of motion of individual particles are reversible; that is, there is no "arrow of time." Once a conglomeration of particles is considered, however, the situation changes. Gas molecules packed together in one end of a box will subsequently spread out and fill the box; they have almost no chance of ever again coming together in their original configuration. The expansion of the gas is an irreversible process, and in thermodynamics irreversible processes cost energy. The lost energy appears as waste heat, which cannot be recovered by returning to the original configuration.

California Institute of Technology physicist and Nobel laureate Richard Feynman entered the debate in 1984 with his development of a model in which individual atoms played the role of parts of a computer. The properties of atoms are described by quantum mechanics. Feynman considered atoms that could exist in either of two quantum states, one corresponding to the binary number 0 and the other to the binary number 1 of digital computer logic. He then devised mathematical operations that, when applied to the quantum states of the atoms, resulted in digital logic functions that were reversible. By contrast, most of the logic operations in conventional computers are irreversible. In the end, Feynman concluded that a reversible quantum mechanical computer was theoretically possible. Realizing the machine in practice, however, would require manipulating individual atoms.   A.L.R.

POLAND. In July 1984, a year after the lifting of martial law, the Polish government of General Wojciech Jaruzelski freed nearly all remaining political prisoners, as part of its announced policy of political "normalization." However, restrictive measures remained in force, and the regime made no significant progress in solving deep-rooted political and economic problems. In October the government suffered a serious blow to its prestige when it was learned that a well-known Warsaw parish priest and supporter of the outlawed Solidarity labor movement had been abducted, tortured, and killed.

Politics and Government. In conjunction with the 40th anniversary of the Polish Communist state on July 22, about 600 political prisoners were freed, including four leading members of the Workers Defense Committee (KOR), whose trial for treason had been suspended a few days earlier, in anticipation of the amnesty. The government continued to promote membership in new state-supported labor unions which met together to form an official federation in late November. Although the new unions could not be seen as a restoration of the free unions of 1980 and 1981, they showed a degree of autonomy by pushing for wage increases and price restraints.

On the other hand, the government continued to crack down on so-called antistate activities. Early in the year, security forces were arresting and interrogating intellectuals believed to oppose the regime, and in June the Polish United Workers (Communist) Party expelled Adam Schaff, an internationally known Marxist scholar and philosopher, after he had criticized the government.

In one case that had attracted wide attention, a Warsaw court in July acquitted two police officers in the May 1983 death of 19-year-old Grzegorz Przemyk, son of a prominent dissident. The youth had been arrested and brought to a police station, where he was reportedly beaten. Taken by ambulance to an emergency medical center, he died of internal injuries two days later. Two ambulance drivers were convicted of negligence by the court; doctors who had treated the youth were also found negligent but were given amnesty.

On October 19, Father Jerzy Popieluszko, a Warsaw priest widely revered as an outspoken proponent of Solidarity, was abducted on a highway near Toruń. Eleven days later, his body was found in a reservoir on the Vistula River, northwest of Warsaw. He had been beaten and thrown, apparently already dead, into the reservoir. In late December four members of the state security police went on public trial in Toruń, charged with kidnapping and murder. The Jaruzelski government condemned the "hideous crime" and took steps to purge the Interior Ministry, which oversees the security police, of suspected hard-liners.

In response to the killing, dissidents formed new groups to monitor police behavior and seek to publicize instances of abuse. These

After more than two years in jail, Solidarity activist Andrzej Gwiazda, freed with hundreds of other political prisoners in a general amnesty marking the 40th anniversary of Communist rule in Poland, flashes a victory sign to Polish television reporters.

groups charged that more than 50 people, most of them Solidarity activists or sympathizers, had been abducted and murdered by police or "unknown perpetrators" since martial law was first declared in December 1981.

The Popieluszko murder heightened tensions between church and state. Earlier in the year, there had been compromises on both sides. When a bishop and some 450 priests went on a bread-and-water fast to express opposition to the government's removal of crucifixes from an agricultural college, the government agreed to let crucifixes be hung in some rooms of the college but not in classrooms. For his part, the Roman Catholic primate, Cardinal Jozef Glemp, transferred an activist priest, the Reverend Mieczyslaw Nowak, from an industrial parish to a rural area; the move was believed by some to stem from an alleged agreement under which

331

the church undertook to discourage antigovernment activities in return for release of political prisoners by the regime.

During the year, more than 1,000 Poles on boat trips to the West, mostly West Germany, defected by jumping ship.

Economy. Bowing to widespread opposition, the government postponed and modified a 15 percent rise in food prices planned for January 1, 1984; price hikes were cut to 10 percent, on a narrowed range of goods, effective January 30. Poland's foreign debt continued to grow— to about $26.5 billion by the beginning of 1984. Although there was a trade surplus in 1983, it resulted from severe governmental restrictions on imports and from expanded exports of raw materials and coal. The overall pattern of Polish exports to the West showed signs of deterioration, with fewer exports coming from industrial sectors of the economy.

Foreign Relations. With the collapse in the economy and a shelving of Poland's application for membership in the International Monetary Fund, the regime turned increasingly to the Soviet Union for trade and economic assistance. During a visit to Moscow in May, Jaruzelski signed a 15-year agreement calling for greater integration between the economies of the two countries. Despite Poland's release of political prisoners in the summer, relations with the United States remained quite frigid. Most major U.S. sanctions against Poland remained in force, including a denial of most-favored-nation trading status. In December, however, following the release of prominent Solidarity members still held in prison after the June amnesty, the United States announced it would no longer block Poland's bid for IMF membership.

See STATISTICS OF THE WORLD.   R.E.K.

PORTUGAL. In 1984, the Socialist government of Premier Mário Soares remained basically popular. However, with inflation running at over 30 percent and unemployment at half a million early in the year, Portugal's economic crisis was serious. It was made more acute by a $14 billion foreign debt and a $1.25 billion balance-of-payments deficit. The government continued drastic austerity measures to reduce the budget and trade deficits. One side effect of the measures was a projected drop in real wages of 5 percent for 1984, which followed an estimated 9 percent fall in 1983.

Portugal was anxious to be admitted to the European Economic Community so as to obtain important economic and trade benefits. A snag, however, developed in December, when Greece threatened to veto Portugal's admission, as well as Spain's, unless the EEC agreed to a five-year, $5 billion aid program for Greek and Italian farmers to protect them from agricultural competition.

In legislation, the Assembly passed a controversial measure early in the year, legalizing abortion in some cases. The Catholic Church had conducted an all-out campaign to defeat the bill, which was supported by the Socialists and Communists but opposed by Social Democrats and Christian Democrats.

At the end of July the Assembly passed a security bill that expanded police powers to deal with internal security threats by allowing tapping of telephones and, in special cases, searches and seizures without a warrant. Passage of the bill followed on the heels of a June police roundup that netted more than 40 suspected leftist guerrillas. The raid was aimed at a group called the Popular Forces of the 25th of April (the date of the 1974 revolution), which had taken responsibility for several murders and bank robberies since 1980. Among those taken into custody was Lieutenant Colonel Otelo Saraiva de Carvalho, a popular leader of the revolution and a presidential candidate in 1976 and 1980.

A Lisbon loan officer, Carlos Lopes, won the marathon at the 1984 summer Olympics in Los Angeles, taking home Portugal's only gold medal.

See STATISTICS OF THE WORLD.   J.O.S.

PRESIDENT OF THE UNITED STATES. Ronald Wilson Reagan, 40th president of the United States, was born February 6, 1911, in Tampico, Ill. Riding a tide of rising popularity, Reagan achieved a victory of historic proportions on November 6, 1984, when he was reelected to a second term with a record of 525 electoral votes, as against only 13 for his Democratic opponent, former Vice-President Walter Mondale. The robust American economy provided the backdrop for Reagan's center-stage performance. Although budget deficits remained

Suited up for a group portrait in Los Angeles, medal-winning members of the United States Olympic team engulf a beaming Ronald and Nancy Reagan in a sea of matching smiles. The president told the athletes they were "heroes."

high, the president was credited with reducing inflation and unemployment. His handling of foreign policy was hotly debated, but throughout the year Reagan stressed that "America is back," a theme first set forth in his January 1984 State of the Union address. Buttressing this message of hope and patriotism with symbols such as the Olympic torch and heroism 40 years ago at Normandy, the president and his supporters argued that under Reagan the United States had regained confidence in itself. For a time during the campaign, questions were raised as to whether, at age 73, the president was vigorous enough to build on his record in the future. The election results, however, indicated that the "age factor" never seriously damaged his image as a basically healthy and strong leader.

The Economy. Most economic numbers looked good for Reagan in 1984. The inflation rate, which had stood at 12.4 percent before he took office in 1981, was running at about 4 percent. For most of 1984 the civilian unemployment rate hovered slightly above 7 percent.

A slowdown in economic growth rate in the third quarter was welcomed by most experts as necessary to prevent higher inflation. Virtually the only economic trouble spots were high interest rates and the federal deficit, which under Reagan had ballooned from $55 billion to $175 billion in three years. Prior to the election, the president refused to spell out details of plans to reduce deficits, beyond contending that economic growth and unspecified spending cuts would probably do the job. He insisted that a future tax increase would be imposed only as a "last resort."

After the election, the Treasury Department offered a sweeping tax simplification plan that would reduce tax rates for individuals and companies and eliminate many tax deductions especially popular with large corporations and wealthy individuals. Reagan hedged on supporting the plan. On December 5, Reagan proposed a broad package of spending cuts for the 1986 fiscal year, totaling $34 billion.

Policy disputes within the administration on economic issues occasionally caused embar-

333

rassment. In May the White House criticized the Federal Reserve for pursuing a "tight money" policy that some presidential aides believed would hurt the recovery. But Martin Feldstein, the chairman of the president's Council of Economic Advisers, backed the Fed publicly. He also announced his resignation from the council, ending a series of policy disagreements with the administration. In an August mixup, Vice-President George Bush said that he could envision some circumstances under which a tax increase might be necessary. The White House immediately said the president had no "secret plan" to raise taxes, as Mondale charged.

Foreign Relations. Throughout the year, the president sought to soften his previously harsh rhetoric about the Soviet Union. Nevertheless, relations between the superpowers—strained by the Soviet walkout from arms control talks in late 1983—continued to deteriorate in early 1984. In May, the Soviet Union announced its withdrawal from the summer Olympics in Los Angeles; the same month, Moscow stated that additional Soviet missile-carrying submarines had been placed off the U.S. coast to counterbalance the deployment of U.S. missiles in Europe.

Reagan entered the November elections as the only president in 50 years not to have met his Soviet counterpart. The president's image as a peacemaker also was damaged when, preparing to give a radio address in August, he jokingly remarked, "My fellow Americans, I am pleased to tell you that I've signed legislation that will outlaw Russia forever. We begin bombing in five minutes." Reagan did, however, agree to meet privately with Soviet Foreign Minister Andrei Gromyko in late September, and in November it was announced that Gromyko and U.S. Secretary of State George Shultz would meet in Geneva in January 1985 to plan an agenda for arms limitation talks.

The most serious foreign policy reversals came in Lebanon. On February 7, with the Lebanese army collapsing, Reagan announced that the U.S. Marines in Beirut as part of a multinational peacekeeping force would be "redeployed" to ships offshore. The retreat seemed hasty and disorganized to many observers, but opinion polls taken later indicated that the president's popularity had not been damaged. On September 20, a truck full of explosives blew up in the new U.S. embassy annex outside Beirut, killing more than a dozen people, including two Americans. Reagan cited

Soviet Foreign Minister Andrei Gromyko joins President Ronald Reagan in the Oval Office for a three-hour conversation, later characterized by the White House as "forceful and direct." The surprise election-year meeting was hailed as a positive step by advisers who had urged the president to soften his unyielding posture toward the Soviet Union.

delays in the construction of safety features at the embassy, noting that "anyone that's ever had their kitchen done over knows that it never gets done as soon as you wish it would," and he placed some of the blame for the security failure on "destruction of our intelligence capacity in recent years." Later, he apologized to former President Jimmy Carter for what Reagan termed misinterpretations of the latter remark.

The Reagan administration's policy of support for El Salvador received a strong boost when moderate José Napoléon Duarte defeated right-winger Roberto d'Aubuisson in elections for the presidency of that country and, later in the year, agreed to meet with rebel leaders. Nicaragua posed more of a problem for the administration. In April, revelations that the Central Intelligence Agency had helped plant mines in Nicaraguan ports provoked criticism in Congress, which then barred further U.S. aid to CIA-backed rebels fighting to topple the Sandinista regime.

During his April 26–May 1 visit to China, Reagan met with Chinese leader Deng Xiaoping and others. Their meetings were cordial, but no major agreements were signed. A minor flap occurred over Chinese censorship of remarks by Reagan in an interview and a speech broadcast on Chinese television. The deleted comments extolled American freedoms and criticized the Soviet Union.

A ten-day trip to Europe in June gave Reagan public relations opportunities. Before attending the London summit, he visited Ireland. Unperturbed by demonstrations against U.S. involvement in Central America, he appeared moved by his visit to Ballyporeen, his ancestral home. In Normandy on June 6, at ceremonies marking the 40th anniversary of D-Day, Reagan tearfully read a poignant letter from the daughter of a D-Day veteran who had died before he could return to Normandy.

Cabinet. Controversy swirled around the cabinet. In January, the president nominated presidential counselor Edwin Meese III for attorney general, to replace William French Smith, who was eager to return to his law practice. But the Senate held up the nomination after allegations were made that Meese had received financial favors in exchange for government

Cabinet of the United States

Vice-President George Bush

Secretary of State George P. Shultz
Secretary of the Treasury Donald T. Regan
Secretary of Defense Caspar W. Weinberger
Attorney General William French Smith
Secretary of the Interior William Clark
Secretary of Agriculture John Block
Secretary of Commerce Malcolm Baldrige
Secretary of Labor Raymond Donovan
  (on leave)
**Secretary of Health and Human
  Services** Margaret Heckler
**Secretary of Housing and Urban
  Development** Samuel R. Pierce, Jr.
Secretary of Transportation Elizabeth Dole
Secretary of Energy Donald P. Hodel
Secretary of Education Terrel H. Bell

Counselor to the President Edwin Meese
**Director of the Office of Management and
  Budget** David Stockman
**Director of the Central Intelligence
  Agency** William Casey
**U.S. Representative to the United
  Nations** Jeane Kirkpatrick
U.S. Trade Representative William Brock

jobs, had improperly received a promotion and an active duty listing in the Army Reserve, and had not testified fully about his involvement in receiving Carter's debate briefing book while acting as chief of staff of Reagan's 1980 campaign. An independent counsel, Washington attorney Jacob Stein, investigated the charges, and Smith agreed to stay on the job pending the outcome. Stein's report, issued in September, absolved Meese of blame, but his nomination was set aside until 1985.

On October 1 it was learned that Secretary of Labor Raymond Donovan had been indicted by a Bronx, N.Y., grand jury with nine other individuals on charges related to an alleged multimillion-dollar defrauding of the New York City Transit Authority in 1978–1980 by the Schiavone Construction Company, of which Donovan was then an executive vice-president and part owner. Donovan, who took a leave pending developments, pleaded not guilty. He

335

was the first cabinet member ever indicted while in office.

After the election, Education Secretary Terrel Bell, UN Ambassador Jeane Kirkpatrick, and Interior Secretary William Clark announced plans to leave their posts.

See also ELECTIONS IN THE UNITED STATES.

J.A.

PRINCE EDWARD ISLAND. See STATISTICS OF THE WORLD.

PRIZES AND AWARDS. The following is a selected listing of prizes awarded during 1984 and the names of the persons who received them. For some awards given in specific fields, see the appropriate subject entry, such as MOTION PICTURES.

NOBEL PRIZES

The 1984 Nobel Prizes were more widely international than in some previous years, with the winners broadly distributed among different countries. Presented on December 10, the prizes carried a cash value of about $190,000 each, with the sum divided among co-winners in the case of shared prizes.

Chemistry. For his contribution to the study of proteins:

R(obert) Bruce Merrifield (1921–), professor at Rockefeller University in New York City. Born in Fort Worth, Texas, Merrifield received his Ph.D. in biochemistry from the University of California at Los Angeles in 1949. Since then, he has taught and conducted research at Rockefeller University. According to the

Nobel committee, Merrifield's primary achievement was the development of solid phase peptide synthesis, a rapid automated method of synthesizing proteins, the key component of living organisms, by assembling peptide chains of amino acids. The method has made possible the systematic study of enzymes, hormones, and antibodies and led to development of important new drugs, as well as to advances in gene technology.

Economics. For devising the standard uniform accounting system used to track and compare the economic development of nations:

Sir Richard Stone (1913–), retired Cambridge University economics professor. Born in London, he studied economics at Cambridge under John Maynard Keynes and, upon Keynes's invitation, became a statistician with the British government. When Cambridge University formed an applied economics department, Sir Richard was named its director. His system of national accounts, which has been adopted by major international organizations, measures national consumption, investment, and government spending and defines their interaction. Sir Richard was knighted in 1978.

Literature. For poetry which eschews all "dogmas and dictators" and "provides a liberating image of the indomitable spirit and versatility of man":

Jaroslav Seifert (1901–), Czechoslovak poet who was greatly admired and respected in his own country, although not well known internationally. He was born in Prague, where he still resides; many of his verses celebrate his native city. Seifert worked as a journalist until 1950, when he devoted himself exclusively to writing poetry. In his youth, he espoused the Soviet revolutionary cause, but, after a trip to the Soviet Union, he became disenchanted and left the Communist Party in 1929. He was a signer of Charter 77, a 1977 manifesto accusing the Czech regime of widespread human rights violations.

Peace. For being a leader of nonviolent efforts to end apartheid in South Africa:

Bishop Desmond Mpilo Tutu (1931–), general secretary of the South African Council of Churches. Born in the Afrikaner town of Klerksdorp, Tutu attended a segregated training college and at first became a teacher. Ordained in the Anglican Church in 1960, he earned degrees in divinity and sociology from London University and served in England for several years as associate director of the Theological Education Fund of the World Council of Churches. In 1975, he was appointed Anglican dean of Johannesburg, the first black to hold the position; in 1976 he became bishop of Lesotho. In 1978, Tutu was the first black to become general secretary of the South African Council of Churches. Under his leadership, the council played an increasingly important role in South African blacks' struggle for civil rights.

Bishop Tutu, who was named in November as the first black Anglican bishop of Johannesburg, continued his practice of speaking out against apartheid, notably in a meeting with President Ronald Reagan and at award ceremonies in Oslo, Norway, in December.

Physics. The prize in physics went to two scientists for their contribution to the discovery of long-sought-after subatomic particles.

Carlo Rubbia (1934–), born in Gorizia, Italy, attended the University of Pisa, New York City's Columbia University, and the University of Rome. In 1960, he joined the staff of CERN, the European Organization for Nuclear Research, near Geneva, Switzerland; since the early 1970's, he has also taught physics at Harvard.

Simon van der Meer (1925–), born in The Hague in the Netherlands, graduated from the

Higher Technical School in Delft. After working in electron microscopy, he earned a degree in physical engineering from Delft's Technical University. He began working at CERN in 1956.

The experiments of Rubbia and van der Meer at the CERN laboratories led to detection of one positive and one negative W particle and a neutral Z particle. Rubbia provided the basic theory behind the discovery, while van der Meer worked out the technical details. Their work confirmed predictions based on theoretical unification of the weak force and the electromagnetic force.

Physiology or Medicine. For pioneering work in immunology:

Niels Kai Jerne (1911–), professor emeritus

The Pulitzer Prize for feature photography was given to Anthony Suau of the Denver Post for this photograph of a widow grieving at her husband's grave on Memorial Day and for a series of pictures showing mass starvation in Ethiopia.

at the Basel Institute of Immunology. Born in London of Danish parents, Jerne holds dual citizenship in Britain and in Denmark, where he grew up. After many years as a researcher, he earned his doctorate in medicine from the University of Copenhagen in 1951. He held positions at the California Institute of Technology and at the University of Pittsburgh, and from 1969 to 1980 he was director of the Basel Institute in Switzerland, which he helped found. Described in the award announcement as "the leading theoretician in immunology during the last 30 years," he laid the foundation for practical advances.

Cesar Milstein (1927–), Cambridge University researcher. Born in Bahia Blanca, Argentina, he was educated at the University of Buenos Aires. Focusing his early research on enzymes, he turned to the study of antibodies in the 1960's after receiving his doctorate from Cambridge, where he now teaches.

Georges J. F. Köhler (1946–), researcher at the Basel Institute of Immunology. Born in Munich, he earned his doctorate in biology in 1974 from the University of Freiburg. From 1974 to 1976, Köhler was a postdoctoral fellow at the British Medical Research Council's Laboratory of Molecular Biology in Cambridge, England. Since 1976, he has been a staff member of the Basel Institute, and he was recently appointed a director of the Max Planck Institute for Immune Biology in Freiburg, West Germany.

Milstein and Köhler were cited for their discovery of a way to produce monoclonal antibodies, which are highly sensitive in seeking out specific targets. These antibodies, now turned out in quantity by the biomedical industry, have many possible uses, as diagnostic tools, as research probes, and in treating certain diseases.

PULITZER PRIZES

The 1984 Pulitzer Prizes were announced on April 16. The fiction award went to William Kennedy for the novel *Ironweed*. Bernard Rands won the music award for his *Canti del Sole* for tenor and orchestra. Winner in the drama category was David Mamet for *Glengarry Glen Ross*. In journalism, the public service award went to The Los Angeles *Times* for its 27-part series, *Latinos*, on Hispanic Americans. Mary

Oliver won the poetry prize for her collection, *American Primitive*, and Theodor Seuss Geisel ("Dr. Seuss") received a special citation for his children's books.

Other Pulitzer Prizes in letters and journalism were as follows:

Biography. Louis R. Harlan, for the second volume of his biography, *Booker T. Washington.*

Commentary. Vermont Royster, editorial writer for the *Wall Street Journal.*

Criticism. Paul Goldberger, senior architecture critic, New York *Times.*

Editorial Cartooning. Paul Conrad, Los Angeles *Times.*

Editorial Writing. Albert Scardino, editor of the Atlanta *Georgia Gazette.*

Feature Writing. Peter Mark Rinearson, Seattle *Times.*

General Nonfiction. Paul Starr, *Social Transformation of American Medicine.*

Photography, Feature. Anthony Suau, Denver *Post.*

Photography, Spot News. Stan Grossfeld, Boston *Globe.*

Reporting, General Local. Long Island *Newsday*, for coverage of the case of the severely handicapped Baby Jane Doe.

Reporting, International. Karen Elliott House, the *Wall Street Journal* Washington bureau, for articles on the failure of the U.S. peace plan in the Middle East.

Reporting, National. John Noble Wilford, New York *Times*, for articles on astronomy and space exploration and research.

Reporting, Special Local. Boston *Globe,* for articles examining race relations in city institutions.

OTHER PRIZES AND AWARDS

Among other awards were the following:

Academy of American Poets. $10,000 fellowship to Robert Francis; Walt Whitman Award to Eric Pankey.

Albert and Mary Lasker Foundation. $15,000 divided by Georges Köhler and Cesar Milstein of the Basel Institute of Immunology for their contribution to development of monoclonal antibodies. $15,000 to Michael Potter of the National Cancer Institute for studies leading to development of monoclonal antibodies; to Henry J. Heimlich, of Xavier University for his method

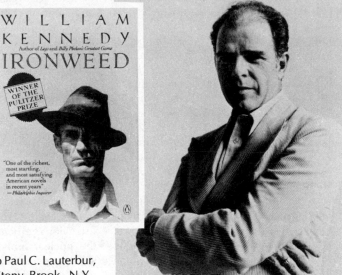

William Kennedy's novel Ironweed, about a former baseball player who becomes an outcast and a murderer, won the 1984 Pulitzer Prize for fiction.

of aiding a choking victim; to Paul C. Lauterbur, of the State University at Stony Brook, N.Y., for contributions toward a new form of medical imaging.

American Academy and Institute of Arts and Letters. $5,000 each to Alice Adams, Herman Cherry, Donna Dennis, Nathan Oliveira, and Tony Rosenthal (art); Amy Clampitt, Don DeLillo, Sanford Friedman, Robert Hass, Lincoln Kirstein, Romulus Linney, Bobbie Ann Mason, and Craig Nova (literature); James Dashow, William Kraft, John Melby, and Ellen Taaffe Zwilich (music). Award for Distinguished Service to the Arts: Roger L. Stevens (chairman of the Kennedy Center for the Performing Arts). Gold Medals: Gordon Bunshaft (architecture) and George F. Kennan (history). Special awards of $5,000 each to Humphrey Carpenter, Denis Santiago, Andrea Lee, W. M. Spackman, and Jamaica Kincaid (literature); to the American Composers Orchestra, Ross Bauer, Richard Campanelli, Kenneth Fuchs, Laura Karpman, Bright Sheng, Larry Stukenholtz, and Gregory Youtz (music); to James Brown (painting); and to Raoul Hague (sculpture). Charles Ives Fellowship ($10,000) to Nicholas C. K. Thorne and Goddard Lieberson Fellowships ($10,000) to Primous Fountain III and Peter Lieberson (music).

American Film Institute. Lifetime Achievement Award to Lillian Gish.

American Institute for Public Service. Jefferson Awards of $5,000 each and medallions to Sally

Ride, William Webster, J. Peter Grace, and Maude E. Callen.

Armand Hammer Foundation. $100,000 award for cancer research (shared) to Michael J. Bishop, Harold E. Varmus, Raymond E. Erikson, and Robert A. Weinberg.

Association of American Publishers, American Book Awards. Prizes of $1,000 each to: Harriet Doerr, for first fiction; Ellen Gilchrist, for overall fiction; and Robert V. Remini for nonfiction.

Bristol-Myers Awards. $50,000 prize for cancer research to Robert A. Weinberg.

Medal of Freedom. Highest U.S. civilian honor, awarded to Whittaker Chambers, Henry ("Scoop") Jackson, Anwar Sadat, and Jackie Robinson (posthumously) and to Howard H. Baker, James Cagney, Leo Cherne, Denton Cooley, Tennessee Ernie Ford, Hector Garcia, Andrew Goodpaster, Joseph Luns, Lincoln Kirstein, Louis L'Amour, the Reverend Norman Vincent Peale, and Eunice Kennedy Shriver.

National Conference of Christians and Jews. Charles Evan Hughes Gold Medal to John Brademas, university president and former Indiana U.S. representative.

Onassis Foundation. $100,000 (shared) to Stewart Young, Francesco Nicosia, and Dillon Ripley.

Samuel H. Scripps–American Dance Festival Award. Prize of $25,000 awarded to Hanya Holm.

Templeton Foundation. $205,000 Templeton Prize for Progress in Religion to the Reverend Michael Bourdeaux.

Wolf Foundation. $100,000 to agriculturalist Robert H. Burris; $100,000 (shared) to mathematicians Hans Lewy and Kunihiko Kodaira.

M.W., P.H. & R.F.

PUBLISHING. The U.S. book publishing industry's upturn continued in 1984, with increased sales in nearly all categories. Familiar titles and authors did well on best-seller lists. There was little growth in overall circulation of newspapers and magazines, but most major companies reported substantial profits. U.S. journalists detected signs of increasing public antagonism toward news media, and some media analysts expressed concern that a court decision against *Hustler* magazine publisher Larry Flynt could discourage free speech. (*See also* CIVIL LIBERTIES AND CIVIL RIGHTS.)

Books. Estimates by the Association of American Publishers for the first seven months of 1984 showed sales of adult trade paperbacks up by more than 6.7 percent over the same period in 1983 and hardbound books up 10.9 percent. Mass market titles rose 4.6 percent, and sales of children's paperbacks increased by an astounding 65.6 percent, according to the AAP. The only downturn was in sales of Bibles and religious titles.

Several previous best-sellers continued to do well; among these were Carole Jackson's grooming guide, *Color Me Beautiful*, and such popular business advice books as *In Search of Excellence, Megatrends,* and *The One Minute Manager.* The best-seller lists featured novels by familiar names ranging from Danielle Steel (*Full Circle*) to Stephen King (*Pet Sematary*) to John Updike (*The Witches of Eastwick*). The most familiar name of all was that of 80-year-old Dr. Seuss (Theodor Geisel), who hit the lists with *The Butter Battle Book*, a parable of the nuclear arms race. Among other books selling especially well were *Eat to Win,* a sports nutrition work by Dr. Robert Haas, and *Mayor,* the candid memoir of New York City's Mayor Edward I. Koch. One of the more remarkable publishing successes was scored by Helen Hooven Santmyer, age 88, whose novel ". . . And Ladies of the Club,'' which she had begun writing in the 1920's, was number one in hardcover fiction for a time.

Doubts were cast on the accuracy of two

Going Strong

New York City's flamboyant mayor, Edward I. Koch, became a publishing sensation in February, when, after only two weeks in print, his autobiography *Mayor* catapulted onto national best-seller lists. The book—highly anecdotal, and sparing of neither friend nor foe—left thousands of readers titillated and almost as many politicians writhing in pain. The author-mayor, a native New Yorker, worked his way through two years at City College by selling shoes, earned a pair of battle stars in World War II, and received a law degree from New York University in 1948. Shortly thereafter he began a political career that included five terms in the U.S. House of Representatives. Elected as mayor in 1977, he was easily reelected in 1981 but pundits were startled by his decision to publish his vitriolic autobiography a year before he was expected to run again. The unflappable mayor just kept on smiling and asking his eternal question: "How'm I doing?"

Edward Koch

books about recent popes, but the consequences could not have been more different. *In God's Name* by David A. Yallop contended that Pope John Paul I, who died unexpectedly in September 1978, after only a few weeks in office, had been murdered. The Vatican called the assertion "absurd." Nonetheless, the book shot toward the top of best-seller lists. By contrast, when *God's Broker* by Antoni Gronowicz, a biography of Pope John Paul II based on purported extensive interviews with the pope, was disavowed by the Vatican, its publisher, Richardson & Snyder, withdrew the book and closed up shop.

Two of the oldest publishers in the United States joined forces in 1984. Macmillan, Inc. acquired The Scribner Book Companies Inc., one of the last of the privately owned, family businesses in publishing. In another industry development of interest, Gulf and Western Industries and Prentice-Hall Inc. announced they had agreed to merge, creating the largest book publisher in the United States. Gulf and Western, through its ownership of Simon & Schuster, was already the nation's sixth-largest publishing house, and Prentice-Hall, which publishes textbooks and professional material for accountants and attorneys, was 11th.

Magazines. The magazine industry appeared stronger than it had in several years. The number of advertising pages was increasing at a faster rate than in 1983 and was expected to be as much as 10 percent higher for the year. Because many magazines raised their ad rates, the percentage improvement in ad revenues promised to be even greater.

Optimism among publishers was not undiluted, however. An industry forecaster predicted in midyear that magazine publishing costs would rise by more than one-third between 1983 and 1986, outpacing an anticipated growth of about 31 percent in ad revenues. The greatest problem, it was said, was paper, whose cost was up sharply over 1983 and was expected to increase by another 10 percent by 1985. Slow circulation growth was also an industry concern. Single-copy sales showed little improvement over lagging totals in the second half of 1983.

The employee-owned U.S. News and World Report, the third-largest newsmagazine in the

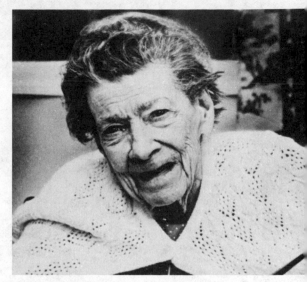

Helen Hooven Santmyer, 88, who had begun writing her long, character-filled novel of Ohio, ". . . And Ladies of the Club", some 60 years earlier, found herself an overnight sensation when the book became the nation's best-selling hardcover work of fiction.

United States, was sold in June to Mortimer Zuckerman, a Boston real estate developer and publisher of the *Atlantic*. In June, St. Louis publisher Jeffrey Gluck sold the *Saturday Review* to a group of Kansas City investors, who paid $300,000 and assumed its debts. A division of Australian publisher Rupert Murdoch's News America Publishing Company in May paid a reported $20 million for *New Woman*, a women's life-style and entertainment monthly. Finally, in November, the Ziff-Davis Publishing Company sold its stable of 24 consumer and trade magazines for an aggregate sum of more than $700 million. CBS Inc. paid $362.5 million for 12 Ziff-Davis consumer periodicals—believed to be the highest price ever paid for a group of magazines. These included such periodicals as *Car & Driver*, *Modern Bride*, *Popular Photography*, and *Stereo Review*. A day after the CBS announcement, it was disclosed that Rupert Murdoch had bought 12 Ziff-Davis trade publications for $350 million.

Many new magazines appeared, including some in the crowded computer field, which saw several titles fail to survive. In March the National Geographic Society introduced *Na-*

By R. FOSTER WINANS

Chicago Milwaukee Corp. shares have been strong lately and could strengthen further this week when the bidding for its Milwaukee Road rail unit begins to take final shape.

The stock, which traded as low as 3 in 1978 after the rail subsidiary began bankruptcy proceedings, jumped as much as 25% in the past month to a high of 120. The shares closed Friday at 117, up 3¾.

The news that got the stock price rolling last month was the entry into the bidding war by Soo Line Railroad, majority-owned by Canadian Pacific Ltd. Soo Line will be bidding against Chicago & North Western Transportation and Grand Trunk, which is owned by Canada's government-controlled Canadian National

Heard on the Street

In a year when the public seemed unusually suspicious of the press, the *Wall Street Journal* suffered an ethical crisis. Front-paging its own embarrassing story, the *Journal* confessed that one of its reporters, R. Foster Winans (left), had enabled speculators to profit by selling them advance news from his influential "Heard on the Street" column. The *Journal*, which fired Winans, noted that the misuse of privileged information was a violation of its formal ethics policy. At the same time, critics asserted that to maintain public confidence in its ethical credibility, the press would have to institute a policy of more vigilant self scrutiny.

---

tional Geographic Traveler, a quarterly that features articles, photographs, and practical information on places of interest to tourists. Available only to the society's members, the new magazine began with a circulation of 600,000. Another newcomer was *World of Sport*, distributed monthly through airlines and hotel chains and aimed at the frequent business traveler.

Newspapers. More U.S. newspapers invested in new equipment, built new plants, and experimented with advanced technologies. Continuing a trend, many papers sought to increase their appeal to readers and advertisers in the face of growing competition from the electronic media by adding special sections and zoned editions and brightening their pages with colorful graphics. The total circulation of U.S. daily newspapers hovered around 62.6 million, only slightly above the 1970 figure. Sunday newspapers, however, continued to grow in number and circulation. Advertising revenues were expected to approach $24 billion in 1984, a 15 percent gain.

The nation's best-selling daily newspaper, the *Wall Street Journal*, increased its circulation, reaching a total of 2 million copies. The Gannett Company's national daily, *USA Today*, which had first appeared in September 1982,

grew even faster. It stood near the 1.3 million mark in October 1984, challenging the number two position of the troubled New York *Daily News*, which had dropped to 1.4 million daily from a onetime peak of about 2 million.

United Press International, for two decades a money-losing operation, strengthened its financial position in several ways. In June, the agency signed a ten-year contract with the British news and information agency Reuters, which agreed to pay $5.76 million for the facilities of UPI's 24 photo bureaus outside the United States. UPI and Reuters clients were to receive photographs from both agencies. In August, UPI agreed on a 13-month austerity program with the Wire Service Guild, representing about 1,000 UPI employees.

Following protests from the press about the Reagan administration's imposition of a news blackout and the barring of journalists from the first two days of the October 1983 U.S. invasion of Grenada, the Defense Department appointed a commission to study relations between the military and the media. In October 1984 the department released the commission's report, which recommended the creation of a pool of reporters, some of whom could be ready at any time to cover the initial stages of a surprise military operation. The department agreed to the formation of an 11-member pool, including representatives of news agencies, radio, television, and newsmagazines; it was later agreed to include one newspaper representative.

Many of the general public appeared to support the administration's original position in excluding reporters, and journalists were concerned by what they perceived as increasing public hostility toward them. Results of a research study published in the *Bulletin,* the official magazine of the American Society of Newspaper Editors, indicated that most newspaper readers strongly supported freedom of the press but gave both newspapers and television low marks for accuracy and fairness.

A scandal involving a *Wall Street Journal* reporter helped underscore the uneasy relationship between press and public. After the Securities and Exchange Commission commenced an investigation of R. Foster Winans, one of the two principal reporters for the *Journal*'s "Heard on the Street" column, which contains tips that often affect stock prices, the newspaper front-paged the whole embarrassing story. Winans, the *Journal* confessed, had sold advance news from the column to speculators, enabling them to make handsome profits. Noting that the reporter's actions were in violation of its ethics policy, the *Journal* fired Winans. In August, he was indicted by a grand jury, with three other defendants, on charges of stock fraud. G.B. & J.L.

PUERTO RICO. In Puerto Rico's gubernatorial election on November 6, 1984, former Governor Rafael Hernández Colón, won 48 percent of the vote and narrowly defeated the incumbent, Carlos Romero Barceló, after a highly personal campaign. This was the third straight gubernatorial contest between Romero Barceló, whose New Progressive Party (PNP) supports statehood, and Hernández Colón, whose Popular Democratic Party (PDP) favors retaining the island's commonwealth status. The PDP also won more than two-thirds of the seats in both houses of the legislature. The election outcome was widely blamed on perceptions of government corruption and inefficiency.

Pope John Paul II visited Puerto Rico on October 12. Some 650,000 people—the largest gathering ever to assemble on the island—joined the pontiff in prayer at a mass in San Juan, where he delivered a homily in Spanish.

The island's economy improved in 1984, with a real growth of 4.7 percent in the gross domestic product, the best rate in five years. Manufacturing and construction were both strong. On the negative side, tourism declined, mainly because of a strong U.S. dollar, which attracted Americans to Europe. The highly subsidized sugar industry was still in the red, and the coffee crop declined.

Ten current and former police officers were charged in February with conspiring to cover up the 1978 murder of two independence activists. Witnesses had testified that the two were shot after surrendering. The defendants said that the two were terrorists who were shot in self-defense. Formal murder charges also were filed, in October.

See STATISTICS OF THE WORLD. A.C.-C.

QATAR. *See* STATISTICS OF THE WORLD. *See also* PERSIAN GULF STATES.

QUEBEC. *See* STATISTICS OF THE WORLD. *See also* CANADA.

RADIO. *See* TELEVISION AND RADIO BROADCASTING.

RAILROADS. *See* TRANSPORTATION.
RECORDINGS. *See* MUSIC.

Religion

In 1984, the U.S. presidential election campaign, and also the resumption of diplomatic ties with the Vatican, stimulated debate over the relation between religion and politics. In South Africa, a black Anglican bishop and apartheid foe won the Nobel Peace Prize. In India, ethnic and religious strife gave rise to massive violence.

During 1984, Pope John Paul II journeyed to Canada and to Asia and the Pacific, spreading the gospel message. Protestant denominations continued steadfast efforts toward interchurch unity. The plight of Soviet Jews remained an international concern.

ROMAN CATHOLIC CHURCH

In 1984 the Vatican strengthened its position in the international community through the establishment of diplomatic relations with the United States; at the same time, however, it experienced a weakening of position in Italy with the signing of a new concordat with the Italian government. Internally, the Church was involved in efforts to preserve dogmatic orthodoxy and work out teachings on social principles.

Diplomatic Realignments. On January 10 the United States and the Vatican established formal diplomatic relations for the first time in 117 years. The White House declared that the step was intended to improve communications, at a time when Pope John Paul II had become increasingly involved in international affairs. The Senate ratified the action, approving President Ronald Reagan's nomination of William A. Wilson as ambassador by an 81–13 vote on March 7. Archbishop Pio Laghi, the apostolic delegate to the Roman Catholic Church in the United States, was upgraded to papal pronuncio. The establishment of relations drew criticism from some religious and civil liberties groups as contrary to the principle of separation of church and state.

A concordat signed by the Vatican and Italy on February 18 continued the status of Vatican City as an independent and sovereign state but markedly lessened the influence of the Catholic Church on civil life in Italy. Under the concordat, replacing the one signed in 1929, Roman Catholicism ceased to be the state religion, and such hitherto purely ecclesiastical matters as Church annulments of marriages were made subject to state confirmation. Also, Rome lost its official designation as a "holy city," a status that had allowed the Church to ban plays, books, and films there.

Liberation Theology. A major controversy erupted over "liberation theology," a radical interpretation of Christian teachings that developed in the 1960's and helped motivate social activism among priests and nuns in Latin America. Proponents of the doctrine, which makes use of Marxist analysis, argue that it is the role of the Church to help bring political and economic change to the developing countries of the world. On September 3 the Vatican issued a document criticizing advocates of liberation theology for identifying the "history of salvation" and "the kingdom of God" with "the human liberation movement." On September 7, Leonardo Boff, a Franciscan theologian from Brazil who is a leading exponent of liberation theology, was summoned to Rome, where he defended his views during a four-hour interrogation by Church authorities.

Latin America. After years of delay, the case of four U.S. Catholic churchwomen murdered in El Salvador in 1980 was closed in May. Five former Salvadoran national guardsmen were convicted of aggravated homicide and sentenced to 30-year prison terms, the maximum allowable under Salvadoran law.

Church-state tensions continued in Nicaragua. In April the country's bishops criticized the Sandinista government for failure to ne gotiate with rebel leaders. The Vatican stepped up pressure on four priests in the Nicaraguan government to resign their posts, and the education minister, Reverend Fernando Cardinal, a member of the Jesuit order (Society of Jesus), was dismissed from the order in December, following his refusal to resign his government position.

United States. Public debate on the role of religion in politics and on the related issue of abortion heated up in June, when New York Archbishop John J. O'Connor declared, in response to a question, "I don't see how a Catholic in good conscience can vote for a candidate who explicitly supports abortion." Several leading Catholic politicians, including New York's Democratic Governor Mario Cuomo, took issue with O'Connor's remark, asserting that moral tests on such issues as abortion were not valid criteria for choosing or rejecting a candidate. Later in the year, O'Connor accused the Democratic vice-presidential nominee, Geraldine Ferraro, a Catholic, of fostering a mistaken impression, in a public statement, that Catholic teaching on abortion was "open to interpretation."

At the annual meeting of the national Council of Catholic Bishops in November, a committee headed by Archbishop Rembert G. Weakland of Milwaukee released the first draft of a proposed pastoral letter on the U.S. economy. It described current U.S. levels of poverty and unemployment as "morally unacceptable" and called for a national commitment and changes in policies to remedy those problems. A few days before, the Lay Commission on Catholic Social Teaching and the U.S. Economy, a group of conservative business and professional leaders headed by former Treasury Secretary William E. Simon, issued a statement in support of the U.S. capitalist system, as the best means of solving economic problems to the advantage of all.

Europe. In October, Father Jerzy Popieluszko, a Warsaw priest noted for his support of Solidarity, the outlawed Polish labor movement, was abducted and murdered. Four security police officers went on trial for the crime late in the year. Also in Poland, the removal of crucifixes from classrooms in an agricultural college touched off a church-state confronta-

tion that gradually widened. Students staged demonstrations, while Bishop Jan Mazur of Siedlce and hundreds of priests went on a bread-and-water fast; a compromise finally allowed crucifixes in some places in the school but not in classrooms.

In June a report by Italian State Prosecutor Antonio Albano charged that the Bulgarian secret services, possibly with Soviet support, had recruited Mehmet Ali Agca to shoot the pope in 1982, in a plot to eliminate papal support for Solidarity. In October, Ilario Martella, an Italian judge, asserted that Agca had not acted alone but had been aided by another gunman, a Turkish terrorist named Oral Celik. Martella said that three Bulgarians and four Turks (including Celik) would be tried on charges of complicity in the assassination attempt.

There were new developments related to the 1982 collapse of the Milan-based Banco Am-

Summoned from Brazil to testify about "liberation theology," Friar Leonardo Boff talks to Rome reporters after defending his views at the Vatican. The radical doctrine, espoused by the Franciscan theologian and other members of the clergy in Latin America, uses Marxist analysis and proposes a greater involvement of the Church with local political movements, particularly in extremely poor regions.

Peripatetic Pope

Like past years, 1984 was a year of pastoral journeys for the most traveled pope in the history of the Church. In May, for instance, John Paul II made an 11-day trip to Asia and the Pacific, highlighted by a canonization ceremony in Seoul, South Korea, for 103 19th-century martyrs. In September he became the first pope ever to visit Canada; during 12 days of travel in that country, he addressed issues ranging from unemployment and Indian rights to abortion and human sexuality. At home, he attended to business—realigning the 17 top posts in the Curia, for example—but he also took time out in July for a ski vacation in the Adamello mountains of northern Italy. Guides said the Holy Father was an "intermediate" skier and that he had not fallen a single time.

Pope John Paul II

brosiano. The Vatican bank, the Istituto per le Opere di Religione (IOR), had holdings in the failed Ambrosiano group, and its management was under investigation for fraud connected with the bankruptcy. On May 25, in Geneva, IOR officials agreed to pay creditors of Banco Ambrosiano $250 million as part of a $406 million settlement, with the balance to come from the sale of Banco Ambrosiano's assets. The creditors agreed to waive further claims against the IOR or the Banco Ambrosiano's successor.

Asia. In early 1984 it was disclosed that John Paul II had requested and obtained the resignations of 21 elderly priests and bishops who had once held church posts in China but had lived in exile for 30 years or more. The resignations cleared the way for possible Vatican negotiations with the Chinese government on the appointment of new resident prelates.

An Italian paper this summer reported the arrest of Archbishop Philippe Nguyen-Kim Diem of Hue, Vietnam, for opposition to a government-formed organization of Catholics. The action heightened Vatican fears that Vietnam might be moving to isolate its 3 million Catholics from Rome.

Tridentine Mass. On October 15, the Vatican announced that the pope would allow limited use of the Latin-only Tridentine Mass, which had been banned in the 1960's. However, regular parish use of the Latin Mass remained prohibited.

Papal Trips. South Korea was the principal stop during an 11-day papal trip to the Far East in May that also included Papua New Guinea, the Solomon Islands, and Thailand. In Seoul, South Korea, before a special canonization ceremony, a 22-year-old South Korean student, later termed "mentally unsound," fired a toy pistol at the pope. In June, John Paul made a six-day visit to Switzerland. The pope urged the Swiss to monitor their powerful financial system against abuses and, on a visit to World Council of Churches headquarters, spoke on behalf of Christian unity.

On September 9, John Paul began a 12-day visit to Canada, becoming the first pope to visit that country. A bomb explosion on September 3 in a Montreal train station, which killed three people, was thought to be linked to the papal visit, and security was tightened. The pontiff was greeted warmly as he traveled from the Maritime Provinces across to Vancouver by way of the Northwest Territories.

In October the pope made a three-day trip to Zaragoza, Spain, the Dominican Republic, and Puerto Rico. His route, approximating that taken by Christopher Columbus in 1492, was timed to inaugurate a "novena of years" leading to the 500th anniversary of Columbus's trip.

Appointments. Cardinal Bernardin Gantin of Benin, on the West African coast, was named prefect of the Vatican's Congregation for Bishops on April 9, becoming the first black African to hold a major post in the Curia. Bishop Bernard F. Law of Springfield–Cape Girardeau in Missouri was named archbishop of Boston on January 24. A week later, on January 31, Bishop John J. O'Connor of Scranton, Pa., was named head of the archdiocese of New York.

J.D.

PROTESTANT AND ORTHODOX CHURCHES Church-state issues during a political year, U.S. foreign policy, South Africa's apartheid, leadership changes, and continuing efforts toward interchurch unity were prevalent Protestant concerns in 1984.

Church, State, and Politics. The relationship between religion and politics became a subject of wide public attention in the United States during the 1984 presidential election campaign. The Reverend Jesse Jackson, a contender for the Democratic presidential nomination and an ordained Baptist minister, frequently quoted Scripture and included religious themes and images in his speeches. As the first serious black contender for the presidency, he was supported by many black churches and their leaders. Debate during the year over the specific issue of abortion at first mainly involved Catholic religious leaders and prominent Catholic politicians, but Protestant preachers, politicians, and academics soon participated as well. Issues such as social welfare and nuclear arms also were often discussed in a religious context.

Lutheran writer Richard Neuhaus predicted that the political-religious conflicts of 1984 would be "a point of reference in years to come in talking about the interaction of politics, religion, and moral judgment." Some observers, however, were disturbed by the dimensions of the debate and believed that the constitutional principle of separation between church and state was not being properly heeded. Many Protestants were concerned over President Ronald Reagan's seeming alliance with various fundamentalist groups, who were

prominent at the 1984 Republican National Convention. Some feared that the United States was being improperly identified as a specifically Christian nation, while others argued that there was no essential difference between current activism on issues such as abortion and school prayer and past church involvement in civil rights and antiwar movements, except for a political shift from left to right.

Questions of foreign policy continued to be a major concern of many church groups. The United Methodist Church, at its General Conference in May, adopted a statement asking the United States to cease military and other destabilizing activities in Central America. The movement to give sanctuary to Central American refugees who could not obtain legal alien status in the United States continued to spread, with more than 150 churches involved.

The reestablishment of formal diplomatic ties between the United States and the Vatican, in January, was opposed by many Protestant leaders and civil libertarians. In September a coalition of Protestant churches, joined by two Catholic groups, filed a suit to nullify the exchange of ambassadors, arguing that it violated church-state separation.

Religion and Education. A proposed constitutional amendment to allow organized, vocal prayer in public schools failed to get out of the U.S. Senate in 1984. Congress did, however, approve a so-called equal access bill, signed by President Reagan in August, that allows voluntary, student-initiated religious, political, and philosophical meetings in public school facilities before or after school.

A case that pointed up basic church-state disagreements over education concerned the Reverend Everett Sileven and the school operated by his Faith Baptist Church in Louisville, Neb. Over a period of seven years, courts several times ordered the school closed because it employed teachers not certified by the state; Sileven was found in contempt of court for defying the orders. However, under a new law signed in April by Nebraska Governor Robert Kerrey, if parents submit a statement declaring that accreditation and approval requirements violate their religious beliefs, they may now set up their own schools for their children, exempted from those requirements.

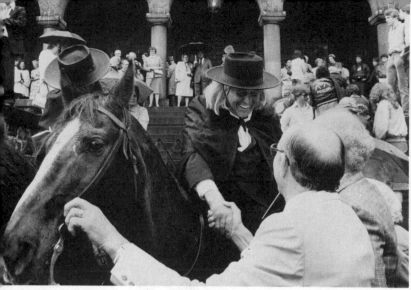

With buoyant greetings to parishioners at Lovely Lane Methodist Church, the Reverend Sidney C. Dillinger ends a 1,380-mile ride from Kansas to Baltimore. Dressed as 19th-century circuit-riding preachers, Dillinger and a fellow Methodist clergyman made the trip to help celebrate the birthday of Methodism, founded 200 years earlier in Baltimore.

© 1984 MARTY KATZ

The schools must comply with compulsory attendance laws; however, the state cannot prohibit schools from employing teachers who do not meet state requirements.

Opposition to Apartheid. In October it was announced that the Nobel Peace Prize was awarded to Bishop Desmond Tutu, a black Anglican cleric and the secretary-general of the South African Council of Churches, for his role as a leader in the nonviolent campaign against apartheid. The bishop declared that the prize honored all those involved in the struggle to eradicate racial inequality in South Africa. Authorities in South Africa have criticized the bishop and his organization. In February, South Africa's Eloff Commission issued a report claiming the council was subversive but did not call for its banning, an action that had been feared by some. Bishop Tutu himself was named in November as the first black Anglican bishop of Johannesburg.

The Lutheran World Federation, at its international assembly in Budapest, Hungary, during the summer suspended two white South African churches from membership for failure to clearly oppose apartheid.

World Council of Churches. The World Council of Churches, international ecumenical agency for 300 Protestant and Orthodox churches, elected a new chief executive, the Reverend Emilio Castro. A Uruguayan Methodist clergyman, Castro was praised for combining a commitment to social justice with a fiery passion for evangelism. He succeeded the Reverend Philip Potter, a West Indian Methodist.

National Council of Churches. At the National Council of Churches, with 31 U.S. Protestant and Orthodox member bodies, Presbyterian laywoman Claire Randall prepared to step down after 11 years as general secretary. Her elected successor, the Reverend Arie Brouwer, former top executive of the Reformed Church of America, was elected to a three-year term to begin in January 1985.

Billy Graham in the Soviet Union. The Reverend Billy Graham, who had received criticism after a Soviet trip in 1982, seemed somewhat careful in the remarks he made at the conclusion of his second tour of the Soviet Union, in September 1984. Graham preached at Russian Orthodox and Baptist churches in Leningrad, Moscow, Tallinn, and Novosibirsk. Afterward, he stated that churches in the Soviet Union were "open and active" but added that some believers "may face definite opposition from their government."

Church Conferenes. The Lutheran World Federation at its summer meeting in Budapest—its first meeting in a Communist country—elected as its new president the controversial head of the Hungarian Lutheran Church, Bishop Zoltan Kaldy. Kaldy has been criticized by some for the adjustments the church has made to the Communist regime in Hungary.

The newly merged Presbyterian Church

348

(U.S.A.), meeting in Phoenix in June for its first full General Assembly since a Civil War split over slavery, chose a southerner, the Reverend James Andrews, as its stated clerk (executive administrator). Texas-born Andrews had served as stated clerk of the southern branch of the church before reunification. His election was an upset victory over William P. Thompson, the northern branch's stated clerk for almost 20 years.

In June the Southern Baptist Convention, reportedly the largest U.S. Protestant denomination, elected Atlanta pastor and television preacher Charles Stanley as president. At its lively annual meeting the SBC also passed a resolution against the ordination of women, which was, however, not binding, since local congregations have the autonomous power to ordain.

In May, the United Methodists held a two-week General Conference in Baltimore, where 200 years earlier the Methodist Church in the United States had been formally established. The 1,000 delegates passed a resolution barring "self-avowed, practicing homosexuals" from the church's ordained ministry. In regional meetings the United Methodists also elected 19 bishops, including two women and five blacks.

Church Unions and Unity. On November 30 a nine-denomination group, the Consultation on Church Union, meeting in Baltimore, capped an effort of more than 20 years when it approved a 40,000-word statement setting forth agreement on key issues involving baptism, creeds, liturgy, and forms of ministry. The document, intended to provide the basis for a possible merger, was sent back to participating denominations for approval. The churches involved were the African Methodist Episcopal Church, the African Methodist Episcopal Zion Church, the Christian Church (Disciples of Christ), the Christian Methodist Episcopal Church, the Episcopal Church, the International Council of Community Churches, the Presbyterian Church (U.S.A.), the United Methodist Church, and the United Church of Christ. Meanwhile, a major international Methodist-Lutheran theological dialogue team concluded five years of talks with a significant call for churches of the two traditions to move toward "full fellowship of word and sacrament"—in other words, a commonality of all aspects of worship. This is further than Lutherans have gone with any other communion.   J.C.L.

JUDAISM

A continuing decline in Jewish emigration from the Soviet Union remained a major concern of world Jewry. From a peak of 51,320 emigrations in 1979, the number of Jews permitted to leave fell to 1,314 in 1983 and 896 in 1984, according to U.S. Jewish officials. There were also further efforts by Soviet authorities to reduce the already limited number of contacts Soviet Jews had with foreigners, partly by intimidating foreign visitors (in July the former president of Israel, Ephraim Katzir, was arrested briefly in Moscow).

In August the U.S. Congress passed a resolution declaring that the Soviet Union had "grossly violated" the Helsinki human rights

"The Precious Legacy," an exhibit of Jewish secular and religious art, is inspected by visitors to New York City's Jewish Museum. Most of the show's 300 items, displayed outside Czechoslovakia for the first time, had been confiscated from the Jews of Moravia and Bohemia by Nazi troops during World War II.

accords of 1975 by refusing to allow Jews to emigrate freely. Earlier, in June, the European Parliament issued a formal declaration on the situation of Soviet Jewry, and French President François Mitterrand raised the question of Soviet Jewry during a visit to the Soviet Union.

For the first time since World War II, the Jewish community in Czechoslovakia got its own rabbi when a young Czech Jew was ordained at the Jewish seminary in Budapest, Hungary. In another first, Rabbi Ernst Lorge, who fled Germany in the 1930's, became the first American rabbi to return to East Germany in a clerical capacity.

In August, Valerian Trifa, former Nazi sympathizer and an archbishop of the Romanian Orthodox Church in America, was deported from the United States for concealing his World War II association with Romania's anti-Semitic Iron Guard movement when he had applied for naturalization.

More than 1,500 people attended the first international gathering of the "second generation"—the children of survivors of the Holocaust—held in New York City at the end of May. The three-day conference was organized by the International Network of Children of Jewish Holocaust Survivors. Another international conference, entitled "Faith in Humankind: Rescuers of Jews During the Holocaust," was convened in Washington, D.C., in September. The two-day conference, attended by over 1,100 people, brought together Holocaust survivors and rescuers, as well as scholars, educators, and religious leaders.   L.G.

NEWER FAITHS

The Reverend Sun Myung Moon, of South Korea, founder of the Unification Church—a Christian sect with Confucian and other, non-Christian elements in its teachings—began serving an 18-month prison sentence in the United States in July, after being convicted of income tax evasion. He was also fined $25,000. Many religious leaders joined in protesting the prosecution of the Reverend Moon, arguing that he was entitled to the traditional tax exemption for religious organizations.

ISLAM

The Muslim pilgrimage, or Hadj, to Mecca in late summer was overshadowed by rumors that a group of Libyan revolutionaries intended to

seize the Great Mosque, which houses Islam's holiest shrines, as a way of marking Libyan leader Muammar al-Qaddafi's 15th year in power. Strong warnings from Saudi Arabia, which at one point refused to allow Libyan pilgrims to land at the port of Jiddah, on the Red Sea, prompted Qaddafi to disown the "plotters" and to urge that Libyan pilgrims conduct themselves peaceably. The pilgrimage took place without violence.

In Nigeria early in the year, members of an extremist Muslim sect, whose founder, Maitatsine, was killed in 1981, rioted in the town of Yola, leaving at least 1,000 people dead and thousands homeless. Sect members regard their founder, and not Muhammad, as the true prophet of Allah and view as heretics those who display material wealth of any kind, even wristwatches. In reaction, state governments in the predominantly Muslim North decreed tighter restrictions on the conduct of outdoor religious preaching.

A letter from Muhammad to the Byzantine Emperor Heraclius (c. 575–641 A.D.), will be permanently displayed in a specially built shrine in Amman, according to a Jordanian announcement. The letter, authenticated by experts, was one of six sent by the prophet heralding the advent of Islam in surrounding nations.

BUDDHISM

In December the Dalai Lama, spiritual and onetime temporal leader of the Tibetan people who has been living in India as head of a Tibetan government in exile, cancelled plans to visit his homeland in 1985; he had been invited by the Chinese government, which has been reopening Tibetan Buddhist temples and returning religious objects seized by authorities during the Cultural Revolution. The Dalai Lama has expressed fears that Tibetans could be punished for enthusiasm they might exhibit in response to his visit.

RELIGIONS OF INDIA AND SRI LANKA

On June 2, the Indian Army stormed the Golden Temple in Amritsar, capital of the northern state of Punjab, killing at least 1,000 Sikh militants according to unofficial estimates, including their leader Jarnail Singh Bhindranwale. Sikhs are members of a religious community founded some 500 years ago by the

Armed Sikhs guard their stronghold, the Golden Temple in Amritsar, before an impending Indian army assault in early June.

mystic Nanak. The religion, a blend of Hinduism and Islam, now has about 14 million members, living mostly in India, mainly in Punjab. They are distinguished by their dress, with the men turbaned and bearded and often wearing weapons. Sikh militants were using the temple as a fortress and base for terrorist attacks, as part of a campaign for political and religious autonomy. Sikhs openly vowed revenge against Prime Minister Indira Gandhi, and on October 31 two of her bodyguards, both Sikhs, shot her to death outside her office in New Delhi, an event which precipitated massive violence against Sikhs.

Tensions between Hindus and Muslims in the southwestern Indian state of Maharashtra erupted into bloody riots during May; more than 250 deaths were reported. That same month, in New Delhi, a Hindu mob sacked the Bangladeshi embassy in protest over the takeover of Hindu properties in Bangladesh, which is predominantly Muslim.

Ethnic conflict between the largely Hindu Tamil minority and the predominantly Buddhist Sinhalese majority continued in Sri Lanka. The Tamil, who make up about 20 percent of the population, seek establishment of a separate state in the northern region of Jaffna. The government initiated "amity talks" involving the two communities, but without apparent result. On one occasion, after Tamils burned a police station and a Buddhist temple, government troops attacked civilian crowds, causing over 200 deaths.

A study published in September showed a significant increase in the number of "dowry killings" among working-class Indians. According to the religiously sanctioned dowry system, the Hindu bride usually brings with her to her husband's home an agreed-upon quantity of cash, jewelry, clothing, and household goods. An increasing number of bridegrooms' families also require additional payments from the bride or her family after marriage. When payment is not forthcoming, the new wife may be murdered by her in-laws; a frequently used method is to douse the clothing of the victim with kerosene and then set her on fire, afterward claiming that the burning was either an accident or suicide. The increase in this type of crime has been attributed by some to social stress consequent upon expansion of the consumer-oriented economy.   C.S.J.W.

REPUBLICAN PARTY. In 1984, for the second time in a row and for the fourth time in 16 years, a Republican presidential nominee swept to victory in November. In carrying 59 percent of the popular vote and 49 states, President Ronald Reagan demonstrated broad support among most demographic groups. Although

351

the GOP remained a minority party in voter registration, Republicans were also heartened by newfound strength among young people and those voting for the first time. However, the party did not achieve the congressional mandate its leaders had hoped for.

Convention and Campaign. With Reagan's renomination a foregone conclusion, the Republican National Convention, held in Dallas on August 20–23, served mainly to showcase key personalities, define the party's principles, and outline themes for the campaign against the Democrats and their presidential and vice-presidential standard-bearers, Walter F. Mondale and Geraldine A. Ferraro.

To counteract the "Ferraro factor," the party allotted prominent convention roles to several women. The keynote address was given by Katherine Davalos Ortega, a Hispanic who held the largely ceremonial office of U.S. treasurer. For the main foreign policy speech the party turned to a maverick Democrat, Jeane

Senator Robert Dole of Kansas (right) meets the press after being elected majority leader of the Senate by his Republican colleagues on November 28. He succeeded Howard Baker of Tennessee (left), who retired from the Senate in 1984.

J. Kirkpatrick, chief U.S. delegate to the United Nations.

The platform, adopted without debate, was conservative even by Republican standards. One plank, drafted over White House objections, opposed any tax increases. Other planks called for constitutional amendments to require a balanced budget and to ban abortions, committed the president to appoint federal judges who opposed abortion, and endorsed voluntary prayer in the public schools.

After Reagan and Vice-President George Bush were renominated on a single roll call, the campaign formally began. In their acceptance speeches and in the ensuing months, Reagan and Bush derided Mondale's pledge to raise taxes, extolled the new spirit of patriotism they saw in America, promised four more years of peace and prosperity, and sought to tie Mondale to the alleged failures of President Jimmy Carter's administration. They contrasted what they portrayed as the negativism of the Democrats with the positive values of Republicanism and Reagan's leadership.

The Election. At the presidential level, this approach apparently worked well. One survey showed that the Reagan-Bush team drew 66 percent of all white votes, 57 percent of all women (despite the presence of a woman on the Democratic ticket), and majorities in every age category. Only among blacks, Hispanics, Jews, and the poor did the Republicans fare badly in the 1984 presidential race.

In legislative races the results were mixed. The GOP lost two seats in the U.S. Senate; in the U.S. House, a Republican pickup of 14 seats (with one other undecided) was not enough to reverse the party's 1982 losses.

Problems and Prospects. In Congress, the president faced possible problems from independent-minded Republicans said to harbor presidential ambitions of their own, including Senator Robert Dole (Kan.)—the new majority leader—and Representative Jack Kemp (N.Y.). Thus far, however, the main contender for the party's 1988 presidential nomination appeared to be Vice-President Bush. A poll taken at the Republican convention showed 48 percent of the delegates and alternates favoring Bush, with 26 percent for Kemp and 16 percent for Howard Baker, Jr. (Tenn.), the Senate majority leader, who declined to run for reelection in 1984.

Polls taken in 1984 showed that increasing numbers of Americans identified themselves as Republicans or leaning toward the Republican Party. One New York Times–CBS News poll, taken in December, found 41 percent so identifying themselves, only slightly fewer than the 43 percent who said they were Democrats or leaning toward the Democrats. However, political analysts differed as to whether such results reflected the beginning of a new U.S. political realignment or were only temporary offshoots of Reagan's popularity.

See DEMOCRATIC PARTY; ELECTIONS IN THE UNITED STATES; PRESIDENT OF THE UNITED STATES.

G.M.H.

RHODE ISLAND. See STATISTICS OF THE WORLD.

RHODESIA. See ZIMBABWE.

ROMANIA. The Romanian government continued to have cool relations with the Soviet Union in 1984. The death of Soviet leader Yuri Andropov in February received less media coverage than in other Soviet bloc countries, and only one day of mourning was declared. Relations between the two nations were strained because Romanian leader Nicolae Ceaușescu continued to support more national autonomy in Eastern Europe. The commands and general staffs of the Warsaw Pact forces held a joint exercise on the territories of Bulgaria, Hungary, and Romania, but on Romanian territory only general staffs of the Romanian Army participated, to play the exercise on paper.

In October, Ceaușescu, in a further attempt to show his independence from the Soviet Union, visited Bonn, West Germany, a short time after East German and Bulgarian leaders had cancelled similar visits apparently because of Soviet pressure. Romania also took part in the summer Olympics in Los Angeles, despite a Soviet-led boycott. Romanian athletes did extremely well there, capturing 20 gold medals, the second highest total after the United States, including four golds won by gymnast Ecaterina Szabo.

After many delays, the 40-mile-long Danube–Black Sea Canal was inaugurated on May 26. The waterway connects the Danube port of Cernavoda with a new Black Sea port, Constanta South–Agigea, and can accommodate two-way ship traffic. It will also be a source of water for irrigation. Work on the $2 billion project had begun in 1949; it was suspended from 1953 to 1975 for economic reasons.

In April when the Romanian-Jewish community, led by Chief Rabbi Moses Rosen, protested anti-Semitic material in a book of poetry, the Bucharest regime ordered withdrawal of unsold copies. Anti-Semitism, endemic in Romania but officially forbidden, does appear in literature. Since all publications must be cleared by Romania's Communist Party, such attacks are apparently supported by high authorities.

See STATISTICS OF THE WORLD. R.A.P.

RUSSIA. See UNION OF SOVIET SOCIALIST REPUBLICS.

RWANDA. See STATISTICS OF THE WORLD.

S

SAHARA, WESTERN. See AFRICA; MOROCCO.

ST. KITTS–NEVIS (ST. CHRISTOPHER AND NEVIS). See STATISTICS OF THE WORLD. See also CARIBBEAN COUNTRIES.

ST. LUCIA. See STATISTICS OF THE WORLD.

ST. VINCENT AND THE GRENADINES. See STATISTICS OF THE WORLD. See also CARIBBEAN COUNTRIES.

SAMOA, AMERICAN. See STATISTICS OF THE WORLD: American Samoa.

SAMOA, WESTERN. See STATISTICS OF THE WORLD: Western Samoa.

SAN MARINO. See STATISTICS OF THE WORLD.

SÃO TOMÉ AND PRÍNCIPE. See STATISTICS OF THE WORLD.

SASKATCHEWAN. See STATISTICS OF THE WORLD.

SAUDI ARABIA. Defense-related issues preoccupied the Saudi government in 1984, as controversies flared over U.S. weapons sales and Saudi involvement in the Iran-Iraq war. Oil production was lagging, but advances were reported in agriculture.

Foreign Relations and Defense. In January the government announced that France would supply the kingdom with an air defense system. The $4.5 billion package included radar complexes and surface-to-air missiles, for which the Saudi military reportedly provided 33 percent of research-and-development money.

The Saudi government encountered greater obstacles in its attempts to acquire arms from the United States. The proposed sale of Maverick air-to-ground missiles and Stinger surface-to-air missiles, although supported by the Reagan administration, was withdrawn in March in the face of congressional opposition.

Two months later, however, Saudi involvement in hostilities in the Persian Gulf war and U.S. fears that the fighting there could jeopardize Western oil supplies galvanized U.S. interest in Saudi defense needs. On May 16 a Saudi-owned tanker was attacked and set afire in Saudi waters; evidence pointed to Iran as the source of the attacking planes. President Ronald Reagan then promised Saudi King Fahd ibn Abdul-Aziz that the United States would provide air cover over the Gulf, if asked to do so. Reagan also invoked emergency powers to initiate the sale of 400 Stinger missiles and a KC-10 air tanker to the Saudi Air Force. On June 5, two Saudi F-15 fighters shot down two Iranian F-4 fighter-bombers that had violated Saudi air space. The Saudi fighters were guided to the interception point by U.S. manned Awacs surveillance planes. Later in the year, a new threat to Saudi security emerged—the mining of the Red Sea along the kingdom's west coast. The mines, dumped by an unidentified party, damaged 19 ships from July to September, including a Saudi-registered merchant ship. A multinational group of naval vessels and mine-hunting helicopters swept the Red Sea in August and September.

Another consequence of the Iran-Iraq war was closer cooperation within the Gulf Cooperation Council (Saudi Arabia, Kuwait, Qatar, Bahrain, Oman, and the United Arab Emirates).

In October, the GCC staged the "Gezira Shield II" joint maneuvers in Saudi Arabia. In November, the GCC agreed to establish a rapid deployment force.

Energy. Low levels of oil production posed major problems for the economy. Production did not rise above 5.5 million barrels per day in the first half of the year. This depressed level (less than half of capacity) led to concern over the availability of associated natural gas supplies (those accompanying oil deposits) for Saudi desalinization, utility, petrochemical, and other plants. The development of nonassociated gas fields remained a government priority; several rich fields were opened during the year.

Late in the year, the Organization of Petroleum Exporting Countries cut the organization's overall production ceiling by 1.5 million barrels per day, and Saudi Arabia agreed to the largest cuts, lowering its quota to 4,353,000 barrels per day. The kingdom had acted previously to protect crude oil exports and to expand the range of petroleum products exported. About 60 million barrels of crude oil were stockpiled in tankers outside the Persian Gulf, as insurance against Iranian closure of the Strait of Hormuz.

Budget. Low oil production contributed to the woes of Saudi financial planners. The riyal, devalued four times in 1983, was reduced twice more before gaining some strength by mid-1984. The kingdom ended fiscal 1983–1984 with expenditures of $63.2 billion, the lowest since 1978–1979. The 1984–1985 budget called for a 17 percent increase in expenditures.

Agriculture and Industry. After several years of aggressive development of agricultural resources, the kingdom became self-sufficient in wheat, eggs, dairy products, and poultry in 1984. Wheat production accounts for 60 percent of cultivated land and benefits from heavy government subsidies. Production reached 1.3 million metric tons in 1983–1984, against local consumption of 800,000 tons. This level was achieved only through intensive irrigation that involved drawing irreplaceable water from deep underground reservoirs. Some experts feared that the country would exhaust its supplies of underground water in the forseeable future.

The petrochemical industry experienced difficulties as its exports met with increasing protectionism abroad. Saudi urea, drawing on cheap feedstock and state-of-the-art production techniques, costs only $140 a ton, whereas the world market price is around $180 a ton. U.S. and Japanese tariff restrictions of Saudi petrochemical products ranged from 9 to 18 percent.

See STATISTICS OF THE WORLD.   C.H.A.

SENEGAL. See STATISTICS OF THE WORLD.

SEYCHELLES. See STATISTICS OF THE WORLD.

SIERRA LEONE. See STATISTICS OF THE WORLD.

SINGAPORE. Elections for Singapore's 79-seat lower house of Parliament were held on December 22, 1984. The ruling People's Action Party (PAP) fielded 26 new candidates, including Brigadier General Lee Hsien Loon, son of the prime minister. Opposition candidates ran in 49 constituencies but won only two seats, one more than in the previous session.

In August, Prime Minister Lee Kuan Yew expressed a desire to relinquish his office by age 65, that is, by September 1988. At a PAP conference the next month, veteran party leaders, with the exception of Lee, quit the party's central committee in favor of younger members. A new cabinet, named on December 31, confirmed in power a group of young leaders. Defense Minister Goh Chok Tong was named to an additional post as first deputy prime minister, and General Lee Hsien Loon was named a junior minister.

To encourage educated women to have more children, tax incentives were granted by the government to mothers with professional or university degrees and three or more children. Children of these women were also given priority in being accepted by the best schools.

The economic recovery of the United States and other industrialized nations helped revive Singapore's growth rate, which was expected to be close to 10 percent for 1984.

See STATISTICS OF THE WORLD.   K.M.

SOCIAL SECURITY. Despite charges and countercharges during the 1984 presidential election campaign about "secret plans" to cut social security benefits, the U.S. social security system stirred relatively little major controversy. Projections indicated that social security trust funds would remain solvent through 1990.

In October, President Ronald Reagan signed legislation overhauling the social security disability system. The bill liberalized eligibility standards and made it more difficult for the government to disqualify recipients. The system had been in turmoil because of the administration's efforts to remove people from the benefit rolls. Of 1.2 million cases reviewed since 1981, benefits were terminated for 490,000 persons who were classified as no longer disabled. However, in more than half of these cases, benefits were restored after the former recipients showed, on appeal, that their removal had been unjustified.

The president and Congress acted to guarantee a cost-of-living increase for social security recipients in 1985. Under existing law, beneficiaries receive an increase only if the Consumer Price Index (CPI) rises 3 percent or more from the third quarter of one year to the corresponding period of the next year. In July, when it appeared that the CPI for the relevant period might increase less than that amount, the president proposed a guaranteed 3 percent adjustment. The Senate quickly went along. The House later acted to pass this legislation even though it was becoming evident that inflation would rise more than 3 percent, making the bill unnecessary.

To help reduce massive federal deficits, the Deficit Reduction Act of 1984 authorized spending cuts totaling $13 billion over three years. About two-thirds of these cuts were in medicare, the health insurance program for the elderly. One provision prohibited any increase in doctors' charges to medicare patients until October 1, 1985, and assessed penalties for noncompliance against any doctor participating in medicare. Also, premiums paid by medicare beneficiaries for insurance coverage of doctors' fees (Part B of medicare) were to be increased sufficiently to finance 25 percent of the program's cost through 1987. The remaining 75 percent of the cost will continue to be paid from general tax revenues. In 1984, Part B premiums were $14.60 a month. Under the Deficit Reduction Act, they were expected to reach $20.50 per month in 1985. The Deficit Reduction Act also liberalized supplemental security income (SSI).   J.A.R.

SOLOMON ISLANDS. See STATISTICS OF THE WORLD.

355

SOMALIA. Somalia faced many of the same problems in 1984 as in previous years. Internally, the government continued to experience armed opposition, with sporadic raids and constant propaganda barrages coming from the Somali Democratic Salvation Front (SDSF), an Ethiopian-supported coalition of Somali rebels attempting to overthrow President Muhammad Siad Barre. The most frequent attacks came in the northern region. The SDSF also called for a general strike against the government on April 8–9. The response was, however, very limited.

A major political development was the death on May 10 of the president's son and possible political heir, Shire Muhammad Siad Barre. Rumors soon started that he might have been driven to suicide by his father, pointing up the latter's political vulnerability and the succession problem posed by his son's unexpected death.

In foreign relations, the government received delegations of Eritrean rebels, hostile to the Ethiopian regime, from time to time; meanwhile, Somalia cultivated cordial relations with its neighbors other than Ethiopia. Extensive talks were held with Djibouti and Kenya during the year, and a Somali military delegation visited Djibouti in May to work out various forms of cooperation. Later, in July, President Daniel arap Moi of Kenya undertook his nation's first presidential visit to Somalia. There was an atmosphere of remarkable cordiality, given the past history of open conflict between the two nations, and the meetings resulted in an important trade agreement and a project for a 280-mile truck road for commercial traffic between the two countries.

The economy continued to suffer severely from the drought devastating the entire region, and imports of staple foodstuffs increased from already high levels, as nearly all economic dealings abroad became negotiations for food.

See STATISTICS OF THE WORLD.   R.B.

SOUTH AFRICA. In 1984, as South Africa implemented provisions of a new constitution giving some nonwhites a role in government for the first time, there was growing unrest within the country. A prominent peaceful foe of apartheid in South Africa, Bishop Desmond Tutu, won the Nobel Peace Prize.

Politics and Government. On September 14, Prime Minister Pieter W. Botha relinquished that post and was sworn in as the country's first state president, a position with expanded, wide-ranging powers. These powers, and the electoral college that chose Botha to fill the office, were established under a new constitution, which also provided for a new tricameral Parliament. There were separate chambers for whites (173 members), Coloureds, or people of mixed race (85 members), and Indians (45 members).

On September 15, President Botha named his new cabinet. For the first time, it included nonwhites; the Reverend Allan Hendrickse of the Labor Party (which represents Coloureds) and Amichand Rajbansi of the National People's Party (which represents Indians) were both appointed ministers without portfolio.

On August 20 the United Democratic Front (UDF), a multiracial alliance formed to oppose the new constitution's failure to provide a political role for black Africans, celebrated its first anniversary with rallies throughout the country, during which voters were urged to boycott elections to the Coloured and Indian chambers of Parliament. In the subsequent Coloured elections, held on August 22, the Labor Party won the majority of the votes, taking 76 out of the 80 elected seats. The turnout was only about 30 percent. About 20 percent of registered voters turned out for the Indian elections six days later; the moderate National People's Party captured 18 of the 40 elected seats, and the progovernment Solidarity Party won 17 seats.

On September 13, five UDF leaders, who had been held under preventive detention laws and then released, sought refuge, with a sixth activist, in the British consulate when police tried to redetain them. The British government declined to evict them; all eventually left, but five of the six were promptly rearrested.

Internal Security. On August 23 a powerful bomb destroyed the Johannesburg offices of the Department of Education and Training. The attack coincided with widespread clashes in all four provinces of South Africa between police and African students, many of whom had been boycotting school since May. The pupils—several of whom were killed—were

Prime Minister P. W. Botha (later president) of South Africa speaks at a ceremony announcing the signing of a nonaggression pact with neighboring Mozambique; seated to the right of Botha is President Samora M. Machel of Mozambique. Under the treaty, each country was constrained from aiding the other's internal enemies.

demanding autonomous students' representative councils and an end to discriminatory education policies. They were also protesting the elections to the tricameral Parliament. The government announced in October that student councils would be established. However, with many students still dissatisfied, boycotts continued in a number of places.

Some 30 people died and many were injured in rioting and police counterattacks that occurred early in September in the African townships of Evaton, Sebokeng, and Sharpeville. The unrest spread to Soweto, where incidents of arson and stone-throwing were reported. On September 11, indoor gatherings were banned in 21 cities and townships until September 30. Over 600 violators were arrested.

On October 5, the minister of law and order announced that units of the South African Defense Force (SADF) would help the police to fight the unrest, which by then had reportedly resulted in 80 deaths. Twelve days later, rioting erupted again in black townships around Johannesburg, and on October 23 thousands of army troops and police raided townships, searching homes and arresting hundreds. A protest strike by large numbers of black townships on November 5–6 resulted in consider-

able loss of life. Subsequently, 800,000 black workers took part in a labor stoppage in the Transvaal; 6,000 of them were fired. In the protracted unrest during the last few months of the year, more than 160 people were reportedly killed.

Bishop Tutu. On October 16, Bishop Desmond Tutu, a black Anglican cleric and general secretary of the South African Council of Churches, was named the winner of the 1984 Nobel Peace Prize. The Nobel committee praised Tutu for being a leader "in the campaign to resolve the problems of apartheid in South Africa." A few weeks later, a synod of bishops selected Tutu to be the Anglican bishop of Johannesburg; he was to become the first black to hold the post. In early December, before going to Norway to accept the award, Bishop Tutu met with President Ronald Reagan in Washington, D.C., and urged the United States to take stronger action to oppose apartheid.

Foreign Affairs. In May and June, Prime Minister Botha visited several Western European capitals, in the first official overseas tour by a South African leader in 20 years. Botha met with British Prime Minister Margaret Thatcher, Chancellor Helmut Kohl of West Germany, and Pope John Paul II, among other leaders.

Relations with the United States hit a sour note late in the year when President Reagan, in an International Human Rights Day address, expressed his country's "grief over the human and spiritual cost of apartheid in South Africa." At the same time, there were demonstrations against South Africa's racial policies in Washington and at least 13 other U.S. cities; more than 50 protestors, including 23 members of Congress, were arrested.

In March, South Africa and Mozambique concluded a nonaggression pact, in which each side promised not to back guerrilla attacks on the other. (See MOZAMBIQUE.)

See STATISTICS OF THE WORLD. See also SOUTH WEST AFRICA. J.F.

SOUTH CAROLINA. See STATISTICS OF THE WORLD.

SOUTH DAKOTA. See STATISTICS OF THE WORLD.

SOUTH WEST AFRICA, or NAMIBIA. Efforts to end the long-standing dispute over South West Africa continued during 1984. In February, South Africa and Angola established a Joint Monitoring Commission to oversee the withdrawal of all South African forces from Angola. The agreement followed "Operation Askari," an incursion by the South African Defense Force (SADF) into southern Angola that began in December 1983. Pretoria had described that operation as a preemptive strike against the South West Africa People's Organization (Swapo), the insurgent group that is fighting for the independence of Namibia and that uses Angola as its base. As part of the February pact, Angola agreed not to let Swapo guerrillas or Cuban troops enter southern Angola as the South African troops withdrew. In June, Angola claimed that South Africa—which admitted losing 21 troops during Askari—was proceeding too slowly with the disengagement. (It continued to lag.) Pretoria said the delay was caused by the infiltration into Namibia of Swapo guerrillas from Angolan bases.

Meanwhile, on March 11, South Africa proposed that a regional peace conference be convened, to be attended by Angola, Swapo, and the so-called internal parties in Namibia that are supported by South Africa. Both Angola and Swapo rejected the offer. Three months later, however, talks on Namibia, sponsored by South Africa and Zambia, began in Lusaka.

Attending were delegates from South Africa, Swapo, and the internal parties. The talks ended inconclusively. There was reportedly disagreement over South Africa's insistence on linking a Namibian settlement to the withdrawal of Cuban troops from Angola, as well as over the status of the internal parties. Talks held in Cape Verde between South Africa and Swapo representatives in July also yielded no settlement. In November, however, the Angolan government reportedly agreed to the principle of a Cuban troop withdrawal as part of a negotiated settlement in Namibia.

On March 1, veteran black nationalist leader Herman Toivo Ja Toivo was released from prison by South Africa after serving 16 years of a 20-year sentence for terrorism. Toivo flew to Lusaka to consult with the Swapo hierarchy in exile and later was named an official member of its leadership. J.F.

SOVIET UNION. See UNION OF SOVIET SOCIALIST REPUBLICS.

SPACE EXPLORATION. U.S. efforts in the exploration of space in 1984 were again dominated by manned shuttle flights. The Soviet Union continued to conduct scientific research from its space station Salyut 7 and also launched two new space probes.

U.S. Manned Flights. In the tenth shuttle mission since the series began, the space shuttle *Challenger* was launched February 3 from the Kennedy Space Center. The crew members were Vance Brand, commander, Robert Gibson, pilot, and Bruce McCandless II, Ronald McNair, and Robert Stewart, mission specialists. McCandless and Stewart, using propulsion backpacks and space suits, spent 12 hours outside the shuttle in two untethered extravehicular activity sessions ("space walks"). Two communications satellites, Westar 6, owned by Western Union, and Palapa B-2, owned by the Indonesian government, were launched from the shuttle but failed to achieve their planned orbit. The *Challenger* completed its mission on February 11, making the first shuttle landing at Kennedy Space Center. This saved about seven days in turnaround time and made it possible to refurnish the shuttle in time for the launch of a mission in early April.

The *Challenger* crew for the 11th shuttle mission (April 6–13), consisting of Robert L.

Crippen, commander, Francis R. Scobee, pilot, and George D. Nelson, James D. Van Hoften, and Terry J. Hart, mission specialists, succeeded, after some hitches, in their primary objective of repairing the orbiting Solar Maximum observatory. In addition, a platform housing 57 experiments to determine the long-term effects of space on materials was also placed in orbit.

The 12th mission was launched on August 30; the *Discovery*, making its maiden voyage, had a crew consisting of Henry W. Hartsfield, commander, Michael L. Coats, pilot, Steven A. Hawley, Richard M. Mullane, and Judith A. Resnik, mission specialists, and Charles D. Walker, test engineer. The only problems encountered were ice formations around a waste water vent and minor oxygen leaks. Three communications satellites (Telstar 3, SBS-4, and Leasat) were successfully launched from the cargo bay and placed in orbit. A 102-foot-tall, 13-foot-wide solar-energy panel, a prototype of future energy-gathering devices in space, was extended and retracted several times. The *Discovery* made a perfect landing September 5 on a dry lake bed runway at Edwards Air Force Base in California.

On the 13th shuttle mission (October 5–13), the *Challenger* crew, commanded by Robert L. Crippen, included the first Canadian to make a space flight, Marc Garneau of the Canadian navy. The crew of seven was the largest ever launched at one time, and also included two women, Sally K. Ride and Kathryn D. Sullivan. The latter made a space walk (the first by an American woman) with David C. Leestma for a test of satellite-refueling procedures. Also on the flight, whose primary purpose was earth observation, were Jon A. McBride, pilot, and Paul D. Scully-Power, an Australian-born oceanographer. Mission assignments included launching an earth-monitoring satellite and making observations of the land, sea, and atmosphere.

The *Discovery* made the 14th shuttle mission (November 8–16), under the command of Frederick H. Hauck. Other crew members were David M. Walker, pilot, and Anna L. Fisher, Joseph P. Allen, and Dale A. Gardner. After successfully launching two communications satellites, the astronauts retrieved the two satellites that had gone astray on the tenth shuttle flight, so that they could be returned to earth and refurnished. This first salvage mission

Working in an open cargo hatch, mission specialist Kathryn D. Sullivan, the first American woman to walk in space, checks the antenna latch during her historic flight aboard the Challenger.

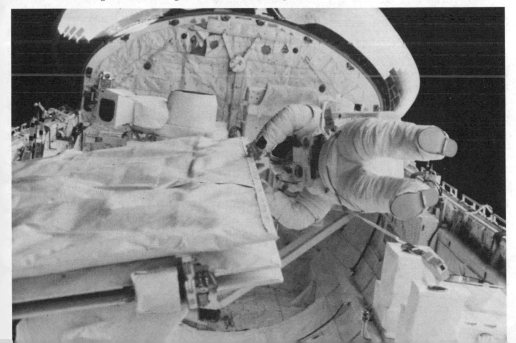

U.S. astronauts Dale Gardner and Joseph Allen (who stands on the remote control manipulator arm of the space shuttle Discovery) propose to put up "for sale" a stray 1,200-pound satellite that they have retrieved from the void and placed in the shuttle's cargo bay.

in space was financed in part by the companies that had insured the satellites, which planned to recover some of their losses by reselling them; it was also a milestone for practical work in space. When an overlooked metal projection prevented attachment of a metal bracket for the mechanical arm to hold one satellite steady, Allen simply held it manually while Gardner attached clamps for stowage in the cargo bay. Retrieval of the other satellite two days later went more smoothly, with Allen serving as a "human bracket" attached to the end of the mechanical arm operated by Fisher.

Other U.S. Activities. A new National Oceanic and Atmospheric Administration satellite was launched in December. In addition to obtaining weather data, it was designed to provide cov-

erage for the Sarsat-Cospas network, a joint U.S., French, Canadian, and Soviet space-based search and rescue system to pinpoint the location of emergency beacons carried on aircraft and ships. Three Soviet satellites continue to provide satellite coverage for this purpose.

The three satellites in the Active Magnetospheric Particle Tracer Explorer (AMPTE) project (one British, one West German, and one American) were successfully launched from Kennedy Space Center by the same booster on August 16. The British and West German satellites were placed in similar orbits. The West German satellite was to provide an active stimulus to the space environment by releasing barium and lithium on seven separate occasions; it was expected that sunlight would transform these chemicals into ionized particles to be detected by the British satellite as distances ranging from a few miles to 600 miles. The U.S. satellite was intended to measure the transfer of the charged particles as the solar wind moved them into the earth's magnetosphere, providing important data on the Van Allen radiation belt around the earth.

Soviet Space Station. The Soyuz T-10 spacecraft, with Leonid Kizim, mission commander, Vladimir Solovev, flight engineer, and research cosmonaut Oleg Atkov, was launched on February 8. The spacecraft docked with the Salyut 7 space station the next day and the crew reactivated the experiments on board. In April, Kizim and Solovev spent five hours outside the station repairing its propulsion system. During their stay in orbit, they and two visiting cosmonauts from the Soyuz T-12 spacecraft spent a total of more than 22 hours in six space walks. Five resupply spacecraft with fuel, provisions, and additional equipment sent to the space station were unloaded by the crew. The three men returned to earth on October 2, after 237 full days in space, surpassing the Soviets' 1982 211-day record.

Soviet cosmonauts Yuri Malyshev (mission commander) and Gennady Strekalov (flight engineer), along with Indian cosmonaut Rakesh Sharma, in the Soyuz T-11 spacecraft, increased the crew of the space station to six when they docked with it on April 3. They returned to earth on April 11 in the Soyuz T-10 spacecraft.

The Soyuz T-12, with a crew consisting of Vladimir Dzhanibekov, mission commander, Svetlana Savitskaya, flight engineer, and research cosmonaut Igor Volk, docked with the Salyut 7 on July 18 and assisted in conducting experiments for 12 days. Savitskaya became the first woman to walk in space when she and Dzhanibekov conducted a three-hour, 35-minute excursion on July 25. They tested a multipurpose tool, which was used to cut and weld metal in space. The crew returned to earth on July 30 in the Soyuz T-11.

Other Projects. Two Soviet spaces probes, Venera 15 and 16, which arrived at Venus in October 1983, continued to orbit the planet and provide radar pictures of its surface, revealing large volcanic features, rolling terrain, and mountains and canyons. Data were also obtained on surface temperature and atmospheric composition of the northern polar regions.

On December 15 and 21, two other Soviet space probes, Vega 1 and 2, were launched on six-month voyages to Venus, from where, after changing direction because of the planet's gravitation, they would travel to rendezvous with Halley's comet in March 1986. Carrying television cameras and scientific sensors, including two U.S.–built comet-dust detectors, the spacecraft were designed to pass unharmed through the thick dust and gas cloud, or coma, in front of the comet and move closer to the comet's solid nucleus. The project had the

Pioneering Soviet cosmonaut Svetlana Savitskaya, who walked in space almost four months before her American counterpart, tests a new hand tool designed to cut and weld metal, during an open space walk on July 25

participation of scientists from the United States as well as from Western and Eastern Europe. Similar probes were expected to be launched by the Western European Space Agency and Japan in mid-1985.

As part of a project sponsored by the United States, Great Britain, and West Germany, West German scientists in late December launched an artificial comet from a satellite 60,000 miles over the Pacific, in a pioneering experiment to demonstrate solar wind behavior.   R.Y.D.

SPAIN. Basque terrorism and foreign policy issues were major concerns of Prime Minister Felipe González Márquez in 1984.

Basque Terrorism. On January 29, the former military commander of Madrid, Lieutenant General Guillermo Quintana Lacaci, was gunned down by terrorists thought to be members of the Basque separatist organization ETA (Basque Homeland and Liberty). A month later, Enrique Casas Villa, a senator and the leading Socialist candidate in upcoming elections for the Basque regional parliament, was killed by two hooded gunmen. A government offer to negotiate with the ETA leadership over ending the terrorist violence was rejected; there was some progress, however, toward stopping Basque guerrillas from using southern France as a sanctuary. In June, France and Spain signed an accord containing a French pledge not to grant refugee status to Basques sought by the Spanish police in connection with terrorist acts. French courts subsequently ruled that Basque terrorists who had taken refuge in southern France could be extradited to Spain.

Regional Elections. In February elections were held to the Basque regional parliament. The Basque Nationalist Party (PNV), which had enjoyed an effective majority in the outgoing parliament, won only 32 of the 75 seats, not enough to rule unchallenged. The Socialists garnered 19 seats to become the second largest party in the region.

In another regional election, in Catalonia, the moderate, nationalist alliance known as Convergencia i Unió won an absolute majority in the Catalan parliament in late April. Just a few weeks after the election, however, Jordi Pujol, head of the regional Catalan government, along with 24 other former board members of the defunct Banca Catalana, was charged with fraud and embezzlement. Pujol denied the charges.

Foreign Affairs. Despite the accord regarding Basque terrorists, relations between Spain and France were not without strains. In March, for example, a French patrol boat fired on two Spanish ships fishing illegally in the French waters of the Bay of Biscay. In all, during the first ten months of the year, some 400 incidents of illegal fishing were recorded. While protesting the shooting incidents, Prime Minister Gonzáles threatened future action against Spanish fishermen violating the law.

On June 3 an estimated 100,000 demonstrators rallied in Madrid, demanding the closing down of U.S. military bases, a binding referendum on NATO membership, and a government declaration of a neutralist foreign policy. Prime Minister González issued a strong statement rejecting neutralism. In October, however, he called for a reduction in U.S. troop levels in Spain and announced he would call a referendum on NATO membership by early 1986, although he continued to support Spanish membership.

On October 19, González met with Libyan leader Muammar al Qaddafi on the Spanish island of Majorca. The meeting, arranged by former Austrian Chancellor Bruno Kreisky, drew criticism in Spain from right-wing parties and leading newspapers.

Labor Accord. On October 9, González, along with representatives of employers and Socialist unions, signed a two-year agreement on labor relations and salaries. The pact was widely seen as aiding efforts to streamline industry through measures that risk substantially raising unemployment (already at the highest level in Europe).

Church-State Dispute. Tension between the Roman Catholic Church and González's Socialist government intensified. On November 18, hundreds of thousands marched in Madrid to protest a law that would impose state controls and ban mandatory religion classes and services in private (mostly Catholic) schools receiving state subsidies. The law, which was passed in March, had yet to be put into effect because of a court appeal over its constitutionality.

See STATISTICS OF THE WORLD.   J.O.S.

Sports

Dwight Gooden, Willie Hernandez, Patrick Ewing, Kareem Abul-Jabbar, Doug Flutie, Martina Navratilova, John McEnroe, Tom Watson, Wayne Gretzky—these were a few of the stars, old and new, whose performances graced the sports world in 1984.

The year 1984 will be long remembered for the enthralling spectacle of the winter and summer Olympic Games (see the following section, SPORTS: THE OLYMPIC GAMES). It will also be remembered as the year when the Detroit Tigers capped a superb season with a World Series crown, when Georgetown University won its first-ever NCAA championship, when the Edmonton Oilers took the Stanley Cup away from the New York Islanders, and when three-year-old Swale collapsed and died after having won the Kentucky Derby and the Belmont Stakes. These and many other sporting highlights are recorded in the pages that follow.

AUTOMOBILE RACING

In the highly competitive world of Formula One racing for the world drivers championship, the major competition was between two drivers from the same team in identical cars. The turbocharged McLaren-Porsches driven by Niki Lauda of Austria and Alain Prost of France dominated the season, winning 11 of the first 15 races to take the constructors championship. Lauda won the Grands Prix of South Africa, France, Great Britain, Austria, and Italy; Prost took the Grands Prix of Brazil, San Marino, Monaco, West Germany, the Netherlands, and Europe. Prost took the final race, in Portugal, but Lauda's second-place finish gave him the championship by a mere half point.

The most important American oval track race was the 68th Indianapolis 500, on May 27. Rick Mears of Bakersfield, Calif., won for the second time, and his average speed of 163.612 miles per hour was the fastest ever at

En route to victory in the 68th Indianapolis 500, Rick Mears, in the yellow car, passes two of his competitors. Mears set a new record for the course with an average speed of more than 163 miles per hour.

Indianapolis. Mears and his car owner earned a record $434,061. Roberto Guerrero, a rookie from Colombia, finished second and Al Unser, Sr., of Albuquerque, N.M., third. The Indy cars competed in 15 other races in the $8 million series run by Championship Auto Racing Teams (CART). The Lola-Cosworth cars driven by Mario Andretti and Danny Sullivan registered eight victories in the first 12 races. Andretti won six of the season's races to take his fourth Indy car championship. Tom Sneva placed second overall.

The National Association for Stock Car Auto Racing (NASCAR) again offered a 30-race Grand National series for late-model sedans. Terry Labonte, driving a Chevrolet, clinched the Grand National title by finishing third in the last race of the season, giving him 4,508 points to 4,443 for Harry Gant (Chevrolet).   F.L.

BASEBALL

A new world championship team and a new commissioner of baseball were the highlights of the 1984 season in the major leagues. The new champions were the Detroit Tigers, who stormed through the American League and then disposed of the San Diego Padres in the World Series. The Tigers were the seventh different team to win the World Series in the past seven years.

The new commissioner was Peter Ueberroth, the man in charge of the successful 1984 Los Angeles Olympics. Shortly after succeeding Bowie Kuhn as commissioner on October 1, Ueberroth got his first test in office when the umpires went on strike prior to the start of the league playoffs. The strike lasted five days before Ueberroth was called in as an arbiter; his settlement of the dispute, announced after the World Series, greatly boosted the umpires' compensation for postseason games.

The Season. The Tigers became the first major league team since the 1927 New York Yankees to occupy first place from the first day of the season until the last. After winning 35 of their first 40 games, they breezed to 104 victories, and manager Sparky Anderson pronounced his team one of baseball's finest ever. They didn't disappoint him in postseason play. After winning the American League East, they disposed of the Kansas City Royals in three games to win the AL playoffs and then clobbered the

Padres to bring home Detroit's first world championship since 1968.

The National League had no team as good as the Tigers, but it had several good stories. The Padres, an expansion team formed in 1969, had never won a title before capturing the National League West this season. In the National League East, the Chicago Cubs, those perennial losers, won their first title of any kind since 1945. The Cubs won the first two games of the playoffs only to lose the final three, and the pennant, to San Diego.

World Series. Coming into the World Series, Detroit was widely expected to make short work of the apparently mismatched Padres—and the Tigers did exactly that, wiping out their National League opponents in five games. After the teams split the first two games, played in San Diego, Detroit reeled off three straight

NATIONAL LEAGUE

Eastern Division	W	L	Pct.	GB
Chicago Cubs	96	65	.596	—
New York Mets	90	72	.556	6½
St. Louis Cardinals	84	78	.519	12½
Philadelphia Phillies	81	81	.500	15½
Montreal Expos	78	83	.484	18
Pittsburgh Pirates	75	87	.463	21½
Western Division				
San Diego Padres	92	70	.568	—
Atlanta Braves	80	82	.494	12
Houston Astros	80	82	.494	12
Los Angeles Dodgers	79	83	.488	13
Cincinnati Reds	70	92	.432	22
San Francisco Giants	66	96	.407	26

AMERICAN LEAGUE

Eastern Division	W	L	Pct.	GB
Detroit Tigers	104	58	.642	—
Toronto Blue Jays	89	73	.549	15
New York Yankees	87	75	.537	17
Boston Red Sox	86	76	.531	18
Baltimore Orioles	85	77	.525	19
Cleveland Indians	75	87	.463	29
Milwaukee Brewers	67	94	.416	36½
Western Division				
Kansas City Royals	84	78	.519	—
California Angels	81	81	.500	3
Minnesota Twins	81	81	.500	3
Oakland Athletics	77	85	.475	7
Chicago White Sox	74	88	.457	10
Seattle Mariners	74	88	.457	10
Texas Rangers	69	92	.429	14½

PENNANT PLAYOFFS

National League—San Diego defeated Chicago, 3 games to 2

American League—Detroit defeated Kansas City, 3 games to 0

WORLD SERIES—Detroit defeated San Diego, 4 games to 1

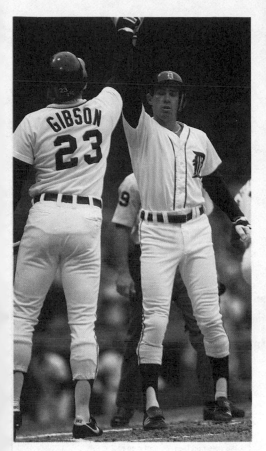

Detroit Tigers outfielder Kirk Gibson (far left) exchanges high-five salutes with teammate Alan Trammell, the World Series Most Valuable Player, after hitting a two-run homer in game five of the Series. With that 8–4 victory over the San Diego Padres, Detroit captured the Series, four games to one. Above, another Tigers hero, pitcher Jack Morris, shows the winning form that helped Detroit to its first world championship since 1968.

victories at home, clobbering the Padres, 8–4, in the fifth game to wrap up the championship. The Tigers' big guns were pitcher Jack Morris, who registered complete-game victories in games one and four; right fielder Kirk Gibson, who hit two home runs in the Series-clinching fifth game; and shortstop Alan Trammell, who was named the Series Most Valuable Player.

Landmarks. Pete Rose, at age 43, became the second player in major league history to make 4,000 hits in a career. His 4,097 hits at season's end left him 94 shy of Ty Cobb's long-standing record. Rose, a part-time player with the Montreal Expos for most of the season, in August was traded to the Cincinnati Reds, where he became a player-manager. The California Angels' Reggie Jackson became the 13th player to hit 500 home runs.

There were three no-hitters, including two perfect games. On April 8, Detroit's Jack Morris no-hit the Chicago White Sox, 4–0, and on April 21, Montreal's David Palmer beat St. Louis, 5–0, in a five-inning, rain-shortened perfect game. Then, on the last day of the season, Mike Witt of the Angels was perfect in a 1–0 win over the Texas Rangers.

Outstanding Players. Perhaps the most remarkable performer in either league was Tiger relief pitcher Willie Hernandez, who chalked up a 9–3 won-lost record, 1.92 earned run average, and 32 saves. For his efforts, Hernandez swept both the American League Cy Young (best pitcher) and Most Valuable Player awards. The National League MVP was Cubs second baseman Ryne Sandberg, who hit .314 with 19 homers, 84 RBI's, and 114 runs scored. Cub starter Rick Sutcliffe, who went 16–1 for Chicago after being acquired from the Cleveland Indians in May, was the unanimous choice for the NL Cy Young award. Rookie of the Year

365

honors went to Seattle Mariners first baseman Alvin Davis (27 homers, 116 RBI's) in the AL and to New York Mets pitcher Dwight Gooden (17–9, 276 strikeouts—a major league record for a rookie) in the NL (see biography at PEOPLE IN THE NEWS).

The AL batting champion was the New York Yankees' Don Mattingly (.343), who edged teammate Dave Winfield in a race that went down to the last day of the season. Tony Gwynne of the Padres hit .351 to take NL batting honors. The AL home run crown was taken by Tony Armas of the Boston Red Sox, who slugged 43 round-trippers; in the NL, Mike Schmidt of the Philadelphia Phillies and Dale Murphy of the Atlanta Braves each hit 36 homers to lead the league. Among the pitchers, the only 20-game winners in the majors were Mike Boddicker (20–11) of the Baltimore Orioles and Joaquin Anjular (20–14) of the St. Louis Cardinals.

All-Star Game. Fifty years to the day after Carl Hubbell struck out five consecutive batters, Fernando Valenzuela and Dwight Gooden combined for six strikeouts in a row, pitching the National League to a 3–1 victory over the Americans. There were 21 strikeouts in all in a game played in the San Francisco twilight. It was the 12th win for the National League in the past 13 years.

Hall of Fame. Five former players were inducted into the Hall of Fame in Cooperstown, N.Y. in August. They were shortstops Luis Aparicio and Pee Wee Reese, pitcher Don Drysdale, catcher Rick Ferrell, and slugger Harmon Killebrew. Ferrell and Reese were voted in by a special veterans' committee.

M.L.

BASKETBALL

Georgetown University won its first-ever National Collegiate Athletic Association championship in 1984. In contrast, the 1984 National Basketball Association champions, the Boston Celtics, won that title for the 15th time.

College. Georgetown's impressive march to the NCAA title was led by intimidating 7-foot center Patrick Ewing. The Hoyas, coached by John Thompson, capped a 34–3 season with an 84–75 defeat of the University of Houston in the title game, held April 2 at the Kingdome in Seattle. With both teams' star centers,

Ewing and Houston's Akeem Abdul Olajuwon, plagued by foul trouble, the game was largely decided by Georgetown's superior bench strength; two Hoya reserves, Reggie Williams and Michael Graham, combined for 33 points and 12 rebounds. Ewing, who had ten points, nine rebounds, and four blocked shots in the championship game, was named the tournament's Most Valuable Player.

NATIONAL BASKETBALL ASSOCIATION
1983–1984 Regular Season

EASTERN CONFERENCE

Atlantic Division	W	L	Pct.	GB
Boston Celtics	62	20	.756	—
Philadelphia 76ers	52	30	.634	10
New York Knicks	47	35	.573	15
New Jersey Nets	45	37	.549	17
Washington Bullets	35	47	.427	27

Central Division	W	L	Pct.	GB
Milwaukee Bucks	50	32	.610	—
Detroit Pistons	49	33	.598	1
Atlanta Hawks	40	42	.488	10
Cleveland Cavaliers	28	54	.341	22
Chicago Bulls	27	55	.329	23
Indiana Pacers	26	56	.317	24

WESTERN CONFERENCE

Midwest Division	W	L	Pct.	GB
Utah Jazz	45	37	.549	—
Dallas Mavericks	43	39	.524	2
Denver Nuggets	38	44	.463	7
Kansas City Kings	38	44	.463	7
San Antonio Spurs	37	45	.451	8
Houston Rockets	29	53	.354	16

Pacific Division	W	L	Pct.	GB
Los Angeles Lakers	54	28	.659	—
Portland Trail Blazers	48	34	.585	6
Seattle SuperSonics	42	40	.512	12
Phoenix Suns	41	41	.500	13
Golden State Warriors	37	45	.451	17
San Diego Clippers	30	52	.366	24

PLAYOFFS

First Round
Boston defeated Washington, 3 games to 1
Milwaukee defeated Atlanta, 3 games to 2
New York defeated Detroit, 3 games to 2
New Jersey defeated Philadelphia, 3 games to 2
Utah defeated Denver, 3 games to 2
Dallas defeated Seattle, 3 games to 2
Phoenix defeated Portland, 3 games to 2
Los Angeles defeated Kansas City, 3 games to 0

Second Round
Boston defeated New York, 4 games to 3
Milwaukee defeated New Jersey, 4 games to 2
Phoenix defeated Utah, 4 games to 2
Los Angeles defeated Dallas, 4 games to 1

Conference Finals
Boston defeated Milwaukee, 4 games to 1
Los Angeles defeated Phoenix, 4 games to 2

Championship Finals
Boston defeated Los Angeles, 4 games to 3

In women's basketball, the University of Southern California became the third school to win consecutive NCAA Division I women's titles by defeating Tennessee, 72–61. The Lady Trojans, who finished with a 29–4 record, were led by Cheryl Miller, who was named the NCAA tournament MVP. Janice Lawrence of Louisiana Tech was awarded the Wade Trophy as the nation's outstanding woman player.

Professional. The Celtics began the 1983–1984 season with both a new coach, former Celtic great K. C. Jones, and new owners. But the change that proved to be a key factor in the championship season was the preseason trade that brought Dennis Johnson to Boston from the Phoenix Suns. The 6'4" Johnson gave the Celtics a new weapon—a guard capable of stopping the league's best post up players. After finishing the regular season with a 62–20 Atlantic Division mark, ten games ahead of the defending-champion Philadelphia 76ers, the Celtics won playoff series with the Washington Bullets, the New York Knickerbockers, and the Milwaukee Bucks to capture the Eastern Conference title and set up a much-awaited match with the Los Angeles Lakers.

In cruising to the Western Conference championship, the Lakers relied heavily on a fast-break offense anchored by 7'2" center Kareem Abdul–Jabbar and directed by superlative guard Farvin (Magic) Johnson. In the championship series, however, Boston's physical style of play and its strong front line, led by championship series MVP Larry Bird, eventually prevailed over the Lakers' speed and finesse game. Still, it was barely enough: the teams split the first six games, with the Celtics winning excruciatingly close overtime contests in games two and four. In the seventh and deciding game, played on June 12 in Boston, the Celtics prevailed, 111–102, to capture the team's 15th NBA crown.

In addition to his tournament MVP award, Larry Bird edged the Knickerbockers' Bernard King in the voting for the league's Most Valuable Player. Other stellar individual performers were Adrian Dantley of Utah, who won scoring honors with an average of 30.6 points a game and was also named Comeback Player of the Year; Moses Malone of the 76ers, who took a

fourth straight rebounding title by averaging 13.4 boards a game; and the Lakers' Abdul–Jabbar, who on April 5 broke Wilt Chamberlain's career scoring record of 31,419 points. Another NBA great, Elvin Hayes of the Houston Rockets, retired after 16 seasons in the league. The 12-time All-Star wound up his career holding league records for games played (1,303), minutes played (50,000), and field goals attempted (24,272) and the third-best career marks in scoring (27,313), field goals (10,976), and rebounds (16,279).

Also during the 1983–1984 season, the Den-

In a duel between two 7-foot centers, Georgetown's Patrick Ewing fires a shot past Akeem Abdul Olajuwon of Houston in the National Collegiate Athletic Association championship game, which Georgetown won, 84–75.

ver Nuggets, who led the league in scoring with an average of 123.7 points per game, were involved in the highest scoring regulation and overtime games in NBA history, both at the McNichol Arena in Denver. On December 13, 1983, the Nuggets edged Detroit, 186–184, in triple overtime in the highest scoring game in NBA history. The combined total of 370 points far surpassed the previous record of 337 points set when San Antonio defeated Milwaukee, 171–166, in triple overtime on March 6, 1982. Then, on January 11, 1984, Kiki Vandeweghe, later traded to Portland, paced the Nuggets to a 163–155 victory over San Antonio, in the highest scoring regulation game. The combined total of 318 points broke the previous record of 316, achieved twice.

Off the court, meanwhile, headlines were made by a change of commissioners, an unauthorized move by the Clippers from San Diego to Los Angeles, and a league-record fine levied against the Portland Trail Blazers. The NBA's new commissioner was David J. Stern, formerly the league's executive vice-president for business and legal affairs; Stern succeeded the retiring Larry O'Brien, who had served in the post since 1975, on February 1. Stern's first year in office was a difficult one. At the end of the 1983–1984 season, the financially troubled Clippers, who had been based in San Diego since the 1978–1979 season, announced that they would play their 1984–1985 games in the Los Angeles Sports Arena. The move was made without the approval of the NBA, which filed suit in federal district court in San Diego, seeking to terminate the franchise or replace it in another city. The suit also sought $25 million in damages from the Clippers and the commission that operates the Los Angeles Sports Arena. Another team in trouble with the league was Portland, which was fined $250,000, the largest penalty in NBA history, for illegally making indirect contact with college stars Pat Ewing and Akeem Olajuwon. Commissioner Stern, who assessed the fine, said the league's investigation had found that Blazer representatives had met with Ewing's coach, John Thompson, and with "friends of Olajuwon," despite the fact that the league bylaws forbid teams from engaging in discussions with underclassmen.   S.G.

BOWLING

During the Fairhaven (Mass.) Classic, Lisa Rathberger, a right-hander from Palmetto, Fla., and the 1983 Women's Bowler of the Year, bettered two all-time scoring records. Her 16-game total of 4,030 beat the men's record of 4,015 set by Carmen Salvino; her 24-game score of 6,013 broke Earl Anthony's record of 5,825.

Bob Chamberlain of Pontiac, Mich., who had never won a tour title, became the Professional Bowlers Association (PBA) national champion by defeating Dan Eberl of Tonawanda, N.Y., 219–191, in the final. Mark Roth of Spring Lake Heights, N.J., won the U.S. Open, and Mike Durbin of Chagrin Falls, Ohio, won the Firestone Tournament of Champions.

The richest stop on the women's tour was the $100,000 Queens tournament, where Kazue Inahashi of Japan defeated Aleta Rzepecki Sill, 248–222, in the final.   F.L.

BOXING

Former world welterweight champion Sugar Ray Leonard, after a two-year retirement following eye surgery, made a brief comeback in a May 11 fight against Kevin Howard in Worcester, Mass. Leonard was floored in the fourth round, but he went on to win a ninth-round technical knockout, after which he retired again—this time, he said, for good. Another ring favorite, Roberto Durán, fought Thomas Hearns in Las Vegas on June 15 for Hearns's World Boxing Council junior middleweight title. Hearns stopped him in the second round, and the 33-year-old Durán returned to his native Panama and retired.

World Boxing Council middleweight champ Marvelous Marvin Hagler of Brockton, Mass., stopped Mustafa Hamsho on October 19 in New York, in the third round of a scheduled 15-round fight. The WBC, which had objected to the flouting of its 12-rounds-only rule, stripped him of title recognition. Hagler filed suit in an effort to regain the title.

After other planned bouts had to be cancelled for lack of financing, International Boxing Federation heavyweight champion Larry Holmes met James (Bonecrusher) Smith of Magnolia N.C., in Las Vegas on November 9. Holmes who had not fought for a year, stopped Smith (not even a ranked contender) in the 12th round, but with difficulty. On December 8, Gerry Cooney had his first real fight in 2½ years, defeating the briefly spirited George Chaplin with a left uppercut in the second round.

Former heavyweight champion Muhammad Ali underwent medical tests in New York City because of problems with slurred speech and a halting gait. Ali's physicians said his condition was "very possibly" the result of punches to the head, but that it could be controlled by drugs. Cases like Ali's prompted the American Medical Association to adopt a resolution in December calling for abolition of professional and amateur boxing.

In the Los Angeles Olympics, U.S. boxers won nine gold medals, one silver, and one bronze in the 12 weight classes. In the world championship challenge bouts in Los Angeles, the United States won six gold medals, Cuba five, and Canada one.   F.L.

FOOTBALL

Controversies raged on and off the field in 1984. Fans argued over whether Brigham Young University, the only unbeaten college team, deserved the national championship despite its comparatively weak schedule. The National Collegiate Athletic Association (NCAA) put the University of Florida's football program on probation. In professional football, the United States Football League (USFL) decided to shift to a fall schedule in direct competition with the National Football League (NFL) and then filed an antitrust suit against the older league. NFL franchise shifts, real and potential, created furors in some cities.

U.S. Pro Football. Actions by the USFL led to growing tension between the two major leagues. The new league captured some top college players. The Los Angeles Express signed Brigham Young quarterback Steve Young to a contract reportedly worth about $40 million through the year 2027. The Pittsburgh Maulers signed running back Mike Rozier of the University of Nebraska, winner of the Heisman Trophy in 1983, and the New Orleans Breakers signed Marcus Dupree, a formidable runner who had left the University of Oklahoma in 1983.

For its second season, played in spring and summer 1984, the USFL expanded from 12 to

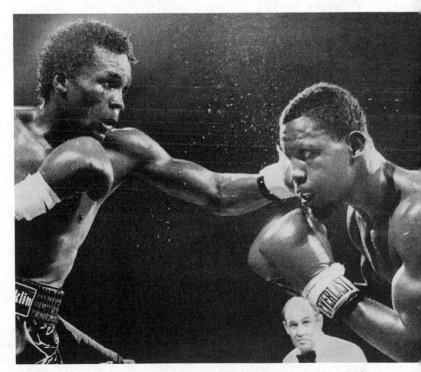

Landing a left hook that signals Kevin Howard's ninth-round TKO defeat, former welterweight champion Sugar Ray Leonard fights his last bout before retiring in May for the second time.

18 teams, and the number of teams losing money likewise rose from 12 to 18. Attendance at USFL games averaged less than half that at NFL games, and USFL television ratings were less than half the levels for the NFL. In the USFL championship game on July 15, the Philadelphia Stars defeated the Arizona Wranglers, 22–3. Jim Kelly, rookie quarterback for the Houston Gamblers, was named Player of the Year.

The USFL retrenched for 1985, merging six teams into three, allowing three other teams— including the Stars—to move, and permitting Chicago to remain inactive for a year. The Stars were to play in College Park, Md., in 1985 and in Baltimore thereafter.

Television revenues from ABC and the cable network ESPN had paid each USFL team only $1 million a year. (In contrast, the NFL's contracts with CBS, NBC, and ABC paid each of its teams $14 million a year.) In hopes of snagging juicier TV contracts and greater fan interest during the traditional football season, the USFL voted in August to play in the fall beginning in 1986. When the USFL was unable to negotiate a contract with a major network, it filed a $1.32 billion antitrust suit against the NFL, accusing the latter of conspiring to control

"the business of major league professional football."

In the NFL, one franchise dispute was settled when the U.S. Supreme Court declined to hear the league's appeal of a lower-court ruling upholding the shift of the Raiders from Oakland to Los Angeles. In March, Colts' owner Robert Irsay, saying he was unhappy with facilities and declining attendance, moved the team from Baltimore to Indianapolis. In December, the league and the city of Philadelphia acted to avert the possibility that the Eagles would be moved to Phoenix by owner Leonard Tose, who reportedly was $40 million in debt.

Individual achievements highlighted the regular NFL season. Dan Marino of the Miami Dolphins set single-season records of 48 touchdown passes and 5,084 yards passing. Eric Dickerson of the Los Angeles Rams set a one-season rushing record of 2,105 yards. Walter Payton of the Chicago Bears became the NFL's career rushing leader with 13,309 yards.

Divisional champions included Miami (14–2), the Denver Broncos (13–3), and the Pittsburgh Steelers (9–7) in the American Conference and San Francisco (15–1), the Washington Redskins (11–5), and Chicago (10–6) in the National Conference. In the playoffs, in the "wild card" games, the Seattle Seahawks defeated the Raiders, 13–7, and the New York Giants defeated the Rams, 16–13. In conference semifinals, the results were: Miami 31, Seattle 10; Pittsburgh 24, Denver 17; San Francisco 21, New York 10; and Chicago 23, Washington 19. In conference finals, on January 6, 1985, San Francisco defeated Chicago, 23–0, and Miami routed Pittsburgh, 45–28. San Francisco overwhelmed Miami, 38–16, in Super Bowl XIX on January 20.

Canadian Football. The Winnipeg Blue Bombers defeated the Hamilton Tiger Cats, 47–17, November 18, 1984, in Edmonton, Alberta, in the Canadian Football League's Grey Cup championship game. Winnipeg overcame a 14-point first-quarter deficit to win its first championship since 1962.

College Football. On June 27 the U.S. Supreme Court upheld a lower court ruling ending the NCAA's traditional exclusive control over the telecasting of college football. Existing NCAA television contracts were nullified, and new arrangements were made involving various groups. As a result, conferences, individual colleges, and packagers presented seemingly unlimited telecasts, but to smaller audiences.

Brigham Young (12–0), led by quarterback Robbie Bosco, was the only major college team to finish the regular season undefeated. The last regular season polls by the Associated Press and United Press International ranked BYU first. In the Holiday Bowl on December 21, Michigan (6 5) outplayed Brigham Young most of the way. Although BYU won, 24–17, on a touchdown pass in the last two minutes, its lackluster showing meant Oklahoma (9–1–1) might still win the national title with an impressive victory over Washington (11–1) in the January 1 Orange Bowl. However, Washington won, 28–17. The final wire service polls ranked Brigham Young first and Washington second. In other major bowl games, Nebraska defeated Louisiana State, 28–10 (Sugar Bowl); Southern California downed Ohio State, 20–17 (Rose Bowl); and Boston College beat Houston, 45–28 (Cotton Bowl).

The Heisman Trophy was awarded to Doug Flutie, Boston College's 5 foot, 9 3/4 inch quarterback, the first college player to pass for more than 10,000 yards. In the play of the year, on November 23 in Miami, Flutie passed to Gerard Phelan in the end zone (the ball traveled 64 yards) as time ran out, giving the BC team a 47–45 victory over the University of Miami.

In October, the NCAA notified the University of Florida that its football program had committed 59 infractions of NCAA rules and proposed placing the school on probation. While Florida appealed the proposed sanctions, which included a ban on bowl games, the Southeastern Conference refused to let Florida play in a bowl, possibly denying Florida (9–1–1) a shot at the national title. The sanctions were later finalized.   F.L.

GOLF

The 1984 season was one of the most competitive and financially rewarding in recent memory. Familiar figures in the golf world—Jack Nicklaus, Tom Watson, Raymond Floyd,

Running back Walter Payton of the Chicago Bears blasts through the Denver Broncos' defense in a September game in which he became football's all-time leader in combined yardage gained.

Kathy Whitworth watches yet another ball roll to victory during a triumph-studded season. Three 1984 tournament wins boosted her total to 87, surpassing previous record-holder Sam Snead's all-time high of 84.

In the U.S. Open, Fuzzy Zoeller defeated Greg Norman in an 18-hole play-off, 67–75. Spain's Severiano Ballesteros won his second British Open. The PGA Championship went to Lee Trevino, in his first win in three years.

On the LPGA tour, Kathy Whitworth's three tournament wins brought her total to 87, an all-time record. Hollis Stacy won her third Women's U.S. Open with a one-stroke victory. Amy Alcott won four tournaments, as did Patty Sheehan, whose triumphs included the LPGA Championship. Whitworth, Betsy King, and Japan's Ayako Okamoto all scored three victories. In the du Maurier Classic in Toronto, rookie Juli Inkster won by a stroke.   T. McC.

GYMNASTICS

In the Los Angeles Olympics, the U.S. men's team upset China, the 1983 world champions, for the team title, while U.S. women finished a close second to Romania for their team title.

Diminutive superstar Mary Lou Retton demonstrates the form that made her the biggest winner in the women's gymnastic events at the summer Olympics.

and others—had to share the spotlight with relative unknowns such as Fred Couples, Gary Koch, Greg Norman, and Peter Jacobsen. Four golfers exceeded $400,000 in earnings, and five others won more than $300,000. For the first time ever, five member of the Ladies Professional Golf Association (LPGA) won more than $200,000.

Tom Watson, three-time winner (Tucson Match Play title, Tournament of Champions, and Western Open) and leader of the money list, with $476,260, gained the Player of the Year title for a record sixth time. Another Watson, Denis Watson, a native of South Africa, started a winning streak in August, during which he captured the Buick Open, the World Series of Golf, and the Las Vegas Invitational (for total winnings in all three of $360,000.) Calvin Peete won the Vardon Trophy for the fourth consecutive year.

Ben Cranshaw, who had gone his entire career—12 years— without a major title, beat Tom Watson by two strokes to win the Masters.

372

Laffit Pincay, Jr., rides Swale to victory in the Belmont Stakes on June 9. Eight days later, the three-year-old horse, which had also won the Kentucky Derby, died, probably of a heart attack.

Mary Lou Retton, 16, of Fairmont, W. Va., upset Ecaterina Szabo of Romania for the women's all-around championship. Koji Gushiken of Japan won the men's all-around, with Peter Vidmar of Los Angeles finishing second. The United States won more gymnastics medals than any other nation—five gold, five silver, and six bronze. U.S. male gymnasts had not won an Olympic gold medal since 1932, and the women had never won any medal. (*See also* SPORTS: THE OLYMPIC GAMES.)

Earlier in the year, Retton and Vidmar took the all-around titles at the American Cup competition; at the U.S. Gymnastic Federation championships the titles went to Retton and Mitch Gaylord of Van Nuys, Calif.   F.L.

HARNESS RACING

Historic Freight, who until 1984 had never won a race, took the 59th and richest ($1,219,000) Hambletonian at the New Jersey Meadowlands. The Roosevelt International Trot was won once again by a French trotter, Lutin d'Isigny of France, by a record margin (seven lengths) and in world record time of 2:30.

Nihilator won the $1,080,500 first prize in the Woodrow Wilson Pace, setting a world record for two-year-old pacers. Among three-year-olds, On the Road Again took the Can Pace, Colt Fortysix won the Little Brown Jug,

and Troublemaker captured the Messenger Stakes.   W.L.

HORSE RACING

For racing fans, the most memorable event of 1984 was the sudden collapse and death of Swale on June 17, after the outstanding colt had won the Kentucky Derby (by 3¼ lengths) and the Belmont Stakes. A son of 1977 Triple Crown winner Seattle Slew, the three-year-old Swale had amassed $1,538,622 in earnings and was valued at an estimated $40 million. Exhaustive tests never fully determined the cause of the colt's death, although veterinarians attributed it to some form of heart attack.

The early season favorite, Devil's Bag, never fulfilled his promise. The undefeated two-year-old of 1983 finished an unimpressive fourth in the Flamingo (won by Time for a Change) and never even ran in any Triple Crown races. Withdrawn from the Derby because of a small-bone fracture, he was retired on May 7 and syndicated for stud duty. Although Swale took two of the three Triple Crown races, he ran a distant seventh in the Preakness, which was won by Gate Dancer, the fifth-place finisher in the Derby. Gate Dancer ran a disappointing sixth in the Belmont, but returned to win both the Omaha Gold Cup and the Super Derby at Louisiana Downs.

373

Slew o'Gold won the fall championship series at Belmont, consisting of the Woodward Stakes, the Marlboro Cup, and the Gold Cup. The $1 million bonus he received as the first horse to win the series raised his career earnings to $2,858,534—the second highest figure in the records of racing. A five-year-old named Fit to Fight became only the fourth horse ever to win the Handicap Triple Crown, made up of the 1-mile Metropolitan, the 1¼-mile Suburban, and the 1½-mile Brooklyn handicaps.

John Henry won $600,000 in his second victory at the Budweiser-Arlington Million in Chicago, kicking his lifetime earnings to $5,482,797. But the incredible nine-year-old gelding's most impressive run was in the $625,250 Turf Classic at Belmont. "Ole John" easily beat the 1983 Horse of the Year, All Along, and edged out the four-year-old Win to claim a neck victory in 2:25⅕, a stakes record.   W.L.

ICE HOCKEY

The Edmonton Oilers made the 1983–1984 National Hockey League season memorable by breaking the New York Islanders' four-year grip on the Stanley Cup. Edmonton, led by Wayne Gretzky, already said by some to be the best player ever, defeated the Islanders four games to one to take their first NHL title. They had joined the NHL when it and the World hockey Association merged in 1979. New York had hoped to equal the string of five straight titles won by the Montreal Canadiens between 1956 and 1960. After splitting the first two games of the 1984 finals, the Oilers won the next two and captured the clincher, 5–2, before a wildly emotional home crowd May 19, as Gretzky scored two first-period goals and later added an assist.

Edmonton also dominated in the regular season, with 57 victories against only 18 losses and five ties, for a total of 119 points. The season produced a new attendance record of almost 12 million spectators. Fans liked the new sudden-death rule, which reduced the number of ties.

For the fifth year in a row, Gretzky was named Most Valuable Player and, with 205 points, also led the league in scoring. Other award-winners for the regular season included Rod Langway of the Washington Capitals, who received the Norris Trophy as the best defenseman for the second time; Tom Barrasso of the Buffalo Sabres, who won the Calder Trophy as best rookie and the Vezina Trophy as best goalkeeper; and Mike Bossy of the Islanders, who won the Lady Byng Trophy for sportsmanship combined with outstanding play.

The Soviet Union steamrolled all opposition to win the gold medal at the 1984 winter Olympics. Czechoslovakia and Sweden won the silver and bronze medals, respectively; Canada placed fourth.   B.V.

NATIONAL HOCKEY LEAGUE
1983–1984 Regular Season

PRINCE OF WALES CONFERENCE

Patrick Division	W	L	T	Pts.
New York Islanders	50	26	4	104
Washington Capitals	48	27	5	101
Philadelphia Flyers	44	26	10	98
New York Rangers	42	29	9	93
New Jersey Devils	17	56	7	41
Pittsburgh Penguins	16	58	6	38

Adams Division				
Boston Bruins	49	25	6	104
Buffalo Sabres	48	25	7	103
Quebec Nordiques	42	28	10	94
Montreal Canadiens	35	40	5	75
Hartford Whalers	28	42	10	66

CAMPBELL CONFERENCE

Norris Division	W	L	T	Pts.
Minnesota North Stars	39	31	10	88
St. Louis Blues	32	41	7	71
Detroit Red Wings	31	42	7	69
Chicago Black Hawks	30	42	8	68
Toronto Maple Leafs	26	45	9	61

Smythe Division				
Edmonton Oilers	57	18	5	119
Calgary Flames	34	32	14	82
Vancouver Canucks	32	39	9	73
Winnipeg Jets	31	38	11	73
Los Angeles Kings	23	44	13	59

STANLEY CUP PLAYOFFS

Division Semifinals
N.Y. Islanders defeated N.Y. Rangers, 3 games to 2.
Washington defeated Philadelphia, 3 games to 0.
Montreal defeated Boston, 3 games to 0.
Quebec defeated Buffalo, 3 games to 0.
Minnesota defeated Chicago, 3 games to 2.
St. Louis defeated Detroit, 3 games to 1.
Edmonton defeated Winnipeg, 3 games to 0.
Calgary defeated Vancouver, 3 games to 1.

Division Finals
N.Y. Islanders defeated Washington, 4 games to 1.
Montreal defeated Quebec, 4 games to 2.
Minnesota defeated St. Louis, 4 games to 3.
Edmonton defeated Calgary, 4 games to 3.

Conference Finals
N.Y. Islanders defeated Montreal, 4 games to 2.
Edmonton defeated Minnesota, 4 games to 0.

Championship Finals
Edmonton defeated N.Y. Islanders, 4 games to 1.

ICE SKATING

At U.S. Figure Skating Championships in January, Scott Hamilton breezed to his fourth U.S. men's title, while Rosalynn Sumners narrowly took the women's title. Hamilton went on to victory in the Olympics over Canadian champ Brian Orser; Katarina Witt of East Germany took the women's figure skating gold. Yelena Valova and Oleg Vasiliev of the Soviet Union won the pairs. Jayne Torvill and Christopher Dean of Great Britain led all the way in the Olympic ice dancing competition. Hamilton, Witt, and Torvill and Dean again were gold medalists at World Figure Skating Championships in Ottawa. Canadians Barbara Underhill and Paul Martini took the pairs.

Oleg Bogiev of the Soviet Union was declared world speed skating champion at the men's world competition in Göteborg, Sweden; Karin Enke of East Germany was the women's champion in competition in the Netherlands. Gaetan Boucher of Canada was declared the men's champion at World Sprint Speed Skating Championships in Trondheim, Norway. Enke was the women's champion.

See also SPORTS: THE OLYMPIC GAMES.

I.A.A.

SKIING

In the 1984 winter Olympics, the Americans surprisingly won five Alpine medals, the best Alpine performance of any nation. The Finns, Norwegians, Swedes, and Eastern Europeans dominated Nordic events as usual. Finland's Marja-Liisa Hämäläinen became the first cross-country skier to win three individual races in a single Olympics. Finland's Matti Nykänen and East Germany's Jens Weissflog snagged all the gold and silver jumping medals. Gunde Svan won the 15-kilometer gold, carried his Swedish teammates to a gold in the men's relay, won the silver in the 50 km, and picked up a bronze in the 30 km. (*See also* SPORTS: THE OLYMPIC GAMES.)

In the World Cup, Switzerland's Pirmin Zurbriggen won the overall men's crown, and Erika Hess of Switzerland the women's. Downhill champions were Switzerland's Urs Raeber and Maria Walliser; giant slalom champions were Hess and Sweden's Ingemar Stenmark. The slalom title went to Marc Girardelli of Luxembourg and Tamara McKinney of the United States. Combined champions were Hess and Liechtenstein's Andreas Wenzel.

The World Cup giant slalom in Colorado

World Champion Skater

In January, Scott Hamilton took his fourth straight U.S. men's figure skating title in a brilliant performance in Salt Lake City. He skated less brilliantly in the Olympics—but still did well enough to win the gold in men's figure skating, and he went on to win his fourth straight world title, in Ottawa, before announcing his retirement from amateur competition. (Hamilton signed a contract with the Ice Capades in May, and later began appearing as a skating commentator for CBS-TV.)

The diminutive (5'3", 115 pounds) Hamilton suffered as a child from Schwachman syndrome—a rare disease that prevents proper digestion and is often associated with stunted growth. Exercise was recommended as part of his therapy, and at age nine he started skating. A classic skating technician, he has been praised especially for his compact moves, his triple-double jump combinations, the lightness of his landings, and the brilliance of his footwork.

Scott Hamilton

Erika Hess zooms down the slope toward the World Cup overall crown. The Swiss skier also captured the women's giant slalom and combined titles.

was the final competition for "America's best skier," Phil Mahre and his twin brother Steve. After a disappointingly slow finish for the run, the 26-year-old Phil reaffirmed his decision to retire, and Steve announced that he would retire along with Phil.   R.N.

SOCCER

France ruled international soccer, winning the European championship in June and the gold medal in the Olympics. The French victory in Los Angeles was the first Olympic soccer title for a country outside Eastern Europe since 1948; it came as a result of the Soviet-bloc boycott of the games. With the reluctant approval of the International Olympic Committee, many countries fielded professional players for the first time. In the Olympic final, witnessed by a record (for North America) crowd of 101,799 persons, France defeated Brazil, 2–0.

The United States narrowly missed advancing to the Olympic quarterfinals, but it did move up to the second round in 1986 World Cup qualifying-round competition. France became a favorite for 1986 by defeating Spain in the European final, 2–0, in Paris. Uruguay won the South American championship by defeating and then tying Brazil. Liverpool of England took the European Cup with a win on penalty kicks over Italy's Roma, after the teams had played to a 1–1 overtime tie. The flow of stars to Italy continued, with Argentina's Diego Maradona getting a record fee of $7.5 million for moving to Napoli.

By the end of the 1984 season, the North American Soccer League had dwindled to nine teams, from 24 four years earlier, and after the season the Tulsa and Vancouver teams folded. It was uncertain whether the league could continue operating in 1985. The Chicago Sting won the NASL title with 2–1 and 3–2 victories against the Toronto Blizzard. The San Diego Sockers won the NASL indoor title by sweeping three games against the New York Cosmos. The Major Indoor Soccer League title went to the Baltimore Blast, victors over the St. Louis Steamers, four games to one. In U.S. college soccer, Clemson won the NCAA Division I title, edging out Indiana, which had won the previous two years.   P.G.

SWIMMING

U.S. swimmers dominated the Olympics, capturing nine of the 15 events for men and 11 of the 14 for women. (The women were aided very significantly by the absence of Soviet and East German competition.) World records for men were set in the Olympics by Alex Baumann of Canada (200-meter and 400 individual medley), American Steve Lundquist (100-m breaststroke), and Jon Sieben of Australia (200-m butterfly). West Germany's Michael Gross broke the world record for the 200-m freestyle in the West German championships and afterward in the Olympics; Gross also set a world record at the Olympics for the 100-m butterfly.

Rick Carey of the United States won both Olympic golds in backstroke. Some U.S. women who won multiple individual events were: Tracy Caulkins (200-m and 400-m medley), Mary T. Meagher (100-m and 200-m butterfly), and Tiffany Cohen (400-m and 800-m freestyle).

At the post-Olympic Friendship '84 Games in Moscow, Soviet swimmer Sergei Zabolotnov set a new world record for the 200-m backstroke. East German women set records for the 100-m breaststroke (Sylvia Gerasch), 400-m

The French soccer team (wearing blue jerseys) defeated Spain, 2–0, in Paris to win the European championship.

freestyle relay, 400-m medley relay, and 100-m backstroke (Ina Kleber). East German women also bettered Olympic times in other events.

Californian diver Greg Louganis swept the men's 3-m springboard and 10-m platform titles in the U.S. Olympic trials and the Olympics. He also won firsts in the U.S. indoor and outdoor championships.   F.L.

TENNIS
A relative calm descended on the world of professional tennis, as superstars Martina Navratilova and John McEnroe dominated the sport despite some upsets.

Early in the year, Czechoslovakia's Hana Mandlikova beat Navratilova, 7–6, 3–6, 6–4, in the final of an Oakland, Calif., tournament. It halted Navratilova's winning streak at 54 matches, one shy of the record 55 held by Chris Evert Lloyd. Navratilova immediately embarked on another incredible winning streak, this time reaching a record total of 74. Her tying mark of 55 was reached against Evert Lloyd in the U.S. Open final in September, which Navratilova won, 4–6, 6–4, 6–4.

Having won Grand Slam titles at Wimbledon and the U.S. and Australian Opens in 1983,

Soviet swimmer Sergei Zabolotnov hoists a triumphant fist after breaking the 200-meter backstroke world record at the post-Olympic Friendship '84 Games in Moscow. Zabolotnov's 1:58.41 shaved more than half a second from American backstroker Rick Carey's record of 1:58.86 in the U.S. Olympic trials.

377

The tennis world's dazzling John McEnroe, shown here in action at the U.S. Open, won that tournament for the fourth time.

Navratilova came to the French Open in May 1984 hoping to hold all the world's top tennis crowns at once. She succeeded, defeating Evert Lloyd in the final by a lopsided 6–3, 6–1 score. Evert Lloyd mounted a stronger challenge in the final at Wimbledon; however, Navratilova prevailed, 7–6, 6–2. The end of Navratilova's winning streak came in the semifinals of the Australian Open on December 6, when she was upset by Czechoslovak teenager Helena Sukova, 1–6, 6–3, 7–5. Evert Lloyd went on to defeat Sukova in the finals, by a score of 6–7, 6–1, 6–3.

The McEnroe juggernaut started rolling in January when he defeated Ivan Lendl in the final of the Volvo Masters. Later, entering the French Open with a perfect 42–0 match record for the year, McEnroe seemed likely to take the trophy. However, Lendl eventually turned the match around with his sizzling passing shots and took his first Grand Slam crown, 3–6, 2–6, 6–4, 7–5, 7–5.

There was no such upset at Wimbledon, where McEnroe, the defending champion, barreled past Jimmy Connors in the finals. At the U.S. Open, two extraordinary semifinal matches—Lendl's 3–6, 6–3, 6–4, 6–7, 7–6 defeat of Australian Pat Cash and McEnroe's victory over Connors, 6–4, 4–6, 7–5, 4–6, 6–3—sparked the men's competition. In the anticlimactic final, McEnroe easily downed Lendl, 6–3, 6–4, 6–1.

Mats Wilander of Sweden won the men's title in the Australian Open, beating Kevin Curren in the final. In Davis Cup play, the United States defeated Australia in the semifinal but was beaten in the final by Sweden, 1–4.

R.J.L.

TRACK AND FIELD

Aided by a Soviet-bloc boycott, the United States took the most Olympic medals in track and field (40), followed by Britain (with 16). Of 16 golds won by the United States, Carl Lewis earned four of them, in some brilliant performances (see biography in PEOPLE IN THE NEWS). Sebastian Coe of Great Britain took the 1,500-meter race in an Olympic record time of 3 minutes, 32.53 seconds, and Britain's Daley Thompson won the decathlon with an Olympic record 8,797 points. Brazil's Joaquim Cruz took the 800 m, and Said Aouita of Morocco won the 5,000 m, both in Olympic record times. Carlos Lopes of Portugal was the surprise winner of the men's Olympic marathon. Among U.S. women, Joan Benoit was the Olympic marathon winner, and Evelyn Ashford took the 100-m dash. Valerie Brisco-Hooks of Los Angeles won individual golds for the 200-m and 400-m dashes; her time of 21.81 seconds in the former was the third fastest in history. Perhaps the most memorable event, however, was the 3,000-m final in which Mary Decker was injured in a collision with Zola Budd. (See SPORTS: THE OLYMPIC GAMES.)

Outside of the Olympics, Sergei Bubka of the Soviet Union broke world records for the pole vault three times indoors and four times outdoors. East Germany's Uwe Hohn set a world javelin record of 343'10", bettering the previous record by more than 16 feet. Evelyn Ashford of the United States lowered the women's world record for the 100-m dash to 10.76 seconds in August. Tatyana Kazankina of the Soviet Union also set new world marks in August: 5:28.72 for 2,000 m, and 8:22.62 for 3,000 m. Among other athletes to break world records were Yuri Sedykh of the Soviet Union and Zhu Jianhua of China (whose 7'10" high jump in July was his third world record in a year). F.L.

After breaking his own record by clearing 19'3½" in June, Soviet pole vaulter Sergei Bubka said, "I am not yet at the top of my form," a prophecy which proved entirely accurate: In the next two months, he improved the world outdoor record again—twice.

French yachtsman Yvon Fauconnier (left) joins in a celebration of his victory in the Plymouth-to-Newport Transatlantic Race, which he won after coming to the rescue of a competitor whose catamaran had capsized. He was given 16 hours credit for the rescue.

YACHTING

In the summer Olympic sailing competition, held at Long Beach, Calif., U.S. yachtsmen took three gold medals (in the sailing and Flying Dutchman classes and in Stars) and four silver, more total medals than any other sailing team in Olympic history. Stephan Van den Berg of the Netherlands, a five-time world champion, won the Windglider class in its Olympic debut, and Russell Coutts of New Zealand won the Finn class. Teams from Spain and New Zealand also took gold medals.

In the London Observer Single-handed Transatlantic Race, run from Plymouth, England, to Newport, R.I., Yvon Fauconnier of France, sailing his trimaran, *Umupro Jardin V*, was declared the overall winner, after judges gave him a 16-hour time credit for aiding in the rescue of a competing ship in distress. In the Southern Ocean Racing Conference, or Southern Circuit, the 39-foot sloop *Diva*, skippered by Berend Beilken of West Germany, became the first European yacht to win top honors. D.M.P.

SPORTS: THE OLYMPIC GAMES

The 1984 Olympic Games in both Sarajevo and Los Angeles generated their share of excitement and record-setting performances, despite a Soviet-led boycott of the summer games. The Soviet Union and East Germany dominated the winter games, while U.S. athletes were dominant in Los Angeles.

Well organized by the host countries of Yugoslavia and the United States, the 1984 Olympic winter and summer games provided dramatic entertainment for spectators and glory for participating athletes from around the world. However, a Soviet-bloc boycott of the summer games, a mirror image of the 1980 U.S.–led boycott, cast some doubt on the future of the Olympic movement.

Winter Games. At the XIV Olympic Winter Games, staged February 7–19 in Sarajevo, Yugoslavia, the major winners were the Soviet Union, East Germany, and Yugoslavia—the first two because they won the most medals and the most gold medals respectively, the Yugoslavs because they organized and presented the games almost without fault.

Critics had feared that Yugoslavia would not be able to build adequate facilities in time, but the people of Sarajevo came through. For the summer games, Los Angeles officials made sure local residents would bear no financial burden; Sarajevo residents, in contrast, willingly gave 2.5 percent of their salaries for four years to help finance the winter games. Facilities proved to be first rate; the only major problem was the snow. It snowed for 100 consecutive hours, and huge drifts and high winds forced almost daily postponements of Alpine skiing events.

Of the 117 medals awarded, the Soviet Union won 25, East Germany 24, Finland 13, Norway nine, and the United States and Sweden each eight. Of the 39 gold medals, East

Britain's Jayne Torvill and Christopher Dean overwhelmed the judges in the ice dancing competition during the Winter Olympics. In capturing the gold medal, they received an unprecedented 19 perfect scores.

Marathon Champion

In 1983, Joan Benoit of Freeport, Me., had set a world record of 2:22.43 in the Boston Marathon. Less than a year later, her right knee locked during a practice run, jeopardizing her prospects of even competing in the first women's Olympic marathon. But, after other treatment failed, Benoit elected to undergo arthroscopic surgery on the knee shortly before the Olympic trials in May. She made an extraordinary recovery, went on to win the trials in 2:31.04, and in August won an Olympic gold medal in a swift 2:24.52. Benoit, who was 27 at the time of her Olympic victory, first took up running at the age of 16, to strengthen herself after a skiing accident.

Joan Benoit

Germany won nine, the Soviet Union took six, and the United States, Finland, and Sweden four each. East Germany was especially dominant in certain sports; its athletes won both gold and both silver medals in bobsledding and all four gold and all four silver medals in women's speed skating.

The individual star was Marja-Liisa Hämäläinen, a shy, 28-year-old Finnish physiotherapist. Sweeping the three individual women's cross-country races, she became the only athlete to win three golds. In speed skating, Karin Enke of East Germany took two golds and two silvers, while Gaetan Boucher of Quebec took two golds and a bronze. The Soviets put on an overwhelming performance to take the gold medal in ice hockey. In the ice dancing competition of figure skating, Jayne Torvill and Christopher Dean of Great Britain easily won their expected gold; en route, they received 19 perfect scores of 6.0. Scott Hamilton of Denver, also an overwhelming favorite for a gold, won the men's figure skating competition, and Katarina Witt of East Germany edged out Rosalynn Sumners of Edmonds, Wash., for the women's title.

Alpine skiing brought some surprises. Two of the world's top competitors, Ingemar Stenmark of Sweden and Hanni Wenzel of Liechtenstein, were ineligible because they had directly accepted endorsement money. Austria, the traditional Alpine leader, was limited to one medal, Anton Steiner's bronze in the men's downhill. The most successful nation overall was the United States, with three gold and two silver medals. Bill Johnson of Van Nuys, Calif., who had never won an important international race until 3½ weeks before the Olympics, became the first American man to win an Olympic gold in Alpine skiing and the first to win any kind of medal in the downhill.

The United States took both the gold and the

Breaking his own world records, swimmer Alex Baumann took two Olympic gold medals for Canada in the individual medley events.

U.S. track star Carl Lewis left Los Angeles with four gold medals, captured in the 100-meter dash, the 200-meter dash, the long jump, and the 400-meter relay.

Los Angeles Memorial Coliseum for the 3½-hour opening ceremonies. The audience saw—and took part in—a Hollywood extravaganza, complete with doves, fireworks, and planes swooping to skywrite the five-ring Olympic symbol. Gina Hemphill, the late Jesse Owens's granddaughter, brought the Olympic torch into the Coliseum and handed it to 1960 decathlon champion Rafer Johnson, who lighted the Olympic flame.

The United States won medals in all but three of the medal sports, shut out only in rhythmic gymnastics, soccer, and team handball. It won 83 gold medals, breaking the record of 80 set by the United States (in 1904) and the Soviet Union (in 1980). In addition, the United States won 61 silver and 30 bronze medals. Next in gold medals were Romania with 20 and West Germany with 17. In total medals, West Germany won 59, Romania 53, Canada 44, and Great Britain 37. China, fielding a full team for the first time in over 30 years, won 32 medals, 15 of them gold.

The most celebrated hero may well have been Carl Lewis of Willingboro, N.J. (see biography in PEOPLE IN THE NEWS). The sprinter and long jumper won four gold medals in track and field. They came in the same events in which the great Jesse Owens won four gold medals in the 1936 Berlin Olympics. In gymnastics, powerful Li Ning of China came away with six medals. Mary Lou Retton, the dynamic, 16-year-old crowd favorite from Fairmont, W. Va., Ecaterina Szabo of Romania, and Koji Gushiken of Japan won five each, and Mitch Gaylord of Van Nuys, Calif., took four. In swimming, Michael Gross of West Germany and Nancy Hogshead of Jacksonville, Fla., each won four medals.

Lewis and Szabo were the only athletes who won four gold medals. Those who won three golds were Li Ning in gymnastics, Valerie Brisco-Hooks of Los Angeles in track and field, Ian Ferguson of New Zealand in kayaking, and five U.S. swimmers: Hogshead, Tracy Caulkins of Nashville, Mary T. Meagher of Louisville, Ky., Rowdy Gaines of Winter Haven, Fla., and Rick Carey of Mount Kisco, N.Y.

Jeff Blatnick of Schenectady, N.Y., became the first-ever U.S. winner of a medal for Greco-Roman wrestling, when he won in the super-

silver medal in two events: the men's slalom, where the top finishers were the twin brothers Phil and Steve Mahre of Yakima, Wash., and the women's giant slalom, where the gold and silver went to Debbie Armstrong of Seattle and Christin Cooper of Sun Valley, Idaho, respectively. Jure Franko won a silver in the men's giant slalom, giving Yugoslavia its first medal in winter Olympics history.

Summer Games. The games of the XXIII Olympiad, held from July 28 to August 12, proved a huge athletic and financial success. The competition attracted more than 7,800 athletes from a record 140 nations. But among the missing were some of the world's amateur athletic powers—the Soviet Union, East Germany, Czechoslovakia, Bulgaria, Hungary, Poland, and Cuba. The Soviets cited inadequate security as a major reason for the boycott, but they may have been motivated more by a desire to retaliate for the U.S.–led boycott of the 1980 Olympics in Moscow.

A capacity crowd packed the 93,000-seat

Ecaterina Szabo, shown poised upon the balance beam, took five medals in gymnastics, four of them gold, home to Romania.

dersen-Schiess staggered into the stadium, obviously dehydrated, and she trudged and teetered the final one-and-a-fraction laps. As she finished, medical personnel rushed her off for treatment, and in two hours she had recovered. Joan Benoit of Freeport, Me., was the women's marathon winner. Carlos Lopes of Portugal, running in only his third marathon ever, was the upset winner of the men's event.

The women's 3,000 m will long be remembered for an incident in the final. It involved Mary Decker of Eugene, Ore., the world champion, and 18-year-old Zola Budd, a native of South Africa (which is banned from Olympic competition) who had just became a British citizen. With just over three laps remaining and Decker in the lead, Budd pulled in front. The two made contact; Decker fell, injured a hip, and was out of the race. Decker's dreams of an Olympic gold medal—thwarted in 1976 by injury and in 1980 by the U.S. boycott—again had failed to become a reality. She blamed Budd for cutting her off without having taken a sufficient lead, but track officials exonerated Budd, who finished seventh. The winner, almost unnoticed, was Maricica Puică of Romania.   F.L.

heavyweight class, less than two years after having undergone surgery and radiation treatment for Hodgkin's disease.

Edwin Moses of Laguna Hills, Calif., history's best 400-meter hurdler, won the men's gold medal, as he did in 1976. (The final was Moses's 105th consecutive victory.) Greg Louganis of Mission Viejo, Calif., brilliantly swept the men's 3-meter springboard and 10-meter platform diving. Tracie Ruiz of Bothell, Wash., won gold medals in both the solo and duet events of synchronized swimming, a new Olympic sport. Daley Thompson of Great Britain repeated his 1980 Olympic decathlon victory and missed the world record by one point. His countryman Sebastian Coe overcame a history of respiratory problems and repeated his 1980 Olympic victory in the men's 1,500-meter run.

One unlikely star was Gabriela Andersen-Schiess of Sun Valley, Idaho, a 39-year-old with dual citizenship who ran for Switzerland in the first Olympic women's marathon. An-

Mary Decker lies in pain on the grass, minutes after she fell in the women's 3,000-meter race. Decker, who stumbled when she came into contact with runner Zola Budd, suffered a hip injury and the anguish of knowing she would not win an Olympic medal

SRI LANKA. Despite government efforts to reach a peaceful settlement, ethnic violence continued to plague Sri Lanka in 1984. In January, President J. R. Jayewardene called a conference of national reconciliation. All major political parties, including the leading opposition groups—the Sri Lanka Freedom Party (SLFP), the Communist Party, the Tamil United Liberation Front (TULF), and the All Ceylon Tamil Congress—participated. The talks continued for months, but nothing substantial emerged. The government proposed giving the Tamil minority local control at the district council level, whereas the Tamil parties wanted control of a much wider area combined into a single jurisdiction with a Tamil majority. In December the government unveiled a power-sharing plan aimed at ending the ethnic violence, but it encountered a cool reception and was withdrawn.

Meanwhile, the killing continued. In April, clashes between security forces and Tamil guerrillas resulted in at least 22 deaths, followed by the retaliatory burning of a police station and a Buddhist temple (the Sinhalese majority is mostly Buddhist, while most Tamils are Hindus). This in turn led to attacks by the army on civilian crowds, reportedly causing more than 200 deaths.

On August 11, several soldiers were killed when their truck was destroyed by a bomb south of Jaffna. The army retaliated by going on a rampage, killing, burning, and looting. On November 30, Tamil separatists raided two prison settlements, reportedly killing 80 peo-

Opposite page: Some outstanding stamps of 1984. Top row (left to right): Australia, France, and Jamaica commemorate the games of the XXIII Olympiad in Los Angeles. Second row: The Falkland Islands recognizes the 19th Universal Postal Congress; Malta, Norway, and Switzerland all mark the 25th anniversary Europa issue. Third row: Great Britain publicizes the London Economic Summit; the first stamps of the Federated States of Micronesia; Bahamas honors the Conference of Heads of Government of the Caribbean Community. Fourth row: The United States commemorates the Summer Olympic Games, the 400th anniversary of the Roanoke Voyages, Horace Moses, John McCormack, and Smokey the Bear. Fifth row: The United Nations commemorates the International Conference on Population with this special issue released in New York, Geneva, and Vienna.

ple; at least 68 Tamils were then killed in clashes with police. By mid–December, hundreds of people had died in three weeks of political violence.

Relations with India remained tense. The Sri Lankan government asserted that Tamil guerrillas were being trained and protected in the southern Indian state of Tamil Nadu. On several occasions, Sri Lankan military forces fired on ships they believed to be carrying invasion forces of Tamil guerrillas from India, killing about 35 people in all.

See STATISTICS OF THE WORLD.   T.F.

STAMPS, POSTAGE. The Olympic Games, notable anniversaries, and ecology and conservation problems were among themes emphasized on postage stamps during 1984.

United States Issues. The U.S. Postal Service issued 44 commemorative stamps in the 20-cent denomination and special stamps in other denominations to recognize important persons, special events, or particular themes. Individuals honored included black historian Carter Woodson, author Herman Melville, Junior Achievement founder Horace Moses, athletes Roberto Clemente and Jim Thorpe, and stateswoman Eleanor Roosevelt. Douglas Fairbanks and John McCormack were featured in issues of the performing arts series. Sheets consisting of blocks of four different stamps were issued to mark both the winter Olympics, held in Sarajevo, Yugoslavia, and the summer Olympics in Los Angeles, and on the topical subjects of orchids and dogs. Also given recognition were the 25th anniversaries of Alaskan and Hawaiian statehood and of the opening of the St. Lawrence Seaway; the 50th anniversaries of the National Archives, the Federal Deposit Insurance Corporation, and the Credit Union Act of 1934; and the 400th anniversary of the Roanoke Voyages of early American explorers. Other subjects featured included conservation, wetlands preservation, the Louisiana World Exposition, Smokey the Bear, Hispanic Americans, and the Vietnam Veterans Memorial.

Regular annual issues included a "Love" stamp and two Christmas stamps, one with a secular and one with a religious theme. Six new definitive stamps were issued in denominations of 7.4, 10, 11, 20, 30, and 40 cents. Postal stationery released during the year included four commemorative postal cards and an envelope with wrap-around design.

Worldwide Issues. The subject most widely commemorated on postage stamps was the summer Olympics, at Los Angeles. Other major events recognized by many postal administrations were the 25th anniversary of the Conference of European Posts and Telecommunications Administration (Europa), the London economic summit, and the Universal Postal Union Congress in Hamburg, West Germany.

Several political entities that had been granted postal independence produced their first stamps; these were the Marshall Islands and the Federated States of Micronesia (formerly the Caroline Islands), both part of the U.S. Trust Territory of the Pacific Islands, and the Cayes (Keys) of Belize (formerly British Honduras).

United Nations Issues. The UN Postal Administration issued five commemorative sets. The themes were the International Conference on Population, World Food Day, World Heritage–UNESCO, a future for refugees, and International Youth Year 1985. The three UN postal facilities shared in issuing the stamps in each set—thus, New York, Geneva, and Vienna each issued, simultaneously, two of the six stamps in the World Heritage series; each stamp bore the currency denomination of the country in which it was issued.

On September 21 the UNPA released the fifth group of 16 stamps in its continuing flag series. These were 20-cent denominations issued only in New York, in sheets of 16 stamps, each sheet showing four different flags in blocks of four. The countries represented were, in the order printed, Burundi, Pakistan, Benin, Italy, Poland, Papua New Guinea, Uruguay, Chile, Tanzania, United Arab Emirates, Ecuador, Bahamas, Paraguay, Bhutan, Central African Republic, and Australia.

Stamp Market. Prices for investment-quality stamps continued to decline, but at a slower rate than during the previous two years. Stamp auctions throughout the world reported increased participation and stronger competitive bidding.   J.W.K.

STATE GOVERNMENT REVIEW. The renewed health of the U.S. economy in 1984 was reflected in state economies and, in turn, in the tax actions of some states. New laws to improve education, protect children, and reduce the number of alcohol-related driving accidents were prominent among those passed. In the November elections, Republicans made modest inroads in the traditional Democratic control of state legislatures but made negligible progress in gaining control of governors' mansions.

State Finances. In 1984, most states, buoyed by economic recovery and a backlog of spending cutbacks and tax hikes, were in good financial shape. New Hampshire and Vermont experienced a deficit in fiscal 1984, but many other states, including New Jersey, California, Minnesota, Texas, and Wisconsin, had healthy budget surpluses. The total net surplus for all 50 states came to $5.3 billion, compared with $2.1 billion in 1983. At least seven states— Delaware, Michigan, Minnesota, Nebraska, Rhode Island, Pennsylvania, and Wisconsin— took the opportunity to reduce personal income taxes, and another state, Ohio, mailed rebate checks to taxpayers.

Education. In response to growing criticism of public education nationwide, many states formed task forces to review their educational systems. At least half the states significantly increased aid to education; in Texas alone, $847 million in revenues from increased taxes were targeted for educational improvements, and South Carolina and Tennessee increased their sales taxes by 1 percent for the same purpose. Increased pay for teachers was approved by a dozen legislatures. Other educational reforms to win approval included expanded kindergarten programs, reduced class size, more stringent high school graduation requirements, standardized testing programs for students and teachers, improved teacher training, merit pay, and career ladder programs for teachers.

Children. Measures to protect children were a major legislative concern, reflecting public reaction to allegations of widespread sexual abuse and exploitation of children and to widely publicized cases of missing children. Clearinghouses for information on missing children were authorized by new laws in Florida, Illinois, Kentucky, and Minnesota. Washington began a statewide identification program to photograph and fingerprint its children, and another dozen states toughened laws on child pornography or sexual abuse.

Several states passed laws to enforce better collection of child support payments. California enacted unique legislation requiring the noncustodial parent to contribute a level of child support at least equal to state welfare payments; the law was designed to ensure a "survival" level of income to children whose parents divorce.

Consumer Legislation. Since first adopted by Connecticut, "lemon" laws, requiring motor vehicle manufacturers to repair or replace defective new vehicles, have become increasingly common, with at least a dozen states passing such measures in 1984. Timesharing (usually of vacation property) was further regulated in Hawaii and Rhode Island. Pennsylvania funded loans to homeowners in danger of foreclosure because of economic reverses, and Minnesota extended protection against home foreclosures until July 1985.

Driving. Higher fuel taxes were passed in several states. New Jersey voted to allocate part of its gas tax revenues to highway work, and Indiana extended its tax to the gasoline-alcohol mixture known as gasohol. Texas no longer could lay claim to the lowest gasoline tax in the nation, having doubled its rate to 10 cents. Connecticut approved a decade-long $5.5 billion road and bridge repair program, funded by an increase in the gas tax scheduled to reach 23 cents per gallon in 1991. Alabama approved a $405 million highway bond program.

By the end of the year nearly every state had legislation requiring children of a certain age to use seat belts when riding in cars. New York enacted the nation's first mandatory seat-belt law for adults; New Jersey and Illinois also enacted seat-belt measures (the latter was signed in January 1985). In July, Secretary of Transportation Elizabeth Dole announced that air bags would be mandatory in new cars by 1989 unless enough states passed federally approved seat-belt laws. Interestingly, however, New Jersey intentionally designed its law *not* to meet federal guidelines, because legislators felt carmakers should have to install air bags.

Stronger laws to discourage drunk driving were enacted in many states. Penalty provisions

Ann and David Collins of San Francisco search for their son Kevin, who disappeared in February. Growing concern over the problem of missing children led to legislation in many states, authorizing clearinghouses for information on child abductions or tightening penalties for sexual abuse of children.

included higher fines, mandatory jail terms, immediate license suspension, and loss of license. In some cases refusal to take the blood alcohol concentration test was made admissible as evidence in court. Victims of drunken drivers were made eligible for aid from victims' compensation funds in Missouri and Wisconsin, and special youth driver licensing, providing for restriction or loss of driving privileges for young people convicted of alcohol-related offenses, passed in at least eight states.

Minimum 21-year-old drinking ages were adopted by four more states—Arizona, Ne-

387

braska, Rhode Island, and Tennessee—bringing the total to 23 states. The minimum drinking age for beer and wine was raised to 19 by South Carolina and South Dakota. Congress passed a law requiring all states to raise the drinking age to 21 or face loss of 5 percent of federal highway funds for 1987 and 10 percent for 1988, but states reacted angrily to this federal pressure, and South Dakota filed suit against the order.

Health and Social Measures. Several states passed legislation permitting the use of the "living will," stating that an individual does not wish to be kept alive by extraordinary medical intervention, and a dozen states passed laws aimed at controlling hospital, medicaid, or other health costs. Welfare payments were increased in at least five states. Measures to curb domestic abuse also passed in at least five states, with Kansas and Tennessee increasing marriage license fees to fund shelters for victims of domestic violence.

Hazardous waste cleanup and measures to ensure clean water supplies dominated the environmental agenda of many states, with Maryland and Virginia funding a major program for cleanup of the Chesapeake Bay. In law enforcement, victims' rights laws passed in at least five states and computer crime statutes in several. Provisions to restrict the use of the insanity defense were enacted in a few states, and the authority of local goverments to pass gun control laws was restricted by at least four states.

Election Results. In the November 6 elections, Republicans were able to gain approximately 320 new seats in state legislatures around the United States, but Democrats still retained legislative control in most states. Before the election, Democrats had a legislative majority in both houses of 33 states, with control split between the two chambers in five other states. After the election, Democrats had majority control in 28 states, with control split in ten others.

In governors' races, Republicans did little to change the pattern of Democratic dominance. Of 13 governorships at stake, four (North Carolina, Rhode Island, Utah, West Virginia) changed hands from Democrat to Republican control, while three (North Dakota, Vermont,

Washington) went from Republican to Democratic control. The GOP thus had a net gain of one, giving them only 16 of the 50 executive mansions.

Among races of particular interest, U.S. Representative James G. Martin (R) handily defeated Attorney General Rufus Edmisten to win the North Carolina governorship, previously held by Democrat James Hunt, who had relinquished his office in an unsuccessful drive to capture the Senate seat of Republican conservative Jesse B. Helms. And in Vermont, former Lieutenant Governor Madeleine Kunin (D) very narrowly defeated Attorney General John Easton (R) to win the governorship and became one of two current woman governors. (The other was Democrat Martha Layne Collins of Kentucky.) Incumbent Governor John Spellman (R) was defeated in Washington by businessman Booth Gardner (D), and North Dakota Governor Allen Olsen (R) was outpolled by State Representative George Sinner (D). But in West Virginia, former Republican Governor Arch A. Moore, Jr., made a comeback, beating Democrat Clyde M. See, Jr., by a small margin to win the governorship vacated by successful Senate candidate John D. (Jay) Rockefeller IV. In Rhode Island, Edward DiPrete, the mayor of Cranston, was elected as the state's first Republican governor in 16 years.

Tax and gambling were among the leading issues in over 200 statewide ballot proposals decided by voters in November 6. The "tax revolt" touched off by the 1978 passage of Proposition 13 in California appeared to have given way to a countertrend, as voters in at least four states, including California, defeated new tax-limiting proposals. State lotteries as a source of revenues were approved by voters in four states (California, Missouri, Oregon, and West Virginia), but casino gambling was defeated in two others. A number of controversial national issues also appeared on state ballots. Among them, a ban on the use of state funds for abortions was accepted by Coloradans but defeated by Washingtonians. In West Virginia, voters approved a constitutional amendment permitting voluntary prayer in public schools. Oregon voters approved the death penalty. South Dakotans voted not to call for a U.S.–Soviet nuclear freeze.   E.S.K.

SUDAN. Domestic tension heightened in 1984 in the wake of a penal code revision by President Jaafar al-Nimeiry in late 1983 to bring it into line with Islamic law (sharia). The new system included bans on alcohol and gambling and cruel punishments for relatively minor crimes—for example, cutting off hands for theft. Armed opposition to the regime increased in generally non-Muslim southern Sudan, and a French-run canal project to recover swampland and provide water for Sudan and Egypt was suspended because of guerrilla attacks.

The traumatic response to the imposition of Islamic law—along with strikes by doctors, university teachers, and public workers seeking wage increases—led Nimeiry to declare a state of emergency on April 29. Considerable power was granted to the armed forces. A new cabinet was announced on May 2, and martial law courts were set up. On September 29, claiming that order had been restored, Nimeiry lifted the state of emergency and suspended the Islamic courts. In October, the government reportedly reached a provisional peace agreement with the southern rebels.

Nimeiry blamed much of the internal turmoil on hostile neighbors such as Libya and Ethiopia. In March a plane—said by Sudanese officials to be a Soviet-built TU-22 from Libya—dropped bombs on the central city of Omdurman, killing five people. The United States and Egypt warned Libya not to repeat the bombing raid; the Libyans denied responsibility. Egypt, with which Sudan had a defense pact, dispatched army advisers, and the United States sent two Awacs surveillance planes to Egypt to monitor Sudanese and Egyptian airspace. The Awacs planes were quietly withdrawn a few weeks later.

Trade agreements were signed with a number of countries, including China and Romania. Sudan's foreign debt of $9 billion was too large for the country to manage; in May, at a creditors' meeting in Paris, 1984 repayments were rescheduled.

See STATISTICS OF THE WORLD.   R.E.B.

SUPREME COURT OF THE UNITED STATES. In 1984, the U.S. Supreme Court handed down important decisions in several fields, including discrimination, criminal law, and separation of church and state. (See also BLACKS IN THE UNITED STATES; CIVIL LIBERTIES AND CIVIL RIGHTS; and WOMEN.)

Church and State. Perhaps no decision received more attention than that in *Lynch* v. *Donnelly*, the nativity-scene case from Pawtucket, R.I. Writing for the 5–4 majority, Chief Justice Warren E. Burger held that a city-sponsored crèche displaying the birth of Christ did not violate the so-called establishment clause of the First Amendment, which prohibits government from fostering religion. The Court majority reasoned that all governmental presentations with religious origins must be viewed in context; otherwise, a public museum would risk censure for hanging a painting depicting some faith's particular tenet. The test, said the chief justice, was whether the display constituted a "purposeful or surreptitious effort to express some . . . subtle governmental advocacy of a particular religious message," a test which, he said, the nativity scene passed. The dissenters, led by Justice William J. Brennan, Jr., decried the majority's use of "context" to overlook what they held was an impermissible government endorsement.

VCR's. A second 5–4 ruling was *Sony Corporation of America* v. *Universal City Studios Inc.*, in which the majority, in a decision written by Justice John Paul Stevens, found that the use of video cassette recorders, or VCR's, in the home to tape television programs did not subject the recorders' manufacturers to liability for copyright infringement. Showing substantial deference to congressional dominance in the areas of copyright law, Justice Stevens was hesitant to find an infringement by VCR manufacturers when their product could be used in so many nonprohibited ways. Justice Harry A. Blackmun, writing for the dissenters, believed the majority's decision ignored the purpose behind the copyright laws, which he said was to ensure that artists enjoy control over their creations in order to encourage them to create.

Criminal Cases. The Court decided several cases related to the search and seizure clause of the Fourth Amendment. In *United States* v. *Leon* and *Massachusetts* v. *Sheppard*, the Court articulated a "good faith" exception to the so-called exclusionary rule, which prohibits the introduction at a trial of evidence seized in

Amber Tatro, an eight-year-old Texan with spina bifida, waits outside as the Supreme Court hears the case brought by her parents against her school district, which had refused to provide for her catheterization as needed. Of broad interest to rights-for-the-handicapped activists, the case was unanimously decided in Amber's favor.

violation of Fourth Amendment's prohibition of unreasonable search and seizure. Justice Byron White's majority opinion in *Leon* reasoned that the exclusionary rule could not have the desired effect of deterring illegal police activity if the officers involved believed in good faith that they were acting within the law. Thus, the Court held, if officers are operating under an apparently valid warrant which is later determined insufficient, the fruits of

their search should not be suppressed. Three justices dissented. Justice Brennan (joined by Justice Thurgood Marshall) did so on the grounds that the courts should be enforcing constitutional protections and not yielding to cost-benefit analyses. Justice Stevens asserted that a search cannot be "unreasonable" under the Fourth Amendment yet "reasonable" under police belief.

Other search and seizure cases contained implications beyond the Fourth Amendment. The Court ruled, 5–4, in *Hudson* v. *Palmer* that random, unannounced prison shakedowns did not violate inmates' rights because the inmates could have no "legitimate . . . expectation of privacy" in their prison cells. In *Block* v. *Rutherford*, in addition to affirming shakedown procedures, a 6–3 majority held that a denial of "contact visits" to people being held in jail before trial was reasonable means of interdicting possible contraband from the outside world.

In *New York* v. *Quarles*, the Court, by a 5–4 vote, created an exception to the *Miranda* requirement that detainees be advised, before being interrogated, of their rights to remain silent and have a lawyer. The exception would permit pre-warning questioning—in this situation, about the location of Quarles' gun—if the officers believed that the detainee posed a threat to the "public safety." In *Berkemer* v. *McCarty*, the Court, by an 8–1 vote, held that the *Miranda* rule is not triggered by a simple roadside stop of an alleged traffic violator unless the officer has placed the driver in custody.

In *Nix* v. *Williams*, a 7–2 majority permitted the admission during trial of information obtained in violation of a detainee's right to counsel, provided the prosecution proves by a preponderance of the evidence that the information—here, the location of a murder victim's body—would have come to light "inevitably" in any event. In *Pulley* v. *Harris*, the Court determined, by a 7–2 majority, that a state need not review a death sentence to determine if the punishment was "proportional" to that imposed in other, similar prosecutions.

Freedom of the Press. In *Keeton* v. *Hustler Magazine*, the Court held unanimously that a periodical with regular circulation in a given state can be sued in that state for libel, because of an article in the magazine, even though both the plaintiff and the magazine's headquarters are outside the state. In *Bose Corporation v. Consumers Union of the United States*, the justices ruled, 6–3, that an appellate court, in reviewing a libel judgment against a news organ, must include in that review a careful examination of whether the record supports with convincing clarity the necessary finding of actual malice. The three dissenting justices all believed that a finding of actual malice was a question of fact to be determined at the trial level and not in an appellate review.

Rights of the Handicapped. The Court held unanimously that, under a federal law requiring public schools to provide "related services" as well as education for handicapped students, a school system must make arrangements to administer catheterization when necessary. The case, *Irving Independent School District v. Tatro*, involved a girl suffering from spina bifida whose parents sued when the school district declined to provide for catheterization.

J.F.H., III

SURINAME. See STATISTICS OF THE WORLD. *See also* CARIBBEAN COUNTRIES.

SWAZILAND. See STATISTICS OF THE WORLD.

SWEDEN. In 1984, the Social Democratic government of Olof Palme presided over continued economic growth and reductions in inflation and unemployment. By May, industrial output was at record levels, inflation was running at about 6 percent, and unemployment was under 3 percent. The trade surplus for the first six months was over $1.6 billion. Swedish exports, expected to show a 15 percent increase for the year, accounted in large part for substantial increases in industrial profits.

Government officials urged union leaders to practice wage restraint. They pointed particularly to the potential benefits of the new regional wage-earner funds, which came into effect on January 1, 1984. The funds, drawn from additional corporate and payroll taxes and controlled by labor unions, were earmarked to buy stock in Swedish companies. The system continued to be opposed by employers, and the Swedish Employers' Confederation, the principal employers' association,

filed suit challenging the system's constitutionality.

Wildcat strikes initially portended rank-and-file opposition to wage restraint. In mid-March, unions for blue-collar public-sector workers signed collective agreements that provided for an average increase of 8.4 percent over a two-year period. Other unions signed varying agreements for similar increases. In an informal policy meeting in June, government spokesmen and representatives of the unions and employer groups agreed to seek a maximum wage increase of 5 percent in 1985 and to resume centralized wage negotiations.

Delegates from some 35 nations, including the United States, Canada, and most European countries, attended an East-West conference on confidence and security-building in Stockholm. Prime Minister Palme was later criticized by Swedish conservatives for not being forceful enough about continuing Soviet submarine incursions into Swedish waters when he met with Soviet Foreign Minister Andrei Gromyko at the conference. Palme has taken a low-key approach, to avoid worsening relations with the Soviets. Meanwhile, major political parties reached an agreement to increase military appropriations, so as to improve coastal defenses and purchase military equipment abroad.

See STATISTICS OF THE WORLD. M.D.H.

SWITZERLAND. Many of the major developments in Switzerland during 1984 concerned banking and finance. The sanctity of the secret Swiss bank account was preserved in May,

Vanishing Breed

If you're ever trapped in an avalanche in the Swiss Alps, don't expect to be rescued by a gigantic, shaggy Saint Bernard dog with a keg of brandy around its neck. Saint Bernards (named after the hospice and monastery where they were first used as rescuers 300 years ago) have now been replaced by German shepherds, who are more agile and take up less space in a rescue helicopter. Incidentally, to spoil another illusion, the noble Saint Bernards, with all their talent for digging up people in the snow and reviving them, never did carry those storied brandy kegs.

The first woman elected to Switzerland's ruling Federal Council, Elisabeth Kopp, 47, is sworn in at an October ceremony in Bern. Because the position is rotated annually among the council's seven members, Kopp, a supporter of feminist and environmentalist causes, will be president of Switzerland at some point before the end of 1991.

when voters rejected a proposed constitutional amendment that would have opened records to tax authorities and judges. The measure called for banks to cooperate in investigating domestic and international cases of tax evasion and other currency crimes. The measure's opponents claimed that abandoning the secrecy law would drive away foreign investors.

The Federal Tribunal ordered in May that three Swiss banks help the U.S. Securities and Exchange Commission in an investigation of insider trading violations. The case involved a $5 million profit investors made in Santa Fe International Corporation stocks and options before public announcement of the the corporation's 1981 sale to the Kuwait Petroleum Corporation. (In Switzerland, insiders may make such trades, but may not leak information to outsiders.) The banks later named the persons who traded the stock through their secret accounts—in the first time the Swiss had ever assisted an SEC inquiry.

In October, for the first time ever, a woman obtained a seat on the Federal Council, when the Federal Assembly chose Radical Democrat Elisabeth Kopp to fill a vacancy on the government's executive body.

A boycott against Nestlé Alimenta S.A. ended after it agreed to revamp the marketing of its infant formula in the Third World to comply with World Health Organization guidelines. Nestlé had been accused of selling formula without regard for its correct use. In September, Nestlé said it would buy the U.S.–based Carnation Company, a dairy and food concern, for $3 billion.

The legal battle in the Marc Rich tax fraud case continued. Rich and his partner Pincus Green had been indicted in 1983 in the United States for tax evasion, fraud, and racketeering. The Swiss-based commodity trading firm they owned also was indicted, as was a U.S. subsidiary. In September the Swiss government refused to extradite the two for trial in the United States. U.S. prosecutors then negotiated with the indicted firms, which pleaded guilty to criminal tax charges and agreed to pay $150 million (mainly for taxes and interest) to the U.S. government. The firms were free to do business in the United States, but Rich and Green remained subject to arrest should they return from Switzerland.

See STATISTICS OF THE WORLD. J.F.S.

SYRIA. Syria saw its influence grow in Lebanon in 1984; at home, the regime of President Hafez al-Assad had to contend with political infighting and an economy strained by heavy military spending.

Lebanon. The withdrawal of U.S. and other Western forces from Lebanon in 1984 simplified the chaotic situation there, at least from Syria's point of view. During late 1983 and early 1984 there had been sporadic clashes between Syrian-backed forces in Lebanon and U.S. Marines (there as part of a multinational Western peacekeeping force) and U.S. planes and ships offshore. On January 3, the Syrian government freed a U.S. Navy flier whose jet had been downed during an attack on Syrian positions in Lebanon; at the time, Syria expressed hopes that the United States would withdraw its forces. U.S. domestic opposition to the American military presence also was growing. In early February, President Ronald Reagan decided to "redeploy" the U.S. Marines to warships offshore. U.S. support for the Lebanese government of President Amin Gemayel was now waning. Other members of the multinational peacekeeping force also withdrew and the Lebanese Army disintegrated, with most of its Muslim soldiers refusing to fight other Muslims. Gemayel had to turn to Damascus for help in ending the civil war and reestablishing the legitimacy of his government.

In late February, Gemayel traveled to Damascus for talks with Assad. The Syrians demanded that the Gemayel government cancel its 1983 peace agreement with Israel, which called for the withdrawal from Lebanon of both Syrian and Israeli forces, and that it share power more equitably with Muslim leaders. On March 5, Lebanon formally abrogated its pact with Israel; Syria in turn pressured its Muslim allies to drop demands for Germayel's resignation and to cooperate in seeking a solution to the civil war.

A broader-based Lebanese government, formed in April, reorganized the army and imposed a cease-fire in Beirut. Sporadic fighting continued inside and especially outside the capital, however. Late in the year, new Lebanese troops were deployed in Beirut and in Tripoli, Lebanon, in a Syrian-supported effort to strengthen and extend government control.

Succession Struggle. As health problems plagued President Assad, potential successors began to jockey for position, and early in the year, pictures of the main rivals for power were plastered all over the capital. Particularly prominent were those of Rifaat Assad, the president's brother, who had accumulated power through control of the Defense Companies, an elite force charged with protecting the regime. In late February, displeasure with government

Syrian President Hafez al-Assad (right) confers with his younger brother, Rifaat, in May before sending him on a mission to Moscow. Rifaat's subsequent prolonged stay in Geneva prompted speculation that Assad had banished him forever; but he returned to Syria in November and assumed a new title.

appointments apparently led Rifaat to redeploy his forces around Damascus. On March 11, President Assad shuffled his cabinet and named three vice-presidents, including his brother (as vice-president without portfolio).

During the next several weeks there were two reported confrontations between Rifaat's Defense Companies and rural forces; both showdowns apparently ended without violence. On May 28, Rifaat Assad and his main rivals were sent to Moscow, supposedly to meet with Soviet leaders. Rifaat remained abroad for some time; he was said to have been exiled, but he denied these reports. In October it was reported that President Assad had transferred most of the soldiers in Rifaat's Defense Com-

panies to regular army units. On November 11, however, Rifaat was named vice-president for national security, and on November 26 he returned to Damascus.

Economy. Syria's economy continued to suffer from the massive defense bill. For 1984, defense spending was projected at $3.2 billion, about 30 percent of the total budget and a rise of 20.5 percent over the 1983 figure. The cost of the military presence in Lebanon was about $250,000 a day. Arab Gulf states, except Saudi Arabia, were not meeting their military aid commitments to Syria. Even Libya, a longtime friend, provided less help than in the past.

See STATISTICS OF THE WORLD. See also PALESTINE LIBERATION ORGANIZATION.   A.D.

T

TAIWAN. Taiwan had an eventful political year in 1984. In May, Chiang Ching-kuo, at 74, began his second six-year term as president of the Republic of China (ROC). He selected Lee Teng-hui, governor of Taiwan Province, a native of Taiwan and 13 years his junior, to be the vice-president, in place of Shieh Tung-min, who was retiring. In June an economist and banker, Yu Kuo-hua, was appointed premier. He was a surprise replacement for former Premier Sun Yun-suan, who had been groomed by President Chiang to take over as president but who suffered a stroke in February. Many other changes also were made in the leadership of the ROC government and the Kuomintang (Nationalist Party).

On August 15 authorities released two prominent political prisoners. Lin Yi-hsiung, a former member of the Taiwan Provincial Assembly, jailed after attending a human rights rally in December 1979, received a commutation of his 12-year sentence. Reverend Kao Chun-ming, general secretary of the Taiwan Presbyterian Church, who was charged following that same rally, was released on parole.

On May 19, U.S. Senator Claiborne Pell of Rhode Island delivered a speech on the Senate

floor appealing to the Kuomintang authorities to end martial law, in force since 1949, and move toward a democratic political system. Meanwhile, U.S.–Taiwan ties were threatened by improving relations between Peking and Washington that threatened to isolate Taiwan further internationally.The conclusion of a Sino-British agreement on the future of Hong Kong also put political and psychological pressure on the Kuomintang leadership; Peking apparently viewed the Hong Kong agreement as a model for reunification with Taiwan as well.

One bright note for Taiwan was its economic performance. Gross national product growth in 1984 showed signs of reaching 10 percent; per capita income was expected to exceed $3,000 per year, up from $2,683 in 1983.

See STATISTICS OF THE WORLD.   P.H.C.

TANZANIA. Tanzanians sensed that an era was coming to an end after President Julius K. Nyerere announced in March 1984 that he would not seek reelection in 1985. Rashidi Kawawa, the secretary-general of the ruling Chama Cha Mapinduzi (CCM) party, and Prime Minister Edward Sokoine were immediately perceived as the two likeliest candidates to succeed Nyerere, but on April 12, Sokoine was killed in an automobile crash while returning to Dar es-Salaam from Dodoma. Sokoine was replaced as prime minister by Foreign Minister Salim Ahmed Salim, one of Africa's most experienced and influential diplomats, who thus became a potential successor to Nyerere.

Proposed constitutional changes designed to tighten Zanzibar's unity with Tanganyika triggered demands for the greater autonomy for Zanzibar, and on January 29, Zanzibar President Aboud Jumbe, seen by some as too subservient to Nyerere, was forced to resign. His replacement by strongly pro-union Ali Hassan Mwinyi brought several other government resignations, but a semblance of calm was restored after elections on April 19 saw Mwinyi's appointment ratified by 87.5 percent of the Zanzibar electorate.

Tanzania took some steps toward increased austerity. The government decreed a downward "readjustment" of the shilling in June, followed by producer price increases, designed to encourage the production of food and export crops. A massive agricultural development plan, focusing on 17 food crops and seven cash crops, was announced in February, and large development projects in progress or under study envisioned the rehabilitation and extension of the transportation infrastructure, including rail and harbor facilities.

In May, the presidents of Uganda, Kenya, and Tanzania signed a final agreement settling the financial problems arising from the 1977 collapse of the East African community. In November, President Nyerere was elected to the chairmanship of the Organization of African Unity at a summit meeting in Ethiopia.

See STATISTICS OF THE WORLD.   E.B.

TECHNOLOGY. In 1984, pioneering magnetic-levitation vehicles were put into service, newly developed supermagnets were launched into production, and pocket-size satellite transceivers and a satellite-guided automobile navigation system were being developed. Plans were made for a fully automated factory employing robots for production.

Magnetic-levitation Train. Around midyear, Great Britain inaugurated its first commercial system using the wheelless train suspended in a magnetic field. These maglev (magnetic-levitation) vehicles provided service on a quarter-mile rail link between the Birmingham airport and a nearby rail station. In this system, electromagnets beneath 20-foot-long maglev cars lift the vehicles upward toward two steel suspension rails, while electronic-control circuits prevent the magnets from touching, so that the vehicles are suspended in air. The maglev trains are propelled by linear-induction motors, which have one component (the stator) built into the vehicle; another component (the rotor)

A wheelless train that floats above the track at high speed has been developed by Japan Airlines for future airport-to-city transportation. Shown here in a trial run, the magnetic-levitation train, which has a design speed of 187.5 miles per hour, is propelled by a linear-induction motor. Another model was introduced in Britain.

is an aluminum plate laid along the entire track.

A variety of maglev trains have also been under development in Japan and various other countries since the 1960's. The U.S. government has provided funds for a study on the feasibility of a magnetic-levitation system between Los Angeles and Las Vegas, and systems were being considered for other urban corridors in the United States.

Low-cost Supermagnets. High-strength permanent magnets of superior quality have in the past required costly materials, such as cobalt, that are not abundant in the United States. However, research conducted independently in Japan and the United States recently resulted in the discovery of a new way to make supermagnets—at about half the cost of cobalt magnets—by adding small amounts of boron to iron-based rare-earth alloys. Early in the year, several U.S. companies, including General Motors, announced plans to produce the new supermagnets, using a variety of techniques to process the alloys. GM planned to use the magnets in a new cranking motor for its 1986 cars; such a motor would be half the size of ordinary motors with copper-wire coils and would weigh about 50 percent less.

Magnetic Bearings. Ball bearings are used in everything from roller skates to mammoth industrial equipment, so as to smooth the rotation of wheels, axles, and gears. But energy must be expended to overcome friction in bearings, and elaborate lubrication systems are needed for large equipment. Recently, however, a frictionless but costly substitute for the ball bearing has been installed in some industrial equipment. The new bearing, developed by Société de Méchanique Magnetique, a small French firm, suspends a spinning shaft in a magnetic field. Since mechanical contact, friction, and vibration are eliminated, bearing shafts can be rotated at exceptionally high speeds—up to 800,000 revolutions per minute. A computerized sensor notices whenever the spinning shaft begins to move off center, and the magnetic field suspending the shaft is then adjusted to center it again. Very costly versions of the bearing have been installed in large turbines and compressors, but smaller, less-expensive magnetic bearings were also ex-

A Sound Idea?

If you're really determined to get rid of your pet's fleas or ticks, without powders, baths, or sprays, inventor Frank J. Bianco of Miami may have the answer: a battery-powered ultrasonic pet collar. It's no muss, no fuss, and it sells for $69.95. The Microtech Flea & Tick Collar, marketed by BioTechnology Inc., does its job with a high-frequency sound that reportedly is out of hearing range for humans and most pets but, according to Bianco, drives pests into flight. Is it just another expensive gadget that doesn't really work? Bianco claims otherwise and cites a money-back guarantee if the fleas don't take off for parts unknown after five days of electronic harassment.

pected soon, from the Japanese, who were cooperating with the French firm in development.

Advanced Automotive Technology. A blend of mechanical and microcomputer technologies helped to improve comfort and safety, and reduce emissions in some cars introduced in 1984. Ford's Lincoln Mark VII and Continental featured air-suspension springs on each wheel to automatically level the cars and provide a smoother ride. In this system, wheel-height sensors feed signals to a computer that actuates a compressor and pumps air to the proper air springs. Mercedes–Benz introduced an antilock braking system for a 1985 model, and the Mark VII also had this feature, which prevents cars from skidding out of control during panic stops. The antilock systems utilize sensors that detect the speeds of front and rear wheels. Signals sent from the wheels to electronic controls cause a hydraulic pump to cycle the brakes rapidly on and off when wheels start to lock up during sudden stops. Antiskid braking is already available in some expensive European cars.

Electronic fuel injection, also a feature on many costlier models, was being adapted to some economy cars by U.S. firms. Unlike the more expensive injection systems, which feature a fuel injector in each engine cylinder, the economy approach uses a single injector mounted on the carburetor. This so-called throttle-body injector is controlled by a computer that receives signals from numerous sensors. Detroit engineers expect cleaner exhaust emissions to satisfy strict federal standards—and also provide smoother driving and easier cold weather starting.

Food Irradiation. The discovery that some citrus fruits and grain products on grocery shelves contained detectable levels of ethylene dibromide, a cancer-causing chemical that had been sprayed on fruits and grains to eliminate insect infestations, has prompted renewed calls for food-irradiation programs in the United States. Gamma rays or electron beams can pasteurize or sterilize food and extend its shelf life or prepare it for indefinite storage. While microorganisms and insects are destroyed by irradiation technology, no radiation remains in foods or their containers after the process. Irradiation can also be used to reduce the levels of nitrates and nitrites in cured meats such as bacon. In mid-1983 the U.S. Food and Drug Administration authorized the use of irradiation treatment for spices and opened the door for possible use in other foods. Critics charged that widespread irradiation was unjustified because not enough is known about what chemicals may be created in irradiated foods.

Satellite Guidance. Proposals and prototype equipment for the use of satellites in automobile navigation and pocket-size communication devices have appeared recently. The pocket-size satellite transceivers, now under development, would be part of the Geostar Satellite system proposed by space futurist and Princeton University physicist Gerald K. O'Neill. The portable Geostar transceiver, which appears like a hand-held calculator with an alphanumeric keyboard in mockup form, could beam brief bursts of computer-like data to communications satellites in stationary orbits. The data, messages entered on the keyboard, could be relayed by the satellites to other transceivers anywhere in the United States. In addition, since three satellites would receive Geostar transmissions, persons using the system could have their positions pinpointed by triangulation techniques. Messages beamed back to an individual could then direct the receiver to a specific location—or alert police nearby in an emergency.

As O'Neill and other Geostar officials demonstrated and sought to promote their system, Chrysler unveiled a concept car with a navigation system also linked to satellites. The Chrysler system, perhaps a $500 option on 1988-model cars, will rely on 18 government navigation satellites, several of which were already operating in 1984. An antenna built into the car roof would be used to obtain a position fix for a vehicle from at least four of the satellites. This information could then be displayed on a color television screen along with maps covering any location in the United States. The maps are stored on an optical video disc.

"Factory of the Future." In October, General Motors announced plans to develop an experimental automated "factory of the future," using robots in place of human production workers. The factory, to be located in Saginaw, Mich., would be the first in the United States in which all production is directed through a central computer. In the facility, used to manufacture a variety of axles, about 50 robots would move parts within specified manufacturing and assembly cells, while driverless carts move parts from cell to cell. Machines would be flexible, able to adjust promptly to parts of different sizes. A limited number of human workers would be employed for maintenance and other skilled tasks. The factory was expected to be in partial operation by the end of 1985 and in full operation by the end of 1987.   J.R.F.

TELEVISION AND RADIO. Two quadrennial events—the Olympic games and the U.S. presidential elections—dominated media coverage in 1984. Meanwhile, new shows came and old ones went, and a multimillion-dollar libel suit went to trial, pitting CBS against a well-known U.S. general.

Summer Olympic Success. Even before the A. C. Nielsen Company released its final ratings for the ABC broadcasts of the 1984 summer Olympics in Los Angeles, researchers for the network were proclaiming that the $325 million the network had risked to provide 180 hours of coverage would be money well spent. The network was apparently right. The Soviet-led boycott had led some observers to predict that the games would lose much of their dramatic value, but nearly one out of every four American households tuned in to the first few days of the event, and it was estimated that 180 million people in the United States watched at least some part of the games. These figures contrasted sharply with the disappointing ratings earned by the winter Olympics, also carried by ABC.

ABC sold virtually all of its commercial time for the summer games—roughly $435 million for the 180 hours, with sponsors paying $500,000 for one minute of prime time. The Olympic's coverage won praise from many television critics, but there was criticism over what many observers considered to be a bias toward American athletes. Juan Antonio Samaranch, president of the International Olympic Committee, was among those who charged early in the games that ABC's coverage was slanted toward the American audience. He withdrew his criticism after a meeting with Roone Arledge, ABC's president for news and sports, when he understood that the network provided foreign countries only with video coverage of the Olympic events, leaving them to supply all of their own narration and commentary.

Judging from the lofty ratings, American viewers had no objections to ABC's intense concentration on events that took place in a small area of Southern California. The network utilized all of its technical resources, including electric-powered vans and motorcycles for closeups of marathon runners and fiber optics to transmit the pictures back to the Hollywood broadcast studios. Scuba divers helped in covering water polo, diving, and synchronized swimming, using cameras encased in waterproof housings.

The Conventions. For the first time since 1952, the networks elected not to provide gavel-to-gavel coverage of the Democratic and Republican presidential conventions. Part of the reason was the relative lack of news value in the events themselves. The networks, which spent a combined total of some $50 million on their relatively streamlined coverage of the two conventions, still found only disappointment in the ratings. The four-day Democratic convention in San Francisco in July attracted a nightly household average of only 17.2 million homes. The Republican convention in Dallas the following month fared little better, drawing about 19.1 million homes. The highest rated convention broadcast was NBC's coverage of the Thursday session in which President Ronald Reagan delivered his address accepting the nomination, but even so, that telecast ranked only 39th out of the week's 58 network programs. Republican convention coverage for

Dynasty Dynamo
As the ruthless and seductive Alexis Carrington Colby on ABC's prime-time soap opera Dynasty, British actress Joan Collins, since 1981, has delighted millions of viewers as she brings misery and mayhem to the show's Denver oil tycoons. Now a certified superstar at the age of 51, she has posed for Playboy, signed a multiyear contract to promote the Revlon perfume Scoundrel, and written Past Imperfect, a best-selling autobiography (published in the United States in 1984) in which she openly discusses her own marriages and romantic entanglements, involving such people as actors Warren Beatty and Ryan O'Neal and movie executive Darryl F. Zanuck. She is a veteran of over 50 mostly forgettable British and U.S. films, including two steamy blockbusters—The Stud and The Bitch—based on successful novels by younger sister Jackie.

Joan Collins

the other nights of that week ranked among the lowest-rated shows.

CBS anchorman Dan Rather insisted that the networks had a "professional obligation" to provide full coverage of the conventions. But Rather's predecessor in the CBS anchor booth, Walter Cronkite, contended that the growth of the Cable News Network and the Cable Satellite Public Affairs Network (C-SPAN) "may relieve the responsibility that has been put on the commerical networks' shoulders for full coverage." CNN and C-SPAN, both born just four years ago, offered convention coverage for the 34 million homes wired for cable. C-SPAN was, however, the only network to provide full coverage. The Public Broadcasting Service limited itself to two-hour editions of the *MacNeil/ Lehrer Report* each night from the convention sites.

Election Coverage. The other big political event in broadcasting was the series of debates between the Democratic and Republican candidates for president and vice-president. Democratic nominee Walter F. Mondale had proposed that he and President Reagan meet six times before the cameras, but, after negotiations, two meetings were set between the presidential contenders and one between the candidates for vice-president. Mondale and Reagan met October 7 in Louisville, Ky., to discuss domestic issues. Vice-President George Bush and the Democratic vice-presidential nominee, Representative Geraldine Ferraro, met in Philadelphia on October 11, and Reagan and Mondale met again on October 21 in Kansas City to debate foreign affairs. The debates were far more popular with viewers than were the conventions: an audience estimated at more than 80 million people tuned in to each of them. Walter Mondale's perceived victory in the first debate appeared to give his campaign a significant, if temporary, boost. Results in the other debates were less decisive.

On election night, the suspense ended early; all three networks had projected a victory for Ronald Reagan by 8:31 P.M. Eastern standard time, although polls were still open in New York, California, and many other states. (CBS actually announced Reagan the winner shortly after 8 P.M.) Congress had previously passed nonbinding resolutions calling for projections of the presidential winner to be withheld until all polls closed, in the belief that early projections discouraged voters who had not yet cast their ballots.

Prime Time and the Ratings Game. According to the A. C. Nielsen survey, CBS won the ratings title for the 29-week 1983–1984 season. ABC finished second in prime-time ratings, and NBC was third for the ninth consecutive year. The final ratings were: CBS, 18.1; ABC, 17.2; NBC, 14.9. (A rating denotes the percentage of U.S. television households tuned into a given network or program.) Audience size for both CBS and NBC was down by 1 percent over the season, while ABC's audience was down 3 percent. Some consolation could be drawn from the fact that the decline was the smallest since the 1979–1980 season. In recent years audiences have tended to turn from the networks to a variety of other forms of home video entertainment.

Dallas, the long-running prime-time soap opera on CBS, was the number one show in the 1983–1984 season ratings, with *60 Minutes*, the CBS "news magazine," running second. The remainder of the top ten, in order of popularity, were *Dynasty*, ABC; *The A-Team*, NBC; *Simon & Simon*, CBS; *Magnum, P.I.*, CBS; *Falcon Crest*, CBS; *Hotel*, ABC; *Knots Landing*, CBS; and the *ABC Sunday Night Movie*. All of the drama series in the top ten were either action-adventure programs or evening soap operas, leading some critics and industry observers to talk about the possible imminent death of situation comedy as a television staple. This feeling was buttressed by the finales of two more longtime favorites: *Happy Days*, which had looked back at the 1950's through rose-colored lenses for 11 seasons, and *One Day at a Time*, a nine-season veteran that had ventured into the more contemporary territory of divorce, single-parent families, and the working (and dating) mother.

The top-rated miniseries of the 1983–1984 season were, in order, *Master of the Game*, CBS; *Chiefs*, CBS; *Celebrity*, NBC; *George Washington*, CBS; and *Kennedy*, NBC. Popular miniseries during the new fall season included *Ellis Island* and *Woman of Substance*. As miniseries became more frequent events, some critics discerned a decline in their quality, with a greater proportion of lavish soap operas and greater influence of soap opera's dramatic values, even in the historical series.

As the new fall season opened, CBS scored a first-round victory in Nielsen ratings, aided particularly by big audiences for two prime-time soap operas (*Dallas* and *Falcon Crest*), which ranked number one and two; both serials resolved plot cliffhangers that had been dangling all summer. There were signs that comedy might not be as moribund as predicted, as three NBC comedies—*The Cosby Show, Cheers,* and *Family Ties*—all placed initially in the top ten. While CBS and NBC generally held their

Bill Cosby makes a point with TV daughters Keshia Knight Pulliam (left) and Tempestt Bledsoe, two of the five children costarring with the popular comedian in The Cosby Show, a new NBC situation comedy that quickly found a slot in the Nielsen ratings top ten.

own, ABC was off to a slow start; its new, highly touted *Call to Glory* series had been going downhill since its early debut in August, and in the first round of Nielsen ratings ABC had only one show in the top ten—the season premiere of *Dynasty*. Later in the season, the impact of special programs was discernible; for example, in the third week of November the second and final segment of NBC's *Fatal Vision*, about a former Green Beret convicted of murdering his family, ranked first, and George Lucas's first television movie, *The Ewok Adventure* (ABC), ran second.

One ABC television movie, at the beginning of the fall season, attracted praise and also did quite well in the Nielsen ratings. It was *Heartsounds*, a clear-eyed exploration of a doctor's last five years of life following a massive heart attack. Based on Martha Weinman Lear's book, the movie featured superb performances by Mary Tyler Moore and James Garner.

Several fall series on public television took advantage of the medium's potential as an educational tool. *The Constitution: That Delicate Balance, The Brain,* and *Heritage: Civilization and the Jews* were all critical successes that appealed to a general audience; in addition, they were designed as "telecourses" that could be taken by students at participating colleges if certain additional requirements were met.

Awards. The Peabody Awards were presented in New York City in April. A special Peabody was awarded to Don McGannon, president of the Westinghouse Broadcasting System. Another special Peabody went to the Cable News Network, a part of the Turner Broadcasting Company. Among the more noteworthy of the shows honored with a Peabody was *What Have We Learned, Charlie Brown?*, in which the *Peanuts* characters, touring the French countryside, find themselves on the coast of Normandy, site of the D-Day landings in World War II. Other awards went to *Marion McPartland's Piano Jazz,* PBS Radio; *Romeo and Juliet on Ice,* CBS-TV; *He Makes Me Feel Like Dancin',* NBC-TV; *The Grand Ole Opry,* WSM Radio, Nashville; *Studebaker: Less Than They Promised,* WBBM-TV, Chicago; *Give Me That Bigtime Religion,* WBRZ, Baton Rouge, La.; *60 Minutes* episode, "Lenell Geter's in Jail,"

CBS-TV; *The Plane That Fell From the Sky,* CBS-TV; *The Jeffersonian World of Dumas Malone,* KMAL Radio, Washington, D.C.; *The Woman Who Willed a Miracle,* ABC-TV; and *Nova:* "The Miracle of Life," WGBH, Boston.

In the 36th annual Emmy awards, presented by the National Academy of Television Arts and Sciences, NBC's *Hill Street Blues* was honored as the outstanding drama series in the 1983–1984 season. NBC's *Cheers* was named the outstanding comedy series. *Concealed Enemies,* a dramatization of the Alger Hiss–Whittaker Chambers case on PBS's *American Playhouse,* was tapped as the outstanding limited series. Tom Selleck was named the best lead actor in a drama series for *Magnum, P.I.* Tyne Daly won as the best lead actress in a drama series, *Cagney and Lacey.* For her work in *The Dollmaker,* Jane Fonda took honors as the best actress in a limited series or special. Laurence Olivier was honored as best actor in a limited series or special for *King Lear.*

Revamping the Law. In 1934, President Franklin D. Roosevelt signed into law the Communications Act, which created the Federal Communications Commission. Fifty years later, the FCC was heavily involved in trimming back its regulations. For example, in April the FCC eliminated a rule concerning regional concentration of ownership, ending the prohibition against owning three broadcast stations when two of them are within 100 miles of the third. In July the FCC voted to increase from seven to 12 each the number of radio stations and television stations a company is allowed to own. (However, implementation of the rule regarding TV stations was delayed until at least April 1985.) These changes, along with others previously instituted, were seen as enlarging the First Amendment rights of broadcasters. At the same time, many argued that reductions in the agency's regulatory powers were diminishing the accountability of the media to the public.

In October Congress passed and the president signed a bill to establish a federal policy for cable television and to limit local control over cable franchises. While localities will still award franchises, they will not be able to take them away without good cause, their control over programming will be limited, and they

Tyne Daly (right) was named best actress in a drama series for her portrayal of MaryBeth Lacey, partner of Sharon Gless's Christine Cagney in Cagney and Lacey, *the critically acclaimed CBS show about a pair of tough but feminine New York City cops.*

will eventually be prevented from regulating rates.

The Continuing Revolution. Executives of the commercial networks had to contend with growing competition from cable services and from increasingly popular videocassette recorders, or VCR's. Network advertisers in particular voiced a concern about "time shifting," the industry phrase for taping a program on a VCR for later viewing. When the tape is seen, viewers can use a remote control device to eliminate commercials. VCR owners can also avoid advertisements by renting first-run motion pictures long before they are available on network television (or on the cable services).

Another burgeoning television phenomenon, the backyard dish antenna—so called because

401

it resembles a huge saucer—was proliferating in record numbers. Since 1979, the number of dish owners in the United States had grown from 5,000 to more than half a million. The dish antenna receives signals directly from broadcast satellites, bringing in programs on 150 channels. The transmissions received are intended to be picked up by giant antennas owned by local broadcast stations and cable companies, but the owner of the dish antenna, which now costs around $2,000, pays a fee to nobody.

Westmoreland vs. CBS. Not only for awards and high ratings was CBS in the news in 1984. The trial of a $120 million libel suit filed against CBS by General William C. Westmoreland, commander of U.S. forces in Vietnam from 1964 to 1968, began in New York City on October 11, with the general taking the stand on November 15. Westmoreland contended

that in a CBS documentary aired on January 23, 1982, entitled "The Uncounted Enemy: A Vietnam Deception," he was falsely accused of having conspired to conceal the true strength of enemy forces in Vietnam from President Lyndon B. Johnson, the Congress, and the Joint Chiefs of Staff. After the program first appeared, the general had demanded an apology from CBS; when it was not forthcoming, he filed suit in September 1982.

The case attracted attention because it was expected to reexamine the war in Vietnam (also uncovering extensive newly declassified information), to scrutinize the news gathering procedures of CBS, and to raise basic issues as to the scope of First Amendment protection afforded to the news media. The time and money spent by both sides in gathering facts for the case may have been the most extensive for any libel suit in history.

General William C. Westmoreland (left) and then-Defense Secretary Robert McNamara are briefed on the demilitarized zone in this 1967 photograph taken during the Vietnam war. In a $120 million libel suit brought against CBS, the general charged that the network, in a 1982 documentary, "The Uncounted Enemy: A Vietnam Deception," had knowingly presented false information about his veracity in reporting enemy troop strength to the government. Documentation for the suit, which went to trial in federal court in October, included 400,000 pages of evidence.

Nostalgia Radio. For countless dance band fans, 1984 began with a special treat, a four-hour radio special devoted to the big bands. This Big Band Salute, carried by 200 stations around the United States, offered listeners the music of such greats as Benny Goodman, Glenn Miller, Duke Ellington, Count Basie, Stan Kenton, Tommy and Jimmy Dorsey, and Woody Herman. It was but one of many signs of a growing radio phenomenon, as more and more stations turned to a "nostalgia" format, featuring the popular music of the 1930's, 1940's, and early1950's.   D.F.

TENNESSEE. See STATISTICS OF THE WORLD.

TEXAS. See STATISTICS OF THE WORLD.

THAILAND. While retired General Prem Tinsulanond continued as prime minister of Thailand in 1984, General Arthit Kamlangek, the commander in chief of the army and the supreme commander of the armed forces, strengthened his position as Prem's probable successor. Arthit appeared frequently before civilian groups and astutely maneuvered strong supporters into key positions in the military. He also gained the support of a group of influential young officers, even though he had helped defeat an attempted coup d'état led by these officers in 1981.

During the summer and fall, the Thai government was shaken by Prem's prolonged illness and subsequent hospitalization. (He was suffering from a lung ailment.) Another disruption was the atmosphere of insecurity created by the arrest in July of 22 suspected members or sympathizers of the Communist Party of Thailand (CPT), followed by the arrest of noted social critic Sulak Sivaraksa.

The Vietnamese occupation of Cambodia continued to be the main focus of Thai foreign policy. In a year marked by frequent armed clashes between Thai and Vietnamese troops along the Thai–Cambodian border, representatives of Thailand and Vietnam were unable to initiate a dialogue aimed at finding a non-military solution to the problem.

In April, Prem led a group of Thai officials and businessmen on visits to the United States, Canada, Yugoslavia, Denmark, and West Germany. A goal of the trip was to encourage trade with Thailand. Prem also wished to gain reaffirmation of U.S. support for Thai security

and increased military sales, particularly of F-16A fighter aircraft, to Thailand. No decision was announced regarding the aircraft, but the United States did sell 40 M-48 tanks to the Thais, thereby doubling their tank force.

The government continued to fight inflation successfully, but difficulties persisted with the balance of trade, which had reached a record $3.87 billion deficit in 1983. The government curbed credits for imports, ordered commercial banks to limit credit expansion to 18 percent, emphasized growth of exports, and, in November, devalued the baht by more than 17 percent. These efforts, and higher values for rice, rubber, maize, and textile exports, were expected to reduce the 1984 deficit.

Thailand was also faced with soaring budget deficits, which were projected to reach a record high of $1.5 billion in fiscal 1985. Nevertheless, the gross domestic product was expected to grow by an estimated 5.5 percent in 1984, only slightly below the 5.8 percent rate of 1983.

See STATISTICS OF THE WORLD.   A.R.

THEATER. The American theater presented a mixed picture in 1984. Gross revenues reached a record $227 million for the 1983–1984 Broadway season, but attendance had declined 6 percent from the previous season. Only 36 new productions had opened, down from 50 the season before. Resident professional companies across the United States continued to enliven and enrich the theater.

Broadway. Tom Stoppard's *The Real Thing* got the year off to an exhilarating start. The play, with an Anglo-American cast headed by Jeremy Irons and Glenn Close, won high praise for its author, its performers, and its director, Mike Nichols. The first American original play of the year was *Glengarry Glen Ross,* David Mamet's searing look at a group of foul-mouthed, predatory Chicago real estate salesmen. One of the most enthusiastically received new plays was David Rabe's *Hurlyburly,* a sardonic look at adult delinquency in Hollywood, with Mike Nichols once more directing.

Peter Ustinov visited Broadway rather briefly in April as the great Ludwig in his own comic fantasy, *Beethoven's Tenth.* Another April offering was *The Golden Age* by A. R. Gurney, Jr., suggested by Henry James's *The Aspern*

Papers. Although it starred Irene Worth as the onetime darling of the 1920's literary set, the Gurney distillation received a cool critical reception and failed to achieve a run. A generally harsh critical verdict also was handed down on Arthur Kopit's *End of the World,* which starred John Shea, Barnard Hughes, and Linda Hunt in a mock-detective play with a deeply serious theme: the threat of nuclear destruction.

An American classic returned to Broadway with the revival of Arthur Miller's *Death of a Salesman,* staged by Michael Rudman. The production, starring Dustin Hoffman as a desperately jaunty Willy Loman, together with Kate Reid and John Malkovich, was enthusi-

Dustin Hoffman, effectively made up as the middle-aged Willy Loman, was heaped with praise for his performance in a revival of Arthur Miller's Death of a Salesman.

astically received, and it reopened in September after its original spring and summer run. In a contrastingly escapist vein, the Circle in the Square had a new success with Noel Coward's once slightly scandalous *Design for Living,* the first Broadway revival of the 1933 hit. Jill Clayburgh, Frank Langella, and Raul Julia starred.

The Royal Shakespeare Company arrived in October with a cast headed by Derek Jacobi and Sinead Cusack in a repertory consisting of William Shakespeare's *Much Ado About Nothing* and Edmond Rostand's *Cyrano de Bergerac.* On a smaller scale, Ian McKellen, one of Britain's foremost actors, gave a bravura display of the histrionic art in his one-man show, *Acting Shakespeare.* On the American side, Whoopi Goldberg presented her one-woman show of stand-up, black-oriented comedy and political satire, called, appropriately enough, *Whoopi Goldberg,* and supervised by Mike Nichols.

With several new plays opening in the fall, Broadway experienced a modest upturn in activity. *Ma Rainey's Black Bottom,* by August Wilson, featured Theresa Merritt in a drama with music, about the legendary blues singer. Italian playwright Dario Fo's farce about bureaucracy and politics, *Accidental Death of an Anarchist,* opened in November starring Jonathan Pryce, Patti LuPone, and Bill Irwin. It closed after a brief run, however. Janis Paige and Kevin McCarthy shared top billing in Lawrence Roman's comedy *Alone Together.*

The most talked-about Broadway musical of the year was *Sunday in the Park With George,* by composer-lyricist Stephen Sondheim and author-director James Lapine. Inspired by French painter Georges Seurat's 1886 masterpiece *A Sunday Afternoon on the Island of La Grande Jatte,* the musical in its first act dealt with Seurat (Mandy Patinkin); Dot, his mistress-model (Bernadette Peters); and the creation of the painting. At the stunning conclusion of the act, the life-size, finished artwork has been assembled with actors, stage sets, and lighting. The second act, set 100 years later, focused on the fortunes of Seurat's descendant in the 1980's. Although critical response was mixed, *Sunday in the Park* was praised for its innovativeness and won popular acclaim.

Other musicals included *Shirley MacLaine*

The cast of Sunday in the Park with George, a musical based on the life of French painter Georges Seurat, creates a live replica of the artist's masterpiece, A Sunday Afternoon on the Island of La Grande Jatte. The work of composer Stephen Sondheim, with James Lapine directing, Sunday opened with Bernadette Peters (far right), as Seurat's mistress and Mandy Patinkin as Seurat.

on Broadway, in which the recent Oscar winner (see biography in PEOPLE IN THE NEWS) dazzled New Yorkers with her singing, dancing, and clowning, and The Rink, by Terrence McNally (book) and the songwriting team of John Kander and Fred Ebb; it starred Chita Rivera and Liza Minnelli in a tough, sentimental saga about a mother-daughter reunion in an abandoned roller-skating rink scheduled for demolition.

Awards and Honors. The 1984 Pulitzer Prize for best American play went to David Mamet's Glengarry Glen Ross, which also won the New York Drama Critics Circle Award for best American drama. The Critics Circle selected The Real Thing as the season's best play and Sunday in the Park With George as best musical. The critics also honored Samuel Beckett with a special citation for the body of his work. Antoinette Perry (Tony) Awards were won by The Real Thing for best play and by the Jerry Herman–Harvey Fierstein collaboration La Cage aux Folles for best musical. For outstanding performances, the Tony voters chose Jeremy Irons and Glenn Close (The Real Thing), George

Hearn (La Cage aux Folles), and Chita Rivera (The Rink). Directorial honors went to Mike Nichols for The Real Thing and Arthur Laurents for La Cage aux Folles.

Off Broadway. It was a stimulating year for Off Broadway theater. The Public Theater presented a series of plays by Eastern European dramatists—among them, dissident Czech playwright Vaclav Havel's A Private View. Woza Albert! was a spirited South African import that speculated on what would happen were Jesus Christ to visit that racially divided country today. Wendy Wasserstein's Isn't It Romantic proved to be a successful, touching comedy about mothers, daughters, and the struggle for freedom from dependency. A new Beth Henley play, The Miss Firecracker Contest, was a comedy about Southern oddballs. Another new play that enjoyed a lengthy run was Dennis McIntyre's Split Second, a drama about a black policeman's crisis of conscience.

Revivals and musicals provided interest as well. A succession of impressive Samuel Beckett plays included revivals of Rockaby and Footfalls—performed on the same bill by Billie

Whitelaw—as well as *Endgame*. Lanford Wilson's sprawling slice-of-life drama *Balm in Gilead*, first produced Off Off Broadway in 1965, was staged in a successful revival by John Malkovich. Off Broadway musicals included *A . . . My Name Is Alice,* a feminist revue by Joan Micklin Silver and Julianne Boyd, and the Jewish Repertory Theater's *Kuni Leml*, based on the Avrom Goldfadn Yiddish farce. Critical opinion was divided over the New York Shakespeare Festival's innovative English-language version of Puccini's *La Bohème,* produced by Joseph Papp and directed by Wilford Leach, with Linda Ronstadt as one of the production's three Mimis. *Diamonds,* a celebration of baseball featuring the work of more than 30 contributors and staged by Harold Prince, opened in December.

Musical Comedy at the Opera. The New York City Opera received a $5 million gift to establish a musical-comedy season, beginning in 1986. The City Opera—which will continue its regular operatic schedule—has occasionally performed pieces primarily associated with Broadway; in 1984, the company put on *Sweeney*

Todd, the Stephen Sondheim musical that opened on Broadway in 1978.

Regional Theater. Regional professional theater continued to flourish and to be an increasingly important source of new plays.

The Yale Repertory Theater of New Haven premiered Athol Fugard's *The Road to Mecca* and Wole Soyinka's *A Play of Giants,* as well as *Ma Rainey's Black Bottom.* The Actors Theater of Louisville's Humana Festival of New American Plays, now in its eighth year, presented Emily Mann's *Execution of Justice,* based on San Francisco's Dan White murder case, and other new scripts. *Jonestown Express* by James Reston, Jr., based on the 1978 Guyana tragedy, was mounted by the Trinity Square Repertory Company of Providence.

Cleveland's Great Lakes Shakespeare Festival honored Thornton Wilder with a weekend symposium, in connection with which it presented the American premiere of *The Alcestiad* (1955), Wilder's final full-length play. Los Angeles playgoers saw premieres of, among others, Mark Medoff's *The Hands of Its Enemy* and John Guare's *Woman and Water.*

Glenn Close and Jeremy Irons won Tony awards for their roles in Tom Stoppard's tale of infidelity, The Real Thing, *directed by Mike Nichols.*

At the Guthrie Theater in Minneapolis, Peter Sellars amalgamated Maxim Gorki's *Summerfolk* (transplanted to the present-day United States) with Gershwin music, creating a four-hour-plus entertainment entitled *Hang On to Me*. In September, the 26-year-old Sellars, much in the news because of his controversial productions of plays and operas, assumed the post of artistic director of plays to be presented jointly by the American National Theater Academy (ANTA) and the Kennedy Center in Washington, D.C. Sellars's long-range task is the creation of an American national theater company.   J.B.

TOGO. *See* STATISTICS OF THE WORLD.

TONGA. *See* STATISTICS OF THE WORLD.

TRANSPORTATION. Economic recovery in 1984 improved the fortunes of commercial transportation businesses battered by recession and deregulation earlier in the decade. Railroad traffic was consistently higher than in 1983, and the industry's income skyrocketed in the first half of the year. The shipping industry was boosted by strong U.S. import levels and a new regulatory reform law. Trucking companies appeared to have completed the transition to a deregulated environment, and the industry on average benefited from tax relief signed by President Ronald Reagan in July. Airline performance improved in 1984, with some carriers reporting record earnings.

BUS INDUSTRY

The bus industry was the exception to the general trend toward increased profits, as stiff competition from airlines and a resurgence in auto travel prevented carriers from winning back passengers. The Interstate Commerce Commission (ICC) reported that net income for the ten largest carriers declined from 1982's meager $6.9 million profit to a $24.6 million loss in 1983, partly as a result of a seven-week strike late in the year against the largest bus company, Greyhound Lines. Bus companies were not expected to make significant improvements in 1984, as ridership levels appeared to remain stagnant.

RAILROADS

Final 1983 statistics released by the ICC indicated that total freight traffic in ton-miles rose 3.5 percent above 1982 levels, while net carrier operating income for major railroads reached $1.3 billion, up from about $800 million in 1982. Railroad officials were expecting even better figures for 1984.

Santa Fe–Southern Pacific Merger. The Southern Pacific Company and Santa Fe Industries, the parent holding companies of the Southern Pacific Transportation Company and the Atchison, Topeka & Santa Fe Railway Company, announced a merger, aimed at creating a single 26,000-mile system, to be known as the Santa Fe Southern Pacific (SFSP). The new road would compete directly in many markets with the newly formed Western rail giant, the Union Pacific System. ICC approval was required before Southern Pacific's operations could actually be integrated into the new company.

Conrail. The Department of Transportation (DOT) took action to sell now-profitable Conrail. The government-owned freight railroad, which had absorbed more than $7 billion in subsidies since its creation in 1976, went into the black, apparently for good, in 1981. Conrail had $313 million in net income in 1983 and forecast net income ranging between $450 million and $500 million for 1984.

Conrail's improved financial status attracted a host of prospective buyers. However, the complexity of the transaction hindered negotiations. Transportation Secretary Elizabeth Hanford Dole announced in early September that the original list of 15 bidders had been winnowed down to three. Under consideration were $1 billion-plus offers by Norfolk Southern Corporation, the southern railroad holding company; by Alleghany Corporation; and by a group of investors headed by hotel magnate J. Willard Marriott, Jr., and members of the Bass family of Texas.

Bankruptcy. The Chicago, Rock Island & Pacific Railroad faded into history in June as its remaining rail assets were taken over by the new Chicago Pacific Corporation, a real estate holding company, ending a nine-year bankruptcy proceeding.

Deregulation. The ICC continued to free more traffic from rate regulation, exempting poultry, meat, and dairy products, new highway containers and trailers, frozen foods shipments, and miscellaneous agricultural commodities. The ICC also eased burdens for carriers operating in Texas when the federal agency stripped

407

Miami's gleaming new Metrorail, gliding past the palm trees at 70 miles an hour, was one of several public transportation projects undertaken by cities determined to reduce problems caused by clogged and pollution-producing highways. Some experts doubted that Metrorail could attract enough passengers—at $1 a ride—to cover its costs, but rail officials were optimistic. "Anyone in his right mind," said one, "will at least try it."

the powerful Railroad Commission of Texas of its authority to regulate rail shipments moving solely within the state. That action was taken when the state commission refused to bring its railroad rules into conformity with federal regulation, as required by law.

Railroads and Trucking. The ICC ended restrictions against railroads that sought to buy trucking companies or to provide new trucking services not directly related to their railroad operations. The Denver & Rio Grande Western Railroad became the first carrier to receive nationwide trucking authority, although most major railroads by the end of the year had acquired at least regional trucking rights or were providing intermodal trucking services not regulated by the ICC. Norfolk Southern became the first major railroad to try to take advantage of the relaxed rail-truck purchase rules. That railroad asked the ICC to approve its proposed $315 million purchase from PepsiCo of profitable North American Van Lines, which is the nation's fifth largest general freight trucking company and a major household goods hauler.

Amtrak. The government-owned National Passenger Railroad Corporation (Amtrak) was plagued by a series of accidents in July, claiming a total of 11 lives. In one of the worst accidents, on July 7, a Montreal-bound train was derailed after heavy rains had undermined an embankment; it plunged into a gully in rural Vermont, leaving five people dead and about 150 injured. In another serious accident, on July 23, two trains collided in Queens, N.Y.; one passenger was killed and more than 100 injured. There were indications that a signalman had minute amounts of marijuana and cocaine in his urine, but officials believe the amounts were too small to warrant the conclusion that drug use was a factor in the accident. However, the Federal Railroad Administration has been increasingly concerned about both alcohol and drug use among railroad employees, and the agency has proposed new rules to require routine testing of employees for alcohol and drug use.

High-Speed Trains. The federal government provided $1.25 million for a feasibility study on a high-speed rail system between Los Angeles and Las Vegas, which supporters hoped to build by 1991. However, an ambitious plan for what would have been America's first high-speed rail system, between Los Angeles and San Diego, was scrapped because of a lack of available capital. Opposition to the project had been voiced by residents of small towns along the routes, and there was skepticism that the system could attract enough ridership to be profitable.

MASS TRANSIT

An 11-mile portion of Miami's planned 21-mile-metrorail system finally opened in May, after numerous delays and cost overruns, with the rest expected to open in 1985. Planning and preparations continued for a 150-mile system in Los Angeles County, to be partially funded by a half-cent sales tax. In San Francisco, a $1.3 billion extension of the Bay Area Rapid Transit (BART) system was planned, and the city's famous cable cars returned to the streets after a 20-month, $60 million rehabilitation program.

SHIPPING

The tide came in for the shipping industry, as new U.S. shipping reform legislation gave carriers more operating flexibility and economic recovery filled their cargo holds. Pressures to discount shipping rates eased substantially in most trade lanes, although a heavy eastbound traffic imbalance kept rates low in the U.S.–Pacific trades. Rate wars on container traffic on all trade routes were expected to develop, as the result of fleet expansions by major steamship lines.

Shipping Act of 1984. On March 20, President Reagan signed into law the long-awaited Shipping Act of 1984, the first comprehensive revision of maritime economic and operation regulations since 1916. From the carriers' standpoint, one of the law's major benefits was to reduce threats to many of their business activities from antitrust proceedings by the Department of Justice, which during the 1970's had successfully prosecuted many carriers for such violations. The law also permits U.S. ship lines to participate in international conferences to set rates jointly, allows individual shippers and carriers to enter into service contracts for rate discounts, preserves open membership for conferences serving the United States and the

right of independent rate and service action by individual lines, eliminates time-consuming Federal Maritime Commission review of conference agreements, and gives the FMC new powers to retaliate against foreign ship lines or governments that attempt to restrict competition from U.S.–flag carriers. The FMC spent much of the year promulgating regulations to implement the law; these were to be completed in 1985.

Sea-Land. Sea-Land Service, still the world's largest privately owned shipping company,

Bound for Vancouver, the 31,000-ton freighter Aqua City *leaves Yokohama under a pair of computer-controlled sails designed to reduce the vessel's fuel consumption by harnessing power from the wind. The Japanese builders of the unique ship hoped the* Aqua City *would usher in a new age of fuel-efficient ocean transport.*

with assets and annual sales both in excess of $1 billion, was spun off from its parent corporation, the R. J. Reynolds Industries conglomerate, in June. Renamed Sea-Land Corporation, the company enjoyed strong business in early 1984 and announced a $100 million fleet modernization plan.

Shipyards. U.S. shipyards remained apprehensive about their future as a result of the Reagan administration's decision to cease subsidizing commercial vessel construction. When Exxon Shipping Company ordered two tankers at $250 million from National Steel and Shipbuilding Company, it was the first major commercial shipbuilding order in three years. It seemed evident that shipyards would have to seek work from the Navy to remain in business.

Barge Industry. The major news in the barge industry was an ICC decision to approve CSX Corporation's proposed acquisition of American Commercial Lines Inc., the largest operator on the U.S. inland waterways and a subsidiary of the Texas Gas Resources Corporation, which CSX had acquired in 1983. It was the first merger in U.S. history between a major railroad and a barge line. The barge industry, fearful that CSX's move would encourage other railroads to buy barge lines competing for their bulk commodities business, had filed suit against the merger, but a federal appeals court upheld the ICC decision late in the year.

TRUCKING

The trucking industry's financial performance improved, and traffic levels were higher around the United States, although only some carriers fared well, while others struggled. Final ICC statistics for 1983 indicated that the net income of the 100 largest U.S. trucking companies had risen to $360 million, more than four times the level of 1982 (which was said to be the worst year in the industry's history). The carriers' net income continued to rise in small increments in the first half of 1984.

Tax Relief. In July, President Reagan signed legislation increasing the diesel fuel tax to 15 cents per gallon, as a means of producing revenues for the Highway Trust Fund, in place of higher truck registration taxes. Owner-operators, who had staged a brief but violent strike in early 1983 to protest higher registration fees, received temporary tax exemptions.

Deregulation. The ICC continued to loosen its regulatory authority over the industry. The agency relaxed restrictions on equipment leasing between trucking companies, corporate truck fleets, and owner-operators; allowed truckers to offer tariff rates to specific shippers; permitted contact carriers to serve entire industries rather than seeking rights to serve only individual shippers; eased rules for acquiring temporary trucking authority; and allowed truckers to raise their rates in seven days or to reduce them in one day, provided that the action was taken by an individual carrier. Responding to congressional pressure, however, the agency rejected a proposal to withdraw antitrust immunity for joint rate-setting by truckers on shipments weighing less than 1,000 pounds. The proposal had been advanced by less-than-truckload shippers who claimed rate-setting bureaus had taken advantage of immunity to gouge them with high shipping rates, while other truckers hauled full truckloads at discount rate levels.

AVIATION

The upswing in air travel that began in the spring of 1984 continued through the summer, in part because a strong dollar overseas made international travel more attractive to more Americans. The surge in air traffic, however, led to increasing delays at airports, primarily because of scheduling difficulties.

As problems intensified during the summer, over a dozen major carriers, led by Eastern Air Lines, received an antitrust exemption from the Department of Justice and the Civil Aeronautics Board to allow the airlines to discuss coordinating flight schedules to reduce backups at the most delay-plagued major airports. In October the CAB approved an agreement among the major airlines that would spread out flights more evenly over peak hours. The new schedules went into effect November 1.

Braniff Flies Again. Braniff, which declared bankruptcy in 1982, took to the air again in March 1984, with a new corporate parent, the Hyatt Hotels Corporation. The airline's original plan was to focus on business customers. However, losses were heavier than expected, and in September, Braniff announced it would become a low-cost carrier offering unrestricted discount fares.

Waiting to be cleared for departure, planes line up at New York's LaGuardia Airport, one of the six most seriously clogged U.S. terminals. Competing for customers, many airlines overscheduled flights during peak travel times.

Bankruptcies. Continental Air Lines, which in 1983 had filed for reorganization under federal bankruptcy law, was successful in winning a series of legal battles, including a decision by a bankruptcy judge that the airline was justified in scrapping its contract with the pilot's union. (After failing to win wage concessions, Continental had laid off virtually all its employees at the time it filed for reorganization, then began hiring back a lower number at far lower salaries.) More legal skirmishes were anticipated before Continental files a comprehensive reorganization plan in 1985. In the meantime, the airline's finances slowly improved.

Bankruptcy claimed Miami-based Air Florida in July. During the late 1970's, Air Florida flourished as an intrastate carrier, and in the wake of deregulation, it expanded into the Northeast and the Caribbean and began flights to London. But deregulation led to stiff competition and fare wars on these routes, and the airline lost $135 million over the last three years. A takeover by Chicago-based Midway Airlines enabled Air Florida planes to return to the air under new auspices in October.

Innovations on Planes. October 15 saw the launching of an experimental new service on airborne commercial jetliners: pay telephones. The equipment, supplied by Airfone Inc., was introduced on 20 planes, with considerable expansion of the service expected in the following months. However, the future of the service was placed in doubt when the Federal Communications Commission in mid-November voted against assigning permanent frequencies for air-to-ground phone calls.

In late October the U.S. Department of Transportation ordered the installation, within three years, of fire-resistant seat covers in all large airliners flying in U.S. airspace. The new seat covers, required on planes having 30 or more seats and weighing at least 12,500 pounds, should give passengers more time to evacuate an aircraft during a fire.

New Commercial Aircraft. The A-320, a new 150-seat, fuel-efficient, narrow-body jet, is the leading candidate to replace such aging transports as Boeing 727. Pan American World Airways announced in September that it would purchase 28 jetliners, including 16 A-320's,

TRINIDAD AND TOBAGO

from the French-based European consortium Airbus Industrie. In all, Airbus had more than 50 firm orders for the A-320, with delivery of the commercial jets scheduled to begin in the late 1980's.

During the first quarter of 1984, McDonnell Douglas concluded a deal with American Airlines for the largest commercial jet transport order in U.S. history. Earlier, McDonnell Douglas had gambled by leasing 20 MD-80's (also known as DC-9 Super 80's) to American, taking the risk that American might return them. But the airline signed up to buy 67 of the twin-engine transports, with an option to purchase another 100. Industry analysts placed the deal's value at over $1 billion. McDonnell Douglas followed this coup with another important sale, which kept alive the DC-10 production line, originally scheduled to be shut down in 1984. Federal Express bought six of the jets, and McDonnell Douglas was reportedly discussing further sales with other airlines.

See also AUTOMOBILE INDUSTRY.

R.J.K. & R.B.

TRINIDAD AND TOBAGO. *See* STATISTICS OF THE WORLD. *See also* CARIBBEAN COUNTRIES.

TUNISIA. On January 6, 1984, after more than a week of rioting in the capital and elsewhere sparked by the government's decision to double food prices, Tunisia's president-for-life, Habib Bourguiba, announced that the price increases would be rescinded. According to official records, the rioting left 89 dead and 938 wounded (unofficial estimates put the figures higher). Between 800 and 900 people were arrested. The government's initial decision to raise prices had been a response to harsh economic realities. Roughly three-quarters of the government's huge budget deficit was attributable to subsidization of food staples such as bread, semolina, and noodles; the prices of these products had not been changed since the early 1960's.

The bread riots exposed serious conflicts within the regime. On January 7, Bourguiba fired the minister of the interior, Driss Guiga, on the ground that he had actively conspired to exploit the riots in an effort to unseat Premier Muhammad M'zali. Guiga, who fled the country, was later tried in absentia and convicted of high treason. A number of rioters were also tried. After death sentences for eight youths

The twin engine MD–80, from the McDonnell Douglas Corporation, was chosen by American Airlines in a $1 billion purchase deal involving 67 of the planes; it was said to be the biggest order for commercial jets in U.S. aviation history.

were read on May 26, widespread public appeals induced Bourguiba to intervene as a moderating figure. On June 19 he commuted the death sentences to forced labor for life.

Prior to the riots, two secular political parties, the Movement of Democratic Socialists and the Movement of Popular Unity, had acquired legal status. Both acted with moderation during the riots, thereby remaining in the good graces of the ruling Destour Socialist Party.

Despite the government's efforts to promote regional peace, tensions persisted between Libya and Tunisia, with several border skirmishes in mid-May. Earlier that month, Tripoli had accused the Bourguiba government of complicity in a coup against Libyan leader Muammar al-Qaddafi; Tunisia, in response, temporarily withdrew its ambassador.

See STATISTICS OF THE WORLD.   K.J.B.

TURKEY. Prime Minister Turgut Özal and his ruling Motherland Party, which came to power by winning the November 1983 parliamentary elections, passed a crucial test of popular support by finishing first in local elections on March 25, 1984. Özal's conservative party took 41.3 percent of the vote and a majority of the mayoral and city council seats. The election campaign was marred by scattered violence, primarily in rural areas. Several people were killed and more than 100 injured.

Internal Security. Although guarded efforts by the press and some politicians to secure an amnesty for political prisoners were unsuccessful, the Council of Ministers, in July, decided to lift martial law from 26 of Turkey's 67 provinces. Meanwhile, complaints of overcrowding, poor living conditions, and torture in Turkey's prisons continued. In January the European Commission on Human Rights announced it had gathered evidence showing that the military government that ruled Turkey from 1980 to 1983 had tortured and otherwise mistreated hundreds of political prisoners.

Despite the claim that Turkey had returned to democracy, freedom of expression was still limited. Popular newspapers were temporarily shut down for violating martial law regulations, and union activity was curtailed. In August, 56 persons were put on trial for publishing and distributing a petition calling for an ending of the use of torture, the reinstitution of demo-

cratic rights, and changes in the 1982 constitution.

Economy. Prime Minister Özal embarked on a program designed to open up the economy to international market forces and make Turkey a more competitive trading country. Consumer imports were now freely permitted, although they were subject to heavy duties. Restrictions on the possession of foreign currency and on foreign travel were also lifted, and the government raised interest rates on bank deposits to encourage savings and curb speculative land and gold investment. The Turkish trade deficit for the first ten months was down 4.6 percent from 1983 levels.

According to official statistics, economic growth in 1983 was somewhat disappointing, with gross national product rising 3.2 percent, less than the targeted rate. Inflation in 1984 was running at around 40 percent; unemployment late in the year was 16.5 percent.

Foreign Affairs. Turkish-Greek relations almost reached a breaking point in early March when Turkish warships in the northern Aegean apparently fired on a Greek naval vessel and several Greek fishing boats. Greece recalled its ambassador and placed its military on alert, but later accepted Turkey's explanation that the Turkish ships were conducting artillery practice in international Aegean waters and that shell fragments had fallen on a Greek observation vessel that had entered the area.

Turkey's exchange of ambassadors with the newly declared Turkish Republic of Northern Cyprus in April led to another angry protest by Greece. Turkey continued to be the Cypriot Turks' sole supporter, offering them generous aid and protecting them with about 20,000 troops stationed on the island. U.S. congressional sentiment resulted in the reduction of military aid to Turkey to $700 million from the $759 million requested by President Ronald Reagan for fiscal year 1985.

As part of its "multidimensional foreign policy," Turkey has been solidifying ties with neighboring Muslim countries. Among other actions, Prime Minister Özal visited Iran, Iraq, and Libya and signed a trade agreement in Tehran.

See STATISTICS OF THE WORLD.   P.J.M.

TUVALU. See STATISTICS OF THE WORLD.

U

UGANDA. Renewed guerrilla activity during 1984 by the National Resistance Army (NRA) belied the claims of the government of President Milton Obote to have solved Uganda's long-standing insurgency problem. The government also was accused of widespread human rights violations.

In January, NRA rebels captured (and later released) 11 Red Cross workers, of whom four were Europeans and seven were Ugandans. In February, NRA forces mounted a large-scale attack against the army and police barracks as well as the local prison at Masindi, some 120 miles north of Kampala, an area that had not previously witnessed rebel activity. The rebels claimed to have killed more than 200 members of the government security forces, while losing only five of their own men. Five weeks later, the NRA released the prisoners it had captured at Masindi, with the exception of 11 Ugandan soldiers who allegedly elected to join the rebels.

In another incident, in January, four Europeans were killed and one wounded in separate attacks by unidentified gunmen near Kampala. The attacks were the most serious against members of the white community since the end of the dictatorship of Idi Amin in 1979. The government blamed the NRA, but the rebel group denied any connection with the killings.

In the summer, a U.S. official charged that, as part of government efforts to crush rebel activity, more than 100,000 civilians had been killed by the military in Uganda, or died of starvation as a result of military policies, since 1981. The Obote government denied the allegations and, in retaliation, suspended an agreement that provided for the training of Ugandan troops in the United States.

A recent upturn in Uganda's economic performance has been due in large part to its strong agriculture. President Obote was able to claim in mid-1984 that, since 1980, tea production had tripled and coffee output had

Ugandan government troops remain alert after retaking the town of Kapeka from rebels in August. Guerrilla activity persisted despite claims by the government that the insurgency problem had been solved.

risen by 92 percent. Food production had improved sufficiently to allow Uganda to export 40,000 metric tons of maize to Tanzania. Uganda's levels of production and exports still remained far below those of the years preceding the Amin dictatorship, but Uganda enjoyed a balance-of-payments surplus for the first time in ten years thanks to increased aid flows.

In June the government released a budget for 1984–1985, providing for a 90 percent increase in spending. The minimum wage for civil servants was increased, along with producer prices for major crops. The president also announced abolition of the dual exchange rate for currency.

See STATISTICS OF THE WORLD.   E.B.

UNION OF SOVIET SOCIALIST REPUBLICS.

The Soviet Union, which had only two significant leadership changes in the 55 years before Leonid Brezhnev died in November 1982, experienced a new transition little more than a year later, when Yuri Andropov died in February 1984. His successor, Konstantin Chernenko, was three years older than Andropov and himself appeared to be ill at times. While Andropov's tenure had given promise of change, Chernenko's election appeared to some to be a step backward.

Death of Andropov. Because Andropov had not been seen in public since August 1983 and was known to be ill, the announcement of his death, on February 9, was not unexpected. Andropov actually accomplished little in his 15 months in office. He replaced some middle-level officials, moved against corruption, and endorsed economic reform. But he removed or demoted only 8 percent of the voting members of the Central Committee. He tried without success to stop the NATO installation of U.S. Pershing II and cruise missiles in Western Europe.

Accession of Chernenko. On February 13 the Central Committee, doubtless ratifying a Politburo decision, named Chernenko general secretary (see biography in PEOPLE IN THE NEWS). In some ways, Chernenko seemed an improbable choice. Chernenko, aged 72, reportedly had emphysema and heart problems, and he looked feeble in public. A former party secretary in Siberia, he had been Brezhnev's chief aide for a number of years and became one of an inner core of five key Politburo members. When Brezhnev died, Chernenko was given the post Andropov had held, secretary for ideology and relations with foreign Communists.

Chernenko's selection as general secretary was announced four days after Andropov died; because Andropov's own selection had been announced only two days after Brezhnev died, it seemed possible that there was a succession struggle.

Political Developments. In any event, the extent of Chernenko's influence in office was not entirely clear. On April 11, he was elected chairman of the Presidium of the Supreme Soviet, or head of state, and a minor publicity campaign was launched to increase his authority. After Foreign Minister Andrei Gromyko and Defense Minister Dmitri Ustinov appeared to overshadow him in March and April, he seemed to take a more prominent role—for example, by hosting a summit meeting with French President François Mitterrand. Then, during the summer, Chernenko virtually disappeared. Speculation in the West about his health was followed by another flurry of actions apparently designed to demonstrate his authority. The head of the military general staff, Marshal Nikolai Ogarkov, was removed on September 6 and replaced by Marshal Sergei Akhromeyev. On September 22, Chernenko received a medal on his 73rd birthday, and he was described as supreme commander-in-chief of the armed forces, a post almost never referred to publicly. On October 16 he gave an interview to the Washington *Post* in which he sought to counter contentions that he was in poor health, but these rumors persisted.

On October 23, a special plenary session of the Central Committee was held to discuss problems in agriculture. Reports had indicated that Mikhail Gorbachev, the Politburo's only specialist on agriculture and a prime contender for high office in the Soviet Union, was studying alternatives to the agricultural system. However, Gorbachev did not speak at the session. In his report, Chernenko advocated continuing the irrigation program Brezhnev had begun.

If Gorbachev suffered a reverse in October, he nevertheless was clearly a rising star. Andropov had made Gorbachev the Central Com-

The open coffin of Soviet leader Yuri Andropov, dead at 69 after 15 months in office, is carried through Moscow's Red Square by a phalanx of high-ranking officials, including Andropov's successor, Konstantin Chernenko (next to honor guard at right of bier), Prime Minister Nikolai Tikhonov (following Chernenko), and Foreign Minister Andrei Gromyko (partly hidden). Western leaders who attended the Communist chief's Kremlin Wall interment included U.S. Vice-President George Bush, British Prime Minister Margaret Thatcher, and outgoing Canadian Prime Minister Pierre Trudeau.

mittee secretary for personnel (traditional responsibility of the heir apparent), for agriculture and light industry, and for supervision of economic planning; Chernenko also gave him responsibility for ideology and relations with foreign Communists. In addition, Gorbachev took on a highly public role in December, when he made a visit to Great Britain, spoke before Parliament there, and conferred with Prime Minister Margaret Thatcher. Gorbachev's presumed chief rival, Grigorii Romanov, got a narrow portfolio from Chernenko: coordination of the defense industry, the machinery industry, the military, and the security organs, with responsibilities overlapping those of Ustinov. Ustinov himself was said to have suffered a stroke in October, and he died in December. He was replaced by a career officer, Marshal Sergei L. Sokolov.

Economy and Defense. Sharp fluctuations in weather make it difficult to speak about trends in Soviet agriculture, and the situation varies from one product to another. Weather in 1983 was reasonably good, and Chernenko reported that that year had seen the greatest total agricultural output ever. But overall agricultural production fell in 1984; and expenditures of foreign currency reserves for imported feed grains remained an enormous drain on the Soviet economy.

Elsewhere, the increase in the rate of economic growth that began in 1982 continued. In the first half of 1984, industrial production was 4.5 percent above the comparable figure of a year earlier. During the same period, oil production fell by one-tenth of 1 percent.

On September 29, the last segment of track was laid for a new 2,000-mile trans-Siberian railroad line. The railroad, known as the Baykal-Amur Mainline (BAM), runs from Ust-Kut northwest of Lake Baykal to Komsomolsk on the Amur River near the Sea of Japan. It lies

100 to 300 miles north of the old Trans-Siberian Railroad, which runs near the Chinese border. Besides its national-security role, BAM will open for development vast mineral and timber resources in southeastern Siberia. Construction, which began in 1974, was hampered by the climate and terrain. More years of work will be required to complete 20 miles of tunnels.

Despite such advances as BAM, long-term development remains the most serious problem with the economy, and a technological lag has hindered the Soviet effort to keep up with the West militarily. Soviet military problems were dramatized in May by an explosion at a naval arms depot near Murmansk, which may have destroyed much of the missile inventory of the Northern Fleet. In November, it was announced that military expenditures in 1985 would increase by 12 percent.

Domestic Policy. Andropov gave the impression that he was determined to push reform. That would have required dramatic changes, such as an increase in prices of some subsidized commodities and an end to virtually absolute job security. Chernenko's acceptance speech, however, featured a pledge for "social jus-

tice"—usually a code phrase for a maintenance of the old social policy. In later statements, Chernenko remained lukewarm in his support for economic reform.

An energy program announced in April assumed unrealistically that petroleum production would grow until the year 2000. In education, the major new development was the addition of a year to the school program, which will consist of 11 years of six-day weeks. In agriculture, reemphasis of the 1965 irrigation decision seemed almost a parody of policy.

Leeway was permitted to dissidents who remained within the system, but those who left it politically were treated harshly. Emigration almost ceased. Restrictions were tightened on Western contacts with dissidents and individuals who had been denied requests to emigrate. The new policy was applied to Andrei Sakharov, the nuclear physicist who had won the 1975 Nobel Peace Prize, and his wife, Elena Bonner. In 1980, Sakharov had been exiled to Gorky, where foreigners are banned, but Bonner had been allowed to travel and meet foreigners. On May 4, the Soviet news agency Tass charged that Bonner had planned to obtain a visa in order to receive medical treatment

A giant track-laying machine lowers a section of rail onto the roadbed of the Baykal-Amur Mainline (BAM), the 2,000-mile-long Siberian rail system called "the project of the century" by its Soviet builders. Completed in September after a decade of herculean labor, BAM was expected to have a major impact on the development of Siberia's vast natural resources

Politburo member Mikhail Gorbachev, who favorably impressed Prime Minister Margaret Thatcher during his visit to Great Britain in December, was regarded as a strong contender for the future leadership of the Soviet Union.

abroad. Sakharov had begun a hunger strike in support of his wife's visa request. On May 30, however, Tass denied Sakharov was fasting, and on August 20, Moscow Radio said he was "alive and well." Bonner reportedly was convicted in August of slandering the state and sentenced to five years of internal exile in Gorky.

Foreign Relations. The deployment of Pershing II and cruise missiles in Western Europe, begun in late 1983, was a major concern in 1984. The Soviets carried out their threat to break off talks on intermediate-range missiles if the deployment began and said they would not talk again until the missiles were withdrawn. With strategic arms reduction talks also broken off, arms-control efforts had come to an impasse. The Soviet boycott of the summer Olympic Games in Los Angeles reflected the new tensions. (*See also* SPORTS: THE OLYMPIC GAMES).

By summer, the Soviet Union began to modify its posture. The first sign came in an appeal to the United States for talks on antisatellite (ASAT) weapons. Later, angry disagreement on the ASAT talks demonstrated that major suspicions must still be overcome. Although the United States accepted a Soviet offer to meet in Vienna in September, the talks were not held. The Soviet Union demanded, as a sign of U.S. seriousness, a matching of its own moratorium on ASAT testing. Refusing, the United States insisted that the talks include offensive weapons as well as the ASAT weapons. The two nations also argued over whether the talks would deal with the militarization of space. However, the Soviet Union accepted an invitation for Gromyko to meet with President Ronald Reagan in Washington in September while Gromyko was attending the UN General Assembly session. Then, in November, the superpowers announced that Gromyko and U.S. Secretary of State George Shultz would meet in Geneva in early January to negotiate an agenda for new talks on arms limitation.

Installation of U.S. missiles in Britain, Italy, and West Germany raised tensions with Western Europe. Chernenko met with French President François Mitterrand, and Gorbachev visited Great Britain late in the year. However, after apparently approving planned visits to West Germany by the leaders of East Germany and Bulgaria, the Soviet Union strongly denounced alleged neo-Nazism and "revanchism" in West Germany—a move to make such visits impossible—and both leaders then postponed their visits.

Relations with China showed dramatic improvement, when the two countries in late December signed a long-term trade pact for 1986–1990 and other pacts to promote cooperation in economic matters and science and technology. Provisions were included for the Soviet Union to assist in modernizing Chinese industrial plants built with Soviet aid in the 1950's. The agreements capped a visit to China by First Deputy Prime Minister Ivan Arkhipov, the highest Soviet official to visit there since 1969. However, China's demands for the removal of Soviet troops from Afghanistan remained an obstacle to closer normalization of relations between the Soviet Union and China.

See STATISTICS OF THE WORLD. See also AFGHANISTAN; MILITARY AND NAVAL AFFAIRS; SPACE SCIENCE AND EXPLORATION. J.F.H.

UNITED ARAB EMIRATES. See STATISTICS OF THE WORLD. See also PERSIAN GULF STATES.

UNITED NATIONS, THE. What many saw as the increasing irrelevance of the United Nations to the challenging political, economic, and social problems of the times was underlined by signs of continuing deterioration in both East-West and North-South relationships in 1984.

Unesco. On December 19, the United States, acting on its threat of the previous year, announced that it would withdraw from Unesco at the end of the month. The U.S. State Department said the agency had failed to act sufficiently to remedy mismanagement, "extraneous politicization," and hostility toward a free press and other democratic values. In November the United Kingdom said it would pull out of the agency at the end of 1985 if no major changes were made, and West Germany stated in December that it would review its membership in 12 months.

Earlier, in March, the 24 industrialized countries of the Organization for Economic Cooperation and Development (OECD) had presented Unesco's controversial director general, Amadou Mahtar M'Bow, with a list of administrative and budgetary changes they wished the organization's executive board to adopt during 1984 for presentation to the next General Conference in 1985. In October the United States requested that the executive board convene in emergency session to consider a sharply critical report on Unesco management by the U.S. Congressional Budget Office. M'Bow countered that the report did not concern the executive board because it was prepared by a single member country.

Arab-Israeli Dispute. Early in the year, the four Western nations comprising the Multinational Force (MNF) in Lebanon withdrew their peacekeeping units from Beirut. France appealed to the UN Security Council to replace the MNF with UN peacekeepers, and a resolution to that effect was approved by 13 Council members on February 29, but it was vetoed by the Soviet Union.

UN Secretary-General Javier Pérez de Cuéllar visited five countries in the region in June to assess possibilities for a wider UN role in Lebanon. He declined, however, to support an Israeli proposal that UN peacekeepers serve as a buffer between Syrian and Israeli occupying forces in eastern Lebanon, on grounds that it might in some way signify the division of Lebanon. The two UN peacekeeping forces already in place—UNDOF in the Golan Heights between Syria and Israel and UNIFIL, in Israeli-controlled areas of southern Lebanon—were both renewed.

In late August the new Lebanese government of national unity asked the Security Council to take action against Israeli occupation policies. A resolution calling on Israel to change its policies was vetoed by the United States on September 6. On October 31 the UN announced that Israel and Lebanon would begin talks on the issues of Israeli withdrawal from southern Lebanon and the security of Israel's northern border. The talks, held at UNIFIL headquarters in Lebanon, opened in November and recessed the following month in an apparent deadlock.

Iran-Iraq War. Four years of war appeared to leave neither party in a position to prevail. Iran charged that Iraq had used chemical weapons in violation of the 1925 Geneva Protocol, to which both countries subscribed. On March 26 a UN investigative team reported that mustard gas and nerve gas had been used on Iranians in the war zone, although it said the extent of use could not be determined. The Security Council on March 30 issued a non binding declaration condemning the use of chemical weapons in the conflict, but naming no names.

Escalation of Iranian attacks on Persian Gulf shipping, in areas beyond the war zones previously claimed by the two adversaries, prompted the states that comprise the Gulf Cooperation Council to ask on May 21 for action by the Security Council. On June 1 the Council voted to condemn attacks on commercial ships and reaffirmed the right of free navigation in international waters and sea lanes, but again it named no names. The vote was 13–0, with Nicaragua and Zimbabwe abstaining.

During his June visit to the region, Secretary-General Pérez de Cuéllar succeeded in negotiating an agreement between the two sides, to be monitored by UN observers, to halt attacks on each other's cities. In September, however, Iranian leader Ayatollah Ruhollah Khomeini declared once more that Iran would make no compromises with Iraq to end the war.

Central America. Nicaragua requested a Security Council meeting on March 30, accusing the United States of responsibility for mining Nicaraguan harbors. Thirteen Council members joined in condemning the U.S. action on April 4, but the resolution was vetoed by the United States (the United Kingdom abstained). Anticipating that Nicaragua would appeal to the World Court, the United States informed the UN secretary-general on April 6 that for the next two years it would not accept the jurisdiction of the court in cases involving Central America. Nicaragua formally petitioned the court on April 9 to call a halt to the mining.

In a preliminary restraining order on May 10, the court ruled unanimously that the United States should halt any attempts to blockade or mine Nicaraguan ports. By a vote of 14–1, with the U.S. judge opposed, the court also ruled that Nicaragua's political independence should be fully respected and not jeopardized by any military or paramilitary activities. On November 26, the court ruled against the United States and affirmed that it had jurisdiction to hear and decide the case.

On a five-nation Mideast tour in June, to assess the prospects for a greater United Nations role in Lebanon, Secretary-General Javier Pérez de Cuéllar visits the UN peacekeeping force headquarters in southern Lebanon, near Israel's border.

South West Africa (Namibia). U.S. diplomatic efforts to effect a settlement in Namibia leading to free elections and independence appeared to bear fruit in February, when South Africa agreed to a phased withdrawal of its troops from Angola in return for an Angolan undertaking not to allow forces of the South West Africa People's Organization (Swapo)—the Angola-based guerrilla movement fighting to end South African rule—to cross into Namibia. A joint South African–Angolan commission, with U.S. observers, was set up to monitor the plan. However, the actual withdrawal remained incomplete late in the year.

On March 19, Cuba and Angola announced agreement on terms for Cuban troop withdrawal—a South African condition for any permanent settlement—including an end to South African support for the anti-Marxist National Union for the Total Independence of Angola, withdrawal of South African troops from Angola, and acceptance of a UN plan for free elections and independence, followed by the withdrawal of South African troops from Namibia.

In mid-May, representatives of Swapo, the so-called Multiparty Conference (representing Namibia's internal parties), and South Africa met in Lusaka, Zambia, but the talks foundered, reportedly on Swapo's insistence that the UN plan not be linked to Cuban troop withdrawal. Subsequently, however, the Angolan government reportedly indicated to U.S. diplomats acting as intermediaries that it would be willing to discuss a Cuban troop withdrawal as part of an overall package including a negotiated settlement on Namibia.

Namibia's South African–appointed administrator-general and Swapo leaders conferred in the Cape Verde islands on July 25, but the meeting quickly reached stalemate. Swapo refused to join in an unconditional cease-fire and to participate in normal political activities in Namibia so that a UN monitoring force would not be needed.

Population Conference. A UN International Conference on Population, held in Mexico City, August 6–14, was designed to build on the World Population Plan of Action adopted at the first such conference, held in Bucharest ten years earlier. The annual growth rate in the world's population had actually declined in the 1970's from 2.03 percent to 1.67 percent, according to a report published earlier by the UN Fund for Population Activities. The report concluded, however, that continued high growth rates in many developing countries were undercutting economic progress. The U.S. delegate, James Buckley, called for less emphasis on population growth rates and more on action to foster economic growth. He also announced that the Reagan administration would deny the use of U.S. funds contributed to the UN Population Fund for any activities related to abortion.

Economic and Development Issues. The 40 or so least developed countries continued to suffer from low prices for their commodity exports, rising protectionism in Western markets, high prices for imported food and for oil imports, and, in sub-Saharan Africa, lower per-capita food production because of unwise economic policies and devastating drought. The least developed countries have little to offer commercial banks and must rely for development aid on the International Development Association (IDA), an affiliate of the World Bank that makes loans available on favorable terms. On January 13, IDA's seventh refinancing was held to $9 billion for the next three years, a 20 percent decline from the previous replenishment, largely because the United States had reduced both the size and the percentage of its contribution.

Conference Center. At the conclusion of a session that was dominated by concern over widespread famine in Africa, the General Assembly on December 18 voted, 122–5, to provide $73.5 million for a new conference center, to be built in Addis Ababa, Ethiopia, for the UN Economic Commission for Africa. The United States and four other Western countries abstained, criticizing the large outlay as inappropriate "at a time of such unprecedented suffering" on the continent. Meanwhile, at a coordination conference on the famine it was predicted that Africa would need 6.1 million tons of food aid in 1985, nearly double the amount received in 1984.

New Member. Brunei (officially Brunei Darussalem) became the 159th member of the United Nations on September 21. **I.C.B.**

United States of America

President Ronald Reagan was reelected in a landslide in 1984, handily defeating former Vice-President Walter Mondale. Reagan was aided by the economy, which boomed ahead, especially in the early part of the year. Inflation remained low, although soaring federal budget deficits caused concern. Lebanon and Central America were the major trouble spots for U.S. foreign policy.

The voting on November 6 climaxed a long political year that had begun in the snows of Iowa and New Hampshire in January and February. Walter Mondale emerged from the primaries as the clear Democratic nominee; with Representative Geraldine Ferraro as his running mate—the first woman ever to run for vice-president on a major-party ticket—he fought a hard campaign but never succeeded in overcoming Ronald Reagan's decisive edge. Public opinion helped precipitate a U.S. disengagement in Lebanon, with a presumed decline in U.S. influence in the region. The Reagan administration followed a high-risk policy in Latin America, trying to hold the line against leftist guerrillas in one country (El Salvador) while apparently seeking to undermine a leftist regime in another (Nicaragua). U.S.–Soviet relations remained generally tense.

DOMESTIC AFFAIRS

"Do you know what wins elections?" Vice-President George Bush (see biography in PEOPLE IN THE NEWS) asked an Ohio campaign crowd, as he slapped his wallet down on the podium. "It's who puts money into this and who takes money out!"

At least in 1984, the presidential election results proved Bush was right about the importance of the economy. With unemployment moderate, inflation low, and the economy booming, more than 90 million Americans went to the polls on November 6, and they cast a resounding vote for the status quo. Reagan easily won a second term as president.

The Republicans lost two seats in the Senate, and the House of Representatives stayed Democratic by a comfortable margin. Nevertheless, Reagan's own electoral victory was an impressive one.

On the road to reelection, the Reagan administration had to weather another huge budget deficit, as well as foreign policy problems. Feminists and civil rights activists saw progress in the historic candidacies of Geraldine Ferraro and Jesse Jackson (see biographies in PEOPLE IN THE NEWS). During the year the United States hosted both the summer Olympic Games and a world's fair; the former event was an athletic and financial success, the latter a fiscal fiasco.

Reagan Reelection. Ronald Reagan and his running mate, George Bush, captured 59 percent of the popular vote and a record total of 525 electoral votes in carrying 49 states. Democratic presidential standard-bearer Walter F. Mondale (see biography in PEOPLE IN THE NEWS), with Representative Geraldine Ferraro of New York as his running mate, managed to carry only his home state, Minnesota, and the District of Columbia. Weakened by his ties to the Carter administration and scarred by a contentious primary campaign, the former vice-president had from the outset only a slim chance to beat Reagan. The president's lead in the polls rarely dipped below double digits, and when it did, Mondale's pledge to raise taxes and nagging questions surrounding the Ferraro family finances helped restore Reagan's commanding margin. Republican Party leaders were disap-

Basking in bipartisan approval, President Ronald Reagan signs a unanimously passed bill requiring states to collect child support payments from absentee parents. Applauding the action are (left to right) Transportation Secretary Elizabeth Dole, Secretary of Health and Human Services Margaret Heckler, and U.S. Representatives Mario Biaggi (D, N.Y.) and Marge Roukema (R, N.J.).

pointed in the shortness of the president's coattails, but they could look forward to four more years in the White House.

See also ELECTIONS IN THE UNITED STATES; DEMOCRATIC PARTY; REPUBLICAN PARTY.

Economic Expansion. Republican candidates were not at all bashful about claiming credit for the strong, steady economic recovery. The gross national product soared during the first six months of 1984, and rose moderately in the last six. During the whole year, as it turned out, GNP increased by 6.8 percent, the biggest gain since 1951. By December, the civilian unemployment rate had dropped to 7.2 percent, down from 8.2 percent a year earlier. Consumer prices were up by only 4 percent. The prime rate was edging downward.

There were some unfavorable economic developments. The rate of job creation during Reagan's first term had been slower than during the Carter years. Furthermore, data released in August 1984 showed that 35.3 million people were living in poverty in 1983—6 million more than when Reagan took office. Still, most Americans could answer affirmatively when asked if they were better off than they had been four years earlier.

The Deficits. The most glaring weakness of the Reagan recovery was the persistence of enormous budget deficits. Even after the enactment at midyear of a four-year package calling for $50 billion in tax hikes and $13 billion in spending reductions, the Reagan administration forecast deficits of more than $160 billion annually through fiscal 1989. After the election these estimates were substantially increased, as administration officials geared up for another round of budget cuts and revenue "enhancements." Meanwhile, the national debt was raised in October to $1,820 billion; it had been $935.1 billion when Reagan took office. Less publicized but also worrisome was the escalating foreign trade deficit, which reached a record $123.3 billion in 1984.

The budget as approved by Congress for the 1985 fiscal year entailed expenditures of $932 billion, revenues of $751 billion, and a deficit of $181 billion. On September 20, House and Senate conferees reached agreement on a 1985 military budget of $292.9 billion, representing a real increase of 5 percent over estimated outlays for 1984; the White House had initially requested a rise of 13 percent. The debate over military procurement took place amid allegations of gross overspending by the armed services on spare parts, including $400 for a hammer and $7,622 for a ten-cup coffee maker. (See also MILITARY AND NAVAL AFFAIRS.)

Scandals and Controversies. On October 2, Labor Secretary Raymond J. Donovan pleaded not guilty to a 137-count indictment by a New York grand jury on charges involving alleged fraud by the Schiavone Construction Company; Donovan was vice-president of the company before he joined the Reagan cabinet. Donovan, who had been investigated in 1982 by a special prosecutor (who found "insufficient credible evidence" that he had violated federal law), took a leave of absence from the cabinet. One of Reagan's chief political advisers, Edwin Meese 3d, nominated by Reagan to be U.S. attorney general, was alleged to have committed several fiscal improprieties, including the failure to report a $15,000 interest-free loan to his wife by a friend who later became a regional director of the General Services Administration. In Meese's case, too, an independent counsel—the new term for a special prosecutor—found no violation of federal law, but the Senate Judiciary Committee had already postponed a decision on the Meese nomination until 1985.

Both vice-presidential candidates became embroiled to some degree in controversies over their financial affairs. The spotlight fell particularly on Ferraro because of her husband's extensive and perhaps questionable real-estate dealings and because, while representing her Queens congressional disrtrict, Ferraro had failed to report the details of her husband's business to Congress, as the Ethics in Government Act of 1978 required. Moreover, as a result of an audit completed in August, Ferraro and her husband had to pay about $53,000 in back taxes and interest. In October, it was

Her gaze still unwavering, the copper-clad, 151-foot-tall Statue of Liberty is caged in the aluminum scaffolding that was erected during 1984 to permit extensive structural repairs. Rehabilitation was expected to be complete by 1986, the 100th birthday of the world's most celebrated symbol of freedom.

revealed that Vice-President Bush had in June paid $198,000 in back taxes and interest stemming from an Internal Revenue Service audit of his 1981 federal income tax return.

Congress and the Courts. In addition to various tax and budgetary measures, Congress passed an anticrime package authorizing preventive detention in certain cases, abolishing the federal parole system, and placing the burden of proof in an insanity plea, in federal cases, on the defendant. Congress also passed laws strengthening warnings on cigarette packs, providing access to public school facilities for voluntary religious meetings, and inducing states to raise the minimum age for drinking alcoholic beverages.

Two new laws were of special interest to women. The first, originally introduced in the House by Ferraro in 1981, made it less difficult for women to claim retirement benefits under private pension plans. The second required all states to pass laws that would facilitate the collection of court-ordered child-support payments. The Supreme Court ruled in July that Jaycees chapters could not constitutionally claim exemption from state laws banning sex discrimination. Civil rights activists were disappointed, however, by a Court ruling that employers may not be compelled to disregard seniority in order to protect the jobs of recently hired minority employees. (See also CONGRESS OF THE UNITED STATES; SUPREME COURT OF THE UNITED STATES; CIVIL LIBERTIES AND CIVIL RIGHTS.)

The Media. To an unusual extent, the media themselves made news in 1984. The Federal Communications Commission abolished limitations on the number of commercials that television stations may broadcast and eliminated minimum time requirements for local and news programming. The FCC also sought to raise and ultimately abolish limits on the number of radio and television stations a company or individual may own, but after opposition arose in Congress the ruling as applied to TV stations was delayed at least until April 1985. In June the Supreme Court ended the National Collegiate Athletic Association's monopoly over broadcast rights for college football. In the ensuing competitive confusion, television ratings for college football declined, as did viewership of professional games. Con-

troversy over excessive violence in films rated PG (parental guidance suggested) led to the inauguration of a new rating, PG-13, indicating unsuitability of film content for pre-teenagers.

Americana. U.S. athletes excelled at the summer Olympics in Los Angeles, capturing 83 gold medals, 61 silver, and 30 bronze. No other nation won more than 20 gold medals. The luster of all that gold was only partly dimmed by the fact that Soviet-bloc nations (except Romania) declined to compete. Almost as remarkable as the performance of the U.S. athletes was the fact that the organizing committee reported a $150 million surplus, most of which was earmarked for the U.S. Olympic Committee and for youth sports programs in southern California. Not so fortunate were the backers of the New Orleans world's fair, which closed in bankruptcy in November; the unpaid bills totaled more than $100 million. The fair was regarded as an artistic success, but attendance ran well below expectations. On a more positive note, fundraisers for the Statue of Liberty and Ellis Island restoration project announced in September that they had reached the $100 million mark in an effort that was expected eventually to yield $230 million.

The Pulitzer Prize–winning comic strip "Doonesbury" returned after a 21-month hiatus, but the 54-year-old "Joe Palooka" strip hung up the gloves. Sometime on November 20, McDonald's reportedly sold its 50 billionth burger; which one of the fast-food chain's 8,000 outlets in 34 countries sold the epoch-making patty remained unknown.   G.M.H.

FOREIGN AFFAIRS

The year 1984 was a fairly quiet one in U.S. foreign relations. After the stunning events of 1983—the downing of a Korean airliner by the Soviet Union, the bombing of the Marine barracks in Beirut, the invasion of Grenada, and the Soviet walkout at the arms talks—the diplomatic moves of 1984 seemed more subdued, though perhaps no less significant. A tense year in Soviet relations ended with an agreement to open preliminary talks at the ministerial level in 1985, and elections favorable to the United States in El Salvador and Grenada brightened the Latin American picture. The U.S. peacekeeping force withdrew from Lebanon as Syria appeared to gain a dominant role in that strife-torn nation.

Soviet Union. Having walked out of the intermediate nuclear force (INF) negotiations and the strategic arms reduction talks (START) late in 1983, the Soviet Union chose not to return during 1984. The United States, for its part, did not budge on the deployment of Pershing II and cruise missiles in Europe, which had provoked the Soviet walkout. But by moderating his rhetoric—there was no more talk of an "evil empire"—President Ronald Reagan sent at least a weak signal to the Soviet Union that relations between the superpowers could thaw a bit.

Immediate hopes that the Soviet Union might moderate its policy were dampened by the death in February of Yuri Andropov, who had led the nation barely more than a year. His successor, Konstantin Chernenko, a party functionary with little international experience, appeared, at least initially, to show little interest in improving relations with the West. A U.S. proposal to break a deadlock at the Mutual and Balanced Force Reductions talks in Vienna, over the number of troops each side has in Europe, was dismissed by the Soviets in April. A draft U.S. treaty on a comprehensive worldwide ban on chemical weapons met a similar reaction. In late June, Chernenko appealed for negotiations "without delay" on a treaty banning the use and development of antisatellite (ASAT) weapons. Accepting, the White House said it would also raise the question of nuclear arms control proposals at the talks. This broadening of the scope of the talks was unacceptable to the Soviets, and Washington in turn found unacceptable Moscow's insistence on an ASAT testing moratorium as a precondition for the negotiations. The talks did not take place in Geneva in September as first planned. But on September 28, Soviet Foreign Minister Andrei Gromyko met with the president, and on Thanksgiving day, two weeks after Reagan's reelection, Washington and Moscow announced that Gromyko and Secretary of State George Shultz would meet in Geneva in January to discuss an agenda for arms talks.

In general, U.S.–Soviet relations were a mixed bag. The Soviet Union and most of its supporters boycotted the summer Olympic games in Los Angeles, ostensibly because of danger to their athletes, more likely in retaliation for a U.S. boycott of the 1980 Moscow Olympics. On the other hand, there were minor advances. A ban on Soviet fishing rights in U.S. waters was lifted, the telephone "hot line" between Moscow and Washington was upgraded, and in September it was announced that the Soviets would be allowed to buy 22 million metric tons of grain per year, nearly double the total allowed in 1983.

Middle East. The presence of U.S. Marines in Beirut was not popular among the American people, especially after the bombing of October 1983 that killed 241 U.S. servicemen. Furthermore, the security situation in Beirut worsened early in 1984. As Lebanon's army crumbled, Muslim militiamen expanded their sphere of authority in the Beirut area. On February 7, in a surprise announcement, Reagan essentially ended the U.S. peacekeeping mission, ordering the Marines to begin withdrawing to ships offshore. Britain, Italy, and France also pulled out their peacekeeping forces. Many viewed Reagan's sudden policy reversal—the administration had said the Marines would not be withdrawn until Lebanon's government was secure—as a setback for U.S. policy and credibility.

Syrian influence in Lebanon rose after the multinational forces withdrew. Even though U.S. influence had become minimal, the U.S. embassy annex outside East Beirut was hit by a suicide truck bombing on September 20. Two Americans and 12 other persons were killed.

The Iran-Iraq war escalated in 1984 with Iraq's apparent use of chemical warfare agents, which the United States strongly condemned. The United States stopped selling chemical compounds to Iraq that could be used to produce these weapons. In April the air war over the Persian Gulf also escalated, as Iraq began attacking tankers in or near Iran's oil terminal at Kharg Island. Iran in turn attacked neutral ships at ports of Arab states supporting Iraq's war efforts. Reagan, in May, citing the escalation, authorized the emergency sale (not requiring congressional approval) of 400 Stinger antiaircraft missiles and a KC-10 air tanker to Saudi Arabia. On June 5, Saudi F-15 fighers,

En route to the inauguration of El Salvador's President José Napoleón Duarte, Senator Jesse Helms (R, N.C.) and Secretary of State George Shultz (second and third from left) are met at San Salvador's airport by U.S. Ambassador Thomas Pickering (left). The following day, Secretary Shultz made a surprise call on Sandinista officials in Nicaragua.

guided by U.S.-manned Awac surveillance planes, downed two Iranian jets.

U.S. and Soviet policy was based on the proposition that neither side should win the Gulf war, although both in fact tilted toward Iraq—the United States in a number of ways, including an effort to cut off the supply of weapons to Iran. The United States made it clear that it had no intention of any uninvited military involvement, but Reagan said that "the free world" would not allow the Strait of Hormuz, at the entrance to the Gulf, to be closed. In November, Iraq and the United States announced that they had agreed to restore diplomatic relations, broken by Iraq in 1967.

Central America and the Caribbean. On January 11, the Reagan-appointed National Bipartisan Commission on Central America—better known as the Kissinger Commission, after its chairman, former Secretary of State Henry Kissinger—asserted that Cuba and the Soviet Union posed a threat to the United States in Central America and called for a five-year, $8 billion aid package for the region.

In El Salvador, the moderate José Napoleón Duarte, whom the Reagan administration supported, was elected president, defeating an extreme rightist, Roberto d'Aubuisson. Duarte's victory altered the mood of Congress. Three days after the election, the Democratic-controlled House of Representatives voted to authorize the administration's entire fiscal 1985 military aid package for the country. The United States also applauded Duarte for meeting with Salvadoran guerrilla leaders later in the year.

The administration met with less success in Nicaragua. In April it was learned that the Central Intelligence Agency had helped mine Nicaraguan harbors; several vessels had been damaged. Other nations and both houses of Congress condemned the CIA's involvement. On May 10 the World Court ruled, 15–0, in a preliminary decision, that U.S. efforts to mine or blockade Nicaraguan ports should be halted. The administration contended that the court had no jurisdiction in the case, but the court ruled to the contrary in late 1984, paving the way for a possible trial. The U.S. House, meanwhile, had cut off official U.S. funding for contras seeking to overthrow the Sandinista regime, but evidence accumulated that the administration sought funds for the contras from other governments and from private U.S. groups.

In the first high-level contact between the two countries since 1981, Shultz met with Daniel Ortega Saavedra of the ruling junta in Nicaragua on June 1. Tensions eased a bit, only to rise in October when it was revealed that the CIA had distributed a manual on guerrilla warfare to anti-Sandinista rebels. The manual, which advocated the creation of martyrs and recommended "selective violence" to "neutralize" Sandinista officials, violated the spirit of an executive order signed by Reagan in 1981 that prohibited even indirect participation in assassinations.

Asia. Premier Zhao Ziyang of China visited Washington in January, and Reagan paid his first visit to China in April. Both visits resulted in relatively minor accords being signed; one of these, on nuclear cooperation, hit a snag when it was reported that China might transfer materials to Pakistan. The accord did not come before Congress for ratification in 1984. China was displeased when the United States limited the amount of Chinese textiles entering the United States. Japan and the United States agreed in April on expanding U.S. beef and citrus exports; Japan also was continuing to increase its defense spending to a limited degree.

The United States pressured the Philippines government to make progress toward democracy and economic reform, and it made clear that those responsible for the 1983 assassination of opposition leader Benigno Aquino should be punished. Relations between the two countries remained close, however.

Europe. Economic recovery in Europe was slow in 1984, and Allied governments' defense budgets edged upward about 2 percent—less than a 1978 NATO pledge of annual 3 percent increases. U.S. officials expressed their concern. The leader of one NATO nation, Prime Minister Andreas Papandreou of Greece, outraged Washington in May when he said that the United States was an imperialist power but

that the Soviet Union was not. In August, Greece cancelled military exercises with the United States.

Africa. The Reagan administration supported efforts to relax tensions between South Africa and its neighbors. Angola and Mozambique both signed nonaggresion agreements with South Africa in 1984. At the same time, however, protests in the United States against human rights abuses in South Africa ultimately led Reagan to issue a call for the white regime there to modify its policies. The Reagan administration generally preferred what it called quiet diplomacy, rather than the open confrontation desired by many Americans, as the means of persuading the South African government to modify its racial policies.   C.A.K.

UPPER VOLTA. See STATISTICS OF THE WORLD. See also AFRICA.

URUGUAY. National elections in Uruguay, the first in 13 years, were held on November 25, 1984. Julio María Sanguinetti of the Colorado Party, a 48-year-old former congressman and cabinet minister, was elected president with almost 40 percent of the vote. He was expected to replace General Gregorio Alvarez, who has ruled Uruguay on behalf of the armed forces since September 1981, on March 1, 1985. Alberto Sánez de Zumarán of the Blanco Party, who was second with about 33 percent of the vote, went to Colorado Party headquarters to embrace the victor. There had been fears that the Blancos might challenge the result because their charismatic leader, Wilson Ferreira Aldunate, had been kept from being a candidate.

The elections had seemed imperiled for a time, as negotiations between the military and civilian political leaders on terms of the transition to democracy made no progress. The armed forces insisted on major constitutional changes that would ensure them a lasting role in any civilian government, while most political leaders remained adamant about ending military rule and reinstating the 1967 constitution.

To break the impasse in negotiations, the government made major concessions that led to an agreement in early August. The accord called for a constituent assembly to be elected on November 25; its mission was to draft changes in the constitution so as to reduce the considerable powers of the armed forces. In return, the political parties agreed to observe a long-standing ban imposed by the military on the civic rights of some 3,500 individuals, including the right to run for political office.

In the months preceding the election, the government eased restrictions on the press, released a number of political prisoners, and hastened the trials of alleged terrorists.

See STATISTICS OF THE WORLD.　　　　A.P.

UTAH. See STATISTICS OF THE WORLD.

V

VANUATU. See STATISTICS OF THE WORLD.

VENEZUELA. Jaime Lusinchi of the Democratic Action Party began a five-year term as president on February 2, 1984. The new president, elected in December 1983, called for a "social pact" among government, business, and labor to stabilize employment, encourage foreign investment, and avoid strikes. He promised that Venezuela would pay its $35 billion foreign debt in full and renegotiate its public sector debt without signing a formal agreement accepting supervision by the International Monetary Fund. In June the National Congress approved a law enabling the president to bypass that body in arriving at an agreement with banks holding the Venezuelan debt.

The previous administration had failed to reach an agreement with the IMF because the latter's demands were regarded as unacceptable; these included devaluation of the bolivar, wage and hiring restraints, and removal of subsidies on gasoline and essential food items. The Lusinchi government found Venezuela's creditor banks unwilling to restructure any of the $27 billion government-held debt until an agreement had been reached on $8 billion that the Venezuelan private sector had borrowed and on which $1 billion in repayments was overdue.

With progress having been made on the private sector borrowings, the bankers began to work with a Venezuelan negotiator in July. By September a tentative agreement was ready on the repayment of Venezuela's public debt. It called for stretching out over 12½ years payments on $20.75 billion, otherwise due by the end of 1985. In late October the bankers

agreed to a 90-day extension of principal payments until the $1 billion in arrears could be paid.

See also STATISTICS OF THE WORLD.　　　L.L.P

VERMONT. See STATISTICS OF THE WORLD..

VICE-PRESIDENT OF THE UNITED STATES. See PEOPLE IN THE NEWS: *George Bush.*

VIETNAM. In 1984, Vietnam continued efforts to establish full control of Cambodia, which it has occupied since 1979, and also took action against an alleged antigovernment conspiracy at home.

The offensive launched by Vietnam during the dry season of December 1983–March 1984 did little to improve Vietnam's position in Cambodia. During that period, in fact, two anti-Vietnamese Cambodian rebel groups—the Communist Khmer Rouge and the anti-Communist Khmer People's National Liberation Front (KPNLF)—had penetrated deep into Cambodia, blowing up fuel depots and attacking provincial centers. These two groups, along with another opposition faction loyal to Prince Norodom Sihanouk, had formed an alliance in 1982 and enjoyed considerable diplomatic support. However, the Hanoi government reportedly made intensive preparations and, beginning in late November 1984, launched a new, unusually intense dry-season onslaught against Cambodian rebels, especially against the KPNLF. Four major rebel camps near the Thailand border were overrun, among them the largest (Rithisen). At Rithisen, some 55 guerrillas and more than 60 civilians were reported killed during action in late December, and over 60,000 civilians forced to flee into Thailand. By the end of the year, KPNLF forces had reportedly retaken part of the Rithisen camp, as both sides suffered heavy casualties. Vietnam also reported numerous border clashes with Chinese forces late in the year, involving heavy casualties as well.

Meanwhile, what was said to be the biggest treason trial in Vietnam since the capture of South Vietnam ended in mid-December. Five men were sentenced to death, three to life in prison, and 13 others to lesser prison terms. (Two of the death sentences were later commuted.) All had been charged with seeking to overthrow the Vietnamese government with Chinese backing. About 100 others were arrested in a campaign against dissidents late in the year and were expected to be tried in 1985.

Vietnamese relations with the United States remained tenuous. In July, the Hanoi government handed over to the United States the remains of eight more American servicemen killed during the Vietnam war. Two months later, in response to an often-made Vietnamese offer, U.S. Secretary of State George Shultz said the United States was willing to accept as many as 10,000 Vietnamese held in reeducation camps. Shultz also announced that the United States was prepared to take in all Amerasian children (those born of Vietnamese mothers and American fathers), along with family members, if they wanted to emigrate. Representatives of the two nations met on the subject in Geneva during October, but progress later appeared stalled because of Vietnam's suspicions that Vietnamese living in the United States and other Western countries were backing organized subversion against the Hanoi government.

See STATISTICS OF THE WORLD. E.B.

VIRGINIA. *See* STATISTICS OF THE WORLD.

VIRGIN ISLANDS. *See* STATISTICS OF THE WORLD.

WARSAW TREATY ORGANIZATION. *See* COMMUNIST WORLD.

WASHINGTON. *See* STATISTICS OF THE WORLD.

WESTERN SAHARA. *See* AFRICA; MOROCCO.

WESTERN SAMOA. *See* STATISTICS OF THE WORLD.

WEST VIRGINIA. *See* STATISTICS OF THE WORLD.

WISCONSIN. *See* STATISTICS OF THE WORLD.

WOMEN. The year 1984 saw both gains and setbacks for women and women's rights. The biggest breakthrough was the nomination of Geraldine Ferraro as Democratic candidate for U.S. vice-president.

Ferraro and Others. On July 19, Geraldine Ferraro, a U.S. representative from Queens, N.Y. (see biography in PEOPLE IN THE NEWS), was officially nominated for vice-president at the Democratic National Convention in San Francisco, becoming the first woman ever to run for that office on a major-party ticket. She ran a spirited campaign, attracting enthusiastic crowds, and was strongly supported by women's groups. In the end, her candidacy did not appear to draw significant numbers of votes to the Democratic ticket, but it was regarded as a major milestone for women, and Ferraro herself appeared to be established as a major figure on the political scene.

Other individual achievers included astronaut Kathryn D. Sullivan, who became the first woman to walk in space; Joan Benoit, winner of the first Olympic women's marathon; the many other female Olympic stars; and Madeleine Kunin, who was elected as Vermont's first woman governor. In U.S. politics, however, it was a mixed year for women. Of ten who ran for the Senate, only one, incumbent Nancy Kassebaum (R, Kan.), was elected. All 20 women incumbents in the U.S. House were reelected, but only two of more than 40 women challengers won House seats.

Equal Rights. In February the U.S. Supreme Court voted, 6–3, to limit the reach of federal law barring sex discrimination in schools. In *Grove City College* v. *Bell*, the Court ruled that Title IX of the 1972 Education Amendments, which prohibits sex discrimination in institu-

Actress/director/producer Barbra Streisand receives the prestigious Woman of Courage Award from the National Organization for Women, as well as a plaque of honor from the city of Los Angeles. Flanking the singing star are Mayor Tom Bradley and Judy Goldsmith, president of NOW. Streisand was cited for "commitment to excellence in her profession as well as her long-standing commitment to equality and human dignity."

tions receiving federal aid, applies only to the specific program or activity receiving federal assistance and not to the institution as a whole. This interpretation of Title IX overturned years of practice under the 1972 law against discrimination in higher education. The House of Representatives on June 26 voted, 375–32, in favor of a bill aimed at neutralizing the ruling's effect, but the bill died in the Senate.

Other major Supreme Court rulings during the year were favorable to women. In *Roberts v. U.S. Jaycees,* the Court ruled, 7–0, that under its antidiscrimination laws a state may compel the all-male Jaycee organization to admit women as members. In August, the national Jaycees, meeting in Tulsa, Okla., overwhelmingly voted to allow women full membership in the 64-year-old organization. The Supreme Court also heard *Hishon* v. *King & Spalding,* a discrimination suit brought by a woman lawyer against an Atlanta law firm that rejected her for partnership. The Court ruled

that law firms are not beyond the reach of civil rights laws. Thus, they may not discriminate on the basis of sex, race, religion, or national origin in promoting young lawyers.

Economic Advances. Two measures affecting the economic status of women were adopted by Congress. One measure, designed to provide methods for collecting child support from delinquent parents (more than half are delinquent in whole or in part), authorizes withholding of salaries, attachment of property, deductions from income tax refunds, and reporting of such debts to credit agencies. The other law guarantees pensions for homemakers whose employed spouses die before retirement and assures that working mothers (or fathers) keep their retirement plan credit if they leave their jobs in order to raise families.

New Bedford Rape Case. A widely publicized rape case ended in March with the conviction of four Portuguese men in two separate trials and the acquittal of two others. The case,

431

Evolution of a Feminist

Germaine Greer, whose first book, *The Female Eunuch*, made her a feminist celebrity in the early 1970's, was back with *Sex and Destiny* in 1984—and reviewers were variously ecstatic, furious, or dumbfounded. In an apparent about-face from *Eunch*, which called on women to express their sexuality freely outside of marriage and family, the new work, subtitled *The Politics of Human Fertility*, focused on children as the purpose of sex, decried "recreational sex" as "the new opiate of the people," and argued for sexual restraint. Critics found it provocative but riddled with contradictions and factual errors. Before her writing success, Greer, born in Australia in 1939, was a journalist and literature professor in England. Her new book, some said, may reflect the impact of her short-lived marriage, a series of abortions, and disappointment over failing when she later wanted a child.

Germaine Greer

involving the alleged gang-rape of a woman in a New Bedford, Mass., bar in March 1983, raised questions about the rights of rape victims. The primary evidence at the trials was given by the woman, a bartender, and two of the defendants. The defense frequently tried to discredit the woman's character and, in effect, blame the rape on her. This attempt was decried by women's groups, who closely monitored the proceedings. The case received extensive media coverage, including live national telecasts of the trials by the Cable News Network. Although the woman was not seen on television, her name was broadcast repeatedly, in violation of the customary policy of news organizations not to disclose the names of rape victims. The woman claimed the resulting notoriety caused her to live in fear and forced her to move to another city.   M.Gr. & D.Y.

WYOMING. *See* STATISTICS OF THE WORLD.

YEMEN, PEOPLE'S DEMOCRATIC REPUBLIC OF. Energy development, especially oil industry investment, consumed 30 percent of the 1984 budget of the People's Democratic Republic of Yemen (South Yemen), as the country continued to pin its economic hopes on petroleum. A Soviet company, which had been conducting seismic tests in the promising Shabwah region, drilled its first test well in January, and the Italian firm Agip sunk two more test wells offshore from Al Mukalla.

The World Bank and Kuwait provided financial support for water and irrigation systems to serve Saywun and Wadi Hadhramaut, in the first stage of a long-term plan to reduce chronic water shortages and raise agricultural production in the area. Work was also begun on a water project for the remote Laboos area northeast of Aden, where water has had to be carried in by pack animal.

Minor cabinet changes and shifts within the ruling Yemeni Socialist Party in May led to rumors of a major shake-up within the South Yemeni government. President Ali Nasser Muhammad was reportedly under increased pressure from Communist hard-liners, led by First Deputy Prime Minister Ali Ahmad Antar, to adopt a more pro-Soviet policy.

In late May, South Yemen joined the Soviet-led boycott of the Los Angeles summer Olympics. In August, at the request of the South Yemeni government, Soviet ships joined in minesweeping operations in the Red Sea, where vessels had been damaged by mines. President Muhammad visited Moscow in October and met with Soviet leader Konstantin Chernenko.

See STATISTICS OF THE WORLD.   C.H.A.

YEMEN ARAB REPUBLIC. The government of President Ali Abdullah Saleh enforced austerity measures with increasing strictness in early 1984. These measures showed some success, as imports declined and tariff income rose. Increased foreign aid and higher than expected remittances from Yemenis working abroad also helped the economy. The measures had been introduced in late 1983, under a new prime minister, Abdel Aziz Abdel Ghani, and other new ministers allied with Abdel Ghani.

Development hopes continued to focus on oil. In February the American-owned Hunt Oil Company discovered oil in its Ma'rib concession. The Yemen Oil and Mineral Company (Yominco), buoyed by the Hunt discovery, began carrying out oil surveys in other parts of the country, as well as surveys for mineral deposits and sources of geothermal energy. Contracts were awarded for the construction of an oil terminal at Salif with a pipeline to Sana. Agricultural development was the nation's second priority; a nine-year, $20 million project was initiated in an endeavor to increase food production in the central highlands by 70 to 100 percent.

During a visit to Moscow in October, President Saleh met with Soviet leader Konstantin Chernenko, and the two countries signed a 20-year treaty of friendship.

See STATISTICS OF THE WORLD.   C. H. A.

YUGOSLAVIA. In 1984 financial problems and internal tensions beset Yugoslavia, which started the year with a mammoth foreign debt of $20 billion. Under an agreement reached in March with the International Monetary Fund permitting foreign debt payments due in 1984 to be rescheduled, Yugoslavia promised to raise interest rates, devalue the dinar, deregulate prices, and impose financial discipline.

Turmoil continued in the predominantly Albanian province of Kosovo, where some 200 "irredentists and counterrevolutionaries" were jailed for one to 15 years after trials during the summer. The government's increasing concern over Yugoslavia's large Muslim population manifested itself as Communist Party leaders in Serbia tried, unsuccessfully, to influence the choice for the important religious post of Belgrade mufti.

Action was also brought against disloyal "rightist elements." In April authorities detained the prominent dissident Milovan Djilas and 27 other intellectuals who had gone to hear him deliver an informal talk in a private Belgrade apartment. Djilas and most of the others were released the next day, but one of those detained, Radomir Radovic, was found dead ten days later in his summer cottage near Belgrade. The police claimed he had committed suicide. In a petition addressed to the minister of the interior, however, 19 Belgrade intellectuals, including Gojko Nikolis, a general under Tito during World War II, declared that Radovic and others had been badly beaten while in police custody and asked for a thorough investigation. In November, six of the dissident intellectuals who had been detained in April were put on public trial.

In governmental and foreign affairs. Prime Minister Milka Planinc was confirmed in her office for another two-year term. Early in the year, Mika Spiljak, then president of Yugoslavia's collective presidency, visited the United States, where he met with President Ronald Reagan and congressional leaders.

Talks aimed at closer links with Albania broke down, but relations with China improved, as high-ranking Chinese officials visited during the year.

A welcome interlude arrived with the Olympic Winter Games, successfully staged by Yugoslavia, in Sarajevo during February. (See also SPORTS: THE OLYMPIC GAMES.)

See STATISTICS OF THE WORLD.   R.A.P.

YUKON TERRITORY. See STATISTICS OF THE WORLD.

Z

ZAIRE. Zaire early in 1984 received new infusions of loans and aid pledges to help shore up its economy. On the political front, President Mobutu Sese Seko was elected unopposed to the office of president for a third term, which began December 5.

Satisfied with the apparent stabilization of the Zairean currency and other austerity measures, Zaire's Western creditors had agreed in December 1983 to allow Zaire to spread debt repayments, amounting to more than $1 billion, over a period of 11 years. In early January 1984, the IMF approved a 15-month standby credit of $235 million, half of which was made immediately available, and a new loan of $356 million repayable over five years. Aid pledges collected after the rescheduling session totaled close to $300 million. It was hoped that these new flows of capital would reactivate the stagnant Zairean economy, whose GDP growth remained near zero through 1983 and the first half of 1984.

In early January, President Mobutu announced his intention to seek another term. There were rumors that Mobutu was seriously ill and hoped to pass on the presidency to his son Niwa. The election was held on July 28–29, and Mobutu, who ran unopposed, was reported by the government to have received 99.16 percent of the votes. The opposition claimed that voter intimidation was responsible for the small number of negative votes.

Terrorist involvement was suspected in explosions in Kinshasa that killed one person and injured five in January and March. Several people, most of them members of the exiled Congolese National Movement–Lumumba (MNC/L), were arrested in May in connection with the bombings. In mid-November, rebels apparently based in Tanzania captured the southeastern town of Moba. The town was taken within a few days by Zairean paratroopers, who reportedly killed 100 rebels.

Although Zaire denied involvement in South African-backed attempts to destabilize the government of Angola, it seemed likely that the guerrillas who attacked a northern Angola town in February had come from, or passed through, Zaire. Relations with Zambia continued to suffer from a rash of border incidents; in a June meeting in Lusaka, Mobutu and Zambian President Kenneth Kaunda agreed to regular high-level consultations in order to reduce tensions.

See STATISTICS OF THE WORLD. E.B.

ZAMBIA. A sluggish economy and a region-wide drought, now in its third year, dominated events in Zambia in 1984. As drought persisted, Zambia was importing at least 20 percent of its food supply. The Red Cross bought local crops in the capital city of Lusaka and trucked them to areas in need. Even so, agricultural products were smuggled out to Zaire, where prices were much higher.

With foreign debt soaring, factories were running at less than 50 percent capacity for lack of foreign exchange to purchase raw materials and spare parts. An austerity program imposed by the International Monetary Fund remained unpopular. Riots at the University of Zambia in February, protesting austerity measures and the arrest of student leaders, led to the closing of the university for almost two months and the expulsion of 3,000 students.

The government's January budget announcement emphasized promoting exports and reducing dependence on mining. Late in May a group of international financial institutions pledged to give Zambia approximately $400 million a year until 1986 to assist in restructuring of the economy.

President Kenneth Kaunda's initiatives in seeking to bring about settlement of the Angolan and Namibian issues made Zambia the focal point of intense diplomatic activity. An accord signed in Lusaka in February established a Joint Monitoring Commission to oversee South Africa's troop withdrawal from Angola. The city also hosted a meeting between leading South African and Angolan officials in May and a conference on South West Africa (Namibia). South Africa's banned African National Congress asked Kaunda to help improve its relations with Swaziland, and a meeting for that purpose was held in Lusaka in August. The following

434

month, Paul John Firmino Lusaka of Zambia was elected president of the UN General Assembly.

See STATISTICS OF THE WORLD.   K.W.G.

ZIMBABWE. The government made conciliatory efforts toward political opponents in 1984, but the year overall was marked by internal unrest and indications of movement toward one-party rule.

Starting in December 1983, several key political detainees were released, including leaders of the opposition Zimbabwe African People's Union (Zapu), white air force officers accused of sabotage, and (in September 1984) Bishop Abel Muzorewa, leader of the opposition United African National Council and of the United Methodist Church in Zimbabwe, who had been detained since October 1983. Meanwhile, in February, troops were sent to Matabeleland province to subdue an armed rebellion. The government, run by Mugabe's Zimbabwe African National Union (Zanu), charged that rebels affiliated with the Zapu opposition or trained by South Africa were responsible for the violence. Violence also flared in Midlands province in June, as gangs of Zanu youths attacked Zapu supporters and burned their homes and offices. Hundreds were injured and at least six were killed.

Mass graves of 4,000 black guerrillas and civilians were discovered in March. The victims had been killed during the war for independence in the 1970's and secretly moved by Rhodesian armed forces to a "dumping ground" in eastern Zimbabwe.

In August, Zanu held its first party congress in 20 years. Mugabe declared his intention to transform Zimbabwe into a one-party Marxist-Leninist state. Pushed by the left wing of his party and a recent Youth League congress, Mugabe said that he planned to call for a general election early in 1985 and that he would interpret a big victory as a mandate for one-party rule. Zimbabwe still depends on Western financial assistance, particularly to support a major land-reform program, so it was expected that Mugabe would be cautious in proceeding. In mid-November, however, he dismissed the last two Zapu members from his cabinet, after blaming Zapu for the murder of a Zanu Central Committee member.

A mass grave is uncovered in Zimbabwe, 100 miles east of the capital, Harare. Government officials claim that graves found at the former shooting range contain the remains of thousands of black people who were killed during Zimbabwe's seven-year war for independence.

A food shortage, brought on by the continuing drought and exacerbated by rapid population growth and a flood of refugees from Mozambique, necessitated the importation of 300,000–500,000 tons of maize, at inflated prices. But by the end of 1984, unexpectedly large increases in farm productivity had helped ease the food crisis.

Foreign exchange and balance of payments remained critical problems, necessitating a government freeze on virtually all foreign payments. The inflation rate was around 20 percent. Real gross domestic product fell some 4 percent in 1983; a similar decline was expected in 1984.

See STATISTICS OF THE WORLD.   K.W.G.

435

THE COUNTRIES OF THE WORLD

Nation Capital	Population	Area of Country (sq mi/ sq km)	Type of Government	Heads of State and Government	Currency: Value in U.S. Dollars	GNP (000,000): GNP Per Capita
AFGHANISTAN Kabul	14,400,000 2,000,000	250,000 647,497	People's republic	President, Revolutionary Council: Babrak Karmal Prime Minister: Sultan Ali Keshtmand	Afghani 0.02	$ NA NA
ALBANIA Tiranë	2,900,000 220,000	11,100 28,748	People's socialist republic	Chairman, Presidium of the People's Assembly: Ramiz Alia Chairman, Council of Ministers (Premier): Adil Çarçani	Lek 0.14	1,930 666
ALGERIA Algiers	21,400,000 2,000,000	919,595 2,381,741	Republic	President: Col. Chadli Benjedid Premier: Abdelhamid Brahimi	Dinar 0.20	42,010 1,693
ANGOLA Luanda	7,800,000 1,200,000	481,353 1,246,700	People's republic	President: José Eduardo dos Santos	Kwanza 0.03	3,320 426
ANTIGUA AND BARBUDA St. Johns	90,000 25,000	171 442	Parliamentary state (C)	Governor-General: Sir Wilfred E. Jacobs Prime Minister: Vere C. Bird, Sr.	East Caribbean dollar 0.37	120 1,333
ARGENTINA Buenos Aires	29,100,000 2,908,000	1,068,301 2,766,889	Federal republic	President: Raúl Alfonsín	New peso 0.022	72,120 2,478
AUSTRALIA Canberra	15,500,000 235,900	2,967,907 7,686,848	Federal parliamentary state (C)	Governor-General: Sir Ninian M. Stephen Prime Minister: Robert Hawke	Dollar 0.86	165,460 10,674
AUSTRIA Vienna	7,600,000 1,531,346	32,374 83,849	Federal republic	President: Rudolf Kirchschläger Chancellor: Fred Sinowatz	Schilling 0.05	77,120 10,147
BAHAMAS Nassau	228,000 135,437	5,380 13,935	Parliamentary state (C)	Governor-General: Sir Gerald C. Cash Prime Minister: Lynden O. Pindling	Dollar 1.005	780 3,421
BAHRAIN Manama	409,000 121,986	240 622	Emirate	Emir: Isa bin Salman al-Khalifah Prime Minister: Muhammed Khalifa bin Salman al-Khalifa	Dinar 2.65	3,240 7,922
BANGLADESH Dacca	99,600,000 3,605,000	55,598 143,998	Republic (C)	President: H. M. Ershad Prime Minister: Atuar Rahman Khan	Taka 0.04	12,840 129
BARBADOS Bridgetown	252,000 7,466	166 431	Parliamentary state (C)	Governor-General: Hugh Springer Prime Minister: Tom Adams	Dollar 0.50	880 3,492
BELGIUM Brussels	9,900,000 994,774	11,781 30,513	Constitutional monarchy	King: Baudouin Prime Minister: Wilfried Martens	Franc 0.018	117,510 11,870

The section on countries presents the latest information available. All monetary figures are expressed in United States dollars. The symbol (C) signifies that the country belongs to the Commonwealth of Nations. NA means that the data were not available. * indicates that the category does not apply to the country under discussion. Footnotes at the end of the section contain more specialized information.

Imports Exports	Revenue Expenditure	Elementary Schools: Teachers Students	Secondary Schools: Teachers Students	Colleges and Universities: Teachers Students
$ 695,000,000.............$ 708,000,000	665,000,000............. 665,000,000	32,937............. 1,006,094	6,114............. 133,498	1,448 22,974
246,000,000[1]............. 267,000,000[1]	1,140,000,000............. 1,130,000,000	25,900............. 555,910	NA............. 156,984	1,015 14,695
10,754,000,000............. 13,182,000,000	13,838,593,000............. 13,733,848,000	88,481............. 3,118,827	40,003............. 1,014,430	7,903 72,200
660,000,000............. 666,000,000	3,974,000,000............. 3,974,000,000	12,622............. 516,131	4,723............. 79,055	333 4,746
137,000,000............. 33,000,000	28,609,230............. 16,984,797	414............. 10,159	358............. 6,927	* *
4,099,000,000............. 7,116,000,000	26,600,000,000............. 29,400,000,000	200,388............. 4,035,404	178,681............. 1,296,839	44,402 498,928
19,393,000,000............. 20,594,000,000	46,623,000,000............. 48,343,000,000	91,280............. 1,688,121	85,340............. 1,095,610	20,822 323,716
19,364,000,000............. 15,431,000,000	43,000,000,000............. 44,500,000,000	27,525............. 400,397	63,678............. 739,702	11,792 127,746
3,085,000,000............. 2,465,000,000	273,600,000............. 288,200,000	NA............. 32,854	1,018............. 28,136	NA 4,396
3,614,000,000............. 3,789,000,000	1,320,414,500............. 1,256,489,200	2,479............. 48,672	844............. 24,233	125 1,314
2,284,000,000............. 765,000,000	1,630,000,000............. 1,000,000,000	188,234............. 8,236,526	111,972............. 2,407,888	12,329 232,780
617,000,000............. 338,000,000	239,700,000............. 263,700,000	1,172............. 31,147	1,231............. 28,818	NA 1,140
54,278,000,000[2]............. 51,929,000,000[2]	26,100,000,000............. 38,000,000,000	46,430............. 842,117	71,170............. 835,524	NA 188,232

Nation Capital	Population	Area of Country (sq mi/ sq km)	Type of Government	Heads of State and Government	Currency: Value in U.S. Dollars	GNP (000,000): GNP Per Capita
BELIZE .... Belmopan	157,000.... 2,932	8,867.... 22,965	Parliamentary state (C)	Governor-General:................ Minita Gordon Prime Minister: George C. Price	Dollar 0.50	$ 160 1,019
BENIN .... Porto-Novo	3,900,000.... 144,000	43,484.... 112,622	People's ...... republic	President:................ Lt. Col. Ahmed Kérékou	CFA franc[3] 0.0023	1,140 292
BHUTAN .... Thimbu	1,400,000.... 16,500	18,147.... 47,000	Monarchy	King:................ Jigme Singye Wangchuk	Ngultrum 0.08	110 79
BOLIVIA .... Sucre La Paz	6,000,000.... 80,000 881,400	424,164.... 1,098,581	Republic	President:................ Hernán Siles Zuazo	Peso 0.0005	3,440 573
BOTSWANA .... Gaborone	1,000,000.... 59,700	231,805.... 600,372	Republic ...... (C)	President:................ Quett K. J. Masire	Pula 0.85	940 1,010
BRAZIL .... Brasília	134,400,000.... 1,173,915	3,286,487.... 8,511,965	Federal .... republic	President:................ Gen. João Baptista de Oliveira Figueiredo	Cruzeiro 0.0007	267,730 1,992
BRUNEI .... Bandar Seri Begawan	200,000.... 49,900	2,226.... 5,765	Constitutional monarchy (C)	Sultan:................ Muda Hassanal Bolkiah	dollar......... 0.4614	4,050 20,250
BULGARIA .... Sofia	9,000,000.... 1,070,358	42,823.... 110,912	People's .... republic	Chairman, Council of State: ..... Todor Zhivkov Chairman, Council of Ministers (Premier): Grisha Filipov	Lev 1.002	37,390 4,154
BURMA .... Rangoon	38,900,000.... 2,400,000	261,218.... 676,552	Socialist ..... republic	President:................ U San Yu Prime Minister: U Maung Maung Kha	Kyat.......... 0.13	6,540 168
BURUNDI .... Bujumbura	4,700,000.... 146,000	10,747.... 27,834	Republic	President:................ Col. Jean-Baptiste Bagaza	Franc 0.0085	990 211
CAMBODIA........... **(PEOPLE'S REPUBLIC OF KAMPUCHEA)** Phnom Penh	6,100,000.... 600,000	69,898.... 181,035	People's ...... republic	President, Council of State:....... Heng Samrin Chairman, Council of Ministers (Premier): Chan Sy	New riel ...... NA	NA
CAMEROON .... Yaoundé	9,400,000.... 456,000	183,569.... 475,442	Republic	President and .... Prime Minister: Paul Biya	CFA franc[3] 0.0023	7,630 812
CANADA .... Ottawa	25,100,000.... 295,163	3,851,809.... 9,976,139	Federal .... parliamentary state (C)	Governor-General:................ Jeanne Sauvé Prime Minister: Brian Mulroney	Dollar 0.76	276,220 11,005
CAPE VERDE .... Praia	300,000.... 39,000	1,557.... 4,033	Republic	President: .... Aristides M. Pereira Premier: Pedro Pires	Escudo 0.0125	100 333
CENTRAL AFRICAN .. **REPUBLIC** Bangui	2,600,000.... 387,100	240,535.... 622,984	Republic	Chairman, Military Committee ..... for National Recovery (President): Gen. André Kolingba	CFA franc[3] 0.0023	770 296
CHAD .... N'Djamena	5,000,000.... 303,000	495,755.... 1,284,000	Republic	President: .... Hissène Habré	CFA franc[3] 0.0023	490 98
CHILE................. Santiago	11,900,000.... 4,132,293	292,258.... 756,945	Republic	President: .... Gen. Augusto Pinochet Ugarte	Peso 0.011	28,890 2,210
CHINA, PEOPLE'S .. **REPUBLIC OF** Peking	1,034,500,000.... 5,597,972	3,705,406.... 9,596,961	People's ...... republic	Chairman, Standing Committee of the National People's Congress: Peng Zhen Premier: Zhao Ziyang	Yuan 0.47	299,770 290
COLOMBIA .... Bogotá	28,200,000.... 4,300,000	439,737.... 1,138,914	Republic	President: .... Belisario Betancur Cuartas	Peso 0.01	36,390 1,290
COMOROS .... Moroni	500,000.... 16,000	838.... 2,171	Federal .... Islamic republic	President: .... Ahmed Abdallah Abderemane Premier: Ali Mroudjae	CFA franc[3] 0.0023	110 220

Imports Exports	Revenue Expenditure	Elementary Schools: Teachers Students	Secondary Schools: Teachers Students	Colleges and Universities: Teachers Students
$ 162,000,000.............$	$ 40,300,000..............	1,207..............	349..............	15
94,000,000	44,500,000	32,986	5,420	113
320,000,000..............	381,841,120..............	7,994..............	1,509..............	234
46,000,000	381,841,120	379,926	87,648	3,003
NA..............	39,731,720..............	897..............	NA..............	37
NA	46,158,910	22,648	1,783	322
514,000,000..............	301,300,000..............	48,894..............	7,143..............	2,797
739,000,000	2,030,000,000	978,250	170,710	51,585
834,000,000..............	387,600,000..............	5,316..............	1,137..............	90
573,000,000	384,700,000	171,914	20,969	1,052
16,313,000,000..............	25,700,000,000..............	863,335..............	180,782..............	120,550
21,366,000,000	25,700,000,000	22,025,449	2,537,949	1,251,116
599,000,000..............	869,190,000..............	1,833..............	1,276..............	51
4,068,000,000	499,050,000	33,308	16,891	436
11,527,000,000..............	15,000,000,000..............	51,581..............	25,666..............	14,909
11,428,000,000	14,980,000,000	994,018	314,753	108,308
268,000,000..............	951,471,000..............	364,451..............	23,853..............	4,522
378,000,000	1,009,364,400	3,711,464	885,621	121,609
186,000,000..............	167,400,000..............	4,623..............	919..............	231
73,000,000	234,000,000	159,729	16,410	1,784
NA..............	NA..............	20,374..............	3,937..............	NA
NA	NA	479,616	99,936	9,228
1,217,000,000..............	1,353,000,000..............	25,289..............	8,374..............	220
942,000,000	1,353,000,000	1,302,974	212,860	9,060
61,325,000,000..............	44,512,560,000..............	119,200..............	139,100..............	52,756
73,797,000,000	53,247,960,000	2,184,919	2,323,228	852,911
68,000,000 ,,,,,,,,,,,	24,300,000..............	1,350..............	317..............	*
4,000,000	27,000,000	54,452	6,600	*
95,000,000..............	101,100,000..............	3,690..............	526..............	405
79,000,000	132,570,000	247,782	38,704	7,547
109,000,000..............	10,800,000,000..............	2,610..............	NA..............	62
58,000,000	24,000,000,000	210,882	19,580	758
2,754,000,000..............	9,040,000,000..............	66,354..............	27,207..............	11,419
3,840,000,000	9,400,000,000	2,185,459	538,309	127,349
21,267,000,000..............	59,500,000,000..............	5,499,400..............	3,171,500..............	236,637
22,255,000,000	61,100,000,000	146,270,000	56,777,800	1,019,950
4,471,000,000..............	4,240,000,000..............	136,381..............	88,905..............	27,985
3,001,000,000	4,510,000,000	4,168,200	1,811,003	279,194
30,000,000..............	6,270,000..............	1,292..............	449..............	*
13,000,000	10,590,000	59,709	13,798	*

Nation Capital	Population	Area of Country (sq mi/ sq km)	Type of Government	Heads of State and Government	Currency: Value in U.S. Dollars	GNP (000,000): GNP / GNP Per Capita
CONGO . . . . Brazzaville	1,700,000 400,000	132,047 342,000	People's republic	President: . . . . Col. Denis Sassou-Nguesso Premier: Auge Edouard Poungai	CFA franc[3] 0.0023	$ 1,840 1,082
COSTA RICA . . . . San José	2,500,000 265,445	19,575 50,700	Republic	President . . . . Luis Alberto Monge Alvarez	Colón 0.02	3,340 1,336
CUBA . . . . Havana	9,900,000 1,951,373	44,218 114,524	Socialist republic	President of the Councils of State and Ministers: Fidel Castro Ruz	Peso 1.14	12,330 1,245
CYPRUS . . . . Nicosia	645,500 . . . . 159,400[5]	3,572 9,251	Republic (C)	President: . . . . Spyros Kyprianou	Pound 1.78	NA
CZECHOSLOVAKIA . . . Prague	15,500,000 . . . 1,185,693	49,370 127,869	Federal socialist republic	President: . . . . Gustáv Husák Premier: Lubomir Štrougal	Koruna 0.16	89,260 5,758
DENMARK[8] . . . . Copenhagen	5,100,000 645,198	16,629 43,069	Constitutional monarchy	Queen: . . . . Margrethe II Prime Minister: Poul Schlüter	Krone 0.097	68,230 13,378
DJIBOUTI . . . . Djibouti	290,000 200,000	8,494 22,000	Republic	President: . . . . Hassan Gouled Aptidon Premier: Barkad Gourad Hamadou	Djibouti . . . . franc 0.0056	180 620
DOMINICA . . . . Roseau	74,000 8,346	290 751	Republic (C)	President: . . . . Clarence A. Seignoret Prime Minister: (Mary) Eugenia Charles	East . . . . Caribbean dollar 0.37	60 810
DOMINICAN REPUBLIC Santo Domingo	6,300,000 1,300,000	18,816 48,734	Republic	President: . . . . Salvador Jorge Blanco	Peso 1.00	7,070 1,122
ECUADOR . . . . Quito	9,100,000 1,110,250	109,483 283,561	Republic	President: . . . . Léon Febrés Cordero Rivadeneira	Sucre 0.02	10,120 1,112
EGYPT . . . . Cairo	47,000,000 . . . 12,000,000	386,661 1,001,449	Republic	President: . . . . Hosni Mubarak Prime Minister: Kamal Hassan Ali	Pound 1.197	28,160 600
EL SALVADOR . . . . San Salvador	4,800,000 429,000	8,124 21,041	Republic	President: . . . . José Napoleón Duarte	Colón 0.40	3,040 633
EQUATORIAL GUINEA Malabo	300,000 37,240	10,831 28,051	Republic	President, Supreme Military Council: Lt. Col. Teodoro Obiang Nguema Mbasogo	Ekuele 0.0033	60 200
ETHIOPIA . . . . Addis Ababa	32,000,000 1,200,000	471,778 1,221,900	Socialist state	Head of State, Chairman, ... Provisional Military Administrative Council and Council of Ministers: Lt. Col. Mengistu Haile Mariam	Birr 0.49	4,530 142
FIJI . . . . Suva	700,000 71,255	7,056 18,274	Parliamentary state (C)	Governor-General: . . . . Penaia Ganilau Prime Minister: Kamisese Mara	Dollar 0.95	1,290 1,842
FINLAND . . . . Helsinki	4,900,000 484,399	130,129 337,032	Republic	President: . . . . Mauno Koivisto Prime Minister: Kalevi Sorsa	Markka 0.17	51,270 10,463
FRANCE . . . . Paris	54,800,000 . . . 2,317,227	211,208 547,026	Republic	President: . . . . François Mitterrand Premier: Laurent Fabius	Franc 0.116	657,560 12,000
GABON . . . . Libreville	1,000,000 250,000	103,347 267,667	Republic	President: . . . . Omar Bongo Premier: Léon Mébiame	CFA franc[3] 0.0023	2,550 2,550

Imports Exports	Revenue Expenditure	Elementary Schools: Teachers Students	Secondary Schools: Teachers Students	Colleges and Universities: Teachers Students
$ 807,000,000.............$ 977,000,000	651,794,000.............. 651,794,000	7,186............. 390,676	5,117............. 187,585	681 6,848
995,000,000.............. 867,000,000	858,700,000.............. 1,210,000,000	12,596............. 347,708	7,157............. 134,358	4,382 60,990
6,293,000,000.............. 5,536,000,000	12,744,340,000.............. 12,739,789,000	86,519............. 1,550,323	61,930............. 1,009,441	10,736 146,240
NA.............. NA	455,700,000[6].............. 616,200,000[6]	2,193[7]............. 48,701[7]	2,953[7]............. 47,599[7]	205 1,608
15,800,000,000.............. 16,507,000,000	48,701,465,000.............. 48,677,130,000	90,380............. 1,904,476	33,227............. 388,561	22,595 179,780
16,762,000,000.............. 16,380,000,000	24,378,000,000.............. 34,744,000,000	64,118............. 442,931	NA............. 370,778	6,702 106,579
139,000,000.............. 77,000,000	107,500,000.............. 161,500,000	358............. 14,121	148............. 3,123	NA 150
47,000,000.............. 24,000,000	24,814,790.............. 22,740,718	887............. 16,540	NA............. 6,779	8 514
1,282,000,000.............. 811,000,000	745,600,000.............. 973,900,000	NA............. 1,105,730	NA............. 249,409	1,435 42,412
1,405,000,000.............. 2,203,000,000	1,420,000,000.............. 2,030,000,000	39,825............. 1,427,627	31,489............. 535,445	10,706 235,274
9,078,000,000.............. 3,120,000,000	6,650,000,000.............. 8,400,000,000	167,821............. 4,662,816	121,999............. 2,929,168	21,680 502,884
883,000,000.............. 704,000,000	436,200,000.............. 677,800,000	17,364............. 834,101	3,080............. 73,030	2,757 35,268
52,000,000.............. 16,000,000	9,726,700.............. 13,186,500	630............. 35,977	165............. 4,523	* *
787,000,000.............. 404,000,000	797,100,000.............. 1,400,000,000	33,329............. 2,130,716	9,962............. 427,597	1,085 14,949
484,000,000.............. 233,000,000	301,300,000.............. 343,200,000	4,058............. 129,298	2,053............. 37,036	166 2,760
12,847,000,000.............. 12,550,000,000	12,000,000,000.............. 11,900,000,000	25,949............. 373,347	33,958............. 444,165	6,192 84,634
105,302,000,000.............. 90,632,000,000	125,800,000,000.............. 131,800,000,000	232,405............. 4,621,670	364,758............. 5,015,447	40,512 1,060,412
724,000,000.............. 2,161,000,000	1,310,584,000.............. 1,310,584,000	3,441............. 155,081	1,510............. 26,750	231 1,663

Nation Capital	Population	Area of Country (sq mi/ sq km)	Type of Government	Heads of State and Government	Currency: Value in U.S. Dollars	GNP (000,000): GNP Per Capita
GAMBIA, THE .... Banjul	700,000.... 49,181	4,361.... 11,295	Republic ...... (C)	President: .... Sir Dawda K. Jawara	Dalasi ....$ 0.28	220 314
GERMAN .... DEMOCRATIC REPUBLIC East Berlin	16,700,000.... 1,173,028	41,768.... 108,178	Socialist .... republic	Chairman, Council of State: ...... Erich Honecker Chairman, Council of Ministers (Premier): Willi Stoph	Mark 0.33	120,940 7,241
GERMANY, FEDERAL REPUBLIC OF Bonn	61,400,000.... 292,000	95,976.... 248,577	Federal .... republic	President: .... Richard von Weizsäcker Chancellor: Helmut Kohl	Deutsche ..... mark 0.317	829,600 13,511
GHANA .... Accra	14,300,000.... 840,000	92,100.... 238,537	Republic ...... (C)	Chairman, Provisional .... National Defense Council: Jerry J. Rawlings	Cedi 0.029	4,770 334
GREAT BRITAIN[9] ..... London	56,500,000.... 6,696,000	94,227.... 244,046	Limited .... monarchy (C)	Queen: .... Elizabeth II Prime Minister: Margaret Thatcher	Pound 1.16	510,310 9,032
GREECE .... Athens	10,000,000.... 885,136	50,944.... 131,944	Republic 	President: .... Constantine Karamanlis Prime Minister: Andreas Papandreou	Drachma 0.01	42,890 4,289
GRENADA .... St. George's	113,000.... 10,000	133.... 344	Parliamentary .. state (C)	Governor-General:............... Sir Paul Scoon Prime Minister: Herbert A. Blaize	East.......... Caribbean dollar 0.37	100 885
GUATEMALA .... Guatemala City	8,000,000.... 1,300,000	42,042.... 108,889	Republic 	President: .... Oscar Humberto Mejía Victores	Quetzal 1.00	8,510 1,064
GUINEA .... Conakry	5,600,000.... 763,000	94,926.... 245,857	Republic 	President: .... Lansana Conté Premier: Diarra Traoré	Syli 0.04	1,660 296
GUINEA-BISSAU...... Bissau	800,000.... 109,486	13,948.... 36,125	Republic 	President, Council of............. the Revolution: Cmdr. João Bernardo Vieira Premier: Vitor Saúde Maria	Escudo 0.012	150 188
GUYANA .... Georgetown	800,000.... 187,600	83,000.... 214,969	Republic ...... (C)	President: .... Forbes Burnham Prime Minister: Ptolemy A. Reid	Dollar 0.27	580 725
HAITI .... Port-au-Prince	5,500,000.... 719,671	10,714.... 27,750	Republic 	President: .... Jean-Claude Duvalier	Gourde 0.20	1,510 275
HONDURAS .... Tegucigalpa	4,200,000.... 500,000	43,277.... 112,088	Republic 	President: .... Roberto Suazo Córdova	Lempira 0.50	2,270 540
HUNGARY .... Budapest	10,700,000.... 2,064,307	35,919.... 93,030	People's .... republic	Chairman, Presidential Council: ... Pál Losonczi Chairman, Council of Ministers (Premier): György Lázár	Forint 0.02	22,550 2,107
ICELAND............. Reykjavík	239,000.... 87,106	39,769.... 103,000	Republic 	President: .... Vigdís Finnbógadóttir Prime Minister: Steingrímur Hermannsson	New króna 0.03	2,970 12,427
INDIA .... New Delhi	740,400,000.... 2,000,000	1,269,345.... 3,287,590	Federal .... republic (C)	President: .... Zail Singh Prime Minister: Rajiv Gandhi	Rupee 0.083	176,660 240
INDONESIA .... Jakarta	161,000,000.... 6,503,449	782,662.... 2,027,087	Republic 	President: .... Suharto	Rupiah 0.001	78,750 490
IRAN................ Tehran	43,800,000.... 5,433,721	636,296.... 1,648,000	Islamic .... republic	President: .... Hojatolislam Sayed Ali Khamenei Prime Minister: Mir Hussein Moussavi	Rial 0.01	69,170 1,579

Imports Exports	Revenue Expenditure	Elementary Schools: Teachers Students	Secondary Schools: Teachers Students	Colleges and Universities: Teachers Students
$ 115,000,000.............$	56,340,000.............	1,808.............	620.............	NA
48,000,000	59,930,000	43,432	9,657	NA
21,524,000,000.............	164,500,000,000.............	168,849.............	NA.............	37,789
23,793,000,000	164,430,000,000	2,203,991	506,412	399,204
151,031,000,000.............	91,700,000,000.............	273,556.............	298,277.............	156,883
168,050,000,000	106,700,000,000	5,044,424	4,300,740	1,151,978
705,000,000.............	2,078,000,000.............	48,397.............	31,812.............	1,103
873,000,000	3,610,000,000	1,295,525	613,710	9,745
100,083,000,000.............	185,700,000,000.............	270,346.............	333,515.............	43,017
91,653,000,000	193,300,000,000	5,133,710	5,360,097	330,619
9,632,000,000.............	8,500,000,000.............	35,750.............	26,921.............	7,932
4,459,000,000	11,000,000,000	922,698	710,169	117,407
54,000,000.............	12,460,000.............	587.............	383.............	77
14,000,000	38,000,000	18,720	9,413	614
1,388,000,000.............	749,100,000.............	23,770.............	8,604.............	2,845
1,120,000,000	1,110,000,000	803,404	156,612	47,555
296,000,000.............	473,625,000.............	2,555.............	3,520.............	650
411,000,000	473,625,000	257,547	101,113	20,739
50,000,000.............	10,493,100.............	3,102.............	213.............	*
12,000,000	17,378,400	76,709	4,256	*
280,000,000.............	399,900,000.............	5,831.............	4,340.............	496
416,000,000	147,963,000	159,749	74,965	2,401
461,000,000.............	176,300,000.............	13,472.............	4,018.............	493
154,000,000	366,500,000	580,127	91,247	4,186
712,000,000.............	385,100,000.............	13,305.............	3,132.............	1,495
654,000,000	574,800,000	543,021	102,964	23,317
8,503,000,000.............	13,200,000,000.............	75,422.............	24,235.............	13,597
8,696,000,000	13,600,000,000	1,162,203	202,788	103,469
815,000,000.............	536,000,000.............	1,732.............	2,387.............	575
751,000,000	516,700,000	25,924	26,506	4,035
12,839,000,000.............	19,130,000,000.............	1,599,182.............	1,341,155.............	244,448
7,408,000,000	21,400,000,000	68,602,224	26,831,109	5,038,369
16,352,000,000.............	16,600,000,000.............	787,400.............	385,186.............	46,668
21,146,000,000	18,400,000,000	25,537,053	5,721,815	296,326
12,549,000,000.............	25,100,000,000.............	154,577.............	96,395.............	15,453
12,587,000,000	29,900,000,000	5,020,686	2,356,878	115,811

Nation Capital	Population	Area of Country (sq mi/ sq km)	Type of Government	Heads of State and Government	Currency: Value in U.S. Dollars	GNP (000,000): GNP Per Capita
IRAQ Baghdad	15,000,000 3,236,000	167,925 434,924	Republic	President and Chairman, Revolutionary Command Council: Saddam Hussein al-Takriti	Dinar 3.22	$ 39,500 2,633
IRELAND, REPUBLIC OF Dublin	3,600,000 543,563	27,136 70,283	Republic	President: Patrick J. Hillery Prime Minister: Garret FitzGerald	Pound 1.13	17,990 4,997
ISRAEL Jerusalem	4,200,000 410,000	8,019 20,770	Republic	President: Chaim Herzog Prime Minister: Shimon Peres	Shekel 0.0016	20,420 4,862
ITALY Rome	57,000,000 2,831,512	116,304 301,225	Republic	President: Alessandro Pertini Prime Minister: Bettino Craxi	Lira 0.0006	391,440 6,867
IVORY COAST Abidjan	9,200,000 1,800,000	124,504 322,463	Republic	President: Félix Houphouët-Boigny	CFA franc[3] 0.0023	10,190 1,108
JAMAICA Kingston	2,400,000 600,634	4,244 10,991	Parliamentary state (C)	Governor-General: Florizel A. Glasspole Prime Minister: Edward P. G. Seaga	Dollar 0.26	2,600 1,083
JAPAN Tokyo	119,900,000 8,334,900	143,751 372,313	Constitutional monarchy	Emperor: Hirohito Prime Minister: Yasuhiro Nakasone	Yen 0.004	1,186,430 9,895
JORDAN Amman	3,500,000 1,300,000	37,738 97,740	Constitutional monarchy	King: Hussein I Prime Minister: Ahmad Obaidat	Dinar 2.68	3,880 1,108
KENYA Nairobi	19,400,000 1,150,000	224,961 582,646	Republic (C)	President: Daniel arap Moi	Shilling 0.07	7,280 375
KIRIBATI (GILBERT ISLANDS) Tarawa	60,000 17,921	332 861	Republic (C)	President: Ieremia T. Tabai	Dollar 0.86	30 500
KOREA, DEMOCRATIC PEOPLE'S REPUBLIC OF P'yŏngyang	19,600,000 1,800,000	46,540 120,538	People's republic	President: Marshal Kim Il Sung Premier: Kang Song San	Won 1.06	17,040 869
KOREA, REPUBLIC OF Seoul	42,000,000 9,454,825	38,025 98,484	Republic	President: Chun Doo Hwan Prime Minister: Chin Iee Jong	Won 0.0013	66,090 1,573
KUWAIT Kuwait	1,600,000 60,525	6,880 17,818	Constitutional emirate	Emir: Sheikh Jabir al-Ahmad al-Sabah Prime Minister: Sheikh Saad al-Abdullah al-Salem al-Sabah	Dinar 3.36	30,600 19,125
LAOS Vientiane	3,700,000 100,000	91,429 236,800	People's republic	President: Prince Souphanouvong Premier: Kaysone Phomvihan	New kip 0.10	290 78
LEBANON Beirut	2,600,000 1,000,000	4,015 10,400	Republic	President: Amin Gemayel Prime Minister: Rashid Karami	Pound 0.16	NA
LESOTHO Maseru	1,500,000 45,000	11,720 30,355	Constitutional monarchy (C)	King: Moshoeshoe II Prime Minister: Chief Leabua Jonathan	Loti 0.58	740 493
LIBERIA Monrovia	2,200,000 208,600	43,000 111,369	Republic	Head of State and Chairman, People's Redemption Council: Gen. Samuel K. Doe	Dollar 1.00	1,010 459

Imports Exports	Revenue Expenditure	Elementary Schools: Teachers Students	Secondary Schools: Teachers Students	Colleges and Universities: Teachers Students
$ NA	$ 61,915,700,000	94,000	33,514	6,515
NA	61,915,700,000	2,615,910	1,033,418	102,430
9,182,000,000	7,340,000,000	14,636	20,965	4,088
8,612,000,000	10,200,000,000	419,998	300,601	49,313
8,386,000,000	27,000,000,000	39,401	NA	13,981
4,931,000,000	29,690,000,000	605,933	193,219	88,786
80,367,000,000	116,400,000,000	269,279	493,513	- 43,220
72,681,000,000	159,400,000,000	4,435,217	5,308,595	1,097,954
2,090,000,000	1,730,000,000	24,441	4,026	220
2,235,000,000	1,730,000,000	954,190	172,280	12,470
1,518,000,000	477,855,000	8,783	6,473	567
738,000,000	749,070,000	363,420	234,867	6,892
146,992,000,000	209,400,000,000	470,991	554,078	213,000
146,676,000,000	165,800,000,000	11,826,573	9,745,517	2,422,915
3,030,000,000	2,060,000,000	14,303	12,153	1,125
579,000,000	2,080,000,000	454,391	248,643	30,076
1,683,000,000	1,860,000,000	92,762	15,726	NA
979,000,000	2,410,000,000	3,698,246	388,216	10,282
18,000,000	13,609,382	447	108	NA
3,000,000	14,539,770	13,383	1,766	741
899,000,000	27,872,346,000	100,000[4]	100,000[4]	NA
843,000,000	27,872,346,000	2,561,674	2,000,000	NA
26,192,000,000	12,600,000,000	122,727	113,185	20,900
24,445,000,000	11,800,000,000	5,586,494	4,396,984	615,452
6,969,000,000	11,450,000,000	8,035	15,342	1,143
16,298,000,000	12,560,000,000	148,983	181,882	12,435
85,000,000	119,000,000	14,983	3,705	118
9,000,000	215,200,000	463,098	82,618	1,157
374,000,000	NA	22,646	21,344	2,300
122,000,000	NA	405,402	287,310	85,087
NA	181,335,000	4,782	940	162
NA	181,912,500	235,604	22,546	1,682
428,000,000	399,600,000	9,099	1,129	190
477,000,000	420,100,000	227,431	54,623	3,789

Nation Capital	Population	Area of Country (sq mi/ sq km)	Type of Government	Heads of State and Government	Currency: Value in U.S. Dollars	GNP (000,000): GNP Per Capita
LIBYA............. Tripoli	3,700,000.... 1,000,000	679,362.... 1,759,540	Socialist republic	Revolutionary Leader (Head of State): Col. Muammar al-Qaddafi Secretary-General, General People's Congress: Muhammad az-Zarrouk Ragab	Dinar....... 3.38	$ 26,080 7,049
LIECHTENSTEIN...... Vaduz	26,400.... 4,900	61.... 157	Constitutional monarchy	Sovereign:.................... Prince Hans Adam Chief of Government: Hans Brunhart	Swiss franc ... 0.427	NA
LUXEMBOURG .... Luxembourg	366,000.... 78,900	998.... 2,586	Constitutional monarchy	Grand Duke:.................... Jean President: Jacques Santer	Franc 0.02	5,790 15,820
MADAGASCAR .... Antananarivo	9,800,000.... 525,000	226,658.... 587,041	Socialist republic	President: Cmdr. Didier Ratsiraka Prime Minister: Lt. Col. Désiré Rakotoarijaona	Franc 0.002	2,970 303
MALAWI .... Lilongwe	6,900,000.... 98,718	45,747.... 118,484	Republic (C)	President:............... Hastings Kamuzu Banda	Kwacha 0.73	1,250 181
MALAYSIA .... Kuala Lumpur	15,300,000.... 937,875	127,317.... 329,749	Federal constitutional monarchy (C)	Supreme Head of State: Sultan Mahmood Iskander Prime Minister: Datuk Seri Mahathir bin Mohamad	Ringgit 0.43	26,110 1,706
MALDIVES .... Male	173,000.... 29,500	115.... 298	Republic 	President:............. Maumoon Abdul Gayoom	Rupee........ 0.25	40 231
MALI................ Bamako	7,600,000.... 419,237	478,766.... 1,240,000	Republic	President:................ Brig. Gen. Moussa Traoré	Franc 0.0012	1,340 176
MALTA............... Valletta	356,000.... 13,950	122.... 316	Republic ...... (C)	President:.................. Agatha Barbara Prime Minister: Carmelo Mifsud-Bonníci	Pound........ 2.25	1,310 3,680
MAURITANIA .... Nouakchott	1,800,000.... 135,000	397,955.... 1,030,700	Islamic republic	President and Chairman, Military Committee for National Salvation: Lt. Col. Mohamed Khouna Ould Haidalla Prime Minister: Lt. Col. Mohamed Khouna Ould Haidalla	Ouguiya 0.02	710 394
MAURITIUS .... Port Louis	1,000,000.... 148,389	790.... 2,045	Parliamentary state (C)	Governor-General:............... Seewoosagur Ramgoolam Prime Minister: Anerood Jugnauth	Rupee 0.07	1,230 1,230
MEXICO.............. Mexico City	77,700,000.... 9,377,300	761,604.... 1,972,547	Federal republic	President:................ Miguel de la Madrid Hurtado	Peso 0.005	160,230 2,062
MONACO .... Monaco	27,000.... 4,000	0.58.... 1.49	Constitutional monarchy	Prince:....................... Rainier III Minister of State: Jean Herly	French franc .. 0.12	NA
MONGOLIAN **PEOPLE'S** **REPUBLIC** Ulan Bator	1,900,000.... 1,565,000 461,000	604,250....	People's .... republic	Presidium Chairman: Jambyn Batmönh	Tugrik 0.30	1,100 579
MOROCCO .... Rabat	23,600,000.... 367,620	172,414.... 446,550	Constitutional monarchy	King:....................... Hassan II Prime Minister: Muhammad Karim Lamrani	Dirham 0.12	17,960 761
MOZAMBIQUE........ Maputo	13,400,000.... 785,510	309,496.... 801,590	People's ...... republic	President:................ Samora M. Machel	Metical 0.02	2,800 209
NAURU .... Yaren	8,400.... NA	8.... 21	Republic ...... (C)	President:................ Hammer DeRoburt	Australian ..... dollar 0.86	NA

446

Imports Exports	Revenue Expenditure	Elementary Schools: Teachers Students	Secondary Schools: Teachers Students	Colleges and Universities: Teachers Students
$ 8,382,000,000..............$ 15,576,000,000	NA.............. 13,019,106,000	28,229.............. 603,759	21,026.............. 280,215	1,340 15,267
NA.............. NA	123,960,000.............. 123,780,000	95.............. 1,899	92.............. 1,831	NA NA
NA.............. NA	1,350,000,000[10].............. 1,410,000,000[10]	1,449.............. 27,510	1,801.............. 24,984	168 404
540,000,000.............. 316,000,000	685,400,000.............. 685,400,000	23,937.............. 1,311,000	5,088.............. 131,863	557 22,857
312,000,000.............. 230,000,000	218,600,000.............. 306,800,000	12,540.............. 809,862	931.............. 18,006	190 2,000
13,987,000,000.............. 13,917,000,000	7,070,000,000.............. 9,510,000,000	63,479[11].............. 1,675,340[11]	43,797[11].............. 987,624[11]	4,052 39,947
28,000,000.............. 9,000,000	25,292,330.............. 36,488,130	49.............. 2,662	26.............. 712	* *
332,000,000.............. 146,000,000	237,000,000.............. 266,000,000	7,214.............. 298,831	3,004.............. 70,625	489 5,281
733,000,000.............. 363,000,000	471,665,340.............. 485,941,630	1,567.............. 32,448	2,229.............. 27,673	224 1,674
273,000,000.............. 232,000,000	204,000,000.............. 240,000,000	2,183.............. 90,530	646.............. 20,248	110 477
438,000,000.............. 373,000,000	390,800,000.............. 491,600,000	6,177.............. 123,666	3,101.............. 82,748	242 1,213
8,136,000,000.............. 21,399,000,000	59,750,000,000.............. 74,680,000,000	375,220.............. 14,666,257	250,890.............. 4,741,850	73,760 934,111
NA.............. NA	166,309,000.............. 199,803,400	400[4].............. 1,017	400[4].............. 2,065	* *
566,000,000.............. 416,000,000	1,490,000,000.............. 1,480,000,000	4,482.............. 141,306	10,215.............. 237,190	1,033 11,826
4,315,000,000.............. 2,059,000,000	5,378,000,000.............. 7,899,000,000	63,157.............. 2,411,000	38,252.............. 885,028	2,561 74,465
792,000,000.............. 303,000,000	514,000,000.............. 594,000,000	17,030.............. 1,387,192	2,831.............. 102,745	244 836
NA.............. NA	83,416,742.............. 95,426,887	.... 	129[4].............. 600	* *

447

Nation Capital	Population	Area of Country (sq mi/ sq km)	Type of Government	Heads of State and Government	Currency: Value in U.S. Dollars	GNP (000,000): GNP Per Capita
NEPAL Kathmandu	16,600,000 393,494	54,362 140,797	Constitutional monarchy	King: Birendra Bir Bikram Shah Deva Prime Minister: Lokendra Bahadur Chand	Rupee 0.06	$ 2,300 138
NETHERLANDS, THE Amsterdam	14,400,000 700,759	15,770 40,844	Constitutional monarchy	Queen: Beatrix Prime Minister: Ruud Lubbers	Guilder 0.32	167,980 11,665
NEW ZEALAND Wellington	3,200,000 342,000	103,736 368,676	Parliamentary state (C)	Governor-General: Sir David S. Beattie Prime Minister: Robert D. Muldoon	Dollar 0.63	25,460 7,956
NICARAGUA Managua	2,900,000 902,000	50,193 130,000	Republic	Coordinator, Junta of the Government of National Reconstruction: Cmdr. Daniel Ortega Saavedra	Córdoba 0.10	2,400 828
NIGER Niamey	6,300,000 343,600	489,191 1,267,000	Republic	President, Supreme Military Council: Col. Seyni Kountché Prime Minister: Oumarou Mamane	CFA franc[3] 0.0023	1,890 300
NIGERIA Lagos	88,100,000 4,200,000	356,669 923,768	Federal republic (C)	President: Gen. Mohammed Buhari	Naira 1.38	76,170 865
NORWAY Oslo	4,100,000 448,775	125,182 324,219	Constitutional monarchy	King: Olav V Prime Minister: Kaare Willoch	Krone 0.12	57,640 14,058
OMAN Masqat	1,000,000 6,000	82,030 212,457	Sultanate	Sultan and Prime Minister: Qabus bin Sa'id	Rial 2.89	5,440 5,440
PAKISTAN Islamabad	97,300,000 378,000	310,404 803,943	Federal republic	President and Chief Martial Law Administrator: Gen. Muhammad Zia ul-Haq	Rupee 0.07	29,800 306
PANAMA Panamá	2,100,000 388,638	29,762 77,082	Republic	President: Nicolás Ardito Barletta	Balboa 1.00	3,580 1,704
PAPUA NEW GUINEA Port Moresby	3,400,000 140,000	178,260 461,691	Parliamentary state (C)	Governor-General: Kingsford Dibela Prime Minister: Michael Somare	Kina 1.07	2,570 755
PARAGUAY Asunción	3,600,000 474,122	157,048 406,752	Republic	President: Gen. Alfredo Stroessner	Guarani 0.004	4,970 1,380
PERU Lima	19,200,000 4,900,000	496,224 1,285,216	Republic	President: Fernando Belaúnde Terry Prime Minister: Luis Percovich	Sol 0.0003	19,980 1,041
PHILIPPINES Manila	54,500,000 1,630,485	115,831 300,000	Republic	President: Ferdinand E. Marcos Prime Minister: César Virata	Peso 0.06	39,010 716
POLAND Warsaw	36,900,000 1,628,900	120,725 312,677	People's republic	Chairman, Council of State: Henryk Jabłoński Chairman, Military Council of National Salvation, and Chairman, Council of Ministers (Premier): Gen. Wojciech W. Jaruzelski	Zloty 0.009	139,780 3,788
PORTUGAL Lisbon	10,100,000 812,385	35,553 92,082	Republic	President: Gen. António Ramalho Eanes Prime Minister: Mário Soares	Escudo 0.007	24,750 2,450
QATAR Doha	276,000 190,000	4,247 11,000	Constitutional emirate	Emir and Prime Minister: Sheikh Khalifa bin Hamad al-Thani	Riyal 0.27	6,540 23,700
ROMANIA Bucharest	22,700,000 1,861,007	91,699 237,500	Socialist republic	Head of State and President, State Council: Nicolae Ceauşescu Chairman, Council of Ministers (Premier): Constantin Dăscălescu	Leu 0.22	57,030 2,512

Imports Exports	Revenue Expenditure	Elementary Schools: Teachers Students	Secondary Schools: Teachers Students	Colleges and Universities: Teachers Students
$ 765,000,000 ....$ 271,000,000	202,000,000 404,800,000	27,805 1,067,912	16,376 512,434	2,311 38,539
61,573,000,000 65,662,000,000	47,200,000,000 55,300,000,000	57,536 1,333,342	103,369 1,394,939	28,500 350,778
5,279,000,000 5,272,000,000	6,892,339,200 7,750,974,400	22,658 381,262	NA 352,427	7,694 76,643
776,000,000 406,000,000	624,900,000 771,800,000	13,318 472,167	2,720 139,743	1,299 27,179
442,000,000 333,000,000	187,026,400 187,026,400	4,298 187,251	961 45,846	224 1,435
20,846,000,000 19,739,000,000	13,960,000,000 15,982,000,000	NA 12,556,881	NA 1,826,629	5,748 115,166
13,500,000,000 17,979,000,000	24,238,968,000 20,622,613,000	46,604 394,510	NA 355,567	7,624 78,401
2,492,000,000 4,058,000,000	2,300,000,000 2,300,000,000	3,959 91,895	1,733 15,280	* *
5,341,000,000 3,075,000,000	3,864,996,000 4,482,756,000	147,000 6,601,227	129,035 2,244,500	6,074 148,451
1,412,000,000 304,000,000	1,060,000,000 1,400,000,000	12,361 337,522	8,138 171,273	2,065 41,234
974,000,000 734,000,000	506,100,000 873,000,000	9,935 300,536	2,289 49,334	578 2,883
506,000,000 262,000,000	492,000,000 67,000,000	17,525 504,377	9,830 110,095	1,945 20,812
2,709,000,000 2,909,000,000	3,510,000,000 3,200,000,000	80,331 3,117,055	37,383 1,151,748	13,468 233,420
8,086,000,000 4,781,000,000	6,520,000,000 7,740,000,000	264,241 8,033,642	85,779 2,928,525	40,022 1,182,103
9,931,000,000 10,951,000,000	41,540,000,000 48,928,000,000	212,050 4,167,313	139,412 1,673,869	55,941 609,997
8,245,000,000 4,608,000,000	3,570,380,800 4,731,596,800	65,124 1,220,527	21,847 499,557	10,723 91,373
1,456,000,000 3,384,000,000	3,690,000,000 3,470,000,000	2,037 28,472	1,369 14,360	261 2,025
9,836,000,000 11,714,000,000	18,500,000,000 17,200,000,000	156,817 3,236,808	48,082 871,257	14,592 192,769

449

Nation Capital	Population	Area of Country (sq mi/ sq km)	Type of Government	Heads of State and Government	Currency: Value in U.S. Dollars	GNP (000,000): GNP Per Capita
RWANDA Kigali	5,300,000.... 141,000	10,169.... 26,338	Republic	President: Maj. Gen. Juvénal Habyarimana	Franc 0.01	$ 1,340 253
SAINT KITTS– NEVIS Basseterre	40,000.... 14,700	104.... 269	Parliamentary state (C)	Governor-General: Sir Clement Arrindell Prime Minister: Kennedy Simmonds	East Caribbean dollar 0.37	50 1,250
SAINT LUCIA Castries	120,000.... 45,000	238.... 616	Parliamentary state (C)	Governor-General: Allen Lewis Prime Minister: John G. M. Compton	East Caribbean dollar 0.37	120 1,000
SAINT VINCENT AND THE GRENADINES Kingstown	138,000.... 388 22,782	150....	Parliamentary state (C)	Governor-General: Sir Sydney Douglas Gun-Munro Prime Minister: James Mitchell	East Caribbean dollar 0.37	70 507
SAN MARINO San Marino	21,200.... 4,400	24.... 61	Republic	Co-Regents: Renzo Renzi Germano De Biagi	Italian lira 0.0006	NA
SÃO TOMÉ AND PRÍNCIPE São Tomé	89,000.... 964 25,000	372....	Republic	President and Prime Minister: Manuel Pinto da Costa	Dobra 0.02	40 449
SAUDI ARABIA Riyadh	10,800,000.... 680,000	830,000.... 2,149,690	Monarchy	King and Prime Minister: Fahd ibn Abdul-Aziz	Riyal 0.28	117,240 10,855
SENEGAL Dakar	6,500,000.... 978,553	75,750.... 196,192	Republic	President: Abdou Diouf Premier: Habib Thiam	CFA franc[3] 0.0023	2,530 389
SEYCHELLES Victoria	66,000.... 23,000	108.... 280	Republic (C)	President: France Albert René	Rupee 0.14	110 1,666
SIERRA LEONE Freetown	3,900,000.... 274,000	27,699.... 71,740	Republic (C)	President: Siaka P. Stevens	Leone 0.40	1,140 292
SINGAPORE Singapore	2,500,000.... 2,413,900	224.... 581	Republic (C)	President: C. V. Devan Nair Prime Minister: Lee Kuan Yew	Dollar 0.47	12,800 5,120
SOLOMON ISLANDS Honiara	263,000.... 20,842	10,983.... 28,446	Parliamentary state (C)	Governor-General: Sir Baddeley Devesi Prime Minister: Solomon Mamaloni	Dollar 0.76	150 570
SOMALIA Mogadisho	5,700,000.... 400,000	246,201.... 637,657	Republic	President and Chairman, Council of Ministers: Maj. Gen. Muhammad Siad Barre	Shilling 0.06	1,240 218
SOUTH AFRICA,[13] REPUBLIC OF Cape Town Pretoria	31,700,000.... 711,500 942,851	471,445.... 1,221,037	Republic	President: Pieter Willem Botha	Rand 0.73	81,840 2,582
SPAIN Madrid	38,400,000.... 3,188,297	194,897.... 504,782	Constitutional monarchy	King: Juan Carlos I Prime Minister: Felipe González Márquez	Peseta 0.006	214,300 5,580
SRI LANKA (CEYLON) Colombo	16,100,000.... 585,776	25,332.... 65,610	Republic (C)	President: Junius R. Jayewardene Prime Minister: Ranasinghe Premadasa	Rupee 0.04	4,460 277
SUDAN Khartoum	21,100,000.... 1,000,000	967,499.... 2,505,813	Republic	President and Prime Minister: Maj. Gen. Jaafar al-Nimeiry	Pound 0.77	7,390 350
SURINAME Paramaribo	370,000.... 200,000	63,037.... 163,265	Republic	President: Desi Bouterse Prime Minister: Wim Udenhout	Guilder 0.56	1,070 2,892
SWAZILAND Mbabane	600,000.... 38,640	6,704.... 17,363	Monarchy (C)	Queen: Ntombi Prime Minister: Prince Bhekimpi Dlamini	Lilangeni 0.73	480 800

Imports Exports	Revenue Expenditure	Elementary Schools: Teachers Students	Secondary Schools: Teachers Students	Colleges and Universities: Teachers Students
$ 279,000,000............$ 81,000,000	161,400,000............ 184,400,000	11,912.............. 704,924	887.............. 10,667	229 1,266
45,000,000.............. 19,000,000	24,370,346.............. 20,222,202	NA.............. NA	141.............. 3,350	8 40[12]
46,000,000.............. 15,000,000	43,036,994.............. 56,370,314	942.............. 30,610	220.............. 4,879	51 437
61,000,000.............. 32,000,000	33,425,151.............. 31,874,042	1,210.............. 21,854	243.............. 5,084	41 259
NA.............. NA	87,370,000.............. 87,370,000	132.............. 1,535	112.............. 1,228	* *
25,000,000.............. 9,000,000	6,740,000.............. 17,700,000	527.............. 14,162	NA.............. 3,145	* *
40,654,000,000.............. 79,118,000,000	60,776,000,000.............. 73,840,000,000	50,511.............. 926,531	26,788.............. 348,996	6,598 56,252
974,000,000.............. 477,000,000	690,600,000.............. 690,600,000	9,178.............. 392,541	3,493.............. 87,755	638 12,373
88,000,000.............. 20,000,000	65,800,000.............. 65,800,000	405.............. 9,978	288.............. 5,143	28 144
298,000,000.............. 111,000,000	201,800,000.............. 398,200,000	7,943.............. 250,480	2,720.............. 60,285	289 1,594
28,153,000,000.............. 21,833,000,000	4,680,000,000.............. 3,140,000,000	9,463.............. 291,649	9,298.............. 169,538	1,927 21,022
76,000,000.............. 66,000,000	26,279,916.............. 46,291,921	1,148.............. 28,870	257.............. 4,030	* *
221,000,000.............. 185,000,000	219,100,000.............. 219,100,000	8,693.............. 271,139	1,405.............. 22,691	324 2,899
13,460,000,000 14,054,000,000	15,200,000,000.............. 17,400,000,000	164,149[4].............. 4,480,493	164,149[4].............. 1,225,153	16,708 98,577
29,194,000,000.............. 19,735,000,000	27,100,000,000.............. 37,400,000,000	205,550.............. 3,608,854	NA.............. 3,912,777	37,468 630,463
1,786,000,000.............. 1,062,000,000	855,700,000.............. 1,710,000,000	60,835.............. 2,081,391	58,755.............. 1,258,002	2,017 36,628
1,354,000,000.............. 624,000,000	2,510,000,000.............. 3,570,000,000	43,451.............. 1,464,227	18,831.............. 384,194	6,497 26,996
511,000,000.............. 429,000,000	289,400,000.............. 441,500,000	3,068.............. 85,060	1,867.............. 34,372	118 900
NA.............. NA	211,110,000.............. 325,550,000	3,278.............. 112,019	1,292.............. 23,198	163 1,399

Nation Capital	Population	Area of Country (sq mi/ sq km)	Type of Government	Heads of State and Government	Currency: Value in U.S. Dollars	GNP (000,000): GNP Per Capita
SWEDEN . . . . Stockholm	8,300,000 649,680	173,732 449,964	Constitutional monarchy	King: Carl XVI Gustaf Prime Minister: Olof Palme	Krona 0.12	$ 123,770 14,912
SWITZERLAND . . . . . . Bern	6,500,000 143,800	15,941 41,288	Federal . . . . republic	President: . . . . Leon Schlumpf	Franc 0.43	122,850 18,900
SYRIA . . . . Damascus	10,100,000 1,201,000	71,498 185,180	Socialist republic	President: Lt. Gen. Hafez al-Assad Prime Minister: Abdel al-Raouf al-Kassem	Pound 0.26	14,660 1,451
TAIWAN or . . . . **FORMOSA** **(REPUBLIC OF** **CHINA)** Taipei	19,200,000 2,500,000	13,892 35,981	Republic	President: Chiang Ching-kuo Premier: Yu Kuo-hua	New Taiwan . . dollar 0.03	38,200 1,990
TANZANIA . . . . Dar es-Salaam	21,200,000 900,000	364,900 945,087	Republic . . . . . . (C)	President: Julius K. Nyerere Prime Minister: Salim Ahmed Salim	Shilling 0.08	5,260 248
THAILAND . . . . Bangkok	51,700,000 5,500,000	198,456 514,000	Constitutional monarchy	King: Bhumibol Adulyadej Prime Minister: Gen. Prem Tinsulanonda	Baht 0.04	36,900 714
TOGO . . . . Lomé	2,900,000 275,000	21,925 56,785	Republic 	President: Gen. Gnassingbe Eyadéma	CFA franc[3] 0.0023	1,010 348
TONGA . . . . Nukualofa	99,000 20,564	270 699	Constitutional monarchy	King: Taufa'ahau Tupou IV Prime Minister: Prince Fatafehi Tu'ipelehake	Australian . . . . . dollar 0.86	50 505
TRINIDAD AND . . . . **TOBAGO** Port of Spain	1,200,000 61,160	1,981 5,130	Republic . . . . . . (C)	President: Sir Elliis E. I. Clarke Prime Minister: George M. Chambers	Dollar 0.42	6,720 5,600
TUNISIA . . . . Tunis	7,000,000 1,000,000	63,170 163,610	Republic	President: Habib Bourguiba Prime Minister: Muhammad M'zali	Dinar 1.33	9,300 1,329
TURKEY . . . . Ankara	50,200,000 1,877,755	301,382 780,576	Republic	President: Gen. Kenan Evren Prime Minister: Turgut Özal	Lira 0.003	70,210 1,398
TUVALU . . . . **(ELLICE ISLANDS)** Funafuti	7,300 . . . . NA	10 26	Parliamentary state (C)	Governor-General: Sir Penitala Fiatau Teo Prime Minister: Tomasi Puapua	Australian . . . . . dollar 0.86	5 685
UGANDA . . . . Kampala	14,300,000 458,000	91,134 236,036	Republic . . . . . . (C)	President: Milton Obote Prime Minister: Erifasi Otema Alimadi	Shilling 0.003	2,890 202
UNION OF SOVIET . . . . **SOCIALIST** **REPUBLICS** Moscow	274,000,000 8,396,000	8,649,534 22,402,200	Federal . . . . socialist state	Chairman, Presidium . . . . of the Supreme Soviet: Konstantin Chernenko Chairman, Council of Ministers (Premier): Nikolai A. Tikhonov	Ruble 1.26	1,212,000 4,423
UNITED ARAB . . . . **EMIRATES** Abu Dhabi	1,500,000 516,000	32,278 83,600	Federal . . . . state	President: . . . . Sheikh Zayed bin Sultan al-Nahayan Prime Minister: Sheikh Rashid bin Saeed al-Maktloum	Dirham 0.27	26,910 17,940
UNITED STATES . . . . . . **OF AMERICA** Washington, D.C.	236,300,000 623,000	3,618,770 9,372,569	Federal . . . . republic	President: . . . . Ronald W. Reagan Vice-President: George Bush	Dollar . . . . *	3,701,200 15,663

Imports Exports	Revenue Expenditure	Elementary Schools: Teachers Students	Secondary Schools: Teachers Students	Colleges and Universities: Teachers Students
$ 26,100,000,000	$ 33,800,000,000	40,204	61,759	NA
27,441,000,000	50,200,000,000	666,679	606,833	198,798
29,117,000,000	9,290,000,000	NA	NA	5,911
25,595,000,000	8,870,000,000	450,942	459,590	81,530
4,015,000,000	3,510,000,000	55,346	31,916	1,332
2,026,000,000	4,720,000,000	1,555,921	604,327	112,577
18,888,000,000	7,990,000,000	69,143	70,688	17,452
22,204,000,000	8,870,000,000	2,202,904	1,620,165	358,437
1,134,000,000	1,070,000,000	81,153	3,218	1,068
445,000,000	1,410,000,000	3,359,966	78,965	4,031
10,232,000,000	5,050,000,000	304,400	71,446	25,045
6,368,000,000	6,820,000,000	7,370,846	1,912,621	472,995
391,000,000	227,420,000	9,193	2,855	291
177,000,000	227,420,000	506,356	128,175	3,638
47,000,000	14,897,347	818	NA	26
5,000,000	14,883,627	19,744	12,795	128
2,558,000,000	2,689,848,000	6,363	NA	412
2,387,000,000	2,895,322,500	181,863	76,180	4,940
3,108,000,000	2,790,000,000	27,375	14,328	3,647
1,852,000,000	2,790,000,000	1,054,027	293,351	30,150
9,348,000,000	15,990,000,000	212,456	95,827	20,643
5,694,000,000	14,880,000,000	5,656,494	2,225,533	269,864
2,800,000	NA	44	10	*
360,000	3,001,250	1,226	250	*
293,000,000	507,300,000	36,442	3,775	681
345,000,000	537,300,000	1,223,850	77,929	6,192
80,267,000,000	446,166,000,000	2,321,000	NA	317,152
91,331,000,000	445,914,000,000	21,714,000	20,708,300	5,236,000
9,419,000,000	6,120,000,000	5,424	2,499	76
16,836,000,000	5,080,000,000	88,617	32,362	1,015
269,878,000,000	666,500,000,000	1,351,000	1,100,000	822,000
200,538,000,000	841,800,000,000	27,448,000	14,556,000	11,569,899

Nation Capital	Population	Area of Country (sq mi/ sq km)	Type of Government	Heads of State and Government	Currency: Value in U.S. Dollars	GNP (000,000): GNP Per Capita
UPPER VOLTA (BURKINA FASO) Ouagadougou	6,700,000 247,877	105,869 274,200	Republic	Head of Government: Thomas Sankara	CFA franc[3] 0.0023	$ 1,490 222
URUGUAY Montevideo	3,000,000 1,500,000	68,037 176,215	Republic	President: Julio María Sanguinettí	New peso 0.02	8,260 2,753
VANUATU (NEW HEBRIDES) Vila	130,000 14,598	5,700 14,763	Republic (C)	President: Ati George Sokomanu Prime Minister: Rev. Walter H. Lini	Vatu 0.01	40 307
VENEZUELA Caracas	18,600,000 1,658,500	352,144 912,050	Federal republic	President: Jaime Lusinchi	Bolivar 0.07	65,080 3,499
VIETNAM Hanoi	58,300,000 2,500,000	127,242 329,556	Socialist republic	Chairman, Council of State (President): Truong Chinh Chairman, Council of Ministers (Premier): Pham Van Dong	Dong 0.10	7,750 133
WESTERN SAMOA Apia	161,000 33,170	1,097 2,842	Constitutional monarchy (C)	Head of State: Malietoa Tanumafili II Prime Minister: Tupuola Efi	Talà 0.47	NA
YEMEN, PEOPLE'S DEMOCRATIC REPUBLIC OF Aden	2,100,000 272,000	128,560 332,968	People's republic	President: Chairman of the Presidium of the Supreme People's Council, and Prime Minister: Ali Nasser Muhammad al-Hasani	Dinar 2.92	910 433
YEMEN ARAB REPUBLIC Sana	5,900,000 278,000	75,290 195,000	Republic	President: Col. Ali Abdullah Saleh Prime Minister: Abdel Aziz Abdel Ghani	Rial 0.20	3,310 561
YUGOSLAVIA Belgrade	23,000,000 1,470,073	98,766 255,804	Federal socialist republic	President: Veselin Djuranovic President, Federal Executive Council (Prime Minister): Milka Planinc	Dinar 0.008	62,930 2,736
ZAIRE Kinshasa	32,200,000 3,500,000	905,567 2,345,409	Republic	President: Mobutu Sese Seko First State Commissioner (Prime Minister): Kengo wa Dondo	Zaire 0.03	6,280 195
ZAMBIA Lusaka	6,600,000 538,469	290,586 752,614	Republic (C)	President: Kenneth D. Kaunda Prime Minister: Nalumino Mundia	Kwacha 0.62	3,490 529
ZIMBABWE (RHODESIA) Harare	8,300,000 656,000	150,804 390,580	Republic (C)	President: Rev. Canaan S. Banana Prime Minister: Robert G. Mugabe	Dollar 0.86	6,260 754

1. Figure excludes trade with members of Soviet bloc.
2. Figure includes data for Luxembourg.
3. "CFA" stands for Communauté Financière Africaine.
4. Combined figure for elementary and secondary education.
5. Excluding Turkish sector of Nicosia.
6. Excluding budget of the Turkish sector (Turkish Republic of Northern Cyprus), which was balanced at $51,785,900 in 1982–1983.
7. Figures for Greek schools only.

Imports Exports	Revenue Expenditure	Elementary Schools: Teachers Students	Secondary Schools: Teachers Students	Colleges and Universities: Teachers Students
$ 346,000,000..............$ 56,000,000	142,200,000.............. 159,900,000	3,700.............. 201,595	818.............. 27,539	116 1,281
647,000,000.............. 1,015,000,000	2,670,000,000.............. 8,870,000,000	14,768.............. 331,247	NA.............. 180,678	3,847 36,298
64,000,000.............. 31,000,000	3,724,000,000.............. 3,724,000,000	NA.............. NA	NA.............. 2,284	* *
6,667,000,000.............. 15,924,000,000	22,700,000,000.............. 19,300,000,000	88,493.............. 2,156,815	45,888.............. 820,660	27,025 299,773
838,000,000.............. 430,000,000	1,002,309,000.............. 1,002,309,000	217,493.............. 7,923,495	156,164.............. 3,703,199	15,183 137,002
50,000,000.............. 13,000,000	16,030,860.............. 12,555,051	NA.............. NA	1,913[4].............. 19,785	79 654
1,527,000,000.............. 779,000,000	651,093,100.............. 959,121,450	10,078.............. 212,795	2,194.............. 66,681	246 2,517
1,758,000,000.............. 47,000,000	1,580,000,000.............. 1,740,000,000	10,576.............. 460,630	1,172.............. 35,726	NA 4,058
11,104,000,000.............. 9,038,000,000	9,510,000,000.............. 9,730,000,000	59,391.............. 1,431,582	131,348.............. 2,426,164	24,171 448,755
480,000,000.............. 569,000,000	1,156,000,000.............. 1,331,000,000	NA.............. 3,919,395	NA.............. 704,332	2,782 26,700
831,000,000.............. 1,059,000,000	724,200,000.............. 1,200,000,000	19,868.............. 996,597	4,236.............. 94,930	412 9,192
1,430,000,000.............. 1,273,000,000	1,600,000,000.............. 2,940,000,000	36,734.............. 1,714,266	6,148.............. 149,018	483 1,873

8. Figures generally include data for Greenland and Faero Islands.
9. Figures include data for Northern Ireland.
10. Included in figure for Belgium.
11. Figure is for peninsular Malaysia.
12. Enrollment figure includes nondegree programs.
13. Data generally exclude the homelands that have been granted independence. Population of the homelands (including homeland citizens residing in South Africa) is: Bophuthatswana, 1,400,000; Ciskei, 721,000; Transkei, 2,500,000; Venda, 340,000.

THE STATES AND OUTLYING AREAS OF THE UNITED STATES

State Capital	Population	Area (sq mi/ sq km)	Per Capita Personal Income	Governor Lieutenant-Governor	Revenue Expenditure	Roads (Miles)
ALABAMA Montgomery	3,959,000 182,406	51,705 133,915	$ 9,242	George Wallace (D) William Baxley (D)	$ 4,159,000,000 4,181,000,000	87,240
ALASKA Juneau	479,000 19,528	591,004 1,530,693	17,194	William J. Sheffield (D) Stephen McAlpine (D)	5,583,000,000 3,034,000,000	9,085
ARIZONA Phoenix	2,963,000 854,990	114,000 295,259	10,656	Bruce E. Babbitt (D) *	2,888,000,000 2,966,000,000	78,286
ARKANSAS Little Rock	2,328,000 167,331	53,187 137,753	8,967	Bill Clinton (D) Winston Bryant (D)	2,238,000,000 2,159,000,000	76,764
CALIFORNIA Sacramento	25,174,000 292,600	158,706 411,047	13,257	George Deukmejian (R) Leo T. McCarthy (D)	34,421,000,000 35,492,000,000	176,665
COLORADO Denver	3,139,000 500,000	104,091 269,594	12,770	Richard D. Lamm (D) Nancy Dick (D)	3,174,000,000 3,216,000,000	75,708
CONNECTICUT Hartford	3,138,000 135,100	5,018 12,997	14,895	William A. O'Neill (D) Joseph L. Fauliso (D)	3,846,000,000 3,498,000,000	19,442
DELAWARE Dover	606,000 27,000	2,044 5,295	12,665	Pierre S. du Pont 4th (R) Michael N. Castle (R)	1,066,000,000 1,005,000,000	5,249
DISTRICT OF COLUMBIA *	623,000	69 178	15,744	Mayor: Marion S. Barry, Jr. (D)	1,976,000,000 1,976,000,000	1,102
FLORIDA Tallahassee	10,680,000 113,843	58,664 151,938	11,593	D. Robert Graham (D) Wayne Mixson (D)	8,338,000,000 8,757,000,000	97,186
GEORGIA Atlanta	5,732,000 428,153	58,910 152,575	10,379	Joe Frank Harris (D) Zell B. Miller (D)	5,376,000,000 5,523,000,000	104,253
HAWAII Honolulu	1,023,000 365,017	6,471 16,759	12,114	George R. Ariyoshi (D) John Waihee (D)	1,843,000,000 1,826,000,000	4,107
IDAHO Boise	989,000 104,596	83,564 216,431	9,555	John V. Evans (D) David Leroy (R)	1,009,000,000 1,021,000,000	67,442
ILLINOIS Springfield	11,486,000 99,637	56,345 145,933	12,405	James R. Thompson, Jr. (R) George H. Ryan (R)	11,879,000,000 12,031,000,000	133,672
INDIANA Indianapolis	5,479,000 707,655	36,185 93,720	10,476	Robert D. Orr (R) John M. Mutz (R)	5,099,000,000 5,148,000,000	91,676
IOWA Des Moines	2,905,000 191,506	56,275 145,752	10,705	Terry E. Branstad (R) Robert Anderson (D)	3,271,000,000 3,449,000,000	112,487
KANSAS Topeka	2,425,000 120,269	82,277 213,097	12,247	John W. Carlin (D) Tom Docking (D)	2,428,000,000 2,403,000,000	132,209
KENTUCKY Frankfort	3,174,000 25,973	40,409 104,660	9,397	Martha Layne Collins (D) Steven Beshear (D)	4,252,000,000 4,225,000,000	68,429

The material in the following tables is the latest available. As before, it should be noted that the symbol * indicates that the category is not applicable to the area mentioned, and that NA means that the data were not available. The Office of Territorial Affairs was helpful in supplying some data for the table on Outlying Areas.

Railways (Miles)	Aircraft Departures	English-language Daily Newspapers	Public Elementary Schools (K–8): Teachers Students	Public Secondary Schools (9–12): Teachers Students	Colleges and Universities: Institutions Students
4,299	42,153	29	20,000 509,952	19,400 214,085	59 166,375
536	171,556	7	3,100 63,211	2,500 26,202	15 24,754
1,801	92,078	17	19,900 359,229	8,900 151,067	28 205,169
2,708	18,216	30	11,500 304,443	12,000 128,122	35 76,032
6,476	504,721	132	104,600 2,801,818	65,800 1,263,668	272 1,885,757
3,320	183,436	29	15,000 379,599	14,000 165,610	46 167,977
484	28,945	24	18,900 335,997	12,800 150,473	47 162,367
236	80	3	2,500 59,527	2,900 33,119	8 32,061
50	114,145	1	2,900 64,096	2,000 26,409	19 88,553
3,384	347,912	47	46,500 1,038,998	35,500 445,736	81 426,570
5,042	271,127	22	34,700 739,178	22,300 314,511	78 191,384
0	87,737	5	5,000 110,202	3,100 51,822	12 48,121
2,381	29,926	12	5,400 145,416	4,800 57,557	9 42,758
9,639	282,429	85	67,800 1,286,858	36,400 593,431	158 659,623
5,608	58,438	74	25,500 663,547	25,200 335,995	74 251,826
4,906	38,452	39	14,600 337,728	16,400 167,255	60 143,105
7,580	36,638	46	14,500 282,879	11,800 124,195	52 138,453
3,453	29,076	23	21,000 457,505	11,200 193,579	57 144,154

State / Capital	Population	Area (sq mi/ sq km)	Per Capita Personal Income	Governor / Lieutenant-Governor	Revenue / Expenditure	Roads (Miles)
LOUISIANA Baton Rouge	4,438,000 241,483	47,752 123,676	$10,270	Edwin W. Edwards (D) Robert L. Freeman (D)	$ 5,785,000,000 5,773,000,000	56,676
MAINE Augusta	1,146,000 22,000	33,265 86,156	9,847	Joseph E. Brennan (D) *	1,361,000,000 1,307,000,000	21,902
MARYLAND Annapolis	4,304,000 31,740	10,460 27,092	12,994	Harry R. Hughes (D) J. Joseph Curran (D)	5,591,000,000 5,416,000,000	27,005
MASSACHUSETTS Boston	5,767,000 562,994	8,284 21,456	13,264	Michael Dukakis (D) John Kerry (D)	7,883,000,000 7,771,000,000	33,772
MICHIGAN Lansing	9,069,000 128,338	58,527 151,585	11,466	James J. Blanchard (D) Martha W. Griffiths (D)	11,441,000,000 11,506,000,000	117,396
MINNESOTA St. Paul	4,144,000 269,240	84,402 218,600	11,913	Rudy Perpich (DFL) Marlene Johnson (DFL)	6,095,000,000 6,385,000,000	130,834
MISSISSIPPI Jackson	2,587,000 204,195	47,689 123,515	8,098	Bill Allain (D) Brad Dye (D)	2,724,000,000 2,725,000,000	70,442
MISSOURI Jefferson City	4,970,000 33,619	69,697 180,515	10,969	Christopher S. Bond (R) Kenneth J. Rothman (D)	4,003,000,000 3,966,000,000	118,403
MONTANA Helena	817,000 23,938	147,046 380,846	9,949	Ted Schwinden (D) George Turman (D)	1,088,000,000 944,000,000	71,703
NEBRASKA Lincoln	1,597,000 177,340	77,355 200,349	11,212	Robert Kerrey (D) Don McGinley (D)	1,561,000,000 1,576,000,000	91,828
NEVADA Carson City	891,000 32,022	110,561 286,351	12,451	Richard Bryan (D) Robert Cashell (R)	1,102,000,000 1,110,000,000	43,442
NEW HAMPSHIRE Concord	959,000 30,765	9,279 24,031	12,021	John Sununu (R) *	789,000,000 822,000,000	14,412
NEW JERSEY Trenton	7,468,000 92,362	7,787 20,169	14,122	Thomas H. Kean (R) *	9,254,000,000 9,215,000,000	33,490
NEW MEXICO Santa Fe	1,399,000 48,953	121,593 314,923	9,640	Toney Anaya (D) Mike Runnels (D)	2,773,000,000 2,272,000,000	53,715
NEW YORK Albany	17,667,000 100,048	49,108 127,189	12,990	Mario M. Cuomo (D) Alfred B. DelBello (D)	26,513,000,000 25,533,000,000	109,639
NORTH CAROLINA Raleigh	6,082,000 154,211	52,669 136,412	9,787	James B. Hunt, Jr. (D) James C. Green (D)	6,123,000,000 6,180,000,000	92,587
NORTH DAKOTA Bismarck	680,000 44,500	70,702 183,118	11,666	Allen I. Olson (R) Ernest M. Sands (R)	1,142,000,000 1,119,000,000	85,904
OHIO Columbus	10,746,000 570,588	41,330 107,043	11,216	Richard F. Celeste (D) Myrl H. Shoemaker (D)	10,170,000,000 10,416,000,000	110,845
OKLAHOMA Oklahoma City	3,298,000 427,714	69,956 181,185	10,963	George Nigh (D) Spencer Bernard (D)	4,237,000,000 3,697,000,000	109,946
OREGON Salem	2,662,000 91,400	97,073 251,417	10,740	Victor G. Atiyeh (R) *	3,356,000,000 3,445,000,000	121,408
PENNSYLVANIA Harrisburg	11,895,000 53,264	45,308 117,347	11,448	Richard L. Thornburgh (R) William W. Scranton 3rd (R)	12,973,000,000 12,353,000,000	117,103
RHODE ISLAND Providence	955,000 155,717	1,212 3,140	11,670	J. Joseph Garrahy (D) Thomas R. DiLuglio (D)	1,421,000,000 1,402,000,000	6,275
SOUTH CAROLINA Columbia	3,264,000 104,000	31,113 80,582	9,187	Richard W. Riley (D) Michael S. Daniel (D)	3,344,000,000 3,216,000,000	62,731
SOUTH DAKOTA Pierre	700,000 11,973	77,116 199,729	9,847	William J. Janklow (R) Lowell C. Hansen 2nd (R)	793,000,000 794,000,000	73,018

Railways (Miles)	Aircraft Departures	English-language Daily Newspapers	Public Elementary Schools (K–8): Teachers Students	Public Secondary Schools (9–12): Teachers Students	Colleges and Universities: Institutions Students
3,250	74,936	24	23,800 / 555,978	18,700 / 219,688	32 / 174,656
46	9,499	8	7,800 / 146,848	4,500 / 65,138	29 / 44,012
1,133	32,710	16	18,100 / 461,794	19,700 / 237,407	56 / 229,936
1,112	91,464	47	22,000 / 596,990	30,000 / 311,994	118 / 417,830
3,787	126,771	47	40,100 / 1,156,597	37,100 / 604,924	91 / 513,033
6,342	95,111	28	19,400 / 471,670	21,200 / 243,520	70 / 210,713
2,703	19,632	22	13,700 / 326,998	11,200 / 141,296	41 / 105,974
5,677	160,051	44	24,010 / 546,751	24,300 / 255,784	89 / 243,672
3,675	36,186	11	5,000 / 106,869	3,900 / 45,466	16 / 35,959
4,736	30,533	19	8,100 / 186,265	8,100 / 82,744	31 / 93,507
1,492	86,605	8	3,900 / 96,812	3,500 / 54,292	7 / 39,936
461	2,847	8	5,300 / 107,349	4,800 / 52,848	26 / 48,524
1,506	62,917	28	41,800 / 776,608	31,500 / 395,912	61 / 322,797
2,075	33,533	19	6,900 / 189,968	7,300 / 78,664	19 / 60,413
4,281	306,367	82	73,800 / 1,761,336	80,300 / 957,342	294 / 1,014,863
2,818	106,629	55	34,200 / 768,755	22,300 / 328,060	127 / 295,771
4,767	24,026	10	4,700 / 81,171	2,800 / 35,507	17 / 35,446
6,999	138,750	91	53,400 / 1,258,642	41,600 / 601,603	136 / 521,396
3,627	42,997	46	17,900 / 423,140	16,000 / 170,685	44 / 162,825
2,941	42,478	21	15,000 / 308,964	9,500 / 139,220	45 / 149,924
6,761	157,452	100	47,200 / 1,157,356	55,500 / 626,613	202 / 517,879
0	8,314	7	4,700 / 89,467	4,100 / 49,895	13 / 68,339
2,524	26,822	17	20,100 / 424,362	12,000 / 184,156	60 / 132,394
2,037	26,822	12	5,300 / 85,990	2,700 / 37,907	20 / 35,015

459

State Capital	Population	Area (sq mi/ sq km)	Per Capita Personal Income	Governor Lieutenant-Governor	Revenue Expenditure	Roads (Miles)
TENNESSEE	4,685,000......	42,144......	$ 9,549....	Lamar Alexander (R)	$ 3,953,000,000....	83,497
Nashville	455,252	109,151		John S. Wilder (D)	3,813,000,000	
TEXAS	15,724,000......	266,807......	11,685....	Mark White (D).................	14,691,000,000....	268,253
Austin	396,440	691,026		William P. Hobby (D)	13,189,000,000	
UTAH	1,619,000......	84,899......	8,993....	Scott M. Matheson (D)	1,862,000,000....	43,735
Salt Lake City	163,697	219,888		David S. Monson (R)	1,756,000,000	
VERMONT............	525,000......	9,614......	9,979....	Richard A. Snelling (R)..........	738,000,000....	13,942
Montpelier	8,277	24,900		Peter Smith (R)	720,000,000	
VIRGINIA..............	5,550,000......	40,767......	12,116....	Charles S. Robb (D)	5,772,000,000....	64,683
Richmond	218,237	105,585		Richard J. Davis (D)	5,683,000,000	
WASHINGTON........	4,300,000......	68,139......	12,177....	John Spellman (R)	5,621,000,000....	83,291
Olympia	28,790	176,478		John A. Cherberg (D)	5,893,000,000	
WEST VIRGINIA	1,965,000......	24,231......	9,159....	John D. Rockefeller 4th (D).......	2,468,000,000....	34,999
Charleston	63,968	62,759		*	2,351,000,000	
WISCONSIN	4,751,000......	56,153......	11,352....	Anthony S. Earl (D)...........	6,296,000,000....	108,110
Madison	172,263	145,435		James T. Flynn (D)	6,202,000,000	
WYOMING............	514,000......	97,809......	11,911....	Ed Herschler (D)	1,366,000,000....	36,709
Cheyenne	47,283	253,325		*	1,002,000,000	

OUTLYING AREAS OF THE UNITED STATES

Area Capital	Population	Area (sq mi/ sq km)	Status	Governor Lieutenant-Governor	Revenue Expenditure	Roads (Miles)
AMERICAN SAMOA.....	33,800....	77....	Unorganized,........	A. P. Lutali...................	$ NA....	94
Pago Pago	2,732	199	unincorporated territory	Eni Hunkin	71,415,573	
GUAM	110,800....	209....	Unincorporated	Ricardo J. Bordallo	185,800,000....	419
Agaña	881	541	territory	Edward D. Reyes	NA	
PUERTO RICO..........	3,300,000....	3,515....	Commonwealth	Carlos Romero Barceló	3,895,000,000....	10,456
San Juan	433,901	9,103		*	3,819,000,000	
TRUST TERRITORY..... OF THE PACIFIC ISLANDS[1] Capitol Hill, on Saipan Island	120,400.... NA	533.... 1,380	UN Trust .... Territory	High Commissioner: .... Janet J. McCoy	114,100,000.... NA	64
VIRGIN ISLANDS	101,500....	133....	Unincorporated	Juan Luis	225,600,000....	532
Charlotte Amalie	11,756	344	territory	Julio Brady	225,300,000	

1. The Northern Mariana Islands in 1984 were an internally self-governing part of the Trust Territory of the Pacific Islands. The government of the Northern Marianas was headed by Gov. Pedro P. Tenorio and Lt.-Gov. Pedro A. Tenorio. The capital was Susupe, on Saipan Island.

Railways (Miles)	Aircraft Departures	English-language Daily Newspapers	Public Elementary Schools (K–8): Teachers Students	Public Secondary Schools (9–12): Teachers Students	Colleges and Universities: Institutions Students
2,890	96,738	28	24,500 / 590,839	14,800 / 237,425	79 / 200,183
13,011	428,672	109	92,800 / 2,149,813	74,000 / 835,846	156 / 716,297
1,691	47,392	5	9,100 / 275,145	5,800 / 95,038	14 / 97,048
142	7,305	9	3,000 / 64,181	3,600 / 27,273	21 / 30,573
3,487	57,985	38	33,100 / 682,630	23,200 / 293,097	69 / 286,015
4,281	116,298	25	18,400 / 507,515	16,100 / 231,700	50 / 278,680
3,604	17,428	23	12,700 / 266,950	9,300 / 108,165	28 / 82,375
3,977	77,483	35	28,800 / 503,871	23,400 / 280,959	64 / 275,325
1,978	13,882	9	4,000 / 74,396	3,300 / 27,269	9 / 21,235

Railways (Miles)	Aircraft Departures	Daily Newspapers	Public Elementary and Secondary School Teachers	Public School Students: Elementary Secondary	Higher Education: Institutions Students
0	500	1	378	5,596 / 2,473	1 / 856
0	2,800	1	1,290	17,528 / 7,389	2 / 3,168
60	5,219	4	24,761	492,908 / 191,015	39 / 129,708
0	2,400	0	1,970	30,159 / 8,316	2 / 1,329
0	5,141	2	1,732	17,587 / 5,485	1 / 1,990

THE PROVINCES AND TERRITORIES OF CANADA

Province Capital	Population	Area (sq mi/ sq km)	Per Capita Personal Income	Premier Lieutenant-Governor
ALBERTA Edmonton	3,360,300 551,314	255,285 661,185	$14,025	Peter Lougheed Frank Lynch-Staunton
BRITISH COLUMBIA Victoria	2,863,000 65,258	366,255 948,596	13,811	William R. Bennett Robert Gordon Rogers
MANITOBA Winnipeg	1,051,500 602,000	251,000 650,087	11,987	Howard R. Pawley Pearl McGonigal
NEW BRUNSWICK Fredericton	696,403 43,723	28,354 73,436	9,229	Richard B. Hatfield George F. G. Stanley
NEWFOUNDLAND St. John's	579,400 86,576	156,185 404,517	8,580	Brian Peckford William A. Paddon
NORTHWEST TERRITORIES Yellowknife	48,000 10,000	1,304,903 3,379,684	13,014[1]	Commissioner: John H. Parker
NOVA SCOTIA Halifax	847,442 114,594	21,425 55,491	10,090	John M. Buchanan Alan R. Abraham
ONTARIO Toronto	8,625,107 599,217	412,582 1,068,582	13,842	William G. Davis John Black Aird
PRINCE EDWARD ISLAND Charlottetown	123,000 15,500	2,184 5,657	8,894	James M. Lee Joseph Aubin Doiron
QUÉBEC Québec	6,521,600 176,600	594,860 1,540,680	12,021	René Lévesque Gilles Lamontag
SASKATCHEWAN Regina	1,003,300 172,900	251,700 651,900	12,372	Grant Devine Frederick Johnston
YUKON TERRITORY Whitehorse	24,000 14,814	186,300 482,515	13,014[1]	Commissioner: Douglas Bell

1. Figure is the combined average for the Northwest Territories and Yukon Territory.

The material in this table has been prepared with the assistance of Statistics Canada. It should be noted that all dollar figures are in Canadian dollars.

Revenue Expenditure	Motor Vehicle Registrations	Railways (Miles)	Radio and Television Stations	Daily Newspapers	Elementary and Secondary Schools: Teachers Enrollment	Postsecondary Education: Institutions Enrollment
$ 9,400,000,000 9,600,000,000	1,720,008	5,760	69 19	10	24,649 471,000	23 60,000
7,719,000,000 8,390,000,000	1,998,295	4,531	86 5	20	28,824 531,000	28 57,000
2,969,000,000 3,456,000,000	651,999	3,996	32 17	6	12,324 216,000	15 25,000
2,403,000,000 2,500,000,000	349,342	1,633	28 2	5	7,767 145,000	13 16,000
1,923,000,000 1,955,000,000	185,827	906	33 10	3	7,819 143,000	7 11,000
554,400,000 550,700,000	17,042	130	9 1	0	690 13,000	0 0
2,381,000,000 2,770,000,000	511,574	1,223	34 9	6	10,825 174,000	24 25,000
26,800,000,000 24,700,000,000	3,992,278	9,549	201 27	47	95,112 1,843,100	52 279,000
435,000,000 464,200,000	65,574	253	6 3	3	1,365 25,000	3 2,000
22,500,000,000 25,000,000,000	2,671,451	5,171	166 14	11	71,986 1,149,000	91 242,000
3,010,000,000 3,280,000,000	670,072	7,696	39 10	5	11,247 212,000	6 21,000
152,000,000 148,000,000	18,237	58	3 2	0	250 4,400	0 0

KEY TO
SIGNED ARTICLES

Here is a list of contributors to this Yearbook. The initials at the end of an article are those of the author, or authors, of that article.

A.C.–C., ANGEL CALDERÓN–CRUZ, A.B., M.S.
Director, Office of Planning & Development, Center for Energy & Environment Research, University of Puerto Rico. Co-author, *Contemporary Caribbean Issues.*

A.D., ALASDAIR DRYSDALE, PH.D.
Assistant Professor, University of New Hampshire.

A.L.R., ARTHUR L. ROBINSON, PH.D.
Senior Writer, Research News Section, *Science* Magazine.

A.P., ARTURO PORZECANSKI, PH.D.
International Economist, Morgan Guaranty Trust Company. Author, *Uruguay's Tupamaros: The Urban Guerrilla.*

A.R., ANSIL RAMSAY, A.B., PH.D.
Professor of Government, St. Lawrence University. Editorial Board Member, *Asian Survey.*

A.V., ARTURO VALENZUELA, B.A., M.A., PH.D.
Professor of Political Science and Chairman, Council on Latin American Studies, Duke University. Author, *The Breakdown of Democratic Regimes: Chile; Political Brokers in Chile.*

B.B.S., BONNIE BARRETT STRETCH, A.B., M.S.
Writer on Art, Antiques, and Photography. Associate Editor, *Art & Auction.*

B.G.V, BRUCE G. VANDEN BERGH, A.B., M.S., PH.D.
Associate Professor of Advertising, Michigan State University.

B.J., BRUCE JUDDERY, A.B.
Canberra Branch Secretary, Australian Journalists Association.

B.R., BEA RIEMSCHNEIDER, A.B., M.A.
Editor in Chief, *Archaeology.* Associate Trustee, American Schools of Oriental Research.

B.V., BOB VERDI, A.B.
Columnist, *Chicago Tribune.*

C.A.K., CHRISTOPHER A. KOJM, A.B., M.P.A.
Senior Editor, Foreign Policy Association. Editor, *U.S. Defense Policy.*

C.B., CHRISTIE BARTER, A.B.
Music Editor, *Stereo Review.*

C.H.A., CALVIN H. ALLEN, JR., A.B., M.A., PH.D.
Associate Professor of History, School of the Ozarks, Mo.

C.L.K., CHARLES L. KIMBELL, B.S.
Physical Scientist, U.S. Bureau of Mines.

C.S.J.W., CHARLES S. J. WHITE, B.A., M.A., PH.D.
Professor and Chairman, Department of Philosophy and Religion, The American University; former Director of the Center for Asian Studies.

D.B., DON BOHNING, A.B.
Latin American Editor, Miami *Herald.*

D.D.B., DARALICE D. BOLES, A.B., M.ARCH.
Associate Editor, *Progressive Architecture.*

D.F., DON FREEMAN
Television Editor and Columnist, San Diego *Union* and Copley News Service.

D.F.A., DONALD F. ANTHROP, PH.D.
Professor of Environmental Studies, San Jose State University. Author, *Noise Pollution.*

D.G.S., DAVID G. SAVAGE, A.B., M.S.
Education Writer, Los Angeles *Times.*

D.L.L., DAVID L. LEWIS, B.S., M.S., M.A., PH.D.
Professor of Business History, Graduate School of Business Administration, University of Michigan.

D.M.P., DAVID M. PHILIPS, A.B.
Boating and Yachting Writer, Providence *Journal.*

D.P., DON PERETZ, A.B., M.A., PH.D.
Professor of Political Science, State University of New York at Binghamton. Author, *Middle East Today.*

D.R., DIANE ROBACK, A.B.
Free-lance Writer and Reviewer. Contributor, *Publisher's Weekly.*

D.R.F., DAVID R. FRANCIS, B.J., A.B.
Business Editor, *The Christian Science Monitor.*

D.R.W., DONALD R. WHITAKER, A.B.
Economist, Office of Policy and Planning, National Marine Fisheries Service. Contributor, *Fishing Gazette, Commercial Fisheries Review.*

D.S., DAVID STAINES, A.B., A.M., PH.D.
Associate Professor of English, University of Ottawa. Author, *Tennyson's Camelot: The Idylls of the King and Its Medieval Sources.*

D.S.M., DONALD S. MACDONALD, PH.D.
Research Professor of Korean Studies, School of Foreign Service, Georgetown University. Former State Department Foreign Service Officer.

D.W., DAVID P. WERLICH, A.B., M.A., PH.D.
Professor of History, Southern Illinois University. Author, *Peru: A Short History.*

D.Y., DONALD YOUNG, A.B., M.A.
Yearbook Staff Editor.

E.B., EDOUARD BUSTIN, PH.D.
Professor of Political Science, Boston University. Author, *Lunda Under Belgian Rule.*

E.C.R., EDWARD C. ROCHETTE, B.S.
Executive Director, American Numismatic Association.

E.H.B., ELIZABETH H. BECKER, A.B.
Free-lance Writer. Former Indochina Correspondent, Washington *Post.*

E.J.F., ERIK J. FRIIS, B.S., M.A.
Editor and Publisher, *The Scandinavian–American Bulletin.*

E.J.G., ELLEN J. GREENFIELD, A.B., M.A.
Free-lance Writer. Former Textiles Editor, *Women's Wear Daily.*

E.P., EUL–SOO PANG, A.B., M.A., PH.D.
Associate Professor of History, University of Alabama at Birmingham. Author, *Bahia in the First Brazilian Republic: Coronelismo and Oligarchies 1889–1934.*

E.S.K., ELAINE S. KNAPP, A.B.
Editor, *Council of State Governments.*

E.S.R., EUGENIA S. ROBBINS, A.B.
Free-lance Writer and Editor. News Editor, *Art Express.* Coauthor, *Henri de Toulouse-Lautrec.*

E.W., ED WARD
Free-lance Writer, Rolling Stone Press.

F.D.S., FREDERICK D. SCHNEIDER, PH.D.
Professor of History, Vanderbilt University.

F.L., FRANK LITSKY, B.S.
Assistant Sports Editor, New York *Times.*

G.B., GEORGE BLOOSTON, A.B., M.A.
Free-lance Writer. Regular Contributor, *Publisher's Weekly.*

G.H., GARY HANSEN, B.S., M.S., PH.D.
Professor of Economics, Utah State University. Director, Utah Center for Productivity and Quality of Working Life.

G.L., GEORGE LAMSON, PH.D.
Professor of Economics, Carleton College, Northfield, Minn.

G.M.H., GEOFFREY M. HORN, A.B., M.A.
Free-lance Writer. Coauthor, *Bible Stories for Children.*

H.C.H., HAROLD C. HINTON, PH.D.
Professor of Political Science and International Affairs, George Washington University. Editor, *The People's Republic of China, 1949–1979: A Documentary Survey.*

H.W.H., HARRY W. HENDERSON, A.B.
Free-lance Writer. Former Writer-Economist, U.S. Department of Agriculture.

I.A.A., IAN A. ANDERSON, A.B.
Publications Director, U.S. Figure Skating Association.

I.C.B., IRIRANGI COATES BLOOMFIELD, A.B., M.A., PH.D.
Lecturer, Boston University. Researcher and Writer.

I.K., INDULIS KEPARS, B.A.
Chief Reference Librarian, Australian Studies, National Library of Australia.

J.A., JONATHAN ALTER, A.B.
Associate Editor, *Newsweek.*

J.A.P., JOHN A. PETROPULOS, PH.D.
Professor of History, Amherst College. Author, *Politics and Statecraft in the Kingdom of Greece.*

J.A.R., JAMES A. ROTHERHAM, A.B., M.A., M.A.L.D., PH.D.
Deputy Associate Director, Committee on the Budget, U.S. House of Representatives.

J.B., JOHN BEAUFORT
Contributing Drama Critic, Christian Science Monitor.

J.C., JAMES CARPER, B.S.
Managing Editor, *Professional Builder/Apartment Business.*

J.C.L., JEAN CAFFEY LYLES, A.B.
Associate Editor, *The Christian Century.* Editorial Consultant, *The Christian Ministry.*

J.D., JOHN DAMIS, PH.D.
Professor of Political Science, Portland State University. Consultant, U.S. Department of State.

J.E.S., JOHN E. SHIELDS, A.B.
Editor, *Congressional Digest.*

J.F., JULIE FREDERIKSE, A.B.
Southern Africa Correspondent, National Public Radio.

J.F., Jr. JOHN FORAN, JR., A.B., M.A.
Graduate Fellow in Sociology, University of California, Berkeley.

J.F.H., JERRY F. HOUGH, PH.D.
Professor of Political Science, Duke University. Staff Member, Brookings Institution. Author, *Soviet Leadership in Transition.*

J.F.H., III, JEREMIAH F. HEALY, III, A.B., J.D.
Associate Professor, New England School of Law, Boston. Free-lance Writer.

J.F.J., JAMES F. JEKEL, M.D., M.P.H.
Professor of Epidemiology and Public Health, Yale University Medical School. Former Epidemiologist, Centers for Disease Control.

J.F.S., JOANNE F. SCHNEIDER, A.B., M.A., PH.D.
Visiting Assistant Professor of History, Wheaton College.

J.G.D., JOHN G. DEEDY, A.B., M.A.
Former Managing Editor, *Commonweal.* Contributor, New York *Times, U.S. Catholic, Informations Catholiques Internationales.*

J.H., JOHN HAY, A.B.
Reporter, *Ottawa Citizen.*

J.H.B., JAMES H. BUDD
Free-lance Writer Based in Mexico. Correspondent, Ziff–Davis Magazines and Gemini News Service.

J.J.Z., JOSEPH J. ZASLOFF, A.B., M.A., PH.D.
Professor of Political Science, University of Pittsburgh. Specialist in Southeast Asian Affairs.

J.K., JON KRAUS, PH.D.
Professor of Political Science, State University of New York, Fredonia.

J.L., JOHN LUTER, A.B.
Professor and Chairman, Journalism Department, University of Hawaii. Former Coordinator, Advanced International Reporting Program, Columbia University Graduate School of Journalism.

J.O.S., JAMES O. SAFFORD III, A.B., M.A., PH.D.
Instructor of History, The Shipley School, Bryn Mawr, Pa.

J.P.B., JOHN P. BURNS, B.A., M.A.
Lecturer in Political Science, University of Hong Kong.

J.P.F., JOHN P. FORDE, A.B.
Staff Writer, *American Banker.*

J.R., JANET RALOFF, B.S.J., M.S.J.
Policy and Technology Editor, *Science News.*

J.R.F., JOHN R. FREE, A.B.
Senior Editor, *Technology, Popular Science.* Former Associate Editor, *Radio Electronics.*

J.S.I., JACQUELINE S. ISMAEL, A.B., M.A., PH.D.
Associate Professor of Social Welfare, Faculty of Social Sciences, University of Calgary. Author, *Kuwait: Social Change in Historical Perspective.*

J.T.S., JAMES T. SHERWIN, A.B., L.L.B.
Vice-Chairman and Chief Administrative Officer, GAF Corporation. Former New York State, Intercollegiate, and U.S. Speed Chess Champion and International Master.

J.W.K., JOHN W. KAMPA, B.S.
Former Editorial Board Member, *Minkus World-Wide Stamp Catalog and New American Stamp Catalog.*

K.F.R., KARL F. REULING
Managing Editor, *Ballet News.*

K.J.B., KIRK J. BEATTIE, A.B., M.A.
Researcher in Egyptian Politics.

K.M., KENT MULLINER, B.S., M.A.
Executive Committee, Malaysia/Singapore/Brunei Studies Group. Assistant to the Director, Ohio University Libraries.

K.W.G., KENNETH W. GRUNDY, A.B., M.A., PH.D.
Professor of Political Science, Case Western Reserve University.

L.A.K., LAWRENCE A. KLETTER, A.B., M.A., J.D.
Certificate in Middle Eastern Studies, Columbia University. Associate, Nutter, McClennen & Fish.

L.D., LARRY DIAMOND, A.B., M.A., PH.D.
Assistant Professor of Sociology, Vanderbilt University.

L.G., LOIS GOTTESMAN, A.B., M.A.
Research Analyst, American Jewish Committee.

L.J.R., LEIF J. ROBINSON
Editor, *Sky & Telescope.*

L.L.P., LARRY L. PIPPIN, A.B., M.A., PH.D.
Professor of Political Science, Elbert Covell College, University of the Pacific.

L.R., LINDA RICHTER, A.B., M.A., PH.D.
Assistant Professor of Political Science, Kansas State University. Author, *Land Reform and Tourism Development: Policy-Making in the Philippines.*

L.R.H., LINDLEY R. HIGGINS, P.E., A.B., M.S.
Consulting Engineer. President, Piedmont Publications. Author, *Handbook of Construction Equipment Maintenance* and *Maintenance Engineering Handbook.*

L.S.G., LOVETT S. GRAY, A.B.
Free-lance Writer and Consultant. Former Editor, National Council on Crime and Delinquency.

L.W.G., LOWELL W. GUDMUNDSON, A.B., M.A., PH.D.
Assistant Professor of History and Associate Director of the Latin American and Caribbean Center, Florida International University.

L.Z., LAWRENCE ZIRING, B.S., M.I.A., PH.D.
Director, Institute of Government and Politics, Professor of Political Science, Western Michigan University. Author, *Pakistan: The Enigma of Political Development* and *The Middle East Political Dictionary.*

M.B.R., MARK B. ROSENBERG, A.B., M.A., PH.D.
Associate Professor of Political Science, Associate Dean of International Affairs, Florida International University. Associate Editor, *Caribbean Review.*

M.C.H., MICHAEL C. HUDSON, A.B., M.A., PH.D.
Professor of International Relations and Political Science, Seif Ghobash Professor of Arab Studies, Georgetown University. Author, *Arab Politics: The Search for Legitimacy.*

M.D., MICHAEL DIRDA, A.B., M.A., PH.D.
Daily Book Review Editor, *The Washington Post Book World.*

M.D.H., M. DONALD HANCOCK, PH.D.
Professor of Political Science, Vanderbilt University.

M.G., MURIEL GRINDROD, A.B.
Author, *Italy, Rebuilding of Italy.*

M.Gr., MILTON GREENBERG, A.B., M.A., PH.D.
Provost, The American University. Coauthor, *The American Political Dictionary, Political Science Dictionary.*

M.G.G., M. GRANT GROSS, A.B., M.S., PH.D.
Director, Division of Ocean Sciences, National Science Foundation. Author, *Oceanography: A View of the Earth.*

M.G.W., MARTHA G. WISEMAN, A.B.
Yearbook Staff Editor.

M.H., MARJORIE HOLT, A.B.
Yearbook Staff Editor.

M.L., MIKE LITTWIN
Sports Writer, Los Angeles *Times.*

M.S.B., MICHAEL S. BAKER, A.B., M.A.
Japan Foundation Research Fellow and Ph.D. Candidate, Columbia University.

M.W., MARGARET WILLY, F.R.S.L.
Lecturer, City Literary Institute, London. Lecturer, Morley College, London. Poetry Collected in *The Invisible Sun, Every Star a Tongue.*

M.W.T., MARIAN W. TAYLOR, A.B.
Yearbook Staff Editor.

N.M.R., NATHAN M. REISS, PH.D.
Associate Professor of Meteorology, Cook College, Rutgers University.

N.P., NEAL PRONEK, B.B.A.
Managing Editor, *Tropical Fish Hobbyist.* Former Editor, *Pet Industry.*

N.P.N., NANCY PEABODY NEWELL, A.B.
Coauthor, *The Struggle for Afghanistan.*

P.G., PAUL GARDNER
Free-lance Writer. Author, *The Simplest Game, Nice Guys Finish Last.* Commentator, ABC National Soccer Telecasts.

P.H., PATRICIA HOWE, A.B.
Yearbook Staff Editor.

P.H.C., PARRIS H. CHANG, PH.D.
Professor of Political Science, Chairman

of Asian Area Studies, Pennsylvania State University. Author, *Power and Policy in China.*

P.J.M., PAUL J. MAGNARELLA, A.M., PH.D.
Professor of Anthropology, University of Florida. Author, *Tradition and Change in a Turkish Town, The Peasant Venture.*

P.L.W., PENELOPE L. WANG, A.B., M.A.
Senior Editorial Assistant, *Newsweek.*

P.W., PETER WINN, A.B., PH.D.
Associate Professor of History, Tufts University. Senior Research Fellow, Research Institute on International Change, Columbia University.

R.A.M., ROBERT A. MORTIMER, A.B., M.A., PH.D.
Professor of Political Science, Haverford College. Author, *The Third World Coalition in International Politics.*

R.A.P., RICHARD A. PIERCE, PH.D.
Professor of History, Queen's University, Ontario. Author, *Eastward to Empire: Exploration and Conquest on the Russian Open Frontier to 1750.*

R.A.S., ROBERT A. SORENSON, A.B., M.A.
Yearbook Staff Editor.

R.B., RICHARD E. BISSELL, A.B., M.A., PH.D.
Executive Editor, *Washington Quarterly.* Adjunct Professor of Government, Georgetown University.

R.E.K., ROGER E. KANET, A.B., M.A., PH.D.
Professor of Political Science, University of Illinois at Urbana–Champaign. Editor, *Background to Crisis: Policies and Politics in Gierek's Poland.*

R.F., ROSALIE FADEM, B.A.
Yearbook Staff Editor.

R.H., ROBERT HEALY
Associate Editor and Washington Bureau Chief, the Boston *Globe.*

R.J.K., ROBERT J. KURSAR, A.B.
Assistant Editor, *Traffic World* Magazine.

R.J.L., ROBERT J. LaMARCHE, A.B.
Associate Editor, *TENNIS* magazine.

R.J.S., ROBERT J. SHAW, B.S., A.B., M.A.
Free-lance Writer. Author, *Libraries: Building for the Future.*

R.J.W., RICHARD J. WILLEY, A.B., M.A., PH.D.
Professor of Political Science, Vassar College. Author, *Democracy in the West German Trade Unions.* Contributor, New York *Times.*

R.L.B., RICHARD L. BUTWELL, A.B., M.A., D.Phil.
Vice-President for Academic Affairs and Professor of Political Science, University of South Dakota. Author, *Southeast Asia, A Political Introduction; U Nu of Burma.*

R.L.K., ROBERT L. KOVACH, M.A., PH.D.
Associate Dean for Research and Professor of Geophysics, School of Earth Sciences, Stanford University.

466

R.N., RICHARD NEEDHAM, A.B., M.A. Editor, *Ski* Magazine, *The Encyclopedia of Skiing.*

R.O.F., ROBERT O. FREEDMAN, PH.D. Dean and Professor of Political Science, School of Graduate Studies, Baltimore Hebrew College. Author, *Soviet Policy Toward the Middle East Since 1970.*

R.S., ROBERT SCHWARZ, A.B., M.A., PH.D. Professor of Philosophy, Florida Atlantic University. Author, *Sozialismus der Propaganda.*

R.S–S., RICHARD STAHLER–SHOLK, A.B., M.A. Ph.D. Candidate in Political Science, University of California at Berkeley.

R.Y.D., RICHARD Y. DOW, B.S., M.S. Staff Officer, Geophysics Research Board and Space Science Board.

S.-A.R., SALLY-ANN RAY, PH.D. Lecturer in Politics, Canberra College for Advanced Education, Australia.

S.A.W., STANLEY A. WOLPERT, A.B., A.M., PH.D. Professor of History, University of California, Los Angeles. Author, *A New History of India.*

S.E., SANFORD ELWITT, PH.D. Professor of History, University of Rochester. Author, *The Making of the Third Republic.* Contributor, *Journal of Modern History, French Historical Studies.*

S.F., SHIRLEY FLEMING, A.B., M.A. Editor, *Musical America.*

S.G., SAM GOLDAPER Sports Reporter, New York *Times.* New

York Area Chairman, Pro Basketball Writers' Association.

S.L.D., SPENCER L. DAVIDSON Associate Editor, *Time.*

S.M., SIEGFRIED MANDEL, A.B., M.A., PH.D. Professor of English and Comparative Literature, University of Colorado. Author, *Contemporary European Novelists.*

S.M.H., STEPHEN M. HEAD, M.A., PH.D. Lecturer in Zoology, University of the West Indies, Jamaica.

S.R., STEVE C. ROPP, PH.D. Professor of Government, New Mexico State University. Author, *Panamanian Politics: From Guarded Nation to National Guard.*

S.W., SUSAN WALTON, A.B., M.A. Assistant Editor, *Education Week.* Former News and Features Editor, *BioScience* Magazine.

T.F., TISSA FERNANDO, A.B., D. PHIL. Associate Professor of Sociology, University of British Columbia. Co-editor, *Modern Sri Lanka.*

T.G.S., THEODORE G. STAVROU *Yearbook* Staff Editor.

T.H.M., THOMAS H. MAUGH, II, PH.D. Senior Science Writer, *Science* Magazine. Coauthor, *Energy and the Future, Seeds of Destruction: The Science Report on Cancer Research.*

T.I., TAREQ Y. ISMAEL, A.B., M.A., PH.D. Professor of Political Science, University of Calgary. Author, *The Middle East in World Politics: A Study in Contemporary International Relations.*

T.J.O.H., T.J.O. HICKEY Member, Editorial Staff, *The Times* of London.

T.McC., TOM McCOLLISTER, A.B. Sports Writer, Atlanta *Constitution.*

V.L., VINCE LOVETT Public Information Specialist, Bureau of Indian Affairs, U.S. Department of the Interior. Writer, *Indian News Notes,* for Indian Tribal and Organizational Publications.

W.C.C., WILLIAM C. CROMWELL, A.B., M.A., PH.D. Professor of International Relations, American University. Author, *The Eurogroup and NATO.*

W.D.M., WILLIAM D. MARBACH, B.A., M.A. General Editor, *Newsweek.*

W.L., WILLIAM LEGGETT, A.B. Senior Writer, *Sports Illustrated.*

W.M., WILLIAM MINTER, PH.D. Staff Writer, Africa News Service. Author, *Portuguese Africa and the West.*

W.N., WILLIAM NEIKIRK, A.B. Economics Correspondent, Washington Bureau, Chicago *Tribune.*

W.S.M., WALTER S. MOSSBERG, A.B., M.J. Deputy Washington Bureau Chief, *Wall Street Journal.*

W.W., WILLIAM WOLF, A.B. Contributing Editor, *New York* Magazine. Lecturer, New York University and St. John's University. Author, *Landmark Films, The Marx Brothers.*

PICTURE CREDITS

2 Lawrence Manning/Black Star **8** NASA **10** UPI/Bettmann Archive **11** Art by Jo Anne Borne **12** *Top:* NASA; *Bottom:* TASS from Sovfoto **13** General Electric Photo **14–15** *Both:* NASA **16** Boeing Aerospace Company **17** *Top:* McDonnell Douglas Corporation; *Bottom:* NASA **19** *Top:* UPI/Bettmann Archive; *Bottom:* Illustration by Dale Gustafson © 1983 National Geographic Society **20** Art by George Bakacs **23** Robert Holland **24–25** *All:* Don Kincaid **26** *Both:* New York *Post* Photograph © 1984 **27** Ray Fisk/The New York *Times* **28** O. Franken/Sygma **29** New York *Post* Photograph © 1984 **30** Flip Schulke/Black Star **31** NOAA photo by Jack LaCovey **32** Peter Jordan/Gamma-Liaison **33** UPI/Bettmann Archive **34–35** *All:* courtesy National Parks Service **36** Derek Oliver/Canapress Photo Service **37** Dawna Henderson **38** Peter J. Kaplan **39** © 1974 CN Tower Limited **40** *Top:* R. Thompson/Photo Trends; *Bottom:* John deVisser/Black Star **41** Milan Kubik/Canapress Photo Service **42** *Top Left and Right:* Canapress Photo Service; *Bottom:* Photo Trends **43** *Left:* Canapress Photo Service; *Right:* Photo Trends **44** Peter J. Kaplan **45** Dawna Henderson **46** United Press Canada Limited **47** *Both:* George Mason/Canapress Photo Service **48** Jack Jarrie/Canapress Photo Service **50** Michel Philippot/Sygma **51** UPI/Bettmann Archive **52** Sara Krulwich/The New York *Times* **53** Newsday **53** Wide World **54** Baldev/Sygma **56** UPI/Bettmann Archive **58** Wide World **61** Wide World **62** Pierre Perrin/Gamma-Liaison **63** Judith Pszenica/The New York *Times* **64** UPI/Bettmann Archive **68** William E. Sauro/The New York *Times* **69** © National Geographic Society **71** *Top:* Terry Sanders/Museum of Modern Art; *Bottom:* Herman Kokojan/Black Star **72** Richard Payne AIA **75** St. Louis Art Museum **76–77** Metropolitan Museum of Art **80–81** Australian Information Service **83** U.S. Department of Transportation **86** UPI/Bettmann Archive **88** Wide World **92** Marty Katz **94** © 1984 Jose Azel/Contact Press Images **95** *Top:* Sandro Tucci/Gamma-Liaison; *Center:* Matsumoto/Sygma **98** UPI/Bettmann Archive **99** United Press Canada Limited **101** Canapress Photo Service **103** Brian Willer **107** *Left:* Derrick Grubbs/Texas A & M University; *Inset:* Texas A & M University **109–110** UPI/Bettmann Archive **112** J. L. Atlan/Sygma **113** Wide World **114** UPI/Bettmann Archive **116** Parga-Tiempo/Sygma **122** UPI/Bettmann Archive **123** J. P. Laffont/Sygma **125** Manuel Ceniceras/Sygma **126** Hanson William/Sygma **129** Wide World **131** © 1984 Martha Swope **132** © 1984 Susan Cook **134** UPI/Bettmann Archive **137** UPI/Bettmann Archive **138** Wide World **140** © 1984 The Miami *Herald,* reprinted with permission **143–145** UPI/Bettmann Archive **146** Dith Pran/The New York *Times* **148** Shepard Sherbell/Picture Group **151–152** Wide World **153–154** UPI/Bettmann Archive **156** *Clockwise from top left:* Wide World, Kevin Wick/*Time* Magazine, New Jersey Newsphotos, Brent Jones **157** *Left:* Lloyd Taggart; *Right:* Bruce Hoertel **158** Picture Group **160** Claude Urraca/Sygma **163** *Top:* Al Gutierrez; *Bottom:* Jerry Litmann **164** Régis Bossu/Sygma **169** Alen Mac Weeney/Archive Pictures, Inc. **170** *Top Left:* Daniel Simon/Gamma-Liaison; *Top Right:* Vittoriano Rastelli/*Time* Magazine **172–174** Alain Keler/Sygma **176** Wide World **178** Horst Schreiber/*Time* Magazine **180** Syndication International/Photo Trends **182** UPI/Bettmann Archive **186** UPI/Bettmann Archive **187** Robert Rearick, Chief Photographer, Loma Linda University Medical Center **188** Australian Information Service **190** Bruce Hoertel **191** Wide World **194** Wide World **196** Terrence McCarthy/The New York *Times* **197** *Top:* The New York *Times; Bottom:* Joyce Dopkeen/The New York *Times* **199** Santosh Basak/Gamma-Liaison **200** Jacques Langevin/Sygma **201** UPI/Bettmann Archive **204** François Lochon/Gamma-Liaison **206** Jacques Pavlovsky/Sygma **208** UPI/Bettmann Archive **210** ANSA News Agency **211** Antonio Bono/Informazione Fotografica/Gamma-Liaison **213** Greg Davis/The Stock Market **214** Paul Hosefros/The New York *Times* **217** UPI/Bettmann Archive **219** Wide World **223** Wide World **224** The New York Public Library **227** from the *Macmillan Book of Dinosaurs;* artist, John Hamberger **228** UPI/Bettmann Archive **230** © Townsend P. Dickinson, The National Audubon Society Collection/Photo Researchers, Inc. **231** Paul Schuhmann/The Courier-*Journal* and Louisville *Times* **233** Slick (W. E.) Lawson **235** Australian Information Service **236** United Press Canada Limited **238** Kasterine/Camera Press/Photo Trends **240** Thomas Victor, 1983 **241** François Lochon/Gamma-Liaison **242** Courtesy of Viking Press **243** E. T. Masterton **246** © 1984 Bob Straus/Woodfin Camp, Inc. **249–252** Wide World **253** Sygma **254** UPI/Bettmann Archive **255** Michel Phillipot/Sygma **256** Rockwell International **259** UPI/Bettmann Archive **260** *Top:* Wide World; *Bottom:* UPI/Bettmann Archive **262** *Top:* © 1984 Buena Vista Distribution Company, Inc.; *Bottom:* Phototeque **263** S. Schapiro/Gamma-Liaison **265** *Top:* Gamma-Liaison; *Bottom:* Wide World **267** Ross Marino/Sygma **268** *Top:* D. Fineman/Sygma; *Bottom:* Wide World **269** Photo Trends **271** *Top:* Carol Rosegg/Martha Swope Assoc.; *Bottom:* Clive Barda **275** Consulate General of New Zealand **276** *Left:* James Pozarik; *Right:* UPI/Bettmann Archive **278** Urraca/Sygma **279** Clifford D. May/The New York *Times* **283** Tannenbaum/Sygma **284** Wide World **285** *Top:* Alain Mingham/Gamma-Liaison; *Bottom:* Jack Manning/The New York *Times* **286** *Top:* Martha Swope; *Bottom:* UPI/Bettmann Archive **287** UPI/Bettmann Archive **288** Wide World **289** Sapieha/Camera Press/Photo Trends **291** P. Apesteguy/B. Laforet/Gamma-Liaison **292** Wide World **293** *Top:* UPI/Bettmann Archive; *Bottom:* Wide World **294** Wide World **295** Turofsky **296** *Top:* William Karel/Sygma; *Bottom:* UPI/Bettmann Archive **297** Wide World **300** Gianni Giansanti/Sygma **302–304** Wide World **306** UPI/Bettmann Archive **307** Photo Trends **308** Laurent/Gamma-Liaison **309** Steve Schapiro/Gamma-Liaison **310** *Top:* Ray Fairfall/Photoreporters, Inc.,; *Bottom:* UPI/Bettmann Archive **311** *Top:* Wide World; *Bottom:* UPI/Bettmann Archive **312** Nova/Sygma **313** UPI/Bettmann Archive **314** *Both:* UPI/Bettmann Archive **315** Ira Wyman/Sygma **316** Edinger/Gamma-Liaison **317** Syndication International/Photo Trends **318** *Top:* David Madison/Duomo; *Bottom:* © 1984 Martha Swope **319** UPI/Bettmann Archive **320** Paul Chiasson/Gamma-Liaison **321** Sygma **322** Wide World **323** A. Tannenbaum/Sygma **325–326** UPI/Bettmann Archive **327** © 1983 Lucas Samaras/Polaroid Corporation **328** Wide World **329** The New York *Times* **331–333** Wide World **334** UPI/Bettmann Archive **336** Don Hogan Charles/The New York *Times* **337** Anthony Suau/Black Star **339** *Left:* Penguin Books; *Right:* © Joyce Baronio **340** New York *Post* Photograph © 1984 **341** Charles Steinbrunner/Dayton Newspapers, Inc. **342** Wide World **345** UPI/Bettmann Archive **346** Giansanti/Sygma **349** Dith Pran/The New York *Times* **351** Magnum Photos, Inc. **352** UPI/Bettmann Archive **357** Magubane/Gamma-Liaison **359–360** NASA **361** TASS from Sovfoto **363–365** *All:* Focus on Sports **367** Wide World **369** UPI/Bettmann Archive **370–371** Wide World **372** *Top:* Focus On Sports; *Bottom:* Steven E. Sutton/Duomo **373–375** Focus On Sports **376** Steven E. Sutton/Duomo **377** *Top:* © G. Rancinan/Sygma; *Bottom:* TASS from Sovfoto **378** © Paul J. Sutton **379** *Top:* © J. Guichard/Sygma; *Bottom:* Wide World **380–382** *All:* Paul J. Sutton/Duomo **383** *Top:* Steven E. Sutton/Duomo; *Bottom:* Arthur Grace/Sygma **387** James D. Wilson/*Newsweek* **390** UPI/Bettmann Archive **392** Keystone Press Agency, Inc. **393** Wolf Achtner/Sygma **395** Graig Davis/Sygma **398** Charles William Bush/Sygma **400** NBC Photo **401** Photo Trends **402** UPI/Bettmann Archive **404** Inge Morath/Magnum Photos, Inc. **405** © 1984 Martha Swope **409** Martha Swope **408** John Lopinot/Duomo **409** UPI/Bettmann Archive **411** Nik Kleinberg/Picture Group **412** Douglas Aircraft Company **414** Clifford D. May/The New York *Times* **416–417** TASS from Sovfoto **418** Stuart Franklin/Sygma **420** Wide World **423–424** UPI/Bettmann Archive **427** Wide World **431** Wide World **432** Flavia Perrone/Gamma-Liaison **435** UPI/Bettmann Archive

468

INDEX TO THE
1985 YEARBOOK
EVENTS OF 1984

INTRODUCTION

This index is a comprehensive listing of persons, organizations, and events that are discussed in the 1985 Yearbook. Entries in **boldface** letters indicate subjects on which the Yearbook has an individual article. Entries in lightface type indicate individual references within articles. In either type of entry, the letters a and b refer, respectively, to the left and right column of the page cited. If no letter follows a page number, the reference is to text that is printed across the full width of a page. Only the first significant mention of a subject in a given article has been included in the Index.

In a main entry such as **Australia:** 79b, the first number refers to the page on which the article begins. The succeeding lightface page numbers refer to other text discussions in the volume. The first number in lightface entries, when not in numerical order, will similarly provide the most extensive information on the subject. Subtitles following major entries refer to further references on the main subject, as in **Congress of the United States:** 121a; Elections, 154a. In the case of comprehensive articles such as the **United States of America,** reference is made to the page location of the beginning of the article. The discussion of foreign relations of the United States in that article may be augmented by reference to separate articles on the countries and international organizations concerned.

When an entry is followed by the abbreviation **illus.,** the reference is to a caption and picture on the page mentioned. When a text mention and an illustration of the same subject fall within the same article, only the text location is included in the index.

LIST OF ABBREVIATIONS USED IN THE INDEX

NATO   North Atlantic Treaty Organization
OPEC   Organization of Petroleum Exporting Countries
PLO   Palestine Liberation Organization
U.N.   United Nations
U.S.   United States
U.S.S.R.   Union of Soviet Socialist Republics

A

B

473

474

479